MW01096696

UNDER THE GUN

West German and Austrian Latter-day Saints in World War II

Roger P. Minert

To the many Latter-day Saint soldiers
of the West German Mission
whose whereabouts remain a mystery
and to their families who await
a glorious reunion

Published by the Religious Studies Center, Brigham Young University, Provo, Utah, in cooperation with Deseret Book Company, Salt Lake City, Utah
http://rsc.byu.edu/

Printed in the United States of America by Sheridan Books, Inc.

ISBN: 978-0-8425-2798-9
Retail U.S. $29.99

Cover and page design by Jonathon Owen. Page layout by Jonathon Owen and Jeff Wade.
On the cover: Ingrid (*left*) and Isolde Reger of the Saarbrücken Branch survey the ruins of their home shortly after the war. (Ingrid Reger Rankin)

Library of Congress Cataloging-in-Publication Data

Minert, Roger P. (Roger Phillip), 1952– author.
Under the gun : West German and Austrian Latter-day Saints in World War II / Roger P. Minert.
p. cm.
Includes index.
ISBN 978-0-8425-2798-9 (hardcover : alk. paper) 1. Mormons—Germany (West)—Biography. 2. Mormons—Austria—Biography. 3. Church of Jesus Christ of Latter-day Saints—Germany (West)—History—20th century. 4. Church of Jesus Christ of Latter-day Saints—Austria—History—20th century. 5. World War, 1939–1945—Religious aspects—Church of Jesus Christ of Latter-day Saints. 6. World War, 1939–1945—Personal narratives, German. 7. World War, 1939–1945—Personal narratives, Austrian. 8. Germany (West)—Church history—20th century. 9. Austria—Church history—20th century. I. Title.

BX8693.M56 2011
289.3092'243—dc23
[B]

2011025233

CONTENTS

ACKNOWLEDGMENTS

It should be evident that a work of this expanse could not emanate from the hand of one person in less than five years. Such is the case, and I am quite pleased to confess it. First and foremost, I express my gratitude to the hundreds of eyewitnesses who agreed to share their stories. Although recalling wartime events can be a difficult and painful task, eyewitnesses now have the opportunity to see family members, friends, fellow Latter-day Saints—and themselves—memorialized in this volume. None would call themselves heroes, but what they did was very often heroic. It is gratifying to note that less than 5 percent of the surviving eyewitnesses declined to participate in our study; I did not debate their decisions.

I am grateful to the many members of the Church who provided names of friends they thought might qualify as eyewitnesses. Their vigilance led to interviews with persons who otherwise would not have been identified. Other friends directed our attention to published stories and other media that turned out to be of importance to the work.

The staff and missionaries of the Church History Library in Salt Lake City have been most cordial in assisting us in our search for pertinent literature and other items in their collection. I am especially grateful to Bill Slaughter and Matthew Heiss, who opened many doors for us through their enthusiastic support of the research.

Religious Education at Brigham Young University has proffered support in many ways since this project began in earnest in 2005. The principal support has come in the form of funds to pay the wages of student research assistants. Those funds were granted through the Religious Studies Center and the Department of Church History and Doctrine. The David M. Kennedy Center for International Studies at Brigham Young University likewise awarded grants to partially fund my travel in Europe for the purpose of conducting interviews, examining historical venues, and presenting programs on this topic to Church members and friends. Latter-day Saints in Germany and Austria have also come to my aid by identifying eyewitnesses and helping to establish interview times and venues. Several were so kind as to take me into their homes for a night or two as I traversed the two countries. Significant contributions from private individuals allowed me to retain the services of several of the student research assistants mentioned below; in this regard, I offer my particular thanks to the Seattle, Washington, FORE (Friends of Religious Education), represented by D. Richard Dance.

Patty Smith in the Faculty Support Office of Religious Education has been most supportive of this project by allowing her student employees to transcribe more than one hundred eyewitness interviews conducted in English. My colleagues in Religious Education have offered excellent suggestions and critical readings of portions of the text.

Readers and reviewers have been solicited from the ranks of my friends, associates, and eyewitnesses. They have served with distinction in locating text in need of clarification or revision. I express my appreciation to my brother Brian Minert and his wife, Debbie, and to my friends Marion and Guenter Wolfert, Justus Ernst, Ilse Young, Heinz Rahde, Werner Thaller, Mary Petty, and Heimy Taylor.

Thanks also to the staff of the Religious Studies Center, including Robert Millet, Joany Pinegar, Brent Nordgren, and Devan Jensen and his student editorial staff: Jessica S. Arnold, Heidi Bishop, Jacob F. Frandsen, Amanda Kae Fronk, Matt Larsen, Jonathon R. Owen, Rosalind E. Ricks, and Nyssa Silvester. Particular thanks to Jonathon R. Owen and Jeff Wade for design, layout, and image editing.

One of the greatest pleasures of my academic career has been my association with student research assistants. I have engaged sixteen such students in the process of writing this book. What a gratifying experience it is to see them take ownership of significant aspects of the book and to carry out their stewardships with enthusiasm and dedication. The more they were involved with the research, the more they understood that this work begged to be carried to completion—that this book had to be presented to the Church and the world as a monument to the people about whom it is written. I have expressed my gratitude to them collectively and personally, and list them here as well:

Archivist: Mary Wade, Ashley Jones, Sarah Gibby Peris

Interviews in German: Michael Corley, Jennifer Heckmann, Judith Sartowski

Interviews in English: Michael Corley, Jennifer Heckmann, Russell Michael, Judith Sartowski

Interview translation (German to English): Judith Sartowski

Archival research: Colter Kennedy, Kathryn Penfield Price

Memorial Book compilation (English sources): Judith Sartowski, Nicole Gibb Taylor

Memorial Book compilation (German sources): Emily Cox, Julianna Baumann Edlinger, Judith Sartowski

Correspondence: Zach Alleman, Jennifer Heckmann, Mary Wade

Interview text editing: Judith Sartowski, Mary Wade

Book editing: Russell Michael, Mary Wade

Eyewitness contacts: Zach Alleman, Erin Collins, Ashley Jones, Russell Michael, Judith Sartowski

Timeline: Zach Alleman

Webmaster and computer support: Casidy Andersen, Trevor Brown

I am very grateful to my personal mentor and professor Douglas F. Tobler (BYU emeritus), who first employed me in 1975–76 to study the Church in Germany prior to 1945. It was under his tutelage that I first began to consider the fate of the Latter-day Saints whom I readily recognized to be under the gun. When I finally found the opportunity to make the formal study a reality, he immediately expressed his enthusiastic support. Conversations with him on this topic have been most rewarding.

Finally, to my dear wife, Jeanne, I express the thanks of a dependent husband who must constantly use his wife as a sounding board for new ideas and impressions. She heard many of these stories before they were written and has examined the entire text with a careful eye at least twice. She has travelled with me to remote locations and heard my renditions of sad but amazing events and people. She shares my conviction that our readers will be changed when introduced to these stories.

Roger P. Minert
Provo, Utah

INTRODUCTION

Historical Background

The Church of Jesus Christ of Latter-day Saints has a fascinating history that spans more than 170 years and includes peoples of every continent. The missionary effort that began in the German states in the 1840s resulted in the establishment of branches of the Church all over that land by 1900. While many converts in Germany and Austria chose to emigrate to the United States, others remained in the fatherland to help the Church grow and prosper there. Given the religious, cultural, and political traditions of this relatively young Germany (officially established in 1871), being a Latter-day Saint in Europe was not a simple task.

Joining the Church in central Europe made German Latter-day Saints outsiders in their native country in several respects. They no longer worshipped with their Catholic or Protestant neighbors, business colleagues, school comrades, or best friends. But even in their new church, they may have felt like second-class citizens. Instead of wards and stakes, they were organized into branches and districts. Instead of listening regularly to prophets, apostles, seventies, and bishops, they received instruction at the hands of mission presidents and young missionaries from small towns and farms in the American West. Instead of meeting in beautiful neighborhood churches with park-like surroundings, they gathered in taverns, apartment houses, or renovated factory rooms in the smoky industrial districts of large cities.

Nevertheless, they worshipped the same Heavenly Father, prayed in the name of the same Savior, studied the same scriptures, supported the same missionary program, and lived and preached the same gospel to their neighbors.

Emigration to North America before and after World War I (1914–18) had weakened large branches in Germany and Austria and in some locations had made smaller branches defunct. As was the case in other European countries, Latter-day Saint branches in Germany were constantly "starting over."[1] However, as the history of the Church in Germany approached its centennial mark in the late 1930s, emigration had essentially stopped, missionary work had increased, and the branches of the West German Mission (Frankfurt am Main) and the East German Mission (Berlin) were strong and growing slowly. Unfortunately, World War II would seriously weaken the Church in Germany and end for decades its presence in the eastern German territories that became part of post–World War II Poland and the Soviet Union.

The Latter-day Saints in Germany during the Hitler Era (1933–45) found themselves subjected to

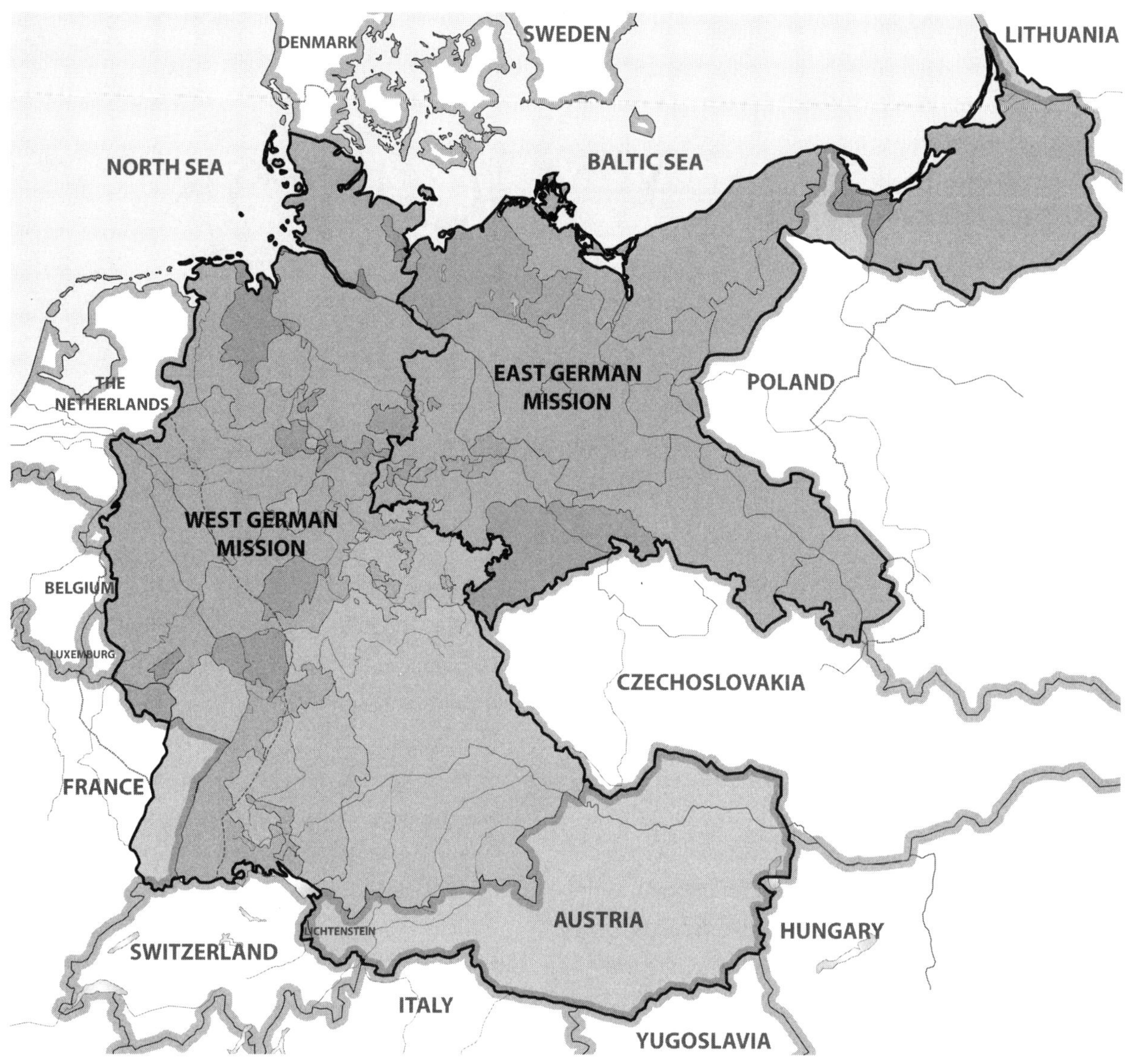

Fig. 1. The missions of the Church in Germany and Austria in 1939.

a unique set of challenges. For the first time, large numbers of Latter-day Saints were citizens of a totalitarian regime. Under a government that convinced or compelled more and more of its citizens to march to the same dark tune, members of a church that exalted the concept of agency were bound to feel at odds with the party line. When Hitler's armies achieved bloodless conquests of Austria (1938) and parts of Czechoslovakia (1938 and 1939), some LDS Germans saw a war coming. By the time the German army invaded Poland on September 1, 1939, Germans were no longer allowed to emigrate. Thirteen thousand Latter-day Saints were trapped and compelled to share the fate of their eighty million countrymen. What happened to them by the time Germany surrendered on May 8, 1945, is tragic—and for some of them the tribulations were far from over. How they reacted to the events of the time is inspiring.

Telling the Story

The history of The Church of Jesus Christ of Latter-day Saints in Gemany during World War II has never been written in more than a few pages. Gilbert Scharffs devoted a chapter to the topic in his book *Mormonism in Germany*.[2] A few dozen autobiographies have been published by eyewitnesses, and those books give excellent detail about the lives of individual Latter-day Saints in specific towns and branches, but most were written for family members and remain essentially unknown.[3] Several diaries written during the war years have survived, but none have been published.[4] Many survivors have written short stories about their experiences; few of these have ever found their way into print, though some have been submitted to the Family History Library and to the Church History Library.

In 1974, I began to focus my German history interest on the Church in that country. From a review of the wartime issues of the Church magazine *Der Stern*, it was clear to me that the Church suffered heavy losses during the Third Reich. I began asking questions to which nobody could offer answers: How many members in Germany and Austria died from 1939–45? How many priesthood holders were lost? How many branch meeting places were damaged or destroyed? How many LDS families lost their homes? What happened to the branches in territories later ceded to Poland and the Soviet Union? What happened to Primary classes, Relief Society work meetings and bazaars, and Young Women and Young Men programs? How was the missionary effort sustained, if at all? Answers to these questions are finally available and are found in the pages of this book.

This story needed to be told—not in general, but in such detail that the experiences of members of every branch of the Church in Germany and Austria could be described. Why had this not been done in the six decades since the end of the war? This one question I can now answer—after thirty-four years of thinking and planning and five years of intense investigation. The effort required to write this history is enormous and daunting. Such a story could be composed only after years of research and with the help of talented student assistants.

Interest in such a history is great. There could be currently as many as forty thousand members of the Church who served missions in Germany and Austria. At least 250,000 Latter-day Saints and others are related to the persons whose stories are featured in this history. The possibility that a German soldier in a photograph taken during the D-Day invasion in 1944 could have been a priest from the Darmstadt Branch, or that a Relief Society president might be among the dead in the aftermath of the Hamburg firebombings of 1943 might motivate readers of World War II history books to think about the conflict from a different perspective.

In 2003, when Brigham Young University invited me to join the faculty of Religious Education as the instructor of Germanic family history, I realized that I now had the opportunity to write this history. I knew that nobody had attempted this work, and I was more convinced than ever that it must be done. Finally, these faithful members of the Church—living or deceased—would have the chance to tell their story.

My goal from the beginning has been to describe in great detail the lives of typical Latter-day Saints. Rather than an investigation of the relationship of The Church of Jesus Christ of Latter-day Saints and the government of Hitler's Germany or the National Socialist (Nazi) Party, this is the story of everyday Saints. How did they maintain a testimony of the everlasting gospel under conditions few large groups of Church members have ever experienced? How did they conduct worship services without priesthood holders, locate each other after air raids, support each other after they lost their homes and loved ones? The remarkable stories they tell answer such questions.

When the foreign missionaries were evacuated from Germany and Austria in August 1939, the leadership of the Church was placed in the hands of local members. All contact with Church leadership in Salt Lake City, Utah, was lost when the United States was drawn into the war in December 1941. How did the leaders of the West and East German

Missions administer the affairs of the Church? How did they communicate with district and branch presidents? Did they continue to hold conferences, print and distribute literature for instruction, keep membership records, promote genealogical research, and do missionary work? These matters are described within the stories of eyewitnesses quoted here and in branch history documents, many of which have likely never been examined before.

Compiling the Data

In order to present this history from the perspective of first-person experience, my assistants and I set out to interview all available surviving eyewitnesses, to locate biographies and autobiographies by and about eyewitnesses, and to study all available documents produced by Church units in the East and West German Missions. It was also decided early on that this history should be augmented with photographs, maps, and historical documents depicting the lives of the Latter-day Saints described in the pages of this book. To accomplish these goals, we needed the assistance of many individuals and the public media.

We immediately began assembling lists of survivors by conducting interviews with people we already knew and asking them to share with us the names of their living relatives and friends. Our list eventually grew to more than five hundred persons (of the nearly 13,400 members of the Church in the two missions in 1939). Interviewees provided not only excellent first-person narratives regarding conditions and events in Germany and Austria during World War II, but also copies of stories of their own lives and the lives of deceased siblings, parents, and friends.

As we began our search for documents produced by Church units such as branches and mission offices, we were enthusiastically supported by the staff of the Church History Library in Salt Lake City. The *Church News* was kind enough to feature an introduction to our research on the cover of the February 11, 2006, issue. This coverage yielded more than three hundred responses from individuals wishing to share their stories or to recommend persons for us to contact. The same article was translated and featured in the German *Liahona* later that year and likewise attracted many responses from readers in Germany and Austria.

Organizing the data collected was, of course, a major challenge. The most efficient way was organizing each member under the name of the branch he or she belonged to on September 1, 1939, when the war began. By the time the war officially ended on May 8, 1945, literally thousands of Saints had changed their branch affiliations. The move (or flight) to different or newly founded branches continued in many cases for years, notably among homeless members and soldiers returning from POW camps.

The Status of the Church in Germany and Austria at the Onset of World War II

1939	**East**	**West**
Elders	402	390
Priests	194	179
Teachers	243	161
Deacons	445	345
Other Adult Males	1,245	939
Adult Females	4,336	3,172
Male Children	384	329
Female Children	358	280
Total	7,607	5,795

Mission	**East (Berlin)**	**West (Frankfurt)**	**Total**
Districts	13	13	26
Branches	75	71	146

Fig. 2. The Selbongen Branch building was constructed in 1929. During World War II, this was the only structure owned by the Church in Germany. The Polish name of the town is Zelwagi, and the building is currently owned and used by the Catholic Church. (Deseret News, *1938*)

From reports compiled in the years before World War II, quite a lot is known about the membership of the Church in the two German missions.[5] The missions were similar in population and in geographical size (see map on page 2).[6] No stakes of Zion had been established in Europe by 1939, thus the Saints were organized in districts and branches. Each German Mission had thirteen districts; each district included from three to eleven branches. The largest district in either mission was Berlin (East German Mission), with ten branches and 1,270 members. The smallest district was Hindenburg (East German Mission), with only four branches and sixty-five members.

The average size of a branch in the Church in Germany in 1939 was slightly more than one hundred members. Each branch had a presidency, clerks and secretaries, a Sunday School, a priesthood group, a Relief Society, a Primary organization, and youth groups. Each district had a presidency, with clerks and leaders for each of the auxiliaries. Districts also had genealogical specialists, choir leaders, and in some cases, recreational specialists.

Across the two German missions only one meetinghouse actually belonged to the Church—a modest but excellent structure erected in 1929 in Selbongen, East Prussia (East German Mission). The typical location for LDS branch meetings was something far less prominent. Even freestanding structures were very rare in the Church in Germany and Austria in those days. Most branches rented rooms in large buildings erected primarily for commercial use. Factories, warehouses, office buildings, and the like were sought out for space. Renovations were usually financed by the branch and resulted in a chapel of appropriate size. In a few cases, rooms used by societies or other churches were rented.

In most cases Latter-day Saint meeting venues included two or more classrooms. Most branch facilities featured restrooms and a cloakroom, but there was never an office for the branch presidency or the clerks. Some locations included a cultural hall, but most cultural activities took place on a stage or a rostrum in the main meeting room. Most chapels were used during the week for auxiliary meetings. A baptismal font—a wonderful feature—could be found in only three branches in all of Germany: St. Georg (in the city of Hamburg), Essen, and Stuttgart (all in the West German Mission).

Decorations in branch chapels were sparse and tasteful. In most cases, one or two modest paintings or photographs adorned the walls. The Savior, Jesus Christ, was the most common subject of those pictures, but contemporary photographs also show small renditions of the Salt Lake Temple and of the Prophet Joseph Smith, or photographs of then Church President Heber J. Grant. Benches were rare; folding chairs could be moved with ease to make room for cultural activities and to facilitate cleaning.[7] Music was provided in most cases by a simple pump organ, but some branches had a piano, and several larger branches actually had both instruments.

Church meetings for smaller groups were usually held in private homes, and attendees could number as high as thirty. This became progressively more common as branches lost their meeting rooms in air raids as the war drew to a close. In 1945, schools became popular meeting venues, and in such cases no signs of the presence of the LDS Church were visible.

District presidencies had no specific physical locations or offices. They conducted their business in the rooms of local branches or in their homes. Each mission rented office space in an affluent neighborhood—the West German Mission at Schaumainkai 41 in Frankfurt am Main and the East German Mission at Händelallee 6 in Berlin.

The standard meeting format in a branch was similar to that of branches and wards in other countries. Sunday School was held on Sunday morning; sacrament meeting took place in the late afternoon or evening. Meetings for the Relief Society, priesthood groups, and the Mutual Improvement Association (MIA) were held on evenings during the week. In most branches throughout the two missions, the Primary held its meetings on Wednesday afternoons, primarily because public schools in Germany dismissed by 1:00 p.m. on Wednesdays. Choirs were integral parts of German branches and districts, so choir practice was usually held weekly on a convenient evening. (German Saints are known for singing the hymns of Zion with great enthusiasm.)

Semiannual conferences were an important and popular part of Church life in Germany in 1939 and throughout most of the war. Mission conferences were common before the war, but could not be held later in the war because of restrictions in travel and resources. Each district held semiannual conferences, and each branch was expected to hold an annual conference. In addition, Sunday school conferences were prominent events, and other auxiliaries promoted their work through regular conferences. The largest events were district conferences. Some lasted from Friday through Sunday and included concerts, dances, and performances by LDS choirs, orchestras, and theatrical groups. These were exciting affairs that drew hundreds of members, who in turn often brought their friends.

German Latter-day Saints as Citizens under Hitler

Adolf Hitler and his National Socialist (Nazi) Party officially (and legally) came to power in January 1933. In August 1934, German president Paul von Hindenburg died, and Hitler combined the offices of chancellor and president. By 1935, he had outlawed the Communist Party and neutralized all other political parties, which gave him control of the parliament (Reichstag). He also won the loyalty of the German military by strengthening the army and the navy and establishing an air force—all in contradiction to the Treaty of Versailles, which had severely restricted the German military following World War I.

In Hitler's Third Reich, Latter-day Saints in Germany and Austria (annexed by Germany on March 12, 1938) were expected to be model citizens like all other Germans. In other words, Saints were to be Germans first and to have no secondary allegiance. Nazi Party programs were developed for every member of society old enough to say "Heil Hitler!" By 1936, everybody was encouraged—and some strongly pressured—to join the corresponding Nazi organization; there were distinct groups for men (Sturmabteilung), women (Frauenbund), boys (Hitlerjugend), girls (Bund Deutscher Mädel), athletes (Sportbund), truck drivers (Kraftfahrerkorps), teachers (Lehrerbund), and so on. Each group had its own uniform and insignia; to belong to none of them was to invite negative attention. Nevertheless, many adult Latter-day Saints were able to slip by without associating with the party, often by making excuses about spending their free time in some kind of humanitarian service or by working overtime.

The two prevailing faiths—Catholic and Protestant—comprised more than 95 percent of the German population in that era. Many smaller churches also existed in Germany but apparently were not large enough to warrant concern on the part of the government or the party; Latter-day Saints fell into this category. The two major churches were too powerful to be successfully attacked by the Nazi Party, while the smaller ones (commonly called *Sekten*, "sects") were disregarded by both the government and the common people. The small number of Latter-day Saints in the Third Reich (just over thirteen thousand among a population of eighty million) may have been an advantage in this regard, because Church units were never large enough to attract attention. Indeed, in many cases, their meeting rooms were located in buildings behind the main structure at that location (*Hinterhäuser*). Signs identifying the existence of the Church were usually small and unobtrusive. One usually had to be an insider to know that the Church existed in a given town or city.

One of the most visible ways in which a citizen could perform his or her civic duties was in the military. Perhaps as many as 1,800 Latter-day Saints in Germany and Austria performed active military service between 1939 and 1945 (but few ever volunteered). Many more served in reserve units, including hundreds who had served in the German army during World War I. There was no option of civil (non-military) service in Hitler's philosophy, and the concept of the conscientious objector was unknown.[8]

Community service was expected and commonly rendered by citizens in Nazi Germany, and LDS Church members were consistent and often willing participants. They collected old winter clothing for soldiers at the front, fed the homeless in soup kitchens, hurried to fight fires and rescue buried victims after air raids, and took refugees into their homes when no other housing was to be found. Of course, those functions were carried out by Germans of all religious persuasions who simply believed in helping because it was the right (patriotic) thing to do (or who feared that non-participation might lead to the conclusion that they did not support the effort).

In a negative sense, being a good citizen in the Third Reich also included assisting the government in identifying and apprehending those persons who were considered enemies of the state, such as criminals, traitors, spies, and malcontents—but principally Jews. Several eyewitnesses interviewed in connection with this history remembered scenes of destruction after the "Night of Broken Glass" (Reichskristallnacht, November 9–10, 1938), when organized Nazis raided Jewish stores and invaded Jewish homes. Some eyewitnesses later saw Jewish neighbors and friends being taken away in trucks, but—like most Germans of the day—had no idea what terrible treatment awaited those Jews under the secret German program termed the "Final Solution of the Jewish Question" (the murder of European Jews). Several Latter-day Saints decided for one reason or another that obedience to Hitler and his state was not required of a good member of the Church. Several died in concentration camps and several more spent time there.[9]

The Socioeconomic Status of Latter-day Saints in the Third Reich

As they had been for decades in Germany, Church members in the Hitler era belonged for the most part to the lower middle class. Many men were skilled laborers of the artisan classes, having learned a trade through an apprenticeship lasting from two to four years. A small number were masters in their trades and crafts. In only a few cases were Latter-day Saints in management positions; there were few if any professionals such as physicians, attorneys, and teachers. For example, mission supervisor Friedrich Ludwig Biehl worked in a dental laboratory. His first counselor, Christian Heck, was a traveling salesman, and his second counselor, Anton Huck, was a retired streetcar operator.

Several members owned their own businesses such as Louis Gellersen of the Stade Branch, who operated a bicycle shop and a gas station. The Hermann Huck family of Frankfurt am Main and the Otto Baer family of Nuremberg each owned a neighborhood grocery store. Eugen Hechtle was a tailor in Mannheim and Hermann Walter Pohlsander, an accountant for the city of Celle. Rudolf Niedermair of the Linz Branch in Austria was a career soldier whose service in the Austrian army began before World War I. He had risen to the rank of major and was a post commander by the time the second war began.

Rare was the Church member who rose to management rank in business or industry, such as Kurt Schneider, the president of the Strasbourg District. As a young man, he was already the director of the Strasbourg division of the Rheinmetall Company and in that capacity enjoyed the services of a fancy company car and a chauffeur.

Because the gospel had been preached primarily in the cities of Germany, very few Latter-day Saints in the Nazi era were farmers. It was simply too difficult to travel to church on Sundays from far away. (The Haag am Hausruck Branch in Austria is a marked exception.) Although many LDS families lived in multistory apartment buildings, they often rented garden space at the edge of town and even kept animals such as chickens and goats. On the other hand, stories of dogs and cats are not common; no eyewitnesses in the West German Mission recalled experiences with pets.

According to the testimonies of surviving eyewitnesses, most Latter-day Saint women were homemakers. When the German economy experienced boom years in the late 1930s, great emphasis was placed on occupational training for girls in the schools. Most teenage LDS girls prepared for gainful employment in the Hitler era, while their mothers often remained in the home. However, the war required a change in status for many of the homemakers when they were required by the government to assume jobs vacated by men who were drafted into the military. Most of these jobs were in the blue-collar sector.

Very seldom did a Latter-day Saint family own a single-family dwelling. Few were wealthy enough to employ domestic servants, own an automobile, or have a telephone in the home. Most had indoor plumbing, but families often shared a restroom (WC) at the end of the hallway with their neighbors. Eyewitness stories about carrying water from the neighborhood well or fountain are not rare, and that option became more common as city water lines were destroyed.

Ration Coupons and Shortages in Wartime Germany

As in most nations heavily involved in World War II, ration coupons were an integral part of life in Germany. Restrictions on most food and luxury items were constant and specialty items often disappeared from the public view. Standing in lines to redeem food coupons consumed a great deal of time, and families often split up to accomplish the task: the mother went to the butcher, one child to the baker, another child to the greengrocer, and so on. However, a ration coupon was no guarantee that the item was actually available. It was a common occurrence that a store ran out of the item and the owner came out to announce to those still in line that there was no more of the foodstuffs they wanted (or he simply closed the door and hung out the *Geschlossen* sign).

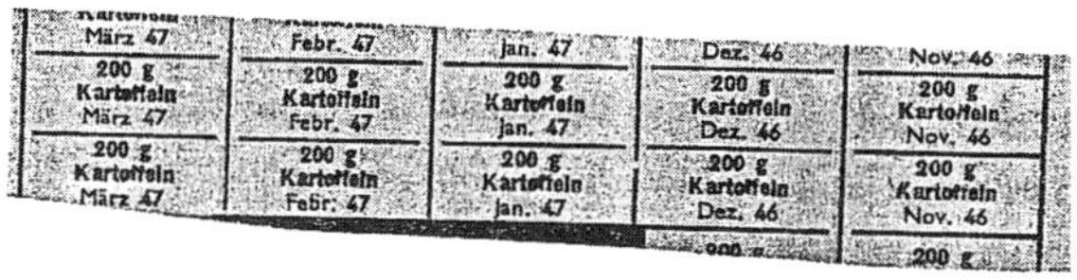

Fig. 3. Ration coupons, each for 200 grams (7 ounces) of potatoes. (J. Ernst)

Toward the end of the war, the German government accomplished near miracles in keeping food distributed throughout the country. Still, ration lines became ever longer, and stories are commonly told of women who refused to leave the lines when the air-raid sirens sounded. They preferred to believe that the raid would not come to their neighborhood, allowing them to complete their purchases and feed their families. Essentially all eyewitnesses who lived in large cities in Germany and Austria reported that they had enough food until the very day the enemy arrived in their neighborhood. Then the food system broke down totally and starvation threatened their existence.

Transportation in the Third Reich

Germany's public transportation systems were excellent during the Nazi period, built for densely populated areas where personal automobile ownership was a rarity. Latter-day Saints often tell of traveling to Church meetings on the bus or the streetcar, but some chose the longer walking time because they could not afford public transportation. Railroad service across the Reich featured only steam locomotives, but some traveled at very high speeds, and timetables were strictly observed during the first years of the war. Latter-day Saints report that there were no general restrictions on travel away from home during most of the war years, though some trains were full of troops and civilians had to wait for later connections on trips that for many reasons took longer than usual: water and coal supplies waned, tracks and bridges were destroyed, and various branches of the government and the military were competing for the use of an ever-decreasing number of trains.

When attacks from the air and invading armies destroyed the trains and tracks, schedules were interrupted and travel became unreliable. People rode in whatever conveyances were available, often in boxcars or cattle cars. During the final year of the war, the railroads were frantically conveying soldiers to the front and wounded soldiers and refugees to the rear. According to eyewitnesses, it was no longer necessary to purchase tickets; passengers fought their way onto the trains, many climbing through windows to get in. Refugees were often compelled to discard their luggage in the scramble to board a train.

Most railroad stations had air-raid shelters because they were prime targets for attacks. Trains moving down the tracks or standing on sidings were under constant attack during the last year of the war, when the German Luftwaffe (air force) could no longer provide sufficient defense. Many Latter-day Saints were in trains attacked by fighter planes, and several lost their lives. At the end of the war and for months afterward, people rode trains under dangerous circumstances; passengers were commonly seen sitting on the roof, standing on the running boards, or clinging to other parts of the train.

By the end of the war, bus and streetcar transportation had been seriously interrupted or curtailed in most German cities. Now and then, a streetcar would run for a few blocks, then passengers would get off and walk down the line for a few blocks where the service would continue again. In cities with subway systems (*Untergrundbahn* or *U-Bahn*), some of the lines survived nicely below the streets and U-Bahn stations were commonly used as air-raid shelters.

Of the few Latter-day Saints who owned automobiles or trucks, most used them as part of their employment. Many of those vehicles were destroyed in air raids. During the last days of the war, surviving personal automobiles were usually seized by the government, the military, or the invaders. Personal property was no longer protected.

Eyewitnesses recalled walking long distances from home to school and to church. Walking times of more than one hour in one direction were not uncommon. For persons in good health, walking was no hardship. Indeed, many branch outings involved *wandern*, the tradition of walking all day through forests outside of town and enjoying a picnic (and a choir practice) along the way. Some eyewitnesses told of being baptized in a pond in the forest, and branch members walked nearly an hour each way to witness the ceremony (at all seasons of the year).

Schools in Nazi Germany

The complex and respected German school system that dated back to the 1870s had been expanded and improved during the early twentieth century. However, the Allied air attacks did not spare schools; programs were often interrupted, abbreviated, and cancelled, and graduations postponed. Some schools in larger cities did double duty, accommodating children from bombed-out schools in split sessions. Many LDS eyewitnesses recalled that the official school starting time was delayed by an hour or two on any morning following a night interrupted by an air raid.

Several eyewitnesses recalled having teachers who were enthusiastic Nazi Party members. (All teachers employed by the state were required to join the party.) Some told of singing the Deutschlandlied (the German national anthem) or the Horst-Wessel-Lied (the official party hymn) every morning. Others recalled army-like inspections (was their clothing in order, hair combed, fingernails cleaned?) and punishments administered when the expected discipline was not maintained.

Entire classes of school children were moved from larger cities to rural areas as part of the children's evacuation program (see *Kinderlandverschickung* in the glossary). Many a teacher was sent with his homeroom class to a distant small town to continue instruction away from the air raids. When schools were damaged or transformed into hospitals later in the war, the children were often pleased at first. Later, they learned of the disadvantages of having less formal instruction.

Religious instruction was provided for Catholic and Protestant students for the first eight grades of public school. Latter-day Saint children were allowed to choose between these two religions where both were available, or to not attend at all. There are no reports of programmatic persecution of LDS students in public schools, though confrontations with fanatic Nazi teachers or religion instructors (usually local Catholic and Protestant parish leaders) did occur now and then.

Most German students left public schools after the eighth grade to pursue an apprenticeship or employment. Few continued formal education, with less than 10 percent planning on attending the university. The majority of LDS youth did not or could not pursue higher education.

Air Raids Over Germany and Austria

As early as the first week of the war, Polish airplanes attacked cities in the German Reich. By 1941, British air raids were launched against most large German cities, especially in the western part of the nation. When the United States joined the war in the European theater in 1942, the Allied bombing campaign became better coordinated, and a standard procedure was developed: the British Royal Air Force conducted their raids under cover of night and the American Army Air Corps flew during the day. In some cities, air raids were rare, perhaps occurring only once or twice. In others, especially where critical war industries were located, raids were more frequent. During the year 1944, the most important cities were subjected to raids every week. Because many large cities in Germany were just a few miles apart, enemy airplanes flying in one direction of the compass had to be considered on their way to one of several cities. Alarms were sounded in all possible target cities. In many communities, false alarms were more frequent than actual attacks.

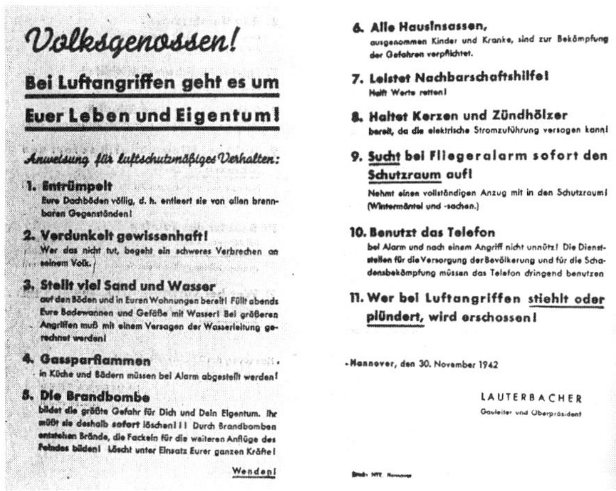

Volksgenossen!

Bei Luftangriffen geht es um Euer Leben und Eigentum!

Anweisung für luftschutzmäßiges Verhalten:

1. **Entrümpelt** Eure Dachböden völlig, d. h. entleert sie von allen brennbaren Gegenständen!
2. **Verdunkelt gewissenhaft!** Wer das nicht tut, begeht ein schweres Verbrechen an seinem Volk.
3. **Stellt viel Sand und Wasser** auf den Böden und in Euren Wohnungen bereit! Füllt abends Eure Badewannen und Gefäße mit Wasser! Bei größeren Angriffen muß mit einem Versagen der Wasserleitung gerechnet werden!
4. **Gassparflammen** in Küche und Bädern müssen bei Alarm abgestellt werden!
5. **Die Brandbombe** bildet die größte Gefahr für Dich und Dein Eigentum. Ihr müßt sie deshalb sofort löschen!!! Durch Brandbomben entstehen Brände, die Fackeln für die weiteren Anflüge des Feindes bilden! Löscht unter Einsatz Eurer ganzen Kräfte!

Wenden!

6. **Alle Hausinsassen,** ausgenommen Kinder und Kranke, sind zur Bekämpfung der Gefahren verpflichtet.
7. **Leistet Nachbarschaftshilfe!** Helft Werte retten!
8. **Haltet Kerzen und Zündhölzer** bereit, da die elektrische Stromzuführung versagen kann!
9. **Sucht bei Fliegeralarm sofort den Schutzraum auf!** Nehmt einen vollständigen Anzug mit in den Schutzraum! (Wintermäntel und -sachen.)
10. **Benutzt das Telefon** bei Alarm und nach einem Angriff nicht unnütz! Die Dienststellen für die Versorgung der Bevölkerung und für die Schadensbekämpfung müssen das Telefon dringend benutzen
11. **Wer bei Luftangriffen stiehlt oder plündert, wird erschossen!**

Hannover, den 30. November 1942

LAUTERBACHER
Gauleiter und Oberpräsident

Fig. 4. These eleven rules were circulated in the city of Hanover to help people prepare for air raids and conduct themselves properly when attacks occurred.

Even in large cities, Germans seldom had access to official, heavy concrete bunkers for refuge from enemy attacks. Many bunkers were constructed in parks, in or near railroad stations, and near large intersections. Nowhere were there enough bunkers to offer protection to everyone. The typical German city-dweller simply sought refuge in his own basement. Of course, those basements had not been constructed to protect people from five-hundred-pound (or heavier) blockbuster bombs, but residents did what they could to fortify the ceilings and walls of the basement. In most cases, entry and exit were through the main hallway or stairway serving the entire building. Shelters in a variety of public buildings and even large private or commercial buildings were clearly marked as *Luftschutzraum* or *LSR* and were open to all.

Air raids were announced by civil defense officials with loud wailing sirens. Systems of two or three different signals were used: one to announce a possible attack, one for a probable or imminent attack, and one for the actual arrival of attackers over the city's airspace. The interim between the first and the last alarms was from ten to twenty minutes or more. Thus there was usually time for people to find shelter, even if it was some distance from the home. Proof positive of a pending strike was seen in the form of illumination flares dropped above the target by advance enemy airplanes. Called *Christbäume* or *Weihnachtsbäume* (Christmas trees) by the Germans, those flares were visible from miles away and heralded death and destruction. Civil defense units sometimes responded by burning decoy flares to mislead the bombers.

Every neighborhood had an air-raid warden. Wardens were sometimes auxiliary policemen but most often were low-ranking members of the Nazi Party. It was their job to see that people vacated their apartments, public buildings, and streets and sought refuge in the shelters. Wardens also reminded people to close their blinds or turn off their lights to achieve total blackout conditions. Heavy fines were levied against violators of this safety standard. It was also the air-raid warden's responsibility to see that all entries to shelters were closed and locked when the final siren was heard. Persons not yet in shelters were then on their own to find places of protection. For a variety of reasons, some people chose to stay in their apartments rather than go to the shelter. In reality, the chances of survival were almost equal wherever they were. On the streets, however, they could be killed by enemy bombs as well as by shrapnel from friendly guns attempting to shoot down the attackers.

Latter-day Saint eyewitnesses tell of preparing for air raids the same way their neighbors prepared. All but the smallest children were expected to carry a bag or a suitcase with the most important survival items as they descended into the basement or hurried down the street to a public shelter. One of the parents usually carried the most valuable family documents, including genealogical papers, family photographs, and books of scripture. Most brought a change of clothing and enough food for the next few hours. There was little time to worry about what was left behind.

Life in the typical air-raid shelter was little more than survival. Some tried to sleep (which was usually impossible because of the noise), while others prayed, read newspapers, or played cards (if there was enough light to do so). Parents tried to entertain or comfort their children. Some sat on chairs, others on the floor—usually in rooms that lacked proper heating or cooling systems. Most were exhausted from lack of sleep and wanted only to return to their homes.

Three means of self-defense were practiced everywhere people gathered in private shelters. First, because apartment houses in most cities were built with no space between them, the basements of any two adjacent apartment buildings shared a common wall. Residents were instructed to make a hole in the wall (*Mauerdurchbruch*) large enough for an adult to crawl through.[10] If the exit of one basement was blocked, the people could escape through that wall into the next basement by removing loose brick or temporary wood structures. Another standard feature in each shelter was one or more barrels of water; if fires had broken out close to the escape route, each person could soak a blanket in the water and put it over his head to prevent suffocation as he exited the shelter. Finally, in the attic space on top of the house, the contents were removed to provide less material for combustion and to make it easier to find and remove incendiary bombs. Such bombs often penetrated the roof and came to rest on the floor of the attic. The timer fuses usually did not initiate fire for several minutes, allowing residents who kept supplies of sand and water in the attic to smother the bombs before they began to burn or douse smaller fires before they spread.

When the all-clear siren sounded, air-raid wardens moved to evacuate the shelters as fast as possible. The main purpose of this maneuver was to prevent the occupants from suffocating in the shelters when smoke became thick or firestorms ensued. In crowded neighborhoods with tall apartment buildings, fires that started in the upper floors soon spread downward and to adjacent buildings. The oxygen feeding those fires was sucked out of the environment, making it hard or impossible to breathe. The upward rush of the air to the fire felt like wind and gave rise to the term *firestorm*. People emerged from the basements and ran down the street in search of open space where air was more plentiful. A technical description of the concept of firestorm is provided by author David Irving from a police report of the city Hamburg:

> An estimate of the force of this fire-storm could be obtained only by analyzing it soberly as a meteorological phenomenon: as a result of the sudden linking of a number of fires, the air above was heated to such an extent that a violent updraught occurred which, in turn, caused the surrounding fresh air to be sucked in from all sides to the centre of the fire area. This tremendous suction caused movements of air of far greater force than normal winds. In meteorology the differences of temperature involved are of the order of 20° to 30° C. In this fire-storm they were of the order of 600°, 800° or even 1,000° C. This explained the colossal force of the fire storm winds.[11]

Following air raids, the fortunate people were those who emerged from the shelters to find that there had been no attack at all. It was also a relief to learn that the damage done was to structures blocks away and that one's own home was intact. However, this relief was often dispelled by the sound of another alarm siren a few hours later.

Culture and Entertainment in Nazi Germany

Despite the privations of the war years, motion picture theaters, opera houses, dance halls, and bars stayed open until they were destroyed or their utilities were cut off.[12] New movies were released and new hit songs were played over the radio. Newspapers were printed in many cities until the day the Allied invaders arrived. Citizens played soccer games and went ice skating, swimming, and hiking. Some Germans and Austrians even continued to take vacations (without leaving the country) for the first few war years. Birthday parties took place, christenings and weddings were celebrated in local churches, and clubs maintained their regular activities as long as possible. Local and national governments did their best to sustain the lifestyle of their citizens during the war and were remarkably successful in the effort. Of course, when the war came to an end and the conquerors ruled, life was reduced to mere subsistence and entertainment was no longer a priority.

The End of Peacetime

When World War II began on September 1, 1939, the majority of Germans believed that Germany's cause was just and that victory was probable, if not certain. Many Latter-day Saints apparently were of the same belief. It is possible that members of the Church in Germany realized before other Germans that the war was not a just cause and that defeat and invasion were possible if not probable. This must have been a frightening prospect.

Several decades ago, Douglas F. Tobler was told by several eyewitnesses that they believed the prophecies of the Book of Mormon, namely that any people fighting against the inhabitants of the "promised land" (identified in LDS scripture as North America) were doomed to ultimate failure. Those eyewitnesses must then have had terrible premonitions when Germany and the United States exchanged declarations of war in December 1941.

Editorial Comments

In chapters in which an eyewitness provided a single interview or document, it may be assumed that all information attributed to that eyewitness was taken from the same source. This allows the elimination of hundreds of repetitious footnotes.

Precise details regarding the sufferings of Latter-day Saints in the following pages have been summarized or even suppressed in some cases. Sufficient allusions are made to the fact that what happened was often much worse than expressed in my descriptions. The presentation of gruesome detail serves no worthy purpose. It is not the goal of this book to emphasize the morbid, the heinous, the perverse, and the inhumane. What the Saints of the West German Mission experienced during World War II was often so terrifying and hideous that the reader may believe the many eyewitnesses who stated simply that "there are no words that could adequately describe what happened." Of course, no such generalizations or simplifications have been made when quotations were taken from interviews and written eyewitness accounts.

The spellings of the names of the following cities are represented in this book by their accepted international variants: Cologne (*Köln*), Hanover (*Hannover*), Munich (*München*), Nuremberg (*Nürnberg*), Vienna (*Wien*), and Strasbourg (*Straßburg*). The name Frankfurt will be used throughout the book to refer to the city on the Main River (not to be confused with Frankfurt on the Oder River in the East German Mission).

Notes

1. Douglas F. Tobler, interview by the author, Lindon, UT, July 25, 2008.
2. Gilbert Scharffs, "Mormonism Holds on during the World War II Years," in *Mormonism in Germany: A History of the Church of Jesus Christ of Latter-Day Saints in Germany* (Salt Lake City: Deseret Book, 1970), 91–116.
3. No such publications are known among the members of the West German Mission, but several have emerged in the East German Mission. An excellent example is by Werner Klein of

the Landsberg Branch, *Under the Eye of the Shepherd* (Springville, UT: Cedar Fort, 2005).

4. Soldier Kurt Ruf of the Stuttgart Branch and young mother Charlotte Bodon Schneider of the Strasbourg Branch kept very detailed wartime diaries that have been preserved.
5. Presiding Bishopric, "Financial, Statistical, and Historical Reports of Wards, Stakes, and Missions, 1884–1955," 257, CHL CR 4 12.
6. Hitler's Germany had about eighty million inhabitants in 1939 and was roughly the size of the state of Texas.
7. Eyewitnesses in several branches recalled rescuing chairs from the ruins of the branch meetings and taking them home for use in group meetings. When branches were evicted from meeting rooms (which happened frequently after 1942), the pump organ was moved to the home of a member who could host meetings.
8. The Jehovah's Witnesses and a break-off group, the Bible Students in Germany (known as die Zeugen Jehovas and die ernsten Bibelforscher), publicly opposed military service and as a group became inmates of prisons and concentration camps.
9. See the story of Heinrich Worbs of the St. Georg Branch of the Hamburg District. The sad fate of the three teenagers of the St. Georg Branch is now well known and has been summarized in the Hamburg District chapter.
10. David Irving, *The Destruction of Dresden* (London: William Kimber, 1963), 42.
11. Ibid., 162.
12. The Berlin Opera House was destroyed and rebuilt twice during the war. No attempt was made to restore it after the third time it was bombed and burned out.

GEDENKBUCH (MEMORIAL BOOK)

For the Lord suffereth the righteous to be slain that his justice and judgment may come upon the wicked; therefore ye need not suppose that the righteous are lost because they are slain; but behold, they do enter into the rest of the Lord their God. (Alma 60:13)

One of the original goals of this study was to compile a list of German and Austrian Latter-day Saints who did not survive World War II. When estimates by previous investigators suggested that approximately 550 Latter-day Saint soldiers and 50 civilians had lost their lives in the two German missions, serious questions emerged.[1] Were not the majority of branches located in large cities—the principal targets of Allied bombing attacks? Would not civilian Church members and meetinghouses also lie beneath the sights of the enemy bombardiers? Would it not be logical to suggest that civilian Saints were killed by invading enemy ground troops? If, in fact, all of the members of the Church units in areas later annexed by Poland and the Soviet Union were driven from their homes, could it not be assumed that some of them would not survive a trek of hundreds of miles to the west, often made in the dead of winter?

From Church records, other written sources, and eyewitness interviews, we have compiled a memorial book (*Gedenkbuch*) with the names of 724 Saints from the West German Mission. For each person, every attempt has been made to show the birth date and place; marriage date and place; spouse; death date, place, and cause; baptism and confirmation dates and places; priesthood ordinations; and military rank of the deceased.

Who is included in the memorial book? The initial goal was to determine which Latter-day Saints died as a direct consequence of the war (what the Germans refer to as *Kriegseinwirkung*). However, it soon became evident that in many cases it was not possible to state that the death of a certain individual was or was not connected to wartime events or conditions. For example, toward the end of the war several diseases such as typhus were prevalent which would otherwise have been rare. Minor illnesses sometimes became major illnesses and causes of death for persons who spent a good deal of time in cold and dank air-raid shelters or out in the open after becoming homeless. The lack of qualified medical personnel and medical facilities certainly contributed to a general decrease in the quality of health care and thus an increase in mortality. Persons who died of heart attacks or strokes may have had their conditions deteriorate more rapidly when hurrying to an air-raid shelter or after receiving news of the death of a soldier. In short, it was decided that no cause of death—including old age or senility—would be excluded from the list of persons who died during the war years.

Each Latter-day Saint who died is found listed in the branch to which the person belonged on September 1, 1939 (except for a very few who moved during the war years). The personal data collected from Church records and eyewitnesses have been compared to public genealogical databases, such as the International Genealogical Index, Ancestral File, and Pedigree Resource File. In many cases, multiple sources offer conflicting data, especially when it comes to name spelling variations and place names.

Who is not included in the memorial book? A great many Latter-day Saints in Germany and Austria in the war era were not married to Church members. Many adult women were the only members of their families to have been baptized. They lost non-LDS husbands, parents, and children, who are not included in our compilation. For example, Erna Kaiser of the Stuttgart Branch later documented no fewer than twenty-four close relatives who were killed in the war, only six of whom were Latter-day Saints. In other words, the sufferings of the Saints regarding the loss of life in their families were in many cases greater than can be reflected in the lists for branches shown in this volume.

Some of those Latter-day Saints who died were inactive and possibly unknown to other branch members. It is possible that several hundred such persons should be listed here, but there is no way of knowing who they were; nobody in the branches knew of their demise.

Finally, I include with some hesitation the names of persons shown in branch records as *vermisst* (missing) or *verschollen* (disappeared). Many of those Saints likely perished under the mountains of rubble resulting from catastrophic air raids over big cities, but no proof is available. If the truth were known, there might be more than one hundred persons in this category. Some persons listed as missing may have been driven from their homes, sought refuge elsewhere, or simply lost contact with the Church.

The details shown in the memorial book section of each chapter do not represent original genealogical research. Entries include data supplied by eyewitnesses, descendants, and friends, taken from branch membership records, LDS Church censuses, and the following public sources:

www.familysearch.org (FS):
Ancestral File (AF)
International Genealogical Index (IGI)
Pedigree Resource File (PRF)
new.familysearch.org (NFS)
www.volksbund.de: This website is maintained by a society dedicated to the preservation of German war graves from the two world wars. The language is German. Searches can be made by the name of the soldier or the place of birth. Some women and civilians are included in this database.

Other abbreviations used in the memorial book lists include:

CHL: Church History Library of the LDS Church

FHL: Family History Library of the LDS Church

The names of persons who provided genealogical data are also found in parentheses.

NOTE

1. Gilbert Scharffs, *Mormonism in Germany: The History of the Church of Jesus Christ of Latter-day Saints in Germany* (Salt Lake City: Deseret Book, 1970), 116.

MAJOR EVENTS OF WORLD WAR II

1939

August

23 The Nazi euthanasia program begins. By the end of the war, seventy thousand mentally and physically disabled Germans are killed.

24–26 American LDS missionaries are evacuated to Denmark and the Netherlands.

28 Food ration cards are introduced in Germany. Meat, dairy, sugar, eggs, bread, cereal, and fruit are limited.

September

1 Germany invades Poland.

2 Willy Klappert of the Frankfurt am Main Branch is the first German LDS soldier to die

3 Great Britain and France declare war on Germany.

8 Friedrich Ludwig Biehl is appointed supervisor of the West German Mission.

29 Germany and the Soviet Union formally divide up Poland.

October

1 Royal Air Force (RAF) airplanes drop propaganda leaflets over Germany.

November

12 Clothing ration cards are issued in Germany.

23 Jews in German-occupied Poland are ordered to wear the yellow Star of David on their outer clothing.

27 German "Aryans" are given twelve months to divorce their Jewish spouses.

1940

January

1 Christian Heck becomes supervisor of the West German Mission.

11 German citizens suffer from coal shortages.

April

9 Germany invades Denmark and Norway.

27 Heinrich Himmler issues orders for the construction of a concentration camp at Auschwitz.

27 German women ages fifteen to forty are required to register with the Employment Ministry.

May
10 Germany invades the Netherlands, Belgium, Luxembourg, and France. Winston Churchill becomes British Prime Minister.
19 The German ports of Hamburg and Bremen are bombed by the RAF.
20 German forces reach the English Channel.
26 British forces start the Dunkirk evacuation.
31 A shortage of doctors causes viruses to spread among the German people.

June
5 German forces launch an attack into France proper.
14 German forces enter Paris.
22 France surrenders to Germany.
26 Germany's meat ration is cut to fourteen ounces per week per person.

July
Hermann Goering, second to Hitler in the Nazi hierarchy, gives Reinhard Heydrich the authority to carry out preparations for a "final solution of the Jewish question" throughout German-occupied Europe.

August
13 The Battle of Britain starts.
25 The RAF conducts its first air raid on Berlin.

September
15 The German Luftwaffe launches a major attack on London.
17 Artur Axmann, the new German youth leader, decrees that all Hitler Youth ages fourteen to eighteen in areas vulnerable to air raids must attend air-raid training on Sunday mornings.
27 Germany, Italy, and Japan sign the Tripartite Pact.

1941

February
12 German Lt. General Erwin Rommel arrives in Tripoli in North Africa.

March
2 German forces enter Bulgaria.
24 Rommel launches his first offensive in North Africa.

April
2 German forces cross Hungary to invade Yugoslavia and Greece.

May
4 Hitler delivers his "Thousand-Year Reich" speech.
7 Joseph Stalin assumes premiership of the Soviet Union.
24 The German battleship *Bismarck* sinks Britain's battle cruiser HMS *Hood.*
27 The British Royal Navy sinks the *Bismarck* in the North Atlantic.

June
22 Operation Barbarossa begins when German forces invade the Soviet Union.

July
9 German forces capture three hundred thousand Soviet troops near Minsk.
10 Stalin assumes the role of commander-in-chief of the Red Army.
12 Britain and the Soviet Union sign a mutual assistance treaty.

August
1 The focus on the Wehrmacht and the armaments industry leaves German citizens without replacement parts for cars and other forms of transportation.

September

1 All German Jews over the age of six are ordered to wear a yellow Star of David with the word *Jude* written on it.

8 German forces lay siege to Leningrad.

October

2 In Operation Taifun, Germany starts the drive on Moscow.

31 German workers are required to "volunteer" to donate twenty-five Reichsmark a week from their wages.

November

22 The German raider *Atlantis* is sunk.

December

7 Japanese forces attack Pearl Harbor.

8 The United States declares war on Japan.

11 Germany and Italy declare war on the United States.

19 Hitler assumes command of the German *Heer* (army).
Only women are serving as missionaries in either German mission.

1942

January

14 German submarines attack shipping vessels off the US East Coast.

26 The first contingent of US troops to reach Europe arrives in Northern Ireland.

February

28 The use of cars for anything but work is banned in Germany.

March

17 Branches throughout Germany celebrate the Relief Society centennial.

19 A gas chamber is first used on human beings at Auschwitz-Birkenau.

21 Severe penalties, including sentences in concentration camps, are announced to deter German citizens from making unnecessary journeys by rail.

May

30 The RAF conducts a thousand-airplane raid on Cologne.

June

4 Mass evacuation of Cologne takes place.

July

4 US bombers fly their first mission in Europe.
British bombers begin attacking Germany's second-largest city, Hamburg, continuing for four straight nights and causing a firestorm that kills thirty thousand civilians.

August

23 German forces reach Stalingrad.

October

27 Helmuth Hübener of the Hamburg–St. Georg Branch (West German Mission) is executed in Berlin for treason.

November

19 Soviet forces counterattack at Stalingrad.

1943

January

14 Allied leaders hold the Casablanca Conference.

27 US bombers conduct the first all-American raid on Germany.

28 All German men between ages sixteen and sixty-five and all women between ages seventeen and forty-five are to be mobilized for military employment.

30 The RAF conducts its first daylight raid on Berlin.

February

2 The German Sixth Army surrenders at Stalingrad; there are 295,000 casualties, including Karl Albert Göckeritz, president of the Chemnitz District (East German Mission).

Hans and Sophie Scholl are arrested on the Munich University campus for distributing pamphlets for the White Rose resistance group.

March

3 Friedrich Biehl, former supervisor of the West German Mission, dies in a fire in Russia.

May

Anton Huck becomes supervisor of the West German Mission

31 Meat rations in Germany are cut to nine ounces.

June

13 German forces in North Africa surrender to the Allies.

July

7 Allied forces invade Sicily.

24 RAF bombings reduce Hamburg to rubble.

25 Benito Mussolini is overthrown and arrested in Italy.

August

17 Regensburg and Schweinfurt are destroyed in air raids.

September

3 More than one million citizens are evacuated from Berlin in one month.

October

13 Italy joins the Allies and declares war on Germany.

23 Martin Werner Hoppe, president of the Breslau District (East German Mission), dies in a field hospital in the Soviet Union.

November

20–22 The office of the East German Mission in Berlin is destroyed in air raids on successive nights.

1944

February

20 Allied air forces launch the "Big Week" air raids over Germany.

March

6 US bombers attack Berlin for the first time.

30 Nuremberg is bombed.

June

6 (D-day) Allied troops land in Normandy, France.

July

20 Claus Graf Schenk von Stauffenberg attempts to assassinate Hitler.

September

10 Heinrich Himmler orders that the families of all deserters be executed.

German civilians begin the evacuation of eastern German provinces.

11 US forces cross the German border near Aachen.

15 US forces take the city of Nancy in Alsace-Lorraine.

25 Hitler calls up remaining sixteen-to sixty-year-old males for military service.

30 Germany's rationing of fish and meat drops to three ounces per person per week plus one-third of an ounce of egg.

October

5 All German hospitals are put under military control.

November

28 Soviet forces cross the Danube River and approach Austria.

December

16 The Battle of the Bulge commences in Belgium and Luxembourg.

1945

January

Millions of German refugees begin the trek west by land and across the Baltic Sea. Latter-day Saint refugees begin to gather in the Paul Langheinrich home in Berlin and the Fritz Lehnig home in Cottbus.

15 The Battle of the Bulge concludes; the Allies prevail.

16 Soviet troops liberate the Auschwitz extermination camp.

28 Soviet forces enter the German province of Pomerania.

30 The German hospital ship *Wilhelm Gustloff* is sunk in the Baltic Sea by a Soviet submarine, and thousands of German refugees perish.

February

1 Soviet forces establish a small bridgehead over the Oder River east of Berlin.

9 "Fortress Königsberg" surrenders to the Red Army; District President Max Freimann is one of several Latter-day Saints who disappear there.

British and Canadian forces penetrate the Siegfried line and reach the Rhine River.

12 German women between the ages of sixteen and sixty are declared eligible for Volkssturm (home guard) service.

13–14 Allied air forces carry out the fire-bombing of Dresden.

March

5 US forces enter Cologne.

German boys sixteen and older are sent into combat.

5 Chemnitz is destroyed by Allied airplanes.

7 US forces cross the Rhine River at Remagen.

20 US forces take Saarbrücken and Zweibrücken.

27 US forces capture Frankfurt.

April

5 Soviet forces take Vienna, Austria.

10 Allied forces enter the city of Hanover.

12 Franklin D. Roosevelt dies in office; Harry S. Truman becomes US President.

15 British forces liberate Bergen-Belsen concentration camp.

16 Soviet forces start the final assault on Berlin.

17 US forces capture Nuremberg.

19 Christian Heck, former supervisor of the West German Mission, is killed near Bad Imnau in southwest Germany.

22 US forces cross the Danube River.

29 US forces liberate Dachau concentration camp.

Hitler designates Karl Dönitz to succeed him as president and Martin Bormann as chancellor.

30 Hitler commits suicide in his underground bunker in Berlin.

May

2 Berlin is surrendered to Soviet forces.

6 "Fortress Breslau" surrenders to the Red Army.
The Dresden District holds a spring conference in Dresden; Russian artillery fire is heard in the distance.
7 In Reims, France, Alfred Jodl signs the surrender of all German forces.
8 (VE Day) In Berlin, Wilhelm Keitel signs the surrender of German forces.
At least 60 percent of the Saints in Germany and Austria are homeless.
14 Heber J. Grant, President of The Church of Jesus Christ of Latter-day Saints, dies in Salt Lake City.

June
5 The Allies (France, Great Britain, Soviet Union, United States) occupy Germany and Austria in four zones.

July
1 American troops evacuate territory conquered in eastern Germany; Soviet troops move in.
East German Mission leaders are granted use of the Wolfsgrün Castle near Zwickau and send LDS refugees to live there.
Mission leaders make the first of two trips through the Soviet Occupation Zone to assess the status of the Saints of the East German Mission.

Fall The first LDS refugees arrive in Langen, near Frankfurt, and establish a colony.

1946

February–November
Apostle Ezra Taft Benson visits the Saints in Europe and arranges for the distribution of welfare supplies from Salt Lake City.

1947

The only surviving LDS branch east of the new German-Polish border is in Selbongen (formerly East Prussia).

1950

The last surviving LDS soldier returns from a Soviet POW camp.

WEST GERMAN MISSION

The River Main flows from east to west through the city of Frankfurt, one of Germany's most important cities. Famous for its role in finance, politics, literature, culture, and transportation, the city had 548,220 inhabitants in 1939. On the south bank of the Main is the quarter known as Sachsenhausen. Some of Frankfurt's finest modern buildings lined that side of the river during the years leading up to World War II. One of those was Schaumainkai 41, the home of both the West German Mission office and the family of the mission president. Located at the corner of Schweitzerstrasse, the front windows of the building offered a fine view of the Main and the main part of the city on the other side of the river.

The missions of The Church of Jesus Christ of Latter-day Saints in the German-speaking nations of Europe were reorganized on January 1, 1938. For several decades, there had been two missions: the Swiss-German Mission, consisting of Switzerland and the western states of Germany, and the Austrian-German Mission, consisting of Austria and the eastern states of Germany. With the new year, three missions were constituted: the Swiss-Austrian Mission (with its office in Basel, Switzerland), the West German Mission (Frankfurt), and the East German Mission (Berlin). In order to balance the populations of the missions in Germany, the Weimar District was moved from the East to the West. Philemon Kelly had been the president of the East German Mission since August 1937 but moved to Frankfurt in January 1938 to assume the leadership of the new West German Mission.[1]

West German Mission[2]	**1939**
Elders	359
Priests	165
Teachers	148
Deacons	317
Other Adult Males	864
Adult Females	2919
Male Children	303
Female Children	258
Weimar District*	337
Total	5670

*Detail not reported

For a few weeks, President Kelly's office was located in the Weber Inn at Weserstrasse 1, but a search began immediately for a more formal setting for the office. The West German Mission history reported the following success on Saturday, February 12, 1938:

Fig. 1. The West German Mission (with districts identified) and the East German Mission of the LDS Church during World War II.

> New Mission Home Occupied. The new permanent headquarters for the West German Mission on Schaumainkai [41] were occupied on this day. All of the ceilings, walls, woodwork, fixtures and floors have been renovated and repaired. Although the office was completely bare at the time of occupation, before the end of the month sufficient furniture, equipment, utensils etc. had been installed to permit the home and office life to run smoothly.[3]

The new location in the upper-class neighborhood on the south bank of the Main River lent an air of respectability to the mission office. The affairs of the mission in general were in excellent condition at the time. Approximately eighty missionaries were serving in the mission in 1938, nearly all of them from the United States. The seventy branches of the Church were grouped in thirteen districts, and all of the auxiliary programs of the Church were functioning in Germany.[4] At the northern end of the mission was the Schleswig-Holstein District, and at the far southeast extent of the mission was the Vienna District.

Fig. 2. The new home of the West German Mission office at Schaumainkai 41 in Frankfurt. The entrance was on the west side (right). The stairs in front of the building lead down to a promenade along the Main River. (G. Blake)

Mission	East (Berlin)	West (Frankfurt)	Total
Districts	13	13	26
Branches	75	70	145

Philemon Kelly's work in Frankfurt lasted only a few months. In August 1938, he was released and succeeded by a dapper young businessman from Salt Lake City, Utah—M. Douglas Wood. Along with his wife, Evelyn, and his daughters Carolyn and Annaliese, President Wood arrived in Frankfurt on June 26, 1938.[5] He had served in the Swiss-German Mission in the early 1920s and was well suited to the task when he returned to Germany.

The Largest LDS Branches in Germany in 1939		
	Branch	Population
1	Chemnitz Center	469
2	Königsberg	465
3	Hamburg–St. Georg	400
4	Dresden	369
5	Stettin	359
6	Leipzig Center	328
7	Nuremberg	284
8	Annaberg-Buchholz	274
9	Berlin Center	268
10	Breslau West	265

Of the ten largest LDS branches in Germany in 1939, only Hamburg–St. Georg and Nuremberg were in the West German Mission.

Adolf Hitler (Germany's chancellor since 1933 and also its president since 1934) had led the country to a position of prominence and power by the time the Wood family arrived in Frankfurt. The nation's international influence was growing (thanks in part to the successful Olympic Games of 1936), its economy was flourishing, the military was increasing in size and strength, and most of the eighty million Germans were participating in their country's recovery from the Great War that had ended in disaster nearly two decades earlier. The 13,400 members of The Church of Jesus Christ of Latter-day Saints were likewise contributing to and benefiting from the prosperity of the nation. Even many of those members who had once dreamed of immigrating to the United States felt increasingly secure in Germany and were becoming convinced that the Saints could be blessed for their efforts in building Zion there.[6]

Reacting to rumblings of impending war, the First Presidency in Salt Lake City directed President Wood to evacuate his American missionaries to the Netherlands or Denmark on September 14, 1938. The missionaries were pleased to return to their assigned areas three weeks later.[7] War had not begun, but tension in central Europe was beginning to mount, and the American missionaries found themselves the object of official curiosity at times. Perhaps the most serious incident was reported in the mission history on October 14, 1938:

> Elders Royal V. Wolters and Allen Luke were sent to Switzerland because the police were on their trail. They had taken some pictures which the government had forbidden to be taken. The pictures were taken while the two of them were laboring in Hannoversch-Münden. They were sent to Brother Johann Kiefer in Saarbruecken, who is a photographer. Upon inspecting Brother Kiefer's records, the police discovered the forbidden negatives and some months later he was arrested. The two elders were traced and would have been involved in the situation, but were transferred to Switzerland just in time to avoid being called in by the police. The investigation of Brother Kiefer and his part in the affair was carried to court in Saarbruecken, and quite some trouble made of it.[8]

Elders Wolters and Luke had taken pictures of military sites. Fortunately, no real damage was suffered by either the missionaries or the Saints, but greater caution was encouraged among the American missionaries. Many of those young men found the Hitler movement and the rearmament of Germany to be fascinating and believed that the developments had nothing to do with the United States.[9]

As Germany's power and influence grew, Hitler initiated a series of "bloodless conquests" in Europe. One of those occurred on March 12, 1938, when the German army marched into Austria and peacefully occupied the entire country. Many of the citizens of this small nation had voted on several occasions since 1918 to be joined to Germany, but the League of Nations had forbidden the move. The German dictator asked no permission to annex the country, and the international community made no attempt to oppose the takeover. Austria's new status in Germany's Third Reich made travel for foreign missionaries between Austria and Switzerland difficult, so the decision was made to add Austria to the West German Mission. This organizational change was made with approval from Salt Lake City on November 1, 1938.[10]

The conference of the West German Mission held in Frankfurt in May 1939 was a wonderful event. The health of the branches and districts is evident from the ambitious program of the conference that lasted from Saturday until Monday, May 27–29. More than a thousand members of the Church registered for the conference, and some came from as far as nine hundred miles away. The different sessions of the conference were held in rented meeting halls in downtown Frankfurt. More than one thousand attended a testimony meeting on Sunday morning, six hundred attended the Relief Society session, and twelve hundred attended the evening session that included the performance of a play entitled *Jesus of Nazareth*. On Monday, the concluding event took place thirty miles to the west, where seven hundred Saints boarded a boat for a cruise on the Rhine River. Several members had to be turned away when the boat was filled to capacity. The mission history includes the following summary statement regarding the conference: "The entire conference was a huge success and far greater in extent and beauty than had even been hoped for. . . . The results of this conference are far reaching and the good it did in cementing bonds of understanding, friendship and cooperation in the work of the Lord in this mission can never [be] told."[11]

Following the mission conference, President Wood conducted a conference for the full-time missionaries. They met in the rooms of the historic Frankfurt city hall (Rathaus-Römer) in the oldest part of the city.

Elder George Blake of Vineyard, Utah, had been serving in the West German Mission since November 1937. In early August 1939, he was

Fig. 3. The Frankfurt city hall was decked out with the flag of the United States in May 1939.[12] (G. Blake)

transferred from the southern German town of Durlach to the mission office. He listed the following persons who lived and worked in the office as of August 18:

> Pres. M. Douglas Wood, his wife Evelyn, his daughters Carolyn (8) and Anna (16).
> J. Richard Barnes, executive secretary
> W. Elwood Scoville, financial secretary
> Elmer Tueller, priesthood support
> Arnold Hildebrand, Mutual Improvement Association (with the help of Evelyn Wood)
> Sister [Hildegard] Heimburg, translation and lesson manuals
> Sister [Ilse] Brünger, translation
> Sister [Berta] Raisch, translation (replacing Sister Brünger)
> Sister [Ilse] Krämer, maid and cook
> Grant Heber [baker], Sunday School and Primary Organizations
> [George Blake, printing, ordering books, genealogy][13]

Elder Blake described the interior of the mission home in these words:

> All six [American] missionaries lived in the attic. The Wood family lived on the second floor. The two secretaries were German ladies and they were . . . on the same or next floor up. . . . The church used the entire building and we were scattered throughout. The mimeograph room was in the basement. The entry was on the west side, not the front. The actual mission office was both the ground floor and the next one up. The ground floor was pretty much the church offices, with a nice waiting room and a large dining room and a couple of rooms for the secretaries. . . . My desk with the mimeograph machine was in the basement. We had one big community dinner on the main floor with a large table, because we had fourteen to sixteen people and a couple of cooks.[14]

Elder Blake's description of the routines in the building is both informative and entertaining:

> As for the rules, they are quite loose. 7:30 in the morning is supposed to be class (only held when apostles or other good men come). 8:00 breakfast. 12:30 dinner. Usually half an hour after dinner for reading newspaper, taking pictures, napping, playing piano etc. 6:30 supper. After supper is free unless one is overworked (which is usually the case). Operas, movies, study, visiting etc. etc. Anna [Wood] usually wants to "quatch" (throw the bull) or wants someone to take her to the movies, but is otherwise O.K.![15]

The West German Mission was experiencing a veritable golden age in the late summer of 1939, but national and international developments soon conspired to slow the Church's progress. On Thursday, August 24, 1939, instructions arrived from the office of Church President Heber J. Grant in Salt Lake City that all American missionaries were to be evacuated from the countries of central Europe. When the message arrived in Germany, President Wood was touring the mission with Elder Joseph Fielding Smith. The two leaders and their wives were in the city of Hannover, where they were contacted on Friday by the mission executive secretary, J. Richard Barnes, from the office at Schaumainkai 41. Elder Smith and President Wood immediately flew to

Frankfurt to assess the situation. The instructions were repeated in more detail on August 25 in a telegram from President Grant to Elder Smith:

> Have issued instructions to mission presidents in Holland, Denmark, Norway and Sweden to prepare to receive missionaries from Great Britain, Germany, France, and have instructed mission presidents in those latter countries to cooperate with American diplomatic representatives in evacuating the missionaries to Holland and Scandinavia. Will you kindly assume general charge and direction of this whole missionary situation.[16]

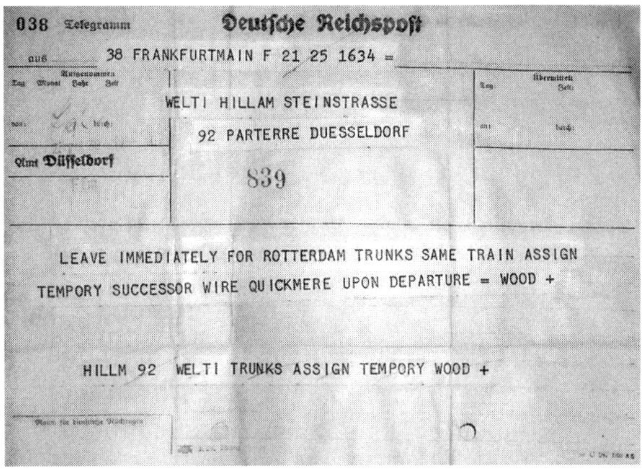

038 Telegramm Deutsche Reichspost

38 FRANKFURTMAIN F 21 25 1634 =

WELTI HILLAM STEINSTRASSE
92 PARTERRE DUESSELDORF

Amt Düsseldorf

839

LEAVE IMMEDIATELY FOR ROTTERDAM TRUNKS SAME TRAIN ASSIGN TEMPORY SUCCESSOR WIRE QUICKMERE UPON DEPARTURE = WOOD +

HILLM 92 WELTI TRUNKS ASSIGN TEMPORY WOOD +

Fig. 4. Elders Hillam and Welti were in Düsseldorf when they received this telegram instructing them to leave for the Netherlands immediately. "Assign tempory [sic] successor" meant that they were to appoint a temporary leader of the Düsseldorf Branch before departing. (C. Hillam)

The following message was sent to the mission office that same day by the United States consulate in Frankfurt:

> CONFIDENTIAL
>
> It has been learned that in view of the present tension in Europe, the American Embassy in Berlin is advising American citizens that it might be best to leave Germany. This advice, of course, does not imply that the Embassy or any officer representing the Embassy or any Consular Office can assume any responsibility in connection therewith, but each one who may act upon this suggestion or advice must do so at his own risk and responsibility.[17]

President Wood decided that a telegram must be sent to each pair of missionaries with instructions to leave for Amsterdam or Copenhagen without delay. The task fell to George Blake, as he recalled years later:

> I was in the office the 24th [25th] of August and it was my job to go to the [telegraph] office to send the telegrams . . . one to each pair. It took me all day long because [the telegraph office] was jammed with official business. So they would take one or two and then they would wait for half an hour and then they'd take another one or two. . . . [President Wood] directed me to tell everyone to either go to Amsterdam or Copenhagen, and then they were supposed to wire back saying they'd received [the message].[18]

Within days, all of the American missionaries serving in the West German Mission had been evacuated to the Netherlands or Copenhagen.[19] Based upon their experience in September and October 1938, the Americans were optimistic that they would soon be allowed to return to Germany to continue their service. However, the matter became doubtful on Friday, September 1, 1939, when the German army invaded Poland. Two days later, Great Britain and France honored their promises to resist Hitler's plans for expansion of power in Europe by declaring war on Germany. What would become known as World War II had begun.

With his characteristic industry, President Wood continued to direct the activities of the mission from Copenhagen, and with the help of Elder Barnes wrote dozens of letters back to Frankfurt. A batch of letters was sent on September 8, 1939. The first was addressed to Friedrich Biehl, a member of the Essen Branch. Brother Biehl was designated the temporary leader of the mission and was authorized to retain all current mission office staff to assist him. Part of his instructions were as follows:

> In localities where branches have diminished to exceedingly small numbers, and especially where there are no priesthood holders, it might be advisable to give up some of the [meeting halls]. . . . We don't want to let our saints down, and we want to keep up their spirit in the gospel, but naturally we can't keep up expenses very long where the income does not justify them.

> In cases such as this kind, it might be advisable to encourage the saints to hold regular meetings in their homes. . . . Some of the brethren from neighboring branches can pay them visits as often as it might be advisable and give them the sacrament. . . . I want to assure you that our faith and prayers are united for the saints there in Germany. As I said before, leaving you is the hardest thing that has come into our lives. We're counting on you, and know that you will come through for us.[20]

Regarding decisions to be made in directing the mission, Wood expressed the following philosophy:

> We feel it much more advisable to hold a strong central control, and try to save some of the expense in the smaller branches. Things will hold together much better with a strong center than if they are left too much to their own. For that reason, the office should be maintained, and some of the smaller branches closed, meetings being held in private homes. However, meetings should be held regularly where it is at all possible.[21]

President Wood then suggested that the rental of meeting rooms in the following cities be terminated as soon as the contracts allowed: Wilhelmshaven, Göttingen, Uelzen, Durlach, Saarbrücken, and Gotha. He recommended that the two branches in Wuppertal (Elberfeld and Barmen) be combined. Elder Biehl was then instructed to direct inquiries until further notice to President Thomas E. McKay, who had moved from Berlin to Basel as the temporary European mission president.

Also on September 8, President Wood wrote a personal letter to each of the five women living and working at Schaumainkai 41. Ilse Brünger was to serve as the mission secretary and office manager,[22] Hildegard Heimburg was to direct the activities of the auxiliary organizations, Berta Raisch was to keep the mission statistics and to help Sister Heimburg with translations and Sister Brünger with finances, Elfriede Marach was to assist Sister Heimburg with the auxiliaries, and Ilse Krämer was to do the cooking and housekeeping. Wood offered each a monthly salary of 50–75 Reichsmark in order to give them official status as employees and to prevent the government from compelling them to take other employment. Within days, each of the women responded affirmatively to the assignment and expressed the hope that the mission president would return soon.[23]

To the disappointment of all, Joseph Fielding Smith eventually announced that the missionaries would not be returning to Germany. Those whose terms of service were nearly completed were to be released, and the rest were to be assigned to missions in North America. Initially, M. Douglas Wood was to go to Sweden to assume the leadership of the mission there.

From Basel, President McKay sent a letter dated September 8, 1939, to be read throughout the West German Mission. The end of that letter reads:

> All who will receive this letter, must not only take care of their own responsibilities but also of those officers, teachers and members who have been called to serve their country.
>
> We pray sincerely to our Heavenly Father, that He might protect and bless those that have been called to arms and that He might strengthen those who have remained at home for the additional responsibilities that rest upon your shoulders.
>
> Don't neglect your personal and family prayers. Live a pure virtuous life, keep the Word of Wisdom, pay your tithing, fast offering and other contributions, visit and participate in all the meetings, keep free from finding fault and bearing false witness, sustain those that have been called to preside and to direct and it is our promise, that the Lord will guide and lead you in all things and that you, even in the midst of afflictions and difficulties, will find joy and satisfaction.
>
> Be always mindful that we are engaged in the work of the Lord and that Jesus is the Christ; He is our head, we are members of His Church and His truth [is] the plan of salvation. His gospel, as it has been revealed to the Prophet Joseph Smith, will be victorious. This is my testimony for you, my beloved brethren, sisters and friends. We love you and leave our blessings with you.
>
> Your Brother
>
> Thomas E. McKay, Mission President[24]

President Wood and his wife then wrote to the Frankfurt office staff to express their sorrow at not being allowed to return. A few days later, they traveled to Stockholm, Sweden, to direct the work of the mission there. In October, they were denied visas to stay and joined the missionaries returning to the United States. Wood's final letter to the Saints in Frankfurt included this message:

> Dear Brethren,
>
> During my absence I have called Brother Friedrich L. Biehl (Riehlstrasse 15 in Essen-West) to be the temporary mission supervisor of the West German Mission. I ask that you all support Brother Biehl in his work with all of your energies.
>
> I hope that you will continue to conduct the business of your branches as you have previously done. The work in the branches should not come to a standstill. Please do not forget that the work of the Lord can only go forward if you cooperate well with each other. You bear the responsibility, so please take this seriously. I trust that you will do your very best. Lead the members by your good example and fulfill your duties faithfully and conscientiously. May the spirit of brotherly love and joyful cooperation be felt everywhere.
>
> We all pray that everything will turn out well. I would be very grateful to you if I could hear from you very soon. May our Heavenly Father bless you in your work. May he bless and protect your dear German homeland.
>
> I send you my most heartfelt greetings and remain with best regards,
>
> M. Douglas Wood
> Mission President[25]

A veteran of the Swiss-German Mission (1934–1937), Friedrich "Fritz" Biehl (born 1913) was only twenty-six years of age and an elder when he became the new *Missionsleiter* (supervisor, not president) of the West German Mission. He spoke fluent English and had an engaging personality. A member of a stalwart Latter-day Saint family, he was dedicated to the work of the Church. His younger sister, Margaretha, described him as "caring, studious, and quiet, but also athletic."[26]

He lived and worked in Essen, about two hundred miles northwest of Frankfurt. Employed in a dental clinic in his home town, he took the train to Frankfurt each Friday after work and spent the weekend there. He attended church on Sunday and then took the train back to Essen late Sunday evening. According to his sister, it was an exhausting schedule, and within a few months Elder Biehl requested that his employer release him so that he could move to Frankfurt to dedicate himself full-time to the work of the Church. His employer kindly granted the request but reminded the young man that if he left Essen, he would be considered unemployed and as such would probably be drafted by the army very soon. Biehl stuck to his decision.

Fig. 5. Mission supervisor Friedrich Biehl of Essen (M. Biehl Haurand)

American missionary Erma Rosenhan (born 1915) spent some time in the Biehl home in Essen and made the following comments in her diary: "Sunday April 30, 1939: After church to Biehls for supper. Talked with Bro. Fritz Biehl. He is very brilliant. Tuesday May 9 1939: Bro. Biehl told me a lot of political jokes. Sister Rohmann complained about that."[27]

Biehl's tenure was short but productive. He wrote the following in his brief autobiography:

> With the beginning of World War II, 1 September 1939, I became the Mission Leader of the West German Mission, with headquarters in Frankfurt/Main. Every Saturday I would [travel] to Frankfurt to take care of any business that needed to be done. Several different Sundays, I visited Fall Conferences in Bielefeld, Hamburg, Hanover, Erfurt, Stuttgart, and Nürnberg. I was drafted into the army on 14 December 1939 so I could no longer function as the mission leader.[28]

As his employer in Essen had predicted, Friedrich Biehl was classified as unemployed by the city government in Frankfurt, and a draft notice

Fig. 6. Mission supervisor Christian Heck (seated in front row left) is shown here as a member of the Frankfurt District choir in 1936. (O. Förster)

from the Wehrmacht arrived in December. With this development, President McKay issued a call to Christian Heck of the Frankfurt Branch to assume leadership of the mission. Brother Heck had served as the editor of the Church's German-language publication, *Der Stern*, and was well versed in the gospel. At the time of his call, he was an unemployed salesman, but he soon found work again. His occupation required frequent travel, which allowed him to visit many of the branches in the mission for the next three and a half years. Brother Heck selected Anton Huck (Frankfurt District president) as his first counselor and Johannes Thaller (Munich District president) as his second counselor.

Heck lost no time in assuming his duties as mission supervisor. His personal records include the following travel schedule for district conferences in the fall of 1940:

29–30 August	Hanover
12–13 September	Bielefeld
19–20 September	Essen
26–27 September	Hamburg
3–4 October	Flensburg
10–11 October	Vienna
17–18 October	Karlsruhe
24–25 October	Weimar
31 October–1 November	Stuttgart
7–8 November	Nuremberg
21–22 November	Frankfurt

Only the Bremen and Karlsruhe Districts were not visited at the time.[29]

According to Luise Heck, her husband, the mission supervisor, "was seldom at home. When my youngest child was born he was at a conference in Nuremberg. He even used vacation time for conferences. My husband recorded everything and kept all of his papers in superb order. . . . He did not have enough time to keep a diary. Every day after work he went to the mission office and worked there until late at night. Most Sundays were devoted to conferences."[30]

All of the five women employed in the mission office at Schaumainkai 41 remained there for various lengths of time. Paying them a stipend (as well as granting them free room and board) was probably effective in allowing them to stay there as employees for some time.[31]

Hildegard Heimburg had served in the Swiss-German Mission (based in Basel, Switzerland) in the 1930s. She was a native of Gotha in eastern Germany but had moved with her family to Frankfurt in 1938. Her younger brother, Karl Heimburg, recalled spending time in the mission office as a volunteer: "I was an auto mechanic apprentice and worked all day long at my trade. In the evening I went to the mission office and did all the printing downstairs in the basement." He also became acquainted with the Wood family before they departed Germany.[32]

Ilse Brünger (born 1912) had joined the Church in 1938 and accepted a call as a missionary within a year. Under M. Douglas Wood, she became the secretary responsible for finances. She wrote the following about the working conditions during the war: "I loved my work. I had a very good relationship with all the district presidents and did most of the correspondence with them. The work was hard; it took long hours, but it was very rewarding. . . . Traveling was nearly impossible, yet we did travel to all [district] conferences."[33] In September 1940, Ilse was drafted to work as a censor in English and French in a military office. Her kind supervisor, a captain, allowed her to continue working in the mission office.

In 1941, government restrictions on paper supplies caused the discontinuation of the Church publication *Der Stern*. In an attempt to maintain communications with the branches, the mission office in Frankfurt published a newsletter entitled *Missions-Echo* from February 16, 1941, to at least April 17, 1941.[34] This four-page publication featured articles by Church leaders, essays by district presidents, and messages from mission leaders and office staff members. The inaugural issue began with this text:

> Today we are introducing to you a new friend, the *Missions-Echo*. This is not to be a replacement for *Der Stern* (the publication of which is only temporarily interrupted) but is designed to remind all of the Saints in the West German Mission that the mission leaders are determined to support and promote the spiritual welfare of the members. . . . This little missive will bring you greetings from the Church every Sunday and will help you to understand better the will of our Heavenly Father. . . . The messages presented in these pages should serve as an echo throughout the mission and enter into the heart of each member and bring blessings and progress.

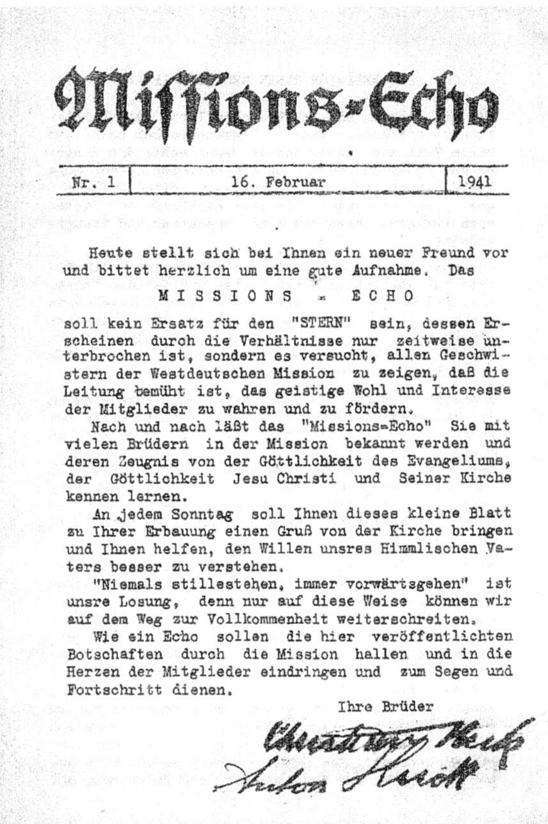

Missions-Echo

Nr. 1	16. Februar	1941

Heute stellt sich bei Ihnen ein neuer Freund vor und bittet herzlich um eine gute Aufnahme. Das

M I S S I O N S = E C H O

soll kein Ersatz für den "STERN" sein, dessen Erscheinen durch die Verhältnisse nur zeitweise unterbrochen ist, sondern es versucht, allen Geschwistern der Westdeutschen Mission zu zeigen, daß die Leitung bemüht ist, das geistige Wohl und Interesse der Mitglieder zu wahren und zu fördern.

Nach und nach läßt das "Missions=Echo" Sie mit vielen Brüdern in der Mission bekannt werden und deren Zeugnis von der Göttlichkeit des Evangeliums, der Göttlichkeit Jesu Christi und Seiner Kirche kennen lernen.

An jedem Sonntag soll Ihnen dieses kleine Blatt zu Ihrer Erbauung einen Gruß von der Kirche bringen und Ihnen helfen, den Willen unsres Himmlischen Vaters besser zu verstehen.

"Niemals stillestehen, immer vorwärtsgehen" ist unsre Losung, denn nur auf diese Weise können wir auf dem Weg zur Vollkommenheit weiterschreiten.

Wie ein Echo sollen die hier veröffentlichten Botschaften durch die Mission hallen und in die Herzen der Mitglieder eindringen und zum Segen und Fortschritt dienen.

Ihre Brüder

Fig. 7. The first edition of the Missions-Echo *appeared on February 16, 1941.*

This message bears the signatures of Christian Heck and Anton Huck. The first issue included a talk by Asahel D. Woodruff and the schedule for district conferences to be held in the spring of 1941.

That Christian Heck also visited small branches is confirmed by the minutes of meetings held in the tiny branch of Bühl, in the southwest corner of the mission. On July 13, 1941, the Saints there must have been a bit surprised to see not only Heck but also the two counselors of the faraway East German Mission, Richard Ranglack and Paul Langheinrich from Berlin. All three spoke during Sunday School.[35] Heck visited the same branch three more times by May 16, 1943, and on one occasion, he sang a solo of the beloved German hymn *Noch Nicht Erfüllt.*

Heck was a man of many talents. For a short time he had served as the editor of *Der Stern.* His daughter Hannelore (born 1939) offered this description: "He was a traveling salesman—an agent. During the depression years, that was [the only kind of work] that was available but it was not actually his occupation. He loved learning and even taught himself English out of books. He also taught himself Italian and French, although I don't know how fluent he was in those two languages."[36]

Annaliese Heck, another daughter, recounted an experience from the year 1938 that embodied her father's dedication to God:

> My parents were very spiritual. They had two children, my sister Hannelore and me, and those were difficult times. My father was a factory representative and wasn't doing very well financially. My parents had said that if my father got a good position with a steady income and he didn't have to travel as much and have so many other expenses, then they would have another child. That was in Easter 1938. And I said, "How can you do that? There will be a war within a year." And my mother said to my father, "Maybe we should rethink that decision to have another child. When we made that covenant with our Heavenly Father, we didn't know there would be a war." Then my father said, "A covenant is a covenant. War or not," and she said that she was ashamed that she had even thought of [changing their plan]. And that is precisely what they did. And then our youngest sister, Krista, was born in 1940; it was very remarkable.[37]

For the leaders of the West German Mission, the war years were not a time to rest. The mission history shows the constant influx of reports from branch and district presidents (mostly from the districts of Schleswig-Holstein, Hamburg, and Bremen). Whereas most of those reports dealt with Sunday School and sacrament meetings, Relief Society programs and district conferences, there were also numerous reports of leaders who had been drafted and therefore needed to be released and replaced. The very first report received during the war was dated Friday, September 1, 1939, and conveyed disappointing news from the distant city of Bremen:

> The meeting hall of the Bremen Branch was confiscated by the German Army. All requests, that at least one room [be] made available to the branch, are mockingly denied. "You are only trying to blunt the intellects of the people," President Willy Deters is told. Meetings in Bremen are held again in the Guttempler Logenhaus at Vegesackerstrasse. However, it is only possible to hold one Sacrament meeting on Sundays. At this time Brother Albert Adler, Brother Erwin Gulla and Brother Johann Wöltjen are called into the military service. The Bremen Branch is now under the direction of district President Willy Deters.[38]

Other reports contained the following information:

> March 16–17, 1940: The Hamburg District held its spring conference, during which five persons were baptized.[39]
>
> October 5–6, 1941: The fall conference of the Bremen District was held. Elders Heck and Huck were among the 153 persons in attendance. "The spirit of God was present in the meetings in rich abundance."[40]
>
> March 22, 1942: During the centennial celebration of the Relief Society, a play was performed in the St. Georg Branch (Hamburg District) meeting hall. The play was written by Inge Baum of the Kassel Branch (who also attended). Sisters from all over the district participated. Five hundred persons were served lunch from the branch kitchen.[41]

A curious document is found among the papers of Erwin Ruf, who was president of the Stuttgart District. Entitled "Decision," the one-page statement

Fig. 8. Christian Heck (seated in the middle of the front row) *represented the West German Mission at a conference of the East German Mission in Berlin in 1942. To his left is East German Mission supervisor Herbert Klopfer.*

is dated January 31, 1942, and appears to have been issued to dispel any doubt regarding Christian Heck's authority to function as the mission supervisor.[42] The translation of the text reads as follows:

> A council convened today consisting of the following brethren: Johann Thaller, president of the Munich District; Hermann Walther Pohlsander of Celle [representing the Hanover District], and Erwin Ruf, president of the Stuttgart District. The council arrived at the following decision:
>
> We hereby recognize Elder Christian Heck of Frankfurt/Main as the current supervisor of the West German Mission until such time as he is released from this office by Church authorities.
>
> It has also been decided that the mission leadership be expanded to include a second counselor. Brother Johann Thaller was nominated.
>
> [signed] Joh. Thaller
> H. W. Pohlsander
> Erwin Ruf
>
> The following brethren accept the above decision:
>
> [signed] Anton Huck
> Christian Heck
>
> As a witness, representing the East German Mission:
>
> [signed] Paul Langheinrich

Because there is no evidence that members of the Church questioned Heck's assignment (who by then had served in that calling for nearly two years), the document was likely produced in order to confirm the position of Heck as the spokesman of the Church in the eyes of the government. The statement may also have proved to the government the claim made by Heck that he needed to travel by rail to points all over western Germany to administer the affairs of the Church.

In the mission office, the Saints were not always unified in their political opinions. According to Ilse Brünger Förster (who married Otto Förster in December 1941), "One evening there was a big misunderstanding in the mission office due to political differences, and I saw things which were too hard for a young convert to understand. I was a young girl, still full of optimism and the hope of a bright future. I was so hurt and felt so sorry for one brother who did not agree politically with another brother and nearly had a heart attack over this conflict."[43]

Fig. 9. Mission financial secretary Ilse Brünger with her groom Otto Förster on December 20, 1941. (O. Förster)

A visit from the Gestapo frightened Ilse in June 1942. Returning with Otto from a visit in Michelstadt, she found that the office had been inspected and sealed by the secret police. The next morning, she was taken from the office to Gestapo headquarters on Lindenstrasse. She recalled the experience in these words:

> At the Gestapo Headquarters I was questioned for six hours or more and then was asked to come back the next morning with a report of all the tithing money that had been collected since 1936 and all the membership records. I told the three people who questioned me that it was impossible to obtain all that information in such a short period of time, but they requested the reports the next morning without any arguments on my part. . . . [Otto and I] sat together all through the night and worked; just before 7 o'clock the next morning the papers were ready. It is a miracle to me that we got it done. . . . I know with all my heart that God gave us this miracle to show us that he was on our side.[44]

Although none of the wartime leaders of the mission told of restrictions placed on the Church by the Gestapo, attempts were made early in the war or perhaps even prior to the war to avoid words or phrases that appeared to be foreign (non-German). As in the East German Mission, the Saints did not sing hymns featuring words such as "Israel" and "Zion"—terms directly linked with the Jewish culture so despised by the Nazis. In the West German Mission, additional linguistic alterations were introduced. For example, the names of groups and meetings were modified.[45] The term for Relief Society was changed from *Frauenhilfsvereinigung* to *Schwesternklasse* (sisters' class). The sacrament meeting was changed from *Abendmahlsversammlung* to *Predigversammlung* (sermon meeting). The term *Gemeinde* (branch) was supplanted in public literature by the word *Verein* (society). The use of the word *Kirche* (church) was even suppressed in some cases in favor of the word *Verein* (society).[46] The foreign word *Distrikt* was also replaced by the German term *Bezirk*.

Christian Heck was a loyal servant of God—a man determined to preserve the Church in Germany when no help from the United States was to be had. For example, at the conclusion of a district presidents conference held in Frankfurt on February 21, 1943, he offered this farewell:

> I wish you well on your trip home, that all of you may return to your districts with a strengthened spirit and that you will take up your work again according to the suggestions made in this conference with renewed courage and that you will use these suggestions and instructions in the future. This is not our work but the work of the Lord. This is not a matter for individuals, and not a matter for many people, but the work of God, given to man for the last time in this dispensation.[47]

On May 17, 1943, Christian Heck responded to a draft notice of the German army and was sent to the Eastern Front. His wife, Luise, recalled:

> Despite all of the opposition he faced, he did his duty until the very end. I recall very clearly—and will never forget for as long as I live—that on that last Sunday (which happened to be our wedding anniversary and Mother's Day) he spent

> the last hours doing the work of the Lord. He had had to make a last-minute trip to Bühl, Baden in order to solve some problems there.[48]

In Christian Heck's absence, the district leaders of the West German Mission met to decide whom to designate as the supervisor of the mission. Their choice was the first counselor, Anton Huck. Huck (born 1872) was too old to be drafted and would thus be likely to be able to remain in this calling for some time. He had already traveled extensively with Heck, was well known throughout the mission, and had even attended at least one conference of the East German Mission in Berlin. While he worked to maintain order at Schaumainkai 41, he was assisted all over the mission by dedicated district presidents, who likewise were constantly on the road to visit branches of the Saints in their respective areas. From the available literature, it is clear that Johann Thaller, president of the Munich District, and Kurt Schneider, president of the Strasbourg District, served as counselors to Huck. Each enjoyed the use of a company automobile for personal activities, which allowed them to travel much more frequently and much further than other district presidents.

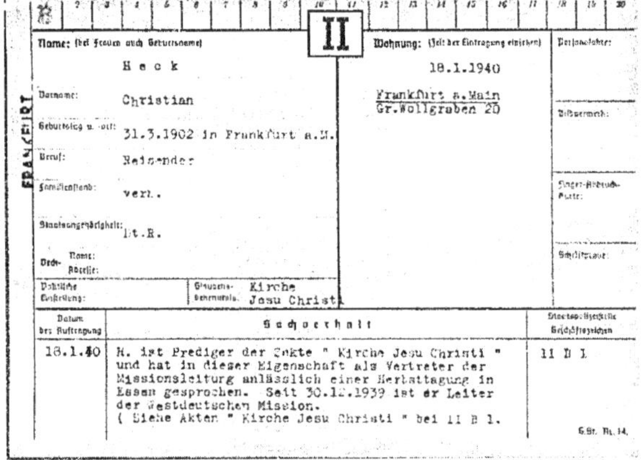
II

FRANKFURT

Name: (bei Frauen auch Geburtsname) Heck

Vorname: Christian

Geburtstag u. -ort: 31.3.1902 in Frankfurt a.M.

Beruf: Reisender

Familienstand: verh.

Staatsangehörigkeit: Dt.R.

Wohnung: 18.1.1940 Frankfurt a.Main Gr.Wollgraben 20

Glaubensbekenntnis: Kirche Jesu Christi

Datum der Auftragung	Sachverhalt	Staatspolizeistelle Geschäftszeichen
18.1.40	H. ist Prediger der Sekte " Kirche Jesu Christi " und hat in dieser Eigenschaft als Vertreter der Missionsleitung anlässlich einer Herbsttagung in Essen gesprochen. Seit 30.12.1939 ist er Leiter der Westdeutschen Mission. (Siehe Akten " Kirche Jesu Christi " bei II B 1.	II B 1

Fig. 10. The official Gestapo record of mission supervisor Christian Heck. He is classified as a traveling salesman. The note at bottom reads, "Heck is a preacher of the sect 'Church of Jesus Christ' and recently spoke at a fall conference in Essen as a representative of the mission leadership. He has been the leader of the West German Mission since December 30, 1939." (Frankfurt City Archive)[49]

Ilse Brünger Förster received a telephone call in July 1943 with the news that many Saints in Hamburg had been bombed out and several killed. She called the Relief Society president of the Frankfurt Branch,

> and within a few hours we were in touch with all the members of the Frankfurt Branch and asked them to help the members in the Hamburg area. I have never seen busier people. Everyone helped with clothing, bedding, and other items. In a very short time relief was on its way to all the members in Hamburg. At that moment I felt that we were all a big family helping and loving one another. I must say that all the things we collected were good things, not just worn out things, but the very best things and that made me feel so wonderful.[50]

In 1943, Anton Huck was for a short time a person of interest to the state police. One morning at 7:30, Gestapo agents knocked at his door and asked to see his historical records. Then they instructed him to dress and accompany them to the mission office. (They also took several Church books and pamphlets from his home.) Upon arriving at the mission office, they found six more agents going through the Church records, "especially our lesson material and our financial records." Huck was required to respond to this question: "Mr. Huck, under your leadership this mission has had a great financial increase. What is the reason for this?" His response: "Before the war we had many unemployed men and women and today they are all working and as you know, we have the law of tithing in our church. Before the war we had to spend money for missionary expenses, to build up branches, to buy furniture, organs and pianos. Today we only pay our current expenses. These are the reasons for an increase in our funds."[51] The agent was apparently satisfied with the explanation. At the end of the day, the Gestapo confiscated several books. Two days later, Huck was asked to report at Gestapo headquarters, where he underwent a lengthy interview. After the interview was properly recorded, he was asked to sign the transcript. When the entire investigation was completed, Huck was asked why he had not joined the National Socialist (Nazi) Party. He explained that he was responsible for seventy-three branches of the Church and had no time for other activities. This reply apparently did not engender the ire of the officials.[52] Perhaps they were not worried about a seventy-one-year-old man who claimed to be a church administrator and worked in a huge building that must have been mostly empty at the time.[53]

Fig. 11. Anton Huck served as the supervisor of the West German Mission for the last two years of the war. (E. Wagner Huck)

Anton Huck was a popular leader, in part because he traveled extensively both within the West German Mission and to events in the East German Mission. Maria Schlimm (born 1923) of the Frankfurt Branch had this recollection of Elder Huck: "We called him 'Papa Huck' and we liked him very much. He was already retired but had worked as a streetcar driver before that. Because he was not working anymore, they could not get him to join the [Nazi] party."[54] Several eyewitnesses had been told that Anton Huck was denied promotions by his employer because of his membership in the Church.

On October 4, 1943, a major air raid destroyed large parts of the city of Frankfurt. Anton Huck's family lost their home in the attack and they moved into rooms in the mission home with what little of their belongings they had been able to rescue from the flames. While the Hucks were sad at having lost their home, Huck now had much more time to devote to the work of the West German Mission. In a report written shortly after the war, he recalled that air raids all over the mission territory had made it impossible to maintain communications, to receive donations, and to record and deposit money safely. On several occasions, the mission received reports that funds had been transferred, but those funds never arrived.

As the war progressed, reports regarding branches in the Alsace-Lorraine province of France (occupied by German troops since 1940) arrived in the mission office. Mention was made of Latter-day Saints in the capital city of Strasbourg on the Rhine River and in Mühlhausen to the south. The general minutes of the Bühl Branch (Karlsruhe District) report a number of activities undertaken by Bühl members and their counterparts across the Rhine in Strasbourg.[55] The first such report was dated March 3, 1942: Anton Huck from the mission office conducted a funeral for a sister Maria Kuester in Strasbourg, and two members of the Bühl Branch attended the service. On April 26, 1943, eleven Bühl Saints and eight from the Strasbourg Branch had a party at the home of the Paul Kaiser family in Grüneberg, near Strasbourg.

In August 1943, a new meeting place for the Strasbourg Branch was dedicated under the leadership of Anton Huck. Eleven members of the Bühl Branch were in attendance, as were forty more members from the branches of Frankfurt, Saarbrücken, Karlsruhe, Mannheim, Pforzheim, and Freiburg. The same Paul Kaiser was the branch president in Strasbourg. On December 12, 1943, Anton Huck presided over a meeting in which a new Strasbourg District was established that included the neighboring branch in Bühl.[56] The only Alsace-Lorraine branches named in the record were those in Strasbourg and Mühlhausen. For the next year, several more activities involving Saints in France and Bühl were reported in the Bühl Branch minutes.

During the last two years of the war, air-raid alarms and attacks made it increasingly challenging to carry on the work of the West German Mission office. Equipment was moved to the rooms on the lower floors. Huck was constantly on the road, presiding over church services where no priesthood holders were present and conducting weddings and funerals in various branches. For example, after he appointed a young woman to see that meetings were held in the Bad Homburg Branch (ten miles northwest of Frankfurt), he attended the Sunday meetings on a regular basis in order to assist with the administration of the sacrament.[57] In accordance with the instructions given to the leaders of the West German Mission in 1940, Huck recalled that he "kept constantly in touch with the leaders of the East German Mission. We exchanged opinions and also things that we were in need of, as much as possible."[58]

Christian Heck had experienced the war in Russia but became quite ill and was sent home in early 1945. It may have been unfortunate that he recuperated there, because as the war drew to a close, he was sent out to fight against the invading American army in southern Germany. It was there that he was shot in the stomach in early April 1945. According to his daughter, Annaliese (born 1925), the operation to remove the bullet was successful, but his heart did not tolerate the stress, and he died in a Catholic hospital in Bad Imnau, Hohenzollern. "We received a wonderful letter from a Catholic nun informing us of my father's death," she recalled.[59] Just forty-three years old, Christian Heck became the third former or current German mission supervisor to die in World War II.[60] He was buried in Bad Imnau, 150 miles south of Frankfurt. In May 1945, a fellow soldier visited Sister Heck, informed her of the fate of her husband, and presented her with his personal effects.

A few years after the war, Luise Heck had this to say about her husband: "I comfort myself with the idea that God could have protected my husband if He had wanted to. As if by a miracle, He brought him safely back from Russia. Would it then not have been possible to protect him in his homeland?"[61]

Of the many meetings held in the mission home in the last year of the war, the sacrament meeting on February 7, 1945, may have been the most memorable, at least in the mind of Carola Walker (born 1922). She recalled that the sirens sounded just as the sacrament was being passed, and they all went downstairs without delay.

> The airplanes started to [drop their bombs] and it did not take long before we realized that we would be hit. The basement was absolutely not a safe place. The windows were above ground and offered only minimal protection together with the sand bags. . . . We knelt down to pray and I was kneeling in front of a wooden box filled with potatoes. . . . We heard the whistling of the falling bombs. I did not breathe. The detonation of the bombs made the walls sway back and forth—like a heavy earthquake. The ground was shaking and we wondered if the walls would straighten out again or if the house would collapse. We would be buried alive. I could not pray. I could not form the words to ask Heavenly Father to protect us. Every fiber of my body was crying out to Him for help. A sister kneeling beside me was praying aloud despite the whistling of the bombs. She was pleading with our Heavenly Father to protect us. I don't remember what she said but it gave me a feeling of comfort. It finally got quiet and we went outside [to] see how serious the damage was. Nothing had happened to the mission home. Beside the building there was a hole, maybe a yard in diameter. A bomb had fallen there and disappeared in the ground but not exploded. If it had exploded, we would have been buried under five stories of stone. The prayer did help.[62]

By early March 1945, the mission office on the south bank of the Main River was home to several dozen Saints from local branches who had lost their homes in air raids. Because the meeting rooms of the Frankfurt Branch at Neue Mainzerstrasse 8–10 had also been lost, Sunday meetings were being held in the mission home as well.[63] It must have been a serious challenge for the adults in the building to locate enough food in a city that had been destroyed to an appalling degree.

The war came to an end at Schaumainkai 41 on March 26, 1945. A resident in the building at the time with his family, Anton Huck was confronted

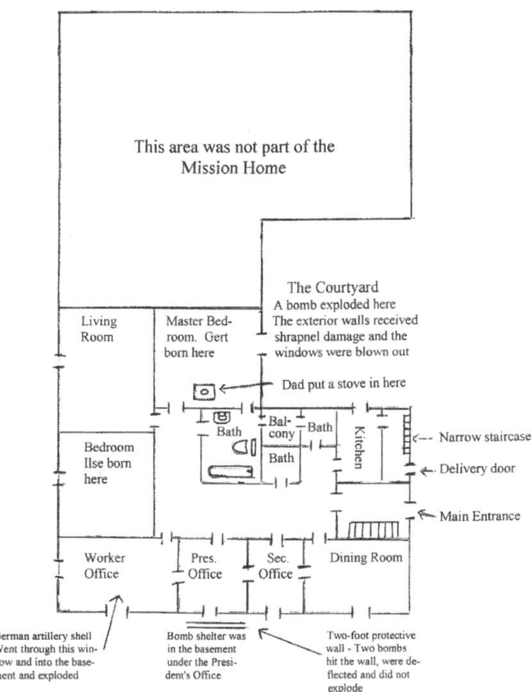

Fig. 12. Otto Förster lived in the mission home at the end of the war. He drew this plan from memory years later. The president's office was on the north side of the building facing the river. (O. Förster)

by American soldiers, who informed him at 6:45 p.m. that all occupants of the building had to be out by 7:00 p.m.; the soldiers ("about fifty of them, many of those were colored") guarding the Main River bridge just across the street were to be quartered in the building. Huck and the other LDS refugees had a very difficult time finding new rooms to inhabit. The few structures in the neighborhood that were intact were filled with people in similar circumstances. According to Huck, the invaders stayed in the building for more than a month. "In our absence much damage was done. All the suitcases, packages, and everything that was wrapped was torn open, ransacked and completely or partly destroyed. . . . It was hard to describe how bad [the damage] was." Despite the collapse of the Third Reich, the presence of the victorious Allies, the loss of Church property, and the scattering of the Saints, Huck wrote in 1946 that "the condition of the mission was spiritually and financially very good."[64]

Ilse Brünger Förster commented on the aftermath of the American occupation of the building:

> We came back only to find that all the beautiful things like china, silverware, crystal, which I had safely brought through the war, were gone. Nothing was left. The furniture that did not get damaged during the bombings was either stolen or completely destroyed maliciously by the soldiers. I cried many tears, but that did not bring back my belongings.[65]

J. Richard Barnes, the American missionary who served as executive secretary to M. Douglas Wood in August 1939, returned to Germany in 1945 as a major in the United States Army. When he found himself in the vicinity of Frankfurt, he immediately sought an opportunity to visit the mission home and determine the status of the Church. A letter he wrote to Thomas E. McKay in Salt Lake City was eventually published in the *Deseret News* under the title "War Leaves Stamp on German Mission."[66] He described his first impression in these words: "To my surprise I found that the mission home and office is still standing, and only slightly damaged. A few broken windows here and there. A bomb had hit in the little 'Hof' formed by the two parts of the building, but had only cracked the wall slightly and left a large crater."

Major Barnes expressed optimism for the future of the Church in Germany and suggested that efforts begin as soon as possible to locate the Saints who were scattered throughout the country. All fourteen districts were still functioning in 1945 under the leadership of Anton Huck, although a few branches had become defunct. The French portion of the fledgling Strasbourg District was returned to the French Mission upon the departure of German troops.

The building at Schaumainkai 41 in Frankfurt continued to serve the West German Mission after the war. The building had survived virtually intact and was used by the mission office until 1952, when new quarters were found across the river on Bettina-Strasse. Today the former mission home serves as the Deutsches Filmmuseum (German Cinema

Museum). Barnes visited the museum in the 1970s and observed that whereas the largest rooms on the main floor had been redesigned and an entrance constructed in the north facade, several offices still looked as they had in 1939.[67] The director of the museum informed the author in 2009 that the entire interior of the building had been renovated in the early 1980s and that none of the rooms look as they did during the war.

Fig. 13. The former West German Mission office at Schaumainkai 41 is now the home of the German Cinema Museum (R. Minert, 2008)

Notes

1. West German Mission History quarterly report, 1938, no. 1, CHL LR 10045 2. Philemon Kelly was succeeded in Berlin by Alfred C. Rees.
2. West German Mission History quarterly report, 1938, no. 6. It was not until August 24, 1938, that Philemon M. Kelly offered a prayer of dedication for the Frankfurt mission office. West German Mission History quarterly report 1938, no. 30.
3. For details on the Church in eastern Germany, see Roger P. Minert, *In Harm's Way: East German Latter-day Saints in World War II* (Provo, UT: Religious Studies Center, Brigham Young University, 2009).
4. Presiding Bishopric, "Financial, Statistical, and Historical Reports of Wards, Stakes, and Missions, 1884–1955," 257, CHL CR 4 12.
5. West German Mission quarterly report, 1938, no. 15. Evelyn Wood became famous years later in the United States for her speed-reading course known as "Reading Dynamics."
6. The 1938 year-end report showed the following: "Members 5190 plus 134 baptisms = 5332; 13 districts; 68 organized branches (48 presided over by local leaders); 89 missionaries; 47 children of record baptized, 87 converts baptized; 1090 full tithe payers, 522 part, 1347 non-tithe payers; 1219 members paid fast offerings (per capita mission average $0.60)." West German Mission quarterly report 1938, no. 46.
7. West German Mission quarterly report, 1938, no. 34.
8. West German Mission quarterly report, 1938, no. 38.
9. The diaries of several Americans who served in the West German Mission in the late 1930s reflect a fascination with the Third Reich. Many felt that Hitler did indeed offer Germans a promising and prosperous future.
10. West German Mission quarterly report, 1938, no. 41.
11. West German Mission quarterly report, 1939, nos. 20–22.
12. It is interesting to note that the flag in this 1939 photograph had only forty-five stars rather than forty-eight. This was the flag flown in the United States from 1896 to 1908, following the admission of Utah as a state. The outdated flag was probably procured by the city around the turn of the century and kept for subsequent events.
13. George Blake, papers, CHL MS 17781.
14. George Blake, papers. In March 1945, the following persons and families also lived in the building: Dr. Richter (second floor), Dominick (third floor), Hecht (fourth floor), caretaker Mr. Armbruester (fifth floor). Each tenant also had a storage room on the fifth floor. Several of those rooms were used as bedrooms for missionaries (Ilse Foerster Young).
15. George Blake, papers.
16. M. Douglas Wood, papers, CHL.
17. Ibid.
18. George Blake, interview by the author, Provo, UT, April 1, 2009.
19. The adventures of many of those missionaries are recounted in Terry Bohle Montague, *Mine Angels Round About*, 2nd ed. (Orem, UT: Granite, 2000). The missionaries were in a hurry to leave at the time but were not in any danger. American citizens were not required to leave the country in August 1939, and indeed several hundred Americans stayed safely in Germany until the two nations exchanged declarations of war in December 1941. Several dozen American citizens were still in Germany in 1942 and were interned in a luxury hotel in Bad Homburg until the war ended. Whereas it is possible that some Germans feared invasion from France or even air raids, none of the American missionaries are quoted as having shared that fear when they departed Germany.
20. M. Douglas Wood, papers.
21. M. Douglas Wood to Friedrich Biehl, September 8, 1939.
22. The sum of 21,000 Reichsmark was held in accounts in several banks at the time. Wood instructed Sister Brünger to withdraw the money and hide it if there was any chance that it would be confiscated by the government. Wood believed that tithing payments would drop substantially as members lost their jobs, but he wanted the mission office to remain open as long as possible.
23. M. Douglas Wood, papers.
24. Thomas E. McKay, papers, CHL B 1381:3.

25. M. Douglas Wood, papers.
26. Margaretha Biehl Haurand, interview by the author, Bountiful, UT, February 16, 2007.
27. Erma Rosehan, papers, CHL MS 16190.
28. Friedrich Ludwig Biehl, autobiography (unpublished), 194; private collection.
29. Christian Heck, papers, 12, CHL MS 651.
30. Luise Heck to Justus Ernst, October 20, 1960; Christian Heck, papers, CHL MS 651.
31. Anton Huck recalled that each of the women was released at the proper time, but it is not known precisely when they came to the mission office. If all of them were indeed released on schedule, none would have been at Schaumainkai by 1942. The Barnes letter of 1945 makes it clear that this did not happen.
32. Karl Heimburg, interview by the author, Sacramento, California, October 24, 2006.
33. Ilse Wilhelmine Friedrike Brünger Förster, autobiography (unpublished, about 1981); private collection.
34. Copies of eleven issues of the *Missions-Echo* were provided to the author by Gustav Karl Hirschmann.
35. Bühl Branch general minutes, 105, CHL LR 1180 11.
36. Hannelore Heck Showalter, telephone interview with the author, March 9, 2009.
37. Annaliese Heck Heimburg, interview by the author, Sacramento, California, October 24, 2006.
38. Annaliese Heck Heimburg, interview by the author, Sacramento, California, October 24, 2006.
39. West German Mission History, March 16–17, 1940, CHL A 2998:217.
40. West German Mission History, October 5–6, 1941, CHL B 1381 5.
41. West German Mission History, March 22, 1942, CHL A 4560:71–72.
42. Stuttgart Germany District general minutes, CHL LR 16982 11.
43. Ilse Brünger Förster, autobiography. Most eyewitnesses would assume that the two were Christian Heck and Anton Huck.
44. Ilse Brünger Förster, autobiography. Ilse claimed that Christian Heck did not assist her in this crisis. "He said that I was the secretary and responsible for everything. That was one of the hardest things for me as a young convert to understand."
45. To date, no literature has been found to explain the reasons for the changes in these terms, but the substitute names are found in the minutes of branches all over the mission.
46. The two dominant churches in Germany at the time (the Roman Catholic and Lutheran Churches) were still slow to grant the Latter-day Saints the status of Church members. See the Stuttgart Branch chapter for an example of interaction between the Lutheran Church and the LDS Church.
47. Christian Heck, papers.
48. Luise Heck to Justus Ernst, October 20, 1960, Christian Heck papers.
49. The author expresses his gratitude to Lutz Becht for locating this document in the archive and providing a digital image.
50. Ilse Brünger Förster, autobiography.
51. Anton Huck, statement, March 17, 1946, CHL LR 10045, vol. 1.
52. The question of Anton Huck's Nazi Party membership is one that has been debated for years. Several eyewitnesses, who requested anonymity when interviewed by the author, insisted that Huck was a party member and that he wore the small, round, party swastika lapel pin on his suit coat. One eyewitness clearly recalled hearing Huck pray for Adolf Hitler in a Church meeting (and being reprimanded publicly by the branch president for doing so). Several persons have stated that it was Anton Huck who required the president of the St. Georg Branch in Hamburg to display a sign with the wording "Juden Verboten" (Jews forbidden) by the entrance to the branch meeting hall (see Hamburg–St. Georg Branch chapter). Just after the war, it was suggested that Huck had visited branches in Alsace-Lorraine (the Strasbourg District included occupied French territory bordering the Rhine River) and recommended that the Saints there (most of whom were French citizens) should support Hitler in his righteous campaigns.
53. Erich Bernhardt (born 1920) was one of many eyewitnesses who were convinced that Elder Huck was an enthusiastic party member. He made the following statement: "The fact is, that I don't know why Br. Huck became a mission president, knowing that he approved the Nazis one hundred percent and there are a whole number of leaders who also were involved. Brother Biehl was not one of those. I don't want to mention any names, but Huck was very well known as a Nazi." Erich Bernhardt, oral history interview, 10, CHL MS 8090.
54. Maria Schlimm Schmid, interview by the author in German, Frankfurt, August 18, 2008; unless otherwise noted, summarized in English by Judith Sartowski.
55. Bühl Branch general minutes, 144, CHL LR 1180 11.
56. Bühl Branch general minutes, 150.
57. See the Bad Homburg Branch section.
58. Anton Huck, statement, March 17, 1946.
59. Annaliese Heck Heimburg, interview.
60. The first was Friedrich Biehl and the second was Herbert Klopfer of the East German Mission, who died in a Soviet POW camp on March 19, 1945.
61. Christian Heck, papers, 75.
62. Carola Walker Schindler, autobiography (unpublished), private collection. Used with permission of Karl Schindler. This event was also recorded in the general minutes of the Frankfurt am Main Branch on February 7, 1945, and mentioned in a report written by J. Richard Barnes a few months later.
63. Maria Schlimm Schmidt, interview by the author in German, Frankfurt am Main, August 18, 2008.
64. Anton Huck, statement, March 17, 1946.
65. Ilse Brünger Förster, autobiography.
66. *Deseret News*, July 2, 1945.
67. John Richard Barnes, recollections, 1985; courtesy Terry Bohle Montague.

Former mission supervisor Christian Heck died from wounds in a Catholic hospital in Bad Imnau just nineteen days before the war ended. Several years later, this stone was placed in the local cemetery for him and another soldier (R. Minert 2010).

BIELEFELD DISTRICT

West German Mission

Of the fourteen districts of the West German Mission, the district centered in Bielefeld, Westphalia, was the eighth largest, with a total of 326 members. Exactly 50 percent of the Saints in the district were females twelve years of age and older. This reflects a trend throughout The Church of Jesus Christ of Latter-day Saints in both German missions. At the same time, only fifty-six men in Bielefeld District's five branches—less than one-half of those over twelve years old—held the priesthood.

Bielefeld District[1]	**1939**
Elders	17
Priests	13
Teachers	9
Deacons	17
Other Adult Males	63
Adult Females	163
Male Children	23
Female Children	21
Total	326

The city of Bielefeld was located near the center of the district territory. The remaining four branches were situated to the north and east of Bielefeld: Herford (eight miles), Minden (twenty miles), Stadthagen (thirty miles), and Münchehagen (thirty-five miles). With the exception of Münchehagen, all of those cities enjoyed excellent railroad connections, which enabled leaders and members to travel to meetings in various locations.

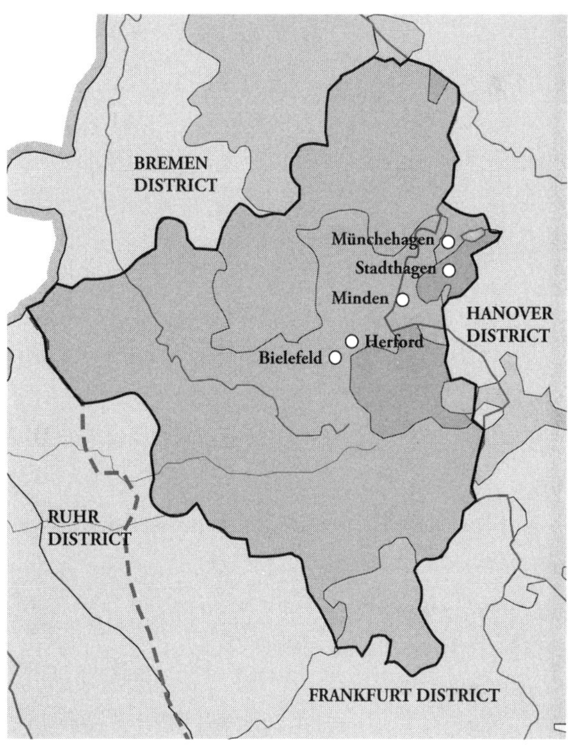

Fig. 1. The territory of the Bielefeld District in northwest Germany.

Fig. 2. Attendees at a district conference in Bielefeld in the early war years. (E. Schmitz Michaelis)

At the onset of World War II, the district was under the leadership of Alfred Hegemeister, who lived in Stadthagen. He had no counselors but was assisted by a secretary, Heinrich Rahde of Heuerssen (Stadthagen Branch). According to the mission directory, more than one-half of the district leadership positions were not filled in August 1939. Members from just two branches filled the remaining district callings. Representing the Bielefeld Branch were Sunday School president Heinrich Recksiek, YMMIA president Martha Klöpper, Primary president Luise Bokermann, and Relief Society president Anna Recksiek. YMMIA president Friedrich Möller belonged to the Stadthagen Branch. All served without secretaries, but there is no reason to believe that the programs of the Church were not in full operation in the Bielefeld District.

The last district conference held before the war took place in the city of Bielefeld on February 26 and 27, 1939. The theme was from John 8: "Know the truth and the truth shall make you free."[2] The history of the Bielefeld Branch described the event in these words: "More than 800 persons participated in the spring conference of the Bielefeld District, including mission president M. Douglas Wood. For the first time, two-color printed invitations were distributed among members and friends."[3]

Werner Niebuhr (born 1916) of the Bielefeld Branch enjoyed only six days with his new bride after their wedding in 1940, while Werner was on leave from his Wehrmacht unit. When he returned to duty, he prayed earnestly for an opportunity to attend the next district conference. But how could he possibly get leave again so soon? One day, his company commander invited him for a drink, but Werner declined, based on his health standards. The officer insisted, but Werner turned him down repeatedly and was surprised to be given three days' leave for his integrity. The leave allowed him to attend district conference, where he was asked by mission supervisor Friedrich Biehl to speak on Sunday afternoon. "I told them how thankful I was

Fig. 3. Surviving members of the Bielefeld District in 1946. (H. Recksiek)

for my testimony of the gospel and how the gospel had helped me so far in my life to understand and do the will of our Father in Heaven," Werner said. After his nearly one-half hour talk, Werner hurried off to catch the train back to his unit. After the war, a Brother Kapp of the Herford Branch thanked Werner for giving that talk, during which Kapp had gained a testimony and decided to join the Church. Werner wrote these words: "I am very thankful that I refused to drink with my captain and he gave me the furlough that I could attend this conference and bear my testimony and bring one brother into the Church."[4]

As was common in the German missions in those years, President Hegemeister not only presided over his own district conferences but also attended conferences in other districts. For example, he was present at the conference of the Ruhr District in 1939.

The records of the West German Mission office in Frankfurt do not include reports from the Bielefeld District for the war years, but it can be presumed that the district president made every effort to visit branches and hold district conferences whenever practicable. According to Bielefeld Branch member Heinz Recksiek, a large meeting hall at the factory where his father, branch president Heinrich Recksiek, lived and worked was made available to the Church for district conferences early in the war.[5]

When World War II came to an end on May 8, 1945, all of the branches in the Bielefeld District were still in existence and holding meetings on at least a sporadic basis.

Notes

1. Presiding Bishopric, "Financial, Statistical, and Historical Reports of Wards, Stakes, and Missions, 1884–1955," 257, CHL CR 4 12.
2. West German Mission quarterly report, 1939, no. 10, CHL LR 10045 2.
3. *Chronik der Gemeinde Bielefeld, 1896–1996* (Bielefeld: Bielefeld LDS Ward, 1996), 49.
4. Werner Niebuhr, autobiography, 1985, 17–18, CHL MS 19617.
5. Heinz Recksiek, interview by Marion Wolfert in German, Salt Lake City, March 22, 2006; summarized in English by Judith Sartowski.

Bielefeld Branch

One of the largest branches in the West German Mission in 1939, the Bielefeld Branch numbered 144 members, fully one-sixth of whom were priesthood holders. The city of Bielefeld, located in the northeast corner of the state of Westphalia, had a population of 126,711 at the time.[1]

The president of the Bielefeld Branch from 1938 until after the war was Heinrich Recksiek.[2] He lived with his family on the grounds of the Ross & Kahn clothing factory at Friedenstrasse 32, where he worked as a mechanic and custodian. Anna Recksiek was the branch Relief Society president during the war and was not employed. Their son, Heinz (born 1924), recalled that both branch and district conferences were held in the meeting hall of the clothing factory on several occasions during the first years of the war.[3] This was an important benefit of the branch president's employment, as was the use of the company automobile.

Bielefeld Branch[4]	**1939**
Elders	7
Priests	4
Teachers	3
Deacons	10
Other Adult Males	25
Adult Females	80
Male Children	4
Female Children	11
Total	144

According to the 1939 directory of the West German Mission, the Bielefeld Branch met in rooms at Ravensbergerstrasse 45. Elfriede Recksiek (born 1925) described the rooms rented in that building:

> There was one large room, and two smaller ones of which we used one as the cloak room. We also had restrooms in the building. The rooms were on the main floor of the building. I also remember seeing a sign of our church in the front of the building that indicated that we met there. We had chairs in our rooms, not benches, but that allowed us to move them around. There was also a raised platform in the front of the room. A choir sang sometimes, and we also had a piano and an organ that we could use to accompany. I would say that we had an attendance of about 50–60 people there on Sunday. I can remember having pictures of Jesus Christ on the wall.[5]

The branch observed the usual meeting schedule, holding Sunday school at 10:00 a.m. and sacrament meeting at 7:00 p.m. Each organization had a full complement of leaders. The MIA and the Primary met on Tuesday evening, and the priesthood meeting was held on Thursday evening. As of July 1939, an English class took place on Wednesdays at 8:30 p.m. and a teacher training class on the first Sunday of each month after sacrament meeting.[6] There was certainly no lack of activities in this branch when the war began. Heinz had this to say about the young people in the branch: "The branch was quite large with many children. We had good relationships and interactions among the young people. Whenever we got together, we had a wonderful and fun time. . . . We had many outings with the MIA."

Elfriede recalled the following about the routine of going to church:

> It took us about twenty to thirty minutes to reach the meeting rooms when we walked. My mother always said that if there are no bombs, we could walk. We walked there in the morning, came back for lunch, and went back for sacrament meeting, which started at 7:00 p.m. Especially in the winter, it was dark and there were hardly any streetlights left [due to the blackout]. But it was safe for us. We also wore a fluorescent button on our jackets so that we would be seen in the dark.

Eleonore Schmitz (born 1936) recalled that as a little girl, she and her younger sister Rosemary sang duets:

Fig. 1. Bielefeld Branch members in the main meeting room in about 1939. (E. Schmitz Michaelis)

> My aunt taught us some hymns, and we had to sing them standing next to the pump organ. Rosemary must have been six, and I was seven. We did it more than once. In one of the hymns, we started singing faster, and the sister who was playing the organ had a hard time keeping up with us.[7]

The history of the Bielefeld Branch reports some of the difficulties experienced by the Saints in that city very early on:

> During the war years, attendance at branch meetings decreased significantly. For this reason, we had to rent smaller rooms on Friedrichstrasse and until November 23, 1941 we rented rooms from Mr. Schlüter on Ravensbergerstrasse. Under those difficult circumstances we moved into other rooms at Am Sparrenberg 8 as of November 30, 1941. At that location we used a large meeting hall and a separate room in the back.[8]

Heinz Recksiek recalled the news of war with Poland in September 1939:

> At that time, I was only fifteen years old and a member of the Hitler Youth. We were more or less obligated to join the Hitler Youth. I remember being told that the Polish people were persecuting the German families who still lived in that [Polish] corridor, which was given back to Poland after World War I. And I remember Hitler saying that we were now justified in attacking Poland. As young men only fifteen years of age, we believed that.

One of the first young men of the Bielefeld Branch to wear the uniform of the Wehrmacht was Werner Niebuhr (born 1916). In June 1941, he found himself among the soldiers invading the Soviet Union. He had expected to experience terrible things in combat, but what he saw in Russia was shocking. He recalled:

> As we tried to shoot at the bunkers we found out that [the enemy] had women and children bound with rope in front of the bunkers so we would not shoot at the bunkers. . . . Something

Fig. 2. Heinz Recksiek (in light shirt) with members of his Hitler Youth unit in about 1938. (H. Recksiek)

> else that the Russians had done that I have never seen before . . . was [the enemy] had put their own soldiers in foxholes, buried them with dirt to the chest, put in front of them pile of ammunition and a rifle so that they could shoot at us and could not retreat when we came. I have never seen anything so inhumane as this before.[9]

Werner's unit moved to many locations along the southern reaches of the Russian Front, including the Crimea, where a belated message from home reached him in February 1942. His wife, Hilda, had given birth to their first child the previous October, but the child was stillborn. Under a new Wehrmacht regulation, Werner was allowed a short leave due to this death in the family.

Shortly after his return to Russia in March 1942, Werner ran into another member of the Bielefeld Branch, Walter Recksiek (born 1919). Walter had volunteered for service in the Waffen-SS, where he had been promised better conditions, equipment, transportation, etc. However, he had found out that service with the Waffen-SS was not all pleasant. Werner recalled Walter's words in Russia: "If I knew then what I know now, I would never have joined the Waffen-SS." It is very possible that Walter's unit had been in the area behind the lines where political prisoners and Jews were being sought out for *Sonderbehandlung* ("special treatment," a euphemism for murder).[10]

Just a few months later, the Recksiek family received the letter feared by every German family in those years: "It is my sad duty to inform you that your son, Walter Recksiek, gave his life for his country near Terekbogen on the morning of September 26, 1942." Unlike many German families, the Recksieks at least were fortunate enough to receive a photograph of their son's grave.

When the war began, Elfrieda Recksiek was in the League of German Girls. "We mostly sang and had to march. We camped outside and cooked together.

Sehr geehrter

Herr R e c k s i e k !

Ich muss Ihnen eine traurige Mitteilung machen. Am 26.9.1942 ist am Terekbogen vormittags Ihr Sohn Walter den Heldentod für sein Vaterland gestorben.

Im Zuge seiner Ausbildung für die aktive Führerlaufbahn war er kurzfristig als MG.-Truppführer zur Sicherung der Feuerstellung eingeteilt. Dort traf ihn bei der Sicherung seiner die Geschütze bedienenden Kameraden aus der Flanke die tödliche Kugel.

Seine Ausbildung stand vor dem Abschluss. Leider hat es das Schicksal nicht gewollt, dass er wieder als Führer vor seine Kameraden treten konnte.

Wir alle, die gesamte Batterie und ich insbesondere, der ich mich sehr um eine gute Ausbildung und sein Fortkommen bemühte, verlieren in ihm einen lieben und von allen geachteten Kameraden. Im Ehrenbuch der Batterie wird sein Name seinen Mitkämpfern stets das Vorbild eines tapferen Soldaten sein, der für Deutschland, damit dieses lebe, das grösste Opfer, sein eigenes Leben gab.

Wir haben Ihren Sohn neben anderen Kameraden des Regiments in Gnadenburg am Terek zur letzten Ruhe gebettet. Eine Aufnahme von seinem Grabe wird Ihnen später zugesandt.

Möge Ihnen die Tatsache, dass er im festen Glauben an unseren Führer und unser Vaterland sein Leben gab, dass auch wir hier alle täglich erneut einsetzen, ein Trost sein und eine Beruhigung, dass er durch Herzschuss fiel, also nicht mehr gelitten hat.

Ich grüsse Sie in tiefem Mitgefühl.

H e i l H i t l e r !

gez. Müller

SS Hauptsturmführer und Batteriechef.

Daß vorstehende(r) Abschrift — Auszug — mit der Urschrift wörtlich übereinstimmt, wird hiermit bescheinigt.

Bielefeld, den 12. 12. 1942.

Der Oberbürgermeister

als Ortspolizeibehörde

2. Polizeirevier

Gebührenfrei

Fig. 3. This letter announced the death of Walter Recksiek in 1942. (H. Recksiek)

Fig. 4. The grave of Walter Recksiek (far left) in the Soviet Union. (H. Recksiek)

I had a lot of fun, and I think the other girls did too. We also had a uniform." When she finished public school at fourteen, she began training as a nanny.

Heinz Recksiek had been drafted just weeks before Walter's death and was in boot camp in Cologne to train as a combat engineer. "My parents visited me, and I wondered why they would come to visit me. Then I realized that they wanted to tell me in person [about Walter]. I admired and adored my older brother, and my parents knew that. He was a wonderful example of a member of the Church."

Fig. 5. Heinz Recksiek as a Wehrmacht soldier. (H. Recksiek)

Regarding his response to the draft notice, Heinz recalled, "The Church always told us that we should serve our country, so that is what I did. My father never agreed with that. At one point, he was close to being put into a concentration camp. He had made a remark about the government to somebody at his work. He had to talk his way out of it."

During the year 1942, Werner Niebuhr was constantly in and out of combat. Although he was not trained as a medic, he often found himself caring for wounded comrades, and it was this kind of service that merited him the Iron Cross Second Class during one engagement. Under challenging conditions, he first developed diphtheria, then typhus, in consecutive months. These illnesses necessitated time away from the front, but this turned out to be a blessing. By the time he returned to his unit, 60 percent of the men had been killed or wounded—all of the men attached to the same mobile artillery piece. Because he continued to be ill, he was sent home for a longer leave. By March 1943, he was back in the Soviet Union.[11]

After eighteen months of training as a nanny, Elfriede Recksiek left Bielefeld to assist the family of Kurt Schneider. Brother Schneider was the president of the new Strasbourg District in southwest Germany, and Elfriede's parents were pleased to have their daughter serve in the home of another

LDS family. The Schneiders had one son and were expecting a second child. It was 1943, and Bielefeld was becoming a dangerous place to live.

Fig. 6. Branch president Heinrich Recksiek with his family before the war. (H. Recksiek)

Fig. 7. Bielefeld Hitler Youth marching in a parade. (H. Recksiek)

In the Soviet Union in 1943, Werner Niebuhr was in perilous situations on several occasions. Once, he worked his way deep into and out of a minefield in order to retrieve the body of a fallen sergeant. On another occasion, he was running between foxholes when three shells landed within fifteen feet of him in quick succession. Each shell was a dud. He recalled, "Each one could have killed me if it had exploded. I cannot be thankful enough that our Father in Heaven saved me on different occasions."[12]

Heinz Recksiek's unit was stationed along the northern flank of the Eastern Front. As a member of the 16th Engineer Battalion, he was soon a corporal and was awarded the Iron Cross for heroism in battle. However, he came very close to being killed there in late 1943:

> There was a grenade that you cannot hear until it is already going off. This one I did not see or hear, so it went off close to where I was standing. Just before it went off, I put my head down, and that was a good thing because I was wearing my helmet. The shrapnel would have hit me right in the chest and head. I was taken to the field hospital, and they operated right there. They found out that something had penetrated my lung. It was quite serious. A day later, they transported me by train to Finland. I stayed there over Christmas, but I was able to send a little note to my parents telling them that I was recuperating. Six weeks later, I was sent to the Harz mountain region [in Germany].

Werner Niebuhr was fortunate to be home for Christmas in 1943, when he saw his infant son, Roland, for the first time. Because he was an elder and had maintained the Church's standards of worthiness, he was able to give a blessing to a Sister Wächter, who was expecting a child and had been told that there were serious complications. He promised her that all would be well, and so it was: the physician's negative prediction was not fulfilled, and the baby was born entirely normal and healthy.[13]

Following the disastrous defeat at Stalingrad in February 1943, the German army began a slow

Fig. 8. Members of the Bielefeld Branch on an outing in the early war years. (E. Schmitz Michaelis)

and agonizing retreat westward toward Germany. Werner's unit was shifted many times during the last two years of the war and eventually traveled south to Bucharest, Romania; west to Vienna, Austria; north to Prague, Czechoslovakia; and then northwest to Poland. From there, they went south again to Romania and west into Hungary. In action again, Werner pondered about how he "had been saved so many times where my life had been spared when it could have gone the other way. Every day my prayer was that my life would be saved that I could go home."[14]

With time, the Allied air campaign against cities in western Germany intensified. The branch history provides this picture of meetings in 1943:

> Only one meeting was being held each Sunday. We held Sunday school and sacrament meeting on alternate Sundays, always ending before 4:00 p.m. so that the members would have time to get home again before the anticipated air raid sirens sounded. In those days, we usually had thirty to forty people in attendance.[15]

Anna Carolina Schmitz instructed her children carefully about the sirens that announced impending danger. In the early years of the war, they simply went down into the basement when the sirens sounded, but on one occasion they had a very close call, according to Eleonore: "Next door to us in the same building was a lady, she was not LDS, but she was pregnant and had just had a baby. So my mother was helping her into the bomb shelter one day, and just as my mother got in, a bomb hit right outside in the street. The air pressure slammed the door into her back, but didn't hurt her very much." After that, Sister Schmitz took her children down the street to a bona fide bunker that was located very close to the rooms where they met for church. They were sitting inside that bunker one day when their apartment house was hit and burned to the ground.

By the summer of 1944, Heinz Recksiek had recovered from his wounds and was part of a reserve unit in western Germany. Again he had a close brush with death:

> We were stationed right next to an Autobahn bridge. We saw the [Allied] planes flying over us right into the heart of Germany. I had a strange feeling and the air was literally vibrating. . . . We went down to seek shelter. . . . A door led to a room in which all of the cables of the bridge were anchored. We were just halfway down the stairway when we heard the bombs falling. Then I heard the voice people had been talking about in Church all the time. It pierced my soul and told me to go back upstairs. That is what I did. Back on top again, I crouched down on the ground and put my arms over my head. When it was over, I uncovered my face and saw that the bridge had ripped out all the cables that were anchored in that room down below. I would have been killed. My buddy had stayed in that chamber. When I looked around, I seemed to be the only man alive.

The Schneiders in Strasbourg had two sons. With the American Army approaching the city in the fall of 1944, Kurt Schneider took his family and their nanny, Elfriede Recksiek, east across the Rhine River to the town of Schönwald in Baden's Black Forest. Elfriede was soon assigned by the government to work in a division of the steel factory where Brother Schneider was employed.

One day in 1944, Werner Niebuhr was shot in the leg and left by comrades during a hasty retreat before a Red Army attack on the Eastern Front. Werner tried to stop the bleeding and walk away from the fight but kept falling. Some resistance was overpowering him. While praying for help, he heard a voice as clear and loud as his own saying, "For you the war is over, and you never have to bear arms again; you will go home." However, resistance was strong as he tried to drag himself away from the enemy. "I heard a voice saying, 'You are a holder of the Melchizedek Priesthood; you can command Satan to leave.' . . . So I commanded Satan to leave up from my body so I could go home and do the things my heart desired." Werner made it back to his friends and was transported away from the fighting, but for several days there was no physician in the area to treat his wound. Several times, he loosened the tourniquet to allow some flow of blood into his leg, fearing that if he did not, his leg would have to be amputated. Eventually, he was treated and had some feeling in his leg, but he could not walk. One month later, he was in a hospital in St. Pölten, Austria, still unable to walk without support.[16]

With her home destroyed and her husband in Russia, Anna Carolina Schmitz moved into a small cabin in a refugee colony recently constructed in the Bielefeld suburb of Brackwede. As Eleonore recalled, they were nearly destitute: "We had a sofa that was being repaired. That was the only thing we saved because it was not in the apartment when the building burned. And we had two suitcases that my oldest sister had taken to the bomb shelter, and they contained my father's clothing. Otherwise, we had nothing." Sister Schmitz spent a great deal of time gathering food from local farmers and forests during the final months of the war, when the food distribution system that had worked so well began to break down. The older children were also constantly on the lookout for food from all possible sources. It was a time of survival that would only become more challenging when the war ended.

On September 30, 1944, Allied bombs totally destroyed the rooms in which the branch was holding meetings. Fortunately, much of the branch property was not destroyed, because it had been distributed among members for safekeeping. Beginning on October 15, 1944, meetings were held in the home of the Wächter family at Lange Strasse 47.[17]

By January 1945, Werner Niebuhr had recovered sufficiently to be sent home for a month. He arrived in January 1945 and found that Hilda and Roland were living out in the country with his aunt. Little Roland did not know his father and at one point asked him to leave. His furlough was doubled when he was surprised to receive a letter granting him another twenty-four days of leave due to bravery under fire. Therefore, he was in Bielefeld until March 1945, when, as he recalled, "practically no German soldier was home." Upon leaving, he sensed his wife's fears and promised her, "Nothing will have happened to me if you don't get a letter [from me] in the next 3 months."[18]

Werner's odyssey took him from Bielefeld to Hanover to Vienna, where complications with his leg led him to another hospital. He was then sent west to Krems and Linz in Austria, where he was told simply to go home. Near Halberstadt in north-central Germany, he was captured by American soldiers. He was first put in a former concentration camp, then moved to Merseburg and Naumburg, where he was released and told to get to the British Occupation Zone in three days. He went to Sangerhausen, then Nordhausen, Hameln, and Bielefeld. He arrived there on Sunday, June 24, 1945—three months and two days after leaving his wife. "How great was our togetherness that I could be home again after this long and terrible time."[19] The following Sunday, Werner joined the surviving members of the Bielefeld Branch meeting in the home of Sister Wächter.[20]

In early 1945, Elfriede Recksiek was allowed to leave the Schneider family and her employment in Schönwald and return to Bielefeld. She found that her home town had been extensively destroyed. The church rooms, too, had fallen victim to Allied bombs, and meetings were being held in the apartments of branch members. Her parents' home had been destroyed, and they had moved in with Elfriede's grandparents just outside of town. The Recksieks did not have a chance to participate in branch meetings again until after the war. For the remainder of the war, Elfriede worked in an office of the German army and lived in Bielefeld with the Schabberhardt family, who were members of the branch.

Heinz Recksiek's unit retreated toward Bielefeld in the spring of 1945, and he was not far from his home town when the group decided to become civilians to avoid capture by the invaders. Up to that point, he had carried the holy scriptures with him, but this was not possible when he discarded his uniform. While he thought he could pass himself off as a civilian, he was undone by a photograph of his brother, Walter. The two boys looked so much alike that the British soldiers who caught up with Heinz on April 20, 1945, thought that he was the one in the photograph and treated him like a soldier. A few days later, he was turned over to the Americans, who put him in a POW camp in southern Germany. He was fortunate to be released just three months later.

On April 4, 1945, the American army entered Bielefeld, and the city surrendered without a fight. No meetings were held the next Sunday, but LDS services continued one week later with the permission of the military occupation authorities. Approximately thirty persons attended.[21]

Fig. 9. Brother Heinrich Recksiek conducted the funeral of Wilhelmine Bokermann, who was killed in a streetcar accident in 1941. (E. Schmitz Michaelis)

Engelbert Schmitz had worked as a tailor in the employ of the city for the first few war years, but eventually the Wehrmacht came for him, and he spent the remainder of the war on the Eastern Front. He was wounded in the arm, and the bullet was never removed. But no real damage was done, and he finally came home to his family in the spring of 1945. Eleonore recalled how her father let his children feel the bullet in his arm. The Schmitz family had been isolated from the Saints in Bielefeld and did not establish contact again until they were given a small attic apartment in town in about December 1945. However, they were together again. Herr Schmitz had been given his former job with the city, and conditions slowly began to improve.

The city of Bielefeld had been attacked from the air twenty-three times; 40 percent of the city was destroyed, and at least 1,349 people had been killed.[22] Ten or more of those were Church members, and the branch history also lists ten soldiers who were killed or were missing in action by the end of the war. Several Saints died of other causes, and the Bielefeld Branch suffered more than any other branch in the West German Mission. Fortunately, those losses did not prevent the branch from prospering during the next few years as the city of Bielefeld gradually came back to life.

In Memoriam

The following members of the Bielefeld Branch did not survive World War II:

Ludwig August Karl von Behren b. Gellershagen, Bielefeld, Westfalen, 5 May or Jun 1911; son of August von Behren and Wilhelmine Marie Macke; bp. 19 Jun 1920; MIA near Moscow, Russia, 18 Dec 1941 (IGI; CR Bielefeld Branch)

Wilhelm Friedrich von Behren b. Gellershagen, Bielefeld, Westfalen, 5 Mar 1913; son of August von Behren and Wilhelmine Marie Macke; bp. 7 May 1923; conf. 7 May 1923; k. in battle Russia 3 Aug 1943 (CR Bielefeld Branch, FHL microfilm 68784, no. 189; IGI)

Henry Albert Bock b. London, England, 27 May 1911; son of Heinrich Friedrich Karl Martin Bock and Annie Jane Price; bp. 8 Aug 1924; conf. 8 Aug 1924; lance corporal; k. in battle Gorodischtsche, near Bolchow, Russia, 22 Feb 1943 (CR Bielefeld Branch, FHL microfilm 68784, no. 220; www.volksbund.de)

Hermann Karl Eberhard Bokermann b. Overberge, Hamm, Westfalen, 26 Mar 1920; son of Karl Wilhelm H. Bokermann and Marie Luise Grappendorf; bp. 8 Sep 1928; d. 5 Oct 1944 (IGI)

Fig. 10. Hermann Bokermann (middle) was killed in 1944. (E. Schmitz Michaelis)

Wilhelmine Margarethe Johanna Bokermann b. Overberge, Hamm, Westfalen, 18 Oct 1924; dau. of Karl Wilhelm H. Bokermann and Marie Luise Grappendorf; bp. 17 Jun 1933; conf. 17 Jun 1933; k. streetcar accident 3 Oct 1941 (CR Bielefeld Branch, FHL microfilm 68784, no. 230; IGI)

Erich Ditt b. Bielefeld, Bielefeld, Westfalen, 21 Dec 1913; son of Heinrich Kraemer and Elisa Ditt; bp. 30 Nov 1930; conf. 30 Nov 1930; ord. deacon 6 Dec 1931; corporal; d. in military hospital 2/571 in Roslawl, Russia, 8 Mar 1942 (CR Bielefeld Branch, FHL microfilm 68784, no. 305; www.volksbund.de; IGI)

Heinrich Friedrich Wilhelm Dröscher b. Heuerßen, Stadthagen, Schaumburg-Lippe, 10 Nov 1901; son of Johann Heinrich F. Dröscher and Engel Marie Karoline Heu; bp. 11 Aug 1928; conf. 11 Aug 1928; ord. deacon 24 Mar 1929; ord. teacher 9 Mar 1930; ord. priest 7 Sep 1930; m. Heuerßen 20 Jun 1925, Engel Marie Sophie Karoline Kirchhöfer; k. air raid Bielefeld, Bielefeld, Westfalen, 30 Sep 1944 (CR Bielefeld Branch, FHL microfilm 68784, no. 84; IGI)

Margarethe Charlotte Galts b. Wittmund, Ostfriesland, Hanover, 22 Mar 1867; dau. of Bernhard Galts and Elisabeth Margarethe Ihnen; bp. 7 May 1923; conf. 7 May 1923; m. 16 Apr 1898, Wilhelm Meier; k. air raid Bielefeld, Bielefeld, Westfalen, 30 Sep 1944 (CR Bielefeld Branch, FHL microfilm 68784, no. 157; CHL microfilm 2458, 346–47)

Engel Marie Karoline Sophie Kirchhöfer b. Reinsen-Remeringhausen, Stadthagen, Schaumburg-Lippe, 23 Mar 1903; dau. of Friedrich Johann Wilhelm

Ludwig Kirchhöfer and Engel Marie Sophie Oltrogge; bp. 11 Aug 1928; conf. 11 Aug 1928; m. Heuerßen, Stadthagen, Schaumburg-Lippe, 20 Jun 1925, Heinrich Friedrich Wilhelm Dröscher; k. air raid Bielefeld 30 Sep 1944 (CR Bielefeld Branch, FHL microfilm 68784, no. 85)

Erhardt Kirchhoff b. Bielefeld, Bielefeld, Westfalen, 15 Aug 1924; son of Wilhelm Kirchhoff and Anna Luise Tosberg; bp. 27 Aug 1932 (CR Bielefeld Branch; IGI)

Lina Luise Christine Marowsky b. Todtenhausen, Minden, Westfalen, 13 Dec 1877; dau. of Christian Marowsky and Lina Mearhoff; bp. 7 Nov 1910; conf. 7 Nov 1910; m. 9 Dec 1911, Karl Bockermann; d. cardiac insufficiency 11 Jul 1941 (CR Bielefeld Branch, FHL microfilm 68784, no. 142)

Franziska Emma Kätchen Mothes b. Hamburg 12 Jun 1880; dau. of Edward Mothes and Marie Johanna M. Friedrichsen; bp. 7 Sep 1928; conf. 7 Sep 1928; d. 13 Jun 1943 (CR Bielefeld Branch, FHL microfilm 68784, no. 98)

Friedrich Heinrich Walter Recksiek b. Schildesche, Bielefeld, Westfalen, 28 Aug 1919; son of Karl Heinrich Recksiek and Anna Katharine Johanna Milsmann; bp. 17 Dec 1927; conf. 20 Dec 1927; ord. deacon 6 Dec 1931; ord. teacher 10 Jan 1928; ord. priest 2 Apr 1939; corporal; k. in battle Nishni-Kurp, Kaukasus, Russia, 26 Sep 1942 (CR Bielefeld Branch, FHL microfilm 68784, no. 207; FHL microfilm no. 271400, 1925 and 1935 censuses; IGI, AF, PRF; www.volksbund.de)

Fig. 11. Walter Recksiek. (H. Recksiek)

Marie Katharine Reick b. Warburg, Paderborn, Westfalen, 12 Jun 1903; dau. of Wilhelm Reick and Helene Schmidt; bp. 16 Jan 1926; conf. 17 Jan 1926; m. 14 Apr 1925, Alfred Passon (div.); d. surgery 9 Jan 1940 (CR Bielefeld Branch, FHL microfilm 68784, no. 232)

Johann Friedrich Heinz Schroeder b. Bielefeld 12 May 1919; son of —— Schroeder and Anna Wegener; k. in battle 1943 (*Chronik der Gemeinde Bielefeld*, FHL microfilm 245258, 1930 and 1935 censuses)

Pauline Simon b. Orchowo, Mogilno, Posen, 25 Jan 1903; dau. of Phillip Simon and Katharine Gruber; bp. 21 Oct 1923; conf. 21 Oct 1923; m. Wilhelm Uibel; d. lung ailment 17 Sep 1944 (CR Bielefeld Branch, FHL microfilm 68784, no. 182)

Hellmut Heinz Steinkühler b. Theesen, Bielefeld, Westfalen, 14 Aug 1927; son of Gustav Adolf Steinkühler and Karoline Sophie Auguste Obermeier; bp. 26 Oct 1935; conf. 27 Oct 1935; ord. deacon 3 May 1942; d. battlefield wounds 6 Apr 1945 (CR Bielefeld Branch, FHL microfilm 68784, no. 252; IGI)

Nephi Uibel b. Bielefeld, Bielefeld, Westfalen, 28 Jul 1925; son of Wilhelm Uibel and Pauline Simon; bp. 19 Aug 1933; conf. 19 Aug 1933; ord. deacon 2 Apr 1939; sapper; k. in battle Normandy, France, 10 Aug 1944; bur. La Cambe, France (CR Bielefeld Branch, FHL microfilm 68784, no. 238; www.volksbund.de)

Karoline Friederike Weber b. Münchehagen, Stolzenau, Hanover, 7 Mar 1884; dau. of Friedrich Weber and Karoline Rode; bp. 2 Aug 1929; conf. 2 Aug 1929; m. —— Koppelmeyer; d. Russia 2 Feb 1942 (CR Bielefeld Branch, FHL microfilm 68784, no. 277)

Friedrich Wind b. Detmold, Lippe, 2 Jun 1864; son of Heinrich Wind and Louise Nolte; bp. 26 Oct 1910; conf. 26 Oct 1910; ord. deacon 21 Jun 1914; ord. elder 16 Sep 1914; m. Minna Luise Wind (div.); d. senility 7 Mar 1941 (CR Bielefeld Branch, FHL microfilm 68784, no. 194)

Notes

1. Bielefeld city archive.
2. *Chronik der Gemeinde Bielefeld, 1896–1996* (Bielefeld, Germany: Bielefeld LDS Ward, 1996), 132. This source lists Brother Recksiek as the branch president as of September 14, 1938, the date on which the American missionaries were evacuated from Germany the first time. However, the directory of the West German Mission shows Elder Dean Griner of the United States in that leadership position as late as July 20, 1939. Whichever record is correct, it is certain that Heinrich Recksiek was the branch president after Elder Griner left Germany on August 25, 1939.
3. Heinz Recksiek, interview by Marion Wolfert in German, Salt Lake City, March 22, 2006; summarized in English by Judith Sartowski.
4. Presiding Bishopric, "Financial, Statistical, and Historical Reports of Wards, Stakes, and Missions, 1884–1955," 257, CHL CR 4 12.
5. Elfriede Recksiek Doermann, interview by the author, Salt Lake City, May 4, 2009.
6. West German Mission manuscript history, CHL MS 10045 2.
7. Eleonore Schmitz Michaelis, interview by the author, Salt Lake City, February 6, 2009.
8. *Chronik der Gemeinde Bielefeld*, 49.
9. Werner Niebuhr, autobiography, 1985, CHL MS 19617, 19.
10. Niebuhr, autobiography, 22.
11. Niebuhr, autobiography, 26–27.
12. Niebuhr, autobiography, 31.
13. Niebuhr, autobiography, 35.
14. Niebuhr, autobiography, 44–45.

15. *Chronik der Gemeinde Bielefeld*, 50.
16. Niebuhr, autobiography, 46–49.
17. *Chronik der Gemeinde Bielefeld*, 50.
18. Niebuhr, autobiography, 53–54.
19. Niebuhr, autobiography, 54–62.
20. Niebuhr, autobiography, 62.
21. *Chronik der Gemeinde Bielefeld*, 51.
22. Bielefeld City Archive.

Herford Branch

The Latter-day Saint branch in the city of Herford, Westphalia, had sixty-four members when World War II began, but with only five priesthood holders, it was not very robust in a city of 42,339 inhabitants. According to the directory of the West German Mission in June 1939, Elder Ferryle B. McOmber of the United States was the branch president and was serving at the time without counselors.[1] Most of the branch leadership positions were not filled at the time, but there was a Sunday School president, a Primary president, and a YWMIA president.

Herford Branch[2]	**1939**
Elders	2
Priests	1
Teachers	2
Deacons	0
Other Adult Males	17
Adult Females	28
Male Children	9
Female Children	5
Total	64

On August 25, 1939, all American missionaries serving in Germany were evacuated from the country and Elder McOmber left with them. His instructions were to designate a local priesthood holder to guide the branch, but there is no record that he informed the mission office in Frankfurt of his choice.

Branch meetings were held in rented rooms at Elverdisserstrasse 13. The branch observed the traditional schedule of holding Sunday school at 10:00 a.m. and sacrament meeting at 7:00 p.m. Relief Society, Primary and Mutual meetings were all held on Tuesday. Choir practice took place at 8:00 p.m. on Sunday.

As of this writing, no eyewitness accounts by members of the Herford Branch can be located.

In Memoriam

The following members of the Herford Branch did not survive World War II:

Louisa Adolphine Hermine Borgstädt b. Herford, Westfalen, 2 Apr 1870; dau. of Hermann Borgstädt and Auguste Wistinghausen; bp. 21 Aug 1927; conf. 21 Aug 1927; m. 3 Oct 1890, Wilhelm Brinkmann; d. gout and rheumatism 12 Mar 1943 (FHL microfilm 68796, no. 1; CHL CR 275 8, no. 1)

Albert Heinrich Gustav Buchtmann b. Herford, Westfalen, 3 Nov 1922; son of Wilhelm Albert Georg Buchtmann and Paula Kleimann; bp. 27 Aug 1932; conf. 27 Aug 1932; d. pneumonia 21 Jun 1945; bur. Schierke, Wernigerode, Sachsen (FHL microfilm 68796, no. 4; IGI; www.volksbund.de)

Hans Karl Hermann Albert Buchtmann b. Herford, Westfalen, 18 Mar 1921; son of Wilhelm Albert Georg Buchtmann and Paula Kleimann; bp. 5 Aug 1929; conf. 5 Aug 1929; k. in battle Budarki, Caucasus, Russia, 4 Jan 1943 (FHL microfilm 68796, no. 3; IGI)

August Wilhelm Burkhardt b. Milse, Bielefeld, Westfalen, 4 Feb 1913; son of Karl Friedrich Burkhardt and Karoline Nebel; bp. 21 Jun 1936; conf. 28 Jun 1936; ord. deacon 7 Mar 1937; ord. teacher 19 Nov 1939; m. Herford, Westfalen, 18 Oct 1935, Maria Anna Luise Moll; lance corporal; d. in POW camp at Iwanowo, Russia, 6 Nov 1945 (FHL microfilm 68796, no. 54; www.volksbund.de; PRF)

Karl Friedrich Wilhelm Danielmeyer b. Schweicheln, Herford, Westfalen, 9 Apr 1918; son of Hermann Danielmeyer and Ida Rosa Graue; bp. 21 Aug 1927; conf. 21 Aug 1927; lance corporal; k. in battle Fela, Krolowez, Russia, 10 Sep or Nov 1941; bur. Kiev, Ukraine (FHL microfilm 68796, no. 10; www.volksbund.de; CHL microfilm 2458, form 42 FP, pt. 37, 346–47; IGI; AF; PRF)

Marie Florentine Friederike Echternkamp b. Herford, Westfalen, 17 or 18 Dec 1873; dau. of Friedrich Wilhelm Echternkamp and Juliane Friederike Brinkmann; bp. 8 Sep 1928; conf. 8 Sep 1928; m. Apr 1898, Friedrich Kassing; d. heart failure 30 Nov 1945 (FHL microfilm 68796, no. 16; IGI)

Maria Wilhelmine Anna Elisabeth Münstermann b. Windheim, Minden, Westfalen, 22 Jul 1864; dau. of Adolf Münstermann and Wilhelmine Rolf; bp. 14 May 1927; conf. 14 May 1927; m. 11 Jun 1910, Theodor Johann Schiersch; 2m. Bünde, Herford, Westfalen, 6 Oct 1882, Caspar Heinrich Kammann; d. 17 Jan 1945 (FHL microfilm 68796, no. 29; IGI)

Friederike Louise Nagel b. Herford, Westfalen, 30 or 31 May 1883; dau. of Ernst Heinrich Nagel and Anna Margarethe Ilsabein Berger; bp. 18 Apr 1937; conf. 18 Apr 1937; m.; d. 1 or 2 Jul (IGI; AF)

Notes

1. West German Mission manuscript history, CHL MS 10045 2.
2. Presiding Bishopric, "Financial, Statistical, and Historical Reports of Wards, Stakes, and Missions, 1884–1955," 257, CHL CR 4 12.

Minden Branch

Minden, a large city of historical and industrial importance located on the Weser River, has been called "the gateway to Westphalia." The city lies twenty miles northeast of Bielefeld and thirty-five miles west of Hanover and had a population of 28,389 people in 1939.[1] According to LDS Church records, the branch consisted of thirty-seven members at the time, nearly one-half of whom were females over the age of twelve. Only four brethren age twelve years or older held the priesthood. The address of the meeting rooms of the Minden Branch at the time is not known.

Hans Otto Deppe (born 1937) recalled holding meetings in the homes of the member families during the war, with the group gathering in his apartment about once each month.[2] Brother Sommer was always available to render priesthood services because he was classified as disabled and thus not fit for military service. Attendance at meetings held in member homes may have been a dozen persons. According to Hans Otto, there was no reason for the Saints in Minden to fear persecution; nevertheless, they kept their windows shut while singing to avoid bothering the neighbors.

Minden Branch[3]	1939
Elders	1
Priests	0
Teachers	0
Deacons	3
Other Adult Males	9
Adult Females	17
Male Children	5
Female Children	2
Total	37

Hans Otto was the youngest of six children. His father worked as a waiter at times and also did odd jobs around town. While most Latter-day Saints in the West German Mission were not enthusiastic about Adolf Hitler and the Nazi Party, some were more vocal than others. Hans Otto's father was perhaps one of them:

> My father was drafted into the military but did not want to go. I remember that we talked about politics quite often in our home. My father was a unionist and we knew that. We also listened to BBC broadcasts and my parents trusted that we would not talk about that outside of our home. My parents did not like the Führer and often told us that.

Hans Otto's father was drafted in 1943 and sent to the Netherlands, where he served only on guard duty. A veteran of both the Western and Russian Fronts in World War I, he had hoped to be spared military service as an older man. Back at home, the Deppe family moved into rooms in the local army barracks along with perhaps one hundred

Fig. 1. In 1931, the LDS branch in Minden was relatively strong, as evidenced by this photograph taken during an outing in a local forest. (H. O. Deppe)

other families short on means. The children were allowed to play in the courtyard that had previously served as the soldiers' training grounds. Hans Otto recalled this fondly: they climbed the trees and even spent time on the meadows along the Weser River. "We could always go swimming or play at the railroad station." Despite the war, little children were still able to enjoy life.

During the air raids that took place over Minden, Sister Deppe and her children joined other occupants in the basement of the massive army post quarters. According to Hans Otto, "The basement had very thick walls with a big iron door. Even our apartments had those doors in front of them. . . . When we sat in the basement, the walls were shaking, and some of the plaster fell down on us. We always took an emergency suitcase with us, and we did not have to walk far to the shelter."

The city of Minden was important for industry and transportation and thus attracted the interest of the British Royal Air Force with increasing intensity as the war neared its conclusion. Hans Otto recalled observing the aftermath of an attack on the Mittelland Canal that runs along the north edge of the city; many boats and small ships had been destroyed. Although points of military significance appeared to be the primary targets, extensive destruction in the city's center also resulted.

Hans Otto recalled having power outages more frequently during the first months of 1945. Although his mother was able to find enough food for the family, there was never more than just enough, and ration cards often did not guarantee the availability of food. There was no water in the apartment, but the children fetched it easily from a well in the courtyard outside.

The war in Minden ended with the arrival of the British Army on April 6, 1945. Apparently, the Deppe family and several others were not quick enough to hang out white flags as a sign of surrender, and a few short artillery bursts were issued by the invaders as warnings. "As soon as we hung out our white sheet, it was quiet," recalled Hans Otto. The British were kind to the people of Minden; most homes were not searched, and the conquerors did what they could to provide employment for local workers. Sister Deppe and her children spent much of their time doing outdoor cleanup and janitorial work.

The city of Minden lost at least 448 civilians during the war and more than 1,300 soldiers. Of the homes in the city limits, 36 percent were damaged or totally destroyed.[4]

Fig. 2. Members of the Minden Branch and friends gathered for this photograph in 1937. (H. O. Deppe)

In 1946, the Deppe family was blessed by the return of their father from a POW camp in Canada. They had known for some time that he had survived the war because he was allowed to send several cards home. However, tragedy struck this family in the death of Victor, a son of Sister Deppe from her first marriage and a half-brother of Hans Otto. Victor had been a soldier in the Wehrmacht and was captured at the end of the war. The family was later informed that while attempting to escape from a Polish POW camp in order to reach home for Christmas 1945, he was captured and punished by beheading.

The Minden Branch was weakened but alive and well when World War II came to an end in May 1945. The members there continued to meet in apartments for some time, and the future brought steady growth among the Saints in that city.

No members of the Minden Branch are known to have died during World War II.

Notes

1. Minden city archive.
2. Hans Otto Deppe, interview by the author in German, Dortmund, Germany, August 8, 2006; summarized in English by Judith Sartowski.
3. Presiding Bishopric, "Financial, Statistical, and Historical Reports of Wards, Stakes, and Missions, 1884–1955," 257, CHL CR 4 12.
4. Minden city archive.

Münchehagen Branch

The town of Münchehagen had only 1,596 residents in 1939, of whom barely a dozen were Latter-day Saints.[1] Located at the northeastern edge of the state of Westphalia, Münchehagen was seven miles directly north of its sister branch in Stadthagen and thirty-five miles northeast of the city of Bielefeld in the district of the same name.

No eyewitness stories of the Münchehagen Branch can be located as of this writing, but the directory of the West German Mission shows the name of Friedrich Möller as branch president with Ernst Wesemann as his first counselor. The only other name appearing in that directory is that of Ernst's wife, Frieda, who was serving as the secretary of the Sunday School.[2] According to the statistical report of the branch filed just months after the German invasion of Poland, Möller and Wesemann were holders of the Aaronic Priesthood.

Branch meetings were held in the Wesemann home, with the address identified simply as

Münchehagen 268.[3] Sunday School took place at 2:00 p.m. and was followed by sacrament meeting at 3:30. No meetings were held during the week; the membership was too small to support auxiliary organizations.

The British army invaded the town without incident in April 1945. The only thing known about the fate of this branch is that Ernst Wesemann lost his life while serving in the Wehrmacht in Russia. It is very possible that the branch organization ceased to exist by 1945 and that the surviving members joined with the Saints in Stadthagen.

Münchhagen Branch[4]	1939
Elders	0
Priests	2
Teachers	2
Deacons	0
Other Adult Males	3
Adult Females	7
Male Children	0
Female Children	1
Total	15

IN MEMORIAM

At least one member of the Münchehagen Branch did not survive World War II:

Fritz Ernst Wilhelm Wesemann b. Münchehagen, Hannover, 18 May 1910; son of Heinrich Wesemann and Karoline Waltemath; bp. 2 Aug 1929; conf. 2 Aug 1929; ord. deacon 6 Apr 1930; lance corporal; d. in field hospital 6/542 at Ljuban 8 Feb 1942; bur. Sologubowka-St. Petersburg, Russia (FHL microfilm 68801 no. 9; www.volksbund.de; IGI)

NOTES

1. Münchehagen city archive.
2. West German Mission manuscript history, CHL MS 10045 2.
3. Smaller towns in Germany had no street names in those days. Addresses consisted solely of house numbers.
4. Presiding Bishopric, "Financial, Statistical, and Historical Reports of Wards, Stakes, and Missions, 1884–1955," 257, CHL CR 4 12.

STADTHAGEN BRANCH

Located twenty miles west of the major city of Hanover, the town of Stadthagen had been home to a strong branch of The Church of Jesus Christ of Latter-day Saints since the early twentieth century. When World War II began, there were sixty-six members in the branch, including nineteen holders of the priesthood, in a town with a population of 28,389.[1] Several leaders in the Bielefeld District called this branch their home, principally district president Alfred Hegemeister.

Stadthagen Branch[2]	1939
Elders	7
Priests	6
Teachers	2
Deacons	4
Other Adult Males	9
Adult Females	31
Male Children	5
Female Children	2
Total	66

According to the directory of the West German Mission in Frankfurt, the president of the Stadthagen Branch in the fall of 1939 was Karl Borcherding Sr. of nearby Ottensen.[3] Heinrich Rahde and Wilhelm Tegmeier Sr. were his counselors. There were at that time leaders and secretaries for all organizations and programs with the exception of the Primary, possibly because only seven children were on the branch rolls.

Church meetings were held in rented rooms on Niedernstrasse 25 as the war approached. Sunday

Fig. 1. The first house on the right is Niederstrasse no. 25 as it appeared in the 1940s. (K. Borcherding)

school began at 9:30 a.m., and sacrament meeting followed at 11:00. All Sunday meetings were held consecutively. The mission office directory indicates that Priesthood and Relief Society meetings were held after the close of sacrament meeting. At that time, no branch meetings were held during the week.

Young Fred Wehrhahn (born 1937) recalled the setting of the meeting rooms:

> The first building was an old horse stable. The people who owned that old farmhouse had had horses at one point. I remember that we always had to enter the rooms through the actual farmhouse—through the *Diele* (hallway). The horse stable had been converted to our meeting rooms. They had cleaned it out and had done some remodeling so we could have more classrooms. . . . It was on the ground floor. I recall that we always had a picture on the wall of the Prophet Joseph Smith. My father would always take the time to tell us about the Prophet Joseph and his visitation by the Father and the Son. We had a pump organ for our music.[4]

According to the official branch minutes, worship services and other branch activities carried on without interruption during the first years of the war. For example, on February 18, 1940, seven members of the Stadthagen Branch traveled to Bielefeld to attend the district conference.[5] In June, all Sunday meetings were moved to the morning hours. By October, when Sunday School was changed to 1:00 p.m. and followed by sacrament meeting, the average attendance had declined from twenty to thirteen.[6]

The branch Christmas party of 1941 was attended by forty persons. By the summer of the next year, Sunday meetings were again held in the forenoon, but only ten persons were still coming faithfully. In October, the meetings were again moved to the afternoon. There are no explanations given for the schedule changes.[7]

Attached to the Stadthagen Branch but too far away to attend very often were perhaps a dozen

Latter-day Saints living in the town of Alverdissen, about twenty miles south. Werner Jacobi (born 1928) recalled the following about the group there:

> In Alverdissen, we sometimes had up to twelve people. We would meet in members' homes. I remember the Franzheimer family and lady who we called Tante Minna. . . . We had [musical instruments] to sing with. We attended district conferences now and then in Bielefeld or Stadthagen. My parents had all scriptures in our home—I knew of the Book of Mormon, and we also made sure that we read in it regularly.[8]

Werner was a member of the Jungvolk and later the Hitler Youth. He enjoyed the activities of both organizations and was especially talented in sports. He believed there was a specific reason for his athletic prowess: "Because I kept the Word of Wisdom, I was always the best—best at the 100 meter dash and the long jump. Because of that, nobody made any fun of me or caused any trouble. I was simply the best in all those athletic activities." Werner's father objected to Hitler's politics and complained about the Hitler Youth program but could not prevent his son from participating in the program.

Fig. 2. The structure in which the branch met during the war stood behind house no. 25—almost exactly where the small, white building in this picture now stands. (K. Borcherding)

Several older members of the Stadthagen Branch passed away during the war, and their funerals were reported in the branch meeting minutes, but only once is a military death found, namely on February 15, 1942: "Fritz Bothe died of wounds at the Russian Front."[9] The minutes were apparently kept for the most part by Heinrich Rahde. Very complete, neat, and correct, the entries contain specific details on each meeting's attendees by member category (priesthood holders, women, children, and friends). Brother Rahde was clearly dedicated to his calling as branch secretary.

Fred Wehrhahn's parents were Karl and Alwine. The family lived in the town of Ehlen, about two miles southwest of Stadthagen. Brother Wehrhahn had worked as a miner but was then employed in a glass factory in Obernkirchen. Shortly after the war began, he was drafted into the Wehrmacht, and his wife and children moved into an apartment house in Obernkirchen.

Fig. 3. The Wehrhahn family early in the war. (F. Wehrhahn)

Even little children can have distinct memories, as was the case with Fred Wehrhahn: "My father was drafted in 1939. Even though I was only two years old, I can still remember that vividly. My father had gotten permission to come home because my mother was ready to give birth to my little sister. I admired him for his uniform and for carrying a gun on his belt. That made an impression on my mind."

Young Heinz Rahde (born 1927) recalled his midwar service in the Hitler Youth. Along with the obligatory political instruction, the boys were taught a strict code of conduct and were kept constantly busy:

> We mainly learned about the life of Hitler, about his movement and his goal. The other time was devoted to sports, hiking, camping, reading maps and compasses. We took trips, roamed through the forests, learned first aid, all the things [American boys] learn in Scouting. . . . It kept us off the street. . . . Once a month we had Sunday morning meeting. They were always arranged at a time when church was held.[10]

Fortunately, Heinz rarely had to miss church meetings. He had been taught gospel principles by his parents and recognized some of the danger signs as he was called upon to serve his country at home and away. At the young age of sixteen, he was commuting about ten miles from his home in Heuerssen to the city of Wunstorf to attend a secondary school. In 1943, Heinz and his classmates were assigned as *Luftwaffenhelfer* (air force assistants) and trained to operate an antiaircraft battery. Under the command of one of their schoolteachers, they took up quarters on the outskirts of the huge city of Hanover. It was there that Heinz witnessed war at its most horrific on the evening of September 8, 1943. His account conveys the emotion of the experience of a young man trying in vain to defend his homeland:

> [Illumination flares] were dropped. . . . [Enemy] planes were all over. We received orders to just shoot in any directions, wherever the noise came from. We rotated the guns continuously and fired as fast as we could. . . . The initial shock was hardly over when a fantastic firework appeared in the sky. Phosphorus bombs were [dropped]. They exploded high in the skies, and the burning tongues of flames danced down. . . . Wherever you looked, there were dancing little flames, dropping slowly down to earth. . . . We were spellbound, standing in awe and fear and desperation, knowing that in minutes, every little inch of the ground would be engulfed in flames. It was a horrible spectacle.[11]

Tens of thousands of residents of Hanover perished in that attack. Heinz Rahde and his friends were compelled to see the aftermath of the bombing with their own eyes when they were transported into town to help rescue persons buried alive or to recover bodies. He would not soon forget the sight: "It was like landing on the moon. Every building was destroyed. There was nothing left of a once proud city, no houses, no anything. . . . We didn't find any people alive."

Fig. 4. Heinz Rahde on leave at home in the uniform of the Reichsarbeitsdienst. (H. Rahde)

Fig. 5. Heinz Rahde's young antiaircraft battery comrades. The boys were pupils of the Hölty School in Wunstorf. (H. Rahde)

Although not officially soldiers, members of Heinz Rahde's antiaircraft unit were constantly in harm's way, and several were killed during air raids. In addition to the physical dangers, men and boys in uniform were subjected to moral dangers as well. Heinz recalled many instances when girls with loose morals entertained the boys. Alcohol and tobacco were in use all around him, but he clung to the teachings of the Church. He did not explain his health code and thus took some chiding from his comrades. On one occasion, his commanding officer complimented him in a rather surprising fashion. His account of the experience reads:

> During a party in the mess hall, he commanded, "Rahde, stand up!" There I stood. I did not know what he wanted. He said, "Rahde is a Mormon. He does not drink, he does not smoke. If you tease him again, I will punish you." I was a bit ashamed of myself. . . . Then he said, "Rahde, from now on, it is your assignment to bring your friends back to the battery compounds, whenever they go out and have too much to drink." I did. I never had more friends since. They all wanted me to go with them.[12]

The Saints of the Stadthagen Branch were few in number but were not forgotten by the leaders of the West German Mission. On April 12, 1942, Anton Huck (first counselor to mission supervisor Christian Heck) attended meetings in Stadthagen and ordained Friedrich Behling an elder. One year later, both Elders Heck and Huck were in Stadthagen to hold a special meeting. By then, the average attendance had increased to about fifteen persons. On July 11, 1943, the Relief Society held a conference to which twenty-three members and friends came. The theme was "keeping the Sabbath day holy."[13]

"We had very many air raids in our area," according to Fred Wehrhahn. "It started in 1942 and got more severe as time went on. At first, we would always hear an 'attention getter' and the sirens would go off. As the planes came closer, the sirens would go off again. When we heard two long, loud sounds, it meant that we had to find a shelter somewhere. Three sounds meant that they were here."

Small deeds of compassion on the part of young Heinz Rahde would return blessings upon his head later on. As an air force assistant, he came into contact with Russian POWs. They were assigned to clean the mess kits of the German soldiers, and Heinz was in the habit of leaving portions of his meals for them, knowing that they were underfed. On one occasion, his commanding officer noticed the clandestine act and asked Heinz, "What did you put in your mess kit?" "Food," answered Heinz. "They're hungry." The officer patted him on the shoulder and said, "Don't do that again. If I reported you, it could cost you your life." One Russian prisoner eventually wrote a note and gave it to Heinz with this comment: "When Germany loses and you need some help from the Russians, show them this little note."[14] Heinz preserved the note with care.

Karl Wehrhahn was among the Wehrmacht soldiers trying to stave off the Allied invasion of France in Normandy in June 1944 and was captured there by British soldiers. He later told his son, Fred, that while he and other German soldiers were being guarded by a nervous British soldier, the young man accidentally fired his weapon, inflicting a mortal wound on the soldier standing next to Karl, who had been praying that no such incident would occur.

Heinz Rahde was seventeen in 1944 when a call came to national service in the Reichsarbeitsdienst (RAD). This duty was almost like a vacation when compared with the high-stress, no-rest duty he had rendered in ground-to-air combat. His RAD unit was stationed in the village of Münchehof, just fifty miles southeast of his home. A bright young man and a good student, Heinz became a trainer responsible for instructing boys fifteen and sixteen in the use of radar equipment. He enjoyed the assignment, the natural beauty of the setting, and the proximity to home.

An opportunity for advancement and prestige presented itself while Heinz was at Münchehof. His performance was so good that he was invited to join an officers' training program. However, he turned down repeated invitations. He later came to the conclusion that the Lord must have been with him in making that decision: "All of my friends left [to join the program]. They were sent to Russia, and over 80 percent of them died. . . . I could stay in Germany, training incoming recruits on our antiaircraft instruments. I felt I was a good teacher."[15]

The year 1944 was one of slight growth for the Stadthagen Branch. On February 20, three members of the Kirchhöfer family (Edith, Ursula, and Heinz) were baptized in a ceremony held in connection with a district conference in Bielefeld. By this time, many members of the branch had left town to serve in the military or in other government assignments to the extent that the Thanksgiving program held on October 8 was attended by only eleven persons.[16]

Fred Wehrhahn recalled being treated differently because of his religion:

> As soon as people at school found out that we were members of the Church, we were quite frankly treated as second-class citizens. They were careful about it, but even as a child, I realized that I was not treated the same as others were. Even the people in our neighborhood knew that we were [Latter-day Saints], especially because my dad always liked sharing the gospel with others. I still had friends in the neighborhood to play with, and it did not matter much to them. But I have to say that it was not the kind of persecution that made us suffer.

On November 26, the Sunday School had to be canceled due to air-raid alarms. On Christmas Day, district president Alfred Hegemeister from Stadthagen visited the branch meetings and guided a discussion about moving the meetings to Sunday morning, because the local Volkssturm (home guard) was conducting training on Sunday afternoons. The members of the branch voted to decline the suggestion.[17]

As the war drew to a close, the Saints in Stadthagen continued to hold their meetings as best they could. On March 18, 1945, a branch anniversary celebration was held, and nineteen persons attended. Three weeks later, the minutes note that no meetings could be held because American soldiers had conquered the surrounding county of Schaumburg-Lippe. British troops moved into the town on April 15, and again church meetings were canceled. The next entries are of postwar events, such as on May 20, when Sunday School was scheduled for 9:30 a.m., to be followed by sacrament meeting. Although church services had been canceled on several occasions, the branch secretary continued to make his entries without interruption.[18]

Werner Jacobi had finished public school in 1943 and began an apprenticeship as a plumber and electrician. He rode his bike every day to Barntrup, a town three miles to the south. His services there were valuable because so many young men had left their masters' shops to serve in the military. Werner was still there when the war drew to a close, and he was drafted into the Volkssturm. Given some training with weapons, he was eventually sent with other citizen soldiers toward Berlin. "We were supposed to march to Berlin in order to defend Hitler. We only made it as far as Rinteln [twelve miles north of Alverdissen] because somebody had destroyed a bridge, and then we had to walk back home. After that, the British army came to our area. There was no fighting." At age seventeen, Werner was very fortunate to avoid dangerous military service.

In the spring of 1945, the Soviet army was driving toward Berlin, and an order came that Heinz Rahde's unit was to race to the German capital to join in the defense of the city. Heinz and two close friends, Günther Abeler and Ali Behrens, deliberated and decided that they were not going to Berlin—they were going home! They found civilian clothing, gathered a supply of food, and headed for the forest. Despite moving toward home with great caution and keeping out of the open, they suddenly found themselves staring down the cannon barrel of an American tank. After the initial terror of facing the enemy for the first time, the boys were interrogated and were about to be shipped off to a POW camp. When he saw several freed Russians sitting on the tank, Heinz recalled the note and displayed it with high hopes. The Americans were impressed and instructed him, "Go home to your mother."[19] He must have been very grateful for the training he had received in treating his fellowman properly.

On the way home, Heinz and his friends traveled under cover of the forests until one day, when he felt inspired to go into the open. This seemed foolish to his friends, because they had watched from afar as enemy truck after truck transported German soldiers to POW camps. Nevertheless, Heinz wanted to leave the forest. Günther inquired, "Heinz, did you pray about it?" "Yes!" "Then I go with you." Moments later, they were invited by a local farmer to hide in a barn. While they did so, American soldiers searched the forest they had left and rounded up many German prisoners. Heinz recalled recognizing the hand of the Lord in this escape.[20]

Finally, the boys found themselves looking down the hill at Heinz's village of Heuerssen and were pleased that no damage had occurred. While sneaking into the backyard, Heinz set off a burglar alarm that sounded like a small bomb. Fortunately, only the family and the neighbors reacted and were thrilled to see Heinz. "What a joy that was! I was home. I cannot describe the feeling. Home, with mother, father and sister." His sister took food to his friends at the outskirts of town, after which they headed in different directions to their respective homes.[21]

There would be one more confrontation with the conquering Americans, but this one was quite harmless. A few days after arriving home, Heinz was still hiding, hoping to avoid being taken away to a POW camp. He had never officially belonged to the Wehrmacht, but in those days, any man in uniform could be considered a soldier and incarcerated. One day, some American soldiers in a tank showed up in front of the Rahde home and called for Heinz. It turned out that the town's mayor had identified him as the only one who could speak English. The soldiers were looking for a guide through the local forest to hunt deer. Heinz joined them, and they even gave him a gun. "For the first time I began to trust our enemy."[22]

Fred Wehrhahn was approaching his eighth birthday when World War II came to an end. He recalled the chaos and insecurity of the times:

> I remember that soldiers often came to our home and asked for civilian clothing. They would leave all their uniforms with us. We were told to prepare ourselves for the Russians to come in when the war came to an end. We packed bare necessities to put on our little wagon, and we were just waiting to hear who would come. In the end, it was the Americans. Even as old as I was, I had already heard stories about the Russians and how ugly they were to people. We also heard some things about the Americans.

As it turned out, Fred and his family were not in danger when the conquerors arrived:

> When the Americans then came in with their jeeps, they were loaded with clothing and would give it to us to use. I still remember how nice some of those soldiers were to us and how they smiled. They tried in their own way to communicate with us that they were our friends. I got some chocolate from them once, and I got really sick from it because my stomach was not used to it anymore. We were nothing but skin and bones. The Americans took over one of the homes and made it their communication center. I remember that we heard of what they did with the food when they were full and did not want it anymore—they buried it. But we dug it out and hid it underneath our shirts because we were so hungry. I got caught one time, but I wasn't punished. All my friends ran away, but the sergeant caught me by the neck. He looked at the can that we had found that they buried. He took me on his jeep and didn't take me home until late at night. I had to go on all his rounds with him.

When World War II ended, Heinz Rahde was only seventeen years old, but he had experienced the horrors of war. He emerged unscathed physically as well as spiritually. Having been perhaps in greater danger of losing his good standing in the Church than losing his very life, he had withstood all temptations and conducted himself as a worthy Latter-day Saint. He had been preserved by the hand of the Lord and was pleased to acknowledge that fact.

The small group of Saints in Alverdissen had survived the war. Their little town was untouched by the conflict, and the British conquerors did no harm as they came through in April 1945. Nevertheless, the times had been difficult in many regards, and in the recollection of Werner Jacobi, "We were very happy that the war was over."

By the summer of 1945, Karl Wehrhahn had been moved to a POW camp in Canada. Coincidentally, he was then only about fifty miles from his brother, who had emigrated from Germany in the early 1920s. Unfortunately, Canadian officials denied the two any opportunity to meet during Karl's stay in the region. The brothers would never see each other again.

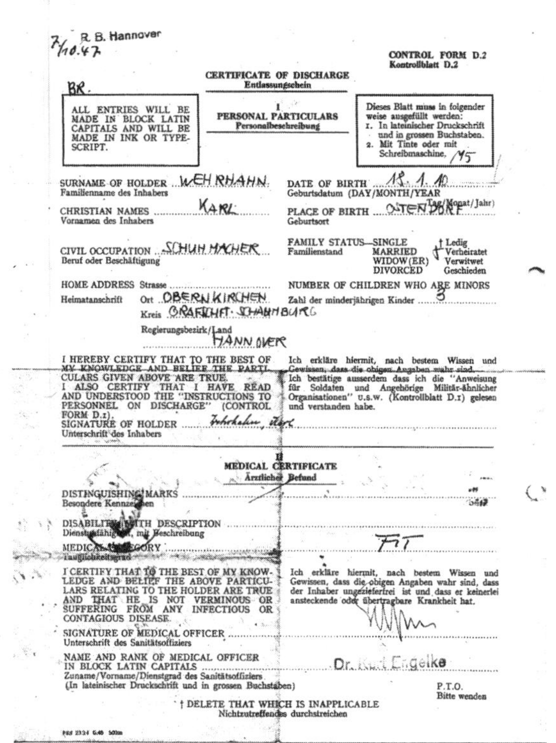

7/10.47 R. B. Hannover

CONTROL FORM D.2
Kontrollblatt D.2

CERTIFICATE OF DISCHARGE
Entlassungschein

BR.

ALL ENTRIES WILL BE MADE IN BLOCK LATIN CAPITALS AND WILL BE MADE IN INK OR TYPESCRIPT.

I
PERSONAL PARTICULARS
Personalbeschreibung

Dieses Blatt muss in folgender weise ausgefüllt werden:
1. In lateinischer Druckschrift und in grossen Buchstaben.
2. Mit Tinte oder mit Schreibmaschine. /45

SURNAME OF HOLDER / Familienname des Inhabers: WEHRHAHN

DATE OF BIRTH / Geburtsdatum (DAY/MONTH/YEAR Tag/Monat/Jahr): 18. 1. 10

CHRISTIAN NAMES / Vornamen des Inhabers: KARL

PLACE OF BIRTH / Geburtsort: OSTENDORF

CIVIL OCCUPATION / Beruf oder Beschäftigung: SCHUHMACHER

FAMILY STATUS—SINGLE / MARRIED / WIDOW(ER) / DIVORCED; Familienstand † Ledig / Verheiratet / Verwitwet / Geschieden

HOME ADDRESS / Heimatanschrift: Strasse ... Ort OBERNKIRCHEN; Kreis GRAFSCHAFT SCHAUMBURG; Regierungsbezirk/Land HANNOVER

NUMBER OF CHILDREN WHO ARE MINORS / Zahl der minderjährigen Kinder: 3

I HEREBY CERTIFY THAT TO THE BEST OF MY KNOWLEDGE AND BELIEF THE PARTICULARS GIVEN ABOVE ARE TRUE. I ALSO CERTIFY THAT I HAVE READ AND UNDERSTOOD THE "INSTRUCTIONS TO PERSONNEL ON DISCHARGE" (CONTROL FORM D.1).

Ich erkläre hiermit, nach bestem Wissen und Gewissen, dass die obigen Angaben wahr sind. Ich bestätige ausserdem dass ich die "Anweisung für Soldaten und Angehörige Militär-ähnlicher Organisationen" u.s.w. (Kontrollblatt D.1) gelesen und verstanden habe.

SIGNATURE OF HOLDER / Unterschrift des Inhabers: Wehrhahn, Karl

II
MEDICAL CERTIFICATE
Ärztlicher Befund

DISTINGUISHING MARKS / Besondere Kennzeichen

DISABILITY WITH DESCRIPTION / Dienstunfähigkeit, mit Beschreibung

MEDICAL CATEGORY / Tauglichkeitsgrad: FIT

I CERTIFY THAT TO THE BEST OF MY KNOWLEDGE AND BELIEF THE ABOVE PARTICULARS RELATING TO THE HOLDER ARE TRUE AND THAT HE IS NOT VERMINOUS OR SUFFERING FROM ANY INFECTIOUS OR CONTAGIOUS DISEASE.

Ich erkläre hiermit, nach bestem Wissen und Gewissen, dass die obigen Angaben wahr sind, dass der Inhaber ungezieferfrei ist und dass er keinerlei ansteckende oder übertragbare Krankheit hat.

SIGNATURE OF MEDICAL OFFICER / Unterschrift des Sanitätsoffiziers

NAME AND RANK OF MEDICAL OFFICER IN BLOCK LATIN CAPITALS / Zuname/Vorname/Dienstgrad des Sanitätsoffiziers (In lateinischer Druckschrift und in grossen Buchstaben): Dr. Karl Engelke

P.T.O.
Bitte wenden

† DELETE THAT WHICH IS INAPPLICABLE
Nichtzutreffendes durchstreichen

Fig. 6. The official release papers for POW Karl Wehrhahn. (F. Wehrhahn)

Karl Wehrhahn did not return to his family until 1947, having been absent from them with rare exceptions since 1939. When he arrived home, he learned that he almost missed seeing his son Fred alive again because of a bizarre incident that occurred a few months after the war:

> I remember that [cleanup crews] took out the ammunition out of the woods that were close to our housing complex. They detonated them and destroyed them that way. I nearly was killed during one of those explosions. I was outside helping my mother to saw some logs for firewood. We had been told that when they started exploding those bombs, they would indicate that with a siren so we would know when to go inside to be safe. We kept ignoring it because we really needed the wood that day. A piece of shrapnel came flying through the air and passed me very close to my head. It hit the house and left quite a lot of damage. My mother was so pale—she dropped the saw and demanded that I go with her immediately. We then went inside to be safe. I would say that the piece of metal was about a foot in diameter.

Karl Borcherding Sr. had served his small branch well as its president during the entire war. When the fighting ended and nearly all of the soldiers of the Stadthagen Branch came home, he gathered the members of the branch together to begin a new phase of church life.

In Memoriam

The following members of the Stadthagen Branch did not survive World War II:

Friedrich Conrad Wilhelm Bothe b. Wendthöhe, Stadthagen, Schaumburg-Lippe, 30 Aug 1920; son of Friedrich Wilhelm August Bothe and Ernestine Stahlhut; bp. 10 May 1929; conf. 10 May 1929; ord. deacon 7 Jan 1940; rifleman; d. in field hospital 906 at Witebsk, Weißrussland, 15 Feb 1942 (FHL microfilm 68805, no. 8; FHL microfilm 245288, 1930 census; www.volksbund.de; IGI)

Johann Heinrich Otto Desenis b. Beckedorf, Grafschaft Schaumburg, Hessen-Nassau, 12 Jun 1861; son of Otto Desenis and Anna Knolle; bp. Minden, Westfalen, 31 Aug 1918; conf. 31 Aug 1918; ord. deacon 12 Oct 1919; ord. teacher 17 Apr 1921; m. 19 Jul 1891, Anna Sophie Charlotte Engelking; five children; d. senility 13 Dec 1944 (CR Bielefeld Branch; FHL microfilm 68805, no. 19)

Anna Sophie Charlotte Engelking b. Beckedorf, Grafschaft Schaumburg, Hessen-Nassau, 16 May 1867; dau. of Hans Heinrich Konrad Engelking and Engel Marie Sophie Charlotte Meier; bp. 31 Aug 1918; conf. 31 Aug 1918; m. 19 Jul 1891, Johann Heinrich Otto Desenis; five children; d. senility 24 Jan 1942 (CR Bielefeld Branch, FHL microfilm 68805, no. 18; 68784, no. 2; IGI)

Friedrich Johann Wilhelm Ludwig Kirchhöfer b. Reinsen, Stadthagen, Schaumburg-Lippe, 12 Nov

1861; son of Christian Ludwig Kirchhöfer and Anne Sophie Karoline Oltrogge; bp. 6 Nov 1926; conf. 6 Nov 1926; ord. deacon 17 Jun 1928; ord. teacher 7 Apr 1929; ord. priest 25 Jan 1931; m. Heuerßen, Stadthagen, Schaumburg-Lippe, 26 Apr 1891, Engel Marie Sophie Oltrogge; d. bronchitis and heart ailment 20 May 1940 (FHL microfilm 68805, no. 34; 1925 and 1930 censuses, no. 271379; IGI; AF)

Friederike Karoline Charlotte Maier b. Rolfshagen, Grafschaft Schaumburg, Hessen-Nassau, 12 Mar 1860; dau. of Johann Friedrich Willhelm Maier and Karoline Justine Kinne; bp. 11 Oct 1924; conf. 11 Oct 1924; m. Obernkirchen, Grafschaft Schaumburg, Hesseb-Nassau, 15 May 1880, Karl Heinrich Friedrich Tünnermann; 2m. 8 Apr 1908, Wilhelm Albes; d. old age Rolfshagen, 5 May 1943 (FHL microfilm 68805, no. 1; CR Bielefeld Branch, FHL microfilm 68784, no. 28; FHL microfilm 25708, 1930 census; IGI)

Engel Marie Sophie Oltrogge b. Heuerßen, Stadthagen, Schaumburg-Lippe, 19 Jun 1866; dau. of Johann Heinrich Konrad Oltrogge and Engel Marie Charlotte Hardekopf; bp. 7 May 1927; conf. 7 May 1927; m. Heuerßen, 26 Apr 1891, Johann Friedrich Wilhelm Ludwig Kirchhöfer; d. stroke Reinsen, Stadthagen, Schaumburg-Lippe, 17 Jun 1940 (CR Bielefeld Branch, FHL microfilm 68784, no. 74; IGI)

August Heinrich Friedrich Christian Römbke b. Seelenfeld, Minden, Westfalen, 25 Apr 1859; son of Johann Konrad Dietrich Römbke and Sophie Schröder; bp. 14 Oct 1922; conf. 14 Oct 1922; ord. deacon 22 Jul 1923; ord. teacher 6 Jul 1926; ord. priest 20 Mar 1931; m. Stadthagen, Schaumburg-Lippe, 8 Jan 1887 to Sophie Karoline Dorothee Schäfer; d. stroke 9 May 1941 (CR Bielefeld Branch, FHL microfilm 68784, no. 11; FHL microfilm 68805, no. 46; IGI)

Sophie Karoline Dorothie Schäfer b. Lachem, Hameln, Hannover, 16 or 17 Aug 1867; dau. of —— and Dorothie Rosine Schäfer; bp. 11 Sep 1921; conf. 11 Sep 1921; m. 11 Jan 1887, August Heinrich Friedrich Christian Römbke; d. lung disease, Stadthagen, Schaumburg-Lippe, 4 May 1940 (FHL microfilm 68805, no. 47l; CR Bielefeld Branch, FHL microfilm 68784, no. 7)

Friedrich Wilhelm Ludwig Scheper b. Stadthagen, Schaumburg-Lippe, 14 Nov 1885; son of Ernst Scheper and Gustine Thies; bp. 17 Dec 1926; conf. 17 Dec 1926; m. 2 Jan 1909, Anna Christine Nagel; d. pulmonary tuberculosis 19 May 1940 (CR Bielefeld Branch, record no. 50, FHL microfilm 68805)

Karoline Sophie Vehling b. Wendthagen, Stadthagen, Schaumburg-Lippe, 16 Nov 1867; dau. of Ludwig Vehling and Auguste Runge; bp. 9 Feb 1929; conf. 9 Feb 1929; m. Heinrich Wilhelm Hartmann; d. senility 2 Feb 1944 (CR Bielefeld Branch, FHL microfilm 68784, no. 109; IGI)

August Friedrich Wehrhahn b. Ostendorf, Rinteln, Hessen-Nassau, 24 May 1867; son of Heinrich Karl August Wehrhahn and Mathilde Henriette Schwoone; bp. 3 Jun 1933; conf. 3 Jun 1933; ord. deacon 28 Feb 1937; ord. priest 7 May 1939; m. 7 Apr 1888, Minna Antoinette Dorothee Tebbe; three children; m. 15 Dec 1894, Engel Wilhelmine Justine Schmidt; thirteen children; m. 24 Mar 1920, Luise Requardt; d. peritoneal cancer, Engern, Hessen-Nassau, 24 Dec 1939 (FHL microfilm 68805, no. 67; IGI)

Anne Sophie Dorothee Wills b. Beckedorf, Rinteln, Hessen, Nassau, Hessen-Nassau, 11 Jun 1855; dau. of Johann Heinrich Wilhelm Wills and Christine Sophie Charlotte Dühlmeyer; bp. 11 Sep 1921; conf. 11 Sep 1921; m. Blyinghausen, Schaumburg-Lippe, 4 Nov 1880, Heinrich Friedrich Wilhelm Bredthauer; d. 1 Feb 194. (IGI; CR Bielefeld Branch, FHL microfilm 68784, no. 6; FHL microfilm 25728, 1925 census)

NOTES

1. Stadthagen city archive.
2. Presiding Bishopric, "Financial, Statistical, and Historical Reports of Wards, Stakes, and Missions, 1884–1955," 257, CHL CR 4 12.
3. West German Mission manuscript history, CHL MS 10045 2.
4. Fred Wehrhahn, telephone interview with the author, April 30, 2009.
5. Stadthagen Branch general minutes, 183, CHL LR 8676 11.
6. Ibid., 193, 200.
7. Ibid., 226, 234, 241.
8. Werner Jacobi, telephone interview with the author in German, April 13, 2009; summarized in English by Judith Sartowski.
9. Stadthagen Branch general minutes, 230.
10. Heinz Rahde, autobiography (unpublished), 19.
11. Ibid., 20.
12. Ibid., 22.
13. Stadthagen Branch general minutes, 232.
14. Rahde, autobiography, 25.
15. Ibid., 24.
16. Stadthagen Branch general minutes.
17. Ibid.
18. Ibid.
19. Rahde, autobiography, 25.
20. Ibid., 26.
21. Ibid., 27.
22. Ibid., 28.

BREMEN DISTRICT

West German Mission

Bremen was the smallest district in the West German Mission in three respects: the number of branches, the number of members, and the area covered. The principal branch was in the port city of Bremen itself. Small branches were found in Wilhelmshaven (forty miles to the northwest) and in Wesermünde-Lehe (thirty-three miles to the north, two miles north of the North Sea port of Bremerhaven). A very small number of Saints lived in Oldenburg (twenty-five miles west of Bremen), but they were not sufficiently numerous to sustain a branch and were asked to travel to Bremen to participate in meetings there.[1] The district territory covered only a few hundred square miles but included areas near the North Sea and the Netherlands where no Latter-day Saints lived.

Bremen District[2]	1939
Elders	8
Priests	6
Teachers	4
Deacons	19
Other Adult Males	40
Adult Females	127
Male Children	9
Female Children	8
Total	221

The Bremen District had too few members to provide district leadership in all Church programs when World War II began. Willy Deters was called as the district president on April 7, 1939, and served until after the war.[3] Georg Schulze served as the president of the Sunday School and the genealogy specialist, and Auguste Adler was the district Relief Society president. All three were residents of Bremen.

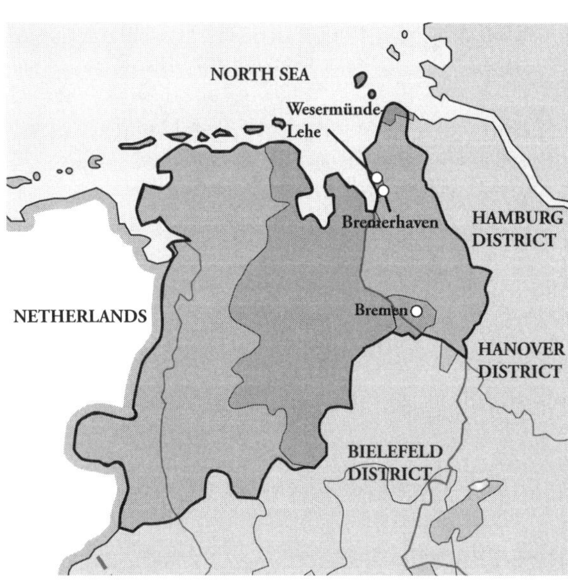

Fig. 1. The Bremen District in the far northwest corner of Germany.

Gerald Deters (born 1934) described his father, Willy, as "a very short man, but a dynamic speaker. He had a loud voice and was well liked by the members. I was proud to hear him speak in church." The fact that he was hard of hearing became a benefit to him when the Wehrmacht called him for a physical examination. When he was questioned about his health, he repeatedly asked, "What did you say?" convincing the army doctors that he was not suited for military duty.[4]

The last prewar conference of the Bremen District was held on April 8–9, 1939. A report sent to the mission office in Frankfurt included this comment: "Because of the beautiful weather and the Easter holiday the conference was poorly visited, but the Saints were happy with the messages presented there."[5] The first report filed by President Deters after the war began in September 1939 makes it clear that the war had already caused subtle difficulties for the Church in the port cities closest to the bases of the British Royal Air Force:

> Sun December 31, 1939: The fall conference of the Bremen District could not be held this year since it was impossible to secure a meeting hall. The conditions in the branches in the Bremen District are generally good. Those members who have always fulfilled their obligations to the Church still do even under these trying circumstances. We have not yet felt any of the effects of the war in Bremen. Whenever possible we hold our meetings. Because of the air-raid danger the windows are shaded and the attendance in our night meetings has dropped. Many of our members dread to go on the streets in the darkness.[6]

The next two reports sent by Willy Deters to the mission office likewise dealt with district conferences:

> March 23–24, 1940: The spring conference of the Bremen District was held on this and the preceding day. The visitor was Elder Christian Heck, acting mission president.[7] Considering the circumstances the conference was well attended, 207 being in attendance. The work in the district and the branches is going forward. Even if there are not too many present in the night meetings, all the meetings are held regularly. On Sunday mornings, even after our members have spent hours in the air-raid shelters, they are present in the Sunday School.[8]

> October 24, 1940: The fall conference of the Bremen District was held. Mission counselor Anthon [sic] Huck was the visitor from the mission office. All the meetings were held during the daytime. This was necessitated by the constant air-raid danger. The conference was attended by 180 persons.[9]

The faithful Willy Deters traveled to Frankfurt in February 1941 to participate in a conference for district presidents. He reported that it was unlikely that a district conference could be held due to constant air raids that often interrupted branch meetings. All evening meetings had been moved to daytime. Two weeks later, President Deters called three new district missionaries: Wilhelm Stelzig, Herbert Baarz, and Kurt Menssen. By July 1941, conditions in the Bremen region had improved and a belated spring district conference was held with 147 persons in attendance.[10]

In October 1941, a district conference was held and 153 persons attended, including mission supervisor Christian Heck and his counselor Anton Huck from Frankfurt. The same mission leaders returned on May 10, 1942, for the spring conference. Saints from the outlying branches overcame substantial difficulties to travel to Bremen. A total of 144 members and twenty-three friends attended the conference.[11]

Willy Deters' report to mission leaders on January 1, 1943, reveals a bit of discouragement:

> The fourth year of the war has started. What has the new year in store for us? The conditions in the branches are becoming increasingly more difficult. The lack of food is more and more noticeable. The constant air raids make the people nervous and irritable. There are only the real faithful Saints coming to the meetings now. However, these are in sufficient numbers to carry on the work.[12]

The spring conference in 1943 was held in Lehe, a small town just north of Bremerhaven. Christian Heck was again in attendance and this comment was included in the report submitted to Frankfurt: "In spite of all the sufferings the members showed a fine spirit of cooperation. The spirit of the Lord was present in rich abundance."

Willy Deters was one of the most faithful submitters of periodic reports in the West German Mission. Over time, his accounts paint a picture of a Third Reich coming down around him in flames. All three of the branches within his stewardship were located near ports critical to the German war effort and Allied bombers pounded the cities mercilessly for several years. The district president's last three reports are increasingly bleak, but he firmly believed that the Latter-day Saints were not about to give up:

> January 1, 1944: The year 1944 has come and this awful war is still going on. Life is very difficult now. The last bit of strength of the people has to be offered to the frantic war god. The life in the branches is getting increasingly more difficult. The brethren have to work day and night and don't find the time to visit the meetings. The food rationing is more severe now. The propaganda is talking of a speedy victory but no one believes this any more. Traveling now is connected with great danger. Bombers attack trains day and night. All the meetings of the branches in the Bremen District are held regularly, so far as possible under the circumstances. The attendance has dropped drastically. But the spirit has not suffered.[13]

> December 31, 1944: Everything is driving to a climax. The stress on body and soul is gigantic. The air raids are increasing with unbelievable fury. The cities of Bremen, Wesermünde and Wilhelmshaven are just ruins. In spite of all the trials our meetings are still being held, even if they have to be interrupted frequently by air raids. The faithful Saints meet in cottage meetings with only 8 to 10 members present. So closes the year of trials, 1944. But we still know that God lives and that the restored gospel still is the truth.[14]

> January 1, 1945: Hell has opened its fiery portals. It is almost impossible to visit the branches. Planes attack trains constantly. No rest can be found at night. In the branches of Wesermünde and Wilhelmshaven meetings are held regularly. Sometimes, these are interrupted. It is almost impossible to hold meetings in Bremen. However, meetings are held infrequently. There are no more members left in Bremen who still have their homes. . . . Many of the brethren are called into the armed services that are either very young, 15, or over 50 in the organization called Volkssturm, so that they might save the fatherland. Reasoning has now changed into madness.[15]

These last messages sent to Frankfurt by President Deters reveal his determination to keep his small flocks safe and to see that meetings were conducted. However, reports with such negative wording would have caused Willy Deters great difficulty had government officials or fanatical Nazi Party members seen them. Suggestions that conditions were anything but positive were considered defeatism and treason in those days. On March 1, 1945, Deters reported that communications with the mission office were disrupted and that he could communicate with branch leaders in Wilhelmshaven and Wesermünde-Lehe only by mail. His last sentence that day reads, "Now we have no one to turn to for help except the Lord. I have given instructions to the branches that all the tithing money should be banked."[16]

Willy Deters lost his own home to the Allied bombs in 1944, but he had previously moved his family just south of the city to Verden on the Aller River. Fortunately, he survived the invasion of the British army and was able to return to Bremen in the summer of 1946. There he resumed his work as the district president by gathering his flock and rebuilding the Church in that region.

Notes

1. See the Bremen Branch chapter for more about the few Latter-day Saints in Oldenburg.
2. Presiding Bishopric, "Financial, Statistical, and Historical Reports of Wards, Stakes, and Missions, 1884–1955," 257, CHL CR 4 12.
3. West German Mission manuscript history, CHL QR 1939:14.
4. Gerald Deters, interview by the author, Bountiful, UT, July 2009.
5. West German Mission manuscript history, CHL QR 1939:15.
6. West German Mission manuscript history, CHL B 1381:4.
7. Heck's official title was Missionsleiter (mission supervisor).
8. West German Mission manuscript history, CHL QR 1381:4.

9. Ibid.
10. West German Mission manuscript history, CHL B 1381:6, A 2999:6, B 1381:5.
11. West German Mission manuscript history, CHL B 1381:6.
12. Ibid., 6.
13. Ibid., 7.
14. Ibid., 7.
15. Ibid., 8. Had this kind of report reached the police at the time, Elder Deters would have almost certainly been punished for such defeatist comments.
16. Ibid., 8.

Bremen Branch

One of the principal port cities of the old Hanseatic League was Bremen, where 424,351 people lived in 1939.[1] This beautiful city on the Weser River was also home to a relatively strong branch of 158 Latter-day Saints.

The meetings were held at the time in the Guttemplerloge on Vegesackerstrasse. The branch observed the traditional meeting schedule of Sunday School at 10:00 a.m. and sacrament meeting in the evening. Other meetings were held on evenings during the week.

Bremen Branch[2]	1939
Elders	5
Priests	3
Teachers	2
Deacons	15
Other Adult Males	29
Adult Females	93
Male Children	6
Female Children	5
Total	158

The branch leadership in July 1939 consisted of president Erwin Paul Gulla and his counselors, Georg Friedrich Schulze and Johann Hinrich Wöltjen. The branch directory shows that an American missionary was the superintendant of the Sunday School but that all other leadership positions were held by members of the branch.[3]

On Friday, September 1, 1939, the branch history reported numerous challenges faced by the Bremen Branch on the first day of the war:

> The meeting hall of the Bremen Branch was confiscated by the German army. All requests, that at least one room [be] made available to the branch, are mockingly denied. "You are only trying to blunt the intellects of the people," President Willy Deters is told. Meetings in Bremen are held again in the Guttemple Logenhaus at Vegesackerstrasse. However, it is only possible to hold one sacrament meeting on Sundays. At this time Brother Albert Adler, Brother Erwin Gulla and Brother Johann Wöltjen are called into the military service. The Bremen Branch is now under the direction of district president Willy Deters.[4]

Helene Deters (born 1904), the wife of the district president, recalled that British air raids over Bremen began almost immediately. Earlier, Hermann Goering, one of Hitler's inner circle and head of the German air force, claimed that if an enemy airplane could drop a bomb on a German city, people could call him Meyer.[5] Generally a very happy young mother, Sister Deters had reason to be concerned about their safety during the many ensuing air raids against that important city: "There were no [air-raid] shelters at that time, and we huddled in our small cellar for what little protection it offered. Our house was so small that a little bomb could have easily destroyed the whole thing." During one of the first air raids, she and Willy sat in a shelter without their son, who they believed was safe at another location. "Willy and I sat there hand in hand expecting the worst. But we were calm and ready to go [die] if that was the Lord's will."[6]

There is little information regarding the location of the branch meeting rooms after the Saints were required to vacate their rooms on Vegesackerstrasse. However, they indeed had found rooms, as evidenced by the report sent to the West German Mission office in Frankfurt on January 1, 1941. Some windows in the main meeting room had been damaged by recent air raids, "but the brethren have been able to repair them."[7] Young Gerald Deters (born 1934) recalled meeting in the upstairs room of a restaurant. The building was very close to the Deters home at Wiedstrasse 42 and was not particularly impressive.[8]

When the attacks on Bremen increased in frequency and severity, the government recommended that mothers take their children to safer places. In January 1941, Willy Deters sent his wife and their son south all the way across the country to Straubing, Bavaria, where they were taken in by her sister, Emma Suelflow, and her husband, Otto. Life there was much easier in many aspects, but Gerald had difficulty understanding the local dialect, which caused some problems in school, and Otto did not treat them kindly. During their year in Straubing, they were totally isolated from the Church, and Willy was able to visit them only once. In Gerald's recollection, "It was just great to see him again, and we spent a most beautiful week in the Bavarian mountains, going on many hikes, and enjoying the magnificent scenery of that area. The time went too quickly."[9]

Back in Bremen in early 1942, the Deters family did their best to weather the storm. In their absence, Erwin Gulla had been released from the military and had served as the branch president in Wilhelmshaven and then again in Bremen. The meeting rooms had been confiscated at least once for a few weeks, then returned to the Saints.

It was good to be together again, but life in Bremen was becoming primarily a question of survival for the Deters family. Helene was working as a bookkeeper, and this allowed the family to enjoy a comfortable lifestyle, but there was rarely time for entertainment, as Gerald wrote: "For the next six months or so our routine was very simple: Mutti and Pappi went to work during the day, and I went to school. We came home, ate our supper, and then went to the air shelter for the night. It was really something to look forward to every day."[10]

On one occasion, the Deters family was visited by a branch member on leave from the Eastern Front. When Gerald learned of the constant attacks, he said that he had never experienced an air raid and wondered what it would be like. A few hours later, he found out. The roar of enemy airplanes was heard (even though no sirens sounded), and everybody ran for a large concrete bunker down the street. The bombs began to fall even before they reached the shelter, so they took refuge elsewhere. The next morning, the guest stated that it was quieter in Russia and that "he could hardly believe that we were going through this type of experience nearly every night."[11]

In early 1943, Willy Deters was transferred to his company's facility in Verden, twenty miles southeast of Bremen. Helene was fortunate to find employment at the same place, and the family moved into a small home on Brunnenweg. From there it was a short train ride back to church in Bremen, but on occasion the air raids made it impossible for them to make the trip. Gerald Deters recalled enjoying the small-town atmosphere and playing cowboys and Indians with local boys in the forest.

Fig. 1. The Deters family moved into the right half of this two-family home on Brunnenweg in Verden in 1943. They lived there for six years. (G. Deters)

Among the members of the Bremen Branch were several persons living in the city of Oldenburg, twenty-five miles to the east. Gustav Christmann and his family moved there from Heilbronn (Stuttgart District) in connection with his military assignment. Frida Bock came during the war to join the company of the state theater as a soprano. Other members there were Wübbedina Koeller and Wilhelmine Grunow and her mother and sister. They were able to attend meetings in Bremen until the last months of the war, when crucial railroad bridges were destroyed and the trip became too dangerous.[12]

The Saints in Bremen were in constant danger, as was reflected in the branch history on May 31, 1943:

> (Very heavy air raid on Pentecost): One bomb hit the house of the Bornemanns. It dug a deep hole in the middle of the cellar where these Saints and other occupants of the apartment house were staying. Luckily, it was a dud and did not explode so that they were able to leave the cellar unharmed. Here again is a wonderful manifestation of the protecting power of the Lord.[13]

Fortunately, important events in the lives of individual members could still take place in that environment. Gerald Deters was baptized in an indoor pool in the city of Bremerhaven on October 3, 1943. But the years of his childhood passed, and he was automatically inducted into the Jungvolk, the first phase of the Hitler Youth program, in the fall of 1944.

Willy Deters was required to join the National Socialist Party due to his employment. He wore the required swastika pin on his collar but was an outspoken opponent of the party and did not attend meetings. According to Gerald, Willy had to be admonished by his wife on many occasions to keep his voice down when he criticized the government, especially when they were out in public. Because his hearing was bad, he compensated with a voice that he likely did not know was loud. Despite his objections, his son Gerald attended meetings of the Jungvolk that took place at least twice a week.

Gerald was an enthusiastic member of the Jungvolk—very much what the government hoped he would become. He later wrote about marching in parades and going to movies where scenes of heroism under fire were common. Fortunately, his dreams of becoming a tank commander or serving aboard a PT boat or a submarine would never have time to become reality, for the war would soon be over.

Fig. 2. Willy Deters with his wife, Helene, and son, Gerald, after the war. (G. Deters)

The Führer, Adolf Hitler, narrowly escaped an attempt on his life on July 20, 1944, when a bomb was placed in a conference room just a few feet from where he was standing. Gerald Deters recalled being shocked to hear of the assassination attempt in a radio broadcast later that day: "We were so relieved to hear that he was safe. . . . Knowing how my dad felt about Hitler [he disapproved], I think he was not surprised to hear that somebody tried to murder him."[14]

The night of August 18–19, 1944, was a very hard one for members of the Bremen Branch, according to the branch history:

> The meeting hall of the Bremen Branch was destroyed on the night of August 18, 1944. Ninety-five percent of the members of the Bremen Branch have lost their homes, including all their belongings. All the property of the branch, chairs, tables, dinnerware, etc., which had been given to the members for safekeeping in their homes, has been completely destroyed. All the homes, where branch property was stored, were destroyed.[15]

The Deters family had transferred some of their property from the apartment at Wiedstrasse 42 to the house in Verden by then, but most of their belongings were in Bremen that night and subsequently were destroyed. In those days, it was still possible for German citizens to appeal to the government for reparations payments after air raids, and Willy Deters did precisely that. In a six-page report, he detailed the property lost when an incendiary bomb reduced the home and its contents to ashes. The report lists ninety-eight specific items (or types of items)—including the obligatory portrait of Adolf Hitler, which was valued at 12 Reichsmark. The declared value of the items inventoried was approximately two thousand Reichsmark, even though some items had no listed replacement value.[16]

Following the attack, the members of the Bremen Branch could not find rooms in which to hold their meetings. They began to meet in groups of eight or ten wherever they could. By January 1945, Willy Deters reported to the mission leaders that it was almost impossible to hold meetings in Bremen. From Verden, he could hardly ever find a train to take his family to Bremen or to go even farther north to visit the branches in Wesermünde-Lehe and Wilhelmshaven.[17] For the Deters family, church attendance was essentially on hold.

In April 1945, the British army approached Verden and was still encountering resistance from German soldiers determined to defend the fatherland. Gerald recalled that his father took the family to a farm about four miles from Verden, where it appeared to be safer, but his calculations were faulty: the family soon found themselves in the worst possible position—precisely between the attackers and the defenders. One night, the family huddled in a barn, sitting atop a pile of potatoes and praying for deliverance, while the opposing forces exchanged round after round of artillery fire and rockets. According to Gerald, "that was probably the night when we really learned how to pray, [even though] we had done it before. It was the most horrible night." A few hours later, the British tanks rolled into view, and the war was over for the Deters family. They moved back to Verden on April 20, 1945—Adolf Hitler's birthday.[18]

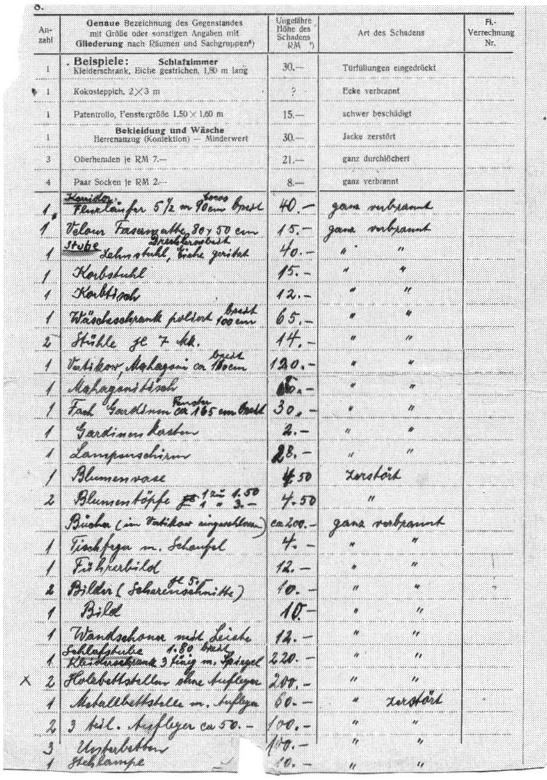

Anzahl	Genaue Bezeichnung des Gegenstandes mit Größe oder sonstigen Angaben mit Gliederung nach Räumen und Sachgruppen	Ungefähre Höhe des Schadens RM	Art des Schadens	Fl.-Verrechnung Nr.
1	Beispiele: Schlafzimmer Kleiderschrank, Eiche gestrichen, 1,80 m lang	30.—	Türfüllungen eingedrückt	
1	Kokosteppich, 2×3 m	?	Ecke verbrannt	
1	Patentrollo, Fenstergröße 1,50 × 1,60 m	15.—	schwer beschädigt	
1	Bekleidung und Wäsche Herrenanzug (Konfektion) — Minderwert	30.—	Jacke zerstört	
3	Oberhemden je RM 7.—	21.—	ganz durchlöchert	
4	Paar Socken je RM 2.—	8.—	ganz verbrannt	
1	Korridor: Flurläufer 5½ m 90 cm breit Cocos	40.–	ganz verbrannt	
1	Velour Fasermatte 80 x 50 cm	15.–	ganz verbrannt	
1	Stube: Lehnstuhl, Eiche geritzt Drechslerarbeit	40.–	" "	
1	Korbstuhl	15.–	" "	
1	Korbtisch	12.–	" "	
1	Wäscheschrank poliert Breite 100 cm	65.–	" "	
2	Stühle je 7 Mk.	14.–	" "	
1	Vertikow, Mahagoni ca 110 cm breit	120.–	" "	
1	Mahagonitisch	[illegible]	" "	
1	Fach Fenster Gardinen ca 165 cm breit	30.–	" "	
1	Gardinenkasten	2.–	" "	
1	Lampenschirm	28.–	" "	
1	Blumenvase	4.50	zerstört	
2	Blumentöpfe 1 zu 1.50, 1 " 3.–	4.50	"	
	Bücher (im Vertikow eingeschlossen)	ca 200.–	ganz verbrannt	
1	Tischfeger m. Schaufel	4.–	" "	
1	Führerbild	12.–	" "	
2	Bilder (Scherenschnitte) je 5.–	10.–	" "	
1	Bild	10.–	" "	
1	Wandschoner mit Leiste	12.–	" "	
1	Schlafstube: Kleiderschrank 3 türig m. Spiegel 1.80 breit	220.–	" "	
x 2	Holzbettstellen ohne Auflagen	200.–	" "	
1	Metallbettstelle m. Auflage	60.–	" zerstört	
2	3 teil. Auflagen ca 50.–	100.–	" "	
3	Unterbetten	100.–	" "	
1	Stehlampe	10.–	" "	

Fig. 3. Willy Deters submitted an inventory of personal property lost when the family's apartment was destroyed in an air raid. The government compensated citizens in part for their losses. (G. Deters)

Two reports sent from Bremen to the mission office in Frankfurt in the late summer of 1945 reflect the spirit of revival among the Latter-day Saints in Bremen once peace was established:

> August 25, 1945, Sunday: Ten U.S. soldiers visited the meeting in Bremen. The joy was great when we found that Elder . . . Robins, a

missionary who had labored in Bremen, was among this group. This was for us, as well as for the brethren from America, cause for great joy. After six years of war and destruction we again had brethren from Zion among us.[19]

September 16, 1945, Sunday: With the help of Col. Horace W. Shurtleff, a meeting hall for the Bremen Branch has been secured in the Wilhadistrasse 1. Starting this day regular meetings were held there. This first meeting was attended by 55 persons. The attendance is increasing constantly.[20]

By April 26, 1945, when the British army entered the city, Bremen had been bombed in 173 attacks that took the lives of at least 4,125 people. Sixty-two percent of the dwellings had been destroyed, and the city had lost 12,996 of its residents in military service.[21] Although most of the Latter-day Saints were among those who had lost their homes, they had been able to stay in or return to Bremen and were soon busy improving the condition of the branch there.

The suffering of the Saints in Bremen is described in depth in the letters written by Relief Society members to Ellen Cheney of San Diego in the years after the war. Sister Cheney directed a program to provide food and clothing to the surviving members of the Bremen Branch. In their letters of thanks, they told about their experiences and feelings. For example, Elli Ellinghaus wrote the following on December 8, 1946:

The Lehmkuhls lost everything during the war. Even their dearest, there [sic] only 20 year old boy was lost in Russia. Yes the last years of the war were for us very very hard. Many times in our troubles we cried to God for help. . . . We have had help from the Lord many times when we did not know where to turn to, there was some unexpected help for us.[22]

Lina Schubert wrote this message to Sister Cheney on November 16, 1946:

Whoever went through the war here with the many bombings, knows how much was lost to the flames. Many nerves are shocked as a result. Many are poor, they have no bed, no home, everything lost, and for what? Then all the prisoners of war who have not been returned. Why do they keep them? . . . It is a bad place to live here now, the need for food is great, there is nothing at all to buy.[23]

Sister Schubert wrote again on April 26, 1947:

I have waited so long for the return of my boy who is still a prisoner of war in Egypt. It will soon be his fifth summer there and I can tell how much he misses his family. We can only hope that his wish will soon be fulfilled. . . . It was two years ago today that our enemies appeared in our city. We spent two full days in the air raid shelters and when we came out, our city looked like a desert. Everything was destroyed. There was no water, no power, no gas, no coal, no food. Nothing but destruction everywhere. The people who didn't believe in God were moaning and groaning. May God bless us if we but stay on the straight and narrow path and do no evil.[24]

The sadness of these letters and many others with similar content is overshadowed by the gratitude expressed by the surviving Bremen Saints for the protection they received from their God and the brotherhood and sisterhood they shared during the difficult war years.

In Memoriam

The following members of the Bremen Branch did not survive World War II:

Heinrich Adler b. Bremen 6 Jun 1926; son of Heinrich Adler and Anna Auguste Drönner; bp. 22 Jun 1934; conf. 22 Jun 1934; ord. deacon 18 Aug 1940; k. in battle Russia 15 Jul 1944; bur. Orglandes, France (CHL microfilm 2458, form 42 FP, pt. 37, 90–91; FHL microfilm no. 68785, no. 111; www.volksbund.de)

Wilhelm Albert Adler b. Bremen 28 Feb 1913; son of Heinrich Adler and Anna Augusta Drönner; bp. 19 Dec 1922; conf. 19 Dec 1922; ord. deacon 8 Jan 1928; ord. teacher 1 Jun 1930; ord. priest 23 Apr 1934; ord. elder 6 Sep 1936; m. 30 Jun 1934, Anna Bodnau; rifleman; k. in battle 28 May 1940; bur. Noyers-Pont-Maugis, France (FHL microfilm 68785, no. 2; www.volksbund.de)

Mathilda Andermann b. Geestemünde, Berden, Hannover, 24 Mar 1891; dau. of Friedrich Andermann and Mathilde Behrens; bp. 21 Sep 1934; conf. 21 Sep 1934; m. 24 Mar 1923, Ernst Kassner; d. abdominal cancer 6 Jun 1940 (FHL microfilm 68785, no. 253)

Hermine Katharine Margarethe Behrens b. Neuenburg, Oldenburg, 13 Mar 1863; dau. of Johann Friedrich Behrens and Hella Margarethe Meyer; bp. 26 Apr 1928; conf. 26 Apr 1928; m. 21 Jun 1899, Johann Friedr. Ortgiesen (div.); d. cardiac insufficiency 2 Jan 1942 (FHL microfilm 68785, no. 152; IGI)

Aug. Emilie Karoline Boeck b. Nörenberg, Gaatzig, Pommern, 8 Nov 1863; dau. of Wilhelm Boeck and Karoline Giese; bp. 20 Jul 1918; conf. 20 Jul 1918; m. —— Kolbe; d. heart attack 28 Jan 1944 (FHL microfilm 68785, no. 26)

Karoline Elise Minna Dauelsberg b. Stolzenau, Berden, Hannover, 11 Feb 1866; dau. of Christian Gerhard Fr. H. Dauelsberg and Auguste Reymann; bp. 31 Aug 1906; conf. 31 Aug 1906; m. 7 May 1892, Ernst Heinrich Jäkel; d. stroke 5 Apr 1942 (FHL microfilm 68785, no. 29)

Tjaltje DeJong b. Opende, Gröningen, Netherlands, 2 Jan 1893; dau. of Andreas DeJong and Sjonkje Ras; bp. 10 Aug 1922; conf. 10 Aug 1922; m. —— Dittrich; d. pneumonia 15 Feb 1942 (FHL microfilm 68785, no. 90; FHL microfilm 25755, 1930 census)

Marianne Hammerski b. Klonia, Konitz, Westpreussen, 2 Jul 1865; dau. of Josef Hamerski and Clara Florentina Zielinski; bp. 20 Aug 1939; conf. 20 Aug 1939; m. Wilhelmsburg, Hamburg, 6 Oct 1894, Johann Hermann Christoph Wesseloh; 7 children; d. senility Bremen 17 Nov 1941 (FHL microfilm 68785, no. 292; IGI)

Mathilde Katharine Rudolfine Klempel b. Valpariso, Metropolitana, Chile, 7 May 1873; dau. of Otto Samuel Klempel and Hanna Ernestine Lina Fleissner; bp. 18 Jun 1926; conf. 18 Jun 1926; d. heart attack 2 Dec 1940 (FHL microfilm 68785, no. 108; IGI)

Hermann Albert Koslowski b. Bremen 22 Feb 1913; son of Max Koslowski and Auguste Schwettling; bp. 28 Jun 1923; conf. 28 Jun 1923; k. in battle Artemowsk, Russia, 1943 (CHL microfilm 2458, form 42 FP, pt. 37, 170–71; FHL microfilm 68785, no. 38)

Emilie Lohwasser b. Neudeck, Österreich, 8 Mar 1868; bp. 31 May 1924; conf. 1 Jun 1924; m. 16 May 1890, Ludwig Fleischer; d. senility 14 Feb 1941 (FHL microfilm 68785, no. 82)

Sophie Marie Mühlenbruck b. Kirchboitzen, Fallingbostel, Hannover, 13 Feb 1872; dau. of Hermann Mühlenbruck and Louise M. Dorothea Grosse; bp. 29 Oct 1907; conf. 19 Oct 1907; m. 6 Apr 1895, Heinrich Thom; k. air raid Bremen 23 Apr 1945 (CHL microfilm 2458, form 42 FP, pt. 37, 122–23; FHL microfilm 68785, no. 64)

Julianne Gesine Wilhelmine Paul b. Spain 14 Jun 1873; dau. of Julius Paul and Sophie von Südwenz; bp. Hamburg 31 May 1924; conf. 1 Jun 1924; d. 22 Jul 1943 (FHL microfilm 68785, no. 79; IGI)

Karl Günter Rau b. Heilbronn, Mittelfranken, Bayern, 6 Oct 1935; son of Gustav Christmann and Else Rau; k. air raid Bremen 17 Apr 1945 (CHL microfilm 2458, form 42 FP, pt. 37, 122–23; FHL microfilm 68785, no. 286; IGI)

Bruen Schroeder b. Mahndorf, Achim, Hannover, 3 Jan 1883; son of Bruen Schröder and Gesche Kuhlmann; bp. 10 May 1913; d. 18 Mar 1942 (CHL CR 375 8 2458; IGI)

Bruno Gerhard Schulze b. Bremen 5 May 1902; son of Georg Friedrich Schulze and Hermine Wagner; bp. 3 Mar 1911; conf. 3 Mar 1911; m. 5 May 1927, Marichen Dreke; k. air raid Bremen 24 Jun 1944 (CHL microfilm 2458, form 42 FP, pt. 37, 90–91; FHL microfilm 68785, no. 58)

Emmi Eliese von Hefen b. Strohauserdeich, Rodenkirchen, Oldenburg, 1 Mar 1869; dau. of Cornelius von Hefen and Marie Schroeder; bp. 5 Jul 1921; conf. 5 Jul 1921; m. —— Freudenberg, d. 2 Jul 1943 (FHL microfilm 68785, no. 16)

Geertje Wagener b. Bunde, Weener, Ostfriesland, Hannover, 27 Aug 1874; dau. of Koene Harms Wagener and Weldelke Bruns; bp. 5 May 1908; conf. 5 May 1908; d. heart attack 17 Oct 1941 (FHL microfilm 68785, no. 67; IGI)

Johann Hermann Christoph Wesseloh b. Fintel, Hannover, 17 Sep 1867; son of Johann Wesseloh and Gesche Windeler; bp. 20 Aug 1937; conf. 10 Aug 1937; m. Wilhelmsburg, Harburg, Hannover, 6 Oct 1894, Marianne Hammerski; 7 children; d. intestinal cancer Wandsbek, Altona, Schleswig-Holstein, 29 or 30 May 1942 (FHL microfilm 68785, no. 293; IGI)

Katharina Wissenbach b. Gundhelm, Schlüchtern, Hessen-Nassau, 24 May 1860; dau. of Franz Wissenbach and Margaretha Hummel; bp. 20 Aug 1938; conf. 20 Aug 1938; m. 12 Aug 1888, Heinrich Lüdecke; d. senility 22 Feb 1941 (FHL microfilm 68785, no. 306; IGI)

Betty Wöltjen b. Rautendorf, Osterholz, Hannover, 18 Mar 1889; dau. of Johann Hinrich Wöltjen and Margarethe Adelheid Viehl; bp. 15 Jun 1929; conf. 15 Jun 1929; m. 27 Apr 1912; 2m. 21 Feb 1921, Ernst Otto Emil Greier; 3m. 25 Jun 1938, Ferdinand Martin Tubbe; k. air raid Bremen 26 Nov 1943 (CHL microfilm 2458, form 42 FP, pt. 37, 58–59; FHL microfilm 68785, no. 154; IGI)

Johann Hinrich Wöltjen b. Rautendorf, Osterholz, Hannover, 25 Apr 1887; son of Johann Hinrich Wöltjen and Margarethe Adelheid Viehl; bp. 6 Jun 1925; conf. 6 Jun 1925; ord. deacon 1 Aug 1926; ord. teacher 28 Oct 1928; ord. priest 1 Jun 1930; m. Bremen 18 Oct 1913, Berta Henschel; six children; d. pleurisy Bremen 11 Mar 1945 (FHL microfilm 68785, no. 96; IGI)

Catharine Marie Wübbenhorst b. Sandhorst, Aurich, Hannover, 12 Mar 1864; dau. of Johann Christian Wübbenhorst and Marg. Folina Götz; bp. 10 Jun 1916; conf. 10 Jun 1916; m. 18 Dec 1893, Heinrich Bengson; d. heart attack 15 Jan 1942 (FHL microfilm 68785, no. 8)

Notes

1. Bremen city archive.
2. Presiding Bishopric, "Financial, Statistical, and Historical Reports of Wards, Stakes, and Missions, 1884–1955," CHL CR 4 12, 257.
3. West German Mission branch directory, 1939, CHL LR 10045 11.
4. West German Mission manuscript history, CHL B 1381:3.
5. Germans would soon be telling countless jokes featuring "Herr Meyer" in an obvious reference to Goering.
6. Helene Albetzky Deters, autobiography (unpublished), private collection.
7. West German Mission manuscript history, CHL B 1381:5.
8. Gerald Deters, interview by the author, Bountiful, UT, July 1, 2009.
9. Gerald Deters, autobiography (unpublished), private collection.
10. Ibid.
11. Ibid.
12. Erwin Büsing, "Beitrag zur Geschichte der Gemeinde Oldenburg von 1946 bis 2007" (unpublished), private collection.
13. West German Mission manuscript history, CHL B 1381:7.
14. Gerald Deters, interview. The incident occurred at Hitler's headquarters for the Eastern Front, near Rastenburg, East Prussia. The bomb was planted by Claus Graf Schenk von Stauffenberg, who was executed for treason later that same day in Berlin.
15. Ibid.
16. *Sachschaden-Antrag*, submitted by Wilhelm Deters to the city of Bremen on September 1, 1944; private collection.
17. West German Mission manuscript history, CHL B 1381:8.
18. Gerald Deters, interview.
19. West German Mission manuscript history, CHL B. 1381:9.
20. West German Mission manuscript history, CHL B. 1381:10.
21. Bremen city archive.
22. Elli Ellinghaus to Ellen Cheney, December 8, 1946; used by permission of George and Lorene Runyan.
23. Lina Schubert to Ellen Cheney, November 16, 1946; used by permission of George and Lorene Runyan.
24. Lina Schubert to Ellen Cheney, April 26, 1947; used by permission of George and Lorene Runyan.

Wesermünde-Lehe Branch

The home of the Wesermünde-Lehe Branch was, in general, the city of Bremerhaven. Thirty-eight miles downriver from Bremen, the community is located at the mouth of the Weser River at the North Sea. The members of this branch lived closer to the enemy air bases during the war than any other Church members in Germany. This fact alone made life in the area very challenging.

The meetings of this branch were held in a building at Poststrasse 123, but no description of the rooms is available. More than one-half of the branch members were females twelve and over and only four members were children. Priesthood leadership was present; there were three elders in the branch. It is also evident from the records of other branches in the district that visitors from Bremen and Wilhelmshaven were seen in this small branch on numerous occasions. The small number of members would explain why the mission directory of August 1939 shows that Mutual and Relief Society were the only groups holding meetings during the week.[1] Sunday School took place at 10:00 a.m. and sacrament meeting at 7:00 p.m. each Sunday.

Wesermünde-Lehe Branch[2]	**1939**
Elders	3
Priests	0
Teachers	1
Deacons	4
Other Adult Males	4
Adult Females	21
Male Children	2
Female Children	2
Total	37

The following comments are taken from the West German Mission manuscript history:

> October 29, 1939: Karl Kinast was ordained an elder and called to be branch president following the departure of the missionaries.[3]

> October 25, 1942: A branch conference was held in the Wesermünde Branch which, under the circumstances, was well attended; forty-two persons attended. A wonderful spirit was in all the meetings.[4]

> November 29, 1942: In Wilhelmshaven, which is in constant danger of enemy attacks, a branch conference was held. In spite of two air raids that interrupted the meetings, the spirit of God was present in rich abundance. The attendance was seventeen.[5]

> June 17, 1944: The Wesermünde Branch meeting hall was destroyed. The Bremen District spring conference had been planned to be held in the Wesermünde chapel on June 25. All the preparations had been made in vain. Since another meeting hall could not be found in Wesermünde, one room in the ruins of this building was used to hold meetings.[6]

The last entry in the branch general minutes referring to the war was recorded on July 5, 1945. President Deters of the Bremen District had found a way to travel again and visited the Wesermünde-Lehe Branch that day. The clerk wrote, "The meetings are still being held in the ruins of the former meeting hall. In spite of this the attendance is constantly increasing. Branch President Kinast has done a wonderful work here. . . . He has stayed on the job and done his best."[7] The man mentioned was Karl Kinast, who had been serving as the second counselor to the branch president, an American missionary, just before the war began.

The port facilities of Bremerhaven were attacked on a great many occasions during the war by the British Royal Air Force and the U.S. Army Air Corps. It can be assumed not only that the branch meeting rooms at Poststrasse 12 were damaged, but that the homes of several members were damaged or destroyed. Whatever the damage was, they were still holding meetings in the summer of 1945 and were likely joined soon by LDS refugees from the East German Mission.

In Memoriam

The following members of the Wesermünde-Lehe Branch did not survive World War II:

Friedrich August Wilhelm Biermann b. Stadthagen, Schaumburg-Lippe, 13 Oct 1910; son of Heinrich Friedrich Wilhelm Biermann and Sophie Karoline Wilhelmine Huckemeier; m. Cuxhaven, Hamburg, 1933, Emmy Geimplinger; d. 8 Oct 1943 (FHL microfilm 25723, 1925 and 1930 censuses)

Ludwig Blass b. Trier, Trier, Rheinland, 2 Jun 1876; son of Karl Ernst Gabriel Blass and Klara von Schmoll; bp. 2 Feb 1928; conf. 2 Feb 1928; ord. deacon 4 Sep 1932; m. Johanna Kühn; k. air raid Bremen 24 Jun 1944 (FHL microfilm 68785, no. 130; FHL microfilm 25725, 1930 census)

Dieter Danklefsen b. Friedrichstadt, Schleswig, Schleswig-Holstein, 28 Aug 1940; son of Paul Heinrich Danklefsen and Anita Martha Elisabeth Brassat; d. dysentery 19 Oct 1942 (FHL microfilm 68808, no. 569; FHL microfilm 25751, 1935 census; IGI)

Notes

1. West German Mission branch directory, 1939, CHL LR 10045 11.
2. Presiding Bishopric, "Financial, Statistical, and Historical Reports of Wards, Stakes, and Missions, 1884–1955," 257, CHL CR 4 12.
3. West German Mission history, CHL LR 10045 2; West German Mission manuscript history B 1381:3.
4. West German Mission manuscript history, 6.
5. Ibid.
6. Ibid., 7.
7. Ibid., 9.

Wilhelmshaven Branch

The smallest branch in the Bremen District was located in the North Sea port city of Wilhelmshaven. About forty miles northwest of the city of Bremen, Wilhelmshaven could be reached via railroad in an hour. Only twenty-six members of The Church of Jesus Christ of Latter-day Saints were associated with this branch when the war began.

Brother Rodewald was the branch president in July 1939 and remained in that position until November 10, 1940.[1] On that date, he was released and replaced by Erwin Gulla during a meeting attended by the presidents of the Bremen and Hamburg Districts (Willy Deters and Alwin Brey, respectively). That same day, the following comment was added in the branch records: "In all cities of the district the conditions brought about by constant air raids grew increasingly worse."[2] The proximity to the British air bases across the North Sea had already proved inconvenient and dangerous.

Wilhelmshaven Branch[3]	1939
Elders	0
Priests	3
Teachers	1
Deacons	0
Other Adult Males	7
Adult Females	13
Male Children	1
Female Children	1
Total	26

Brother Gulla was released as the president and replaced by Alfred Passon on November 11, 1941.[4] No eyewitness accounts of members in this branch could be located at the time of this writing. The only indications of the status or activities of the branch are found in the general minutes.

Two additional entries in the branch minutes are of particular interest and make it clear that the members of the branch were not simply surviving during the final month of the war. On April 6, 1945, President Alfred Passon requested permission from district president Willy Deters to baptize five persons into the Church. The permission was granted.[5] Not three weeks later, President Passon requested permission for another baptism, namely for Sister Henny Haubock. It would seem that the few branch members living in the vicinity of Wilhelmshaven were quite willing to talk about their church even while the Third Reich was collapsing around them.

The port and city of Wilhelmshaven suffered an estimated 60 percent damage. The city was home to 103,842 people in 1939, but many left during the war in search of safer living conditions. At least one hundred air raids took place, and 510 residents are known to have been killed in those attacks before Polish troops entered the city as conquerors on May 6, 1945. The toll in military personnel killed (12,996) likely included soldiers and sailors stationed at the port.[6]

In Memoriam

The following members of the Wilhelmshaven Branch did not survive World War II:

Hermina Katharine Margarete Behrens b. Neuenburg, Oldenburg, 13 Mar 1860; dau. of Johann Friedrich Behrens and Hella Margarete Meyer; bp. 26 Apr 1928; conf. 26 Apr 1928; m. 21 Jun 1891, Johann Friedrich Ortgiesen (div.); d. heart failure 2 Jan 1942 (FHL microfilm 68808, no. 1; IGI)

Karl Friedrich Wilhelm Werner b. Kade, Jerichow, Sachsen, 4 Oct 1861; son of Wilhelm Werner and Louise Reck; bp. 3 Jul 1928; conf. 3 Jul 1928; ord. deacon 17 Nov 1929; ord. teacher 7 Apr 1940; ord. priest 22 Feb 1942; k. street car accident 8 Jan 1943 (FHL microfilm 68785, no. 213; IGI)

Katharina Wissenbach b. Gundhelm, Schlüchtern, Hessen-Nassau, 24 May 1860; dau. of Franz Wissenbach and Margaretha Hummel; bp. 20 Aug 1938; conf. 20 Aug 1938; m. 12 Aug 1888, Heinrich Lüdeke; d. 22 Feb 1941 (FHL microfilm 68808, no. 51; IGI)

Notes

1. West German Mission branch directory, 1939, CHL LR 10045 11.
2. Wilhelmshaven Branch general minutes, vol. 5, CHL B 1381.
3. Presiding Bishopric, "Financial, Statistical, and Historical Reports of Wards, Stakes, and Missions, 1884–1955," 257, CHL CR 4 12.
4. Wilhelmshaven Branch general minutes, 5.
5. Ibid., 9.
6. Wilhelmshaven city archive.

FRANKFURT DISTRICT

West German Mission

Twenty-five miles east of the confluence of the Rhine and Main Rivers, the city of Frankfurt am Main lies in a significant position to support transportation and commerce in southwestern Germany. Around Frankfurt are clustered several major cities, and this concentration of population may have attracted the first missionaries of The Church of Jesus Christ of Latter-day Saints to the region in the 1840s. The Lutheran Church has dominated in the region since the mid-1500s, but the Reformed Lutheran and Catholic Churches are also present, as well as many small synagogues and several Huguenot congregations.

Frankfurt District[1]	1939
Elders	31
Priests	11
Teachers	8
Deacons	36
Other Adult Males	88
Adult Females	332
Male Children	27
Female Children	18
Total	551

As World War II approached in 1939, the Frankfurt District was relatively strong, consisting of six congregations and a total of 551 members. The principal branch was, of course, in the city of Frankfurt, with others located in Bad Homburg (nine miles to the west), Offenbach (six miles to the east), Michelstadt (twenty-five miles to the southeast), Darmstadt (eighteen miles to the south) and Mainz (twenty-five miles to the west). Indeed, the branches were grouped so closely that the leaders of the Frankfurt District could travel by train within one hour to every branch except Michelstadt, which was situated deep in the Odenwald Forest.

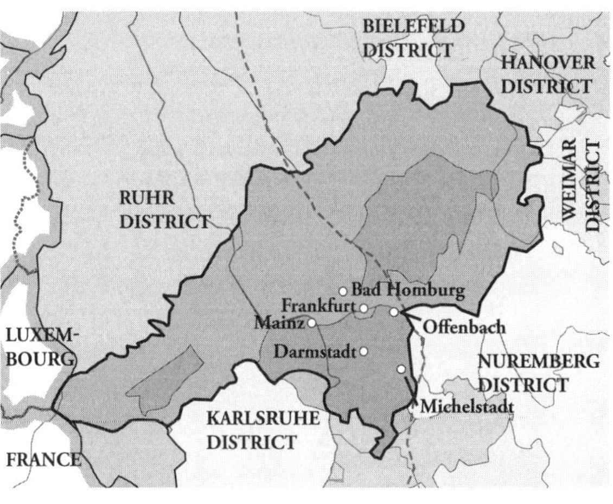

Fig. 1. The territory of the Frankfurt District in southwest Germany. No Latter-day Saints lived in the southwest and northeast areas of this district.

Fig. 1. The circles show (from left) the locations of the West German Mission home at Schaumainkai 41, the Frankfurt Branch meeting rooms at Neue Mainzerstrasse 8–10, and the town of Bad Homburg.

The territory included within the district was extensive and covered many regions where no Latter-day Saints were known to have lived when the war began, including all of the state of Hesse-Nassau to the North (with the exception of Kassel County), all of the state of Hesse, the district of Rhine-Hesse to the southwest, and all of the Rhineland south of the city of Cologne (bordering on France, Luxembourg, and Belgium). There had probably never been any missionary activity in the area west of the city of Mainz, and no branches had existed in that territory.

The average number of elders in the district was only five per branch, while there was probably an average of thirty adult women in each branch. These five branches were certainly not rich in children, with an average of only eight each. As was the case all over the West German Mission at the time, the Saints in this district tended to be older people, but most represented families that had not been acquainted with the Church for more than two generations. Many of the members on the rolls in 1939 had joined the Church since the end of World War I.

The district president in early 1939 was Anton Huck (born 1872), a member of the Frankfurt Branch. A modest man by occupation (a retired streetcar operator), he was likeable and by all reports very dedicated to serving in the kingdom of God on the earth. With the departure of the American missionaries on August 25, 1939, President Huck became the second counselor to the new mission supervisor, Friedrich Biehl of Essen. His replacement as district president was Friedrich Wagner. The next district president was Hans Förster, also of the Frankfurt Branch, who was called on July 9,

1944. He apparently was still serving in this office when the war came to an end in May 1945.

District conferences in Frankfurt were important to the Saints, as they were all over Germany. Those conferences were held at least through the fall of 1944, despite the increasing lack of rentable rooms. In 1943 and 1944, conferences were held in Darmstadt and even in Strasbourg, to the south and west and well beyond the borders of the district. The influence of Kurt Schneider was likely a factor there, because he served as a counselor to Anton Huck in the last year of the war.[2]

When Germany began to pick itself up as a conquered territory in the summer of 1945, the only Saints in the Frankfurt District who still had meeting rooms of their own were those in Michelstadt. The other five branches had been bombed out, burned out, or turned out and were holding meetings as groups in the homes of various members. It would be many months before all of the branches had adequate meetings places again.

A conservative estimate would have at least 50 percent of the members of the Church in this district homeless when the war ended. Hundreds more had been compelled to leave the larger cities due to air raids, and many of them would not be able (or allowed) to come home for another year or two. Dozens left during the war for reasons unknown and were never seen again, as reflected in the efforts of branch clerks to establish their locations as late as 1950. At least a few of the Saints were killed at home or abroad, and the news of their deaths simply never reached the ears of other Latter-day Saints who survived.

As sad as the state of affairs in this district was, the Saints there went about the task of rebuilding their lives and their branches as soon as the gunfire subsided and the smoke cleared. Contributing to the effort were hundreds of refugee Saints who had arrived from as far east as Königsberg and Danzig (areas soon ceded to Poland and Russia). By the fall of 1945, a Mormon colony had formed and was growing steadily in the city of Langen (on the road between Frankfurt and Darmstadt). In just a few years, the Saints there would number more than three hundred.

Notes

1. Presiding Bishopric, "Financial, Statistical, and Historical Reports of Wards, Stakes, and Missions, 1884–1955," 257, CHL CR 4 12.
2. Having both an automobile and a chauffeur, President Schneider was likely the most mobile leader in the West German Mission at the time. He visited Saints all over his own Strasbourg District and in the Karlsruhe and Stuttgart Districts. He also made it to Frankfurt on several occasions.

Bad Homburg Branch

The Taunus Mountain range begins just a few miles northwest of Frankfurt and runs to the west and north for fifty miles. At the eastern edge of those mountains, just eight miles from downtown Frankfurt, is the city of Bad Homburg, known for the curative powers of its fine mineral water springs. When World War II began, 18,541 people called this small city their home.[1] Only twenty-three of those were members of the LDS Church.

With only a few deacons in the branch, the Saints in Bad Homburg depended on the missionaries from the United States for priesthood leadership. The last prewar branch president was Leland B. Blatter. He and his companion, Douglas N. Thompson, were likely the heart of the branch, but they departed with all other Americans serving in the West German Mission on August 25, 1939. The only local member of the Church whose name is included in the branch directory of July 1939 is Marie Molitor, the secretary of the Sunday School.[2]

In August 1939, this small branch held its meetings in rented rooms on the second floor of a building at Luisenstrasse 26. No description of the venue is available. Sunday School began at 10 a.m. and sacrament meeting at 8:00 p.m. The only other meeting held at the time was MIA on Wednesdays at 8:00 p.m.

Bad Homburg Branch[3]	**1939**
Elders	0
Priests	0
Teachers	0
Deacons	4
Other Adult Males	3
Adult Females	13
Male Children	0
Female Children	3
Total	23

The minutes of meetings in the Bad Homburg Branch have survived and offer important information about the activities of the branch during the war. On the first Sunday after the departure of the missionaries, Anton Huck, the president of the Frankfurt District, conducted the meetings and made assignments for ongoing service in the absence of adult priesthood holders. He called Sister Gertrud Glaser to be the temporary leader of the branch and the other members sustained the assignment. Sister Karoline Müller was asked to assume leadership of the adult class, and Sister Marie Gerecht was to support Sister Braun in teaching the children's class. Average attendance at meetings in those days was fifteen persons.[4]

During the fall of 1939, meetings of the Bad Homburg Branch were conducted by Anton Huck, Hans Förster, Valentin Schlimm, and a Brother Faust from Frankfurt. The average attendance at sacrament meeting in the first months of the war was six persons. The Christmas program was a great success with thirty-five persons attending.[5]

Gertrud Glaser (born 1919) had only been a member of the Church since April 1938. Her call to "lead" the branch could be interpreted as an indication that she was faithful in attending her meetings and in carrying out assignments. In her autobiographical writings, she described the reasons why the three adult males in the branch were not called to lead: one was in the military, one had seizures, and one had problems with the Church's health code. "We were a very small branch," she explained.

Gertrud's prime responsibility was to see that meetings took place in Bad Homburg on a regular schedule. Because the brethren could not come from Frankfurt every week, she likely saw to it that the sisters of the branch met to sing, pray, and study the scriptures and other Church literature together. Sister Glaser was a domestic servant in the home of the Hermann and Lieselotte Rüdiger family. The Rüdigers apparently did nothing to prevent Gertrud from attending church meetings on Sundays.[6]

Apparently no records of meetings in Bad Homburg were kept from October 1940 to January 1944, since no pages are missing from the minutes book. As of January 28, 1944, Kerna Kraus was serving as the clerk but explained in her record that she was doing so as a substitute (*in Vertretung*).[7] The entry made one month later offers significant detail regarding branch activities:

> February 28, 1944: Monthly report for February 1944; tithing funds totaling 30 RM were collected, 25 RM forwarded [to mission office] and 5 RM returned to Sister Luise Rück. Mission leader Anton Huck visited the Bad Homburg Branch on February 29, most of all for Sister Rode. She is again in the hospital after a very serious accident. She is recovering and her faith is *extremely strong*. Her time will soon be completed.

Alwine Rode passed away on March 24, having been a member of the Church since 1923. Her funeral was conducted by Pastor Ohli of the local Lutheran Church. August Gerecht had been asked to go to Frankfurt and bring back one of the elders to conduct the service, but air raids prevented him from fulfilling the request. Apparently this led to ill feelings among the sisters, who believed that Sister Rode had been neglected. Marie Gerecht chose not to attend meetings for awhile, offended by the negative comments made about her husband. Fortunately the matter was settled soon thereafter.[8]

Several members of the Bad Homburg Branch traveled to district conferences in Frankfurt and Darmstadt during the war. The branch records show that six members participated in a district conference in Darmstadt in early 1944, and two even made the long trip (150 miles) to Strassburg in occupied France for the district conference on June 3–4, 1944. One month later, four brethren came to Bad Homburg from Frankfurt to present a program commemorating the death of Joseph Smith one hundred years earlier.[9]

In the spring of 1944, Gertrud Glaser's service in the Rüdiger home was terminated after six and one-half years, and the government assigned her to work for a dentist named Sofie Beil in Oberursel. Although Dr. Beil also allowed Gertrud time off on Sundays to attend church, Gertrud did not worship with the Saints in Bad Homburg (just two miles to the northeast), but rather traveled about seven miles to Frankfurt. Gertrud recalled that the Bad Homburg Branch was closed when she moved to Oberursel, and the lack of branch minutes after July 1944 confirm this.

> Events of the summer of 1944 included a rare treat—the baptism of three persons. Emmilie Vogt was baptized on July 22 along with her daughters, Gertrud and Lieselotte, at the Main Bath House in Frankfurt/Main near the Eisener Steg Bridge. It must have been a happy occasion for the members of this small branch.[10]

If the reasons for the long trip to church in Frankfurt on Sundays included spending time with the branch president, nobody need assume anything untoward. Hermann O. Ruf, a native of Stuttgart, had moved to Frankfurt with his military employment and was a widower.[11] In the fall of 1944, Gertrud and Hermann began to discuss marriage, but his military commitments prevented the plan from being carried out until December 9. Gertrud wrote the following about her feelings at the time:

> Because of [Hermann's] military service, we were able to spend only a short amount of time together [after the wedding]. But those were hours of happiness, peace and joy. The war brought times of sacrifice and deprivation. Toward the end, the streetcars were no longer in service and I had to walk from Ginnheim [in northwest Frankfurt] to the meetings in the mission home on the south side of the Main River.

Gertrud Glaser Ruf's story does not indicate when Hermann left Frankfurt, but he was a POW under the Americans for at least seven weeks before returning to his young wife on June 22, 1945. She was living at the time with the Schlichtegroll family (also members of the branch). Regarding the wonderful reunion, Gertrud wrote, "Now we could begin our life together with the few earthly possessions we had."

The branch minutes do not include any information for the crucial last months of the war. The first postwar comments are dated September 1945 and describe the reorganization of the branch:

> Mr. Schrott found a beautiful room for the branch. We will move in on September 1 at Höhestrasse 12 (main floor). The lessor is the Red Cross of Bad Homburg. For the next six months the rent will be 60 RM per month. For the summer half-year, 50 RM. Elders from the Frankfurt/Main branch will conduct our meetings.[12]

The survival of this small branch during World War II can be attributed to two groups of members—the sisters of the branch who carried out their duties in the absence of local priesthood leaders, and the brethren from Frankfurt who made many trips to Bad Homburg to see to the needs of the few Latter-day Saints there.

In Memoriam

The following members of the Bad Homburg Branch did not survive World War II:

Hans Johann Ludwig Gerecht b. Köppern, Bad Homburg, Hessen-Nassau, 30 Dec 1921; son of August Gerecht and Maria Elisabeth Günther; bp. 28 Aug 1937;

conf. 28 Aug 1937; m. Frankfurt/Main, Hessen-Nassau, 24 Jul 1943, Gerda Berta Rode; k. Albania, April 1945 (NFS; www.volksbund.de)

Heinz Edler Gottlieb von Hayn b. Frankfurt/Main, Hessen-Nassau 15 or 19 Apr 1915; son of Albert Philipp von Hayn and Mathilde Luise Schick; bp. 7 Nov 1924; conf. 7 Nov 1924; lieutenant; k. in battle northeast of Kriwoi Rog, Ukraine, 15 Nov 1943 (CHL microfilm 2458, Form 42 FP, pt. 37, all-mission list 1943–46, 186–87; district list 298–99; FHL microfilm 68791, no. 837; www.volksbund.de)

Alwine Morenz b. Elberfeld, Wuppertal, Rheinprovinz, 17 Sep 1885; dau. of Gustav Theodor Moranz and Anna Maria Catharina Alwine Klein; bp. 15 Apr 1923; conf. 15 Apr 1923; m. Elberfeld 30 Mar 1912 to Heinrich Jakob Rode; 2 children; d. cardiac asthma, Bad Homburg, Hessen-Nassau, 24 Mar 1944 (NFS)

Mathilde Louise Schick b. Bad Homburg vor der Höhe, Hessen-Nassau, 14 May 1882; dau. of Johann Heinrich Schick and Marie Elisabeth Engel; bp. 7 Nov 1924; conf. 7 Nov 1924; m. abt 1900, Albert Philipp von Hayn; 7 or 8 children; d. stroke Bad Homburg vor der Höhe 27 Nov 1939 (FHL microfilm 68791, no. 841; Frankfurt District Book I; IGI; PRF)

Notes

1. Bad Homburg city archive.
2. West German Mission manuscript history, CHL MS 10045 2.
3. Presiding Bishopric, "Financial, Statistical, and Historical Reports of Wards, Stakes, and Missions, 1884–1955," 257, CHL CR 4 12.
4. Bad Homburg Branch general minutes, 89, LR 10901 11.
5. Ibid, 96.
6. Gertrud Glaser Ruf, autobiography (unpublished, 2003), private collection.
7. Bad Homburg Branch general minutes, 96.
8. Ibid., 108, 120–21. Hermann Ruf, president of the Frankfurt Branch, dedicated Sister Rode's grave on November 12, 1944.
9. Ibid., 109.
10. Ibid., 125.
11. See the Frankfurt Branch chapter for details about the service of Hermann O. Ruf. His brother, Erwin, was the president of the Stuttgart District.
12. Bad Homburg Branch general minutes, 132.

Darmstadt Branch

The annual summer festival of the city of Darmstadt is called *Heinerfest*, a reminder of the historically high frequency of the name Heinrich (nickname Heiner) among local males. The city had been home to the capital of the Grand Duchy of Hesse for several centuries and is located at the northern end of the Bergstrasse, the road that runs south to Heidelberg along the western edge of the Odenwald Forest. Darmstadt had 110,552 inhabitants when World War II began.[1]

Darmstadt Branch[2]	1939
Elders	6
Priests	3
Teachers	3
Deacons	2
Other Adult Males	7
Adult Females	50
Male Children	8
Female Children	2
Total	81

With six elders and eight Aaronic Priesthood holders, this branch was quite strong. As was true throughout the Frankfurt District, adult women constituted the majority (62 percent) of the membership of the Darmstadt Branch. However, the six elders may have been inactive at the time, because the branch president in June 1939 was a missionary from the United States. The first counselor, Christian Lang, became the branch president when the missionaries left on August 25, 1939.

Church meetings were held in rented rooms at Wilhelm Glässing Strasse 9, just a few blocks south of the city center. Georg Marquardt (born 1918) recalled going up a staircase in the back of the building to the meeting rooms on the second floor.[3] Karl-Heinz Sommerkorn (born 1931) recalled that as a child, he climbed a winding staircase to the meeting rooms above in what he called "a long building."[4] Sunday School began at 10:30 a.m. in those days, and the members returned to church at 7:15 p.m. for sacrament meeting. On Wednesday evenings, they met again—for MIA and genealogy classes at 8:00 p.m. and for Relief Society and priesthood meetings at 9:00 p.m.

The Marquardt family lived on a small farm near Gadernheim, about ten miles south of Darmstadt. The route to church was a challenging one because public transportation did not connect the two locations directly. Members of the Marquardt family often walked the entire distance to church over country roads through the Odenwald Forest. Georg's father, Johannes Marquardt, had joined the Church in 1903, and his mother joined after World War I. When it was not possible to make the trek to Darmstadt, the family held meetings in their home.

The Wehrmacht called Georg Marquardt just after Poland was conquered in the fall of 1939. Following training in nearby Heidelberg, he was sent home for the winter and called up again in July 1940. Among various domestic stations was Schwetzingen, a town close to Mannheim, and Georg took advantage of the opportunity to attend the branch there. The fact that he had a driver's license may have played a role in his assignment to a tank unit, and further duty saw him in Amiens and Versailles, France, before he was moved to Italy.

Georg was fortunate to avoid injury from the enemy during the war, but his own troops accidentally shot him during a New Year's Eve party in France. According to his recollection,

> Somebody upstairs was playing with a gun. Suddenly we heard a shot; it went through the thin ceiling and hit me just when I was about to go to bed. They transported me to the military hospital and told me not to move because the bullet hit me near my spinal cord. But when I moved a little, we saw that the bullet was lying on the floor. It was a harmless ricochet. It was unbelievable.

The Sommerkorn family lived in Arheilgen, a northern suburb of Darmstadt. The father, Karl-Ludwig Sommerkorn, was employed in the construction of the new Autobahn from Frankfurt to Darmstadt. Because he worked for the government, he was required to be a member of the Nazi Party and to attend regular meetings. "But that was too hard for my father, since he was working all day long," recalled Karl-Heinz.

At age ten, Karl-Heinz was inducted into the Jungvolk along with his classmates. However, this only lasted a few years, because his father was killed in Russia, and the family left Darmstadt. Karl-Ludwig Sommerkorn was drafted into the Wehrmacht in February 1942 and sent to the Eastern Front. Two of the letters he wrote from a location near Leningrad in early March 1943 have been preserved:

> Eastern Front, March 4, 1943
> My dearest sweetheart and children,
> It is Thursday at 3 p.m. Finally I have a real roof over my head again. I have been running around since eight last night. Now I am sitting on my bed that has only a straw sack for a mattress. Sweetheart, you could hardly imagine how tired I am. The roads are frozen over and we have to walk on them with our baggage.[5]

Frau
Marg. Sommerkorn
Darmstadt-Arheilgen

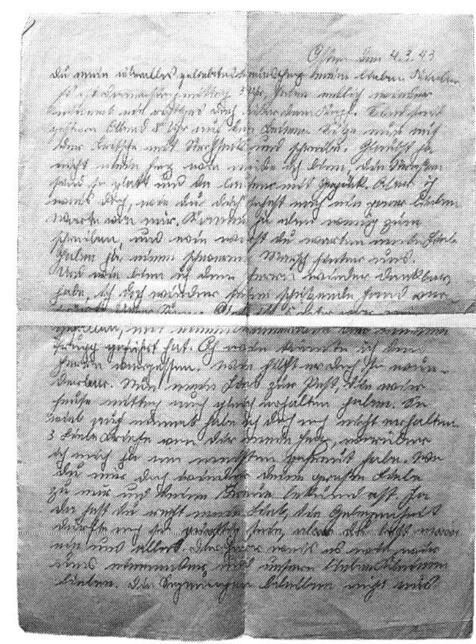

Fig. 1. Soldier Karl-Ludwig Sommerkorn wrote this letter to his wife on March 4, 1943. He was killed in battle two days later. (K.-H. Sommerkorn)

This letter contains many references to Karl-Ludwig's faith, such as the following: "Oh, how could I ever forget my Lord? He has helped me so very much. . . . The Lord knows how much we love each other and our children. His blessings are ever-present." One of the main themes (as with most soldiers' letters) is that he wants nothing more than to go home to his family. A tradition among German soldiers was to acknowledge the arrival of packages from home. In order to know which packages arrived and which did not, the families numbered them. In this letter, Brother Sommerkorn gave his report: "The following packages have arrived: 6, 7, 8, 9, 10, 11, 12, 13, 14, 15, 16, 17, 21, 23, 25, 27, 28, 29 and 30. So several are missing. But I'm fortunate that we are here. Had they arrived yesterday evening, I wouldn't have been able to take them all with me."

The very next day, Karl-Ludwig Sommerkorn wrote to his wife again. He expressed anew his sadness about being so far from home, his concerns for the welfare of his family, and his desire to see them all again soon. He repeated his sentiments about God: "My dearest wife, sometimes I think I can't stand it anymore. But you know that I trust in the Lord and He gives me more strength. Every day He holds His protective hand over me. . . . And I know that you too will not forget the Lord. . . . I know that the Lord will give us the opportunity to be together again."

The following day, March 6, 1943, Brother Sommerkorn was at his post during a Red Army artillery barrage that lasted all day. His commanding officer wrote this report a few days later: "An artillery shell landed right next to him and Karl received shrapnel wounds all over his upper body. He was immediately unconscious and died soon thereafter. The next day, he was buried at the Gulren Utschif Cemetery not far from Naraja, Russia. We have taken a picture of his grave and will send it to you as soon as it is developed."

Margarethe Sommerkorn took her children and left Darmstadt in January 1944 to live with an aunt, Marie Grünewald, in Schönau, Saxony (in eastern Germany). She lost all contact with the branch until after the war and was not able to attend church in Saxony. The surviving Sommerkorns were sad at the loss of their husband and father, but they were fortunate to have left Darmstadt before another tragedy struck.

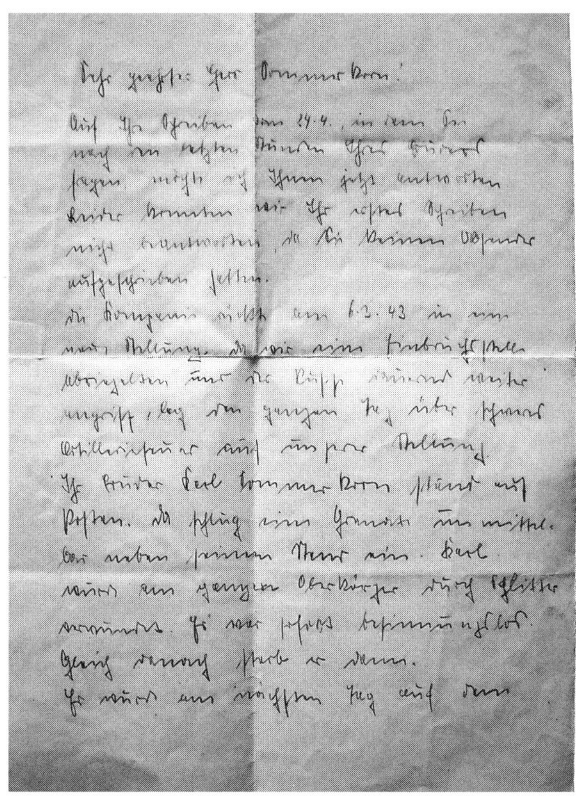

Fig. 2. The company commander sent this letter to Karl-Ludwig Sommerkorn's brother soon after the battle. "He was struck by shrapnel all over his upper body, was immediately unconscious and died in a matter of minutes." (K.-H. Sommerkorn)

Although there had already been thirty-four air raid alarms in Darmstadt, the world seemed to come to an end in that city when the British Royal Air Force attacked during the night of September 11–12, 1944. Chosen as a prime target for a firebombing, the city still had a downtown featuring many very old wood structures lining narrow streets. A combination of explosive and incendiary bombs dropped that night produced a holocaust that lasted several days and took the lives of more than eleven thousand people. The core of the city of

Darmstadt essentially disappeared overnight, and 80 percent of the rest of the city was destroyed.[6]

A short history of the Darmstadt Branch was written in connection with the dedication of the new church building in 1965. In an apparent attempt to avoid negative images at a time of celebration, the history offers only one substantive statement about the war: "The terrible air raid on Darmstadt on September 11, 1944, cost the lives of several members of the branch, including branch president Christian Lang."[7] Brother Lang had sought refuge in the basement of his home along with his wife, Anna Barbara, and reportedly one or more daughters. It may be that several other members of the branch were with them when their apartment house was destroyed and the Langs were killed. Annaliese Heck of the Frankfurt Branch was in Darmstadt shortly after the catastrophic air raid and remembered seeing the body of Sister Lang:

> Those were horrible, horrible attacks. And I had to climb over bodies [afterward]. One of them was Sister Lang, the older Sister Lang. I could not believe it. Those people had stayed in their basements too long, and fumes developed there, and when they came out, they were overwhelmed, and they dropped dead [from asphyxiation]—right in the street.[8]

While stationed near Nattuno, Italy, Georg Marquardt was pleased to meet another LDS soldier, Eugen Keller of the Stuttgart Branch. They had become acquainted quite by chance when Eugen noticed that Georg was holding a church book and asked him where he got it. Georg explained his religious affiliation, and the two were immediately good friends. For the next while, they met as often as the situation permitted and maintained their friendship after the war. This is one of the rare instances when soldiers of the West German Mission were able to spend time together away from their home branches.

Georg also had opportunities to speak with others about his church while in Italy. He was once invited to visit a local family. The hostess inquired about his religion. "She wanted to know what we believed in, and I tried to recite as many articles of faith as I could remember from my childhood and youth. I knew that being an example to the people was very valuable [But] we could not talk much about the Church because I knew that people were watching me."

While on leave near Mannheim and Darmstadt, Georg continued to attend Church meetings whenever possible. He recalled that there were always adult priesthood holders in attendance to see to all necessary ordinances.

When the American army invaded the Odenwald Forest, there was slight action near the Marquardt farm at Gadernheim. One artillery shell fell into their home but fortunately did not explode. A member of the Church living there as a refugee safely removed the shell from the home. The Marquardts did not lose any property and were not forced to leave their home. The American Third Army entered Darmstadt on March 25, 1945, and encountered nothing but white flags and deserted streets.[9]

The war ended peacefully for Georg while he was stationed in the Po River Valley in Italy. He was not taken prisoner officially but was interned at an airfield a few days after the cease-fire on May 8, 1945. For some reason, his captors released him after a very short time, and he was able to return to Gadernheim in July 1945. Regarding his experiences away from home and church for four years, he commented, "My testimony was my comfort in those years. Having the Church in our lives was the highest and most positive feeling, and it kept us alive."

Just before the war came to an end, Margarethe Sommerkorn decided to take her children and flee the oncoming Soviet soldiers by heading from Saxony south into Czechoslovakia. According to her son, Karl-Heinz:

> We had not heard many good things about the Russians, and we were scared. My aunt did not want to go with us, but my mother took her children and left. We were walking through

> the [Erzgebirge] mountains and ran right into the Russians. They didn't bother us, but we turned around and went back to my aunt in Schönau. Later we learned that the people in Czechoslovakia were even worse [to Germans] than the Russians.[10]

Sister Sommerkorn later acquired a small wagon and her family began the journey on foot back to Darmstadt (nearly three hundred miles). They found that the church rooms had been destroyed, but they were able to join with the surviving Latter-day Saints who were holding meetings in schools. The branch was alive, but had been seriously weakened through the loss of at least a dozen of their members, nearly all of whom had been killed in that one terrible air raid.

Fig. 3. Only the walls of this Lutheran church remained after the night of September 11–12, 1944. The plaque reads, "In memory of our dead: May they rest in peace." (R. Minert, 1971)

In Memoriam

The following members of the Darmstadt Branch did not survive World War II:

Philipp Becker b. Fränkisch Crumbach, Hessen, 17 Sep 1867; son of Johann Jakob Becker and Maria Elisabeth Daum; bp. 23 May 1897; conf. 23 May 1897; ord. deacon 18 Sep 1904; m. Darmstadt, Hessen, 18 Mar 1893, Elisabeth Kessel; 5 or 6 children; d. nephritis Darmstadt 23 or 25 Jul 1941 (FHL microfilm 68791, no. 7, Frankfurt District Book II; IGI, AF)

Edith Bossecker b. Darmstadt, Hessen, 28 or 29 Jul 1942; dau. of August Walter Otto Eduard Bossecker and Johanna Jährling; k. air raid Darmstadt 11 or 12 Sep 1944 (CHL microfilm 2458, form 42 FP, pt. 37, 298–99; IGI)

Emma Albertine Dassmann b. Herborn, Limburg/Lahn, Hessen-Nassau, 1 Feb 1883; dau. of Johannes Christian Dassmann and Emilie Haas; bp. 31 May 1913; conf. 31 May 1913; m. Philipp Jährling; k. air raid Darmstadt, Hessen, 12 Sep 1944 (FHL microfilm 68787, no. 18; CHL Microfilm 2458, form 42 FP, pt. 37, 298–99; SLCGW, IGI) Anna Maria Emig b. Roßdorf, Darmstadt, Hessen, 20 Oct 1863; dau. of Nikolaus Emig and Maria Keller; bp. 15 Aug 1920; conf. 15 Aug 1920; m. —— Reitz; d. senility and stomach complications 13 Nov 1940 (FHL microfilm 68791, no. 243; IGI, AF, PRF)

Melani Franke b. Grüna, Chemnitz, Sachsen, 10 Apr 1892; dau. of Franz Emil Franke and Pauline Fleischmann; bp. 8 Nov 1908; conf. 8 Nov 1908; m. —— Stauss; k. air raid Darmstadt, Hessen, 12 Sep 1944 (FHL microfilm 68787, no. 75; IGI)

Anna Waldburga Jäger b. Steinbach, Gießen, Hessen, 7 Dec 1872; dau. of Johann Adam Jäger and Anna Waldburga Schäfer; bp. 17 Apr 1925; conf. 17 Apr 1925; m. —— Egner, k. air raid Darmstadt, Hessen, 12 Sep 1944 (FHL microfilm 68787, no. 13; IGI, AF, PRF)

Maria Anna Jäger b. Zürich, Switzerland, 21 Mar 1911; dau. of Anna Jäger; bp. 15 Oct 1925; conf. 15 Oct 1925; k. air raid Darmstadt, Hessen, 12 Sep 1944 (FHL microfilm 68787, no. 20)

Johanna Jährling b. Darmstadt, Hessen, 19 May 1912; dau. of Philipp Jährling and Emma Albertine Dassmann; bp. 5 Aug 1920; conf. 5 Aug 1920; m. Darmstadt 24 Dec 1938, August Walter Otto Eduard Bossecker; 1 child; k. air raid Darmstadt 11 or 12 Sep 1944 (FHL Microfilm 68787, no. 19; CHL microfilm 2458, form 42 FP, pt. 37, 298–99—lists mother's name as "Lehmann"; IGI)

Christian Lang b. Pfungstadt, Hessen, 11 Jun 1870; son of Christian Lang and Margarethe Meyer or Meier; bp. 14 Jun 1908; conf. 14 Jun 1908; ord. deacon 19 Oct 1922; ord. teacher 6 Oct 1924; ord. priest 13 Dec 1925; ord. elder 14 May 1933; m. Darmstadt, Hessen, 26 Jun 1895, Anna Barbara Löb; 5 children; k. air raid Darmstadt 12 Sep 1944 (FHL microfilm 68787, no. 25; CHL microfilm 2458, form 42 FP, pt. 37, 298–99; SLCGW)

Katharina Lang b. Pfungstadt, Hessen, 26 or 27 Jan 1872; dau. of Christian Lang and Margarethe Meyer or Meier; bp. 18 Nov 1924; conf. 18 Nov 1924; m. 10 Oct 1931, Johannes Mahr; k. air raid Darmstadt, Hessen, 12 Sep 1944 (FHL microfilm 68787, no. 46; CHL microfilm 2458, form 42 FP, pt. 37, 298–99; SLCGW; AF)

Anna Barbara Löb b. Unter Schönmattenwag, Seppenheim, Hessen, 24 Sep 1875; dau. of Peter Karl Löb and Maria Cramlich; bp. Darmstadt, Hessen, 11 Jun 1907; conf. 11 Jun 1907; m. Darmstadt 26 Jun 1895, Christian Lang; 5 children; k. air raid Darmstadt 12 Sep 1944 (FHL microfilm 68787, no. 26; CHL microfilm 2458, form 42 FP, pt. 37, 298–99; SLCGW)

Karl-Ludwig Sommerkorn b. Arheilgen, Darmstadt, Hessen, 29 Sep 1908; son of Heinrich Philipp Sommerkorn and Philippine Gilbert; bp. 15 Mar 1923; conf. 15 Mar 1923; ord. deacon 2 Apr 1928; ord. teacher 2 Nov 1930; ord. priest 29 Nov 1931; ord. elder 24 Nov 1937; m. Darmstadt, Hessen, 18 Oct 1930, Margarethe Dieter; 3 children; corporal; k. in battle Nagatkino 6 Mar 1943; bur. Korpowo, Russia (FHL microfilm 68787, no. 71; www.volksbund.de; IGI)

Fig. 4. Karl-Ludwig Sommerkorn was killed in Russia on March 6, 1943. (K-H. Sommerkorn)

Notes

1. Darmstadt city archive.
2. Presiding Bishopric, "Financial, Statistical, and Historical Reports of Wards, Stakes, and Missions, 1884–1955," 257, CHL CR 4 12.
3. Georg Marquardt, telephone interview with Jennifer Heckmann in German, January 14, 2009; summarized in English by Judith Sartowski.
4. Karl-Heinz Sommerkorn, interview by Michael Corley, South Jordan, UT, February 29, 2008.
5. Karl-Ludwig Sommerkorn to his wife, March 4, 1943; used with the permission of Karl-Heinz Sommerkorn.
6. Data provided by the Darmstadt city archive.
7. Darmstadt Branch, "Ein Plan . . . Wird Wirklichkeit!" September 12, 1965.
8. Annaliese Heck Heimburg, interview by the author, Sacramento, CA, October 24, 2006.
9. Darmstadt city archive.
10. Many thousands of German soldiers and civilians would later testify to inhumane treatment at the hands of Czechs and people of other nations conquered and occupied by German forces before and during the war.

Frankfurt Branch

For centuries, the city of Frankfurt am Main in southwestern Germany has played an important role in commerce and transportation among the German states. It was also the center of politics in the Holy Roman Empire, and dozens of emperors were crowned in the cathedral there (though they ruled elsewhere). As World War II approached, this city of 548,220 was the home of the nation's largest railroad station and the largest airport and was the point of departure for the first completed stretch of the new autobahn highway system.[1]

Frankfurt Branch[2]	1939
Elders	19
Priests	4
Teachers	4
Deacons	16
Other Adult Males	39
Adult Females	160
Male Children	11
Female Children	8
Total	261

The Frankfurt Branch met in the summer of 1939 in rented rooms at Neue Mainzerstrasse 8–10, just a few blocks north of the Main River and very close to the office of the West German Mission at Schaumainkai 41 (on the south side of the river). Among the 261 members of the branch were nineteen elders—a wealth of leadership when compared to other branches in the mission in those days. As was true in most Church units, more than half of the members were females over the age of twelve.

Since its inception in 1894, the branch in Frankfurt had moved time and again in an attempt to find suitable rooms in which to meet and worship. The history of the branch indicates that the rooms at Neue Mainzerstrasse 8–10 were in a Hinterhaus by a photography store. Erna Huck (born 1911) recalled that the meeting rooms were on the second floor and that there were several classrooms for children and teenagers.[3] Photographs of the rooms show a picture of Jesus Christ flanked by pictures of the prophets Joseph Smith and Brigham Young. The branch sang hymns accompanied by a pump organ. Several eyewitnesses recalled a modest sign on the street indicating the presence of the branch at that address.

Maria Schlimm (born 1923) recalled the following about the building at Neue Mainzerstrasse 8–10 and the schedule of the meetings:

> It was a large building with many offices. [We rented] a large room and four smaller rooms for other classes. Upon entering the main door, you could see the wardrobe and some benches where we waited until the meeting started. There was a large painting in the [chapel] showing Christ and Joseph Smith in the first vision. The member who painted it worked in an art museum. . . . There was a rostrum at one end of the chapel; it was not large enough for the choir but we used it for theatrical plays on special occasions.[4]

"Those were very nice rooms, and they reminded me of an office," recalled Hannelore Heck (born 1929). Her description continues:

> The rooms were a fairly good size, and it was nice for us to have Sunday School and sacrament meeting in different places. I think it was more of an office than an apartment building. We used the building often, holding MIA on Wednesday nights, Relief Society on the first Sunday of the month, genealogy class on the second Sunday, and Primary on Tuesdays at 2 p.m. We walked to church so many times during the week.[5]

According to young Hermann Walker (born 1929), "We had a lot of fun in that building because it had two entrances. One was just the regular entrance upstairs. We had to walk through several classrooms and then enter what we called the chapel. We also had a stage up in the front and behind that stage was another door that led to the stairs again. We used this door for socials and whenever we performed plays. . . . None of the rooms we met in [at various addresses] looked like chapels we use today."[6]

Carola Walker (born 1922) recalled that perhaps one hundred persons attended church meetings on a typical Sunday.[7] Her parents, Friedrich and Martha Walker, had a little apartment on the outskirts of the city, so it was not easy for them to attend church. Otto Förster (born 1920) recalled an attendance of perhaps fifty to sixty people. His family walked to church from Koblenzerstrasse, about thirty minutes away. According to Otto, "The Church had use of the rooms all week long. We didn't have to share the rooms with anyone."[8]

A native of Gotha in Thuringia, Karl Heimburg (born 1924) moved with his family to Frankfurt in 1938. Moving from a small branch in a small city to a very large branch in one of Germany's largest cities, Karl noticed a distinct difference: "When we came to Frankfurt, there was a big branch; it was a totally different church with a complete Church organization. There was sacrament meeting, Sunday School, priesthood meeting, Relief Society, MIA, Primary—everything. It was like a big family."[9]

At the age of fourteen, Maria Schlimm joined the League of German Girls. "I always liked it because nothing bad happened there. We did handwork, crafts, gymnastics, and choir. But there was nothing political attached to it. Whenever Hitler came to town, we had to wear our uniforms and stand by the side of the street so that he could see us."

Annaliese Heck (born 1925) had a very different experience in the Hitler Youth program: "I had resisted the program a lot because they also met on Sundays some times." Fortunately for her, she was invited to join an orchestra because she played the violin and the viola. "At least we didn't have to march around."[10]

When the West German Mission conference was held in 1939, the members of the Frankfurt Branch were called upon to help set up the meeting venues. As was the custom for mission and district conferences all over Germany in those days, members of the local branch also took into their apartments members who were close friends or had traveled from far away and lacked the funds to stay in hotels. On the Monday following the last conference sessions on Sunday, several hundred Saints joined together for a cruise down the Rhine River.[11]

Otto Förster had spent two and a half years in the Hitler Youth but discontinued his involvement when he became an apprentice electrician working in Königstein (about ten miles west of Frankfurt). His work with the Siemens Company was critical to the war effort, so he could not be drafted by the Wehrmacht early in the war. This protected status allowed him to remain at home, attend church, and pursue a relationship with a young lady in the mission office—Ilse Brünger of the Herford Branch in the Ruhr District.

Just before the war, newlyweds Hermann and Erna Huck purchased a small grocery store at Rotlinstrasse 53 and operated it under the name Lebensmittel Huck. Their customers were the residents of the apartment buildings within a few blocks and included several Jewish families. The store featured such expected products as coffee and wine, but when asked about the quality of such products, the Hucks had to admit that they had no idea how such items tasted. The customers knew that the shop's owners did not drink coffee or alcohol.

As the persecution of the Jews intensified, the Hucks came under pressure from certain neighbors to stop allowing Jews in their store. One woman made it a point to greet the Hucks with a hearty "Heil Hitler!" each time she entered the store, and it was likely that woman who applied the greatest pressure. However, Hermann Huck was not to be intimidated, and he continued to sell to Jews. To avoid endangering both himself and his customers, he met them after hours and provided them whatever he could. This was a difficult undertaking, because he was only allowed to sell items in exchange for ration coupons, and Jews had a very hard time obtaining ration coupons from city authorities.

After the American missionaries departed Germany on August 25, 1939, the only full-time missionaries still in service were in the mission office at Schaumainkai 41.[12] That preparations for war were underway among the populace is clear from a letter written by secretary Ilse Brünger to President M. Douglas Wood on August 28 (just after he arrived in Copenhagen, Denmark, with his evacuated missionaries): Sister Brünger had given the Frankfurt Branch 47.60 Marks to pay for blackout paper to cover the windows of the meeting rooms as required under civil defense laws.[13]

Hans Mussler (born 1934) lived in the spa city of Baden-Baden when the war began. With his mother, Frieda, and his sister, Ursula, Hans first attended church in the Bühl Branch a few miles distant. When his father, Franz Schmitt, was offered a choice for his next assignment, he selected Frankfurt over a small town near Lake Constance. According to daughter Ursula (born 1929), Herr Schmitt wanted to assure little Hans a "proper education."[14] Hans became not only a member of one of the largest LDS branches in all of Germany but also a member of another important institution—the Musisches Gymnasium. Admission was only via recital, and competition was stiff. According to Hans, there were two such state-run schools—one for boys in the Frankfurt suburb of Niederrad and another for girls in the city of Leipzig.[15] Both schools were exclusive, and the pupils were required to live in the buildings.

After the fall of France in the summer of 1940, Otto Förster was sent by his employer to Dunkirk, where the Germans were repairing harbor facilities damaged by the retreating British and French. As he recalled:

> They had blown out the hinges of the two main gates of a lock. When I got there the gates were just hanging in the water. The first gates were

> operated by hydrometrical motors. So they sent me out there to check out the controls. I was part of a construction unit. When the British left, they also just dumped all they had left (such as vehicles) into the locks. That gave them a little more time. We used cranes to get them out, and it took us about a week. I was there for twelve to fourteen days. Then I went home and found an order to report to the military. I had gone to Dunkirk as a civilian because it was a work assignment.

Otto's first assignment with the air force was in Thuringia, where he was to be trained for work with antiaircraft guns. However, a call went out for drivers, and he already had a driver's license (a rare possession in those days; his premonition a few years earlier that he might need one someday paid off). "While others had to practice shooting cannon, I was driving around Thuringia sightseeing, which was much easier."

Hermann Huck was the son of Anton Huck, then the president of the Frankfurt District and later the supervisor of the entire mission. As typical store owners, the young Huck family lived in rooms just behind their business that fronted the street on the ground level of the building. They enjoyed their lifestyle, but it did not last long. By September 1940, Hermann was drafted into the Wehrmacht, and they had to close down their store. Erna was allowed to stay in the building but lost the kitchen and had to make do with one bedroom in the apartment, where her son was born later that year.

Fig. 1. Hermann Huck as a Wehrmacht soldier. (E. Wagner Huck)

The first tragic loss of life among the Latter-day Saints in Germany and Austria during World War II involved the Frankfurt Branch. Corporal Willy Klappert (born 1914), a deacon in the Aaronic Priesthood, was killed on September 2, 1939—the second day of the war—in the town of Jegiorcive, Poland. He was therefore the first of hundreds of LDS men to lose their lives while wearing the uniform of the German armed forces. By the time the war was finally over and German POWs were released from camps all over the world, several other members of the Frankfurt Branch had perished.

The minutes of meetings held by the Frankfurt Branch during the years 1939–45 give valuable insights into the life of the branch and its members. In those minutes we read that Ludwig Hofmann assumed the role of branch president when the missionaries left town. The average attendance at Sunday meetings in 1940 was fifty-five members and friends. The clerk indicated that the winter of 1939–40 was long and hard and that the members endured shortages in coal supplies.[16]

According to the branch records, a "severe air raid" over Frankfurt on July 8, 1941, resulted in "great damage" within the city. There is no mention of damage to the meeting rooms at Neue Mainzerstrasse 8–10. However, on March 8, 1942, the meetings had to be cancelled because there was no heat in the rooms. For the year 1942, the average attendance had decreased to forty. On August 2 of that same year, branch president Ludwig Hofmann died; he was buried in the Rödelheim Cemetery in northwest Frankfurt in a ceremony over which district leaders presided. New branch leaders were called on August 16, 1942: Hermann Ruf (a native of Stuttgart) was the president, Hans Förster was the first counselor, and Valentin Schlimm was the second counselor.[17]

In 1941, Otto Förster was again in France. Due to long hours of stressful driving and poor nutrition, he became seriously ill and spent several months in field hospitals before being sent to a hospital in Brussels, Belgium. Eventually, his condition was considered sufficiently serious to merit him a release from active duty. For the rest of the war, he was classified as "fit for domestic [non-combat] duty only."

Heiratsurkunde F 1

(Standesamt Frankfurt am Main III Nr. 424)

Der [illegible] Otto Hugo Förster, [illegible],
wohnhaft zu Frankfurt am Main
geboren am 22. März 1920
in Schönberg bei Kronberg, [illegible]
(Standesamt Oberhöchstadt Nr. 18),
und die [illegible] Ilse Friederike Wilhelmine Brünger, [illegible],
wohnhaft zu Frankfurt am Main
geboren am 11. September 1912
in Herford, Westfalen
(Standesamt " - Stadt Nr. 648),
haben am 20. Dezember 1941 vor dem Standesamt Frankfurt am Main die Ehe geschlossen.

Vater des Mannes: Friedrich Wilhelm Förster, wohnhaft zu Bad Homburg
Mutter des Mannes: [illegible] geborene Mauermann wohnhaft zu Frankfurt am Main
Vater der Frau: Hermann Heinrich Peter Brünger, [illegible] wohnhaft zu Herford
Mutter der Frau: [illegible] Luise, geborene Nagel, wohnhaft zu Herford
Vermerke:

Stadt Frankfurt a.M. Gebühr
Frankfurt am Main, den 20. Dezember 1941
Der Standesbeamte
(Siegel)
Graf

Zur Vervollständigung und Erleichterung der Familienbuchführung wird empfohlen, die Familienahnentafel, Seiten 36 bis 44 auszufüllen und beglaubigen zu lassen.

Eheschließung der Eltern:
des Mannes am 1. 11. 1902
(Standesamt Dresden III Nr. 742)
der Frau am 1. 10. 1909
(Standesamt Herford-Stadt Nr. 159)

Fig. 2. Marriage record of Otto Förster and Ilse Brünger on December 20, 1941 (O. Förster).

Ilse Brünger was eight years older than Otto and later wrote of her feelings during the courtship: "I liked him too, but since he was younger, I was not too serious at first. I prayed about him and then I felt that God approved of him. . . . Then he was drafted. Only those who went though the same agony of not hearing, not knowing where he was, if he was still alive or not, can understand the fear and terrible thing war brought to nearly every family." Ilse had many friends in the branch, which was helpful because her family was very close to disowning her due to her membership in the Church.[18]

By November 29, 1942, the branch meetings had been moved up the street to rooms at Neue Mainzerstrasse 68; a district conference held at that location featured a full-house contingent of members from the six branches.[19] This address apparently remained unchanged until January 1944.

"I remember vividly that our parents always made sure that we knew that whatever we talked about at home should not leave home," recalled Hannelore Heck. "Our beliefs were our beliefs, and my father didn't think it was wise that the Nazi Party would find out about those. From the time I was very small, I realized that the less I said, the better off I was. We knew that they would take our daddy away from us if we said anything and that he would get killed." At the age of ten, Hannelore was inducted into the Jungvolk with her classmates, but she did not like the activities, which she described as "boring and stupid." It appears that her particular group was disorganized, because nobody came to the Heck home to learn why Hannelore missed so many meetings.

Fig. 3. The main meeting room of the Frankfurt Branch in 1939. Future mission supervisor Christian Heck is seated front right. (E. Wagner Huck)

Cooler heads prevailed in Hannelore's school. She recalled:

> I had wonderful teachers—especially my history teacher. She would put up a huge map of the world, and Germany would be marked with a distinct color. But what we learned from that was not how special Germany was but how small it really was compared to the world. She never said a word but only hung up the map at the beginning of class and then again at the end. We didn't have to be told what she was thinking—we knew it. Her message was that some insane man was trying to fight the entire world.

Erna Huck enjoyed her life as a stay-at-home mother in Frankfurt until the air raids over the city became more severe and frequent. With the public air-raid shelters too far away to be convenient, the Hucks joined their neighbors in the basement of their apartment house when the sirens began to wail. She recalled,

> There was only one small room about twelve by fifteen feet in size, and there were fourteen of us. It felt like we were in a mousetrap. My little boy was the only child in the group. Usually the raids came late at night when it was totally dark [under blackout conditions], but later they also attacked in broad daylight. Sometimes we went downstairs two or three times in a single night. We always took our important papers along—our marriage certificates, photographs, financial papers, etc.

Hans Johann Uhrhahn had served as a full-time missionary in Germany in the 1930s. After returning to Frankfurt, he married Luise Haug, and they had two children—Wolfgang (born 1936) and Vera (born 1941). By the time Vera was born, Walter was well established in a large construction firm that was nationalized just after the war began. Brother Uhrhahn soon found himself traveling to many locations all over eastern Europe, where his company carried out contracts for road and bridge construction. Wolfgang recalled, "My mother told me later that I had been in thirteen countries including Poland, Hungary, Yugoslavia, and Greece. My father worked with payroll matters and also functioned as the liaison between the company and the local government. He was never in the military but often wore a uniform because he was representing the German government."[20] As conquerors, German civilians and paramilitary operatives were usually treated poorly by the occupied peoples, but Wolfgang recalled vividly that "people in countries like Romania, Bulgaria, and Ukraine welcomed us with open arms."

The Uhrhahn family rented an apartment on the main floor of a building at Waldschmidtstrasse, a few blocks east of the center of town, but the family was usually far from home. Luise Uhrhahn was determined to travel with her husband in order to spend as much time with him as possible, and because of his civilian status the government did not object. Wolfgang and Vera received their schooling at home, wherever home happened to be. Brother Uhrhahn was so successful in employment that the family often stayed in expensive hotels in large cities. This was not typical of a German family at the time, nor was it common for Germans to have several weeks of vacation each year, as the Uhrhahns did. It became their habit to spend vacations in alpine winter sports locations.

Karl Walker (born 1935) had vivid memories of the radio in his home during the war: "My mother listened to BBC quite a bit although it was forbidden. One time, I was home alone and turned it on. I remember how angry she was when she found

Fig. 4. Priesthood brethren of the Frankfurt branch. (E. Wagner Huck)

out, and I never did it again. She also stopped listening to it—maybe because she was afraid that I would talk to somebody about it outside the home." Regarding the incessant national broadcasts, Karl recalled, "The radio always aired special reports of victories everywhere. People got more and more excited about the whole thing. The reports were called Sondermeldungen (special announcements), and they always started with [military] music. I also remember hearing Hitler talk on the radio. He always pronounced the word Soldat (soldier) very distinctly. The sentence was always "Wir kämpfen bis zum letzten Soldat! (We'll fight to the last soldier!)."[21]

After doing an apprenticeship as a mechanic, Karl Heimburg was drafted into the Wehrmacht on October 10, 1942, and assigned to a motorized unit:

> We were classified as forward reconnaissance; in other words, we had to move ahead of the tanks quickly. We were kind of like the gypsies, we would escort convoys someplace because they didn't know the way. We would protect them from surprise attacks; we would open up the ways for the tanks to break out [if they were surrounded]. When the tanks broke through, we pulled out and went elsewhere. We were in the middle of a mess all the time.

By January 1943, Karl was on the Eastern Front. It was the aftermath of the crushing defeat of the German Sixth Army at Stalingrad, but Hitler was determined that his army was not to retreat from the interior of the Soviet Union. Karl was part of several offensive and many defensive campaigns all year long. Beginning in May, he was trained as a driver for the Mark IV tank. "It weighed twenty-eight tons and was a good tank," he explained. The action on the Eastern Front that year was so frequent and so intense that "our days were thirty-six hours long, not twenty-four, and that was that."

Karl was wounded on several occasions. Once he had seven pieces of shrapnel removed from his leg. On another occasion a bullet penetrated his side but did so little damage that he did not notice it during the heat of battle. Once a bullet pierced his right hand. Fearing that he would lose touch with his comrades, he refused to be sent to a hospital. However, a serious infection set in, and he was compelled to go to the hospital after all. Later there was no problem in rejoining his unit.

Everywhere he was stationed while away from home, Karl Heimburg was the only LDS soldier around. He found that most German soldiers had no interest in discussing religion. "It was always a neutral thing. Sometimes a Lutheran pastor presided over the service, sometimes a Catholic priest." On the matter of prayer, he stated,

> You said your prayers whether you wanted to or not. Sometimes they were very short. It was not only me but almost everybody [who prayed]. There were times when you saw people actually sitting down in prayer. You knew they were praying. And sometimes they'd be in the middle of a battle; in fact, in the middle of a mess it was actually easier to pray. To me it was the only thing we could get help from. At the moment, it was all you really needed.

While in the Soviet Union, Karl noticed the devout faith of the older generation. "I didn't see a single home that didn't have a prayer altar. There was always a little candle burning and a picture of Jesus and his mother. You could tell that the [older] people still had faith."

Karl's belief in the Word of Wisdom came in quite handy when he sold his tobacco and alcohol rations to other soldiers. "I never saw a [German soldier] who didn't drink and smoke," he recalled.

After a year of furious action, Karl Heimburg contracted malaria and yellow jaundice in November 1943. While he languished in a hospital in Vienna, Austria, for ten weeks, his weight dropped from 180 pounds to 98. When his mother arrived from Frankfurt to visit him, his comrades hurried to dress him in many layers of clothing in an attempt to hide his emaciated condition from his mother. "She never knew," he recalled.

In January 1943, bombs struck Sister Huck's neighborhood as she and her three-year-old son huddled with neighbors in the basement shelter underneath her apartment. The building across the street burned to the ground, as did the building behind theirs. For a while, it seemed as if they would not be able to exit the shelter that night, but they were able to crawl through an escape hole into the basement of the adjacent building and eventually made it out into the street. All of the windows in their building were broken, but the building survived. Nevertheless, Sister Huck decided to evacuate Frankfurt with her son. Along with her father, Friedrich Wagner, she took her son to the home of her aunt in the small town of Hirsau near Pforzheim, about one hundred miles south of Frankfurt. She was allowed to store her furniture in one room at her Frankfurt address.

Anneliese Heimburg recalled the precautions taken by city officials to protect residents from disaster in the case of air raids. Each apartment building was to have a barrel of water in the basement along with a supply of blankets. In the case of a fire in the building or the neighborhood, each person was to soak a blanket in the water and put it over his or her head before leaving the shelter. This tactic proved successful in the prevention of suffocation. In addition, a small hole was to be cut into the wall of each adjacent building to allow for additional escape routes.[22] Annaliese recollected that "the government carried out a big rat-extermination program before the war because they figured that if bombings started, there would be corpses and pestilence, and they wanted to prevent that."

Home on leave from Braunschweig, Otto Förster returned just two days before the birth of his daughter, Ilse, on March 9, 1943. Because Otto's wife, Ilse, was still an employee of the West German Mission and was living in the office building at the time, the baby was born in Ilse's bedroom. The air raids over the city at the time were so dangerous that Sister Förster chose to take her baby home to her family in Herford, where the child stayed in relative safety until the end of the war. The mother returned to the mission office to continue her tireless service to mission leaders Christian Heck and Anton Huck.[23] Fortunately, she was allowed to quit her job in the military censorship office.

Otto Förster was next transferred to Steyer, Austria, where he supported antiaircraft crews defending automobile factories against American aircraft based in Italy. As he recalled, "I had to go to Linz to get supplies for our group. Whenever I was in Linz, [the enemy] bombed Steyer; and when I was in Steyer, they bombed Linz. The Lord was watching out for me."[24]

In 1943, Elsa Heinle (born 1920) was working a second job as a streetcar conductor. She had been trained in tailoring, but her country needed her and other young women to take over the civilian jobs of men called into the military. Operating the streetcar under total blackout conditions was challenging. Because Elsa could not see the passengers, she called out to them to ask if anybody else wanted to get on or off. Then she rang a bell to signal the driver that he could start.

Elsa was still living with her parents, Karl and Lena Heinle, in 1943. When the air-raid sirens sounded, they each carried a small suitcase downstairs to join their neighbors in the basement shelter. As the war went on, they found it easier to simply go to bed with their clothes on rather than to get dressed and undressed several times within a few hours. In the basement they had just enough light to see, but Elsa recalled once knitting a little jacket for her friend's baby. She clearly recalled a momentous air raid just before Christmas in 1943:

> I was a streetcar conductor and rode line 16. On December 20, 1943, I worked the late shift until 1:00 a.m. . . . We arrived at the last station when the sirens went off, and it was a blessing that there was a shelter we could go into. [Afterwards] I walked around the corner to see if my house [at Neuer Wall 19] was still standing. All I saw was that it was destroyed. I knew that my parents were in the [public] shelter, but I still started screaming at the top of my lungs. Somebody came up to me and told me that my parents were still alive and that I should stop screaming. In that [basement] shelter, four people died. I was told that the bomb hit the basement and then lifted up the house, which then collapsed.[25]

Fig. 5. This clock belonged to the Heinle family of the Frankfurt Branch. When their apartment building collapsed, the clock fell two stories into the basement. Upon locating it amid the rubble, the family found that the clock showed only a few scratches from the experience. (R. Minert, 2008)

Fig. 6. Another piece of furniture rescued from the rubble by the Heinle family. (R. Minert, 2008)

After air raids, survivors often went around the neighborhood to see if anybody needed help. With this in mind, Elsa once went down the street to look for her friend's mother. The woman's body was found in the rubble underneath a huge cabinet. When Elsa told somebody that she had to write to her friend about the death of her mother, she was admonished by police to state that her friend's mother had "died for Germany."

From the branch records it appears that the new leaders felt the need to improve attitudes and behavior among the Saints there. On July 11, 1943 (eleven months after they were called to lead the branch), the presidency introduced these "new rules for the branch":

> 1. Know that you are in a holy place where the word of God is spoken by His servants.
> 2. Loud laughter and inappropriate conversations have no place here.
> 3. There should be no talking at all in the chapel—before or after the meeting.
> 4. Find a seat in the front rows; pray in silence for divine inspiration that His servants will proclaim the word of the Lord.
> 5. If you are called upon to pray, then pray concisely and seriously without using many words.
> 6. In the testimony meeting, keep it short; do not rob your neighbor of his time.
> 7. In the discussion classes, keep your comments short and to the point; political statements are not allowed.
> 8. If you are talented, take part in the program and inspire the rest of us.
> 9. Be dignified when partaking of the sacrament and remember the Lord, our Savior.
> 10. After the benediction leave the room with gratitude in your heart. Other rooms may be used if conversations are absolutely necessary.
> 11. Be punctual for all worship services and leadership meetings.
> 12. Be sure that your name is on the roll for each class so that you will take part in the Kingdom of God.
> 13. Only priesthood holders are to handle the sacrament trays.
> 14. Value and support the priesthood holders because they have a weighty responsibility.
> 15. Only call upon the elders if you are seriously ill.
> 16. Do your very best to live a life pleasing to God and do your best to apply what you hear here in your daily life, then you will receive a crown of glory.[26]

The clerk noted that "the above principles were accepted by all attendees by the raising of the right hand."

It would appear that the focus of the new rules was the improvement of worship services. The new branch leadership must have felt that reverence in the meetings needed to improve and that prayers, testimonies, and comments were becoming unnecessarily long. Item 7 suggests that members were making political statements, but no eyewitness accounts substantiate this; perhaps the guideline was made as a preventative measure. At the time, the average attendance in Sunday meetings was holding relatively steady at forty-five.

Being loyal to the Church and to the government at the same time was not an easy task for many Latter-day Saints, and there were discussions about politics within the walls of the church on occasion. Maria Schlimm recalled that in one such discussion, her mother expressed her opinion. Another member, who supported the government and the Nazi Party, remarked that if Sister Schlimm were not a member of the Church, he would have reported her to the authorities. On the other hand, Maria did not recall that the government caused the branch any problems at all.

Sometime in 1943, the Uhrhahn family lost their apartment to an air raid. Fortunately, the family was away from home at the time. Sister Uhrhahn's father called her at their vacation apartment and informed her that all of their belongings had been lost. When Hans Johann Uhrhahn returned to work following their vacation, his wife took the children to her mother's ancestral village of Hohenfeld in Bavaria. From there they continued to follow him to work sites in southeastern Europe. It was a nomadic lifestyle, but they preferred it to that of many of the families in the Frankfurt Branch, who were separated for months or even years at a time.

Hans Mussler's music school was damaged in an air raid on Christmas in 1943, and he was allowed to leave town until the school could be called into session again. His mother and sister had left the city a few months earlier after their apartment was destroyed and were then living in Mühlacker near Pforzheim, two hours south of Frankfurt. Hans joined them there. In early 1944, the school reopened at a different location—the former convent at Untermarchtal, near Ulm in southern Germany. Hans was then isolated from both his family and his church, but he was enjoying his musical studies nonetheless.

By the end of the year 1943, air raids over Frankfurt were beginning to threaten the branch with increasing frequency. The clerk indicated in December that "the members were spared," and on January 2, 1944, many expressed their gratitude to God for surviving "heavy raids" in recent attacks.[27] Conditions deteriorated just weeks later, as reflected in the minutes: "January 29, 1944: In one of the worst raids on Frankfurt, the branch rooms at Neue Mainzerstrasse 68 were burned to the ground. It happened on Saturday at 10 a.m. Due to the many raids, many members have moved out of town."[28] There is no indication in the record just when the Saints began holding meetings at that address, but for the next while, they met in the mission home.

The clerk made the following sad entry in March 1944: "9/10ths of the city has been destroyed in air raids. The majority of the members lost their homes and the branch records were destroyed in the fires." As is clear from subsequent entries in the minutes, not all branch records were lost. The comments of March 24, 1944, demonstrate the determination of branch leaders (and members alike) to preserve the life and function of the branches, as well as Church property:

> March 24, 1944: Branch President Hermann Ruf was staying in the hotel Deutscher Hof and had left his briefcase with the branch records there. The terrible fire that began downtown at 8 p.m. on March 23 became a fire storm and [eventually] spread to that hotel. The next day at about 10 a.m. Brother Ruf ran into the hotel that was already burning and got to the second floor, where he was able to rescue from the flames the briefcase with the membership records. This was only possible with the help of the Lord.[29]

Fig. 7. Hermann Ruf was the president of the Frankfurt Branch for much of the war. (G. Ruf)

The year 1944 may have been a very long one for Hermann Ruf, because his fortunes vacillated from sorrow to happiness. In January or February, his family's apartment was destroyed. On April 4, his wife, Frida, died of a kidney ailment after giving birth to a daughter on March 31. Frida was buried in Frankfurt on April 11 and her newborn daughter, Dorothea Gisela, died two days later. On December 20, President Ruf married Gertrud Glaser, whom he had met while attending meetings as a priesthood visitor in the nearby Bad Homburg Branch. Following the obligatory marriage ceremony in the city hall, mission supervisor Anton Huck presided over a modest church ceremony that was described by the branch clerk in these words: "Despite air-raid alarms that delayed the ceremony, it was a spiritual and uplifting occasion." At the time of his wedding, Hermann Ruf was in uniform but at home between assignments. Valentin Schlimm had been designated temporary branch president on November 15.[30]

Following a recuperation furlough in Frankfurt, Karl Heimburg was shipped to his unit, which was temporarily stationed in Munich. From there it was back to the Eastern Front, which had since moved from Russia west into Poland. Karl arrived just in time to participate in an intense enemy counterattack that resulted in serious losses to the German side. It was August of 1944. "We had super, super equipment, but the [soldiers] didn't know how to use it properly. They were all young kids. We had 120 recruits in our company who had never seen live guns fired. I wasn't afraid of the Russians, but I was afraid for our own guys if the Russians ever attacked us." The Red Army did attack—on January 17, 1945. Karl was separated from his unit for seven hours. Given a motorcycle and told to catch up with his unit, he headed in what he thought was the right direction, but he never saw his comrades again. "All of a sudden there were all of these people around me, a handful of whom spoke a foreign language. They said 'Come on!' and they liked me so much that they kept me for four years and seven months!" Karl joked. He became a Soviet POW, and life changed immediately in many ways.

A great number of German schoolchildren lost school time due to air raids. Finishing the eight years of public school was crucial for boys and girls, so the city government went to great lengths to replace damaged or destroyed schools. In the case of Hermann Walker, this meant sending his entire class to the village of Lollar, forty miles north of Frankfurt. As with so many children in Hitler's Germany, Hermann was isolated from his family and his LDS friends for about a year. In his case, school attendance was particularly important, because he had developed talents in physics and chemistry and hoped to continue his education.

"My father had lots of inspiration," recalled Annaliese Heck. Christian Heck had been the mission supervisor since the drafting of Friedrich Biehl by the Wehrmacht in 1939. In about 1943, he was offered employment by the government in occupied territories such as Czechoslovakia, possibly

Fig. 8. This monument near Frankfurt's city hall reminds pedestrians of the thousands of residents who were killed in air raids over the city and as soldiers at the front (R. Minert, 1979).

because he knew English and had also studied French and Italian. He apparently recognized this as a dangerous job, because several Nazi Party leaders and military officials had been killed by partisans in that area. He ultimately turned down the offer, then went home and told his wife that the party would get back at him by having him drafted. He was correct in his assumption and was in uniform in early 1943.

Before leaving for military service, Brother Heck decided to rent an apartment for his family in Kelkheim, about twelve miles west of Frankfurt and far from major industries and population centers. The family was able to move some items of great value (such as documents) to that location before their apartment was destroyed on March 18, 1944. By that time, his second daughter, Hannelore, had been moved with her school class to the town of Bensheim, about thirty-five miles south of Frankfurt.

Hannelore Heck recalled seeing bright skies over Frankfurt from Bensheim after major air raids. "The city was burning, and I knew that my family was in jeopardy." After one terrible raid, she had to wait for an entire week before she learned that they were safe. On the other hand, she happened to be home the night their neighborhood was hit and their apartment destroyed. She recalled their escape from the burning building:

> We threw wet blankets over our heads so that we wouldn't get burned. We ran to the river [a few blocks south] to get some fresh air and to be near the water just in case we were in danger [i.e., if the flames came nearer]. . . . The entire downtown burned—it was not the first air raid on the city, but one of the first big ones. We lost all of our possessions except for what we carried in our

Fig. 9. This public air-raid shelter in northwestern Frankfurt was painted to represent an apartment house that had been attacked and was burning, apparently in an attempt to deceive enemy dive-bombers looking for targets. (R. Minert, 1973)

> suitcases. We had some clothing and some other valuable personal items like genealogical papers.

As was the case with other Wehrmacht soldiers, Christian Heck was granted a furlough of two weeks to help his family resettle after they lost their home. He took them to Bensheim, where Hannelore was, and they began to look for rooms. The housing shortage in Germany at the time was acute and it seemed as if nothing was available to refugees. At one point, Brother Heck stood for a moment deep in thought and then said, "Let's go ask at that house," pointing to a building near the railroad station. Sure enough, the owner had rooms to rent. They were assigned one large room and one small room with a bathroom downstairs. Annaliese attributed the discovery to her father's inspiration.

As a POW of the Soviets, Karl Heimburg had some terrifying experiences. He and his comrades were marched as far as seventy-five miles in a day, and some of them made the trek with no boots. They were robbed of their valuables and any good articles of clothing. For days on end, they consumed nothing but snow. Those prisoners who fell down were simply shot. On one occasion, their captors drove by in American vehicles, dumped gasoline on some of the prisoners and set them on fire. On another occasion, Karl watched as Soviet tanks veered off the road now and then to run over and crush German POWs. During one stint in a camp in Estonia, only seven thousand of eighteen thousand German prisoners survived.

Back in Frankfurt, Karl's mother was not aware that her son was a prisoner in Russia. In fact, she received an odd letter from Karl's company commander stating that Karl was missing and asking her to contact the army if she knew the whereabouts of her son. The letter did not suggest that Karl was dead. It would be nearly three more years before Sister Heimburg learned that her son was alive.

Babette Rack (born 1909) was the mother of five little children when the war began. Like so many other mothers, she essentially raised her children alone after her husband was drafted into the army. In 1944, Sister Rack's situation changed drastically, as she recalled:

> I was bombed out on March 18, 1944. All we had left were the clothes on our backs—not even a teaspoon or bedding. For seven hours, we sat in an air-raid shelter on Schwanenstrasse in the Ostend neighborhood, unable to get out; the exit was blocked by debris. By the time we got out, the entire neighborhood along the Zeil [street] was burning. That afternoon, they put us up in the prison on Starkestrasse—not in the cells but in the hallways. We spent two days there. Then they sent us to the Liebfrauen School gymnasium. From there I was evacuated to Birklar in Giessen County. There was no place to attend church nearby and that was my situation for quite a while.[31]

For the Rack family and many other families all over Germany and Austria, one of the worst aspects of the war was their isolation from the Church.

Several families in the Frankfurt Branch experienced close calls during air raids. For example, Hermann Walker recalled, "One time, my mother and sister went upstairs again after [the raid] was over and found the bedroom on fire. Our furniture was damaged. The bomb had gotten stuck. They poured two buckets of sand over it and that [put it out]." Fortunately, the family had followed government instructions and prepared to fight fires on their own. Professional firefighters were rarely available under such circumstances.

The air raid of March 22, 1944, was not as merciful to the Walker family or to Hermann personally, as he recounted: "Our house was hit very badly. I lost my friend in that air raid. Three houses totally collapsed. There were two bombs—one fell on the street, and the other one hit the house in which my friend lived. It went all the way down to the basement and exploded there. My friend was not a member of the Church, but he was a very good friend."[32]

In about 1944, Maria Schlimm was sent to live with her mother's friends in Sprendlingen, a small town about seven miles south of Frankfurt.

She had already spent two years away from home with relatives and was twenty when she arrived in Sprendlingen. Wanting very much to continue attending church meetings, she rode her bike back to the city on several Sundays.

The meeting rooms at Neue Mainzerstrasse 8–10 were destroyed during one of the many air raids after 1939, but the branch had already been asked to leave. The Saints met at several different locations near the center of town, such as in an unknown location on Hochstrasse, in a building on the corner of Neue Mainzerstrasse and Neuhofstrasse, in the Weissfrauen School on Gutleutstrasse, in the Rumpelmeier Kaffeehaus next to the city theater, and finally in the West German Mission office at Schaumainkai 41 on the south bank of the Main River.[33]

In Hirsau, refugees Erna Huck; her son, Jürgen; and her father, Friedrich Wagner were far from their home branch, but there was a branch of the Church in Pforzheim, twelve miles to the south. There was no direct public transportation to Pforzheim on Sundays, and it was too far for little Jürgen Huck to walk. However, Friedrich Wagner (an elder and former president of the Frankfurt District) was undaunted and made the trip to Pforzheim on foot, walking three hours each way. This connection to the Church ceased when the inner city of Pforzheim was reduced to rubble in a single air raid in April 1945. The Hucks and Friedrich Wagner could not attend another LDS Church meeting until 1947.

Still working in the mission office in 1944, Ilse Brünger Förster was informed by the government that she was required to take on additional employment. She was fortunate to find a job just around the corner, one requiring her to work only three hours per day for a transportation company. "The owner of the company soon found that he could trust me," recalled Ilse, "so I did all the correspondence on my own and he paid me a good salary. In everything I did, I felt God's hand."[34]

Otto Förster's unit was transferred to the Netherlands in September 1944 to help defend the region near Arnhem against the Allied invasion launched under the code name Market Garden. Arriving after the Germans had crushed the invasion, Otto was moved into Germany. Driving his truck to transport supplies to German defenders during the Battle of the Bulge in December, he was attacked from behind by dive bombers. He saw people at the sides of the road scatter in all directions, but he did not know that they (and his truck) were under attack until his soldier passengers told him about it a few minutes later.[35]

At Christmas time in 1944, Otto found himself close to Herford and stopped in to see his daughter and his relatives. They had been bombed out and moved to another town a dozen miles away, where he was fortunate to find them. His arrival came as a total surprise, which was the case a few days later when Ilse arrived from Frankfurt, also unannounced. They were thrilled to spend a day or two together before he returned to his post west of the Rhine River.[36]

Toward the end of 1944, the Uhrhahn family was together again in Serbia, living well out of town in a small railroad shed. As the German lines began to crumble, partisans in the region became increasingly bold, and one day the entire Uhrhahn family was surrounded by combatants. Several of the men spoke German and it was apparent that they were bent on destroying a railroad tunnel and capturing a large payroll shipment. Wolfgang recalled that day's events as follows:

> The partisans put [Mother, Vera, and me] in our house and made my father and his workers carry dynamite about one-half mile to the tunnel. They put a box of dynamite on the tracks by the tunnel entry and wanted to run over it with a locomotive and blow up the train and the tunnel. My father pushed the dynamite off to the side and the locomotive got through and somehow word went out to the local German army command to come help us. They got there in time to save us. I even kicked a partisan in the shin because he was trying to molest my mother or something like that. The story of my resistance made it all the way up to the German high command, and my mother got a letter about me being such a brave boy.

Luise Uhrhahn and her children were then sent off to Hohenfeld, Bavaria, and her husband's working conditions continued to deteriorate. In a hectic surprise attack, Hans Johann Uhrhahn and all of his office staff were captured by the enemy. His last letter was somehow smuggled out of the area and reached his wife, and then all communications were cut off. One of the secretaries later escaped and eventually told the story to Luise; apparently there was a break-out and Walter and his comrades scattered in all directions. The secretary saw Walter running toward a forest and he may have escaped, but nothing was ever heard from him again. Despite the desperate hopes and prayers of a loyal wife and adoring children, no word of Walter's condition ever reached the family.

In the last year of the war, some Latter-day Saints in Frankfurt held meetings in their homes on Sundays. Carola Walker recalled doing so in their apartment on the outskirts of town. "Later on, we met in the mission home."

After losing their apartment, Martha Walker and her children stayed with relatives in Frielingen, about eighty miles northeast of Frankfurt. According to her son Hermann, it had taken fully three days in March 1944 to make the relatively short trip to Frielingen after their house was destroyed. "We packed everything we could carry and left [Frankfurt]. The trains moved only at night; they didn't want to be seen by enemy airplanes." Although she saw no fighting on the ground, Carola Walker watched American airplanes over Frielingen: "Whatever wasn't destroyed yet got destroyed then," she explained.[37]

Younger brother Karl Walker did not feel at home in Frielingen: "[Our relatives] were like strangers to me. Even their dialect was different and they made fun of how I talked." The small-town schoolteacher was an ardent supporter of the Nazi Party and required the children to greet her with "Heil Hitler" every morning. "We also had to pray that the Führer might be safe and well and that Germany would gain the final victory," Karl explained. That teacher died and was replaced by one who had to ride the train every morning. "Sometimes she would fall asleep and miss her stop. By the time she got to the classroom, we were usually gone."

The foreign soldiers held as POWs in homes and barns near Frielingen apparently represented a particular fascination for Karl. "We were very curious about the American soldiers, because they indicated that they were hungry and wanted food. They traded things for food. I remember that once when we gave them food, we got a football in return. For us kids, a ball was a ball, so we played soccer with it, but it didn't work too well." Karl explained that there were also French and Russian POWs in the area, but the children did not talk with them. "We were scared of them. The Americans were friendlier."

Louise Hofmann Heck was as dedicated to the Church as her husband, Christian. In Bensheim she was miles from the nearest branch and did her best to keep the faith alive in their little apartment. Then she learned that the Marquardt family of the Darmstadt Branch lived just seven miles away, but those were uphill miles into the Odenwald Forest to the town of Gadernheim. According to Annaliese, "Brother Marquardt was an old man. We knew him because he had a beard and he gave a prayer at every conference. There were no buses operating on Sundays, so we walked to his home. It took about three hours each way. Even though my youngest sister, Christa, was only about four years old, she walked all the way. She didn't have to be carried."

As a soldier, Christian Heck became seriously ill in Russia and was sent to a hospital in Germany. By the time he had recovered, it was early 1945 and he was sent to a unit in southwestern Germany, where they faced the invading French army. In April, he was shot in the stomach and was carried by a comrade to a Catholic hospital, where he was given excellent care. Although he survived major surgery, he died of heart failure on April 19, 1945. That same comrade eventually made his way to Bensheim, where he informed Louise Heck of the death of her husband. Hannelore recalled one of her father's last comments at home: "He said something to me once that stuck with me. 'I'm not going to kill anybody—but somebody will have to kill me.'"

The minutes of the Frankfurt Branch meetings include the following statement on February 7, 1945: "A bomb landed in the yard behind the mission home; there was no real damage."[38] Indeed, the mission home survived the war with only a few broken windows. By the spring of 1945, several families of the Frankfurt Branch had moved into the mission home after losing their own homes. The building was quite large, and there was plenty of room for refugees. The branch clerk added the following statement to the record as the war drew to a close: "March 8 to April 14, 1945: The mission home was occupied by American soldiers. Foreigners got into the basement and stole many valuable items. Later we determined that some important records were missing, leaving significant gaps."[39]

Otto Förster seemed to be leading a charmed life. When his truck broke down in late February 1945, he had to leave it in a repair shop in Bonn. He recalled,

> They told me they would need at least a week to fix it. For a week, with nothing to eat, I decided to go home. I went home to Frankfurt and carried all my papers with me. I went to the main train station, where the military checkpoint was located, and reported there because I wanted to make sure they knew that I wasn't running away.

While he spent the next few weeks in the mission office with his wife, he learned that the invaders had crossed the Rhine, and his return to Bonn was impossible. Changing to civilian clothing, he stayed with his wife and awaited the arrival of the Americans.[40]

Maria Schlimm recalled that in the last months of the war, families whose homes were destroyed or damaged often suffered from shortages or outages of utilities: "Large trucks came to bring water and people waited in long lines. During the night, the water was running at a trickle, and we used the opportunity to fill pots and pans. By the end of the war there was no electricity, and sometimes it was turned on for just an hour."

When the American army approached Frankfurt in March 1945, Maria went with her family east to Hanau to the farm of a branch member's brother. There they hid until they saw black GIs searching the homes for German soldiers. "I had never seen dark skin in my life before but I knew that it existed. I was not scared of them."

Luise Uhrhahn and her two children spent the last months of the war near Hohenfeld. Life in the small town was very quiet in the spring of 1945, but Wolfgang recalled two events of significance. On one occasion, an enemy fighter plane zoomed down toward him while he was playing with friends. In his words, "We were kids, so we thought he wouldn't shoot at us, but we were wrong. I suppose fighter planes can't tell whether you are kids or adults."

Once, a railroad train plunged off of a damaged bridge, and Wolfgang and his friends went out a few days later to see what treasures they might find in it. Wolfgang pulled on the handle of a door, and the entire door came off the hinges. "The door fell on my back. They had to carry me back to our raft and float me back across the river because I couldn't walk." Fortunately he was not badly injured.

Hohenfeld was so quiet that the invading American army caught the local residents totally by surprise. Sister Uhrhahn and Wolfgang were inside the small Gasthaus, where they had been given a room, and four-year-old Vera was playing outside. An enemy tank came around a corner and headed downhill toward the Gasthaus, where the road curved. When the tank's treads began to slide on the wet road, the tank missed the turn and slid off the road straight ahead toward the Gasthaus. The tank's long cannon barrel pierced the wall of the Gasthaus, and the vehicle came to a halt when the treads hit the building's outside wall—with little Vera standing precisely between the treads against the wall, safe and sound.

The war ended in Hirsau with the arrival of French and Moroccan troops in the spring of 1945, but the hardships for refugee Erna Huck did not end. For weeks, the locals were subjected to abuse at the hands of the conquerors. According to Sister Huck,

> The Moroccans raped every female from teenagers to eighty-year-olds. My cousin and I were spared because there was a French woman working in my aunt's home. She went out and offered the home to the French officers [as a place to live] so the common soldiers couldn't come in. The soldiers took our bicycles, cameras, jewelry, etc. (they had watches all up and down their arms) but they didn't harm us. I worked in the house as a cook and served meals [to the French] until they got too "touchy," and then I quit.

When American soldiers inspected the building in which the mission office was housed, they liked both its location next to a major Main River bridge and its condition (being one of the few intact structures in the neighborhood). They commanded the inhabitants to leave within thirty minutes. Otto Förster and his wife found a place to live with several other families in a one-room apartment down the street. Nearly two months later, they were allowed to return to their rooms at Schaumainkai 41. In the interim, Ilse had been hired by the American army to work as a translator because she spoke English and French. With a secure place to live and employment (soon for Otto as well), the Försters retrieved their daughter from Herford and began a new life together in the mission home.[41]

With the war over, Hans Mussler's music school was closed and the pupils simply dismissed. Amid the confusion of the end of the Third Reich and the military occupation, each boy was expected to find his own way home. Although only ten years of age, Hans was ready for adventure and boarded a train headed west toward Ulm. At one point on the journey, he rode atop the train with his little suitcase. "That was very dangerous. There were power lines up there, and you had to keep your head down," he explained. The train did not take him to Pforzheim, so he got off at Heidelberg and went looking for his aunt. Walking past the main cemetery, he saw a sight that could not easily be forgotten: the body of a German soldier hanging upside down from a tree. "It was shocking to see that." Hans did not know at the time that summary executions of suspected traitors were happening all over Germany at the whims of fanatics.

While living in Heidelberg with his aunt, Hans came into contact with several LDS soldiers from the United States, and one of them baptized Hans in the summer of 1945. He was united soon thereafter with his mother, his sister, and his adoptive father, Franz Schmitt, who was eventually released from a POW camp in Great Britain.

Karl Heinle was inducted into the home guard at the end of the war, though he was over sixty at the time. His wife suggested that he leave his nice pocket watch at home because she felt that he would not need it. However, he took it along, and it served a crucial purpose: near Bad Mergentheim he was struck by shrapnel, a piece of which hit the watch and then ricocheted into his stomach. Fortunately he was not badly wounded, but the watch was ruined nonetheless.

When Elsa Heinle learned that her father was in a hospital in Bad Mergentheim, she tried to get there on the train. When this proved to be impossible, she got on her bike and rode there, a distance of nearly eighty miles. American army officials allowed her to visit her father in the hospital, and both were overjoyed at the reunion. When Brother Heinle was released, his wife's relatives in the town took him in until he could safely travel back to Frankfurt.

When the American invaders approached Bensheim, some dangerous things happened. Dive bombers searched for local targets, and on one occasion a pilot shot at Annaliese Heck. She was hurrying to find a place to hide as the sirens wailed but was still in the open when the airplane's guns opened fire. Huge .50-caliber rounds drilled a line of holes in a wall just above her head. "I was the only one near that spot, so I know that he was shooting specifically at me. I have no idea how he could have missed me when I [later] saw all of the holes in the wall."

The Hecks were told by neighbors to flee to the Odenwald Forest. Fearing that looters would take what little property they had left, the Hecks chose to stay in their Bensheim apartment and were fortunate to learn that the conquerors were not bent on destruction. They had previously dropped flyers encouraging the people of Bensheim to surrender without a fight, and the Hecks were determined to do so. However, if they hung out a white flag, they could be accused of treason and shot by local fanatics. Annaliese had the clever idea of washing their white sheets and hanging them out to dry at precisely the right time. "It wasn't my idea," claimed Annaliese Heck. "You know where that idea came from."

Hannelore also clearly remembered the arrival of the Americans:

> I was not scared to see the Americans. We knew that they were approaching. The shooting finally stopped and we were wondering why we could not hear them anymore. But then they [suddenly] came in—and we knew why [we didn't hear them]. They were wearing rubber soles, which made it impossible for us to hear them walking. But there was no fighting. . . . When they came in, we were in the house and waiting to see what would happen, but we were not afraid. Fortunately, I spoke English, which I had started learning when I was ten years old. Some of the soldiers came into our home, and they were quite startled to find English-speaking German girls like my sister and me.

Regarding the war experience in general, Hannelore Heck made this comment: "You pulled yourself together for the sake of others. We tried to be strong for each other so that the other person, and especially our parents, would not feel bad. . . . I didn't want my mother to suffer more than she already had to because of the war and my father being gone."

As in most branches of the West German Mission, the Saints in Frankfurt did their best to continue holding meetings when the war ended. On May 27, the meetings were visited by two American soldiers named Cannon and Taylor. At the time, only about fifteen persons were gathering on Sundays. On July 1, Hermann Ruf was again called to serve as the branch president. The search for a new meeting place also began.[42]

Looking back on the war years, Elsa Heinle recalled that her family often could not get to the meetings until the last months of the war. "There were always priesthood leaders on hand to preside over meetings and to administer the sacrament, but the number of members present declined steadily. We took care of each other and visited each other to see what we could do to help. . . . I had a strong testimony of the gospel and the war did nothing to change that."

Carola Walker, who had been baptized at the age of eight, recalled, "I was always active in the Church. I did whatever I could to help in the branch. That helped me to keep going through the difficult conditions."

At one point during his Soviet captivity, Karl Heimburg heard a call for mechanics. He volunteered and was assigned to drive a truck. This activity took him all over the region as he hauled lumber, coal, cement, "and you name it!" Because he was always good at learning new languages, he picked up Russian quickly and got along quite well in the camps. He even earned a bit of money during his last year as a prisoner. "I fed a lot of people with that money," he said.

Toward the end of June 1949, Karl was released from prison and transported to Frankfurt an der Oder—in eastern Germany, just across the river from Poland. He recalled, "They gave us each ten East German Marks, a pound of sugar, and a telegram to send home." He immediately sent the telegram and then made his way back to his mother and siblings in Frankfurt am Main. Soon after his return, he saw his friend Annaliese Heck for the first time in more than seven years. According to her, "I had never asked his mother whether he was alive, because I was afraid that it might open old wounds." Karl and Annaliese married soon after this reunion.

Hermann Huck had been taken prisoner by the Americans just before the war ended and was later turned over to the French. For quite a while, he could not contact his wife to tell her that he was still alive. He finally learned of his family's whereabouts and joined them in Hirsau. In 1947, they returned to Frankfurt and attempted to claim their previous apartment. They were refused, but then were given twenty-four hours to move their remaining furniture to a different location in the city. They made the move successfully and began a new life in their hometown.

A German court declared Hans Johann Uhrhahn officially dead in the early 1950s. The date established for his death was September 30, 1944. No place of death was specified.

In Memoriam

The following members of the Frankfurt Branch did not survive World War II:

Alfred Ausserbauer b. Buer, Buer, Westfalen, 1 Mar 1924; son of Georg Ausserbauer and Katharina Bach; bp. 14 May 1932; conf. 14 May 1932; k. in battle Normandy, France, 22 Jun 1944 (FHL microfilm 68791, no. 6; CHL microfilm 2458, form 42 FP, pt. 37, 289–99; branch membership record book 2)

Sophie Ausserbauer b. Merlenbach, Forbach, Elsaß-Lothringen, 27 Apr 1914; dau. of Georg Ausserbauer and Katharina Bach; bp. 17 Jul 1922; conf. 17 Jul 1922; m. 20 Mar 1937, Ernst Wilhelm Clemens; d. meningitis 4 Aug 1943 (FHL microfilm 68791, no. 350; book 1)

Olga Amalia Bachmieder b. Weissenhorn, Memmingen, Bayern, 29 Jan 1874; dau. of Joseph Bachmieder and Rosina Viedmann; bp. 16 Sep or Oct 1920; conf. 16 Sep or Oct 1920; m. —— Yoos or Fost; d. stomach cancer 5 May 1940 (FHL microfilm 68791, no. 162; branch membership record book 1; FHL microfilm 68791, no. 279; IGI)

Herbert Brandelhuber k. in battle (E. Wagner)

Wilhelm Breitwieser b. Dieburg, Hessen, 29 Jun 1867; son of Konrad Breitwieser and Katharina Heil; bp. 14 Jul 1914; conf. 14 Jul 1914; d. senility Oberkochstadt, 30 Dec 1944 (FHL microfilm 68791, no. 21; branch membership record book 1; IGI)

Eugen Dommer b. Offenbach, Hessen, 14 Dec 1910; son of Alfred Dommer and Barbara Klesius; bp. 16 Jun 1929; conf. 16 Jun 1929; m. 30 Apr 1935, Erna Maria Becht; k. in battle Hermsdorf, Apr 1945; bur. Halbe, Teltow, Brandenburg (CHL microfilm 2458, form 42 FP, pt. 37, 284–85; FHL microfilm 68791, no. 293; www.volksbund.de; IGI)

Christine Karoline Graf b. Jagsthausen, Neckarkreis, Württemberg, 29 Feb 1856; dau. of Johann Georg Graf and Magdalene Henriette Platscher; bp. 15 Jun 1903; conf. 15 Jun 1903; m. —— Waibel; d. senility 3 Feb 1943 (FHL microfilm 68791, no. 160; branch membership record book 1; IGI)

Maria Grebe b. Caldern, Marburg, Hessen-Nassau, 7 Jul 1874; dau. of Johann Peter Grebe and Katharina Junk; bp. 12 Jul 1923; conf. 12 Jul 1923; m. Braunschweig 1 May 1893, Johann Heinrich Jung; d. 29 Mar 1942 (FHL microfilm 68791, no. 85; branch membership record book 1; see Frankfurt District book 1; LR 2986 11, 153; FHL microfilm no. 271375, 1925 and 1935 censuses)

Frida Maria Haagen b. Buenos Aires, Argentina, 29 Jan 1907; dau. of Friedrich Otto Edward Haagen and Anna Margarete ——; m. Frankfurt/Main, Hessen-Nassau, 9 Jul 1940, Hermann Otto Ruf; d. kidney ailment after birth of daughter 4 Apr 1944; bur. Frankfurt/Main 7 or 11 Apr 1944 (LR 2986 11, 174; IGI)

Karl Hermann Haug b. Frankfurt/Main, Hessen-Nassau, 17 Jan 1916; son of Hermann Gottlieb Haug and Christina Lieb; bp. 28 Feb 1925; conf. 28 Feb 1925; ord. deacon 29 Nov 1931; noncommissioned officer; k. in battle Am Swir bei Gorka, Kuuttilahti, Russia, 24 Oct 1941 (FHL microfilm 68791, no. 45; LR 2986 11, 149; www.volksbund.de; branch membership record book 1; IGI)

Christian Karl Henry Heck b. Frankfurt/Main, Hessen-Nassau, 31 Mar 1902; son of Josef Heck and Anna Katharina Steinbach; bp. 4 May 1912; conf. 4 May 1912; ord. deacon 8 Apr 1923; ord. teacher 7 Dec 1924; ord. priest 1 May 1927; ord. elder 21 Mar 1937; supervisor of WGM 1940–1943; m. Frankfurt/Main 16 May 1923, Louise Johanna Hofmann; three children; corporal; k. in battle Imnau, Sigmaringen, Hohenzollern, 19 Apr 1945 (FHL microfilm 68791, no. 47; LR 2986 11, 178; www.volksbund.de; branch membership record book 1)

Josef Heck b. Mainz, Rheinhessen, Hessen, 16 Jul 1871; son of Karl Josef Heck and Margarete Knaf; bp. 13 Mar 1898; conf. 13 Mar 1898; ord. elder 26 Feb 1905; m. Frankfurt/Main, Hessen-Nassau, 28 Dec 1894, Anna Katharina Steinbach; 6 children; d. Frankfurt/Main 5 or 6 Mar 1945 (FHL microfilm 68791, no. 215; branch membership record book 1; IGI)

Georg Heil b. Stuttgart, Neckarkreis, Württemberg, 1 Oct 1918; son of Johann Wilhelm Heil and Friederika Luise Hohlweger; bp. 29 Mar 1935; corporal; k. in battle Ljadno, Tschudowo, Russia, 3 Apr 1942 (CHL microfilm 2458, form 42 FP, pt. 37, 1949 list, 2:44–45; www.volksbund.de; IGI)

Ludwig Hofmann b. Bürgstadt, Aschaffenburg, Bayern, 3 Oct 1892 or 1894; son of Adalbert Hofmann and Marie Rosine Eckert; bp. 25 May 1925; conf. 25 May 1925; ord. deacon 11 Apr 1926; ord. teacher 24 Apr 1927; ord. priest 7 Oct 1928; ord. elder 22 May 1932; m. 20 Mar 1915, Emilie Katharina Auguste Wolf; two children; d. stomach cancer Rödelheim, Frankfurt am Main, Hessen-Nassau, 2 Aug 1942; bur. Rödelheim, Frankfurt am Main (FHL microfilm 68791, no. 65; LR 2986 11, 155; branch membership record book 1)

Emma Höll b. Achern, Baden, 22 Aug 1879; dau. of Ludwig Höll and Viktoria Oberle; bp. 22 Jun 1912; conf. 22 Jun 1912; m. Frankfurt/Main, Hessen-Nassau, 29 Mar 1901, Christian Albert Vosseler; two children; d. frailty Frankfurt/Main, 23 Apr 1944 (FHL microfilm 68791, no. 154; branch membership record book 1)

Frank Heinrich Thomas Humbert b. Frankfurt/Main, Hessen-Nassau, 27 Aug 1903; son of Wilhelm Humbert and Wilhelmina Elisabeth Stuber; bp. 25 Sep 1915; m. 31 Dec 1926; k. in battle near Minsk, Belarus, 2 Jul 1944 (CHL microfilm 2458, form 42 FP, pt. 37, 298–99; FHL microfilm 68791, no. 183; LR 2986 11, 175; www.volksbund.de)

Waldemar Herbert Kalt b. Seckenheim, Mannheim, Baden, 6 Aug 1911; son of Adam Kalt and Wilhelmine Amalie Luise Frank; bp. 22 Oct 1921; conf. 22 Oct 1921; d. work accident 28 Nov 1939 (FHL microfilm 68791, no. 88; branch membership record book 1; IGI)

Willy Klappert b. Ferndorf, Siegen, Westfalen 25 Jul 1914; son of August Heinrich Gustav Klappert and Auguste Dickel; bp. 1 Sep 1929; conf. 1 Sep 1929; ord. deacon 1 Nov 1938; corporal; k. in battle Jegiorcive 2 Sep 1939; bur. Mlawka, Poland (FHL microfilm 68791, no. 298; www.volksbund.de; branch membership record book 1; IGI, AF)

Camilla Meta Lorenz b. Pirna, Dresden, Sachsen, 13 or 15 May 1893; dau. of Gustav Adolf Lorenz and Klara Walther; bp. 31 Jul 1937; conf. 31 Jul 1937; m. Georg Böhm; k. in air raid Frankfurt/Main, Hessen-Nassau, 25 Sep 1944 (FHL microfilm 68791, no. 291; branch membership record book 1; CHL microfilm no. 2458, 298–99; IGI)

Marie Therese Mellinger b. Bockenheim, Frankfurt/Main, Hessen-Nassau, 8 Jun 1867; dau. of Peter Mellinger and Margarethe Lenz; bp. 8 May 1899; conf. 8 May 1899; m. Frankfurt/Main, Hessen-Nassau, 4 Mar 1891, Ludwig Johann Wilhelm Lehwalder; nine children; d. heart attack 27 Apr 1942 (FHL microfilm 68791, no. 116; branch membership record book 1; FHL microfilm 271386, 1935 census; IGI)

Paula Merle b. Frankfurt/Main, Hessen-Nassau, 29 Jul 1894; dau. of Johannes Merle and Emilie Sophie Nahrgang; bp. 25 Sep 1919; m. 5 Feb 1929, Karl Kühnly; d. asthma and heart condition 21 Jul 1942 (FHL microfilm 68791, no. 93; FHL microfilm 271381, 1930 and 1935 censuses; IGI)

Anna Barbara Müller b. Hütten, Neustettin, Pommern, 28 Apr 1870; dau. of Niklaus Müller and Elisabeth Knauf; bp. 30 Sep 1927; m. —— Makko; k. air raid Frankfurt/Main, Hessen-Nassau, 19 Mar 1945 (CHL microfilm 2458, form 42 FP, pt. 37, 1949 list, 2:44–45; FHL microfilm 245224, 1930 and 1935 censuses; IGI)

Walter Münkel b. Frankfurt/Main, Hessen-Nassau, 10 Jan 1913; son of Jakob Münkel and Emilie Elenore Hartung; bp. 12 Nov 1923; conf. 12 Nov 1923; ord. deacon 29 Nov 1931; d. kidney disease or nervous condition 1 Jun 1942 (FHL microfilm 68791, no. 125; LR 2986 11 154; see Frankfurt District book 1; IGI)

Maria Katherina Rosina Naumann b. Hanau, Hanau, Hessen-Nassau, 8 Aug 1868; dau. of Stephan Naumann and Eva Rosenberger; bp. 16 Oct 1928; m. Johann Glock; d. 31 Oct 1940 (FHL microfilm 68791, no. 330; book 1, IGI)

A. Margarethe Noll b. Simmern, Koblenz, Rheinprovinz, 30 Jan 1861; dau. of Karl Noll and Anna Sahl or Sabl; bp. 26 Jun 1912; conf. 26 Jun 1912; m. Josef Elter; d. senility 26 Jun 1940 (FHL microfilm 68791, no. 39; book 1; IGI)

Heinrich Ludwig Persch b. Kassel, Hessen, 1 May 1879; son of Johann Georg Persch and Theodora Helm; bp. 4 Aug 1932; conf. 4 Aug 1932; d. 12 Oct 1944 (FHL microfilm 68791, no. 388; Frankfurt District book 2)

Margarethe Katharina Emma Repp b. Fischborn, Unterreichenbach, Hessen-Nassau, 15 Mar 1890; dau. of Heinrich Repp and Maria Schärpf; bp. 1 Feb 1926; conf. 1 Feb 1926; m. —— Krieg; d. pulmonary tuberculosis 19 Apr 1942 (FHL microfilm 68791, no. 107; book 1; FHL microfilm 271381, 1925 and 1935 censuses; IGI)

Dorothea Gisela Ruf b. Frankfurt/Main, Hessen-Nassau, 31 Mar 1944; dau. of Hermann Otto Ruf and Frida Maria Haagen; d. Frankfurt/Main, 13 Apr 1944 (Gerhard Ruf; LR 2986 11, 174)

Wilhelm Heinrich Melchior Scheel b. Frankfurt/Main, Hessen-Nassau, 10 Nov 1911; son of Heinrich Scheel and Katharina Krebs; bp. 26 Jan 1924; conf. 26 Jan 1924; m. 8 Feb 1939; noncommissioned officer; k. in Talankino, Russia, 22 Jul 1941 (FHL microfilm 68791, no. 213; LR 2986 11, 145; www.volksbund.de; branch membership record book 1)

Ludwig Schiffler b. Uchtelfangen-Kaisen, Ottweiler, Rheinprovinz, 20 May 1867; son of Johann Valentin Schiffler and Katharina Henriette Ulrich; bp. 15 Mar 1910; conf. 15 Mar 1910; ord. elder 29 Nov 1931; d. senility 15 Feb 1941; bur. Frankfurt/Main, Hessen-Nassau (FHL microfilm 68791, no. 310, branch membership record book 1; IGI)

Elisabeth Schönhals b. Friedberg, Gießen, Hessen 16 Dec 1865; dau. of Johannes Schönhals and Marie Kimball; bp. 7 Nov 1924; conf. 7 Nov 1924; m. —— Bilz; d. senility Köppern, Wiesbaden, Hessen-Nassau, 14 Feb 1943 (FHL microfilm 68791, no. 16; branch membership record book 1; IGI)

Ernst Albert Schubert b. Treuenvolkland(?), Frankfurt/Main, Hessen-Nassau, 8 Feb 1874; son of Karl Schubert and Augusta Paul; bp. 16 Oct 1920; conf. 16 Oct 1920; d. 14 Sep 1939 (FHL microfilm 68791, no. 140; branch membership record book 1; IGI)

Elisabeth Seng b. Hochstein, Rockenhausen, Pfalz, Bayern, 25 Jan 1868; dau. of Heinrich Seng and Magdalena Sauer; bp. 25 May 1925; conf. 25 May 1925; m. —— Kretzer; d. heart failure 10 Feb 1941 (FHL microfilm 68791, no. 106; book 1)

Wilhelm Friedrich Steingrand b. Würzburg, Bayern, 27 Mar 1914; son of Katharina Wagner; bp. 1 Feb 1926; conf. 1 Feb 1926; k. in battle 4 Jan 1941 (FHL microfilm 68791, no. 205; LR 2986 11, 151; book 1)

Wilhelmina Elisabeth Stuber b. Laufenselden, Untertaunuskreis, Hessen-Nassau, 9 Aug 1863; dau. of Johann Philipp Stuber and Catharina Louise Kalteyer; bp. 22 Mar 1903; conf. 22 Mar 1903; m. 27 Sep 1881, Peter Hermann Schuessler; two children; 2m. Frankfurt/Main, Hessen-Nassau, 4 Mar 1903, Wilhelm Humbert; six children; d. Frankfurt/Main, 12 Jan 1941 (FHL microfilm 68791, no. 62; FHL microfilm 162793; 1935 census; Frankfurt District book 2; IGI)

Hans Johann Uhrhahn b. Essen, Essen, Rheinprovinz, 22 Jul 1904; son of Heinrich Uhrhahn and Wilhelmine Kunz; bp. 5 Apr 1919; conf. 5 Apr 1919; m. Frankfurt/Main, Hessen-Nassau, 22 Jul 1929, Cecilie Sophie Lola Louise Haug (FS); two children; d. South of Belgrad, Bulgaria, 30 Sep 1944 (Wolfgang Uhrhahn interview; FS)

Alfons Wahl b. Rulfingen, Sigmaringen, Hohenzollern, 5 Apr 1890; son of Joseph Wahl and Josephine Oft; bp. 12 May 1920; conf. 12 May 1920; k. air raid Frankfurt/Main, Hessen-Nassau, 29 Jan 1944; bur. Waldfriedhof, Frankfurt/Main (CHL microfilm 2458, form 42 FP, pt. 37, 298–99; FHL microfilm 68791, no. 230; www.volksbund.de; IGI)

Augusta Wicki b. Westerhof, Osterrode/Harz, Hannover, 11 May 1871; son of Heinrich Wicki and Eleonora Görgons; bp. 30 Sep 1936; conf. 30 Sep 1936; m. 2 Apr 1912, Friedrich Wöll; d. arteriosclerosis 25 Feb 1940 (FHL microfilm 68791, no. 488; Frankfurt District book 2)

Notes

1. Frankfurt city archive. The autobahn route ran from Frankfurt eighteen miles directly south to Darmstadt. Finished in 1937, it was hailed far and wide as the finest highway in Europe. The autobahn construction was begun between Munich and Salzburg, but that stretch was not finished until 1938.
2. Presiding Bishopric, "Financial, Statistical, and Historical Reports of Wards, Stakes, and Missions, 1884–1955," 257, CHL CR 4 12.
3. Erna Wagner Huck, interview by the author, Salt Lake City, July 6, 2006.
4. Maria Schlimm Schmidt, interview by the author in German, Frankfurt, Germany, August 18, 2008; unless otherwise noted, summarized in English by Judith Sartowski.
5. Hannelore Heck Showalter, telephone interview with the author in German, March 9, 2009.
6. Hermann Friedrich Walker, telephone interview with Jennifer Heckmann in German, March 6, 2009.
7. Carola Walker Schindler, telephone interview with Jennifer Heckmann in German, March 6, 2009.
8. Otto Förster, interview by the author, Salt Lake City, UT, November 28, 2009.
9. Karl Heinz Heimburg, interview by the author, Sacramento, CA, October 24, 2006.
10. Annaliese Heck Heimburg, interview by the author, Sacramento, CA, October 24, 2006.
11. See the photograph by Erma Rosenhan in the Offenbach Branch chapter.
12. See the West German Mission chapter.
13. Ilse Brünger to M. Douglas Wood, August 28, 1939, M. Douglas Wood, papers, 1927–40, CHL MS 10817.
14. Ursula Mussler Schmitt, telephone interview with Jennifer Heckmann in German, March 31, 2009.
15. Hans Mussler, interview by the author, Preston, ID, November 22, 2008. See the Bühl Branch chapter for more on Hans's experience in the Church.
16. Frankfurt Branch general minutes, 144, 151, 155–56, LR 2986 11.
17. Frankfurt Branch general minutes.
18. Ilse Wilhelmine Friedrike Brünger Förster, autobiography (unpublished, about 1981); private collection.
19. Offenbach Branch general minutes, CHL LR 6389 11.
20. Wolfgang Uhrhahn, interview by the author, Cottonwood Heights, UT, February 6, 2009.

21. Karl Walker, telephone interview with Jennifer Heckmann in German, March 13, 2009.
22. See the introduction for more details about such precautions that were carried out all over Germany and Austria.
23. See the West German Mission chapter for more details about Ilse Brünger Förster's work at Schaumainkai 41.
24. Otto Hugo Förster, autobiography (unpublished, 1998); private collection.
25. Elsa Heinle Foltele, interview by the author in German, Frankfurt, Germany, August 19, 2008.
26. Frankfurt Branch general minutes, 167.
27. Ibid., 173.
28. Ibid., 173.
29. Ibid., 174.
30. Ibid., 174–76.
31. Babette Rack, *110 Jahre (1894–2004) Gemeinde Frankfurt*, 112–13, CHL.
32. This was a common occurrence with explosive bombs. In older homes, the roofs and floors on the various levels were often not solid enough to activate the fuse, so the bomb went off only when it hit the concrete floor of the basement; then the entire structure collapsed.
33. Rock, *110 Jahre Gemeinde Frankfurt*, 9.
34. Ilse Brünger Förster, autobiography.
35. Otto Förster, interview.
36. Otto Förster, autobiography.
37. Hermann's sentiments about church attendance were similar to those expressed by many eyewitnesses in this study: "Whoever really wanted to attend church meetings found a way to do it."
38. See the West German Mission chapter for details about that specific air raid. Eyewitness Otto Förster recalled much more damage: all exterior and some interior windows were broken, and two bombs bounced off of the exterior walls without exploding. An artillery shell entered the corner office, tore through the floor into the basement, and exploded.
39. Frankfurt Branch general minutes, 177–78.
40. Otto Förster, interview.
41. Ibid.
42. Frankfurt Branch general minutes, 178–79.

Mainz Branch

The city of Mainz, which had 154,003 residents, was home to a very modest branch of The Church of Jesus Christ of Latter-day Saints in 1939.[1] The branch president in July was an American missionary who served without counselors. After his departure on August 25, the Saints there were dependent upon elders visiting from other cities—principally the leaders of the district of Frankfurt.

According to mission records, the meetings of the Mainz Branch were held in rented rooms at Pfaffengasse 13 in the first Hinterhaus. The Sunday School met at 10:00 a.m. and sacrament meeting began at 7:00 p.m. There were enough active members in 1939 to have Mutual on Thursday evenings, Relief Society on Wednesday evenings, and Primary on Tuesday afternoons. The monthly schedule also included a genealogical class, choir practice, and teacher training.[2]

Mainz Branch[3]	**1939**
Elders	0
Priests	0
Teachers	0
Deacons	2
Other Adult Males	12
Adult Females	39
Male Children	1
Female Children	0
Total	54

As of this writing, no eyewitnesses or documents could be found to tell the story of the Saints in Mainz during the war. Only two civilian members of the branch are known to have died from 1939 to 1945, which is remarkable given that the city suffered fifty-five attacks from the air in which 60 percent of the city was destroyed and 2,800 civilians were killed. According to city records, several thousand soldiers from Mainz lost their lives. The war ended there for all practical purposes when the American army arrived on March 22, 1945.[4]

In Memoriam

The following members of the Mainz Branch did not survive World War II:

Elisabeth Philippa Fischler b. Mainz, Mainz, Hessen, 23 Jan 1892; dau. of Johann Philipp Fischler and Margareta Beck; bp. 27 Jan 1928; conf. 27 Jan 1928; m. Mainz about 1919, Karl Kloshöhn; 3 children; d. lung disease 12 or 13 Dec 1941 (FHL microfilm 68791, no. 268; FHL microfilm 271380, 1930 and 1935 censuses; Frankfurt District book II)

Emma Karolina Philippi b. Wiesbaden, Hessen-Nassau, 9 Dec 1865; dau. of Heinrich Ludwig Wilhelm Philippi and Caroline Luise Charlotte Hartmann; bp. 22 Mar 1914; conf. 22 Mar 1914; m. Frankfurt am Main, Hessen-Nassau, Preussen, 17 Apr 1889, Friedrich Adam Philipp Fach; 4 children; d. senility Nauroth, Wiesbaden, Hessen-Nassau, 2 Jan 1945 (FHL microfilm 68791, no. 39; FHL microfilm 25764, 1925, 1930, and 1935 censuses; Frankfurt District book II; IGI)

Notes

1. Mainz city archive.
2. West German Mission manuscript history, CHL MS 10045 2.
3. Presiding Bishopric, "Financial, Statistical, and Historical Reports of Wards, Stakes, and Missions, 1884–1955," 257, CHL CR 4 12.
4. Mainz city archive.

Michelstadt Branch

The charming little city of Michelstadt is located in the Odenwald Forest about thirty-five miles southeast of Frankfurt. Its main attraction is the beautiful city hall that dates to at least 1484, one of the oldest in all of Germany. The Büchler family brought the gospel to this small city just after the turn of the century, but the branch was not officially established there until 1932.[1]

When World War II began, the Latter-day Saints in Michelstadt were holding meetings in a modest building at Horst Wessel Strasse 22. Annaliese Büchler (born 1929) described the meeting place in these words:

> There was a large room and one smaller classroom, a cloak room, and a restroom. In the large room . . . there was a large table, and behind that, the branch presidency sat. On the side was a smaller table for the sacrament. We made music with a pump organ. With everybody there, we might have been twenty people in all. The building was right by the street, and there was a sign saying that [the branch] met there.[2]

Surnames represented among the branch leaders in the directory dated June 1939 were Walther, Büchler, Megner, Leopold, and Jakob.[3] Eleven of the thirty-seven registered members at the time held the priesthood.

Michelstadt Branch[4]	1939
Elders	2
Priests	2
Teachers	1
Deacons	6
Other Adult Males	2
Adult Females	19
Male Children	3
Female Children	2
Total	37

The meeting schedule for the Michelstadt Branch was similar to that of other branches all over Germany: Sunday School began at 10:30 a.m. and was followed by Relief Society. Sacrament meeting was held at 8:00 p.m. Mutual met on Tuesday evenings at 8:00 p.m., and a genealogy class was held on the third Sunday of the month at 8:00 p.m. There was no Primary at the time. When the war began, the branch president was Jakob Walther, and his counselors were Martin Büchler and Heinrich Büchler.

When Germany attacked Poland on September 1, 1939, Annaliese Büchler was a member of the Jungvolk. About her membership in the Jungvolk, she recalled:

> I liked it. For me it was a wonderful time because we learned new things and had fun with all of our friends. Although we had to wear a uniform

> (a skirt with a white blouse), it was a good time for us. When there was a parade going on, I normally didn't attend, but it also didn't feel like we had to. Sometimes the leaders complained about us missing the meetings. . . . It even occurred that they slapped me because I missed the last meeting. They even came to our home and picked me up.

For Anna Elise Hosch (born 1924), the war was not a serious concern in the little city of Michelstadt. She belonged to the League of German Girls and enjoyed that, but the war was far away until she began to attend school in Darmstadt. She happened to be home on vacation the night her school was destroyed, as she recalled: "I cried because I couldn't comprehend how they could destroy the city in which I went to school. I couldn't go back to school for a while. Later, we could see the fires in Darmstadt from our home [twenty miles distant]."[5]

The year-end report of the Relief Society for December 1940 lends an interesting description to the work done by the sisters in Michelstadt: "Our Relief Society is small but fine. Unfortunately, we have had to restrict our meetings a bit, but otherwise all is in order. We hope that our Heavenly Father will continue to bless, support, and protect our society in the coming year so that we can have a lot of success."[6]

One year later, the same organization submitted this report: "Our Relief Society is still operating. Due to the war and illnesses, only two reports have been submitted. On November 9, 1941, the Relief Society meeting was merged with the priesthood meeting because only two brethren were in attendance. We hope that our Heavenly Father will bless us in all of our efforts."[7]

The war was difficult for a little girl to understand, according to the recollections of Annaliese Büchler:

Fig. 1. The Megner family home in Michelstadt before the war. (O. Megner)

> As a ten-year-old child, I tried to understand what it meant to be in a war. I knew through the propaganda of Adolf Hitler that he wanted to make Germany a greater country.
>
> Even in school we learned that all the countries that had belonged to Germany before should now come back to [the Reich]. Who did not dream of owning a large property in East Prussia somewhere? This was taught to us over and over again.

According to the branch history written in 2007, the meeting rooms were confiscated by the city for use by refugees, but the branch was assigned some empty storerooms in which they met until 1947.[8] Otto Megner (born 1926) recalled that the new rooms were in the basement of the city hall and that his family had to sneak past Hitler Youth gatherings on Sunday mornings on their way to church. He had to apologize for missing the Sunday meetings, but his leaders were not fanatics who complained about his absence.[9]

Fig. 2. The building at what was Horst Wessel Strasse 22. The arrow points to the room in which the Saints met in the early years of the war. (M. Esterl 2008)

While Otto did not have to answer to fanatical Nazis in the Hitler Youth, the same was not true at school. He recalled beginning each day with the singing of the national anthem. "The teacher always came in his SS uniform and often made fun of the members of the Church." Fortunately, the Megners' neighbors did not cause them any problems. Otto had other interesting memories of Michelstadt during the war: "In Michelstadt, we did not feel much of the war. The mailman brought the obituary notices for the families whose sons or husbands had died in the war. [The mailman] was an old man who could not hear very well anymore. People would walk out to the street to find out who had died."

In 1943, seventeen-year-old Otto was called into the Reichsarbeitsdienst and sent to work in the Saarland province bordering occupied France. As he recalled:

> I was working in the Reichsarbeitsdienst in the Saarland, and one day I received orders to report to Frankfurt/Main to be tested to see if I was needed for the air force. I took the train from Saarbrücken to Frankfurt in full uniform. Just as we were entering Frankfurt, the train stopped and could not go on. I had to fight my way [through the aftermath of an air raid] to the army post. The houses next to me on the way were burning. During the examination, I was freezing. There was no heater and I had to stand naked in front of everybody. When that was over, everybody went their way and I had to go back to the train station. I took a train to the [Saarland] again.

In July 1944, Otto Megner was drafted and sent to France for training. In six weeks he was prepared for infantry action and had also learned Morse code. By that time, however, the Allied forces had already landed at Normandy and were making their way eastward through France. Fortunately for Otto and his young comrades (seventeen and eighteen years old), they were not sent to the front but moved slowly in the other direction. Dying for the fatherland had lost much of its appeal by that time. According to Otto, "I would not describe myself as a soldier who really stood behind what the war was about. I did what I was assigned to do without much conviction. Back then, I did not even understand everything that was happening." The war came to an end for Otto when he was taken prisoner on September 11.

"It seemed like we were far away from the happenings in Darmstadt and Frankfurt," recalled Annaliese Büchler back in Michelstadt:

Fig. 3. A wartime photograph of the members of the Michelstadt Branch. (O. Megner)

> We knew about the attacks and heard the sirens. Later in the war, we felt the earth quake and saw the fires, although we were 25 miles away. During the day, we could see the planes fly over us and during the night we could hear them. . . . Once an airplane crashed in a nearby forest. We went out to look at it—it was a horrible sight. It was a British plane with Polish soldiers in it. The dead are buried in the Michelstadt cemetery. They could still be identified.

Although the citizens of Michelstadt were quite safe, the same was not true of their relatives elsewhere. Annaliese Büchler's aunt was killed in an air raid on Frankfurt: "My mother went there with my oldest sister so they could identify her. It was a terrible thing for us to deal with." She remembered that the Michelstadt Saints sent food and other items to the members of the branches in Darmstadt and Frankfurt and that members of those branches came to Michelstadt after losing their homes in air raids. "We knew each other well, having attended district conferences together."

Anna Elise Hosch recalled that her family's home was not destroyed during the war. They were grateful for the Lord's protection and were willing to share their rooms with some of the many refugees who arrived in Michelstadt from Darmstadt and Frankfurt. Her mother was one of the many devout members who had no trouble introducing the Church to strangers. As Anna Elise recollected, "Whenever my mother talked to someone for more than five minutes, she would find a way to talk about the gospel."

Life for POW Otto Megner in France was not pleasant, as he recalled:

> We were all put into a camp and when we arrived, five hundred to a thousand other prisoners were already there. It was an old post of the Foreign Legion in Langres. When I think back to my time in the POW camp, one word still comes to mind: hunger. I also think about lice, not having enough clothing, and seeing no soap for weeks on end. We also did not have medical services. It was a French camp. They really did not like the Germans at all.

When the American army tanks rolled into Michelstadt on March 29, 1945, they were greeted by a sea of white flags and sheets hanging out of windows. The Hosch family was evicted by American officers but restored to their home after a few days by an American soldier who became their friend and intervened on their behalf.

American soldiers searched the Büchler apartment, as Annaliese recalled: "The soldiers looked through our home to see if we owned weapons or hid soldiers anywhere. I remember how they opened our closets and looked through our things. I was pretty angry at them for doing that! But all in all, they were nice and did not take anything from us. My father even hid his binoculars because he was scared that they would be taken."

The final branch report for the year 1945 reads: "With the changes in government it was not possible for us to hold regular meetings. Otherwise there is unity in the organization and we are grateful for the blessings of our Heavenly Father. We hope to make improvements next year."[10] It is interesting to note that whereas the discussion topics in Relief Society meetings at the beginning of the war included "Goethe and the Gospel" and other cultural themes, the topics in the last war year included "Obedience" and "Receiving Blessings from the Lord."[11]

In 1947, Otto Megner ceased to be a POW and became a guest worker. With no jobs available at home, he chose to stay in France. He prospered there and was able to send valuable items to his mother in Michelstadt. He remained in France until 1952. Looking back on the war, he made the following observation: "The entire time I was [in France], I never met another soldier who was LDS. . . . I also did not have the scriptures with me. I relied on prayer and the Spirit. There were many occasions in which it was obvious that I was guided by the Spirit and even angels in order to make the right decisions. I was always a member of the Church at heart." Otto's twin brother and two elder brothers were fortunate to survive their years in the German military and eventually return to Michelstadt.

The city of Michelstadt had 4,093 inhabitants in 1939. Almost all civilians survived World War II unscathed, but 238 men lost their lives in the service of Führer, Volk, and Vaterland.[12] The members of the small but strong branch had fared quite well during the war; none lost their homes and only two (one soldier and one infant) died during those difficult years. The Saints were in a good condition to begin life in a new post-Hitler Germany and looked forward to the day when they would have their own meetinghouse.

In Memoriam

The following members of the Michelstadt Branch did not survive World War II:

Georg Arzt b. Michelstadt, Erbach, Hessen, 7 Jun 1911; son of Peter Arzt and Elisabeth Rausch; bp. 20 Dec 1931; conf. 20 Dec 1931; m. 21 Aug 1940, Anna Grenz; k. in battle 19 April 1945. (CHL microfilm 2458, form 42 FP, ft. 37, 298–99; FHL microfilm 68801, no. 1; IGI; FHL microfilm 68791, no. 384)

Peter Ross b. Gadernheim, Bensheim, Hessen 22 Jul 1941; son of Peter Ross and Eva Marquart; d. intestinal surgery 16 Mar 1942. (FHL microfilm 68791, no. 622; Frankfurt District Book II; IGI)

Notes

1. Michelstadt Branch, "Seventy-Five-Year Anniversary" (unpublished manuscript, 2007).
2. Annaliese Büchler Pils, interview by author in German, Darmstadt, Germany, August 19, 2008; unless otherwise noted, summarized in English by Judith Sartowski.
3. West German Mission branch directory, 1939, CHL 10045 11.
4. Presiding Bishopric, "Financial, Statistical, and Historical Reports of Wards, Stakes, and Missions, 1884–1955," 257, CHL CR 4 12.
5. Anna Elise Hosch Egly, telephone interview with Jennifer Heckmann in German, January 14, 2009.
6. Michelstadt Branch Relief Society minutes, CHL LR 5518 14.
7. Ibid.
8. Michelstadt Branch history.
9. Otto Megner, interview by Jennifer Heckmann in German, Darmstadt, Germany, August 22, 2007.
10. Michelstadt Branch Relief Society minutes.
11. Johann Wolfgang von Goethe was possibly Germany's greatest writer and philosopher.
12. Michelstadt city archive.

Offenbach Branch

Just a few hundred yards from the southeast boundary of the city of Frankfurt, Offenbach lies on the south bank of the Main River. Famous as the center of the leather industry in Germany, the official population of 85,128 in 1939 included 95 members of the LDS Church.[1] The branch was established there in 1900.

Church meetings were held in rented rooms at Ludwigstrasse 38, near the city center. Rosel Goeller (born 1927) recalled the conditions: "Our first meetings were in factories, and I didn't like that because [the rooms were] too old. I didn't like telling my friends where I went to church because everybody else who went to church went to nice chapels or large beautiful buildings. I think there was a sign outside saying that we met in those rooms. There were not many people who attended the meetings—maybe around fifty."[2]

Offenbach Branch[3]	**1939**
Elders	4
Priests	2
Teachers	0
Deacons	6
Other Adult Males	25
Adult Females	51
Male Children	4
Female Children	3
Total	95

The directory of the West German Mission shows a full complement of branch leaders at work in June 1939.[4] Arthur C. Reis was the branch

Fig. 1. A Fasching (Carnival) celebration in the Offenbach Branch in February 1939. (E. Rosenhan)

Fig. 2. Members of the Offenbach Branch joined with other Saints of the West German Mission for a Rhine River cruise at the conclusion of the mission conference on May 19, 1939. (E. Rosenhan)

president and was assisted by counselors Wilhelm Rau and Johann Göller. Elly Wolf was the Young Women leader, Bertha Reis the president of the Primary, and Klara Weilmünster the president of the Relief Society. The meeting schedule was quite typical, with Sunday School at 10:00 a.m. and sacrament meeting at 7:00 p.m. All auxiliary meetings took place on Wednesday evening, with the exception of the Relief Society gatherings on Monday evenings.

Thanks to a dedicated clerk, the minutes of branch meetings in Offenbach were kept with great precision through most of the war. The average attendance at sacrament meetings was twenty-eight in 1939. As in other branches throughout the mission, the clerk noted the number of attendees in several categories: priesthood holders, women, children, and friends.[5]

A rare indication of interaction between local police and branch leaders is reported under the date June 28, 1940: Gestapo agents visited President Reis at an unidentified location (possibly in his home) and asked him the following questions:[6]

> Name of the sect: KJC [*Kirche Jesu Christi*] etc. and *Mormonen*
> Address: same [as before] [had there been a previous inquiry?]
> Members: 93
> Preachers: none (any male member can be asked to speak)
> Leader: Arthur C. Reis, warehouse manager, born in London in 1897
> Meeting times: during the war only Sundays 10–12 and 4–5
> Address of worship: Ludwigstrasse 32 in Offenbach[7]
> Any youth groups? No
> Who is the youth group leader? Nobody
> Any publications? None
> What kinds of meetings are held? Worship services.

A copy of the record was sent to Anton Huck at the mission office on July 20, 1940. Apparently there was no further action during the war on the part of the Gestapo in Offenbach.

In late 1940, the meeting schedule was changed such that all meetings took place on Sundays, "giving all members a better opportunity to attend the meetings."[8] The activities of the branch during the year 1941 suggest that the Saints in Offenbach were doing well in sustaining the programs of the Church. On April 6 they celebrated the anniversary of the Church, "and lots of photographs were taken" by the thirty-nine attendees. On July 24, Karoline and Brigetta Ledermann were baptized in Frankfurt, and a festival for the MIA was held on September 14. That event was especially noteworthy because forty-seven persons attended in a year that saw MIA groups discontinue meetings in branches all over Germany. In contrast, the average attendance at sacrament meeting was holding steady in 1941 at twenty-eight persons. The average declined to twenty-five during 1942.[9]

The Göller family was fortunate to live in an apartment house that survived the war. They were also fortunate that Rosel's father was too old to be drafted (in his seventies) and could stay home with his wife. Some of their nine children had already grown up and left the home. Brother Göller was not a friend of the government, but he and his wife rarely spoke of politics in the presence of their children.

Calendar year 1943 brought significant challenges to the branch in Offenbach. President Arthur Reis became quite ill and was given blessings on several occasions by mission leaders such as Anton Huck. President Reis's extended absence from the meetings may have led to some miscommunication, as reflected in an indignant letter written to him by Wilhelm Humbert on August 26, featuring these lines:

> I have read your letter in great astonishment. I know full well that you are the branch president, but I did not know that you listen to such gossip and thus make accusations against me. You are extremely misinformed. A sister had indicated that you wanted to have certain hymns sung in order to make the meetings more spiritual. Is that my fault? To this date, I have done nothing without your permission. I would have visited you had I not suffered an accident on Monday. We were told that nobody should visit you because it might upset you (that is what they told us on Sunday). In order to avoid this gossip and backbiting, I ask that you immediately release me from all callings. In my office as an elder I do not answer to any women. I want you to understand this very clearly. I have also informed Anton Huck of this matter.
>
> Your brother in the gospel
>
> Please excuse my poor handwriting.
>
> Please read *"Evangeliumslehre"* pages 263–264: I have always acted accordingly

The reference to "women" in Brother Humbert's letter apparently included Sister Elly Wolf, who was president of the YWMIA when the war began and had since been called to work in the Relief Society. She wrote the following to President Reis on October 4:

> Dear Brother Reis,
>
> I am enclosing the book for the Relief Society with the copies sent to me as well as the bank book and wish to be released from all of my callings in the branch. Should anything remain unclear, please write me about it. I have a happy home and thus forbid visits by branch members and will not allow my home to be destroyed by the gossip and backbiting of the branch. I hope you understand this so that I do not have to use legal means to prevent visits. I will send all visitors away, regardless of who it is! . . . I will be sending you my monthly report in the next few days. I am not at home much, because I work for the welfare services. Should there be any unresolved matters with the lesson manuals, you may do with the money what you feel is correct. The balance of the MIA funds and the Gleaner funds should be the same when they are opened again. I will close now and wish you best regards for your life.
>
> Heil Hitler!
>
> Sister Elly Wolff

The reader is left to speculate as to the origin of the conflict, but at the very least it would seem that some amount of gossip had approached the level of slander, and the writers of the letters quoted above felt that they had been victimized and their reputations sullied. There is no indication in the branch records through 1946 that Sister Wolf attended church meetings in Offenbach again, but Brother Humbert returned by 1944.[10]

Shortly after the climax of the crisis, President Reis died following a lengthy illness; branch membership records indicated that his illness was somehow related to air raids. In the apparent absence of a qualified replacement, Brother Valentin Schlimm of the Frankfurt Branch was called to preside in Offenbach. He encountered difficulties within a month when the meeting rooms were damaged and he had to cancel meetings. The average attendance at sacrament meeting for the year 1943 had already declined to twenty-two persons.[11]

The Allied air offensive against Frankfurt and Offenbach intensified in 1944 and the branch clerk made many notations regarding this problem. The meeting rooms were slightly damaged on March 18 and four days later were totally destroyed. By May, the Saints were meeting in the home of a Sister Sorawia at Grosse Marktstrasse 13. Air-raid alarms caused interruptions in meetings on five different Sundays from July through November.

Rosel Goeller recalled the following about the constant air raids and false alarms:

> Air raids were terrifying. I took my Book of Mormon with me when we went into the basement. I would say that we were not completely safe there; it was not like a regular concrete bunker. We sat in the basement until they told us [via the all-clear siren] that we could go back upstairs. It wasn't usually all night long. . . . It was dark in those basements; there was no light. Sometimes, when we came out of the basement, we saw buildings burning.

The report dated August 30–31, 1944, includes a sad event: "Sister Margarethe Leutenbach nee Göller died on the way to the air raid shelter. She will be buried in the new cemetery."[12] Margarethe's younger sister, Rosel, recalled that Margarethe "was running to the bunker from her home, and she collapsed and died." The trip to the shelter was not a simple walk. City dwellers had to deal with inclement weather,

Fig. 3. This branch history book survived for more than six months in the rubble of a building that was destroyed by bombs in November 1944. (Church History Library)

rubble from damaged buildings on damaged streets, the drone of the engines of approaching airplanes, and the worst hazard of all—being under stress or in panic under blackout conditions.

The branch clerk did not identify himself in the detailed accounts of meetings in the Offenbach Branch, but a careful study of the records from 1941 to 1945 suggests that he was Rudolf Buchmann. We have him to thank for his diligence, evidenced perhaps best by his comments under the date November 5, 1944:

> House service and fast meeting:
>
> Branch President Brother Schlimm presided. Opening hymn 221; invocation by Brother Humbert; hymn no. 12; sacrament blessed by President Schlimm and passed by Brother

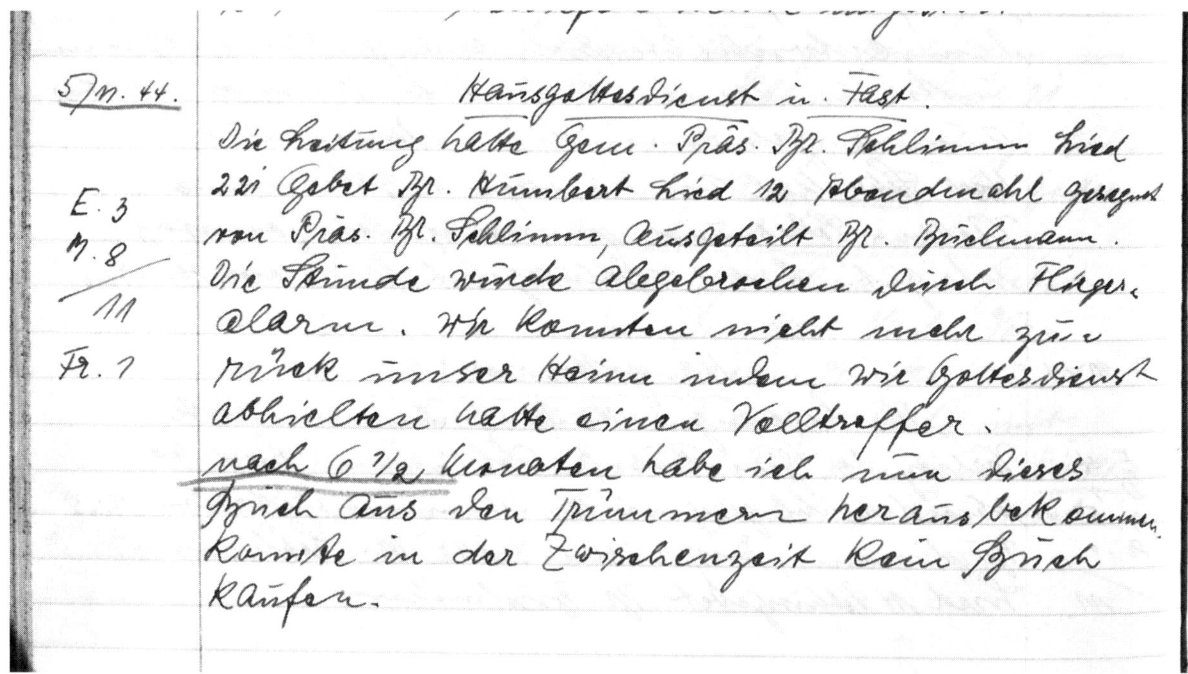
5/XI. 44. Hausgottesdienst in Fast.

E. 3
M. 8
11
Fr. 1

Die Leitung hatte Gem. Präs. Br. Schlimm Lied 221 Gebet Br. Humbert Lied 12 Abendmahl gesegnet von Präs. Br. Schlimm, ausgeteilt Br. Buchmann. Die Stunde wurde abgebrochen durch Flieger-alarm. Wir konnten nicht mehr zurück unser Heim indem wir Gottesdienst abhielten hatte einen Volltreffer. nach 6 1/2 Monaten habe ich nun dieses Buch aus den Trümmern herausbekommen, konnte in der Zwischenzeit kein Buch kaufen.

Fig. 4. This entry in the Offenbach Branch history explains how the book shown above came to be buried under the rubble of a collapsed building from November 1944 until May 1945. (Church History Library)

> Buchmann. The meeting was interrupted by air-raid sirens. We could not come back after the air raid. Our home in which we had conducted the meeting received a direct hit.
>
> After 6 ½ months [May 20, 1945] I was able to rescue this book from the ruins. I had not been able to purchase a new book in the meantime.

While it is clear that the branch clerk was dedicated to his calling of keeping records for all meetings, this man did much more. He must have been very discouraged that his record book was buried in the rubble during the air raid. He tried unsuccessfully to replace the book and found no source of even individual sheets of paper since wartime shortages were acute. During the twenty-eight weeks the branch record book lay buried within the ruins of the building where Rudolf Buchmann lived, the ruins of the building would have been subjected to the winter weather. Germany traditionally receives a minimum of five inches of precipitation per month, and one would assume that the book would be wet or even soaked and rotting from water seeping through the wreckage. The record book may have been kept in a cabinet or a desk drawer that remained intact and watertight. One can imagine that the clerk was overjoyed when his search for this record (and likely other items of branch or personal value) was a success.

Rosel Goeller's recollection of the end of the war is as follows:

> When the Americans came into Offenbach, I was there. I watched the tanks and the soldiers coming in and going from house to house while we were hiding. I was afraid because we had heard rumors [about the American soldiers]. But in the end, the Americans were not too bad to us. It was mostly the [Nazis] who told us that we should not believe the Americans. The soldiers did not come into our home to look for anything.

It is apparent that the members of the Church in Offenbach did their best to continue holding meetings. On June 7, the following report was made:

> [Mission leader Anton] Huck visited the meeting and blessed our temporary branch pres. Wilhelm Humbert. Later he visited the secretary's [Rudolf Buchmann's?] house: "I told him that we had

> a chance to buy a building in which we could meet and bombed-out members could live. He replied that the mission does not purchase buildings, based on the fact that our prophet, Heber J. Grant, had died on May 15 of this year and that he said on his death bed that the Second Coming of Christ will happen very soon, it could not be far away."[13]

It should come as no surprise that after the cataclysmic events of World War II, some Church members believed that the end of the world was approaching. The veracity of such a statement likely cannot be confirmed.

The records of the city of Offenbach indicate that only 467 people died in air raids there, but approximately 40 percent of the city was destroyed during twenty-eight air raids. At least 2,229 soldiers lost their lives. The war ended there for all practical purposes when the American army entered the city on March 26, 1945.[14]

A brief history of the Offenbach Branch offers only one sentence regarding the experience of the members of the Church there during the war years: "Due to the severe lack of living space after the war, the branch had no suitable meeting rooms for one year. Branch meetings and worship services were held in the apartment of Sister Sorawia at Grosse Marktstrasse 13 in Offenbach."[15]

The final comment in the branch records connected with the war was made on July 29, 1945: "A memorial program for the fallen heroes: The new branch president is Valentin Schlimm [of Frankfurt]; Anton Huck was also there."[16] No names of the soldiers are recorded, but lists compiled by the office of the West German Mission include the names of four soldiers from this branch who lost their lives while serving in the Wehrmacht.

In Memoriam

The following members of the Offenbach Branch did not survive World War II:

Margarethe Göller b. Offenbach, Hessen, 17 May 1913; dau. of Johann Martin Göller and Elisabeth Fr. Tron; bp. 27 May 1921; conf. 27 May 1921; m. 12 Oct 1938, Wilhelm Lautenbach; k. in air raid Offenbach 30 Aug 1944 (CHL microfilm 2458, form 42 FP, pt. 37, 298–99; IGI; FHL microfilm 68802, no. 31)

Albert Hausch b. Leimen, Heidelberg, Baden, 10 May 1909; son of Johann Hausch and Katharine Kalbeck; bp. 24 Aug 1934; conf. 24 Aug 1934; k. in battle France 21 Dec 1943 (CHL microfilm 2458, form 42 FP, pt. 37, 298–99; IGI; FHL microfilm 68802, no. 134; FHL microfilm 68791, no. 496)

Johann Karl Hausch b. Leimen, Heidelberg, Baden, 10 May 1909; son of Johann Hausch and Katharine Kalbeck; bp. 1 Oct 1932; conf. 2 Oct 1932; ord. deacon 22 Apr 1934; m. 16 Dec 19—, Anna M. Jacob (Löffel); corporal; k. in battle France 17 Dec 1944; bur. Daleiden, Prüm, Rheinland (FHL microfilm 68802, no. 128; CHL microfilm 2458, form 42 FP, pt. 37, 298–99; FHL microfilm no. 68791, no. 400; www.volksbund.de; IGI)

Otto Kallenbach b. Offenbach, Hessen, 12 Mar 1916; son of Michael Kallenbach and Dorothea Kath. Jacobi; bp. 8 Oct 1925; conf. 8 Oct 1925; lance corporal; k. in battle Dubrowka, Wjasma, Russia, 2 Oct 1941 (FHL microfilm 68802, no. 64; FHL microfilm 68791, no. 949; www.volksbund.de)

Rudolf Kallenbach b. Offenbach, Hessen, 25 Aug 1910; son of Michael Kallenbach and Dorothea Kath. Jacobi; bp. 20 Jun 1925; conf. 20 Jun 1925; ord. deacon 11 Feb 1929; m. 21 Dec 1932 or 1933, Katharina M. Trapp; corporal; k. in battle France 9 Jun 1940; bur. Noyers-Pont-Maugis, France (FHL microfilm 68802, no. 65; FHL microfilm 68791, no. 910; www.volksbund.de; IGI)

Katharina May b. Weiten Gesäß, Erbach, Hessen, 20 May 1861; dau. of Georg May and Dorothea Kropp; bp. 22 May 1941; conf. 22 May 1941; m. Frankfurt/Main, Hessen-Nassau, 15 Mar 1884, Heinrich Koob; four children; d. old age Offenbach, Hessen, 13 Aug 1943 (FHL microfilm 68802, no. 158; FHL microfilm 68791, no. 601; IGI)

Anna Marie Rall b. Offenbach, Hessen, 27 Sep 1861; dau. of Karl A. Rall and Katharina Z. Diez; bp. 31 Jul 1900; conf. 31 Jul 1900; m. —— Hübner; d. senility 28 Mar 1943 (FHL microfilm 68791, no. 76; Frankfurt District book II; IGI)

Albert Rau b. Offenbach, Hessen, 10 Apr 1929; son of Wilhelm Waldefang Rau and Ida Esswein; bp. 10 Oct 1937; conf. 10 Oct 1937; d. injuries from incendiary bomb, Offenbach, 25 Mar 1944 (CHL microfilm 2458, form 42 FP, pt. 37, 298–99; PRF; FHL microfilm 68802, no. 79)

Emma Waltraut Rau b. Offenbach, Hessen, 26 Jul 1941; dau. of Wilhelm Waldefang Rau and Ida Esswein; d. Offenbach cramps, 28 Mar 1942 (CHL LR 6389 11, 156)

Arthur Charles Reis b. London, England, 31 Aug 1897; son of Charles A. Reis and Betha H. Steuck or Steuch; bp. 17 May 1926; conf. 17 May 1926; ord. deacon 13 Feb 1927; ord. teacher 15 Sep 1930; ord. priest 7 Apr 1935; ord. elder 22 Mar 1936; m. 12 May 1928, Minna Frieda Richter (div.); 2m. 28 Mar 1934, Elisabeth K. Heck; d. health complications due to air raid 24 Oct 1943, bur. 28 Oct 1943 (FHL microfilm 68802, no. 84; FHL microfilm 68791, no. 995; IGI)

Kathinka Weber b. Offenbach, Hessen, 21 Oct 1870; dau. of Wilhelm Weber and Maria Geider; bp. 11 Aug 1907; conf. 11 Aug 1907; d. 1941 (FHL microfilm 68791, no. 145; Frankfurt District book II; IGI)

Pauline Mathilda Bertha Zacharias b. Langensalza, Erfurt, Sachsen, 11 Nov 1867; dau. of Christian Heinrich Rudolf Zacharias and Therese Eleonore Klara Wiegand; bp. 27 Jan 1927; conf. 27 Jan 1927; m. Langensalza 12 Aug 1911, Philipp Ludwig Reinhard Houy; d. senility 26 Oct 1943 (FHL microfilm 68791, no. 191; FHL microfilm 162790, 1935 census; Frankfurt District book II; IGI)

Margarethe Zintel b. Worms, Rheinhessen, Hessen, 8 May 1875; dau. of Katharina Zintel; bp. 28 Jun 1939; conf. 28 Jun 1939; m. 25 Mar 1930, Hieronymus Blumöhr; d. cancer 9 Jan 1941 (FHL microfilm 68802, no. 156; FHL microfilm 68791, no. 566)

Notes

1. Offenbach am Main city archive.
2. Rosel Goeller Meyer, interview by the author, Salt Lake City, November 3, 2006.
3. Presiding Bishopric, "Financial, Statistical, and Historical Reports of Wards, Stakes, and Missions, 1884–1955," 257, CR 4 12.
4. West German Mission branch directory 1939, CHL 10045 11.
5. Offenbach Branch general minutes, CHL LR 6389 11.
6. Ibid., 140.
7. Apparently the branch had moved three buildings down the street in the previous eight months, confirming what Rosel Goeller said about various locations.
8. Offenbach Branch general minutes, 143.
9. Ibid., 152–56.
10. The fact that Brother Humbert was asked later during the war to serve as the temporary branch president suggests that he harbored no ill will toward the gossipers.
11. Offenbach Branch general minutes, 170–72.
12. Ibid., 178.
13. Ibid., 182.
14. Offenbach am Main city archive.
15. Johann Ludwig Schneider, collected papers, CHL MS 13829.
16. Offenbach Branch general minutes, 184.

Gustav Horn (born 1930) of Offenbach used this old cigar box for his collection of anti-aircraft shell fragments

HAMBURG DISTRICT

West German Mission

Hamburg had more than 1.7 million inhabitants when World War II began and was thus the largest city in the West German Mission. Three branches existed there at the time—St. Georg, downtown; Barmbek, in the eastern part of the city; and Altona, in the western part. Nearly one thousand Saints belonged to those three branches. No other city in the mission had more than one branch in 1939.

Hamburg District[1]	1939
Elders	71
Priests	24
Teachers	24
Deacons	54
Other Adult Males	147
Adult Females	527
Male Children	55
Female Children	47
Total	949

When the war began, the district president was Alwin Brey (born 1902), a real estate agent dealing with nautical properties. His counselors were Paul Pruess of the St. Georg Branch and Friedrich Sass of the Lübeck Branch. Their church responsibilities included three branches in other cities: Glückstadt (twenty-five miles northwest of Hamburg), Lübeck (thirty miles northeast), and Stade (eighteen miles to the west). Direct connections via railroad made it convenient for Elder Brey and his counselors to visit the outlying branches and for the Saints from those towns to attend district conferences held every six months in the rooms of the St. Georg Branch in Hamburg.

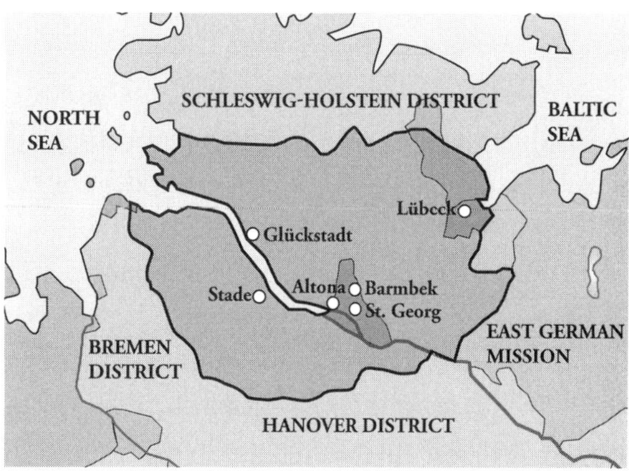

Fig. 1. The Hamburg District consisted of three branches in the city of Hamburg and three more close by.

Alwin Brey was drafted into the German navy at the end of 1941. His first counselor, Paul Pruess, was not in good health, so second counselor Otto Berndt (born 1906) temporarily assumed the leadership of the district. Counselor Friedrich Sass had been drafted into the Luftwaffe and was also no longer able to serve. Otto Berndt had done a short stint in the Luftwaffe but had spent so much time in hospitals with minor illnesses that he was classified as unfit for duty and sent home. He admitted that his health was not seriously impaired, but the change in status allowed him not only to avoid military service for the duration of the war but also to travel without restriction—both evidences to him of God's protecting hand. In any case, it was nice to be home in June 1941, when his wife was expecting their fifth child. President Berndt was able to find employment with a company making metal signs with enamel finishes. (He was able to produce one for the St. Georg Branch and proudly mounted it on the wall by the entrance to the rooms at Besenbinderhof 13a.)[2]

Fig. 2. Alwin Brey, the president of the Hamburg District in 1939, served later in the German navy. (I. Brey Glasgy)

Perhaps the greatest challenge for Otto Berndt as the district president was the philosophical disagreement he had with Arthur Zander, president of the St. Georg Branch. Brother Zander was enthusiastic in his support of the Nazi regime—too enthusiastic, as far as President Berndt was concerned. However, it seemed more important to avoid open conflict that might damage the atmosphere of the St. Georg Branch and perhaps call down the wrath of Nazi Party leaders upon the Church. By 1942, there were problems enough for the Church due to the Helmuth Hübener incident (see below), but Arthur Zander was drafted that year, effectively negating the hostilities between him and Otto Berndt.[3]

The case of the three teenagers of the St. Georg Branch who were convicted of conspiracy to commit treason is by now quite well known. Helmuth Hübener (born 1925), Karl-Heinz Schnibbe (born 1924), and Rudi Wobbe (born 1926) were arrested, charged with conspiring to commit treason against the state, tried before Germany's highest court, and punished. Their story has been told in great detail in several books and needs no elaboration here. Nevertheless, a history of the West German Mission during World War II is not complete without at least a short summary of this sad episode.[4]

Fig. 3. From left: Rudi Wobbe, Helmuth Hübener, and Karl-Heinz Schnibbe were all arrested for distributing antigovernment literature. (Blood Tribunal)

By all accounts, Helmuth Hübener was a bright young man, wise and mature beyond his years. An excellent student bound for a career in government service, he came into possession of a radio in 1941 that enabled him to listen to news reports from the British Broadcasting Corporation (BBC). He quickly came to the realization that the German radio news reports were not telling the full story—especially regarding German military losses. In about July of 1941, he invited (on separate occasions) his two best friends, Rudi Wobbe and Karl-Heinz Schnibbe, to share his discoveries. Listening to BBC broadcasts was strictly forbidden, and the fact that Helmuth transcribed or summarized broadcasts and then typed them out for distribution around town was nothing short of treason in Hitler's Germany. Karl-Heinz and Rudi (both of whom were convinced that Helmuth's political observations were correct) were the runners who placed the handouts in telephone booths, in apartment house hallways, and even on bulletin boards in blue-collar neighborhoods of Hamburg. Copies of some sixty messages were produced and circulated, and the two runners knew from the beginning that they had to be extremely cautious in distributing the literature.

Unfortunately, Helmuth was not as cautious. Convinced of the righteous nature of his cause, he approached another young man at work with the request that he translate the political messages into French. Helmuth hoped that French forced laborers working in Hamburg's factories could read the messages, many of which openly charged Hitler and the government of lying to the German people about the status of the war. Eventually, Helmuth was reported by suspicious coworkers to the foreman, who collected information for the Gestapo. Helmuth was arrested on February 5, 1942. His best friends were picked up just days later—Karl-Heinz on February 10 and Rudi on February 18. The president of the St. Georg Branch informed the branch members of Helmuth's arrest and expressed his dismay in the fact that Helmuth had used the branch typewriter to produce his anti-Hitler messages. (Helmuth was the branch secretary, and the machine was kept in his apartment so that he could type letters to branch members away from home in military service.)

The three best friends were held in a local prison and interrogated for days in the Gestapo headquarters downtown. They had agreed in advance that if caught, they would do their best to shoulder the guilt individually and thus attempt to avoid burdening each other with guilt. Rudi and Karl-Heinz later wrote of the beatings they received and were both convinced that Helmuth had been formally tortured. In the meantime, the families of the three teenagers were questioned by the Gestapo, as were the presidents Arthur Zander and Otto Berndt. At first, the police could not be convinced that Helmuth could produce such sophisticated literature without the help of adults, but eventually they accepted his claim that he alone had written the messages.

The Gestapo theory that the boys had been enlisted by conniving adults was pursued aggressively, and district president Otto Berndt was summoned to Gestapo headquarters as part of the investigation. His description of the setting gives a clear picture of Hitler's police state:

> I rang the bell and the door opened automatically. The hallway was dark and there was nobody there. Suddenly, I heard a voice over the loudspeaker: "Come in. Take three steps forward!" which I did. The door closed behind me and I stood in the dark. Then a light went on and I saw a man sitting there; he took my papers. He wrote my name in a book, then handed me a piece of paper with a number on it and told me, "Sit on the chair with this number on it and wait until you are called. If you walk around or try to look into other rooms, you are breaking the law." I went upstairs to the next floor and sat on the chair with the assigned number. I had not been waiting long when the door next to me opened and I was ordered to enter and take a seat. Until that moment, I had seen nobody but the man at the entry and all doors had opened and closed automatically. The building was like a mausoleum and I couldn't hear anything. . . . It was creepy and I have to admit that my knees were shaking. I entered the room and it was empty except for two chairs and a table between them—that was the extent of the furnishings. A few files and a telephone were on the table. An official about thirty years old ordered me to sit down. I told him that while sitting in the hall I have been more afraid than at any other time in my life. . . . I felt the presence of evil

> and knew that I was in a dangerous situation and could not escape. Before entering the room I had said ("screamed" would be a better word for it) a quick prayer to my Heavenly Father. I cried for help from the depths of my soul; no sound escaped my tongue. When I sat down, all fear left me and I was encompassed by total peace. . . . I knew that God had heard my prayer and that I was under His protection. I noticed that a higher power had taken control over my body and this feeling stayed with me for four days—the duration of my interrogation. There is no other way to explain it; there is no other way that I could have answered all of those questions honestly and quickly and to the satisfaction of the Gestapo.[5]

In his recollection, Otto Berndt was questioned about the teachings of the Church, the relationship of the Church and the state, the philosophy of the Church regarding Jews, and several other topics.

In early August 1942, the three friends were transported by train to Berlin where their case was to be tried before the highest court of the land—a court famous for quick rulings and summary judgments against those who opposed the regime. The boys were provided defense attorneys who did their duty in a most perfunctory manner. The trial of all three began on August 11 and finished that very day. From the onset, Karl-Heinz and Rudi were convinced that a verdict of guilty was assured. Their sentences were indeed severe: Helmuth was sentenced to die; Rudi to spend ten years in prison; and Karl-Heinz, five years. Helmuth's last statement to the judges inspired both Rudi and Karl-Heinz: "You have sentenced me to death for telling the truth. My time is now—but your time will come!"[6] The last two were soon transported back to Hamburg to prison, while Helmuth awaited the results of many appeals made in his behalf for clemency. All appeals were denied, and Helmuth Hübener was executed in Berlin's Plötzensee Prison on October 27, 1942.[7] In the hours before his death, he wrote three letters to family and friends in Hamburg. Only one letter survives, in the possession of the Sommerfeld family; it includes this text:

> I am very thankful to my Heavenly Father that this agonizing life is coming to an end this evening. I could not stand it any longer anyway! My Father in Heaven knows that I have done nothing wrong. . . . I know that God lives and He will be the proper judge of this matter. Until our happy reunion in that better world I remain your friend and brother in the Gospel. Helmuth.[8]

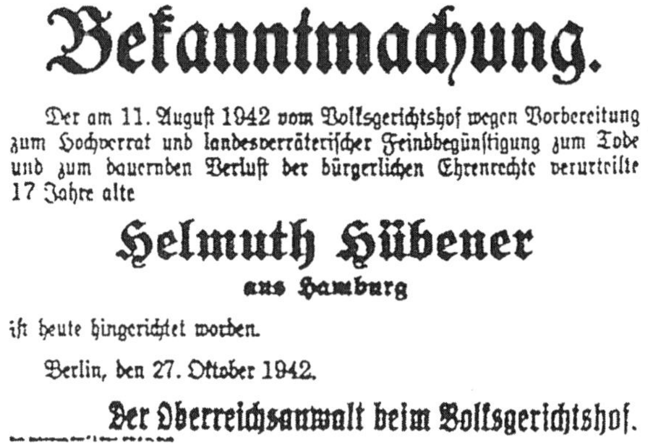

Bekanntmachung.

Der am 11. August 1942 vom Volksgerichtshof wegen Vorbereitung zum Hochverrat und landesverräterischer Feindbegünstigung zum Tode und zum dauernden Verlust der bürgerlichen Ehrenrechte verurteilte 17 Jahre alte

Helmuth Hübener

aus Hamburg

ist heute hingerichtet worden.

Berlin, den 27. Oktober 1942.

Der Oberreichsanwalt beim Volksgerichtshof.

Fig. 4. This notice of Helmuth Hübener's execution appeared in a Kassel newspaper. (J. Ernst)

The reactions of fellow members of the St. Georg Branch were mixed. Most felt sorrow for the young men when their arrest and punishment were announced but were disappointed that such apparently foolish and self-destructive acts could be committed by Latter-day Saints who had been taught to obey laws and give allegiance to governments. Branch meetings were observed by government agents for some time after the incident, and the Church equipment used by Helmuth to produce the handbills was confiscated and not returned.

Rudi Wobbe and Karl-Heinz Schnibbe spent the next year in prison not far from Hamburg. The conditions of their incarceration improved a bit with time, but it was no happy existence. In December 1943, they were sent to occupied Poland and assigned to work in an aircraft repair factory. In January 1945, the Red Army streamed into Germany, and Rudi and Karl-Heinz were marched toward the west along with their fellow prisoners. They were back in the familiar surroundings of their Hamburg prison on February 16. Days later, Karl-Heinz was drafted into the German army and assigned to help stop the Soviet invasion in eastern Germany. Rudi was kept in Hamburg because he had a longer prison sentence to serve.

For the next three months, Rudi watched as more and more prisoners left to serve in the German army, but his own status as a political prisoner guaranteed him a longer stay in prison. It was not until late May that he and the last remaining prisoners were freed by French conquerors. The British occupation authority reviewed his story, were convinced of his innocence, and sent him home on June 2, 1945. He viewed with sadness the ruins of his hometown but was thrilled to see his family again after more than three years.

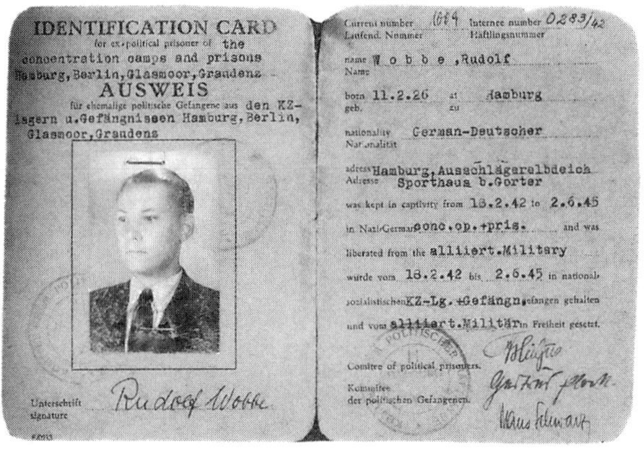
IDENTIFICATION CARD
for ex-political prisoner of the
concentration camps and prisons
Hamburg, Berlin, Glasmoor, Graudenz
AUSWEIS
für ehemalige politische Gefangene aus den KZ-
Lagern u. Gefängnissen Hamburg, Berlin,
Glasmoor, Graudenz

Unterschrift
signature Rudolf Wobbe

Current number 1614 Internee number 0283/42
Laufend. Nummer Häftlingsnummer
name Wobbe, Rudolf
Name
born 11.2.26 at Hamburg
geb. zu
nationality German-Deutscher
Nationalität
adress Hamburg, Ausschläger elbdeich
Adresse Sporthaus b. Gorter
was kept in captivity from 18.2.42 to 2.6.45
in Nazi-German conc.cp.+pris. and was
liberated from the alliiert. Military
wurde vom 18.2.42 bis 2.6.45 in national-
sozialistischen KZ-Lg.+Gefängn. gefangen gehalten
und vom alliiert. Militär in Freiheit gesetzt.
Comitee of political prisoners.
Komitee
der politischen Gefangenen.

Fig. 5. Ruddi Wobbe's identification card indicates that he was a political prisoner under the Nazis. (H. Schmidt Wobbe)

Karl-Heinz was captured by the Soviets in Czechoslovakia in April 1945 and spent the next four years in work camps in Russia. He suffered terrible illnesses, starvation, subzero temperature, mosquitoes, and the torture of being told repeatedly that "we would be going home soon." After losing a dangerous amount of weight in April 1949, he was classified as unfit for work and was sent back to Germany. Following a recuperative stay in a Göttingen hospital, he was released for good in June 1949 and returned to his family in a Hamburg that was finally beginning to rise from the ruins.

In the first few years of the war, the Allies had learned that a combination of explosive bombs and incendiary bombs could produce a disastrous effect known as "firebombing" in major German cities where wood structures were crowded around narrow streets. To be sure, the German military commanders knew this as well, but as the war dragged on, the German Luftwaffe became less and less able to defend the homeland. In July 1943, the British and American bomber forces in England decided that the city of Hamburg should be subjected to an intense campaign of raids within just a few days. Explosive bombs were to be dropped first to burst roof surfaces, doors, and windows, after which incendiaries would be dropped to start fires in the open structures. Four major attacks were carried out on July 25, 28, and 30, and August 3, and the proposed results were achieved—Hamburg burned for days. The heat was so intense and the fires so widespread that thousands died in air-raid shelters of suffocation without being so much as singed by the flames.

In his detailed study of the results of the air war against Hamburg, Hans Brunswig presented information collected by the Hamburg harbor weather service showing that the firestorm produced by the attacks resulted in flames soaring more than four miles into the sky, fed by winds of more than fifty miles per hour (winds caused by the fires sucking oxygen from ambient air on the ground level).[9] Following the success of these attacks, firebombings were carried out against many other German cities, the prime example being the attack of February 13–14, 1945, on Dresden.[10]

The following figures illustrate the extent of the losses in Hamburg during the entire war (about 80 percent of the damage occurring in July 1943). Among the residents and structures listed below were 790 Latter-day Saints, their homes, and their meetinghouses. The following accounts were provided by eyewitnesses regarding their experiences during the firebombings of July–August 1943.

Results of the Allied air war against Hamburg, Germany[11]	
Air-raid warnings sounded	778
Air-raid warnings with enemy airplanes sighted	702
Attacks	213
Airplanes involved in those attacks	Approx. 17,000
Explosive bombs dropped	Approx. 101,000
Incendiary bombs dropped	Approx. 1,600,000
Bombs not effective (fell in water, etc.)	Approx. 50%
Deaths (male 41.8%, female 58.2%)	48,572
Deaths elsewhere from injuries in Hamburg	Approx. 3,500
Apartments not damaged	21%
Apartments with slight damage	19%
Apartments with medium damage	7%
Apartments with serious damage	4%
Apartments totally destroyed	49%
Apartments totally destroyed in all of Germany	22%
Residents in Hamburg in 1939	Approx. 1,700,000
Residents with property loss	Approx. 1,170,000
Residents with total property loss	902,000
Residents with partial property loss	265,000

With her husband serving as a soldier at the Eastern Front, Maria Niemann had recently given birth to a baby girl, and both of them had nearly died in the process. Just months after that trial, Maria's family experienced the horror of the British attacks on Hamburg. Her son Henry (born 1936) was staying with a grandmother across town when the first bombings took place. As he explained, "They just bombed the living daylights out of this town. For hours we were in the basement and people were cry ing and carrying on and every once in a while you were . . . kind of lifted up in your seat because of the shock [of the bombs]."[12] Between attacks, Henry and his grandmother made their way through the fires and the rubble toward his home:

> There were a lot of streets that we had to bypass because the walls of the apartments and the buildings collapsed into the street and you couldn't get through . . . the narrow streets. . . . When we came to my street, there wasn't anybody outside. All the windows were blown out through the shock and the bar tiles were off the roof. . . . I remember that I started crying and then I started running home.

Henry Niemann found his mother in her bed with his sister—both safe and sound. Maria Niemann recalled the following details about the attack that took place the next day:

> I had to go with my children to the basement, and it was hard for me with a baby and my boy. . . . And so I had to call my neighbor. . . . She was a real good friend to me, and she helped and took the baby, and I took my son, and we went down to the basement. Then the bombs came down. It took our roof away, and here I was with a baby in a carriage and my son, and we had no roof. All the windows were out, and the curtains were hanging outside, and the water pipes were hit, and so there was gas mixed with water. What should we do? I cannot stay in my home with the baby.[13]

Emerging from their basement shelter following one of those raids, Maria saw her city burning in every direction and the neighboring houses in ruins: "The sun was shining, but we didn't see it. It was all black." The three of them made their way out of town and were eventually fortunate to find lodgings in the town of Hude, near the coast of the North Sea, about two hours northwest of Hamburg. According to Henry, they remained there for more than three years.

Gertrud Menssen survived the first few attacks with her two little children and found their home still standing. However, she feared that "the next time would be our turn." She was right, and their home was totally destroyed during the night of July 27–28. Fortunately, her husband, Walter, just happened to be home on leave. In Gertrud's recollection:

> When we heard the bombers and bombs falling, we grabbed our children only and my purse with important papers—nothing else—and ran this time to the big bomb shelter on the corner under the school yard. I guess we just knew we would get it this time. While we were in the shelter, men would come in and call out the number of the houses that had been hit. And it did not take very long until they called #86 Hasselbrookstr. That was us! . . . When we finally got out of the shelter in the afternoon, the whole city seemed to be burning. It was so dark and smoky and frightening that we put wet hankies over the children's eyes. Why cry about a household of furniture? . . . We were alive! And we were together! That was all that mattered.[14]

Walter Menssen got his family safely out of Hamburg and saw them onto a train to southern Germany before he was required to report for duty again. It would be more than a year before Gertrud and her (by then three) children would see Hamburg again.

During the worst hours of the raids over Hamburg, Gerd Fricke witnessed terrifying scenes: "I remember that when everything burned, the asphalt on the streets was like liquid, and the women with their children and strollers got stuck and burned to death right there. We saw many horrible things." The Fricke family lost everything they owned for the second time.[15]

Although Rahlstedt was seven miles from downtown Hamburg, the bombs dropped on the city eventually struck Rahlstedt and the Pruess home there. Lieselotte Pruess (born 1926) recalled the tragedy that struck her family's home in July 1943 while they were huddled in the basement:

> My father had been outside watching things. Then he came into the basement and said, "We all have to get out right now! The house is on fire!" We had felt something hit the house, but in all of the commotion, we didn't know what it was. So we ran out into the street and saw that our house was on fire. There was no fire department to help. Then my father and some neighbor men went back in to save some stuff. They brought our piano out too. The house burned to the ground, but we had our piano out in the street. I played the piano, and then my sister played the song "Freut Euch des Lebens" ("Let's All Be Happy"). The neighbors remember that.[16]

The Pruess family evacuated to the town of Thorn in Poland, where they were given housing in some army barracks. Soon thereafter, Rosalie Pruess returned to Rahlstedt with a son, and they managed to make the home livable on a subsistence level.

Harald Fricke (born 1926) wrote the following account of the firebombings:

> I was sixteen years old at the time. We (my mother, my sister Carla, my brother Gerhard, my Grandpa and I) were living at the time on Norderstrasse in [the suburb of] Hammerbrook. We survived the first attack in the basement shelter of our home even though the building above us was totally destroyed. Then we were assigned an apartment on Olgastrasse in the suburb of Rothenburgsort. This narrow street was destroyed one or two days later by the fires that spread throughout the city. Nobody could seem to escape the sea of flames anymore. We were fortunate to be in an apartment at the end of the street and were able to run through the hail of bombs and shrapnel across the street to the underground bunker at Brandhofer Schleuse. When we got there, they first didn't want to let us in because the shelter was full and they were experiencing a lack of oxygen. . . . My darling aunt burned to death in a hospital. . . . Her son Herbert Fricke, a lieutenant in the Hermann Goering Guard Regiment, came home to Hamburg for a few days but he was unable to identify her among the many badly burned corpses. She was buried in a mass grave in Ohlsdorf.[17]

Perhaps the most trying challenge during the terrible air raids of July 1943 in Hamburg was to mothers with small children when the father was away in military service. So it was with Anna Marie Frank (born 1919) of the St. Georg Branch. She sought shelter in the basement of their apartment in the evening of July 27 with her daughter, Marianne (two years old), and her infant son, Rainer. As she anxiously awaited the all-clear signal a few hours later, Sister Frank and the others in the shelter knew that destruction was all around them. When the air-raid wardens opened the doors to the shelter and instructed them to hurry outside, everybody reached for blankets, soaked them in water, and threw them over their heads to prevent suffocation from smoke. Anna Marie Frank could not do this and simultaneously get her two children into the street and to safety, so her neighbors offered to take little Marianne with them. Tragically, when they emerged into the street, the chaos was such that Sister Frank lost sight of the neighbors. Amid the fires, the smoke, and the collapsing buildings, the neighbors and little Marianne disappeared and were never seen again. Anna Marie searched for months in city offices in vain for any trace of her daughter.[18]

District president Alwin Brey just happened to be home on leave from the navy when the firebombings struck his neighborhood. His daughter Irma (born 1926) recalled clearly what happened one night:

> When the alarm sounded that [the British] were coming, we took our stuff that we had packed already and went down to the basement. When we came out, our building was almost completely flat. Our apartment was on the second floor and the inside was full of flames and it burned everything—our furniture and everything, but not just for us, but for everybody who lived in the building. So my dad took us out of the basement. Oh, there were so many dead people lying in the street, and they came with big trucks and picked them all up with forklifts. We were very lucky that my dad got us out. He got a car because he was an officer of the navy, and he got us in those bunkers. They couldn't hurt them. We stayed there, I think, two or three days, and then a little further down off the bunker in the same street my uncle, my mother's brother and his family lived there and they were all killed. Almost everybody on our street was killed, but we made it out alive.[19]

Alwin Brey was able to get his family out of town. They took a train south all the way across the country to the city of Bamberg, in Bavaria. After he found them a small room to live in, he returned to his station in France.

Young Inge Laabs (born 1928) recalled how people referred to Hamburg in July 1943 as "Gomorrah." In her memory she could still picture many buildings burning for days because of the coal supplies in the basements. Her story illustrates the plight of tens of thousands of homeless people in that huge city in July 1943:

> After we lost our home, we lived in an air-raid shelter for a while. When that was no longer possible anymore, we lived in damaged homes. We did not have much to eat and drink at all and could not brush our teeth. We had lost everything and wandered around trying to find a place to stay. Later on, we went to Pomerania (eastern Germany) where my grandparents lived. We could not stay very long because my mother had to return to her work and I to my work training. . . . The time we had to sleep in a railroad car in Friedrichsruh by Hamburg was the hardest. Sometimes, we couldn't even get food with ration coupons.[20]

Arthur Sommerfeld had just returned from working in the Arbeitsdienst program when the firebombings began. He had received a severe head injury when hit by a falling tree and had not recovered entirely, but he came to the rescue when the Sommerfeld apartment began to burn. His mother, Marie Friebel Sommerfeld, begged him to return to the apartment to retrieve their valued genealogical documents. While he was still in the rooms, a phosphorus bomb exploded, and he received burns on over 80 percent of his body. The documents were saved, but he was grievously injured. Fortunately, he survived. Sister Sommerfeld then received permission to evacuate her family to her hometown in the German-language region of Czechoslovakia.[21]

The Guertler family was on vacation in nearby Lübeck-Travemünde when the city of Hamburg was reduced to ashes in July 1943. Daughter Theresa recalled hearing her father describe what he found while on leave from the military after the bombing:

> When he came to our street, he saw the house was totally destroyed. All that was standing was the chimney from the ground floor to the top floor, and on every level, there was a little kitchen corner attached to the chimney where the kitchen stove was still standing. That's how he described it. So when he found out that the house was destroyed, he was hoping that we were in Travemünde, and we were, and then he told us that our house was destroyed.[22]

Fred Zwick (born 1933) was ten years old when the firebombings took place. He recalled clearly the night his home was destroyed:

> We went to the bunker in the early evening and the air raids started, and I heard a lot of explosions. A lot of smoke was coming in through the vents. The reason was that there was a coal yard right next to it, and they had the coal stored right next to the walls of the bunker, and apparently it was set on fire. There was some water available, and the mothers and the adults, they tried to protect their children with wet blankets so we could breathe because the smoke was just very thick. . . . We got out the next day about two o'clock. . . . Our apartment house was totally destroyed. A neighbor lady went to the basement to get the engagement ring of her daughter. She had suffocated but was still sitting at a table there. She was able to retrieve the ring, but as soon as she touched the hand it fell apart.[23]

Figs. 6. and 7. The Zwick apartment at Süderstrasse 244 in Hamburg in 1939 and after the bombings of July 1943. Note the destroyed and abandoned streetcar. (F. Zwick)

Perhaps the most detailed and chilling account of the firebombing was written in 1963 by district president Otto Berndt.[24] With painstaking detail, he recounted the events of the night of July 27–28. As the air-raid warden of his apartment building, he was allowed to stay outside when the sirens wailed and during the subsequent bombing (which he was pleased to do, having a terrible fear of air-raid shelters). (With the exception of his eldest daughter, who lived across town, his family was safe in a small village north of Berlin.) Soon the apartment building was struck and started burning, but he was able to evacuate all of the occupants unharmed and send them on their way to safer locations. Then he attempted to help others. At one juncture, he ran into a shelter to help get the people out, thinking all the while of the many ways he could be killed in doing so. He was urged on by the thought that his own family might be in such a situation some day and that he would want others to rescue them. In the shelter, he found just one boy of about twelve years of age and quickly carried him outside, only to be told by first-aid personnel that the boy was already dead.

Fig. 8. Otto Berndt in about 1937. (K. Ronna)

Returning to his neighborhood to determine the status of his home, he entered his apartment while the flames raged on the upper floors. He gathered critical personal items using sheets as bags and carried them down into the street. After about the fourth trip, he found that the bags in the street had caught fire. He then gave up any attempt to salvage more property and ran down the street as the fires spread from building to building. "All of a sudden, I felt an intense anger toward the pilots of the planes that had dropped the bombs," he admitted.

An hour later, President Berndt came to a city canal and heard people on the other side screaming for help as the flames approached their position. There was no boat available to transport them to his side of the canal, so he found a rope. His idea was to swim across to their side and tie the rope around one person. Helpers on the safe side could then pull the person across while he swam alongside to assure that they did not drown. This he did stark naked, leaving his clothes on the safe side (hoping that sparks flying through air would not ignite them). He managed to help a number of women and old men across the canal for about an hour, then dressed and ran off in the direction of a safer neighborhood. "Not one of them thanked me," he observed. As he ran between burning apartment houses, he saw in the street countless bodies of fire victims, most of which had shrunk to half their size when the heat removed the fluids from their bodies. When he accidentally touched several of them, "they disintegrated and returned to the earth as dust to dust," he recalled.

At about six o'clock the next morning, when the sun should have been on the rise for the new day, Otto Berndt noticed that the clouds of smoke prevented any sunlight from illuminating the city. He had seen no firefighting personnel because the fires were everywhere and the streets were blocked with burned-out vehicles and furniture rescued from the apartments. Survivors were either fleeing for their lives or trying desperately to help others. At one point, he lay down and slept for an hour or two (time had seemed to be totally irrelevant that night) as chaos reigned round about. Sometime before noon, he found himself on a small boat being carried across the Elbe River to safety south of the harbor. His memories of the moment were clear years later:

> As I sat on deck of the boat, I felt my apartment key in my pocket. I thought about the fact that I had once owned a beautiful apartment. Thirteen years of sweat and frugal living—all destroyed in a single night. The only thing I had left was this little key. Then I made a symbolic gesture by tossing the key into the Elbe, thereby separating myself totally from the past and entering into the present and the future. With no burdens, I stood at the threshold of a new life. Only God could know what it would bring.

President Berndt was united with his family in the village of Nitzow, and his daughter Gertrude joined them there. Exempt from military service, he could have stayed there in safety but felt that he must return to Hamburg to direct the Church there. Before he left Nitzow, he visited the East German Mission office in nearby Berlin and was able to purchase many Church books to replace the ones lost by the Hamburg Saints when they were bombed out. Back in Hamburg, the only place he could find to live was in a room in the building in which the Altona Branch held its meetings. He was still living there when the war ended.

An excellent but sad report was written by Hugo Witt, a member of the defunct St. Georg Branch, who made his way from his home in the Hamburg suburb of Wilhelmsburg to church in Altona on the Sunday after the worst of the air raids. This report was submitted to the mission office in Frankfurt on August 15, 1943:

> Following a terrible war catastrophe, namely air raids by British and American planes over Hamburg-Altona, we were able after a short interruption to resume holding meetings in Altona, thanks to the mercy of the Lord, who preserved our meeting rooms. . . . I will try to describe a little of what I personally witnessed or heard about the catastrophe in Hamburg and how it has influenced the life of the Church in Hamburg:
>
> In the night of Saturday–Sunday 24–25 July, Altona was attacked by a large number of airplanes dropping phosphorus, incendiary, and TNT bombs. I did not experience the worst of the attack because I lived out in Wilhelmsburg. When I made my way to Altona to Sunday School with my family, there were no streetcars in operation. The sun was darkened by the clouds of ashes from burning buildings in Hamburg. Then I made my way by bicycle toward the branch rooms in the Klein Western Strasse [37]. When I tried to cross the Elbe Bridge from Veddel toward Rothenburgsort, I found the way blocked. This compelled me to proceed via the road to Freihafen and over the new railroad bridge over the Elbe. All of the sheds were burning in Freihafen, and the path became increasingly difficult. My eyes started to burn from the smoke and the ashes. I was fortunate to make my way to the Messberg in relatively good time.

> Then my progress was slower and slower toward the downtown where many buildings were on fire. . . . It was almost impossible to ride my bicycle because so many people were fleeing. I then passed the harbor piers and made my way toward Altona. Here I had to climb over the rubble from the facades of buildings that had fallen onto the street. Along the way I had to carefully step around the bodies of the victims. At one point I counted 17 people, mostly women and girls. I finally reached the branch rooms, but of course there was nobody there. Then I went to visit the Thymian family, who lived across the street. Everything was chaos there because they had taken in refugees. There was a family with a two-week-old baby, and they were worried about the baby because there was so much smoke in the air. I stayed there for about 45 minutes. Before I left, Hyrum asked me to say a prayer, which I was pleased to do. Then I left.
>
> I stayed with my family in Wilhelmsburg until Wednesday evening. Then we packed our things and followed the masses leaving Hamburg. They had been passing our house day and night with what little property they could rescue. We went to Göddingen and Bleckede on the Elbe and later with other members we went to Pörndorf, near Landshut in Bavaria. Several weeks later I traveled back to Wilhelmsburg to continue my work in the factory. A week later I brought my family home.[25]

President Berndt had plenty of concerns to deal with in the spring of 1945. He had just succeeded in gathering his family members, who had been spread out over the map, and was living with several other refugee families in the rooms of the Altona Branch. The members of the three branches in the city of Hamburg were all meeting in the damaged rooms of the Altona Branch, but most of the Saints were no longer in Hamburg at all. Nevertheless, President Berndt held a district conference in April 1945, and at the conclusion of the conference, he did something quite different. According to his son Otto (born 1929):

> My father said, Brothers and sisters, I feel that we should all hold hands throughout the congregation. Which we did, and we sang the hymn, "Gott sei mit euch bis aufs Wiedersehen" ("God Be With You Till We Meet Again"). I asked my father why we were holding hands. I didn't understand the importance of it. He said to me, "I have the feeling that many of the brothers and sisters that we saw tonight in the meeting, we will never see in this life again." He was right. . . . There were a lot of people there (they came from miles around)—despite the big hole in the ceiling. This is something that will be with me always.[26]

Notes

1. Presiding Bishopric, "Financial, Statistical, and Historical Reports of Wards, Stakes, and Missions, 1884–1955," 257, CHL CR 4 12.
2. Otto Berndt, autobiography (unpublished, 1963), CHL MS 8316; in German, trans. the author.
3. Twenty years later, Otto Berndt made several distinctly critical statements about Arthur Zander, as he did about several other leaders of the West German Mission and the districts. It appears from his story that Otto Berndt expected that Church leaders should avoid any allegiance to Hitler's government while they represented the Church. In other words, they should join him in condemning but not opposing the government.
4. Two excellent versions in English were written by the principals of the story: Karl-Heinz Schnibbe with Alan F. Keele and Douglas F. Tobler, *The Price* (Salt Lake City: Bookcraft, 1984) and Rudi Wobbe and Jerry Borrowman, *Before the Blood Tribunal* (American Fork, UT: Covenant, 1992). The best German account of the affair was written by Karl-Heinz Schnibbe, *Jugendliche gegen Hitler* (Berg am See, Germany: Verlagsgemeinschaft Berg, 1991).
5. Otto Berndt, autobiography.
6. Both Rudi and Karl-Heinz recalled the quotation in very similar words. Both believed that Helmuth had been particularly bold in court in an attempt to absorb the majority of the guilt and thus draw attention away from his best friends.
7. Helmuth was executed on the guillotine. The room (now empty) in which he died is a national monument to victims of National Socialist terror, and the three young men are listed among the many Germans who offered bona fide resistance to the government.
8. Schnibbe, *The Price*, 58.
9. Hans Brunswig, *Feuersturm über Hamburg*, 6th ed. (Stuttgart, Germany: Motorbuch Verlag, 1983).
10. See the chapters on the Dresden branches in Roger P. Minert, *In Harm's Way: East German Latter-day Saints in World War II* (Provo, UT: Religious Studies Center, Brigham Young University, 2009).
11. Brunswig, *Feuersturm über Hamburg*, 380–81, 383, 385, 401, 405.

12. Henry Niemann, interview by Michael Corley, South Jordan, UT, October 31, 2008.
13. Maria Kreutner Niemann, "An Evening with Maria" (unpublished speech, 1988), transcribed by JoAnn P. Knowles, private collection.
14. Gertrud Frank Menssen, autobiography (unpublished), private collection.
15. Gerd Fricke, interview by the author in German, Hamburg, Germany, August 15, 2006; unless otherwise noted, summarized in English by Judith Sartowski.
16. Liesellotte Pruess Schmidt, interview by the author, Salt Lake City, December 1, 2006.
17. Harald Fricke, autobiography (unpublished, 2003), private collection.
18. Anna Marie Haase Frank, interview by the author, Salt Lake City, October 27, 2006.
19. Irma Brey Glas, interview by Michael Corley, Taylorsville, UT, October 10, 2008.
20. Inge Laabs Vieregge, telephone interview with Jennifer Heckmann in Germany, October 2008.
21. Werner Sommerfeld, interview by the author, Salt Lake City, January 19, 2007.
22. Resa (Theresa) Guertler Frey, interview by Michael Corley, Salt Lake City, March 14, 2008.
23. Fred Zwick, interview by the author, Salt Lake City, June 29, 2007.
24. Otto Berndt, autobiography.
25. Altona Branch general minutes, 93–96, CHL LR 10603 11. From Brother Witt's apartment in Wilhelmsburg to Altona (approximately six miles as the crow flies), his route on that occasion was certainly not direct.
26. Otto Albert Berndt, "The Life and Times of Otto Albert Berndt" (unpublished autobiography), private collection.

Altona Branch

A suburb on the western outskirts of the metropolis of Hamburg, Altona has existed for centuries. Legend has it that the name means "all too close (to Hamburg)" (*all zu nah* or *al to na* in the local dialect). The Altona Branch was one of three in Germany's largest port city.

The Saints in Altona met in rented rooms at Kleine Westerstrasse 37.[1] They enjoyed the use of a pump organ there, but no other details regarding the rooms and furnishings are available at this writing. Sunday School began at 10:00 a.m., as it did almost everywhere in Germany, with sacrament meeting at 7:00 p.m. The MIA met on Wednesdays at 7:30 p.m., and the Relief Society met on Mondays at the same hour. When the war began, there was no Primary organization in the Altona Branch.

Following the departure of the American missionaries on August 25, 1939, the branch president in Altona was Wilhelm Stelzig. The branch was relatively strong, with ten elders and twenty holders of the Aaronic Priesthood, but was dominated (like so many branches in Germany) by adult females (57 percent). The average attendance at Sunday meetings during the last months of that year was thirty-five members and friends.

Altona Branch[2]	**1939**
Elders	10
Priests	5
Teachers	1
Deacons	14
Other Adult Males	38
Adult Females	113
Male Children	8
Female Children	10
Total	199

Significant changes were made in the Altona Branch soon after the war began. On November 12, 1939, the sacrament meeting was moved to a time immediately following Sunday School. The reason for this change was not given in the branch records, but the same change had been made in other branches because blackout regulations had made it difficult for the members to get home safely after the late sacrament meeting.[3] While the meetings were held consecutively, the sacrament was to be administered only during the Sunday School meeting.

According to the manuscript history of the branch, the members continued to tell friends about the gospel during the war. For example, on

Sunday, March 17, 1940, five persons were baptized. Five weeks later, the following comment was written: "Civil defense problems were discussed in the priesthood meeting." The question was not whether to continue to hold meetings, but how to do so under blackout conditions and other restrictions.[4]

In the branch conference held on September 8, 1940, President Stelzig reported that the number of tithe payers in the branch had increased from thirty-six to forty-two in the previous twelve months.[5]

Excellent minutes were kept of the worship services and other meetings in the branch, although it is not clear who the clerk was during the war. He recorded the names of the priesthood holders who conducted the meetings and administered the sacrament, as well as all speakers and those who prayed. He also noted the names of the hymns sung and numbers of persons who attended (priesthood holders, women, children, and friends). According to his records, attendance at branch meetings declined somewhat during 1940 and 1941 but hovered above twenty-five through 1942.

Hundreds of thousands of adults from occupied countries were transported to Germany to work in factories after German workers were drafted into the Wehrmacht. Among those were now and then members of the Church from the Netherlands. According to the branch history, "Elder Jan Copier, President of the YMMIA of the Netherlands Mission from Utrecht, visited the branch. He told the Saints, 'When we do the will of our Heavenly Father, we can expect salvation.'"[6] Allowing Brother Copier to attend and participate in meetings could have caused difficulty for the Altona Saints because such fraternization with foreigners—not formally a crime—was not condoned in Germany at the time.

In February 1943, the St. Georg Branch in downtown Hamburg was evicted from its spacious and beautiful rooms at Besenbinderhof 13a. This was a tragic loss, but the Altona Branch was quick to take in as many Church members as it could. Given the destruction of major portions of the Hamburg city center, it was not at all easy for the St. Georg Saints to make their way to Altona. During the air raids and firestorms of July 1943, the building in which the Barmbek Branch met was also destroyed, and they too were invited to go to Altona. With the members of all three Hamburg branches invited to attend, there were still only about fifty persons participating in Sunday meetings.

Trials and blessings occurred during the war just as they did during peacetime. For example, the branch history includes this report under the date July 4, 1943: "Sister Ingeborg Suppan had suddenly lost her sight. She received a priesthood blessing on June 28 and reported today the complete restoration of her sight."[7]

District president Otto Berndt presided over a meeting on August 29, 1943, and for all practical purposes united the three Hamburg branches into one. According to the meeting minutes, there were fifty persons present. Hugo Witt recalled, "At the conclusion of the meeting, we all knelt to pray for our soldiers."[8]

The following events are reported in the branch general minutes for the final fifteen months of the war:

> March 26, 1944: district conference in our rooms.
>
> April 9, 1944: meetings canceled due to air-raid alarms.
>
> Summer 1944: For several weeks, our rooms were confiscated by the NSDAP and used as a collection point for sewing materials. Therefore we could not hold meetings.
>
> December 10, 1944: Advent program held with 66 attendees.[9]

Many meetings held during this period ended with a prayer for the LDS men in the German military, with all members on their knees.

With all three branches meeting in the Altona rooms, it must have been a great trial for the Saints in Hamburg when the rooms were temporarily confiscated by the city government to be used as a collection point of a rag drive in late November 1943.[10]

Fortunately, the interruption appears to have lasted only a week or two. The same action was taken again in June 1944.[11]

The records of the Altona Branch Relief Society include the following statement at the close of 1944: "We can describe the general condition of the society as excellent. All registered sisters are 100% active. The activity of the visiting teachers has had to be neglected due to the prevailing difficulties. The sisters live too far from each other and public transportation is impossible."[12] The records show an average attendance of twenty sisters at the meetings that year. As in other branches throughout Germany, the sisters in Altona continued to carry out their duties, often in the absence of their husbands. The challenges became more daunting with each new day.

On January 28, 1945, Herbert Baarz became the new branch president. The status of his predecessor is unclear.[13] The attendance at meetings had increased to seventy or eighty persons. This may seem to be a small number comprising members of the three Hamburg branches, but by that time, several hundred local Latter-day Saints had been killed, were serving in the military, or had left town with their children to find safer places to live.

The meetings of the Altona Branch were canceled on Sunday, April 8, 1945, due to air raid alarms. The next three Sundays were a time of great uncertainty as the British army approached and invaded the city of Hamburg. The following comments were made by the branch clerk:

> April 15, 22 and 29: I was not able to attend when English troops invaded the area and prevented me from going to Hamburg [from Wilhelmsburg]. In the last major air raid over Hamburg, our one remaining meeting house at Klein Westernstrasse 37 was severely damaged so that meetings could not be held there until August 25. From April to August, meetings were held in the homes of members with an average attendance of seventy persons.[14]

The terror of the war had ended in this huge city, but many other problems remained or emerged out of the rubble of the once-proud Elbe River port. The city was in ruins, transportation and utilities out of order, food and water supplies interrupted. With housing at an all-time low, it was terribly difficult to find places to live or materials to repair the meeting rooms of the Altona Branch. According to the branch general minutes, the first sacrament meeting held in the repaired rooms at Kleine Westerstrasse 37 took place on August 25, 1945, when eighty-nine members and friends assembled for the first time in months.[15] A week later, an American soldier, Col. Clarence Nesley, located the meeting place. As a missionary before the war, he had once served as the district president in Hamburg. While his feelings on that occasion were likely very sad, his visit did indeed herald a time when the Saints would enjoy the communion with Saints from other lands and a connection with the Church leadership in faraway Salt Lake City.

In the summer of 1945, the Altona Branch was alive and well. Members strewn all over Europe began to return, and LDS refugees from the East German Mission would soon swell their ranks. Though damaged, the meetinghouse still stood, and the Saints began to meet and rebuild their branch with dedication.

IN MEMORIAM

The following members of the Altona Branch did not survive World War II:

Karl Friedrich Ferdinand Sennewald Bornholdt b. Hamburg 24 Mar 1865; son of Detlef Bornholdt and Telsche Sass; bp. 6 Sep 1931; conf. 6 Sep 1931; m. 29 Aug 1891, Anna Franziska Schlueter; bur. 25 May 1941 (CHL MS 10603, 8; FS)

Herbert Hermann Hans Moritz Kahl b. Lichterwerda, Sachsen, 17 Mar 1915; son of Hermann Kahl and Martha Meta Barichs; bp. 30 Sep 1927; lieutenant; d. 14 Jan 1943; bur. Cassino, Italy (www.volksbund.de; FHL microfilm 271376, 1930 and 1935 censuses)

Kurt Heinz Kahl b. Lichterwerda, Sachsen, 28 Jan 1917; son of Hermann Kahl and Martha Meta Barichs; bp. 30 Sep 1927; d. 28 Dec 1943; bur. Cassino, Italy (www.volksbund.de; FHL microfilm 271376, 1930 and 1935 censuses)

Metta Katarina Lassen b. Süder Ballig, Hadersleben, Schleswig-Holstein, 16 Mar 1863; dau. of Thomas Lassen and Margarethe Schmidt; bp. 18 Jan 1931; conf. 18 Jan 1931; m. 12 May 1895, Hans Lorenzen; d. heart attack 27 Feb 1942 (CHL CR 275 8 2438, no. 982)

Erich Richard Lehmann b. Cottbus, Cottbus, Brandenburg, 1 Dec 1913; son of Friedrich Wilhelm Lehmann and Marie Konzack; m. Hamburg 19 Oct 1940, Charlotte or Liselotte Holert; d. 15 Jul 1944 (IGI)

Ernst Günther Meyer b. Westerland, Schleswig-Holstein, 27 Oct 1910; son of Tony Elfrieda Kayser or Kaiser; bp. 16 Apr 1920; conf. 16 Apr 1920; d. Hamburg 4 August 1941 (CHL 10603, 118; FHL microfilm 245232, 1930 and 1935 censuses; FS)

Heinrich Friedrich Peter Hermann Palm b. Ochtmissen, Lüneburg, Hannover, 24 Dec 1874; son of Karl Friedrich Gotthard Palm and Catharine Dorothee Margarethe Albers; bp. 23 Aug 1928; ord. teacher; d. 20 or 21 Jan 1943 (FHL microfilm 245250, 1930 and 1935 censuses; IGI, FS, CHL MS 10603, 81)

Sophie Marie Sellmann b. Stassfurt, Neuendorf, Kloster, Sachsen, 10 Aug 1861; dau. of Gottfried Martin Peter Sellmann and Wilhelmine Henriette Balzer; bp. 6 Sep 1931; conf. 6 Sep 1931; m. Neuendorf, Magdeburg, Sachsen, 22 Jul 1883, Carl Eduard Schulze; bur. Altona, Hamburg, 1941 or 1942 or 1943 (FHL microfilm 245260, 1935 census; CHL MS 10603, 114; FS)

Anna Franziska Schlüter b. Neumünster, Schleswig-Holstein, 11 Nov 1867; dau. of Karsten Schlueter and Elise Behrens; bp. 6 Sep 1931; conf. 6 Sep 1931; m. Altona, Schleswig-Holstein, 29 Aug 1891, Karl Friedrich Ferdinand Sennewald Bornholdt; d. Altona 25 May 1942; bur. 29 May 1942 (CHL MS 10603, 54; FS)

Kurt Fritz Wegener b. Hamburg 11 Mar 1918; son of Carl Friedrich Wegener and Amanda Dohrn; bp. 28 Jan 1930; conf. 28 Jan 1930; ord. deacon 4 Jan 1932; k. in battle 16 Aug 1942 (CHL CR 275 8 2438, no. 898)

Notes

1. West German Mission branch directory, 1939, CHL LR 10045 11.
2. Presiding Bishopric, "Financial, Statistical, and Historical Reports of Wards, Stakes, and Missions, 1884–1955," 257, CR 4 12.
3. Altona Branch manuscript history, CHL LR 10603, 2.
4. Ibid.
5. Altona Branch historical notes, CHL A 2998 240.
6. Ibid., CHL A 2999 56.
7. Ibid., CHL A 2999 92–93
8. Altona Branch general minutes, 96, CHL LR 10603, 11.
9. Ibid., 113–21.
10. Altona Branch historical notes, CHL A 2999 103.
11. Ibid., A 2999 113, 115.
12. Altona Branch Relief Society minutes, CHL LR 10603, 14.
13. Altona Branch historical notes, CHL A 2999 124.
14. Ibid., 132.
15. Ibid., 133.

Barmbek Branch

The metropolis of Hamburg was Germany's second-largest city in 1939 with 1,711,877 people. The northeastern districts of the harbor city comprised the Barmbek Branch of The Church of Jesus Christ of Latter-day Saints (one of three LDS branches in that city). With 178 total members (twenty-six of whom held the priesthood), this was a solid branch.

As the war approached in the late summer of 1939, the Barmbek Branch was under the leadership of Alfred Schmidt, a worker in a cigarette factory in Barmbek. His counselors were Friedrich Mahler and Jonni Schacht. All leadership positions in the branch were filled at the time, with the exception of the Primary organization. Sunday School took place at 10:00 a.m. and sacrament meeting at 7:00 p.m. The Relief Society met on Mondays at 7:30 p.m. and the MIA on Wednesdays at the same time.[1]

The meetings of the Barmbek Branch were held in rented rooms at Dehnhaide 141. That street was located near the southwest border of the branch territory, toward the center of Hamburg. Waltraud (Wally) Möhrke (born 1919) recalled this about the meeting rooms: "We had a small Hinterhaus behind a carpentry shop. There was a large room for sacrament meetings and smaller rooms for the various classes."[2]

Irmgard Schmidt (born 1923) described the church rooms in these words:

> We had to walk up steps at the side of the carpentry shop. When we were there during the week, we could hear the woodworking machines running. At the top of the stairs, you were looking straight into the main meeting room where there

> were benches for about one hundred people. To the right were two or three classrooms. Then there were more stairs up to another floor where there was a large empty room that we used for activities. . . . I remember that there were really big windows on the right side [of the hall]. The room had a big stove, and somebody had to go early to get the rooms heated.[3]

Herta Schmidt (born 1925) added a few details to this description: "At the top of the stairs there was a foyer with a cloak room and a restroom. There was a platform at the end of the hall for the branch presidency; it was two steps up, and we had both a piano and a pump organ."[4]

Barmbek Branch[5]	**1939**
Elders	9
Priests	4
Teachers	5
Deacons	8
Other Adult Males	25
Adult Females	108
Male Children	11
Female Children	8
Total	178

President Schmidt's family lived at Volksdorferstrasse 223 in the suburb of Wandsbek, and it took them about an hour to walk to church. According to Irmgard, "Sometimes our mother gave us money for the streetcar, but we would rather walk home and use the money for candy. There was a vending machine on the way home, and we did that lots of times. [Anyway] I never thought that it was a long way to walk." Herta remembered that several branch members came from even farther to the northwest.

The Schmidt family included eleven children, and they were well known in their neighborhood. According to daughters Irmgard and Herta, the family had visitors every Sunday. Before the war, those visitors were often American missionaries. During the war, the Schmidt teenagers and their friends often sang hymns and other songs for hours. With the windows open, the sounds of their piano and their voices could carry for great distances down the street. Neighbors often gathered on the sidewalk in front of the house to listen to the impromptu concerts. "The neighbors thought that we were a little weird," explained Irmgard.

Wally Möhrke explained that there was a sign by the door to the branch rooms announcing "Jews are not welcome here" (*Juden unerwünscht*). "I didn't understand why we had to have that sign there. We had a young Jewish man named Salomon Schwarz who loved to attend [our meetings]. And the other young men were really wonderful to him." Tragically, Salomon was arrested and later died in a concentration camp.[6] He had been one of the very few Jewish Latter-day Saints in all of Germany when the war began.

"As the branch president, my father never acted openly against the Nazis. He felt that it was wiser to be silent, to not fight openly against them," recalled Irmgard Schmidt. When the war began, Irmgard had finished her public schooling and was working for a baker's family. She lived with the family in the suburb of Rahlstedt and did the household work of the baker's wife, who was helping out in the business. Irmgard worked for the family for several years until she married.

Wally Möhrke served as the secretary of the Sunday School as a teenager before the war. She recalled her duties:

> I think there were about 100 members who attended the meeting regularly. . . . I sat at a small table in the front of the room next to the branch presidency. I counted the attendance and wrote it in a small book. Then, I compared the numbers to the Sunday before and the Sunday a year before. I had to read the report out loud every Sunday.

Rita Fischer (born 1925) and her twin sister, Gisela, had joined the government's Jungvolk organization with great enthusiasm in 1936. "We learned a lot of old songs which my mother especially enjoyed. On some Saturdays we had fun going on singing nature hikes. . . . We [went] from door to door in our neighborhood to collect donations [for government programs]. [They] put some pocket change in our tin cans with a slit on top."[7] Another government program that Rita liked was the one that paid for the twins to spend "six wonderful weeks" at a health spa in Heiligendamm on the Baltic Sea coast in 1938. The Fischer family also won a ten-day vacation in the Harz Mountains in 1939. Life for the Fischer family was excellent as war clouds gathered over Europe.

Another inductee into the Jungvolk from the Barmbek Branch was Werner Schmidt (born 1927). Initially rejected because he was too small, he nevertheless wanted to be part of the movement and devised a way to look older: he used electrical tape to simulate a beard, a mustache, and sideburns. When his schoolmates mocked his appearance, he removed the tape but did not realize that the black glue was still stuck to his face. Once he confessed to the ruse, he was asked by the leader whether his father supported Werner. The boy answered honestly in the negative, which could have put his father in a very difficult situation. Fortunately, nothing happened to Werner's father, the president of the Barmbek Branch.[8]

Once in the Jungvolk organization, Werner lost his fascination for the movement and began to disobey orders: "Seven times in all I was sent home for not following orders—orders like 'Lay down!' when there was good mud to lay into." He objected to what he called "the silly reasons" for obeying his leaders. "I loved my freedom too much." As it turned out, the leaders always begged Werner to come back, because the loss of a boy looked bad in the records.[9]

The outbreak of war in September 1939 was shocking and upsetting to Wally Möhrke and her sister Marianne. "We didn't know what a war would be like, could only trust that everything would be all right." The sisters had both finished school and were gainfully employed, and they lived alone after their father, a widower, moved to Berlin. Within weeks, the basement of their apartment building had been shored up to withstand bombs when enemy air raids were anticipated. According to Wally, "They moved some beds and chairs and installed metal doors. They also broke holes through the walls into the neighboring buildings, providing us an escape underground. . . . They also tried out the alarms, and we had to learn the meaning of each siren."[10]

"Finding my mother sitting in her bed crying was an impression I cannot forget," wrote Werner Schmidt. He was twelve, and the war had just broken out. "She knew that her boys would have to go to war. Within days my two older brothers were drafted, and later the third one had to go."[11] Werner could not have imagined at the time that the war would last long enough for him to receive a call to the Wehrmacht as well.

Elsa Anna Kopp lost her husband to the army shortly after the war began. Her children, Edeltraud (born 1930) and Werner (born 1933), grew up essentially without their father, as Edeltraud recalled: "Because Father was gone right when the war started, we got used to just being the threesome that we were—mother, Werner, and I. We didn't really have a father."[12] Sister Kopp worked the graveyard shift in a shoe factory that was so close that she was able to get home in time to feed the children their breakfast and send them off to school.

Herta Schmidt finished her public school the year the war started, then began an apprenticeship as an office worker. After her initial training in that field, she was hired as a typist and stenographer by the company of Bauer und Schauerte. She recalled, "As an apprentice I earned $15 per month. At sixteen, I was a full-time employee, and I still lived at home."

Regarding her association in the League of German Girls (BDM), Herta explained that she did not often go to the meetings, particularly the ones held on Sundays. When her leaders asked about her Sunday absence, she simply explained that she was in church, and she was not punished. Because the family funds did not extend to such items as the BDM uniform, the jacket was provided for Herta. "It was a nice jacket, and I liked it," she recalled. However, she was not interested in marching in parades and was not even impressed when she saw Hitler from only about one hundred feet away at a prewar event. "He was just there. Who cares?"

Wally Möhrke was engaged soon after the war began. Wilhelm (Willi) Sperling was not a member of the LDS Church but a fine man who regularly went to church with Wally. He was drafted in 1940, but the two had already planned to marry; they expedited those plans and married later that year. The official ceremony took place at city hall, as required by law, and then a church ceremony was held in the branch meeting hall. It was there that they exchanged rings. "We knew what the word 'temple' meant, but that seemed to be a concept for [Saints in] America," Wally explained.[13]

With Hamburg under attack by the British Royal Air Force, Wally Möhrke Sperling left the city to spend the winter of 1940–41 in eastern Germany (Silesia). From there she went to Stuttgart to live with her sister-in-law for a few months and then returned to Hamburg. Conditions there had become more dangerous, as she wrote: "Our suitcases with the most important papers and other necessities were always at the ready. Whenever the alarms went off, those were the first things we grabbed."[14]

In the spring of 1940, Rita Fischer graduated from public school, and her parents allowed her and Gisela to participate in the Lutheran Church confirmation ritual with their friends. As Rita wrote, "It gave our [relatives] who were not of the LDS faith the satisfaction that we were Christians."[15] Soon after this event, the twins found assignments on neighboring farms near the town of Ochsenwerder (six miles south of Hamburg), where they could fulfill the requirements of the national Pflichtjahr program. As Rita wrote:

> We could go home every other weekend. The standard salary was only $15 per month with room and board. From our salary Gisela and I spent half of it for the train fares, etc., and the rest we saved for college. The year went by fast. I learned to appreciate my parents and our home with the "bathtub," etc. I never realized that the job of farming was hard work. I am glad I fulfilled my part in having served my Vaterland.

Perhaps the first member of the Barmbek Branch to lose his life in the war was Karl Friedrich Seemann, who was killed in Poland in 1941. His daughter, Ursula Betty Stein (born 1924) had little time to mourn for him; her country needed her. She first served in the Pflichtjahr program on a farm near Posen (Posnan, Poland). Although far from home, she enjoyed the work: "I always had wonderful girls around me, and we did our best to have a good time and help each other out."[16] Regarding the sacrifice of her time to her country, she said: "I didn't question the requirement to leave home. I knew I didn't have much choice. Besides, if I stayed home, maybe something even worse would happen to me."

Herta Schmidt recalled the blackout regulations with which every family had to comply during the war. "We had to darken the rooms every night using a blanket or a sheet or something similar. The warden would come around with a warning if he could see any light [from our windows]."

The Schmidt family lived a considerable distance from downtown Hamburg, and very few bombs fell in their vicinity. "We didn't have a real bomb shelter [nearby]," explained Irmgard Schmidt. "We lived on the ground floor, and our shelter was in the basement. Sometimes when the sirens went off, we just stayed in bed. It was cold in the winter [in the basement], and my bed was warm. We thought, 'We won't get hit.' But you could get fined for doing that."[17] Herta recalled being reluctant to leave their beds: "My father tried to get us out of bed, but it was hard for him." Finally, they gave in and headed downstairs.

While the bombs fell and the antiaircraft guns pounded away, they sat in the basement hoping that nothing would hit their house. "We just sat there, leaning over just in case something came down on top of us," explained Irmgard. "If so, it would hit us on the back. I knew it wouldn't happen, but we sat there in that position anyway." "There was nothing to do. We just sat there and waited," Herta recalled. Werner took the matter somewhat less seriously and appeared in the basement on several occasions in the costume of a fireman or some other odd character. He wrote, "This brought some laughter for us and the other six families from our apartment [building]."[18]

The Fischer twins graduated from the Dankers Business College in April 1942 and were both hired by their father's employer, the Nova Insurance Company. Initially assigned to a position she did not like, Rita was transferred to a different division in the company and was very happy. She recalled that as the war escalated, more and more Hamburg citizens and her fellow employees experienced personal losses: "At work we all got very close to each other. We shared our sorrows of losing our homes, family, and friends." At home, Rita and her family spent many nights in their basement shelter listening to enemy planes roaring overhead and bombs falling upon the city:

> The explosions lifted up the building, and your head and body went down forward almost to the floor. You just hoped the ceiling and walls would hold and you would not be buried under the bricks and rubble. When the lights went out, I was afraid and prayed that the gas and water lines would not break.

Edeltraud Kopp recalled greeting her teacher with "Heil Hitler!" "We used to stand in the school yard and sing the national anthem, too," she recalled. Her brother, Werner, was also taught the Nazi way of life through the Jungvolk program, as he recollected: "I had a uniform and went to the meetings. It was like the Boy Scouts in America. We learned how to shoot. We didn't go camping often because that cost too much money."

"We could never have imagined what awaited us in 1943," wrote Wally Möhrke Sperling. She compared the shaking of the walls when bombs landed nearby to an earthquake. "We never knew what to expect when we went back to our apartment after an alarm." After the worst attacks in July 1943, when entire Hamburg city blocks were on fire, the smoke was so heavy that "we couldn't see the sun. It was day but still dark. . . . About this time [the government] recommended that all expectant mothers leave the city." Wally was awaiting the arrival of her first child, and she found a place to stay with her sister in the town of Eyendorf on the Lüneburg Heath (about thirty miles south of Hamburg). While there, she was informed that the city of Hamburg planned to confiscate her apartment. On a quick trip back to the city, she prevented that action. On September 5, 1943, her son Horst-Dieter was born in Salzhausen.[19]

The terror of July 1943 was shared by Rita Fischer, whose parents were on vacation when Hamburg was subjected to attack after attack. After bombs damaged the adjacent apartment buildings, Rita left home with Gisela and their grandmother. "I took a last look around the home—the windows were all broken—no gas, water, or electricity. It was so windy outside like a firestorm, and Oma was holding on to our bikes. We were walking with the refugees towards the woods."[20] After a night in the forest near Poppenbüttel, Rita and Gisela went back into the city against the flow of refugees heading out. She later wrote:

> The closer we came [to our home] the stronger the firestorm got. . . . We had to pass a railroad underpass and a military hospital where many wounded soldiers and people were laying, moaning in pain. It was just terrible. . . . When we arrived at our house only half of the front lower [level] was standing. . . . A lady gave us a piece of paper and nail, and we wrote: "Gisela, Rita, Oma fine in Poppenbüttel." It was dark, like midnight and the sun was like a red ball in the sky—but it was noon and very windy. Our Oma was convinced our Savior, Jesus Christ, will come—so we were not afraid.

From a local railroad station, the three took the train east to Schneidemühl. The next day, they continued on south and east to Liegnitz in Silesia, where they were met by their cousin Gerda. Four days later, their parents found them there. Having heard about the catastrophe in Hamburg, they had traveled immediately in that direction, were prevented from continuing, then turned east toward Berlin, and eventually contacted a relative to whom the twins had written a card before leaving Hamburg. "The good Lord really watched over us," concluded Rita. Brother Fischer decided that the family should return to Hamburg without delay, and soon the father and his twin daughters were back at work in the insurance company.

The Kopp family apartment suffered slight damage in early air raids but remained quite inhabitable. Young Edeltraud recalled how several of their windows were broken by the air pressure released by bombs not far away; the openings were covered by cardboard or plastic of some kind. Their apartment house was too old to have a safe basement, so the family went around the corner to a different building, where their chances for survival from bombs were greater. By the time of the firebombings of July 1943, Sister Kopp had taken her children to a town east of Berlin, where the war did not promise imminent danger.

President Schmidt's employment in a cigarette factory did not represent any conflict with his religious health standards. On the contrary, the items he helped produce served the family in a very significant way: each employee was given a specific amount of cigarettes in addition to his wages, and the Schmidts used those cigarettes to barter for additional food items. Herta said, "My father received 200 cigarettes weekly, and they were a different brand made especially for the employees. There were some delicatessen store owners who really liked those cigarettes. We never had to go hungry thanks to those cigarettes." Irmgard explained that her father could trade eight cigarettes for one loaf of bread and often gave the bread to needy members of the branch.

Ursula Stein was again away from home while Hamburg suffered in the firebombings; she was in Berlin serving in another civilian function. "I didn't have contact with the Church very much if at all, but I kept my testimony in my heart and didn't lose it." Later, she was stationed with an antiaircraft unit on the outskirts of Bremen, where her assignment was to shoot down enemy aircraft attacking that city. She never felt that her life was in jeopardy there, "because the bombs fell on the downtown."

Wally Möhrke Sperling lost contact with the Barmbek Branch after the branch rooms at Dehnhaide were destroyed in 1943. Constantly away from the city, she traveled to the occupied French province of Alsace-Lorraine in 1944. While on the way there, the train was attacked by dive-bombers, and she survived another terrifying aspect of war. While living in the home of her maternal grandparents in the Lorraine town of Saverne, she heard the sounds of the approaching American army; it was time to return to Hamburg. When she arrived back at her apartment, she determined that the central heating system had been damaged and was inoperable, but she was able to procure a small coal stove that could be vented directly out the window. The electricity was turned on for only a few hours at a time. "But we were home again!"[21]

The Schmidts lived far enough from the Hamburg city center and the harbor that they had little to fear from bombs. However, the air pressure from miles away did break their windows several times, and the utilities were interrupted for days on end. As Irmgard recalled:

> We often had no water for a day or two, and the water wagon would come down our street. The people all came around with their buckets to get water. Naturally we kids didn't bring the water home; we had to have water fights in the streets. That's how bad kids are. And when the stores had no food, the government came around with food baskets. We could go and say "Can I have a basket full of food?"

Regarding the problems with the gas lines, Irmgard recalled a common predicament after they had gone to all the effort of collecting ingredients all day for something to bake. They would put the item in the oven, and the gas would be turned off during the baking. "Then you have no food."

The attitudes of the Saints in Hamburg during the worst air raids of the war deeply impressed young Werner Schmidt, as he later wrote: "Many of the members lost their homes. In the first testimony meeting after that, people who had lost everything got up to say that they had their testimony and their scriptures, [and] genealogy records and that was the most important thing in their mind. The meetings at those times were very special."[22]

Soon after the catastrophic summer of 1943, many schoolchildren were sent away from Hamburg. Such was the case for Werner Schmidt and his classmates, who were transported to the village of Jochenstein on the Danube, where they were quartered in the abandoned barracks of border guards.[23] Among the approximately ninety boys there, Werner was recognized by leaders for his ability to organize and direct activities. He explained how he gained the confidence of his leaders: "I had much training in the Church. . . . [They] were impressed with my straightforwardedness and honesty." Although far from home, Werner recalled, "I had a really good time . . . and [was] well taken care of."[24]

After the Barmbek Branch meeting rooms were destroyed in 1943, the members were asked to go to the Altona Branch building and join there with the hosts and the survivors of the St. Georg Branch, who also had no place to meet. The journey from Barmbek to Altona was a sporadic walk and ride of about eight miles for most of the members. As more of the downtown was reduced to rubble and fewer streetcars were in operation, the journey became very difficult. Both Sunday meetings in Altona were held in the morning, but the Barmbek Saints still had to get up very early in the morning and did not return home until nearly evening.

Due to the difficulty caused by the long trek to Altona, many Barmbek Branch members chose to hold Sunday meetings in a home. President Schmidt invited local members to join his family in their apartment. By this juncture in the war, many members were away in the service of their country, had been killed in the many air raids, or had left town in search of safer places to live.

Georg Nigbur was not a member of the LDS Church, but he was a handsome young man whom Irmgard Schmidt met at an army dance. He had lost a leg to a landmine in Russia but could already get around the dance floor quite well with his artificial leg.[25] Following an engagement that lasted nearly a year, the two were married on September 5, 1944. With the church rooms destroyed, the church wedding ceremony was conducted by Irmgard's father in their home. There could be no honeymoon in those days, so the celebration consisted mainly of a very nice meal with family members and a few friends. "We had real food and small presents," the bride recalled. The newlyweds were given a room in the Schmidt apartment, and Georg went to work for the government.

Toward the end of the war, the Altona building was damaged but still usable. Irmgard Schmidt recalled watching snow fall through a hole in the ceiling into the meeting room. It would have been difficult if not impossible to have any heat under such conditions. Her brother, Werner, described the hole as a skylight that had been shattered: "When it rained or snowed we had to sit on the sides [of the room] where it was dry. To keep warm we kept our coats on and the elderly could sit close to the coal-burning stove. . . . Sometimes the sacrament water was frozen by the time it was passed out. But the spirit was very much present."[26]

By 1944, it was Werner's turn to serve the nation. At seventeen, he was drafted into the Reichsarbeitsdienst and sent to construct military facilities in Czechoslovakia. He was both amused and bored by what he felt were senseless drills and inspections, during which officers, disturbed by tiny infractions or items slightly out of order, would mess up the barracks and order that the procedure be repeated. According to Werner, such practices were stupid: "Stupidity never turned me on, and many things we had to do were on that level."[27]

In January 1945, Werner made the transition from the national labor service to the army:

> I was drafted into the regular army to be trained as a Tiger Tank driver. Most of the boys were 16 or 17 years old and the leaders—like my corporal—were broken-down soldiers from the eastern front. The rifles we had were from the French army, and tanks were not available—that is we had one to climb in and out of and play like we were driving it. . . . The German army wasn't any more what it used to be, and I had no interest to fight for a lost cause and for an idea I didn't believe in. . . . I didn't put my heart and soul into being a soldier.[28]

At about the time Wally Möhrke Sperling returned to Hamburg, her mail connection with her husband was interrupted for several weeks. She wrote, "I was very bothered by [not knowing his whereabouts]. How many times I prayed to my Father in Heaven for help." As it turned out, Willi had been wounded and was temporarily lost, but he showed up at their apartment in Hamburg in early 1945, his uniform still spotted with blood. "I could hardly believe [that he was home]!" she wrote. "I was so very thankful!"[29]

Toward the end of 1944, Gisela Fischer (then eighteen) was drafted into the Luftwaffe, and Rita volunteered for duty in order to stay with her twin. The girls were assigned to the Leck Air Base near the Danish border. On one occasion in March 1945, they were outside sunbathing when enemy dive-bombers dropped out of the sky to attack the field, and Rita jumped into a foxhole. She described the situation in these words:

> The motors from the airplanes got very loud, and above our heads the guns from the airplanes and our artillery gunmen were firing like crazy. The planes were so low that it seemed like I could reach them with my hands. I found myself deep in the hole so that a bullet could not hit me. I prayed very hard to my Heavenly Father and promised him that when I get out of here I would always go to Relief Society. I always went to Church but not to Relief Society during the week.

By Christmas of 1944, Else Kopp and her children were living with relatives in Landsberg/Warthe, about two hours by train east of Berlin. They enjoyed attending church meetings with the Saints in that town, and it was there that her son, Werner, was baptized: "I remember that the people expected the water in the river to feel cold, but for me it didn't. It felt just right." Soldier Edmund Kopp missed this occasion, as he did many other important dates in the lives of his young children after 1939.

Fig. 1. Edmund Kopp spent nearly the entire war away from home. He was killed in 1945. (E. Kopp Biebau)

While in Landsberg, Jungvolk member Werner Kopp saw Adolf Hitler and shook his hand:

> It was in Landsberg on the SA parade grounds. We all had to stand straight in a row when Hitler pulled up. Hitler came and shook my hand. For me, he wasn't a hero—just an ordinary man like everybody else. Even though he was the leader of Germany, he was ordinary. So what? . . . But looking back, Hitler looked like an old man to me. But I was a young boy at the time. I recognized him immediately—he looked just like in all of his pictures.[30]

Soon after this incident, Sister Kopp had to take her children and flee. She first burned Werner's Jungvolk uniform in the heater, then hurried with her children to the railroad station. Edeltraud recalled hearing the Soviet artillery in the distance and seeing panic reign at the station:

> When we got to the train station, all we could see were people and their belongings. Baby buggies and clothes were everywhere. Nobody

> could take the luggage with them because the cattle cars were already full. The official told our mother that the train was full and couldn't take any more people, so she took Werner and shoved him into the train wagon. She did the same with me. She then told the officer, "Don't tell me what I can or can't do! I'm leaving!" and then she got on the train. We stood the entire trip.

The trip to Berlin should have taken two hours but lasted at least eight, according to Werner. Along the way, people got out and collected snow for water. There was no food to eat until they reached Berlin and were cared for by Red Cross volunteers. Eventually, they reached Hamburg and found a basement room to live in. Their apartment had been destroyed in the firebombing, along with all of their property.

With only five rounds of ammunition in his rifle, Werner Schmidt was sent with his comrades to oppose the advance of the British army in northern Germany. Although he had achieved excellent ratings as a marksman in what little training was available, he had no desire to shoot at the enemy or to be shot at by them. One day in April 1945, he was sitting on a haystack reading in his little New Testament when British soldiers fired in his direction. He was able to find a better hiding place and hit upon the idea of firing his five rounds into the air. The reaction was a surprise to him: "The thought to kill any of them never crossed my mind. But I never saw anyone fall faster to the ground, faster than I could run behind the barn, and then all hell broke loose. I was wondering how effective my five bullets would have been if I really would have started to fight against such firepower."[31] Werner evaded the enemy for a few more hours, then became a prisoner of war. His life was never in jeopardy.

When the war ended on May 8, 1945, enemy units had not reached the northernmost part of Germany, where the Fischer twins were stationed. They decided to simply go home to Hamburg, a distance of nearly one hundred miles. They planned to travel by bicycle. They did not see the British soldiers moving in the opposite direction until they crossed the Kiel Canal. Peddling straight ahead and avoiding eye contact with the soldiers, they moved on unhindered and reached Hamburg without incident. It took them about an hour to work their way from the outskirts of the city to their parents' apartment. The story continues:

> We rang the bell from downstairs so we would not give our parents a heart attack. They were happy, and our father asked us how we got here. He was surprised when he heard our story. . . . An elderly lady came downstairs and offered Gisela and me her spare room. We were so grateful for it and thanked our Heavenly Father also for the safe arrival at home.

In the spring of 1945, Herta Schmidt was far from home in Saxony. She and a girlfriend had been transferred to a location near Chemnitz as employees in a war-critical industry. Only eighteen years old at the time, the two girls were in the area between the invading Soviets and the invading Americans. Not wanting to wait until the Soviets arrived (everybody had heard tales of their misdeeds), the girls left their work and began the long trip home—a distance of nearly 250 miles through territory invaded by the armies of three different enemy powers.

> It didn't seem that dangerous because there were people [refugees] from all over Germany going all different directions. In fact, we had packed a suitcase and it was really heavy. We finally just gave it away and walked home with what we were wearing. We had five pounds of sugar that we had gotten from ration coupons, and we gave it to people who let us stay overnight in their homes. . . . We always had to hide when enemy soldiers came by on patrols. It took us about a month to get home.

When Herta and her friend reached the river that had been established as the border between the Soviet and the British occupation zones, they showed the British guards their papers confirming their right to enter the zone and proceed home to Hamburg. The fact that they could make the long journey without tragic experiences is remarkable.

Willi Sperling was assigned home-guard duties, which enabled him to be with his family when the war came to an end in Hamburg in April 1945. As his wife, Wally, later wrote, "Finally we didn't need to worry about air raids anymore; finally there would be no more dangerous interruptions in the night; this we felt was a great blessing. . . . A new phase of our lives began on May 8, 1945." Looking back on those difficult years, she wrote, "How often during the war did I consider the message of 1 Nephi 3:7. . . . This strengthened my testimony of the truth of the gospel. Without my knowledge I wouldn't have been able to bear it. Despite all of the trials, I always had a sense of well-being deep inside."[32]

In September 1945, Werner Schmidt was released from a POW camp in Belgium and returned home to Hamburg. While a POW, he had lost his New Testament in a camp flood. "It was a great loss to me," he said. He had been reminded also of the importance of keeping God's commandments and standards of conduct. At seventeen, he knew little about the facts of life. The conversations of other POWs revealed a lack of respect for women and moral cleanliness that shocked him. In general, he found his peace and comfort in the Lord. He was thrilled to be in his parents' home, but they were reluctant to celebrate while two of their sons were still missing. They eventually returned. The family of branch president Alfred Schmidt lost one son to the war but retained their home and were thus full of hope in postwar Germany.

"I think that the war just melted us [Latter-day Saints] together more than anything," explained Herta Schmidt. "As members we cared for each other like a large family, a branch." Another branch member, Ursula Seemann, echoed the thought: "The life in Church was the reason why we stayed strong and kept going. We were so excited to see each other whenever we had the chance."

In Memoriam

The following members of the Barmbek Branch did not survive World War II:

Peter August Claessens b. Hamburg 21 Nov 1862; son of Carl Kratzel and Johanna Catherina Claessens; bp. 25 Jun 1926; conf. 27 Jun 1926; ord. deacon 9 Oct 1927; d. old age 5 Aug 1943 (CHL CR 275 8 2438, no. 452; FHL microfilm 25741, 1930 and 1935 censuses; IGI)

Waldemar Erwin Drachenberg b. Liebenow, Urnswalde, Brandenburg, 3 Aug 1923; son of Friedrich Drachenburg and Hulda Kopp; bp. 6 Sep 1931; conf. 6 Sep 1931; ord. deacon 1 Oct 1939; paratrooper; corporal; d. in training France, 12 Mar 1943; bur. Mont-de-Huisnes, France (E. Frank; CHL CR 275 8 2438, no. 959; FHL microfilm 25756, 1935 census; IGI; www.volksbund.de)

Mathias Hackner b. Großmehring, Ingolstadt, Bayern, 31 Dec 1856; son of Bartholomäus Hackner and Anna Maria Kaltenecker; bp. 25 Dec 1921; conf. 25 Dec 1921; m. Hamburg 21 Aug 1897, Maria Franziska Mundt; 2 children; d. old age Barmbek, Hamburg, 28 Dec 1942 (FHL microfilm 68783, no. 49; CHL CR 275 8, no. 620; IGI; FHL microfilm 162769, 1930 and 1935 censuses)

Wilhelm Carl Ferdinand Hintz b. Aschersleben, Magdeburg, Sachsenn, 4 Jun 1894; son of Wilhelm Carl Ferdinand Hintz and Emma Becker; bp. 7 Mar 1929; conf. 7 Mar 1929; ord. deacon 5 May 1935; d. tuberculosis 7 Oct 1943 (CHL CR 275 8 2438, no. 141; IGI)

August Kannwischer b. Mücelin, Poland, 19 Sep 1855; son of Christian Kannwischer and Luise Geisler; bp. 5 Nov 1923; conf. 5 Nov 1923; ord. deacon 8 Mar 1925; ord. elder 8 Oct 1934; m. Pauline Krüger; d. old age 25 Jul 1944 (CHL CR 275 8 2438, no. 963, FHL microfilm 271376, 1930 and 1935 censuses)

Paul Fritz Isaak Koch b. Hamburg 20 Sep 1906; son of Karl Friedrich Wilhelm Koch and Auguste Caroline Sirstins; bp. 17 May 1923; conf. 17 May 1923; ord. deacon 14 Mar 1926; d. burns, POW camp, Caen, France, 9 Sep 1945 (CHL CR 275 8 2438, no. 81; IGI)

Edmund Kopp b. Konojad, Strassburg, Westpreußen, 21 Jan 1905; son of Ludwig Kopp and Paulina Karoline Krueger; bp. 6 Nov 1924; conf. 6 Nov 1924; m. Landsberg/Warthe, Brandenburg, 2 Aug 1930, Else Anna Luckmann; 5 children; k. in battle Russia 1945 (E. K. Biebau; FHL microfilm no. 271381, 1925 and 1935 censuses; FS)

Franz Heinrich Köster b. 22 November 1910; son of Franz Friedrich Ernst Köster and Auguste Wilhelmine Abeling; bp. 17 May 1923; conf. 17 May 1923; corporal; d. POW Caen, France, 9 Sep 1946; bur. La Cambe, France (FHL 68783:76; FHL microfilm 271381, 1925 and 1935 censuses; FS; www.volksbund.de)

Gerd Luhmann b. Wandsbek, Schleswig-Holstein, 19 Nov 1925; son of Franz Wilhelm Luhmann and Carla Adele Schröder; bl. 7 Mar 1926; bp. 18 Sep 1933; conf. 24 Sep 1933; d. scarlet fever 11 Mar or Aug 1941 (CHL CR 275 8 2438, no. 83; CHL CR 275 8 2438, no. 376; IGI)

Richard Friedrich Momburg b. Hamburg 26 Jun 1936; son of Alban Otto Momburg and Anna M. Koch; d. stroke 26 Mar 1942 (CHL CR 275 8, reel 2426, no. 99; CHL CR 275 8 2438, no. 325)

Richard Paul Otto Prüss b. Hamburg 25 Jun 1925; son of Richard Rudolf Ernst Prüss and Rosalie Erika Marta Mertens; bl. 6 Sep 1925; bp. 18 Sep 1933; conf. 24 Sep 1933; ord. deacon 1941; corporal; k. in battle Western Front 14 Aug 1944; bur. Champigny-St. Andre, France (CHL CR 275 8 2438, no. 182; www.volksbund.de; IGI)

Fig. 2. Richard Prüss. (H. Pruess Mueller)

Ernst August Schmidt b. Hamburg 26 Jul 1913; son of Alfred Schmidt and Anne Naujoks; bp. 25 Dec 1921; ord. elder; m. Wandsbek, Schleswig-Holstein, 3 Jul 1937, Helene Amanda Teichfischer; 1 child; rifleman; d. in field hospital 2/591 at Smolensk, Russia, 10 Feb 1942 (W. Schmidt autobiography; IGI, PRF; www.volksbund.de)

Johannes Carsten Friedrich Richard Sievers b. Neumünster, Schleswig-Holstein, 5 October 1855; d. Wandsbek, Hamburg, 5 June 1941 (FS)

Karl Friedrich Stein b. Hamm, Westfalen, 18 Oct 1902; son of Wilhelm Stein and Martha Auguste Böse; bp. 27 or 31 Oct 1923; conf. 27 or 31 Oct 1923; ord. deacon 11 Jul 1932; ord. teacher 11 Sep 1933; m. Hamburg 18 Oct 1923, Bertha Wilhelmina Maria Knopf; 1 child; soldier; k. in battle 10 Dec 1942 or Krakow, Poland, 3 Jun 1941 (CHL CR 275 8 2438, no. 158; www.volksbund.de; CHL CR 275 8, no. 826; CHL 68783, no. 182)

Notes

1. West German Mission branch directory, 1939, CHL LR 10045 11.
2. Wally Möhrke Sperling, interview by the author in German, Hamburg, Germany, August 15, 2006; unless otherwise noted, summarized in English by Judith Sartowski.
3. Irmgard Schmidt Nigbur, interview by the author, Sandy, UT, February 20, 2009.
4. Herta Schmidt Wobbe, interview by the author, Salt Lake City, January 23, 2009.
5. Presiding Bishopric, "Financial, Statistical, and Historical Reports of Wards, Stakes, and Missions, 1884–1955," 257, CR 4 12.
6. Karl-Heinz Schnibbe, *The Price* (Salt Lake City: Bookcraft, 1984), 33–34.
7. Rita Fischer Frampton, autobiography (unpublished).
8. Werner Schmidt, autobiography (unpublished), 3.
9. Ibid.
10. Wally Möhrke Sperling, autobiography (unpublished, 2006), 1.
11. Schmidt, autobiography, 4.
12. Edeltraud Kopp Biebau and Werner Kopp, interview by the author, Salt Lake City, May 3, 2009.
13. In fact, the closest LDS temple to Hamburg, Germany, at the time was in Salt Lake City. No members of the Church in the West German Mission are known to have married in the temple before World War II.
14. Sperling, autobiography, 2.
15. The Fischer children were by no means the only LDS teenagers to participate in the confirmation ceremonies of their Lutheran and Catholic friends in those days. The practice might compare with the tradition of the baccalaureate program associated with high school graduation in some communities in the United States.
16. Ursula Betty Seemann, telephone interview with Judith Sartowski in German, March 12, 2008.
17. Block wardens were responsible for seeing that everybody left their apartments and went down into the basements as soon as the alarms sounded.
18. Schmidt, autobiography, 4.
19. Sperling, autobiography, 4.
20. See the description of firestorms in the Hamburg District chapter. See also the Dresden Altstadt section in Roger P. Minert, *In Harm's Way: East German Latter-day Saints in World War II* (Provo, UT: Religious Studies Center, Brigham Young University, 2009).
21. Sperling, autobiography, 4.
22. Schmidt, autobiography, 4.
23. Since the annexation of Austria to Germany in 1938, the border was no longer international and thus not guarded during 1938–45.
24. Werner Schmidt, autobiography, 5.
25. Years later Georg would tease his wife about how she chased him and he could not run away fast enough. He joined the Church after the war.
26. Schmidt, autobiography, 4–5. In those days, LDS branches used small glass cups for the sacrament. Several eyewitnesses have reported breaking ice that had formed in those cups in order to drink the water.
27. Schmidt, autobiography, 6–7.
28. Ibid., 7.
29. Sperling, autobiography, 5.
30. By January 1945, Hitler took up residence in the chancellery in Berlin and was rarely seen in public again. He committed suicide there on April 30, 1945.
31. Schmidt, autobiography, 8–9.
32. Sperling, autobiography, 5.

Glückstadt Branch

Situated on the right bank of the Elbe River twenty miles downstream from Hamburg, Glückstadt was a city of about ten thousand inhabitants in 1939. The branch of Latter-day Saints in that city consisted of only thirty-nine persons, and four were elders. According to the mission directory, all branch leadership positions were filled at that time by members of the Sievers and Teichfischer families.[1]

Glückstadt Branch[2]	1939
Elders	4
Priests	1
Teachers	0
Deacons	1
Other Adult Males	6
Adult Females	18
Male Children	1
Female Children	1
Total	32

When World War II began, the branch was holding meetings in rented rooms at Am Fleth 60, a place the Saints were privileged to call home throughout the war. Hanna Helene Sievers (born 1930) recalled one large room that served as the chapel in the back of the building and two smaller rooms for classes. There was a sign in the front window to the street indicating the presence of the branch in that building. Hanna's family moved into an upstairs apartment in the same building in 1939.[3]

Sunday School began at 10:00 a.m. and sacrament meeting at 7:00 p.m. The Relief Society met on Tuesdays at 7:45 p.m. and the MIA on Thursdays at the same time. A genealogy class was held every first and third Wednesday of the month at 7:45 p.m. There were too few children then to hold Primary.

Hanna provided the following example of the dedication of Glückstadt Branch members: "I remember that my grandparents always came to church—whether it was good weather or bad. Even if it snowed, they put on an extra pair of socks—they always attended church. They walked three miles one way, and the first meeting started at 9:00 a.m. They were strong in the gospel, and all the members helped each other."

According to Hanna's elder sister Marianne (born 1923), some of the members of the branch lived in neighboring towns and came to Glückstadt for meetings from as far away as Itzehoe, ten miles to the north.[4] Because both sisters were required to participate in the League of German Girls, they had to miss church meetings on occasion. "I was not very happy about that," recalled Hanna. "Once the police came and picked me up."

When the war began on September 1, 1939, Marianne had already finished her public schooling and was working in a shoe store. According to her recollection, "I often took people from work to church with me on Sundays. They all knew that I was a member of the church."

Fig. 1. Marianne Sievers. (R. Fock)

Hermann Sievers was a Social Democrat, like so many people in the northern German cities. According to his daughter Hanna, he was not afraid to voice his political opinions, and his outspokenness caused considerable trouble. "Once they dangled him from a bridge and demanded that he deny his faith, but he refused to do so. Another time, they held a gun to his head and demanded the same thing. They even picked him up from work one day and examined his records, then let him go. This all happened during the war."

Life goes on for young and old during wars, and Marianne Sievers fell in love with a lifelong friend and fellow member of the branch, Richard Fock. Her story reads as follows: "We had known each other long before he left to serve in the military. We gave each other a star in the night sky that would remind us of each other. We kept a promise that we would wait for each other." Richard (born 1924) was a priest in the Aaronic Priesthood and recalled that he had fallen in love with Marianne when he was fifteen.[5]

Richard had planned to be a railroad mechanic and in the summer of 1942 completed a three-year apprenticeship. At seventeen, he was just the right age for military service and was told that if he volunteered, he would be assigned to the Luftwaffe (air force). He was also told that if he did not volunteer, he would be drafted into the infantry. He chose the first option, hoping to become a pilot. Unfortunately, he was soon disappointed to learn that he was to serve as an aviation mechanic and would not be flying airplanes. The various stages of his training took him to Giessen, Germany, and then to Warsaw, Poland, and eventually to Kharkov, Ukraine. It was there that he first saw a Russian fighter shot down. He observed in his autobiography, "Later I saw many planes shot down, as well as many emergency landings and accidents, also involving German airplanes. I was glad that I had not become a pilot."[6]

Fig. 2. Richard Fock as a young Luftwaffe recruit. (R. Fock)

Unlike the terrible suffering of their fellow Saints in Hamburg, the members of the Glückstadt Branch did not lose their homes or starve during the war. Hanna Sievers explained that they sometimes came home from shopping trips without specific food items (despite having the required ration coupons). However, the family was fortunate to have a small garden plot and thus avoided starvation. Sister Sievers also worked on a farm now and then and enjoyed the advantages that came with that labor situation.

Unlike the situation in most LDS branches in Germany, attendance in the meetings of the Glückstadt Branch actually increased during the war years. Several families who had lost their homes in the attacks on Hamburg moved north and found places to live in and near Glückstadt. One of those was the family of Adelbert and Anna Koch of the St. Georg Branch in Hamburg. Sister Koch's mother belonged to the Glückstadt Branch. Young Brunhilde Koch (born 1934) recalled seeing perhaps forty people in the meetings on a typical Sunday in 1943–44.[7] The family returned to Hamburg in 1944 and experienced the end of the war there.

Glückstadt was not a large city, but there was a major railroad yard there that attracted the attention of enemy bombers now and then. As Hanna recalled, "The basement of our building was almost impossible to reach, so we went down to the [church] meeting rooms during air raids. There were not many attacks on Glückstadt. Toward the end of the war, one building was hit by an incendiary bomb and burned."

While away from home, Richard Fock was never privileged to meet another LDS soldier, to attend church meetings, or to read the scriptures. He missed this very much and eventually resolved to do the following:

> I swore to myself that as soon as I was released from the military, I would never miss an opportunity to serve the Lord. I was allowed to go home on leave a few times, and I experienced the joy of the reunion and the sadness of separation [from the Saints], even though Marianne would play hymn no. 60 "I Need Thee Every Hour" on the pump organ and I would sing it. That gave us strength and hope for the impending separation.[8]

Richard spent the rest of the war on the Eastern Front, which crept steadily westward toward Germany. He served in dangerous conditions on several occasions but was never in battle and never wounded. On Christmas 1944, he was stationed at an airfield in Poland. One month later, he was at Finsterwalde, near Berlin, and there he decided it was time to marry his sweetheart, Marianne, back home in Glückstadt.

Fig. 3. Marianne Sievers and Richard Fock married just two months before the war ended. (R. Fock)

The marriage of two young branch members must have been cause for a special celebration among the Glückstadt Saints in the spring of 1945, when things were looking very bad for Germany. In the words of Marianne Sievers:

> We got married on March 3, 1945, in the civil registry office after my husband came home on leave from the Luftwaffe. My father had told me a few days earlier when he would come. On the exact day, he came. We had told the people at Church that we would get married on a certain day and everything worked out very well. [District president Otto] Berndt from Hamburg came and married us. We also had a small celebration with cakes. My husband was home for two weeks, and then he had to return to duty.

Richard expressed his sentiments regarding the wedding: "Those were some of the most beautiful days of our life. Our wedding day represented the attainment of a long-awaited goal." On March 16, lance corporal Richard Fock returned to Finsterwalde but was soon moved east to Silesia and was still there when the war ended on May 8, 1945. To avoid capture by the Soviets, he and his comrades worked their way south into Czechoslovakia and west toward the city of Plzen, where they came into contact with advancing American troops. When the Germans hesitated to surrender, the Americans countered with an ultimatum: if the Germans did not surrender by a specific time the next day, they would be refused by the Americans and handed over to the Soviets. This was sufficient motivation for Richard and his friends to give themselves up immediately.[9]

Life as a POW was never pleasant, but Richard was pleased to have a tent to sleep in and enough food to avoid illness and starvation. Unlike hundreds of other German Latter-day Saints in POW camps all over Europe and North America, Richard was released very early by the Americans in Czechoslovakia. By July 22, 1945, he was on his way through Germany toward home. In Bad Segeberg, just a few miles east of Glückstadt, he was issued official release papers by the British occupation administration. Although he traveled the last few miles on foot, Richard Fock was not bothered, knowing the trip would end in the arms of his dear wife and the home of his parents. Within days, he was again employed as a railroad mechanic and could look forward to the fulfillment of other personal goals and to a life of service to his God and his Church.[10]

The British army entered Glückstadt in April 1945. There was no fighting, and the Saints there were not bothered by the invaders. Their homes and meeting rooms were intact, and they busied themselves with the task of taking in LDS refugees from eastern Germany. Conditions in Glückstadt were relatively good as they began a new life in a new Germany.

In Memoriam

The following members of the Glückstadt Branch did not survive World War II:

Hilde Marie Brandemann b. Högelund Kr. Hadersleben, 16 Nov 1889; dau. of Peter Bundessen and Auguste Marie Nielsen; bp. 24 Nov 1929; conf. 24 Nov 1929; missing (CHL CR 375 8, no. 91)

Margaretha Helene Fischer b. Obendeich bei Herzhorn, Schleswig Holstein, 8 Apr 1904; dau. of Johannes Karl Teich Fischer and Helene Sievers; bp. 30 Oct 1924; conf. 30 Oct 1924; m. 21 Apr 1929, Alwin Drier; missing (CHL CR 375 8, no. 92)

Karl Johannes Teichfischer b. Engelbrechtsche Wildnis, Steinburg, Schleswig-Holstein, Preussen, 23 Jun 1874; son of Claus Teichfischer and Anna Gesche Soltau; bp. 18 Sep 1921; conf. 18 Sep 1921; ord. deacon 15 Jan 1924; ord. teacher 29 Aug 1926; ord. priest 25 Mar 1928; ord. elder 1 May 1932; m. Herzhorn, Steinburg, Schleswig-Holstein, Preussen, 4 Sep 1898, Helene Amonda Sievers; 11 children; d. stomach cancer Herzhorn 4 Mar 1941 (Fock; CHL CR 275 8 2438, no. 870; FHL microfilm 245282, 1930 and 1935 censuses)

Walter Tiedemann b. 18 April 1915; son of Johann Jürgen Tiedemann and Anna Catharina Margaretha von Roenn; bp. 10 Jun 1939; conf. 10 Jun 1939; d. 5 August 1943 (FS)

Notes

1. West German Mission branch directory, 1939, CHL LR 10045 11.
2. Presiding Bishopric, "Financial, Statistical, and Historical Reports of Wards, Stakes, and Missions, 1884–1955," 257, CHL CR 4 12.
3. Hanna Helene Sievers, interview by the author in German, Glückstadt, Germany, August 16, 2006; unless otherwise noted, summarized in English by Judith Sartowski.
4. Marianne Sievers Fock, interview by the author in German, Glückstadt, Germany, August 16, 2006.
5. Richard Jürgen Johannes Fock, autobiography (unpublished, 1999), 2.
6. Fock, autobiography, 3.
7. Brunhilde Koch Richter, telephone interview with Jennifer Heckmann in German, October 3, 2008.
8. Fock, autobiography, 4.
9. Ibid., 7.
10. Ibid., 8.

Lübeck Branch

One of only two Baltic Sea port cities in the West German Mission, Lübeck is located forty miles northeast of Hamburg. Famous for its seven church steeples, the city had a population of 154,811 when World War II approached. The branch in that city numbered 109 persons, including five elders and seven men and boys who held the Aaronic Priesthood. Like so many other branches in the mission, this one had a very large number of adult women but few children.

Lübeck Branch[1]	1939
Elders	5
Priests	1
Teachers	4
Deacons	2
Other Adult Males	22
Adult Females	66
Male Children	5
Female Children	4
Total	109

Leonard J. Bingham, a missionary from the United States, was the branch president in Lübeck on August 25, 1939, when he was instructed to depart the city with his colleague Joseph Loertscher. In his account of leaving the city on Saturday, August 26, he made no mention of designating a successor to lead the branch. However, all indications are that Elder Bingham's first counselor, Gottlieb Wiborny, assumed the position of branch president.[2]

When World War II began, the branch was meeting in rented rooms at Mühlenstrasse 68 in Lübeck's downtown. Reinhold Meyer (born 1923) recalled the location as "an old office building. There were three or four rooms upstairs. One was a double room that we used as a chapel, and there were classrooms for the children. There was a sign outside indicating the presence of the Church there. It was an attractive building, and I was not ashamed to go there."[3] He recalled an attendance of perhaps fifty to sixty persons on a typical Sunday.

Fig. 1. Friedrich (Friedel) Sass was the second counselor to Hamburg District president Alwin Brey when World War II began. (J. Sass)

Sunday School was held at 10:00 a.m. and sacrament meeting at 7:00 p.m. The MIA meetings were held on Tuesday evenings at 8:00 p.m., the Primary Organization on Wednesdays at 3:00 p.m., and the Relief Society on Thursday evenings at 8:00 p.m. Reinhold remembered that they took the glass sacrament cups home each week and cleaned them.[4] According to Wilfried Süfke (born 1934), there was a pump organ in the main meeting hall as well as a small stage. He remembered sitting on individual seats (rather than benches) that could be moved to the sides of the rooms to facilitate social activities.[5]

The Meyer family lived at Burgkoppel 33 in Lübeck, and it took them about forty-five minutes to walk to church. Making the trip twice each Sunday meant that the Meyers spent three hours walking. "We never missed meetings," explained Reinhold, "and it was dark when we got home to have our dinner." Frieda Meyer had been a widow since 1924 and raised seven children on her own. Fortunately, she was able to remain a housewife during those years and was faithful in taking them to the meetings.

Reinhold Meyer was employed in the aircraft industry in the early years of the war, helping to produce the Heinkel 111 and Dornier 217 airplanes. He knew that the planes were to be used to bomb the enemy and that the enemy might bomb Lübeck in return. During the first three years of the war, there were numerous air-raid alarms, but the local residents did not take them seriously. According to Reinhold, "We made our basement nice with beds down there. Instead of changing our clothes and running down there every time the sirens went off, we just slept there."

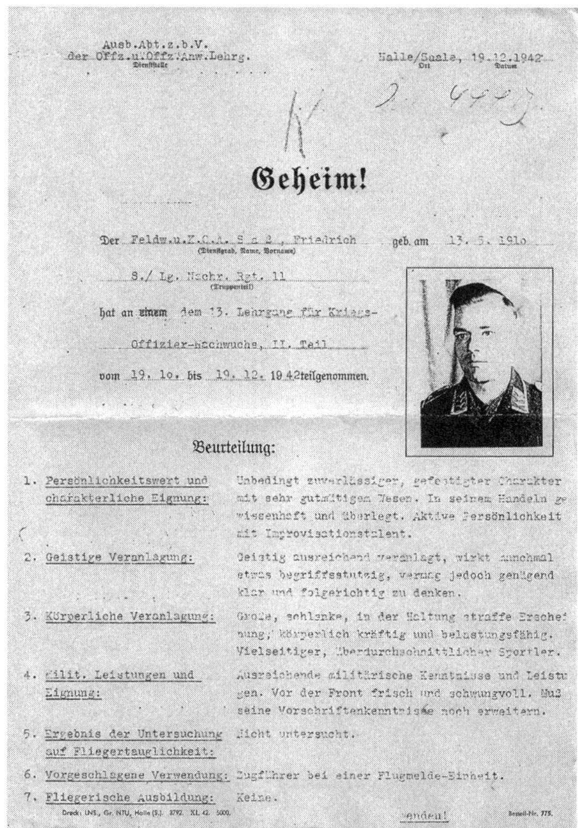

Ausb.Abt.z.b.V.
der Offz.u.Offz.Anw.Lehrg.
Dienststelle

Halle/Saale, 19.12.1942
Ort Datum

Geheim!

Der Feldw.u.K.O.A. Sass, Friedrich (Dienstgrad, Name, Vorname) geb. am 13. 5. 1910

8./ Lg. Nachr. Rgt. 11 (Truppenteil)

hat an ~~einem~~ dem 13. Lehrgang für Kriegs-Offizier-Nachwuchs, II. Teil

vom 19. 10. bis 19. 12. 1942 teilgenommen.

Beurteilung:

1. Persönlichkeitswert und charakterliche Eignung: Unbedingt zuverlässiger, gefestigter Charakter mit sehr gutmütigem Wesen. In seinem Handeln gewissenhaft und überlegt. Aktive Persönlichkeit mit Improvisationstalent.
2. Geistige Veranlagung: Geistig ausreichend veranlagt, wirkt manchmal etwas begriffsstutzig, vermag jedoch genügend klar und folgerichtig zu denken.
3. Körperliche Veranlagung: Große, schlanke, in der Haltung straffe Erscheinung, körperlich kräftig und belastungsfähig. Vielseitiger, überdurchschnittlicher Sportler.
4. Milit. Leistungen und Eignung: Ausreichende militärische Kenntnisse und Leistungen. Vor der Front frisch und schwungvoll. Muß seine Vorschriftenkenntnisse noch erweitern.
5. Ergebnis der Untersuchung auf Fliegertauglichkeit: Nicht untersucht.
6. Vorgeschlagene Verwendung: Zugführer bei einer Flugmelde-Einheit.
7. Fliegerische Ausbildung: Keine.

Druck: LNS., Gr. NTU, Halle (S.). 3792. XI. 42. 5000. Wenden! Bestell-Nr. 775.

Fig. 2. The officer's profile for Friedrich Sass was classified as geheim *(secret). (J. Sass)*

Many residents of the industry-poor city of Lübeck failed to take the air-raid sirens seriously in the early years of the war. Wilfried Süfke recalled the following:

> When we heard the alarms, we did not even go into the basement but stayed in our apartment. . . . It was dangerous and careless of us to do that, but back then it seemed reasonable. [Later] we heard of people who were injured or killed, and then we decided to go into the basement quite often. . . . Being only seven years old at the time, I was not afraid of dying.

The beautiful old city of Lübeck was destroyed to a great extent in a single attack on March 29, 1942. The towers of five of the seven prominent churches were gone, and much of the city's core was reduced to rubble. Fortunately, the Meyers lived far enough from that area to escape harm. The Mühlenstrasse meetinghouse was not destroyed but was soon confiscated by the city government to be used as a place for homeless residents. More than three hundred people lost their lives in the attack. The official report showed that 7 percent of the city's structures were totally destroyed, 10 percent severely damaged, and 41 percent slightly damaged.[6]

Fig. 3. Members of the Lübeck Branch on an outing in a local forest. (J. Sass)

Jürgen Sass (born 1933) recalled with great clarity the night his hometown was so badly damaged:

> The alarm had sounded; we were in the front room dressing when a tremendous explosion rattled doors and windows. As we peeked through the blinds, the sky was lit up by four illuminating devices which had been dropped to serve as target guides for British bomber squadrons. We fled immediately to our shelter, where we were soon joined by our grandmother. . . . Again and again, muffled explosions could be heard through the din of anti-aircraft fire. . . . Suddenly we were startled by a loud whine, followed by an earsplitting explosion which shattered windows and knocked tiles off the roof. A bomb had landed and exploded in a garden plot across the street. That was a close call![7]

When Jürgen Sass was eight years old, his mother, Hedwig, took him to the rooms of the St. Georg Branch in Hamburg, where there was a baptismal font (one of only three in the Church in all of Germany).[8] Jürgen's father, Friedrich (Friedel) Sass, had been stationed there in the air force for several years already and was fortunate to perform his son's baptism on May 23, 1942. Shortly after that event, Brother Sass was transferred to a combat zone.[9]

Figs. 4 and 5. The family of Friedrich (Friedel) and Hedwig (Heidi) Sass in about 1942. (J. Sass)

According to the branch history, "Brother Wiborny guided the branch through the trying and fateful years of the war."[10] No reports regarding him or his family could be found as of this writing. The branch history offers only one paragraph about the status of the Latter-day Saints in Lübeck during the war:

> The members gathered for meetings in the former civil registry office on Mühlenstrasse. Following the bombing of Lübeck in 1942 that destroyed 60% of the city, the meeting rooms were confiscated and the members were again compelled to hold meetings in their homes. At times during the war, meetings were also held in Reinfeld [seven miles east of Lübeck].[11] A book of meeting minutes was kept from January 3, 1943 to April 21, 1946. Walter Meyer usually conducted the meetings, but the names Hans Kufahl and Reinhold Meyer occur in this capacity as well. The average attendance was 10–17 persons, most of whom were members of the extended Meyer family.[12]

According to Reinhold Meyer, the first meetings after the disastrous attack of 1942 were held in a Catholic church ("but only once"), then in the apartment of his elder brother, Walter Meyer. Wilfried Süfke recalled sitting on the floor under such circumstances, but there was enough room. "We didn't have accompaniment on the pump organ any more, but we could still sing the hymns."

Fig. 6. Friedel Sass received the first-place medal for his age-group in the army 10-kilometer run in 1942. He ran the distance in 42:08.5. (J. Sass)

Late in 1942, Reinhold was drafted into the Luftwaffe and was stationed first in Reims, France. Initially, he was classified among the "flight personnel," but by then the number of German airplanes had decreased to the point that he was reassigned. "I never did have to fly, and I'm glad for that. [The Allies] had so many planes. I counted them later on—a thousand planes and I couldn't see any more." Following a short and intense illness, he was assigned to office duty. In 1943, he was transferred to Belgium and trained to drive motorcycles, automobiles, and trucks. Once while he was home on leave, his comrades were all sent to the Soviet Union—a move that cost many of them their lives. Reinhold was spared, at least for a while.

Friedel Sass was transferred to the Eastern Front in 1943 for a very short time, but long enough to have a painfully personal experience. He confided the story to his mother, who often related it to his sons:

> It may have been while he was delivering a message, when he suddenly found himself face-to-face with a Russian soldier. It was a matter of who was going to pull the trigger first, and it was [your] father that did. He said it's something to see somebody a block or so away shooting at you and you shoot back, that's one thing, but to be face-to-face with a living being, that is something else. He must have stayed with that man for a bit [before he died], because he learned that he had three children, just as [your] father did. He left a wife, just as [your] father did. He said it was a very, very traumatic experience.[13]

Specific memories of life in Lübeck during the war remain clear in Jürgen Sass's mind, such as this one:

> I was probably at the most, ten years old, while on the way to my elementary school . . . and there was a field where some construction was going on. [The workers were] forced laborers—probably Poles or Russians—and there was a guard with a gun. Whoever they were, there was a fistfight. . . . [They were] really fighting hard over a strangled cabbage on which all the leaves were already gone. That affected me. . . . I figured, gee, those guys must be starving.[14]

Jürgen Sass saw his father only on rare occasions during the war. Friedel Sass had been drafted in 1939, so his children grew up essentially without him. Jürgen recalled two poignant letters written by his father to Friedel's mother (Jürgen's grandmother). Brother Sass wrote one such letter on his wedding anniversary (September 30) and told of an American artillery barrage that could have killed him. "Please, Lord, if I have to die, not today!" he had thought during the barrage.[15]

Jürgen avoided the Hitler Youth experience for the first year, then volunteered after all: "I felt the need to belong to an organization of other young boys." One occasion must have been quite exciting, namely when the boys were camping and engaging in war games: "American planes flew overhead, and surrounding anti-aircraft batteries began to fire. Our group leader, who was probably not much older than 14, had us stand under trees, while [shrapnel] fragments rained around us. . . . Fortunately, none of us got hit."[16]

Wilfried Süfke was fortunate to have both parents home during the entire war. His father, Walter, was a salesman of agricultural seeds. His mother, Minna, owned and operated a small grocery store on the main floor of the apartment building in which the family lived. According to Wilfried, "Even when the British came in [as conquerors], we were able to keep the store running." Another major advantage in the life of young Wilfried was that he was never sent away from Lübeck as part of the children's evacuation program (Kinderlandverschickung), unlike hundreds of thousands of children all over Germany.

Friedel Sass was a very talented man. A dedicated member of the Church, he was serving as second counselor to Alwin Brey, the president of the Hamburg District, when the war began. From the beginning of his army service, he was selected as an officer candidate and moved steadily up the ranks. The excellent collection of documents preserved by his family attest to the stellar reputation he enjoyed among both superiors and subordinates. He appeared to be a faithful soldier who enjoyed serving his country. The many photos taken of him under both military and civilian circumstances show a man who seemed very happy with his life.

Holger Sass (born 1938) was a child when Allied airplanes coursed over Lübeck in the last years of the war. To him, it was all quite exciting, and he was totally unaware of the danger. "One time, when the sirens sounded to let us know that everything was okay, we could [go outside and] look at the fires. If you're a kid at that young age, it's kind of special."

During the summer of 1944, Reinhold Meyer was involved in a most precarious undertaking. A German V-1 unmanned rocket had plummeted into the French countryside and needed to be disarmed. Reinhold drove an expert he called "Old Gus" to the site and was required to hand him tools during the delicate operation. Just a few seconds after Old Gus removed the firing pin, it popped. "If the device had triggered just a few seconds earlier, I wouldn't be here telling this story," he claimed. However, the device injured Old Gus's hand, and Reinhard helped stop the bleeding. Then the two attached a few pounds of dynamite, retreated to a safe distance, and set off the charge to totally destroy the rocket's lethal payload.

When the Allied landings took place on the beaches of Normandy on June 6, 1944, Reinhold's unit was about a hundred miles inland. They were assigned to construct barriers to hinder the Allied advance, but there were simply no supplies with which to do so. "We just kept moving back, away from them," he recalled. When the Allies entered Paris in August, Reinhold was actually staying in a hotel there and came very close to being captured. His unit quickly moved northeast toward Germany's Eifel forest.

By early 1945, Reinhold Meyer had crossed the Rhine River into the heart of Germany and had moved steadily north and east ahead of the advancing British army. In April 1945, he and his comrades buried their weapons and surrendered to the British. They were moved to Lüneburg and then to Hitzaker on the Elbe River. For several nights, they had no shelter and simply slept in the sand. Once, Reinhold was ordered to latrine duty, which he of course did not like. Because nobody was really paying attention to him, he simply walked away from the distasteful task.

Just days before he was killed in Remiremont, France, Friedel Sass wrote a letter to his mother including the following lines:

> For the second time I have lost all my belongings. . . . Mostly I regret the loss of my briefcase

> with the addresses of my comrades from the Eastern Front, as well as my camera. Yesterday I bought for Jürgen's birthday a wristwatch, Swiss brand, with fifteen jewels. Now I have to see how I can get it home in time for his birthday. Unfortunately, I have not been able to get anything for my other two boys.[17]

Jürgen likely never received that watch because his father was killed a few days later, on October 12, 1944. The family received the sad news one day before Jürgen's eleventh birthday.

Figs. 7 and 8. Friedel Sass was killed in France on October 12, 1944. He lies buried in a German military cemetery. (J. Sass)

During the last days of the war, Holger Sass witnessed what to him was a most confusing incident. Standing near an army warehouse, he noticed that there were small fires inside even before a German officer ordered several of his men to go inside. "We never knew what was in there, but I think they were trying to destroy the stuff so that the [enemy] would not get it," he surmised. "They started a fire in the building, and then some soldiers went back in. They must have known that they would not get out because it was already burning. I think that seeing that [event] would affect anybody."

The British army entered the city of Lübeck on May 2, 1945, six days before the war officially ended.[18] No attempt was made to defend the city. According to young Jürgen Sass, "The subsequent occupation by British troops proved to be rather tolerable. There seemed to be little animosity on either side. . . . Church services . . . were restored, at first in a member's home, later on in schools."

The branch history offers a single sentence regarding the Latter-day Saints in Lübeck in the months following the end of the war: "Many refugees from Selbongen, Königsberg, Stettin and Pomerania (in the East German Mission) made their way to Lübeck and the towns nearby, bringing perhaps as many as 400 members to Lübeck."[19]

As a German soldier, Reinhold Meyer was a priest in the Aaronic Priesthood. While away from home, he could never attend a Church meeting and had no scriptures to read. Only once did he come into contact with another German LDS soldier—a young man from Hamburg's St. Georg Branch—but the experience was not a positive one. "He acted like he didn't know me, but I had stayed in his home once during a district conference in Hamburg. I don't know why he didn't want anything to do with me."

In August 1945, Reinhard was put on a truck and driven to Lübeck. His family had never been told his whereabouts. "My mother had been praying for me. Several times bombs had fallen close to me and could have killed me, but I was protected. And I never fired my gun at the enemy. I never killed anybody."

IN MEMORIAM

The following members of the Lübeck Branch did not survive World War II:

Herbert Emil Derr b. Chemnitz, Sachsen, 22 Nov 1909; son of Emil Derr and Hulda Spindler; bp. 11 May 1918; conf. 11 May 1918; ord. deacon 17 Sep 1928; ord. teacher 16 Jan 1932; naval officer; k. Clisson, Nantes, 13 Aug 1944; bur. Pornichet, France (FHL microfilm 68799, no. 13; www.volksbund.de; CHL CR 275 8 2438, no. 813)

Henriette Maria Helene Dürrkop b. Lübeck 6 Sep 1870; dau. of Jürgen J. H. Dürrkop and Dorothea Horstman; bp. 28 Sep 1923; conf. 28 Sep 1923; m. 11 Nov 1894, Johann Heinrich Friedrich Klinkrad; d. 30 Jul 1944 (FHL microfilm 68799, no. 35)

Heinrich Gottfried Christoff Kock b. Mölln, Lauenburg, Schleswig-Holstein, 24 Apr 1874; son of Heinrich Adolf Kock and Dorothea K. Wilhelmine; bp.

27 Feb 1912; conf. 27 Feb 1912; m. Lütau, Lauenburg, Schleswig-Holstein, 23 Apr 1899, Johanna Marie Sophie Berlin; 10 children; d. heart ailment Lübeck 13 Apr 1944 (FHL microfilm 68799, no. 27; CHL CR 275 8 2438, no. 970; FHC microfilm 271380, 1930 and 1935 censuses; IGI)

Heinz Hugo Helmuth Kock b. Lübeck 29 Dec 1923; son of Heinrich Gottfried Christoff Kock and Johanna Marie Sophie Berlin; bp. 11 May 1934; conf. 4 Jun 1931; d. pneumonia POW camp Russia 17 Nov 1945 (FHL microfilm 68799, no. 116; FHC microfilm 271380, 1930 and 1935 censuses)

Helmut Ludwig Friedrich Heinrich Kock b. Lübeck 18 Feb 1916; son of Heinrich Gottfried Christoff Kock and Johanna Marie Sophie Berlin; bp. 27 Sep 1924; conf. 28 Sep 1924; rifleman; k. in battle Zambrow, Poland, 11 Sep 1939; bur. Mławka, Poland (FHL microfilm 68799, no. 30; CHL CR 275 8 2438, no. 44; www.volksbund.de; FHC microfilm 271380, 1930 and 1935 censuses; IGI)

Marianne Josepha Sophie Lenz b. Lübeck 3 Jan 1908; dau. of Thomas Lenz and Martha Frieda Georgine Krüger; bp. 17 Jun 1929; conf. 17 Jun 1929; m. 2 Mar or May 1936, Walter Spiegel; d. heart failure 23 Nov 1942 (FHL microfilm 68799, no. 42; CHL CR 275 8 2438, no. 817)

Anna Maria Elisabeth Lübcke b. Lehmrade, Lauenburg, Schleswig-Holstein, 31 Aug 1868; dau. of Johann H. Joachim Lübcke and Margaretha M. M. Hardekaper; bp. 1 Jun 1900; conf. 1 Jun 1900; m. 8 Jan 1892, Johann J. H. Burmeister; d. 28 Aug 1943 (FHL microfilm 68799, no. 11; CHL CR 275 8 2438, no. 553; FHL microfilm 25733, 1930 and 1935 censuses)

Dorothea Maria Elisa Agnes Franziska Mecker b. Lübeck 30 Mar 1863; dau. of Johann Joachim Heinrich Mecker and Johanna Regina Henriette Rosenhagen; bp. 8 Jul 1920; conf. 11 Jul 1920; m. Lübeck 5 Oct 1883, Johann Heinrich Friedrich Naevecke; eight children; d. cardiac asthma, angina, and old age 31 Dec 1944 (FHL microfilm 68799, no. 61; IGI)

Edwin Ewald Meyer b. Lübeck 26 Sep 1941; son of Ewald Johann Wilhelm Meyer and Martha H. O. Luth; d. heart attack 27 Nov 1941 or 1944 (FHL microfilm 68799, no. 151; IGI)

Gudrun Adelgund Genovefa Meyer b. Lübeck 9 Dec 1939; dau. of Walter Hans Bernhard Meyer and Cäcilie Sophie Frieda Kost; d. pneumonia Lübeck 5 May 1944 (FHL microfilm 68799, no. 148; CHL CR 275 8 2438, no. 422)

Hermann Johann Karl Meyer b. Eggerstorf, Grevesmühlen, Mecklenburg-Schwerin, 16 Mar 1876; son of Anna S. D. Meyer; bp. 12 Jul 1924; conf. 12 Jul 1924; ord. deacon 3 Sep 1925; ord. teacher 4 Nov 1934; ord. priest 17 May 1936; m. Grevesmühlen, Mecklenburg-Schwerin, 13 Oct 1899, Anna Marie Caroline Johanna Mathilde Tack; three children; 2m. 1 Nov 1919, Friede D. D. Busekist-Best; d. heart attack Lübeck 27 Apr 1941 (FHL microfilm 68799, no. 59; IGI)

Walter Hermann Julius Meyer b. Lübeck 16 Jan 1919; son of Hermann Johann Karl Meyer and Frieda Dorisa Dorothea Best; bp. 3 Jul 1931; conf. 3 Jul 1931; k. in battle Italy 3 Nov 1944 (FHL microfilm 68799, no. 102; CHL microfilm 2458, form 42 FP, pt. 37, 74–75; CHL CR 275 8 2438, no. 59; IGI)

Frieda Maria Berta Ollrogge b. Lübeck 12 Sep 1899; dau. of Heinrich Ollrogge and Dora Rickmann; bp. 3 Jul 1931; conf. 3 Jul 1931; m. 17 Mar 1922, Carl Friedrich Emil Schiemann; d. cramps 6 Sep 1939 (FHL microfilm 68799, no. 105; CHL CR 275 8 2438, no. 14)

Anna Luise L. Plückhalm b. Dambeck, Mecklenburg-Schwerin, 17 May 1914; dau. of Gustav Plückhalm and Martha Bähls; bp. 9 Apr 1928; conf. 9 Apr 1928; missing as of 1 Feb 1946 (FHL microfilm 68799, no. 150; CHL CR 275 8 2438, no. 436)

Heinrich Christian Ernst Rönpage b. Moisling, Lübeck, 28 Aug 1864; son of Hans Heinrich Ernst Rönpage and Sophie M. Maass; bp. 20 May 1910; conf. 20 May 1910; m. Lübeck 25 Jul 1891, Johanna Marie Sophia Faasch; eleven children; d. old age 19 Sep 1940 (FHL microfilm 68799, no. 66; CHL CR 275 8 2438, no. 636; IGI)

Margarethe Helene Wilhelmine Rönpage b. Lübeck 14 Jan 1893; dau. of Heinrich Christian Ernst Rönpage and Johanna Maria Sophia Faasch; bp. 30 Jun 1910; conf. 30 Jun 1910; m. 10 Jun 1915, Ludwig A. J. Wegner; d. 4 Oct 1945 (FHL microfilm 68799, no. 88; IGI)

Friedrich Adolf August Sass b. Lübeck 13 May 1910; son of August Wilhelm Hermann Sass and Frieda Sophie Dorothea Stephan; bp. 3 Jul 1931; conf. 3 Jul 1931; ord. deacon 11 Jan 1932; ord. teacher 7 May 1933; ord. priest 21 Jun 1933; ord. elder 16 Apr 1935; m. Lübeck 23 Sep 1932, Hedwig Wilma Minna Johanna Ront; three children; lieutenant; k. in battle Remiremont, Vosges, France, 12 Oct 1944; bur. Andilly, France (J. Sass; www.volksbund.de; CHL CR 275 8, no. 2443, no. 103; CHL CR 275 8 2438, no. 17; photo, IGI)

Carl Friedrich Emil Schiemann b. Grevesmühlen, Mecklenburg-Schwerin, 30 Aug 1890; son of August Schiemann and Dora Burmeister; bp. 3 Jul 1931; conf. 3 Jul 1931; m. 17 Mar 1922, Frieda Maria Berta Ollrogge; d. stomach surgery 19 Dec 1944 (FHL microfilm 68799, no. 104; CHL CR 275 8 2458, 496; CHL CR 275 8 2438, no. 13)

Emil Friederich Vollrath Steinfeldt b. Lübeck 11 Sep 1908; son of Johannes Heinrich Joachim Steinfeldt and Hedwig Wilhelmine Charlotte Bohnsack; bp. 24 Sep 1921; conf. 24 Sep 1921; m. Grete Hansen (div.); k. in battle Russia 27 Oct 1942 (FHL microfilm 68799, no. 77; CHL CR 275 8, no. 519)

Notes

1. Presiding Bishopric, "Financial, Statistical, and Historical Reports of Wards, Stakes, and Missions, 1884–1955," 257, CHL CR 4 12.
2. Leonard J. Bingham, autobiography, 125, CHL MS 18074. See also West German Mission branch directory, 1939, CHL LR 10045 11.
3. Reinhold Meyer, interview by the author, Salt Lake City, November 3, 2006.
4. West German Mission branch directory, 1939.
5. Wilfried Süfke, telephone interview with the author in German, February 16, 2009; summarized in English by Judith Sartowski.
6. Lübeck city archive.
7. Jürgen Sass, autobiography (unpublished, about 1985).
8. The other baptismal fonts were in the rooms of the Essen and Stuttgart Branches of the Ruhr District, also in the West German Mission.
9. Sass, autobiography.
10. Fred Warncke et al., *Geschichte der Gemeinde Luebeck, 1880–1997* (typescript, 1997), 2, CHL LR 5093 21.
11. There is no explanation for meetings being held at this location. None of the branch leaders listed in 1939 lived in Reinfeld.
12. Lübeck Branch history, 3.
13. The family believes that Brother Sass was awarded the Iron Cross for successfully delivering the message under hazardous conditions.
14. Jürgen Sass, interview by the author, May 25, 2006, Ogden, UT.
15. Sass, interview.
16. Sass, autobiography.
17. As cited in Sass, autobiography.
18. Lübeck city archive.
19. Lübeck Branch history, 5.

St. Georg Branch

As the largest of three branches in the largest city in the West German Mission, the St. Georg Branch was located in the heart of Hamburg, a city of 1.7 million people. With 413 members in 1939, the St. Georg Branch had the largest population in the mission, followed by Nuremberg. It had an outstanding number of elders (thirty-nine) and fifty-four more men and boys who held the Aaronic Priesthood. This was indeed a very strong branch in which nearly all programs of the Church were running at high efficiency when the war broke out.

St. Georg Branch[1]	1939
Elders	39
Priests	13
Teachers	13
Deacons	28
Other Adult Males	54
Adult Females	214
Male Children	28
Female Children	24
Total	413

The location of the meeting rooms was also fortuitous—just a few short blocks from the main railway station and the city hall. Branch historian Hans Gürtler described the rooms at Besenbinderhof 13a in these words:

> How happy we were when the Redding Printing Co. rented us some rooms on the main floor that was not only much larger [than our previous venue] but also isolated and offered us total peace and quiet. . . . The date was January 30, 1910. This would be our location for thirty-five [thirty-three] years. . . . Just before the war we were able to rent small rooms above and next to the main hall. A foyer with a cloak room was added. The crown jewel was the kitchen that was built in the basement."[2]

The entry to the rooms in building 13a was from the street called Besenbinderhof. The Saints went through a portal in the main building, then into an alley and down the so-called Hexenberg (Witch's Mountain) perhaps one hundred feet to the door of the building. The setting outside could not have resembled a traditional German church in any way.

Hertha Schönrock (born 1923) recalled a sign that indicated the presence of the branch in that building and that a baptismal font was constructed on top of the stage in 1940. "It was very rare and we were blessed to have one."[3] Ingo Zander (born 1934), a son of the branch president, was baptized in that font in 1942.[4] The Zander family lived in the suburb of Hamm and needed a good half-hour to get to church with the streetcar and on foot (a trip the family made twice each Sunday). Hertha Schönrock was impressed by the emphasis on reverence in the meetings. "If we came late, they wouldn't let us in. The doors were closed to promote reverence."

The branch presidency in 1939 consisted of Arthur Zander, Franz Jakobi, and Walter Bankowski. Erich Gellersen was the supervisor of the Sunday School; Erich Leiss, the leader of the young men; Paula Schnibbe, the leader of the young women; and Anna Ruthwill, the leader of the Relief Society. The branch directory of August 1939 does not list a leader of the Primary organization (or a meeting time for that matter), even though there were fifty-two children in the branch at the time.[5] Eyewitnesses estimated the average attendance at one hundred to one hundred and fifty persons on a typical Sunday (perhaps one-third of the registered members).

Sunday School began at 10 a.m. and sacrament meeting at 7 p.m. The Relief Society and priesthood groups met on Monday evenings at 7:30 and the MIA met on Wednesdays at the same time. The meeting schedule likewise includes times for a genealogy class and rehearsals for the branch choir and the branch orchestra. Special entertainment was scheduled for a Friday "at least once each month," according to the branch directory of 1939.[6]

Living in the suburb of Wilhelmsburg (across the Elbe River to the south), the Schönrock family had a distance of about four miles to negotiate four times each Sunday if they were to attend all of the meetings of the St. Georg Branch. According to daughter Hertha, "It looked like geese were marching in a line when our entire family was on the way to church. Sometimes it was too expensive for all of us to take the train or the bus to church. When we were older, we spent the time between meetings in the homes of friends."

Hertha enjoyed her experience as a member of the League of German Girls, but she was not an admirer of Adolf Hitler. "I saw him once with my League group when he came to Hamburg, but I never considered him anyone special." Hertha's father, Wilhelm Schönrock, was a communist who sometimes went to a neighbor's apartment to listen to BBC broadcasts. As an electrician, he had worked on the new battleship *Bismarck* and had even participated in the maiden voyage of that famous vessel.

"My life changed drastically in 1938 with the Night of Broken Glass," recalled Karl-Heinz Schnibbe (born 1924). "All of the Jewish businesses were destroyed. I was very angry and decided to leave the Hitler Youth."[7] Soon thereafter, he was called into the Nazi Party headquarters in Hamburg and accused of being a communist (his father was actually a Social Democrat, almost as bad as a communist in the opinion of the Nazis). Karl-Heinz was relieved to be informed that the Hitler Youth no longer had room for him.

Several eyewitnesses recall seeing police officials sitting on the back row during meetings. "We knew who they were," claimed Erwin Frank (born 1923). The men never said anything and never interrupted or tried to cancel the meetings. The Mormon Church apparently meant little to the city government at the time. In general, the neighbors of LDS families in Hamburg also knew little about their Church activities. Erwin's parents had eight children and were interested only in the Church, not politics. According to Erwin, "Back then the big thing was the Nazis and the communists and neither party appealed to us."[8]

"Both of my parents had been out of work," recalled Gerd Fricke (born 1923), "but Hitler turned things around. When my parents found work, they supported him at first." Gerd's father was not active in the Church, but the fact that he joined the SA (the party's organization for men) did not mean that he belonged to the Nazi Party, according to Gerd. During the first years of the war, Gerd worked in a factory where parts for submarines were produced.

Fig. 1. The main meeting room at Besenbinderhof 13a was probably the largest used by any branch in Germany in 1939. The room accommodated up to five hundred people. The baptismal font was constructed on the rostrum (behind the photographer) in 1940. (I. Gellerson Long)

"Back then, we teenagers still found ways to have fun. We were involved in sports and other entertainment. It wasn't all deadly serious."[9]

Just before the war, the family of Richard and Rosalie Pruess of Rahlstedt owned a three-wheeled automobile. According to daughter Lieselotte (born 1926), her father drove as many as six of the family members to church in that vehicle. Rahlstedt is a northeast suburb of Hamburg and fully seven miles from the branch rooms at Besenbinderhof. As a Primary girl, Lieselotte had actually made the trip alone on the bus and the streetcar many times in the mid-1930s. "When I was eight and nine, I took my little sisters too because they begged to go."[10]

Richard Pruess was anything but a Nazi and refused to use the standard greeting of "Heil Hitler!" Nor was he ashamed to receive a Jewish guest in his home. Salomon Schwarz, a member of the Barmbek Branch, visited the Pruess family on occasion—in fact, often enough that the neighbors were aware of him. It was possibly the general respect for Brother Pruess that prevented neighbors (some of whom were "good Nazis") from reporting him to the police for entertaining a Jew in his home. In Lieselotte's recollection, her father removed the *Juden verboten* sign from the church on one occasion; he was accustomed to saying that those who persecute Jews will be punished.

Otto Berndt (born 1929) was inducted into the Jungvolk just months before the war began. He recalled:

> I liked the Hitler Youth because I had the opportunity to go places which I would have never had. We learned the Hitler way and had meetings every week. It actually was indoctrination of the highest order but we were all too dumb to realize what was being done with the youth. After school, we had to assemble and sing the German national anthem and the Horst Wessel song. We did a lot of marching and singing in formation.[11]

Fig. 2. Richard Pruess drove several members of his family to church in this three-wheeled vehicle. (H. Pruess Mueller)

The outbreak of war was not much of a surprise to Erwin Frank and his family. "It got to the point that Hitler didn't seem to be satisfied with what he had. As soon as he marched into one country, he was ready for the next." Erwin's prime concern in the fall of 1939 was not the war; he was only sixteen and had begun his apprenticeship as a galvanizing specialist. He needed four years to prepare for his examination, but his program was interrupted in 1940 by a call to the Reichsarbeitsdienst.

The war began when Karl-Heinz Schnibbe was a young apprentice. He recalled his reaction to the news:

> We heard that Germany had attacked Poland; it was announced over the radio as "special news." I was young and didn't give the matter much thought. When the war started, nobody believed that Germany could lose. I thought that Germany could do anything she wanted because the country was strong and Hitler was a strong personality. Poland was conquered in two and a half weeks, which was unbelievable. I must say though that the older people were worried.

The announcement of the war against Poland also appeared in all German newspapers. Karl Schönrock (born 1929) recalled reading about it as he delivered his newspapers one day:

> We delivered our papers in the afternoon after school (my sister and my brother also had paper routes). . . . I had thirty or forty people to deliver newspapers to. I wasn't scared that Germany was going to war. I felt it was somewhat justified because of an announcement that some Polish troops had attacked the radio station in the [German] city of Gleiwitz. Later on, of course, after the war, they said those were German [criminals] disguised as Polish soldiers.[12]

Werner Schönrock (born 1927) was in the Jungvolk when the war began. He recalled:

> I was a member of the Jungvolk as well as the Hitler Youth later on and I liked going there. In my free time, I liked being involved in sports, especially gymnastics and handball. Because the sports field was right next to our home, we were able to do so much there. We were still able to do all those things during the war though the circumstances got more hazardous.[13]

Werner's athletic field took on a different role as the air raids over Hamburg became more frequent: antiaircraft batteries were set up there, and eventually two bunkers for civilians were erected.

Ingeborg Thymian (born 1930) was baptized in the Elbe River on March 16, 1940. She had wanted to be baptized at the age of eight (two years earlier), but there was a problem. She recalled, "Because I had braided my hair that day, it was always floating on the water. After the third unsuccessful attempt, they told me that they had to baptize me at another date." The successful baptism was conducted despite a different obstacle—ice in the Elbe. A hole was cut in the ice, and Ingeborg was baptized. "We, as children, were always scared that somebody would get sick in the cold water, but Heavenly Father protected us."[14]

The Kinderlandverschickung (children's rural evacuation program) took Astrid Koch (born 1932) away from her family in Hamburg when she was only eight years old. She shared the following recollections:

> When we got to Pulsnitz [in Saxony], there was a big hall in a school and they had something for us to eat. People who wanted to take children in came there and picked out the children. I didn't

> know where I was going. [The people who chose me] were the Hardtmanns; they thought it might be interesting to raise a young child, so they decided on doing that. My twin sisters were also in that town; they were four years older, they were twelve. They went to a different family. My people were very nice, and the people that owned that house [the Erichs] had a daughter my age.[15]

Walter and Gertrud Menssen had married just before the war and were parents by January 1939. Walter (born 1913) was drafted just months after the war began. Gertrud (born 1919) was fortunate to find a nice apartment in his absence. It was there that their second child, a daughter named Edeltraut, was born in May 1941. Because Walter had always wanted a garden, Gertrud found and leased a plot of land measuring sixty by ninety feet in the Hamburg suburb of Horn. They constructed a one-room cottage on the property and spent most of June and July of 1941 there, despite the rain that fell nearly every day that summer. Little did they know that this would become their principal residence in a few years.[16]

Walter Menssen had spent several months in the army in early 1939 and was called in again at the end of that year. When the war began, the Luftwaffe needed men to serve in units all over Europe. Brother Menssen led a charmed life as a soldier, beginning with an assignment just a few miles from his home. He was soon working in the comfort of an office while he watched thousands of air force men be assigned to faraway stations. His health was excellent, with the exception of a short stay in the infirmary. This may have been the reason that he was given the classification of "conditionally fit for duty," which meant that he would not be assigned to locations beyond the borders of Germany.[17]

Werner Schönrock finished his public schooling in 1940 and hoped to join the war effort as a navy man. To his disappointment, he was too small. "They sent me home and told me that I should eat more." A few months later, he reported again and was sent for aquatic training that would render him more fit for duty. This time he became ill, however, and was hospitalized for three months with tuberculosis. It seemed that he was not to serve in Hitler's military.

Fig. 3. Lieselotte and Richard Pruess in the uniforms of the League of German Girls and Hitler Youth respectively in about 1941. (H. Pruess Mueller)

Like hundreds of other LDS men of the West German Mission, Hans Gürtler (born 1901) hoped against hope that he would not be drafted. Already a husband and father of four, he received his call to the Wehrmacht in March 1941. He was first stationed in Harburg, a southern suburb of Hamburg; but in late 1941, he was sent to central Germany for additional training. A man of letters, he was quite opposed to Hitler's regime and expressed this in private by arranging with a comrade to change the wording of the soldier's oath: "Otto Schmidt and I had promised each other that we would not repeat the [words of the] oath correctly, but rather to pronounce a curse on Adolf Hitler, which we then did. Of course, our pious wish went unheard among the loud voices around us, which we wished would happen. After all, we didn't want to cut our own throats." His career as a soldier began most peacefully. For example, during a stay in the Polish city of Posen, he was able to attend a theater play three times in ten days.[18]

Therese Gürtler (born 1929) recalled how her father, Hans, was always writing poems. As an opponent of the Hitler regime, he even wrote poems against the state and the war. Therese and her siblings were aware of this but of course never mentioned it outside of the home. She did remember that one man in the branch found out and threatened to report Brother Gürtler to the Gestapo. Apparently the fact that Hans Gürtler was soon drafted satisfied the man, and the anti-Hitler poet was not denounced.[19]

During the many minor air raids of the early war years, Therese Gürtler spent a lot of time with her family and their neighbors in their basement shelter. As she later explained:

> We usually would bring some games down with us, and it was always something that didn't really scare me. But when you heard the sirens before—when the air raid started, when they were warning us—that was a sound that was so eerie and so frightful. That's really the only thing that I remember being scared of. But for some reason, I was never afraid that we would be bombed, or that we would be hurt, or that we would lose our home. I guess, when you grow up in a family that is living the gospel and believing, there is a feeling of security and safety that is kind of indestructible. You're taken care of by your parents, and you know you'll be fine.

Most LDS children in the Jungvolk told of positive experiences, but that was not the case with Werner Sommerfeld (born 1929); to him, the Jungvolk program was anything but entertaining. He provided the following description:

> Boys of 12 and 13 were taken for intense military training. I can still remember the camps with the ground covered with gravel, where we had to crawl on our elbows from one side of the compound to the other, while they fired bursts of live ammunition over our heads. Many young boys were crying and calling out for their mothers. Some raised a little too high and were injured or killed. . . . My group became trained in anti-tank warfare. We carried bazookas (Panzerfaust) and balanced them under our arms to aim at oncoming tanks. We were expendable.[20]

Karl Schönrock recalled his experience in the Jungvolk, where membership was required of boys and girls when they turned ten: "They mostly indoctrinated us and we were encouraged to read *Mein Kampf* and that was all. As a matter of fact, I still have the book. They didn't give us a copy; I had to buy it. I was maybe twelve when I bought it, and I actually read it, but I didn't understand much of it at that age."

When the air raids over Hamburg became more frequent and intense, the city government required that watchmen be stationed in all larger buildings. Harald Fricke (born 1926) recalled standing guard in the church rooms with his father. Their responsibility was to watch for and report any bomb damage and to fight any fire that might start in the meeting rooms. After each attack, if nothing was out of order at the church, they hurried home to determine the status of their apartment and their family.[21]

Fig. 4. The economy edition of Adolf Hitler's book Mein Kampf *(My Struggle) was seen on many coffee tables in Germany during the National Socialist era. (K. Schoenrock)*

Perhaps the most challenged people in Germany during the war were the young mothers who were left to raise their children alone. Such was the condition of Maria Niemann (born 1911) who dearly missed her husband, Henri, while he served on the Eastern Front for four years. With her young son, Henry (born 1936), she did her best to keep order in life. She recalled:

> We cried for [my husband] and always [awaited] a letter that he was still alive and everything was fine. So, for him it wasn't fine, but I was calmed down and I was happy to hear that he was still alive. . . . He came home for [leave] sometimes and then I was happy to have him for a day and off went his soldier clothes and [on] his private clothes and then I always reminded him . . . that he should take his [identification] papers with him or he would go to jail.[22]

Hertha Schönrock was a spirited young lady who worked in a textile factory. The bombing raids carried out by the British over Hamburg angered her so much "that I was close to enlisting in the army. I sometimes wished I was a boy so that I could do more."[23] Her sister, Waltraud, worked in a different factory where clothing and gowns were produced.

Figs. 5 and 6. Scenes from the St. Georg Branch in happier days. (H. Pruess Mueller)

Johann Schnibbe had been called to be a traveling elder during the early years of the war. He often visited branches in other cities as part of this assignment. Another aspect of his service was visiting four families in the St. Georg Branch. He took his son, Karl-Heinz, along for those visits. As Karl-Heinz recalled, "We either took the streetcar or walked. If nobody was home, my father insisted that we go again the next day and that's what we did. Nobody had a telephone. We were assigned to visit four families and it took about three hours to visit them all."

Like most of the Saints in the West German Mission in the early years of the war, the Richard Pruess family of Rahlstedt sat in the basement of their home while the air-raid sirens wailed and the bombs fell; the public shelter was too far away from their home. According to little Hilde (born 1934), the basement had been reinforced by large wood beams and concrete blocks were stacked outside in front of the basement window.[24]

The government program of evacuating school children from cities under attack took Hilde away from her family several times for a total of nearly two years. She spent more than one year in the southern German town of Wunschendorf. She was home again for a while, then sent back to Wunschendorf. On another occasion, she was sent to Thorn in eastern Germany where she lived in a school along with refugee families. Thorn was a long way from her family and her church.

In August 1941, Erwin Frank was drafted into the national labor force and stationed in France. It was there that he enjoyed a rare privilege, a get-together with his friend Paul Mücke, another member of the St. Georg Branch. The two spent only one afternoon together before Paul returned to his unit. At the completion of the six-month assignment, Erwin returned to Hamburg to the same message thousands of young men received just days after they completed the Reichsarbeitsdienst tenure: a draft notice. Paul was instructed to report for service in the Luftwaffe. It was January 1942.

Eyewitnesses generally agree that several Latter-day Saints in the St. Georg Branch were also ardent members of the National Socialist Party. According to historian Hans Gürtler:

> Essentially all possible political opinions were represented in the branch. It was especially painful that we had National Socialists in our midst—people who idolized Hitler. Despite general caution, we had some disturbances now and then. Even today, we can still recall the negative feelings we had when prayers were said at the pulpit for that Satanic charlatan. Some even dared to put the swastika flag in our hallowed meeting rooms and to use the Hitler salute. On the other hand, it can and should be noted that many of our members only saw the positive aspects of Hitler's regime and could not see behind the scenes. . . . One humiliating concession to the government was a necessary evil—the exclusion of Jews from our meetings.[25]

Branch president Arthur Zander was considered by many eyewitnesses a devout National Socialist. Although most claimed that he did not give political speeches in Church meetings, they did recall that he interrupted meetings so that Hitler's speeches could be played over the radio for the Saints to hear. Indeed the disagreements about politics may have been more distinct in this branch than in any other in the West German Mission. Ingo Zander described his father as "a very dynamic, magnetic person."[26] Perhaps President Zander was also very decisive, because many eyewitnesses identified him as the man who posted the sign "Juden verboten" at the front door and denied entry to such members as Salomon Schwarz, a man with an undetermined degree of Jewish blood. (Brother Schwarz was then taken in by the neighboring Barmbek Branch, where no such sign was posted.) In contrast, some eyewitnesses suggested that President Zander posted the sign in order to curry favor with the local police authorities; he may have believed that without the sign, the branch would be forced to close down entirely.

Fig. 7. "Jews are not allowed!" Signs of this variety were posted all over Germany to make life impossible for Jews who had not yet left the country. (G. Blake)[27]

Like so many children in Germany during the war, young Otto Berndt became an expert on air raids. His recollections are a combination of religious and practical knowledge:

> Whenever we had to go to the bunker because of an air raid, we would all kneel in prayer and ask for protection from what was to come. An air raid would always last two hours. You could set your clock by it. The British bombed during the night and the Americans bombed during the day, so that there wasn't much time to do much of anything [else]. I don't remember being comforted by prayer, but now that I'm older and it's all over with I know that "somebody up there loves me."[28]

Branch historian Hans Gürtler was quite mild in his comments regarding Helmut Hübener, Karl-Heinz Schnibbe, and Rudi Wobbe, the three teenagers tried and convicted of treason in 1942.[29] He referred to their illegal actions as

> the saddest experience in the branch. [These] three younger brethren had listened to foreign radio broadcasts and had copied them using the branch mimeograph machine, then distributed the flyers. It was a serious challenge for the district president [Otto Berndt] to prevent the branch from suffering the worst imaginable punishment. How often the existence of the branch seemed to hang by a thread![30]

The reactions of the Saints to the arrest and trial of the three Aaronic Priesthood holders who defied the government were mixed and emotional (see their story in the Hamburg District chapter). Karl-Heinz Schnibbe recalled that one older man in the branch told him to his face that "he would have shot me personally if he knew what we had done." Most eyewitnesses stated that while they felt sorry for the boys when they were punished, the case had placed the three Hamburg branches in serious jeopardy with the police; the boys were foolhardy to undertake any such resistance and the fact that they used church equipment to support their treasonous activities was inexcusable. The membership records show that Helmut Hübener, Karl-Heinz Schnibbe, and Rudi Wobbe were all excommunicated from the Church shortly after their trial in Berlin (an action that was reversed by the Church's First Presidency a few years later).[31]

After a full year in Saxony, Astrid Koch was returned to her family in Hamburg. However, she had been treated so well in Pulsnitz that she asked her parents to send her back to her host family: "The first thing I told my parents was: 'I want to go back to Onkel and Tante (I called them that) because I loved being there.'" The Kochs sent her back in the summer of 1942 and Astrid lived there until 1946.

By the summer of 1942, Erwin Frank was on the island of Sicily where he worked as a radio operator reporting flights of enemy aircraft toward German positions. He was scheduled to be sent across the Mediterranean Sea to a station in North Africa, but Allied forces gained the upper hand in the region and the move was canceled. Subsequent transfers took him to the islands of Sardinia, Corsica, and Elba.

The air raids that plagued Hamburg were already taking their toll on the populace in 1942—if not in high death counts, then at least emotionally. Gerd Fricke recalled rejecting instructions to go down into the basement when the sirens wailed one night:

> I was too tired to go downstairs, so I stayed in my bed. My mother, my brother, and my sister all went down. I was lying in bed when the roof of our house was blown off. I wasn't fully dressed, so I ran downstairs in a shirt and pants. While we waited in the basement, a bomb fell into our apartment and everything burned, but we got out of the basement safely. That was the first time we lost everything and it happened again [in 1943].

Walter Menssen once returned to his quarters in a Hamburg suburb to find his commanding officer sitting in a chair, reading in one of his American church books. The officer asked him point-blank if he was a Mormon, and the answer was unhesitatingly affirmative. "That is the only reason you are in this office," was the man's response, "because I can trust you." Walter recalled having taken the officer back to his quarters after too many drinks at social affairs on several occasions and knew that statement to be true. The officer then recounted his experiences in the United States and declared that the greatest man he had ever known was one Heber J. Grant, whom he met in a bank in New York City. "He invited me to Salt Lake, and I stayed in his home for two weeks. I was driven around in Salt Lake and saw everything. That is the reason you are here." Once again, a soldier of the LDS Church had been rewarded for living a life of high standards.

Indeed, Walter was tempted on several occasions by comrades who wished to see him deny his standards and smoke cigarettes or drink alcohol. They offered him money to smoke and even spiked his soda drinks, "but a Mormon can smell that alcohol a mile away," he claimed. He used his cigarette rations to pay other soldiers to take over his duty assignments so that he could attend church with his family. "In other words, keeping the Word of Wisdom helped me quite a bit."[32]

Little children seldom understood the reasons for air raids over Hamburg, but they did not enjoy being rousted out of bed in the middle of the night or sitting in dark and cold basements and shelters surrounded by terrifying noises. Regarding the possibility of being hurt or killed under those circumstances, Ingo Zander's observations are typical: "I probably didn't give much thought to dying, but you wouldn't totally dismiss [the possibility] either. I remember once when a classmate didn't show up for school, I went to where he lived. Where his house had been, there was a crater as deep as the house had been high and nobody heard anything anymore of him."

Many children in Germany's largest cities enjoyed the hobby of collecting pieces of shrapnel from the streets on the mornings after air raids. Karl Schönrock of the St. Georg Branch was one of those collectors, as he later explained: "We collected [the shrapnel] from the antiaircraft shells that exploded [above our homes]. In school we compared who had the most and the best-looking ones." Sometimes, Karl and his siblings would go outside during air raids and watch the British flares descend from the sky and the shells of the antiaircraft guns attempting to shoot down the enemy airplanes. With metal raining from the sky, they soon learned that it was better to stay inside during such dangerous activity.

Ingrid Lübke (born 1933) had distinctly sad memories of the air war over Hamburg: "My school was next to a POW camp. One day we had an alarm so we left the school to go to a shelter. When we came back, the school yard was full of bodies [of prisoners] and they even hung in the branches of the trees. It was awful!"[33] Later in the war, she experienced a different type of very personal danger: "Sometimes planes intentionally aimed at us children when we were playing. Once, we ran to the next house that we saw and hid there to be safe. Another time, I was playing outside the shelter and a plane shot at me; [the pilot] saw me and I even saw him and I fell down, but nothing happened to me."

The loss of the meeting rooms in 1943 at Besenbinderhof was painful and very inconvenient. Still very intact, the rooms were needed for more important purposes in the opinion of the city government. After thirty-three years of meetings under what were likely the finest conditions for Latter-day Saints in all of Germany and Austria, the rental contract was canceled and the branch was required to remove the Church property from the building. Historian Hans Gürtler had this to say about the move: "There is no reason to seek the actual cause and perpetrators of the expulsion. At that time, our Church simply did not have the respect it enjoys today [1969] and anybody who did not like us could easily throw stones in our path."[34] The meeting rooms were confiscated in the spring of 1943, and the members were then required to make their way to the home of the Altona Branch—about three miles to the west across town.

Arthur Zander may have wondered what his role was to be as a branch president without a branch, but the Wehrmacht solved this problem by drafting him in 1943. With the destruction of the family's apartment in July 1943, Sister Zander took their three sons and headed for southern Germany. Like so many other families in the St. Georg Branch, the Zanders were absent from town for the rest of the war.

Like tens of thousands of other German schoolchildren, Otto Berndt and his entire school class of thirty-five boys were evacuated to the Czech town of Kubice to spare them the dangers of a Hamburg under constant assault from the sky. For two years, the boys lived in a hotel next to the railroad station in that farming community. Their teacher was with them and was what Otto called "a good egg. We weren't expected to work like slaves. In the morning we had our regular school." For two years, the boys stayed in Kubice. Otto was visited once by his father; otherwise he was totally isolated from his hometown, his family, and his church.[35]

In August 1943, homeless Gertrud Menssen and her two children were sent to Bavaria where they were taken in as refugees on a farm. At first, the host family gave them poor accommodations and treated them as strangers. The guests could not understand the local dialect, suffered from lice ("how sickening!"), and were very homesick for Hamburg, but "the hardest thing was that we were so far away from the church." Eventually, Gertrud learned that the LDS branch in Munich was within reach; a journey of one hour on foot and ninety minutes or more by train took her to the Bavarian capital, where she enjoyed meeting with the Saints a few times. "[The trip] took us the whole day and that was hard with little children and me expecting our third."[36]

Figs. 8 and 9. The Pruess home in Rahlstedt before the bombing (left) and after reconstruction in 1944 (right). The top two floors could not be rebuilt at the time. (L. Pruess Schmidt)

Harald Fricke was evacuated with his family (his mother, brother, and sister) to the part of Poland that had been Germany before 1918. He recalled attending church meetings in the nearby branches of Elbing and Danzig—two cities that could be reached by train from Marienwerder where the family was temporarily housed. "We somehow found out where all the branches met," he recalled. After five or six weeks, Sister Fricke took her children home to Hamburg, where they were assigned another apartment.

As a new recruit, Gerd Fricke went through basic training for six months near Bremen. Just before Christmas 1943, he was transferred to France, but never moved farther west than Luxembourg. He soon became yet another LDS soldier who was harassed because of his health standard: "One time, I was tempted by the other soldiers to drink alcohol. I said that I wouldn't do it, and they wanted to pour it down my throat. I resisted and they later said that I was pretty tough and really knew what I wanted."

The family of Emil and Lilly Koch lost everything they owned in the firebombings of 1943. According to daughter Lilly, the family left town and found a place to live near Dresden in Saxony. However, Brother Koch was a city employee, and he was required to return to Hamburg to work. His daughter Lilly went with him because she had a job in a factory where airplane engine parts were made. The two first lived with relatives, but once they found their own apartment, the rest of the family could return from Saxony to be with them.

Lilly Koch described some of the challenges of being an adolescent during World War II:

> Being a teenager during the war was not a nice situation. I remember that I turned 18 years old during the war and was astonished that many things were already forbidden—like going dancing. That is why we often felt like we were losing contact with our friends and especially with the other members of the Church, because we did not know where all the others were and what we could do. Everything was always destroyed.[37]

The family of former district president Alwin Brey had lost everything when their apartment house burned in July 1943. Brother Brey then took his family to Bamberg in southern Germany where they found a small room to live in. Because there was no branch in that city, Frieda Brey and her children were isolated from the Church. Soon after their arrival in Bamberg, daughter Irma (born 1926) was called to serve a Pflichtjahr on a farm. She lived and worked there with many other girls her age who assumed work normally done by the men who had been drafted. Irma was very homesick but was at least safe from the terrible attacks on Hamburg.[38]

Fred Zwick went with his mother to Polzin, in Pomerania, after their apartment was destroyed. However, his father came on leave and insisted that they return to Hamburg. He told them that the Russians might be invading that area and that he had heard what Russians did to women and children. Back in Hamburg, the only place they could find to live in was a little cottage on a garden property belonging to Fred's grandparents. He described the structure in these words:

> It wasn't too small of a building. It was livable. It had a little store room and a room for a portable potty, and then a kitchen. We had our water pump; the pipe went out through the wall into a shed and then there was a stove in it and a table of course and windows. Next to it was kind of a living room and next to that was a really small bedroom. There was plenty of room for three people.[39]

Waltraud Schönrock's life took an early turn toward adulthood when she became engaged to fellow Latter-day Saint Gerhard Kunkel at the age of seventeen. She was eighteen when they were married on September 25, 1943, and she offered this description of the event:

> It was a simple wedding. Our mother prepared a small dinner at home and that was all. We got married in the civil registry office [in city hall] first, and then we went to church on Sunday. . . . I had a white dress and even a veil. [Gerhard] returned to his unit a few days after our wedding. We didn't have a honeymoon.[40]

After the Koch family lost everything they owned in the firebombings, they traveled to Pulsnitz and were taken in where Astrid had been for more than two years. It was nice for the family to be together again, but that experience was short-lived. Brother Koch was required by his employer (the city of Hamburg) to return to work. The rest of the family stayed until after Christmas and returned to Hamburg in early 1944. Astrid remained with her host family for two more years. In Pulsnitz, she joined with her Lutheran hosts in attending church, and they even wanted her to be baptized as a Lutheran, because her LDS baptism had been postponed. Astrid eventually learned the local dialect and felt very much at home in her Saxon refuge.

Part of Astrid Koch's Pulsnitz experience was her membership in the Jungvolk program. She fondly recalled helping make wood toys for children, for example: "We had to sand them and paint them. And we went on outings and field trips, and we collected magazines from local people. Those were for the wounded so they had something to read in the hospitals. They made half of our school into a hospital. When I was a member of the school choir, we went over to the hospital and sang for them at Christmas."

Fig. 10. The Zwick family acquired this small garden house just before the war and lived in it after they were bombed out. (F. Zwick)

After the horrific summer of 1943, Maria Niemann took her children north to the town of Hude in Schleswig-Holstein. They found a very pleasant apartment there; but according to her son Henry, they had no contact with the church for the next four years. Maria continued to have health crises and was in the hospital again when her husband came home on leave. Although she recognized the hand of God in saving her from the destruction of Hamburg, she was without her husband for four years beginning in 1944. It was an especially discouraging time, during which her father-in-law died. Regarding her absent husband, her prayer often included the same plea: "Heavenly Father, don't let him [have to] kill anybody."[41]

In early 1943, Werner Sommerfeld was sent away from the dangerous life of Hamburg residents. Placed on a farm in Hungary, he was fed by Germans and for the first time in recent memory, he had "enough to eat for an entire year." After a year of life in an area where there was essentially no war, he rejoined his family, but not in Hamburg. His mother had taken the children to Jungbuch, her hometown in Czechoslovakia. Werner was still a small teenager and thus avoided being taken away into military service; he was free to begin an apprenticeship in plumbing. It was about that time that Arthur Sommerfeld was drafted and sent to Russia (despite the severe burns he suffered in July 1943) and that their father, Gustav, was sent to France, where he soon became a prisoner of the British and was moved to England.[42]

Anna Marie Frank (born 1919) had lost her apartment on July 28, 1943, and her two-year-old daughter, Marianne, had disappeared in the smoke and flames of the burning city. Sister Frank was then evacuated to eastern Germany with her son Rainer (only fourteen months old). While there, another disaster befell the family when Rainer contracted diphtheria and died in April 1944. Bereft of both of her children, Anna Marie returned to Hamburg and found a job in a factory and mill where she sewed bags for flour. She worked there through the end of the war and for some time afterward. It was not until 1946 that she learned that her husband, Willy Frank, was a prisoner of war in Yugoslavia. She wrote to him every week from then until his release in 1948.[43]

"After we were bombed out [and lost everything], we lived in the garden plot community," recalled Ingrid Lübke. Her description continues:

> We didn't have electricity, water, or a bathroom. We got our water from a pump, but in the winter it froze and we had to take hot water and pour

> it over the pump so that we could get at least some water. It was also far away and [the bucket] was heavy to carry. When it came to food, it was sparse, but we had an advantage because we had some garden land around our little house. I remember my grandmother telling me one morning: "Look, there are two slices of bread, a little bit of sugar, and some black coffee. That is all I have for today." We ate rutabaga and we ground fish heads so that we could eat them.

Gertrud Menssen's third child, a son named Wolfgang, was born in Bavaria in February 1944. Thinking that Hamburg had been sufficiently destroyed to no longer merit the enemy's attention, Gertrud longed to return and prayed and fasted many times for a confirmation of that plan of action. Her husband had been transferred to a town close to Hamburg and learned that his family could apply for a modular cottage that could be erected on his garden property (to replace the original hut that had since been destroyed). By March, their application was granted and their new cottage constructed. According to Gertrud, "The house was great—it had a big family kitchen and one bedroom just barely big enough for two sets of bunk beds (from a bombed-out shelter) and one crib which was a miracle to find. . . . No plumbing, of course—outhouse only."

Soldier and staff member Walter Menssen was often able to spend weekends with his family. Unfortunately they were still not safe from enemy attacks and he soon dug out a shallow bomb shelter near the cottage. They took a practical approach to life in the last year of the war, as Gertrud recollected: "We did not worry anymore to have to die. We only had one wish every night—that we could all go together. If Walter could be with us, all was fine." In her husband's absence, Gertrud scraped meals together from ration coupons, but had to leave the long lines in front of stores on occasion when the air raid sirens wailed. "It was really bad again, but we lived through it all." They did indeed, and Walter returned shortly after the war to a loving family.[44]

In a most daring move, Walter Menssen forged release papers for two of his brothers-in-law. Because he worked in the air force administration office, he had access to nearly everything he needed to issue papers that would allow his relatives to leave the military early and return home—everything, that is, except the official stamp of that Luftwaffe district. His solution was novel: "I took a fresh egg, cooked it, peeled it, and rolled this egg over an old seal of old papers of mine and then took that egg and put that seal over the new paper I had written." By securing a release for his relatives, Walter may well have saved them a term in a POW camp after the war or even a fate much worse.[45]

In the fall of 1944, orders were given to German soldiers to defend the Mediterranean island of Elba to the last man. Fortunately, Erwin Frank was suffering from malaria at the time and was on the opposite side of the island from the French landing and the combat that ensued. The contingent of three thousand German defenders was soon reduced to three hundred (among them Erwin Frank) who were finally extracted from the island. From that point, Erwin saw only Italy and points north. Whatever the military and the media wished to call the moves of the next few months (such as a "repositioning"), Erwin understood it to be a steady retreat. However, things were not all bleak in his life. On his last wartime visit home, he met and fell in love with a young lady of the Barmbek Branch—Ruth Drachenberg. They were engaged in October 1944.

The St. Georg Branch history includes several comments regarding the few men left in Hamburg as the war dragged on. They were mostly too old to serve in the military, and they took on three, four, or more assignments vacated by the young men who were drafted. However, Hans Gürtler stated in his branch history that the spirit remained very positive among the members as they gathered to worship, and in some respects, the members of the branch grew closer in those challenging times.[46]

As the company clerk, Brother Gürtler traveled frequently during the war but was never in combat and never in danger. In his autobiography, he detailed his route through eastern Europe in

1942–44. He had time to make friendships, carry on extensive correspondence, and write poems to send to his brother Siegfried, an actor and voice talent at the state opera in Bielefeld. In 1943, Hans had moved his wife and their children to the eastern Bavarian town of Cham, where Brother Gürtler sent all possible extra food from his rations (and the booty gained from swapping cigarettes with comrades). Karla Gürtler had lost everything in the destruction of Hamburg but lived in good circumstances with her children in Cham.[47]

Ingeborg Thymian recalled the following about those who attended the meetings in Altona after all three Hamburg branches were united:

> The attendance pretty much stayed the same. What astonished me was that there were many handicapped people in our branch. Even our branch president was blind. We could count the healthy people on one hand. Every other person had some disability, for example having lost a leg or an arm. It was a unique situation and I always wondered why, but I think it must have been because of the war. The branch president also brought his dog with him to the meetings. He would lie next to him at the podium in order to help with anything that his master needed.

"It took us about fifteen or twenty minutes to reach the air-raid shelter from our home," explained Hertha Schönrock regarding air raids during the last year of the war. "We also had to take the stroller with us for Waltraud's baby. One wheel kept falling off, and so it took us even longer. Sometimes, the [illumination flares] were already coming down, and we were still walking." The tension must have been severe at such moments, because the bombers followed the flares marking the target by only a few minutes. One of the raids damaged the roof and the windows of the Schönrock apartment, but eventually there were eleven persons sleeping in the living room.

Even Wilhelmsburg, a suburb south of Hamburg's harbor, was damaged in the attacks. Hertha and Waltraud Schönrock experienced the attacks in terror one night when the British dropped phosphorus bombs, and Waltraud's leg was burned.

> It hurt my leg very badly and I could even stick my fingers into [the holes in] my leg. I sat in water all night, and that relieved the pain. The stairs down to the canal were full of people and . . . they were burning. My husband's pants were on fire, so he jumped into the canal. We saw terrible things. People were sitting by the side of the streets burning. My father and my husband went back the next day to find our grandparents, but they didn't survive.

It was nothing short of remarkable that Richard Pruess found enough building material to restore the lower floors of his Rahlstedt house during the war. "You could hardly get a nail in those days, but we somehow got nails, wood, and glass," recalled Lieselotte. Several Russian POWs were allowed to assist in the reconstruction of the home. The rest of the family out in Poland were worried about the approach of the Red Army from the east and wanted very much to return to Hamburg. A few months later, they did, and "we lived in the basement because there was [almost] nothing upstairs."

Richard Pruess Jr. was a soldier who made a comment often attributed to German LDS young men: "My only wish is that I won't have to kill anybody in this war." His sister, Hilde, heard him make this statement before he left home in the uniform of the Wehrmacht. In August 1944, another sister, Lieselotte, had a remarkable dream:

> My brother [Richard] came to me in a dream. He was a soldier in France at the time. He said, "This is the end for me, but didn't we have beautiful times together? Didn't we have beautiful times when we were little?" In other words, he kind of said good-bye to me. A week or two later, we got the message that he had died. Then I remembered the dream and connected it to the time he died. It was kind of sad when you said good-bye, but the memories he brought to my mind were nice memories.

By the late summer of 1944, former branch president Arthur Zander had been transferred from the Netherlands to France as the Wehrmacht tried to counter the Allied invasion after D-Day. He was wounded, captured there by the Americans, and then shipped as a POW to the United States. He stayed in Oklahoma until the end of 1945 and then was returned to Germany and Hamburg.

For the last year of the war, Irma Brey served in the Reichsarbeitsdienst. Assigned to work in an underground munitions factory, she was frightened by the Russians who worked with her. She lived in army barracks with other young women. All during her service away from home, on the farm, and in the munitions factory, she was totally isolated from the Church.

Life was difficult for Hamburg residents of all ages, but youngsters like Fred Zwick still found happy ways to pass the time. Before the family's apartment house was destroyed, he played with his friends at a kindling wood business next door. They would climb on the wood piles and make structures with bundles of wood. Later, he lived near a park called "ash mountain" with a playground and a swimming pool. "In the winter, we took our sleds there and went sledding down the little hill made of ash," he explained. Fred met some French laborers at a local greenhouse and he played with them. "Somehow they got hold of some sugar once and made candy for us. They were our favorite guys to be with." Life was not all suffering and privation in wartime Hamburg.

The branch history includes some very sad notes about the members in the early months of 1945 as the war drew to a close: "Not only was it a struggle to make the trek for hours to Altona to the meetings, but the winter of 1944–45 was bitterly cold in the rooms. On the coldest days, the water froze in the sacrament cups! The terrible inflation added to the suffering of many members."[48] With the three branches in the city united as one, the attendance was usually about one hundred persons. There were generally only Sunday meetings held in early 1945.

After two years in the Czech town of Kubice with his school class, Otto Berndt was invited in January 1945 to join the army. As a member of the birth class of 1929, he could not be forced to serve, so he chose to attend the Adolf Hitler School east of

Fig. 11. The Zwick family managed somehow to find a Christmas tree in 1944. (F. Zwick)

Prague. In the confusion of the war, he did not stay at that school but returned to Hamburg instead. Back at home, he was ordered to report for military service but was classified as unfit for regular duty. He was handed a rifle and ordered to join the home guard in defending the city. As he recalled, "I was supposed to be an ammo handler for an 88 mm gun. For some reason it never materialized that I was really drafted. My dad told me, 'Don't be a dead hero.'" Rather than look for a fight to join, Otto Berndt and his father traveled to the town of Nitzow, near Berlin, to gather the rest of the family and move them back to Hamburg. It was already clear that the Nitzow area would be included in the, Soviet occupation zone and President Berndt had no intention of leaving his family in that region.[49]

In early 1945, Hilde Pruess was again away from Hamburg, this time living near the home of the Wagner family, members of the branch in Annaberg-Buchholz in the East German Mission. She enjoyed attending church meetings with the Wagners; but when the Soviet army approached the town, Hilde was put on a train all by herself and sent back to Hamburg. She recalled her fears at the time:

> I was eleven years old and had to cross the country by myself. Suddenly, I met a strange lady who said that I could take the last train to Chemnitz.

> I thought she was an angel. I don't remember if I was carrying a suitcase, but I know that I was praying. I just took train after train until I got to Hamburg. When I arrived at my home, my parents didn't recognize me. I had been gone more than a year and was wearing a hat, so my dad didn't know who I was at first.

Lilly Koch described the challenges of attending church in Altona when her family lived in the distant southern suburb of Harburg—well beyond the Elbe River harbors south of Hamburg: "The streetcars were usually not running on Sundays and it was too far to walk, or there were air-raid alarms and we couldn't go. There were still enough priesthood holders to administer the sacrament if we did attend the meetings. Before the war, we had enjoyed special programs and celebrations, but during the war such events were not possible." The Koch family survived the war intact. "During the air raids, we sat in the basement in the corner as a family and prayed to our Heavenly Father to help us," explained Lilly.

In February 1945, political prisoner Karl-Heinz Schnibbe was released from his prison cell on an island of the Elbe River. ("It felt like Alcatraz to me.") He was allowed a short visit with his mother before he was sent to the east to help defend Germany against the Soviet invaders. While with his mother, he spent several precious hours sitting in an air-raid shelter beneath the main railroad station. Among other news, his mother told him that she and his father needed more than three hours to walk through the rubble of the inner city from their home to the meetings in Altona. After their talk, Karl-Heinz left the air-raid shelter and departed immediately for the Eastern Front. He would not see his mother again until 1949.

The last major air raid over Hamburg occurred in March 1945. Karl Schönrock recalled being a bit too far from the concrete bunker when the alarms sounded, but wanting very much to get there:

> The soldiers were just ready to close the door as I came running, and I got in there and only a few minutes later we got a direct hit on that [bunker]. As a matter of fact, it tilted towards the crater. . . . It's a strange feeling when the earth shakes like in an earthquake. And they didn't just drop a bomb here and there; it was carpet bombing. We had about a dozen craters on the soccer field right next to our home. We had one big crater in the backyard which was maybe thirty yards away from the house where it hit our favorite apple tree (the tree disappeared). The crater was big enough to put half a house in, mostly because the ground there was really soft. . . . It looked like the craters of the moon.

In the last months of the war, Inge Laabs learned what it was like to go without the basic necessities of life: "I remember that it was hard to find anything to wear to keep warm. Our shoes were worn and our clothing had holes. We were cold."[50] It was hard for Inge to see her hometown in ruins: "Some parts of the city were closed to pedestrians because so many dead people were lying in the streets." The war ended on Inge's seventeenth birthday, May 8, 1945; but just a few weeks before that, she and her family members were still trying to avoid attacks by dive-bombers. "We couldn't even go out to get water without something dangerous happening. When they attacked us, we jumped into the bushes. We also couldn't make fires to cook or keep us warm." Regarding her attitude toward the death and destruction of the war, Inge stated, "I tried to make the best of everything and turn it into a positive experience. Now I know that I was often protected by my Heavenly Father."

Although he did not qualify for military service, Werner Schönrock came close to losing his life in early 1945. Caught outside in a sudden air raid, he felt a piece of shrapnel hit his hand. He was standing at that moment next to a neighbor who was home on leave from the army. That neighbor sustained such drastic shrapnel wounds that he lost a leg. In the same attack, a bomb fell into the apartment building where the Schönrock family lived, but the damage was not severe. According to Werner, "We were lucky that nothing else happened that day."

The American advance overtook Gerd Fricke's unit in 1945. "One time they attacked us with phosphorus, and I thought I wouldn't survive." A buddy was killed just a few feet from where Gerd was standing. The advancing GIs soon made Gerd a POW. His experience of being incarcerated by the Americans in Germany was very short but not as pleasant as reported by German POWs who spent time in the United States. According to Gerd:

> We slept in a potato field and [the guards] enjoyed seeing us get wet when it rained. [One day] they drove us out of Ulm [in southern Germany] and demanded that we give them everything we owned. Then they allowed us to do whatever we wanted, so many of us simply started to walk home. [The Americans] didn't want to give us a train ticket home, but I protested, saying that I had fought for my country and now I deserved to ride the train home. I rode on a coal car and was filthy when I got home. It was wonderful to see everybody again. My mother hadn't known if I was alive or not because I hadn't been allowed to write home while I was a POW.

Far from the rubble of Hamburg, Sister Niemann and her two children were spared the ravages of war and a dangerous invasion. According to her son, Henry, the war ended in the town of Hude when the last German defenders retreated through the area. "The British came with their tanks and rolled through. They were there and that was it."[51] Henry had just turned nine years old and had little recollection of life without war.

With the British army just twenty miles from Hamburg, Walter Menssen decided that he was through with the war. Discarding his uniform in favor of a civilian suit, he packed his things and was ready to leave his quarters when his commanding officer entered. Thinking that he might be shot as a deserter, Walter was relieved when the man offered him the use of his staff car to go home. "No, I take the motorbike," he replied. "I wish I could do it [go home] too, but I can't," replied the officer. Walter's unit left for the Danish border to the north but ran into the British on the way. The ensuing battle cost many of the men their lives even though the war was long since lost.[52]

For Astrid Koch in faraway Pulsnitz, the war ended when Polish soldiers appeared in town and began to loot. They were driven out by the locals, but soon the Soviet army appeared, and life for Astrid (not yet thirteen) became a little frightening. Her host family took her, and they fled for a few miles but were overtaken by the conquerors. As she recalled:

> We had to be careful because they were after all the girls and women. A lot of people got raped. The niece of the people I stayed with was twelve years old, and she got raped. My hosts must have been scared to death taking care of me. They hid me in a building where they made elastic stuff. When the Russians came back, they went looking for the women and children. We had a man looking out for us, and he told us to hide. So they put us in one kind of a storage room and put boxes and everything in front of the door, but they found out there was a door behind it. So they had us all come out, all of us women and children. A soldier with a big gun told us to stay outside in the sun, but only one woman was raped, and nothing happened to the rest of us.

On May 6, 1945, the commanding officer of Erwin Frank's unit made these comments: "They want us to stay together in case they need us for some action or cleanup, [but] if any of you think you can make it home, you're welcome to try. I can't give you any release papers, so you'll be on your own." Erwin went to the nearest village where he found people who could provide him with civilian clothing and a bicycle. He needed to ride his bike for only one day to reach Hamburg. He was home, but without official release papers from the British occupation authority, he could get neither employment nor ration coupons. In August 1945, he reported to the authorities in Hanover and was given the necessary papers.[53] That month, he married Ruth Drachenberg, and they began a new life without National Socialism.

When the British army entered Hamburg, no attempt was made to defend the city. Ingrid Lübke had positive recollections of her encounters with the "Tommies": "The British came to Hamburg first, and the children ran out to meet them and they gave us chocolate. I didn't know what a roll was or a banana and an orange but we could suddenly buy them again in the grocery stores." All over western Germany, children were treated very kindly by the invading forces, and many LDS eyewitnesses would later tell of such encounters with fond memories.

Three days after returning home (in time to greet his new baby girl), Walter Menssen was arrested by the British, but his charmed life in the service seemed to continue. Despite being terribly hungry and lacking proper facilities on occasion, he was home with his family in a few months and immediately joined the surviving Saints who were meeting in the Altona Branch rooms.[54]

With peace restored and the war ended, the dispersed members of the St. Georg Branch began to return to their devastated city. According to Hans Gürtler:

> From wherever they had been scattered, fled, or sent all over Germany, they came back in the summer of 1945—the families, the mothers with their children, the widows, the flak assistant girls and the brethren who were fortunate to be POWs for just a short time. But many, many did not return. Several men were still missing in action and others still in POW camps.[55]

Hans Gürtler spent the last few months of the war in Hungary and Austria. He was taken prisoner by the Americans near Salzburg in May 1945, and it was then that he first experienced the trials of being a soldier. Going without food, water, or shelter for days on end, he lost his favorite possessions as GIs divested him of most of his personal property. Moved across southern Germany to France, he was handed over to the French and put to work. In St. Avold he experienced what he would call "the worst experiences of my POW time." Although he allied himself with the cultural arts groups in the camp, he worked with a crew of prisoners assigned to remove land mines from the countryside. The danger was severe, and he became seriously ill at least once.[56]

Hans Gürtler's daughter Therese summarized her sentiments about the war and her belief in God in these words:

> We didn't have to maintain a testimony. It was just always there. There was never anything happening that would endanger my testimony, or where I would question that maybe God didn't love me because I had to suffer. I don't have any ill memories of the war. None at all. Only the sound, when the air raid was announced. That is a sound that was frightful. But I don't have any negative memories from the war. So my testimony was never attacked. It was intact.

Marie Sommerfeld and her children were quite safe in Czechoslovakia until the last months of the war, when Germans in that area became personae non gratae. At first, Czech authorities told them to leave, and then the Soviets took over and forced their departure. Loading their things into a two-wheeled cart, they slowly made their way toward the German border. With nothing to eat, they dug for potatoes in nearby fields. Because of the reports of molestation by conquering Soviets, Marie's daughters dressed as boys and tucked their hair into their caps to avoid attracting attention. Werner was brokenhearted when Russian soldiers stole his accordion. Near the city of Dresden, Leni Sommerfeld became separated from the family—apparently abducted by a Russian. As Werner later wrote, "We waited and searched in the city of Dresden, hoping against hope that she would turn up. In the end there was nothing for us to do but to press on for Hamburg." Sister Sommerfeld was suffering from a serious kidney ailment during the entire trip home, and the loss of her daughter was nearly overwhelming. About one month after arriving in Hamburg, Leni showed up and reported that she had managed to escape harm during the separation from her family. The only place the Sommerfelds could find to live was in the basement of an apartment building under construction; there were no doors or windows in the structure. During the winter of 1945–46, they came close to freezing to death, and both Arthur (already home from the Eastern Front) and daughter Mary became seriously ill. Fortunately, everybody survived the trials and Gustav Sommerfeld eventually returned from his tenure as a POW.

Looking back on the difficult experiences of the war, Werner Sommerfeld made this summary statement:

> The German people are good, strong, faithful people, and my mother in particular was a woman of great faith. Many times, she didn't know where she would get food for her five children. She prayed many times and there were many, many miracles in her life where she just found food at the door or somebody just came by with food. And that was not just true with our family. The [Latter-day Saints] trusted in the Lord and lived by faith each and every day.[57]

When Arthur Zander returned to Hamburg in 1946, he found his wife and his three sons living in a tiny (six-by-twelve-foot) garden shed. The structure was so small that according to Ingo, "there were no utilities at all, because it was not designed for people to actually live there. In the morning we had to take out our beds to make way for a table and chairs and at night we reversed the procedure."

As a seventeen-year-old, Harald Fricke had finished his service with the Reichsarbeitsdienst and was drafted into the Wehrmacht. Stationed near the Baltic Sea, his unit was passed by as the Red Army rushed toward Berlin. After the war, he and his comrades were transported as POWs to the city of Stalingrad, where they helped clean up and reconstruct that important industrial center. He recalled some of the trials of the experience:

> At the age of nineteen, I suffered from constant hunger and the lack of proper hygiene. I only survived because a Russian woman doctor sneaked me some medicine and hid me when it came time for physical examinations. Every day German soldiers died in the camp and their bodies were loaded onto small carts and dumped into mass graves. While working near the Volga River during the winter [of 1945–46], the tip of the big toe on my right foot was lost to frostbite and I suffered from thrombosis and other illnesses. This made me incapable of working and I shrank to skin and bones. So they shipped me home which was a great blessing.[58]

When Harald returned to Hamburg, his mother told him that she had constantly prayed that somebody would care about and for her son. The Russian doctor had been that somebody.

In the summer of 1946, Hans Gürtler was released from the POW camp in France and sent to Münster in northwest Germany to be processed out of the military. He immediately made his way back to the northern Hamburg suburb of Rahlstedt, where his family had been living since the end of the war. Not knowing precisely where his family lived, he tossed pebbles against windows after midnight until he woke neighbors who could give directions. He recalled the reunion: "Karla woke up and then . . . she and the children, all of them suddenly wide awake, came down in their pajamas. What a reunion!" They entertained each other with stories as he unpacked the goodies he had brought home—including many poems, a piece of leather, and a chess game. "After six years, I was finally free!" he wrote.[59]

Since March 1941, Karla Gürtler had taken care of four children almost totally by herself. However, she recalled the life of a single mother in positive terms: "Of course it's difficult to be a mother in the war, but everyone was in the same boat. When times got tough, I lived through them the best I could. I had to live for my children. And I think the link to the Church was more intensive during such a time because we needed the faith."[60]

After spending four years away from Hamburg, Maria Niemann finally returned to her apartment in 1946. Although extensively damaged in the air raids, it had been repaired, and refugees were living there when the Niemanns arrived. At first, the refugees insisted that they had forfeited their rights to the apartment by being absent for so long, but city officials intervened and asked the refugees to leave. Maria was home, but she had not heard from her husband since the end of the war. "I prayed and my children prayed," she recalled, "and my daughter put his picture in the window every day and said, 'My father, please come home, I love you.'"[61]

In the summer of 1946, Astrid Koch's mother made her way illegally across the border into the Soviet occupation zone to pick up her daughter in Pulsnitz. There were serious challenges to be overcome when the two made their way back to the British zone, but they managed to do so without injury. After being away from Hamburg for five of the previous six years, Astrid lived with her family in a small apartment her father had found in the rubble of the port city. The Kochs were together again and looked forward to a totally new phase of life.

Frieda Brey and her children had spent three years in the Catholic city of Bamberg in southern Germany. It was a beautiful town, and they enjoyed the peace that prevailed there, but it was a happy day when they returned to Hamburg in 1946. Two years later, former district president Alwin Brey was released from a POW camp and made the trek home to his family.

Willy Frank (born 1915) was captured in Yugoslavia at the end of the war. As a POW there, he wrote to his wife, Anna Marie, every week; but until 1946, he did not know whether she was actually alive. Finally, his message got through via the Red Cross; he was able to write to her and she was able to write back to him. They had lost their two children, and this was a very lonely time for both. One day in 1948, it was announced that his group would be transported to Germany. They rode in boxcars from Yugoslavia to Germany; then they were allowed to ride in first-class coaches for the rest of the trip to Hamburg. For his time and labor as a prisoner of war, he was paid a total of 50 Marks (about thirteen dollars). He had lost nearly half of his weight during his term as a POW.[62]

The war was fully four years in the past when Fred Zwick's father returned from a POW camp in 1949. Sister Zwick had written many letters after the war to locate her husband. It was likely a very sad time for her, but she did not express that openly to her son. As Fred recalled, "Children really weren't included in family affairs or with parents. Children weren't told much." Finally, a connection was established with Fred's father through the Russian Red Cross, and things began to look up. When he returned, his wife and his son were still living in the garden cottage.

"When I came back to Hamburg in 1949, the city was one big heap of rubble," recalled Karl-Heinz Schnibbe. As a political prisoner and then a POW in Russia, he had sacrificed seven years of his young life, but he was happy to be home with his family. "The streets were cleared, and the rubble was piled up on the sides. And everywhere things were being built up and repaired again. I found my street right away."

Perhaps more than any other LDS branch in the West German Mission, the St. Georg Branch was practically broken apart during World War II. After losing their comparatively luxurious meetinghouse, the members had been dispersed all over the continent. Many families were homeless and separated, taking refuge in what they hoped were safe and peaceful locations within Germany. In essentially every case, they were isolated from the Church while away from Hamburg. Those who stayed in the city during the war and could still attend church meetings made the long trek through the rubble of their city to the meeting hall in Altona, where important vestiges of their Latter-day Saint existence were maintained. There were enough older men at home to administer in all priesthood functions. With the war over, the Saints of the St. Georg Branch would need nearly five years to gather home, and their branch was never reconstituted. Beginning in the summer of 1945, they became members of several new branches in and around the city of Hamburg. At least forty members of the branch (10 percent) did not live to see peace return to Germany.

In Memoriam

The following members of the St. Georg Branch did not survive World War II:

Walter Heinrich Johannes Bankowski b. Hamburg 19 Nov 1910; son of Ludwig August Otto Bankowski and Auguste Caroline Sievers; bp. 28 Jan 1930; conf. 28 Jan 1930; ord. deacon 13 Oct 1930; ord. priest 4 Jan 1932; ord. elder 26 Feb 1935; m. Hamburg 24 Mar or Apr 1937, Anna Wittig; d. stomach tumor 19 June 1944; bur. Pomezia, Italy (FHL microfilm 68804, book 1, no. 19; www.volksbund.de; CHL CR 275 8 2438, no. 8; IGI)

Martin Heinrich Friedrich Bergmann b. Fliegenfelde, Stormarn, Schleswig-Holstein, 23 Jun 1887; son of Christian Friedrich Bergmann and Luise Dorothea Anna Kämpfer; bp. 2 Jun 1911; conf. 2 Jun 1911; ord. elder 2 Jun 1927; m. 5 Jun 1943, Caroline Kropp; k. air raid 28 Jul 1943 (FHL microfilm 68804, book 1, no. 37; CHL CR 275 8, no. 317; CHL 10603, 118)

Ilse Johanna Charlotte Blischke b. Burg, Jerichow, Sachsen, 25 May 1911; dau. of Fritz Blischke and Anna Louise Graul; bp. 17 Feb 1925; conf. 17 Feb 1925; missing as of 20 Mar 1946 (FHL microfilm 68804, book 1, no. 31; CHL CR 275 8 2438, no. 231)

Carl Waldemar Bobbermin b. Itzehoe, Steinburg, Schleswig-Holstein, 2 Jul 1911; son of Wilhelm Fr. August Bobbermin and Auguste Krempien; bp. 22 Apr 1923; conf. 22 Apr 1923; k. while deactivating bombs 17 Apr 1947 (FHL microfilm 68804, book 1, no. 42)

Emma Ida Bochnia b. Klein-Lassowitz, Rosenberg, Schlesien, 21 Nov 1901; dau. of Friedrich Bochnia and Bertha Maleck or Malesk; bp. 27 Dec 1931; conf. 17 Dec 1931; m. 21 Nov 1936, Johann Friedrich Paul Haase; k. air raid Hamburg 28 Jul 1943 (FHL microfilm 68804, book 1, no. 139; CHL CR 275 8 2438, no. 64; CHL 10603, 118)

Elke Brey b. Hamburg 19 May 1942; dau. of Alwin Max Brey and Frieda Ocker; d. scarlet fever 27 May 1945 (FHL microfilm 68804, book 1, no. 49; IGI)

Carla Maria Cizinsky b. Hamburg 16 or 18 Aug 1942; dau. of Walter Theodor Wilhelm Cizinsky and Carla Maria Krüger; d. diphtheria 16 Mar or May 1945 (FHL microfilm 68804, book 1, no. 60; CHL CR 275 8 2438, no. 478; IGI)

Alfred Werner Frank Fick b. Hamburg 6 Jul 1925; son of Richard Karl Wilhelm Fick and Grete Anna Elisabeth Schloss; bp. 18 Sep 1933; MIA 1 Jun 1943 (E. Frank; www.volksbund.de; IGI, PRF)

Marianne Sonja Frank b. Hamburg 14 Jun 1941; dau. of Willy Richard Otto Frank and Anneliese Haase; k. air raid Hamburg 27 or 28 July 1943 (FHL microfilm, location by W. Frank; FHL microfilm 68804, book 1, no. 105; CHL CR 275 8 2438, no. 451)

Rainer Willy Frank b. Hamburg 12 Feb 1943; son of Willy Richard Otto Frank and Anneliese Haase; d. diphtheria East Germany 18 Apr 1944 (Haase-Frank; IGI)

Bertha Sophie Marie Gebert b. Tews-Woos, Mecklenburg-Schwerin, 2 Aug 1882; dau. of Wilhelm Gebert and Marie Mahnke; bp. 9 Sep 1911; conf. 9 Sep 1911; k. air raid 27 or 28 Jul 1943 (FHL microfilm 68804, book 1, no. 119; CHL CR 275 8 2438, no. 284; CHL 10603, 118)

Karl Adolf H. Geerken b. Hamburg 28 Mar 1879; son of Heinrich Klaus Geerken and Johanna Dorothea Christ. Gale; bp. 1 Nov 1913; conf. 1 Nov 1913; ord. teacher 2 Nov 1919; ord. priest 7 Mar 1920; ord. elder 25 Jul 1926; k. air raid 27 or 28 Jul 1943 (FHL microfilm 68804, book 1, no. 120; CHL CR 275 8, no. 320; CHL 10603, 118)

Erna Luise Marie Groth b. Hamburg 21 Nov 1894; dau. of Heinrich Johann Groth and Louise Sophie Johanne Törber; bp. 27 Oct 1922; conf. 27 Oct 1922; m. —— Schulz; k. air raid 27 or 28 Jul 1943 (FHL microfilm 68804, book 2, no. 129; CHL CR 275 8, no. 557; FHL microfilm 25778, 1930 and 1935 censuses; CHL 10603, 118)

Rudolf Reinhold Groth b. Hamburg, 2 Jan 1916; son of Adolf Brauer and Erna Luise Marie Groth; bp. 16 Aug 1924; conf. 16 Aug 1924; ord. deacon 13 Oct 1930; ord. teacher 6 Jan 1935; ord. priest 1 Nov 1937; ord. elder; k. air raid 27 or 28 Jul 1943 (G. Fricke; IGI; FHL microfilm 68804, book 1, no. 128; CHL CR 275 8 2438, no. 57; CHL 10603, 118)

Anna Emma Guddat b. Tilsit, Ostpreußen, 26 Oct 1900; dau. of Heinrich Gustav Gudat and Wilhelmine Reszeleit; bp. 8 Sep 1911; conf. 8 Sep 1911; m. 1919, —— Kunkel (div.), 2m. Johannes Ernst Carl Sudrow; k. air raid 27 or 28 Jul 1943 (FHL microfilm 68804, book 1, no. 230; CHL CR 275 8, no. 888; FS)

Otto Bruno Günther b. Hartenstein, Zwickau, Sachsen, 12 Oct 1869; son of Ernst Wilhelm Günther and Marie Heise; bp. 7 Jun 1935; conf. 9 Jun 1935; ord. deacon 6 Apr 1936; ord. teacher 6 Dec 1936; ord. priest 17 Oct 1937; ord. elder 24 Sep 1939; k. air raid 27 or 28 Jul 1943 (FHL microfilm 68804, book 1, no. 129; CHL microfilm 2458, form 42 FP, pt. 37, 74–75; CHL CR 275 8 2438, no. 251; CHL 10603, 118)

Johann Friedrich Paul Haase b. Röslau, Karthaus, Westpreussen, 7 Apr 1892; son of Johann Haase and Auguste Dornburg; bp. 27 Jun 1911; conf. 27 Jun 1911; ord. deacon 22 Oct 1916; ord. teacher 15 Oct 1919; ord. priest 7 Mar 1920; ord. elder 25 Jul 1926; m. 3 Apr 1914 Anna Wilhelmine Wischmann, 2 sons, 2 dau.; m. 21 Nov 1936, Emma Ida Bochnia; k. air raid Hamburg 27 or

28 Jul 1943 (FHL microfilm 68804, book 1, no. 138; CHL CR 275 8, no. 318; CHL 10603, 118)

Juliane Friedel Harms b. Hamburg 25 Apr 1935; dau. of Herbert Ernst Alexander Harms and Frieda Anna Auguste Mücke; d. Hamburg 3 Oct 1940 (FHL microfilm 162775, 1935 census; IGI)

Dora Marie Sofie Heckler b. Hannover, Hannover, 1 Apr 1891; dau. of Emil Wulf Heckler and Dorette Marie Hering; bp. 30 Mar 1924; conf. 30 Mar 1924; d. breast cancer 30 Jan 1944 (FHL microfilm 68804, book 1, no. 146)

Bertha Franziska Anna Herrmann b. Hamburg 18 Jan 1888; dau. of Ernst Heinrich David Herrmann and Helene Auguste Franziska Sperber; bp. 15 Apr 1908; conf. 15 Apr 1908; m. Hamburg 1 Feb 1908, Johann Heinrich Carsten Harms; 1 or 2 children; 2m. 18 Dec 1930, Adolf Haimerl; k. air raid Hamburg 27 or 28 Jul 1943 (FHL microfilm 68804, book 1, no. 151; CHL CR 275 8 2438, no. 576; IGI, AF)

Helmuth Hübener b. Hamburg 8 Jan 1925; son of Emma A. Gudat; bp. Hamburg 27 May 1933; conf. 28 May 1933; ord. deacon Hamburg 3 May 1937; executed for treason Berlin 27 Oct 1942 (Tobler; CHL CR 275 8 2438, no. 994)

Hermann Otto Kluwe b. Berlin, Brandenburg, 5 Dec 1895; son of Martha Kluwe; bp. 30 Sep 1927; conf. 30 Sep 1927; ord. deacon 5 Aug 1928; ord. elder 5 May 1930; m. Hamburg 9 Mar 1935, Tony Elfriede Kayser; d. stomach cancer Oranienburg, Niederbarnim, Brandenburg, 28 Feb 1940 (FHL microfilm 68804, book 1, no. 178; CHL CR 275 8 2438, no. 733; IGI)

Heinrich Gustav Knop b. Koblenz, Rheinprovinz, Preussen, 3 Mar 1874; son Heinrich Wilhelm Knop and Pauline Friederike Bartz; bp. 25 May 1908; conf. 25 May 1908; ord. priest 15 Oct 1919; m. 9 Aug 1901, Frieda Christine Caroline Ihde; d. 9 Feb 1941 (FHL microfilm 68804, book 1, no. 185; CHL CR 275 8 2438, no. 591; IGI)

Karl Otto Friedrich Köhler b. Pritten, Dramburg, Pommern, 5 Apr 1883; son of Karl Kesch and Wilhelmine Friederike Dorothea Köhler; bp. 15 Sep 1906; conf. 15 Sep 1906; ord. deacon 23 Feb 1914; ord. teacher 15 Oct 1919; ord. priest 7 Mar 1920; ord. elder 27 Feb 1921; m. Stettin, Pommern 9 Jun 1906, Elsa Emma Auguste Laabs; 6 children; d. pneumonia Wilhelmsburg, Harburg, Hannover, Preussen, 11 Aug 1943 (FHL microfilm 68804, book 1, no. 197; CHL CR 275 8, no. 321; FHL microfilm 271381, 1935 census; IGI)

Gerhard Karl Paul Köhler b. Wilhelmsburg, Harburg, Hannover, 7 Apr 1921; noncommissioned officer, d. Deksekuli Kurld (near Latvia) 3 Mar 1945; bur. Saldus, Latvia (www.volksbund.de)

Minna Auguste Anna Karoline Konow b. Lauenburg, Lauenburg, Schleswig-Holstein, 4 Mar 1889; dau. of Carl Joachim Friedrich Konow and Bertha Dorothea Elise Kummerfeld; m. —— Kardell; d. 1 May 1940 (IGI; FHL microfilm 271376, 1935 census)

Felix Richard Krause b. Marienthal, Zwickau, Sachsen, 19 Jul 1896; son of Karl August Krause and Maria Hulda Uhlmann; bp. 18 May 1911; conf. 18 May 1911; m. Hedwig Toni Auguste Witt; 2 children; k. in battle France 7 Dec 1944 (FHL microfilm 68804, book 1, no. 214; CHL CR 275 8, no. 667; CHL microfilm 2458, form 42 FP, pt. 37, 74–75; IGI)

Dorothea Lina Krüger b. Wittenberge, Westprignitz, Brandenburg, 16 Jun 1871; dau. of Karl Krüger and Wilhelmine Kaeppen; bp. 17 Aug 1900; conf. 17 Aug 1900; m. Karl Unbereit; k. air raid Hamburg 27 or 28 Jul 1943 (CHL microfilm 2458, form 42 FP, pt. 37, 74–75; CHL CR 275 8 2438, no. 675; FHL microfilm 245289, 1930 and 1935 censuses)

Marie Sophie Lengies b. Hamburg, 20 Aug 1901; dau. of Wilhelm Friedrich Lengies and Johanna Elise Eleonore Ludewig; bp. 10 Sep 1909; conf. 10 Sep 1909; m. 2 Feb 1923, Franz Bohnhorst (div.); missing as of 20 Mar 1946 (FHL microfilm 68804, book 1, no. 42; CHL CR 275 8 2438, no. 306; FHL microfilm 25726, 1930 census; IGI)

Ulrich Ernst Julius Lenschow b. Hamburg, 3 May 1920; son of Heinrich August Christian Lenschow and Emma Erna Karoline Katharine Lenschow; k. MIA Heiligenbeil or Kosselbude or Zinten, Ostpreußen 1 Mar 1945 (Gellersen; www.volksbund.de; IGI)

Herbert Paul Lode b. Hamburg 11 Apr 1918; son of Fritz Lode and Frieda Marie Haase; bp. 26 Nov 1927; conf. 26 Nov 1927; k. in battle Acca, France, 20 May 1940 (CHL CR 275 8, no. 963; Otto Berndt Report A 4560: 71; IGI, AF)

Anna Dorothea Henriette Noack b. Hamburg 18 Dec 1873; dau. of Adolf Carl Eduard Noack and Anna Catharina Margaretha Piening; bp. 8 Jan 1926; conf. 8 Jan 1926; m. Hamburg 25 Oct 1910, Hans Heinrich Becker; 6 children; d. heart attack Husum, Schleswig-Holstein 25 Apr 1944 (FHL microfilm 68804, book 1, no. 17; CHL CR 275 8 2438, no. 347; IGI, AF)

Wilhelmine Resgoleik b. Groß Trumpeiten, Niederung, Ostpreußen, 19 Mar 1877; dau. of Johann Resgoleik and Marie Dalladat; bp. 31 Oct 1909; conf. 31 Oct 1909; m. 26 Jan 1923, Johann E. Carl Sudrow; k. air raid Hamburg 28 Jul 1943 (FHL microfilm 68804, book 2, no. 131; CHL CR 275 8, no. 665)

Hans Heinrich Max Franz Vick Ruwoldt b. Wokrent, Mecklenburg-Schwerin, 9 Feb 1892; son of Heinrich Karl Johann Vick Ruwoldt and Friederike Wilhelmine Sophie Peters; bp. 7 Oct 1926; conf. 7 Oct

1926; ord. deacon 17 Mar 1930; ord. teacher 6 Sep 1931; ord. priest 7 May 1933; ord. elder 3 Jun 1935; m. Alt-Meteln, Mecklenburg-Schwerin 25 Apr 1919, Berta Anna Minna Schmaal; 1 child; k. air raid Hamburg 12 Aug 1943; bur. Ohlsdorf, Hamburg (Otto Berndt report A 4560:71; www.volksbund.de; CHL CR 275 8 2438, no. 484; IGI, AF)

Johannes Ernst Carl Sudrow b. Röbel, Mecklenburg-Schwerin, 7 Feb 1865; son of Johann Heinrich Christian Sudrow and Marie Sophie Friederika Fleischer; bp. 22 Apr 1923; conf. 22 Apr 1923; ord. deacon 8 Dec 1923; ord. teacher 10 Oct 1926; ord. priest 6 Jan 1935; ord. elder 7 Jun 1936; m. Pauline Emma Louise Viebeck; k. air raid Hamburg 27 or 28 or 29 Jul 1943 (FHL microfilm 68804, book 2, no. 130; CHL 10603, 118)

Louise Sophie Johanna Törber b. Klein Hundorf, Mecklenburg-Schwerin, 21 Dec 1873; dau. of Friedrich Törber and Dorothea Berg; bp. 27 Oct 1922; conf. 27 Oct 1922; m. Heinrich Johann Groth; k. air raid 27 or 28 Jul 1943 (FHL microfilm 68804, book 1, no. 127; CHL CR 275 8, no. 558; CHL 10603, 118)

Emilie H. Gertrud Unbereit b. Hamburg 4 Jan 1902; dau. of Karl Unbereit and Dorothea Lina Krüger; bp. 9 Mar 1911; conf. 9 Mar 1911; k. air raid Hamburg 27 or 28 Jul 1943 (CHL microfilm 2458, form 42 FP, pt. 37, 74–75; CHL CR 275 8 2438, no. 676; FHL microfilm 245289, 1930 and 1935 censuses; IGI)

Karl Unbereit b. Hamburg 5 Dec 1903; son of Karl Unbereit and Dorothea Lina Krüger; bp. 17 Mar 1912; conf. 17 Mar 1912; k. air raid Hamburg 27 or 28 Jul 1943 (CHL microfilm 2458, form 42 FP, pt. 37, 74–75; CHL CR 275 8 2438, no. 677; FHL microfilm 245289, 1930 and 1935 censuses)

Bertha Wiedemann b. Seifersdorf, Liegnitz, Schlesien, 28 Apr 1871; dau. of Franz Wiedemann and Magdalena Poppe; bp. 24 Feb 1924; conf. 24 Feb 1924; m. —— Schmidt; d. dropsy 10 Jan 1945 (FHL microfilm 68804, book 2, no. 94; CHL CR 275 8, no. 917; IGI)

Heinrich Wilhelm Worbs b. Nieder Baumgarten, Boltenhain, Schlesien, 21 Nov 1875; son of Heinrich Wilhelm Worbs and Rosa Helene Kuttig; bp. 29 Sep 1922; conf. 29 Sep 1922; ord. teacher 13 Mar 1927; ord. priest 14 Jun 1942; d. pneumonia from concentration camp 8 Oct 1945 (FHL microfilm 68804, book 2, no. 171)

Notes

1. Presiding Bishopric, "Financial, Statistical, and Historical Reports of Wards, Stakes, and Missions, 1884–1955," 257, CHL CR 4 12.
2. Hans Gürtler, "Geschichte der Gemeinde St. Georg" (unpublished history, 1969), 46; private collection.
3. Hertha Schoenrock Hoffmann, interview by the author, Salt Lake City, August 21, 2009. The font of the St. Georg Branch meeting rooms was one of only three in all of Germany.
4. Ingo Zander, interview by the author, West Jordan, UT, March 2, 2007.
5. West German Mission branch directory, 1939, CHL LR 10045 11.
6. West German Mission manuscript history, CHL MS 10045 2.
7. Karl-Heinz Schnibbe, interview by the author in German, Salt Lake City, February 3, 2006.
8. Erwin Frank, interview by the author, Salt Lake City, November 17, 2006.
9. Gerd Fricke, interview by the author in German, Hamburg, Germany, August 15, 2006; unless otherwise noted, summarized in English by Judith Sartowski.
10. Lieselotte Pruess Schmidt, interview by the author, Salt Lake City, December 1, 2006.
11. Otto Albert Berndt, "The Life and Times of Otto Albert Berndt" (unpublished autobiography); private collection.
12. Karl Schoenrock, interview by the author, Ogden, UT, May 30, 2006.
13. Werner Willi Schönrock, telephone interview with Jennifer Heckmann in German, March 17, 2008.
14. Ingeborg Thymian Schaaf, interview by Jennifer Heckmann in German, Göppingen, Germany, August 18, 2006.
15. Astrid Koch Fischer, interview by the author, Salt Lake City, March 24, 2006.
16. Gertrud Frank Menssen, autobiography (unpublished); private collection.
17. Walter Menssen, autobiographical interview, 1974; private collection.
18. Therese Gürtler, autobiography (unpublished).
19. Therese Gürtler Frey, interview by Michael Corley, Salt Lake City, March 14, 2008.
20. Werner Sommerfeld, autobiography, (unpublished); private collection.
21. Harald Fricke, interview by the author in German, Hamburg, Germany, August 15, 2006.
22. Maria Kreutner Niemann, "An Evening with Maria" (unpublished speech, 1988), transcribed by JoAnn P. Knowles; private collection.
23. Herta Schoenrock Hoffmann, interview by the authors, August 21, 2009, Taylorsville, UT.
24. Hilde Pruess Mueller, interview by the author, Salt Lake City, August 9, 2007.
25. Gürtler, "Geschichte der Gemeinde St. Georg," 33.
26. According to Ingo, "I asked my father once if he was a Nazi, and he said 'no.'"
27. Blake indicated that this particular sign was not posted at any LDS meeting location.
28. Berndt, "Life and Times of Otto Albert Berndt."
29. See the Hamburg District chapter for details on this sad episode in the history of the St. Georg Branch.

30. Gürtler, "Geschichte der Gemeinde St. Georg," 35. As it turned out, the fate of the three boys was not generally known. Eyewitnesses from other branches in the West German Mission state that they never heard of Helmut Hübener until decades after the war. It is possible that only the mission leaders knew and felt it inappropriate to spread the sad report.
31. The apparently harsh action by Hamburg Branch and District leaders was considered to be a political necessity of the time and nobody was reprimanded.
32. Walter Menssen, autobiographical interview.
33. Ingrid Lübke Rutz, telephone interview with Judith Sartowski in German, February 20, 2008.
34. Gürtler, "Geschichte der Gemeinde St. Georg," 35. There is no suggestion that the Helmut Hübener affair had anything to do with the loss of the rooms at Besenbinderhof. With increasing damage to the city, such rooms were needed by government agencies and war-critical industries.
35. Berndt, "Life and Times of Otto Albert Berndt."
36. Gertrud Frank Menssen, autobiography.
37. Lilly Rosa Auguste Koch Eloo, telephone interview with Jennifer Heckmann in German, March 7, 2008.
38. Irma Brey Glas, interview by Michael Corley, Taylorsville, UT, October 10, 2008.
39. Fred Zwick, interview by the author, Salt Lake City, June 29, 2007.
40. Waltraud Schoenrock Kunkel, interview by the author, Salt Lake City, August 21, 2009.
41. Niemann, "Evening with Maria."
42. Werner Sommerfeld, autobiography.
43. Anna Marie Haase Frank, interview by the author, Salt Lake City, October 27, 2006.
44. Gertrud Frank Menssen, autobiography.
45. Walter Menssen, autobiographical interview.
46. Gürtler, "Geschichte der Gemeinde St. Georg," 33–34.
47. Hans Gürtler, unpublished autobiography, n.p.
48. Gürtler, "Geschichte der Gemeinde St. Georg," 37. See the Altona Branch chapter for descriptions of damage to the meetinghouse roof and skylights that resulted in such cold conditions.
49. Berndt, "Life and Times of Otto Albert Berndt."
50. Inge Laabs Vieregge, telephone interview with Jennifer Heckmann in Germany, October 2008.
51. Henry Niemann, interview by Michael Corley, South Jordan, UT, October 31, 2008.
52. Walter Menssen, autobiographical interview.
53. Walter Menssen claimed to have provided forged release papers for Erwin, but this account makes no mention of such papers.
54. Walter Menssen, autobiographical interview.
55. Gürtler, "Geschichte der Gemeinde St. Georg," 37.
56. Hans Gürtler, unpublished autobiography, n.p.
57. Werner Sommerfeld, interview by the author, Salt Lake City, January 19, 2007.
58. Harald Fricke, autobiography (unpublished, 2003); private collection.
59. Hans Gürtler, unpublished autobiography, n.p.
60. Karla Schreiner Gürtler, interview by the author, Salt Lake City, July 12, 2007.
61. Niemann, "Evening with Maria."
62. Willy Frank, interview by the author, Salt Lake City, October 27, 2006.

Stade Branch

Situated in the flatlands about two miles west of the Elbe River, Stade was a city of 88,548 when World War II approached.[1] Ten miles from the huge port of Hamburg, the city was home to a very small branch of Latter-day Saints, not even twenty people. With so few members of the Church in Stade, the list of branch leaders is far from complete. Prominent family names were Gellersen, Tiedemann, and Peters.

Stade Branch[2]	**1939**
Elders	4
Priests	0
Teachers	1
Deacons	1
Other Adult Males	2
Adult Females	8
Male Children	2
Female Children	0
Total	18

Louis Gellersen, the owner of a gas station and bicycle shop, was the branch president and was assisted by Christian Tiedemann and Willy Peters. The branch held its meetings in rented rooms on the main floor of a building at Grosse Schmiedestrasse 4. Sunday School took place at 10:00 a.m. and sacrament meeting at 12:30 p.m. There was no official Primary or Relief Society at the time, but members met for MIA every third Thursday of the month, and a genealogy class was held every fourth Thursday, both at 8:00 p.m. One rare characteristic of the Stade Branch was that the president could be reached by telephone at Stade 2664.[3]

Fig. 1. Members of the Stade Branch in about 1933. (I. Gellersen Long)

Even before it began on September 1, 1939, the war had ill effects on the Stade Branch. We read the following in the branch history:

> From August 23 to September 16 [1939] we did not hold any meetings due to the political conditions among Germany, Poland and England. The priesthood holders had responsibilities to the people and the [government], so the meetings had to be cancelled. In addition, no evening meetings could be held because of the blackout regulations.[4]

Young Inge Gellersen (born 1928) recalled her experience with the Jungvolk program and national politics in school:

> When I was ten years old, I was inducted into the Jungmädel, but my father didn't let me go. I think I went twice with a friend, but I didn't like it. They held the meetings in a school; we sang songs, and even the national anthem. We sang the anthem every morning in school, our hands up [in the Hitler salute]. My father never bought me a uniform for the Jungmädel. . . . If you don't have a uniform, you don't want to be in a group when everybody else is wearing one.[5]

Inge recalled the meeting rooms: "The Stade Branch met in one large room and a smaller room. They were separated by a curtain. The children had their own section. . . . There was a sign in the window that said that those were the rooms of the Church. It also stated the meeting schedule and times." Her memories also reflected the vast difference between the LDS setting and the local Lutheran Church: "My mother invited everybody to Church if they seemed interested. One day, she invited a boyfriend of mine. I thought I would die!" Inge's elder brother Manfred (born 1922) recalled their mother's missionary spirit: "She was a kind of district missionary. She went around the whole city twice inviting people to come to church."[6]

Inge also recalled politics in the branch rooms:

> There were pictures on the wall in our room. . . . Next to our Joseph Smith picture was one of Hitler. One day, some [government] officials sat in to listen to testimony meeting. Everybody got up and bore their testimony—even me, as a child. The first person to get up was Brother Tiedemann, and he bore a strong testimony and even said something nice about the Nazis—how well they treated us Mormons. . . . Before they left, they clicked their heels and said, "Heil Hitler!" They told us to be careful what we said and did, but after that meeting they left us alone.

The branch history gives insight into the affairs of this small group of Saints. For example, the clerk noted, "No meetings were held from January 7, 1940, to February 25, 1940, because of the terribly cold temperatures." On April 28, 1940, meetings were canceled due to illness (the same was the case on three other Sundays from 1939 to June 1941 for various reasons and on Sundays when district conferences were held in Hamburg). By June 1941, the attendance had already dropped to about half.[7] This means that only a handful of members were still gathering to worship together by the time the war was halfway over.

Fig. 2. Baptisms in the Stade Branch were conducted in this small canal just north of town. (I. Gellersen Long)

According to Inge Gellersen, Willy Peters had made nice benches for the meeting rooms, but during the war he asked to be released as the second counselor in the branch presidency so that he would be able to attend meetings of the Nazi Party. Sister Peters continued to attend church meetings faithfully.

The Gellersen home at Freiburgerstrasse 54 was located next to and behind the bike shop. At some point during the war, the government took Brother Gellersen's new bicycles; after that, his only business was the repair of older models. His gas station also closed down.

The Gellersen family walked about half an hour to church downtown. Manfred recalled, "We made the trip there and back twice each Sunday. At times the wind blew so hard that we had to walk backwards against it." During the week, Sister Gellersen cleaned the church rooms and also provided wood and coal from the family supply to heat the rooms on Sunday. As Inge recalled, "She didn't want to take the wood and coal there on Sunday because she might get her clothes dirty on the way." According to Manfred, his mother was once cleaning the rooms when some men came in and offered her a job cleaning other rooms in the building. Her response was, "I'm Frau Gellersen. We run a service station, so I don't need a job. This is my church, and I'm doing this for free." Sister Gellersen also put up exhibits in the front window on such themes as the Word of Wisdom, the Book of Mormon, and baptism for the dead. Manfred recalled, "My brother had to paint all of the posters for those exhibits."

A trained automobile mechanic, Manfred Gellersen told his father one day that he was thinking of volunteering for the army. His father's response left a distinct impression: "You don't volunteer. You wait until you're called. I've been there! I know!" Louis Gellersen had taken part in Germany's losing effort in World War I. When Hitler ordered the attack on the Soviet Union in June 1941, Brother Gellersen informed his son, "The war is lost!" In September, Manfred's draft notice arrived. He reported to work the next day in his Sunday suit to announce that he was quitting in order to answer the call to the Wehrmacht, although he had no other option.

Manfred was assigned to a duty that reflected his occupational training. "If you can service automobiles, you can service tanks," he was told. By April 1942, he was in the Soviet Union. He recalled, "I got tired of fixing tanks at 75 degrees below zero." (Temperatures actually reached only about 40 below.) Fortunately, his observance of the LDS health standards rescued him from such duties. Of the 150 men in his company, he was the only one who did not drink alcohol, but he ended up mixing huge batches of brew for his comrades with hot water, rum, and sugar. One night, an officer angry with his drunk driver got Manfred out of bed to drive for him because Manfred was the only one not drunk. "I ended up doing that the whole time," explained Manfred.

In the fall of 1942, Manfred was assigned to Armored Assault Regiment 203, working with the Mark III tank. His unit moved within thirty miles of Moscow before the vehicles froze up in the extreme cold. "We would have won the war [against the Soviet Union] if we'd reached Moscow, but the good Lord interferes with guys like Hitler. We were stuck in the mud, and then it froze, and we had to abandon all of our stuff. (Oil doesn't freeze, it just gets thick like fat.) Then we moved south, and they gave us all new equipment." Manfred's unit was sent toward Stalingrad, where they were to help rescue the encircled German Sixth Army. "But the Romanians and Italians didn't fight, so we couldn't help [our German comrades]. We had to move back from Stalingrad, so they shipped my unit back to Germany."[8]

On one occasion, Manfred narrowly avoided being killed or captured by the Soviets. He and a comrade were sent to pick up a load of ammunition and accidentally drove their small vehicle into the midst of fifteen enemy soldiers at an intersection. Reacting with lightning speed, Manfred made a hard right turn and drove past a house, crashing into a fence. His friend was thrown from the vehicle, and Manfred jumped out and ran for cover while fifteen Soviet soldiers fired their machine guns. They missed, but Manfred encountered one more soldier behind the house. Both instinctively bolted in opposite directions, and Manfred was free to make his way back to the German position, ashamed at having left his comrade behind, along with his commander's suitcase, maps, and other property. Fortunately, when he arrived at his headquarters, his abandoned comrade was already there, safe and sound.

The people of Stade were very fortunate that the city was not the home to critical war industry. Aside from watching and hearing enemy aircraft fly over on their way to Hamburg and other major cities, the residents of Stade went on with their affairs as best they could. The few Latter-day Saints there were sufficiently well off that they were able to respond quickly when the following appeal arrived from the mission office in Frankfurt:

> According to general newsletter no. 2 of the West German Mission dated June 27, 1943, as well as by the request of the Hamburg District Presidency, a request is being made of all members to voluntarily donate anything they can—be it money, clothing or other items—for the relief of the members of the Ruhr District, especially the branches in Barmen and Elberfeld, who have lost their homes in recent air raids. The following items were then collected and prepared for shipment to the district leaders in Hamburg:
>
> Brother Louis Gellersen 200 Marks
> Brother Christian Tiedemann 20 Marks
> Emma Hagenah 5 Marks (nonmember friend)
> 225 Marks total
>
> The following items were donated by Sister Helene Gellersen of Stade:
>
> [coats, underwear, sweaters, pants, blankets, jackets, pens, paper, cutlery, soap, cups, etc.]
>
> Stade on July 9, 1943
>
> Louis Gellersen, branch president[9]

Fig. 3. A very old view of the city of Stade. (I. Gellersen Long)

Like most teenage girls in the Third Reich, Inge Gellersen was called upon to serve for one year in the Pflichtjahr program. She described the experience in these words:

> When I was thirteen years old, I had to serve a Pflichtjahr. I went to a farm in Depenbeck, and when I saw the house for the first time I realized that it must be a huge farm. They had cows and a big and beautiful apple orchard. There were a French POW and a Belgian POW, a Russian forced laborer and a Polish girl named Helena. I got up early every morning before the "madame," as the French and Belgian soldiers called her. . . . The madame cooked the dinner,

> but my task was to prepare breakfast for everybody. I worked mostly in the house, but sometimes they would send me outside to help with the hay. The lady was required to give her workers food for breakfast, lunch, and dinner. Sometimes it wasn't very much. She also sent me into town with the ration coupons and told me what to get.

The madame allowed Inge to go home every other Sunday, and she rode her bicycle the ten miles each way. On one occasion, an overzealous policeman stopped her on the road because she was using her headlight after dark. He chastised her for this violation of the blackout laws, insisting that she could be attacked by an enemy airplane. He then fined her 25 Marks, but she earned only 20 Marks every two weeks and did not have that much money with her. The policeman dutifully came to her home to collect the money and recommended that she make her bicycle trips in daylight.

One of the dangers of life in Hitler's Germany was the possibility of making an innocent statement in the presence of a fanatical party member. Inge recalled how this happened to her mother:

> One day a man came to pick up his bike. My mother gave it to him and then looked up to the sky and said, "Oh, we have a blue sky again! Why are we still fighting in this war?". . . She meant that [the enemy] would come and bomb the city again at night. The man looked at her and said, "I'm a friend of your husband, and I won't tell anybody what you just said." But then he showed us that he was from the secret police. He threatened that he could take her away without giving her the opportunity to say good bye to anybody. "But I'm your husband's friend, and I'll let you off this time. But you have to promise me to never say anything like that again." My mother was a changed person after that. She had always listened to the English BBC radio broadcasts, but she stopped listening to it for fear that somebody would come to take her away.

On leave at home in 1944, Manfred Gellersen was ordained an elder by his father. After returning to the Eastern Front, he was involved in several serious engagements and was awarded the Iron Cross (both First and Second Classes). He was also wounded twice but recovered fully each time. In early 1945, he was stationed in East Prussia near the Baltic Sea coast. The Red Army pushed the German troops against the coast but did not complete the campaign because the Soviets were in a hurry to reach Berlin and end the war. Near the small port of Pillau, Manfred and several others put out to sea in a small craft and were fished out of the water by German sailors who transported them west to the harbor at Swinemünde. Working his way west toward home across northern Germany, he narrowly avoided capture by the advancing British army.

The branch history does not include any irregular statements during the last two years of the war. The Saints in that north German city were truly fortunate in that only one of their number died in the war, and nobody was homeless when the war came to an end. By then, the attendance at meetings had decreased to ten persons, but there is no explanation for this phenomenon.[10] The final entry in wartime reads, "On May 6 our branch meeting rooms were confiscated by the [British] occupation authorities. From now on we will have to hold our meetings in homes."

Manfred Gellersen actually made it all the way home to Stade without spending a day in a POW camp. Moving across the flatlands of the Elbe River basin was difficult, but he stayed in ditches and out of sight until he was able to sneak into his own home like a burglar around three in the morning to surprise his family. However, once at home he could not show himself without the proper release papers. He soon reported to the local British military office, where he was instructed to go to a local POW camp to receive his release papers. As a civilian, he then visited his 1941 employer to ask for his job back, but the employer refused to hire him. Fortunately, there were plenty of jobs for a good mechanic, and Manfred began a new life with his family.

Looking back on his military experiences and his many medals, Manfred explained that he was not a hero. "The heroes are all dead," he declared. "I never had to shoot my weapon at anybody, but they shot at me plenty often!" He never attended a Church meeting away from home, because there simply were none close to his duty locations. Conversations about religion were extremely rare, he explained, "because there was no religion in the German army I knew. And there were no Nazis either. Just soldiers. We just thought about winning the war." Regarding the challenge of remaining a worthy priesthood holder at the front, he stated, "I had plenty of opportunities to fool around [and do sinful things], but I had a good foundation from home."

The British had taken Stade without firing a shot, relieving the residents of the danger of any last-minute deaths trying to save Nazi Germany. Inge recalled her first interaction with the invaders: "They would stand next to their trucks and yell things like, 'Hi, Blondie!' I only spoke a little school English, and we had never learned about the word 'Hi!' so I wasn't sure what they wanted to say. One time, they yelled, 'Hi, Blondie! The war is over! We're going home!' All I could answer was, 'Yes, go home!'"

The Stade Branch was still without an official home at the end of the summer of 1945 as the members continued to collect themselves again from the long conflict. "There were only a few of us left by then," recalled Inge, "my parents and I and the Tiedemanns." Their numbers grew over the coming months and included LDS refugees from the eastern provinces of Germany that had been ceded to Poland.

In Memoriam

Only one known member of the Stade Branch did not survive World War II:

Ernst August Tiedemann b. Schölisch, Stade, Hannover, 29 Sep 1911; son of Christian Ferdinand Friedrich Tiedemann and Margarethe Adele Catharine Marie Bröcker; bp. 18 Jul 1929; conf. 18 Jul 1929; m. 20 Jun 1933, Sophia Richter; k. in battle Eastern Front 21 Apr 1944. (FHL microfilm 68805 no. 7; CHL CR 275 8 2438, no. 829; IGI)

Notes

1. Stade city archive.
2. Presiding Bishopric, "Financial, Statistical, and Historical Reports of Wards, Stakes, and Missions, 1884–1955," 257, CHL CR 4 12.
3. West German Mission manuscript history, CHL MS 1004 2.
4. Stade Branch history, 236, CHL LR 5093 21.
5. Inge Gellersen Long, interview by the author, Bountiful, UT, April 10, 2009.
6. Manfred Gellersen, interview by the author, Salt Lake City, November 3, 2006.
7. Stade Branch History, 241, 243, CHL LF 5093 21.
8. The attack on Stalingrad in the late fall of 1942 was to be supported by many divisions of soldiers from Germany's allies, but when those divisions failed to move forward, the German Sixth Army was isolated and surrounded from the west by the Red Army. By the time the survivors surrendered in early February 1943, as many as 295,000 men were lost. Many Germans came to believe that the disaster of Stalingrad heralded the end of the Third Reich.
9. Stade Branch History, book 2, 10, CHL LR 5093 21.
10. Ibid., 17.

HANOVER DISTRICT

West German Mission

The areas included within the Hanover District of the LDS Church in 1939 were essentially the southeastern portion of the former kingdom of Hanover, the old duchy of Braunschweig (Brunswick) to the east, and the northernmost counties of the former Prussian province of Hessen-Nassau. Surrounding Church districts were the Ruhr on the west, Bremen on the northwest, Hamburg on the north, Frankfurt on the south, and the East German Mission on the east.

Hanover District[1]	**1939**
Elders	21
Priests	15
Teachers	14
Deacons	25
Other Adult Males	69
Adult Females	242
Male Children	18
Female Children	19
Total	423

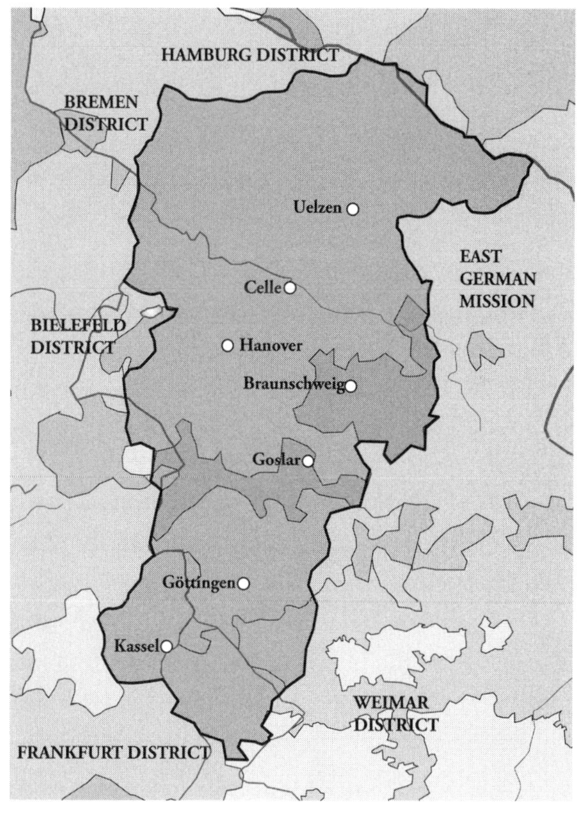

Fig. 1. The Hanover District in north central Germany.

The district was based in the city of Hanover, the political, industrial and cultural center of the region. There were a large LDS branch there and other branches in the cities of Braunschweig (thirty-five miles east), Celle (twenty-two miles northeast), Göttingen (a hundred miles south), Kassel (125 miles south) and Uelzen (sixty miles northeast). A group too small to be a formal branch was holding meetings

Fig. 2. Members of the Hanover Branch met with other Saints for an outing at Langelsheim in the Harz Mountains in 1937. Later district president Willi Wille is at the rear behind Margarete Horn (third from right). Walter Horn of Goslar (third from left) stands next to his daughters Evelyn (left) and Irene. (E. Horn Pruess)

in Goslar (forty miles southeast of Hanover). The branches of the Hanover District were spread across a larger territory than any other district in the West German Mission when World War II approached.

The president of the district in August 1939 was Willi Wille of the Hanover Branch. His only counselor at the time was Hans Bahe of the same branch. Four members of the distant Kassel Branch were district leaders: Konrad Göttig (Sunday School), Maria Schade (Primary), Fritz Diederich (Young Men), and Anny Kersten of Melsungen, ten miles south of Kassel (Young Women). Hermann W. Pohlsander of the Celle Branch was the genealogical specialist and Marie Wernecke of the Uelzen Branch was the president of the Relief Society.[2]

Evidence of enthusiastic activity in the district can be seen in the reports filed by the West German Mission office in Frankfurt in early 1939. For example, a district conference was held in the Künstler Haus in Hanover on March 4–6 (Saturday through Monday), a total of 710 persons attended, and one friend and five children were baptized.[3] The Monday gatherings were most likely social events such as theater performances, dances, hikes through the local woods or visits at cultural or historical sites (as was the custom throughout Germany).

On Friday, March 31, 1939, the annual Gold and Green Ball was hosted by the Hanover Branch in their rooms at Gellertstrasse 10. Eighty-five members of the district attended the event, as did mission president M. Douglas Wood from Frankfurt.[4]

By 1941, Hermann Walter Pohlsander (born 1897) was serving as the substitute president of the Hanover District. It is not known what happened to

Fig. 3. District president Hermann Walter Pohlsander. (H. Pohlsander)

Willi Wille (born 1909), but he was likely drafted into the military. Within a year, Pohlsander was the district president and as such was called to a meeting in the mission home in Frankfurt where the question of succession to mission supervisor Christian Heck was discussed. Pohlsander was of the opinion that it was inappropriate for district presidents to release mission supervisor Heck, who had been drafted by the Wehrmacht and was thus no longer able to carry out his duties. He was able to convince only one other district president, Otto Berndt of Hamburg, of his position, and Berndt joined him in voting against the other ten district presidents of the West German Mission who selected Anton Huck as the new mission supervisor. However, before they left, the two dissenting voters expressed their support for Huck in order to maintain good feelings in the mission at a time when many Germans no longer believed that Hitler could win the war.[5]

From the general minutes of both the Hanover and Celle Branches, it is clear that district conferences were held in Hanover twice each year throughout most of the war. Because the rooms rented by the host branch were too small, larger facilities were used for conferences. For example, on August 29–30, 1942 (Saturday and Sunday), the conference was held in the Haus der Väter in Hanover. According to the minutes of the Hanover Branch, the leaders of the West German Mission presided and Paul Langheinrich, second counselor to the supervisor of the East German Mission, was also in attendance.[6]

The district conference held on March 5, 1944, was a fine affair—this time only one day of meetings. Visitors included mission supervisor Anton Huck from Frankfurt and district presidents Pohlsander (Hanover) and Hegemeister (Bielefeld). Rooms at Volgersweg 54 (close to the original Gellertstrasse 10 rooms) were rented for the meetings, and 177 persons (twenty of whom were called "friends") attended from as far away as Goslar, Kassel, and Frankfurt. The theme of the conference was "The Apostasy and the Restoration of the True Gospel."

The last wartime district conference took place on September 17, 1944. Despite the increasing destruction of the city and the fact that many members had left town (soldiers and mothers with small children), the attendance was still 132 persons, including Anton Huck from the mission office. "Seek ye first for the Kingdom of God" was the theme for the members, who were apparently determined to keep the Church alive in Hanover. Their leaders were definitely trying to do so.[7]

Still functioning as district president when the war ended on May 8, 1945, Hermann Walter Pohlsander and his wife had fled Celle for the safety of the suburb of Garssen. Pohlsander was an accountant for the city, and this may have allowed him to avoid service in the German army. As a postscript of the war, he wrote short descriptions of the status of many of the branches in the Hanover District as of August 1945. Things looked rather bleak, and several branches had lost their meeting places, but hopes were bright for a new start for the Church on the north German heath.[8]

Notes

1. Presiding Bishopric, "Financial, Statistical, and Historical Reports of Wards, Stakes, and Missions, 1884–1955," 257, CR 4 12.
2. West German Mission manuscript history, CHL MS 1004 2.
3. West German Mission quarterly reports, 1939, no. 11, CHL LR 10045 2.
4. West German Mission quarterly reports.
5. Otto Berndt, autobiography (1963), CHL MS 8316, C 14.
6. Hanover Branch general minutes, 126, CHL LR 3594 11.
7. Ibid., 168–69.
8. See the individual sections for the branches of this district on the pages below.

Braunschweig Branch

A city of cultural and political importance for centuries, Braunschweig was also home to a branch of The Church of Jesus Christ of Latter-day Saints in 1939. There were officially seventy-one Saints registered when World War II approached, but only nine were priesthood holders, and the official list of branch officers bears but one name: Willi Wille (district president) as the acting branch president.

Braunschweig Branch[1]	**1939**
Elders	2
Priests	3
Teachers	0
Deacons	4
Other Adult Males	13
Adult Females	39
Male Children	6
Female Children	4
Total	71

The directory of the West German Mission indicates that a home worship service was held each Sunday at 10:30 a.m. at Gördelingerstrasse 18 (third floor).[2] It is not known precisely who lived at that address (presumably a member of the Church), and no eyewitnesses from the branch can be found as of this writing.

In Memoriam

The following members of the Braunschweig Branch did not survive World War II:

Gustav Braun b. Schneiderin, Gerdauen, Ostpreußen, 9 Sep 1865; son of Gottfried Braun and Louise Groneberg; bp. 19 Aug 1924; conf. 19 Aug 1924; ord. deacon 21 Jun 1925; ord. teacher 11 Aug 1926; ord. priest 29 Apr 1928; ord. elder 24 Oct 1937; m. Amalie Wilhelmine Holzstein 26 Dec 1898; d. Braunschweig 11 Jan 1945. (FHL microfilm 68809, no. 4; IGI)

Elizabeth Glorius b. Lenterode, Heiligenstadt, Sachsen, 27 Dec 1882; dau. of Fieligg Glorius and Elizabeth Müller; bp. 26 Jul 1921; conf. 26 Jul 1921; d. pulmonary tuberculosis 15 Feb 1943 (FHL microfilm 68809, no. 24; IGI)

Paul Albert Gottlieb Janitschke b. Nowawes, Teltow, Brandenburg, 3 May 1869; son of Heinrich Janitschke and Emilie Bertholt; bp. 11 Aug 1928; conf. 11 Aug 1928; ord. deacon 11 Nov 1928; m. Antone Knebel 21 Jul 1917; d. dropsy 24 Jul 1943 (FHL microfilm 68809, no. 30)

Elli Lotz b. Braunschweig, 19 May 1919; dau. of Sophie Berta Sprenger; adopted by Conrad Lotz; bp. 26 Jun 1930; conf. 26 Jun 1930; m. Walter Veit 28 Mar 1939; d. childbed fever 4 Sep 1939 (FHL microfilm 68809, no. 39)

Anna Wilhelmine Wagner b. Steinkunzendorf, Reichenbach, Schlesien, 16 Aug 1866; dau. of August Wagner and Johanne Christiane Neumann; bp. 4 Aug 1914; conf. 4 Aug 1914; d. 5 Jun 1941 (FHL Microfilm 68809, no. 32)

Notes

1. Presiding Bishopric, "Financial, Statistical, and Historical Reports of Wards, Stakes, and Missions, 1884–1955," 257, CHL CR 4 12.
2. West German Mission manuscript history, CHL MS 1004 2.

Celle Branch

Located twenty-two miles northeast of the city of Hanover, Celle was a beautiful and historic Lower Saxon city in 1939. The branch of the Church there was one of the smallest in the West German Mission and for years consisted of one family and a few friends.

Branch president Hermann Walter Pohlsander (born 1897) was a dedicated member of the Church, as apparently were the members of his immediate family, namely his wife, Bertha, his daughters, Ingrid and Alheit (Heiti), and his sons, Hans-Achim and Herm-Gerdt. In accordance with the practice in the West German Mission, Brother Pohlsander kept careful minutes of all meetings, which of course were held in the family home at Mühlenstrasse 11a in Celle. The minutes indicate that Brother Pohlsander conducted each meeting and blessed the sacrament. Hans-Achim passed the sacrament, and Heiti played the pump organ. The parents alternated in giving the lessons, and prayers were given by various family members. The minutes also indicate the numbers of the hymns sung during those meetings. The names of members of the Ross family (refugees from the Schneidemühl Branch of the East German Mission) appear beginning in 1940. The branch president also wrote the names of all visitors from other branches, the district, and the mission. These visitors brought joy and variety to the Sunday activities of these isolated Saints.

Celle Branch[1]	**1939**
Elders	1
Priests	1
Teachers	0
Deacons	0
Other Adult Males	2
Adult Females	7
Male Children	3
Female Children	1
Total	15

In October 1939, Hermann Walter Pohlsander was called to be a counselor to Willi Wille, the president of the Hanover District. He was set apart by mission supervisor Friedrich Biehl on November 5, 1939. The calling required him to travel frequently and at times attend conferences in cities well beyond the boundaries of the district. Even on such Sundays, he dutifully noted in his minutes why no services were held in his home in Celle.

"We held the meetings of the Church in our home in the Mühlenstraße 11a," recalled Hans Achim Pohlsander (born 1927).[2] "It was located in the city center. We lived on the second floor while the landlord lived on the ground floor. We had a pump organ in our living room, but we didn't hear any complaints from the neighbors about the noise." Hans recalled that the landlord was the local Nazi Party leader and worked in the same office as Hans's father, but the two men kept out of each other's way when it came to politics.

Hans's sister Ingrid (born 1923) recalled moving the furniture around every Sunday to accommodate the branch members, most of whom were members of her family. The branch population actually increased during the war, as she explained: "Members from eastern Germany came as refugees and met with us."[3]

Regarding the possibility of disturbing the neighbors with their singing, Ingrid said: "They didn't seem to mind, even when we played the pump organ. And we children never made noise anyway. My father was a very stern, strict man. He demanded obedience. Often, he wouldn't have to look at us or say anything—we got the message. If we misbehaved, he would take us up into the attic. But that was [the typical German father] at the time—strict obedience and strict punishment."

Fig. 1. The Pohlsander family of Celle. From left: Heiti, Bertha, Hans-Achim, Herm-Gerdt, Hermann Walter, Ingrid. (I. Pohlsander Perkins)

In Ingrid's recollection, the branch meetings were very simple: her father presided and conducted and blessed the sacrament, which her brother Hans passed to those present. The family met in private each Sunday evening as well. "Then my father would teach us the gospel," she explained. "My basic knowledge of the gospel came from those meetings."

Hans recalled the following about the attendees at church meetings in his home:

> Our family attended the meetings, and a few other individuals joined us. I also remember a Sister Schütte who came from Bremen. She came to live in Celle to escape the air raids on her city. She was single. We got to give talks quite regularly and we participated actively in all the meetings. Richard Müller from Danzig was a soldier in an officer training course. Toward the end of the war he became a POW of the British and was released and stayed with us for a little while until he could find better accommodations.

President Pohlsander also recorded comments on events, such as the invasion of Poland on September 1, 1939.[4] On the same page, he wrote of the visit of Elder Joseph Fielding Smith and mission president M. Douglas Wood with their wives in Hanover on August 24. One of the saddest reports was the illness and death of young Herm-Gerdt (born 1933). His father made this entry on February 20, 1940:

> After four physicians and two healing practitioners failed, and despite repeated blessings and the fasting and prayers of his parents, his brothers and sisters and other members of the Church, all hopes of a recovery vanished. I gave him a blessing this afternoon, February 20, 1940, that our Father in Heaven would allow him a peaceful death. And so, our dear, good little Herm-Gerdt peacefully passed away this evening at 8 p.m. after [months of] serious suffering and struggling.[5]

Finding a place to bury the little boy was a challenge because the local cemetery belonged to the Lutheran Church. Brother Pohlsander was fortunate to be granted permission to bury Herm-Gerdt next to a grandmother and a great-grandmother in the cemetery in Celle-Neuenhausen. Members of the Hanover Branch joined the Celle Saints in celebrating the boy's short life.[6]

The general minutes include the following items of interest in the Celle Branch during the first few years of the war:

> June 16, 1940: Alheit Elsabein Pohlsander was baptized in a public bath in Hanover.[7]
>
> August 9, 1940: Johannes Kaufmann and Gertrude Ross were married.
>
> September 29, 1940: Philipp Lühring returned to activity in the Church after six years.
>
> March 23, 1941: a bomb landed in the street in front of the Pohlsander home; no damage was done.
>
> November 9, 1941: Fritz Todebusch of Dortmund visited the meeting.
>
> May 24, 1942: mission supervisor Christian Heck visited the branch. [He came again on April 26, 1943.]
>
> December 19, 1943: Albert Gahn was baptized in the bathhouse in Celle.

Fig. 2. The home of the Hermann Walter Pohlsander family at Mühlenstrasse 11a in Celle. The living room that was used for church meetings was on the second floor to the left. The girls' bedroom was the top window. (I. Pohlsander Perkins)

At the close of 1942, Brother Pohlsander added this comment to the minutes of the meetings:

> The old year is now ending. All of the difficulties we faced when the year began have been resolved and many of the wishes and hopes we had then have since been fulfilled. May all of the Saints master the year 1943 and may the blessing of our Father in Heaven be with all of us and may His kingdom come with power![8]

Young Hans Pohlsander had been a member of the Jungvolk since the age of ten and was advanced into the Hitler Youth at age fourteen. He remained associated with the group until the last month of the war. The activities were not particularly exciting, but at least they did not interfere with church meetings. For a young man in such a small group of Saints, church meetings held in other towns were especially interesting, as he recalled:

> During the war, we went to district conferences in Hanover. They were usually held in a school building, which I can't recall exactly. The district conferences were nice occasions to get together. On several occasions, I went with my father when he visited branches of the district. I went with him to Goslar on at least one occasion and Braunschweig also. The meeting facility was bombed out in Braunschweig. I knew Walter Horn and his family from Goslar.

Ingrid also recalled the district conferences—including the time when she and Heiti were asked to speak. Despite that nerve-racking experience, "We always had a great time at district conferences," explained Ingrid. "It was an adventure, but I didn't really get to know the youth of other branches very well because we were [geographically] isolated."

The two sisters were fortunate to avoid involvement with the League of German Maidens. Ingrid explained that because their family was so large, she and Heiti were justified in staying home to help their mother, who likewise was not required to leave the home for employment. According to Ingrid, Brother Pohlsander made a comfortable living as an accountant for the city. The family enjoyed indoor plumbing and a small water heater that facilitated the Saturday evening bath. "We enjoyed a very nice lifestyle."

The landlord, Herr Hornbostel, lived with his family on the ground floor. Also a city employee but a member of the Nazi Party, he differed significantly from Brother Pohlsander on political questions, recalled Ingrid.

> But they kept out of each other's way. I don't know how my father avoided the pressure of joining the party. At least twice, he was called in by the Gestapo and questioned [about the Church], but nothing came of it. He and my mother would discuss political issues of the day with us children, but we knew we could not repeat outside what was said in our home. When we joined the Hornbostels in the basement during air raids, we had to be very careful not to criticize the government.

Regarding the activities of youth during the war, Ingrid recalled:

> Whenever we wanted to do something fun, we would go to the park and feed the ducks. It wasn't a time to have fun or to attend parties—it was a time to stay alive. I didn't go on any dates during the war. We were the only Mormons in the city, and I didn't want to date other people, not even other Christians. I didn't even wonder if my father would approve of it, because it never came to that.

Hans finished his public schooling at the age of fourteen and was accepted into a secondary school (a Gymnasium). This was a great privilege but came to an end prematurely due to the war. By the fall of 1944, Hans was one of only three remaining students who had not yet been drafted. The school then shut down, and the three remaining students were assigned to work in local businesses to replace workers away at war. "I was an office errand boy in a factory," recalled Hans.

Enemy air raids did not harass the old city of Celle until the end of the war, as Hans recalled. He and his family did not have access to a concrete bunker when the sirens sounded; thus they took refuge in their basement. "But we didn't feel very safe there," Hans said. Alarms were a common occurrence, but the only real attack Hans could recall occurred on about April 4, 1945. It was a devastating attack and took the lives of a family in the Celle Branch. The Kaufmanns had married during the war and had a little boy by 1945. All three were killed in that attack.

President Pohlsander made this entry in the branch minutes:

> April 4, 1945: It was Sunday and the sun shone brightly when suddenly, the air raid sirens began to wail around town. A few minutes later, the bombers appeared over Celle. During this terrifying attack—that cannot be described in words—many people were killed and a great deal of property was destroyed. Our dear Kaufmann family was killed in a brutal fashion, namely Sister Gertrud Kaufmann nee Ross, her husband Hermann Kaufmann and their little boy, Tilo, who had celebrated his first birthday just the day before. The funeral took place on the morning of Monday, April 16 [*sic*], 1945, at the forest cemetery. At three p.m., Hermann Walter Pohlsander dedicated the graves. . . . May the earthly remains of this dear Kaufmann family rest in peace until their resurrection.[9]

Fig. 3. These old structures on the Stechbahn in Celle survived the war. (R. Minert, 1979)

One of the ongoing mysteries of World War II is the question of who was aware of the atrocities committed in concentration camps within Germany. The question of what went on there bothered some Latter-day Saints as well. Hans Pohlsander recalled this unforgettable experience:

> We recognized that there was something going on in Bergen-Belsen [twelve miles northwest of Celle] very late in the war. They also had a POW camp for Russian soldiers close by, and we knew that they were terribly mistreated. They died of starvation and illness, and we knew that. I didn't see working parties from that camp, but I think my father encountered that. Only later did we find out about the concentration camp. . . . In that [April 4] air raid, another terrible thing happened. In the train yards, there was a train load of concentration camp prisoners on their way to the camp in Bergen-Belsen. In the course of the air raid, they escaped from their train, which resulted in many of them being killed in the air raid. The survivors were hunted down that evening by the police and the SS. Thousands of them were killed. It was a great tragedy. I think I saw two or three [bodies] of the prisoners who were killed.[10]

Some of the last war-time entries made by President Pohlsander in the branch minutes are these:

> December 3, 1944: Soldier Richard Müller of the Danzig Branch [East German Mission] visited us today [the first of several visits].
>
> February 4, 1945: Elfriede Bauer, a refugee from Schneidemühl, gave her testimony. Her mother is with her.
>
> March 30, 1945: The branch president visited refugees from the Breslau Branch [East German Mission] living in nearby Wietze.[11]

Just as the Third Reich was crumbling in every regard, the country called upon young Hans Pohlsander; he was drafted into the home guard—a force consisting of old men and boys. Fortunately, his military service lasted barely one month and was uneventful, as he explained:

> Two days after the air raid [of April 4], my unit of the Volkssturm left Celle, and for the next four weeks or so, we were constantly withdrawing, always a few miles ahead of the British advance. When Germany capitulated on May 8, we were simply dismissed and told it was over. They told us to find a way home on our own. That happened in northern Germany, near Stade. I was

> picked up by a British military patrol and taken to a POW collection point, and once I was there a British officer came around and asked, "Is there anyone around here claiming to be a civilian?" I did. I had already discarded my uniform and was wearing civilian clothing. I was physically underdeveloped and didn't look my age. I showed him my military ID, which didn't have an entry in it after I had been called up. The officer released me. It took me another two weeks to get home because I had to walk back to Celle.

When Hans arrived at home, he found that his family had been spared tragedy and were in good health. They had taken refuge on a farm near the village of Garssen (two miles north of Celle) just after the bombing of April 4 and were still there when the British invaders entered Celle. In May, the Pohlsanders returned to Celle. They were very happy to find that their home had survived the bombing undamaged and that Brother Pohlsander's treasures had not been discovered: he had buried boxes full of genealogical documents in the backyard, determined to safeguard his collection from enemy soldiers on the lookout for valuables of all kinds.

On the farm, Ingrid saw British soldiers for the first time. She recalled hearing on the radio that the enemy should be feared and resisted, and her family did not even hang out white sheets. What appeared to be black soldiers turned out to be white soldiers with black paint on their faces, she recalled. The soldiers took up quarters in the Hornbostel home, but soon left, complaining that the home was too small for their needs. Ingrid had studied English in a secondary school and was thus able to converse with them on a basic level. "They took my brother's electric train and my sister's pretty doll, but other than that, they didn't destroy anything." While the soldiers were in the home, the family lived with another family in the laundry room at the back of the building.

It is unfortunate that even this small group of Saints could not live through the war without frightful tragedies. Nevertheless, the Pohlsanders, the other surviving Celle Branch members, and the refugees from the East German Mission (whose numbers increased throughout the summer of 1945) looked forward to a new life free of tyranny.

In Memoriam

The following members of the Celle Branch did not survive World War II:

Johannes Ludwig Kaufmann b. Bischhofshagen, Westfalen, 30 Jun 1912; son of Julius Karl Kaufmann and Anna Marie Gross; m. Celle, Hannover, 9 Aug 1940, Gertrud Margarete Ross; 1 child; k. air raid Celle 4 Apr 1945 (IGI)

Thilo Kaufmann b. Celle, Hannover, 7 Apr 1944; son of Johannes Ludwig Kaufmann and Gertrud Margarethe Ross; k. air raid Celle 4 Apr 1945 (FHL microfilm 68809, no. 32; IGI)

Hermann Gerdt Jan Pohlsander b. Celle, Hannover, 4 Jul 1933; son of Hermann Heinrich Walther Pohlsander and Bertha W. D. S. Schöneberg; d. lymphatic leukemia 20 Feb 1940; bur. Celle-Neuhausen 24 Apr 1945 (FHL microfilm 68809, no. 24; IGI)

Gertrud Margarete Ross b. Schneidemühl, Posen, 20 Sep 1917; dau. of Adolf Wilhelm Ross and Wilhelmine Marie Anna Klingenhagen; bp. 27 Feb 1927; m. Celle, Hannover, 9 Aug 1940, Johannes Ludwig Kaufmann; 1 child; k. air raid Celle 4 Apr 1945 (FHL microfilm 68809, no. 27; IGI)

Notes

1. Presiding Bishopric, "Financial, Statistical, and Historical Reports of Wards, Stakes, and Missions, 1884–1955," 257, CHL CR 4 12.
2. Hans Pohlsander, telephone interview by the author, December 2, 2009.
3. Ingrid Pohlsander Perkins, interview by the author, Payson, UT, January 20, 2010.
4. Celle Branch general minutes, 149, CHL LR 1519 11.
5. Brother Pohlsander did not identify the illness that took the life of this child, but he said that Herm-Gerdt's red blood cell count was "one million rather than more than 5,000,000." It was likely leukemia. Celle Branch general minutes, 154.
6. Celle Branch general minutes, 156.
7. The entries cited were taken from the Celle Branch general minutes, 160, 162, 164, 168, 175, 181 (also 188), and 193.
8. Ibid., 185.
9. Ibid., 205.
10. The concentration camp Bergen-Belsen is probably best known as the place where Anne Frank died in 1945.
11. Celle Branch general minutes, 201–3.

Göttingen Branch

Famous for its outstanding university, the city of Göttingen lies near the southern border of the old kingdom of Hanover, approximately one hundred miles south of the city of Hanover. The railroad from Hanover to Frankfurt connected the two cities and made it easy for members of the Church in Göttingen to attend district conferences in Hanover.

One of the smallest branches in Germany when the war began in 1939, Göttingen had a single elder, and most of the members were older women. According to the mission directory of August 1939, the only meeting held in the branch was Sunday School, which took place at 10:00 a.m.[1] The location of the meeting hall was Schildweg 5 in a Hinterhaus. The term "cottage meeting" was used, suggesting that the address was that of a member of the branch.

Göttingen Branch[2]	**1939**
Elders	1
Priests	0
Teachers	0
Deacons	1
Other Adult Males	4
Adult Females	11
Male Children	0
Female Children	1
Total	18

The branch president, Bruno Regenscheit, is the only person named among the leaders of the Göttingen Branch. Nothing else is known about this small group of Latter-day Saints as of this writing because no eyewitnesses or documents can be located.

No members of the Göttingen Branch are known to have died in World War II.

Notes

1. West German Mission manuscript history, CHL MS 1004 2.
2. Presiding Bishopric, "Financial, Statistical, and Historical Reports of Wards, Stakes, and Missions, 1884–1955," 257, CHL CR 4 12.

Goslar Group

When World War II began in September 1939, the only members of The Church of Jesus Christ of Latter-day Saints living in Goslar were the family of Walter Horn. With his wife, Rosilie, and three daughters, Walter had moved to Goslar from Weimar, where the family had been faithful members of the branch. The family was motivated to move because Nazi Party leaders in Weimar were putting pressure on Brother Horn to join the Party. It occurred to him that he might escape that pressure by moving to Goslar, where he found other employment. According to his daughter, Evelyn (born 1932), the tactic worked: "Once we got to Goslar, the party there did not come looking for my father."[1]

Evelyn's earliest memories in Goslar include seeing Jewish residents with the garish yellow Star of David on their coats. She recalled telling her girlfriend that it was not nice to make the people wear that star because it made them nervous when people saw it. When she told that to her mother, Sister Horn panicked and said, "Don't you ever dare say this to anybody or else they will pick up your father and take him away!" After that, Evelyn worried every time there was a knock at the door that somebody was coming to arrest her father.

The Horns held church meetings in their home. Walter and Rosilie taught their children the gospel, and they sang the hymns of Zion. "We rented a pump organ and eventually owned it," recalled

Fig. 1. Walter Horn (left rear, with shirt and tie) was probably considered conservative when he participated in this company outing to the Baltic Sea in 1943. (E. Horn Pruess)

Evelyn. "When we held our testimony meeting, we just went around the table, and everybody gave their testimony—young and old." Brother Horn taught his family from several different church books, such as *The Voice of Warning* by Parley P. Pratt. As the district president of the Sunday School, Brother Horn was an expert in Church literature.

The Horns were joined early in the war by Sister Kramer and her daughter, Hilda, so the group of Saints grew from five to seven. The family sometimes traveled from Goslar to Hanover (forty miles away) to conferences and other church activities. Evelyn was baptized in a public bathhouse in Hanover along with several other persons from the district.

Walter Horn was employed by the Greifwerke, a company that made stationery items for the government. As a small man, he was classified as unfit for military service, something neither he nor his family ever regretted. In many ways, the war seemed far away from this historic city at the foot of the Harz Mountains, but Evelyn Horn knew that there was a war going on. The military hospitals established in local hotels offered clear evidence of that. As she recalled:

> We were encouraged in school to take our families and visit the soldiers. So on Sunday afternoons we would go and visit the soldiers, and then later on they made it even a school thing that we had to just go with recorders or violin or whatever and sing for them or play music. I remember that one time I just couldn't stand to see those people suffer, and I was just sick. . . . There was one man who had just been dragged out from under a burning tank, and you couldn't see anything [because he was all wrapped up], and it smelled awful in there.

On many occasions, Evelyn and her sisters saw soldiers who were well enough to walk around

Fig. 2. Winter 1943: the Horn girls (from left, Annegret, Irene, and Evelyn) with their mother, Rosilie, grandmother Anna Gluth (whose home had been bombed in Hanover), and visiting Luftwaffe soldier Hans Beyer. (E. Horn Pruess)

town, but even that was a frightening sight. She recalled seeing soldiers who had severe facial injuries. Skin was grafted from an arm to the face, and a soldier would walk around town with his arm tied to his face. "I've always been happy-go-lucky, but I thought, 'Oh these poor guys!' It was terrible. Sometimes, one side of the face was already healed, and it was all just red and the other side still [looked terrible]."

For the three Horn girls, growing up in wartime meant restrictions in the types of entertainment available. However, their parents knew how to entertain their daughters. According to Evelyn, "we were a family of readers. We read a lot. When we couldn't get new books, my mother went through all of our books and picked out the ones we could read. I read lots of books that were written for adults."

The air raids that made life unbearable in larger cities were not a problem in Goslar, but on occasion enemy planes flew by Goslar on the way to other targets, and that set off the local sirens When the sirens wailed, the Horns went down into their dank basement and listened to the radio until the all-clear was sounded. "They never bombed us, so eventually, nobody worried if people didn't all come to the basement," claimed Evelyn Horn. Nevertheless, the Horns always took a briefcase with their most important personal and genealogical records.

The war ended in Goslar in mid-April 1945 with the arrival of the American army. The city's mayor asked that the residents hang white sheets out of their windows. Evelyn recalled the day:

> All of a sudden, somebody came running down the street yelling, "They're here! They're here!" . . . We all ran down to the end of the street and waved to them, and they threw chocolate and all kinds of stuff around. . . . They were smiling

> and waving, and people were waving [back], and it was liberation. . . . The next morning we had a surprise: there were all kinds of pamphlets glued and stapled on the buildings [with curfew restrictions] in German.

The Horn family spent the war years in relative peace, and the war came to an end for them in an equally peaceful way. In the following months, LDS refugees from the East German Mission moved into the area around Goslar, and soon group leader Walter Horn found himself branch president.

District president Hermann Walter Pohlsander wrote the following in his report to the West German Mission office in August 1945:

> The dependent branch of Goslar, which is connected with the Braunschweig Branch, has only 7 members, consisting of the Horn family in Goslar and Sisters Kraemer Sr. and Jr. in Oker. The meetings are held in the home of Elder Walther Horn. The branch is small but very fine. At this time there are also members of the East German Mission [refugees] in Oker.[2]

No known members of the Goslar group died during World War II.

Notes

1. Evelyn Horn Pruess, interview by the author, Salt Lake City, December 1, 2006.
2. Goslar Group general minutes, CHL LR 3260 2.

Hanover Branch

Formerly the capital of the Prussian province of the same name, the city of Hanover was home to 470,950 people as World War II approached in the late summer of 1939.[1] One of the largest branches in the West German Mission was meeting at the time in rented rooms at Gellertstrasse 10. Doris Fraatz (born 1927) had this recollection of the facility:

> The rooms were used as a dance school during the week. Brother and Sister Wille lived in the same building. Willy Wille was our district president at that time. It was quite a large building. Downstairs in the dance school were benches and a wardrobe. We used those rooms also. The large room of the dance school was the room in which we held our meetings. We put up single chairs for everybody to sit on. There was also a podium in the front of the room. . . . Classes also met in the living room or the bedrooms of the Wille apartment. The dance studio was on the main floor of the building. I think we even had a central heating system at that time. . . . I remember that we would meet outside in the backyard for classes in the summer. We also had a restroom inside. For Primary meetings, we met in a different home sometimes because the dance studio was closed for us during the week. There might have been one hundred and fifty people in attendance on a typical Sunday.[2]

Doris added these comments about goings-on in the meetings:

> In Primary they would ask us if we knew of any poems that we could recite, and if we could, we had to do it during sacrament meeting. All the young children sat on one side of the room, based on their age either in the very front or the following rows. I remember that my mother always looked around to make sure that we were behaving. Whenever we were fidgety, my mother would wave, and as soon as she did that, we knew what she meant—we had to sit still.

Hanover Branch[3]	**1939**
Elders	12
Priests	9
Teachers	8
Deacons	12
Other Adult Males	43
Adult Females	128
Male Children	3
Female Children	11
Total	226

Fig. 1. The Hanover Branch Sunday School children in the summer of 1938. Several of the children were not members. (H. Reschke)

The mission directory compiled in the summer of 1939 shows a full complement of leaders. The branch president was an American missionary (Edward J. Wirthlin), but all other leaders were local Saints.[4] Apparently, all Church programs were in operation in this branch. As was common all over the mission, well over half the branch membership were females over twelve years of age.

The schedule of meetings suggests that the Hanover Branch members saw each other several times each week. The Sunday School met at 10:00 a.m., and sacrament meeting began at 7:00 p.m. Because of the central location of the meeting rooms, most members went home for dinner between Sunday meetings, then returned in the evening. Mutual was held on Tuesdays at 8:00 p.m., Primary on Wednesdays at 4:00 p.m., and Relief Society on Thursdays at 8:00 p.m.

Doris Fraatz recalled walking the two miles from her home on Wörthstrasse to the church. After Sunday School, the family went home for dinner, then returned for sacrament meeting in the evening. This meant about eight miles (about two hours) of walking each Sunday, which was quite common for members of the Church in that large city.[5]

Following the evacuation of the American missionaries from Germany on August 25, 1939, Hans Bahe was called to be the president of the Hanover Branch with Stanislaus Kubiak and Richard Krafft as his counselors.[6] A few weeks later, mission supervisor Friedrich Biehl visited the branch along with three district presidents.[7] The life of the branch continued without substantial disturbances through 1939, and sacrament meeting attendance averaged forty-two persons. The average declined to about thirty-six attendees for 1940 and thirty-four in 1941.

Doris Fraatz completed public schooling at age fourteen and could have continued, but the advanced school was too far from home. In Hanover, she worked under the Pflichtjahr program, serving the nation for one year. As she recalled, "The family I worked for owned a radio store, and they had two children. I was very fortunate to be able to work for them. They also did not live very far away from us, so I was able to go home after work. [At that time] I was the Sunday School teacher for the eight-year-old children in our branch." When the service year ended, she found employment with the local Continental Tire Company, a job that would last until the last few weeks of the war.

Max Reschke was not a follower of Adolf Hitler. His daughter, Annegret (born 1936), recalled once seeing Hitler drive by in a parade and hearing her father say, "I will never support that man!" Having been wounded during World War I, Max was fortunate to be exempt from the draft during the next war. He was also a director in a pharmaceutical company, an industry quite indispensible to the war effort. The family was pleased to have their father in town during the entire war.[8] Brother Reschke's life was, however, not without challenges; he spent some time in a Gestapo camp for hiding a Jewish friend in his home.[9]

President Bahe was drafted by the Wehrmacht in January 1942, which necessitated a change in branch leadership. The new presidency consisted of Richard Krafft, Stanislaus Kubiak, and Karl Blombach.[10]

With more than two hundred members, the Hanover Branch was in a position to offer support for smaller branches nearby. On several occasions before the war and whenever possible during the first few years of the war, Saints from Hanover traveled to rural areas to enjoy walks, picnics, and other activities. For example, on the Monday after Easter in 1942, thirty members of the Hanover Relief Society traveled west to Stadthagen (Bielefeld District) to present a program commemorating the centennial of the Relief Society.[11]

The Hanover Branch was confronted with bad news in April 1942, when their rental contract at Gellertstrasse 10 was canceled. Fortunately the branch leaders were able to find a new place to meet about one mile to the northwest, namely in the Fischer Gesellschaftshaus at Weissekreuzstrasse 10. That building was less than one mile from the center of town and thus a good location for most of the members.[12] However, the Fischer building was likely no longer available that fall, because the general minutes report meetings being held in the homes of various members around town. Attendance dropped to about twenty-five persons in those months.

Fig. 2. The branch performed Snow White *in 1938. (H. Reschke)*

Being a child during the war was not always easy. Nevertheless, German children were like their counterparts in other nations at war when it came to making their own lives more enjoyable. The following is from the recollections of Annegret Reschke: "Toys, the kind one would buy in a store, were rare because few were available. Yet our imaginations knew no bounds. We would fashion dollhouses out of old boxes, and paper dolls were cut from old magazines. Our childhood was different but happy nonetheless, because we were children—resilient and optimistic."[13]

Life became more difficult for Annegret when school began. When she was asked to introduce herself and identify her religious affiliation on the first day, she decided to mention the name "Mormons" instead of the full name of her church. Unfortunately, the term *Mormonen* sounded to the other children like *Mongolen* (Mongolians), and a wave of mockery met Annegret's ears. At that moment, a very kind teacher stepped forward to correct the misunderstanding. As Annegret recalled, "She asked me to come to the front of the room and sit in her chair. Then she directed each child to come forward, shake my hand, and apologize for calling me a *Mongole*. I have never forgotten her kindness."[14]

Anton Huck, first counselor to mission supervisor Christian Heck, visited the branch in May 1942. Such visitors were welcome throughout the mission, but on this occasion it may have been requested by the branch president. The branch general minutes indicate that President Huck called three sisters to repentance. He was assisted in this difficult task by district president Hermann Walter Pohlsander and branch president Richard Krafft. The minutes do not report the results of the encounter, but the recorder ended his account of the affair with this sentence: "May the heavens be merciful to these three unteachable and errant sisters!"[15]

Throughout Germany, LDS branches had hosted a wide variety of cultural programs since the early 1930s. Many such programs could no longer be offered once the war started, but the minutes of the Hanover Branch include reports of two *Wunschkonzerte* ("concerts by request"). On November 28, 1942, a concert was presented in

Haus der Väter and attended by 116 persons ("including several children"). The report does not indicate what was presented, but the review was enthusiastic: "The Spirit of the Lord was in attendance to a great degree and the attending friends expressed their gratitude many times." Visitors came from as far away as Goslar (the Horn family).[16]

The Saints in Hanover must have felt like vagabonds when they were required to move again in December 1942. The new location for their meetings was Markstrasse 64, just one block from the city hall. Elder Pohlsander presided over the first meeting at that location and offered a dedicatory prayer for the facility. Two weeks later, the branch held a Christmas celebration that was enjoyed by thirty persons.[17] Despite the many changes of venue for meetings in 1942 and the holding of some meetings in families' apartments, attendance in sacrament meetings averaged thirty-five persons.

Fig. 3. The M-Men and Gleaners of the Hanover Branch. (H. Reschke)

During the summer of 1943, Doris Fraatz and her family spent substantial time at their tiny garden property at the outskirts of town. On one occasion, the air-raid sirens began to wail and there was not time to reach the bunkers. According to Doris, "While lying on the floor of our little cabin, I heard my father cry out, 'They got me!' I remember my mother repeatedly asking: 'Papa, are you still alive?' The cigarette factory nearby was burning—we could see it and hear it. My father had gotten a piece of shrapnel in his chest. It went through the cabin walls, but what was a blessing—my father wore suspenders that day."

As the Allied air war increased in intensity, the city of Hanover became a favorite target. The first mention of air raids in the branch general minutes is a positive note written after the attack on July 26, 1943: "The city of Hanover was punished by an air raid, but our meeting rooms at Marktstrasse 64 were spared any damage."[18] Unfortunately, time ran out for the building just three months later, as we read:

> October 10, 1943: No Sunday School or sacrament meeting was held today because our meetinghouse was totally destroyed in an air raid during the night of October 8–9. . . . So far none of the members of the Church of Jesus Christ of Latter-day Saints has been killed. However, some have lost everything and others have suffered lesser damages. The Lord, our Heavenly Father, has been merciful to His children. So far, he has sent His protecting angel to watch over us. The Lord has heard the prayers of His children.[19]

Hans Bahe was one of the many LDS men who had to leave a wife and little children to answer the call of the Wehrmacht. His wife, Margaretha, cared for her two daughters, Erika (born 1937) and Sylvia (born 1938), in a Hanover that was beginning to unravel. Sylvia recalled that they became so accustomed to the air raids that her mother could hear the planes approaching even before the alarms sounded. "We didn't even get undressed [to go to bed] anymore. We just stayed in our clothes, so we were the first ones to get to the shelter downstairs in our basement."[20] Eventually, the Bahe apartment was partially burned, and Sister Bahe and her daughters were taken to the town of Holtensen near Göttingen. They would be isolated from the Church for the rest of the war.

It may be that the spirit of the Saints in Hanover was suffering slightly in November 1943, because the general minutes indicate that President Pohlsander felt it necessary to encourage them to stop criticizing and judging. "He told the members to use their agency for good and to merit eternal exaltation." At the same time, some members were doing very well, such as Sister Helena Grahn, whose husband, Albert, had been a friend of the Church for years. He spoke in a testimony meeting, thanking God for saving him and his family from the air raids and expressing the desire to be baptized as soon as possible.[21]

Fig. 4. A branch picnic in the summer of 1939. (H. Reschke)

The bad news increased with the air raids of late 1943. The following lost everything in the final days of November: the Kubiak, Wille, and Böker families, as well as Sister Grahn and Sister Barthelt. The Liebig family and Sister Stockhausen suffered damage to their homes.[22] Despite the challenges of the time, the average sacrament meeting attendance remained at about thirty-four persons for the year 1943.

A new home was found for the branch at Volgersweg 54 in downtown Hanover. The building had been rented for a district conference on March 5, 1944, and by April an ongoing contract had been negotiated. The spirit of permanence was again felt as evidenced by the fact that district president Pohlsander pronounced a dedicatory prayer in the presence of thirty-eight persons. In a unique entry, the clerk indicated that President Pohlsander took the opportunity that day to convey greetings from the leadership of the East and West German Missions, as well as from Denmark and Switzerland. He also spoke of a message received from Christian Heck, the former West German Mission supervisor, then serving on the Eastern Front.[23]

The following recollection of Doris Fraatz seems to best fit the rooms at Volgersweg:

> I remember that we also met in a cheap restaurant for a while as a branch. The smell was terrible, and the brethren had to go before the meetings to clean up so that we could hold the meetings there. It smelled like beer every time. This restaurant was in the city center, and we went there after we lost our rooms in the Gellertstrasse.

At age seventeen in 1944, Doris might have been hoping for a more exciting social life, but this was not the case, as she recounted:

> We could not really have fun as children or teenagers in the war. The bombings were constant. Dancing and dating were not our regular interests, but the districts and branches made sure that the young people had something they could do together. . . . All the young boys were gone and had to serve in the war. What social life I had was connected with the Church.

In the village of Holtensen near Göttingen, Margaretha Bahe and her daughters lived in a few spare rooms on a farm. According to her eldest daughter, Erika, Sister Bahe worked in a dairy; she printed the wrapping papers for butter. The farmers resented the presence of the city folks and did not do any more for them than necessary. Margaretha had no way to get to church meetings in Göttingen (just a few miles away), so she held a Sunday School with her little girls each week. As Erika recalled, "We pretty much followed the pattern of the Church, except that we didn't have the sacrament or the priesthood. We read from the Book of Mormon, and we sang the hymns. We were a very musical family."[24]

Everyday life for the residents of Germany's larger cities was becoming increasingly challenging. Between air-raid alarms, they were struggling to attend school and get in a full workday, as well as collect enough food to eat from various small stores.

Horst Reschke recalled clearly some of the problems with food:

> [Storing food] was called hoarding and was forbidden. But we became adept at scrounging for food and fuel. We would follow a horse-drawn wagon loaded with sugar beets. The cobblestone road bounced some of the sugar beets off the wagon. We took them home to boil and make syrup to be used instead of sugar. We also swept up horse manure as fertilizer in our garden. A family member who worked for the potato authority provided improved access to that precious commodity. My mother became an expert in the many ways in which potatoes could be served, including fried in Postum when fat was lacking.[25]

Fig. 5. The Hanover Branch when the war began. (H. Reschke)

Horst's sister Annegret added these comments regarding food:

> We would send the first person to the bakery at 4:00 a.m. He would wait until the next person came. If you weren't in line by 8:00 a.m., you got bread that wasn't even made out of flour.[26] Bread was supposed to be rationed, but it wasn't. They followed the rules when it came to meat though. We rarely ever got butter. For milk, we had to go to a different place, and it was like skim milk. In one air raid, the water line was damaged, so we didn't have water supply for a number of weeks. Every day, there would be a big water truck where we filled up our buckets. We were very frugal with how we washed our hands or flushed the toilet. This went on until they fixed the water line. The ration cards would not guarantee us anything.[27]

By the fall of 1944, the schools in Hanover were in such bad condition that the three Reschke children were sent to different cities to schools still functioning: Horst to Hildesheim (eighteen miles away), Dieter to Ronnenberg (six miles), and Annegret to Sarstedt (fourteen miles). All three were on their way just after 6:00 a.m. each school day. The trip was difficult enough (especially after a night interrupted by air-raid alarms or attacks) but was made even worse when the commuter trains they rode were attacked by British and American dive-bombers (who by then enjoyed total air superiority over Germany). On one occasion, an attack came and the driver ordered everyone to get out and go to a shelter down the hill a few yards. As the last one out, Annegret found that the shelter door was slammed shut just before she got there. When she desperately pounded on the door, the shelter official opened it—not to let her in, but to let her best friend, Inge, out. "Now there we were, two frightened, little girls, exposed to the enemy. Instinctively, we scrambled back up the embankment and into the streetcar to at least have some cover."[28] On the floor, they rolled from side to side depending on the direction from which the planes attacked. They survived the experience unscathed.

Fig. 6. The Hanover Branch Sunday School. The slogan reads, "Bring a friend to Sunday School!" (H. Reschke)

Not only was she living in a strange village without her husband, but Margaretha Bahe also gave birth in Holtensen to her third daughter, Ilona, in 1944. It was a difficult exile, and the approaching Christmas could have been a dismal experience for the Bahe family. Erika recalled that her mother was determined to observe some of the customs of the season and one day walked to the city of Göttingen on her errand of mercy:

> She went from store to store trying to procure some ingredients to make cookies, and everybody would shake their heads and say, "No, we can't help you." And then finally she turned back and passed a Catholic church, and she had taken the stroller with the idea that if she got too tired, she could lean on it when she walked and hopefully find some foodstuff. She rested right at the side of the church, and she started to sob and prayed, "[Lord], I'm not even going to have the makings for cookies to celebrate your birth." And within minutes, a priest came out of the church, and he looked at her and said, "My child, why are you crying?" And she told him her plight, and he said, "Wait just a minute." He disappeared for what seemed like an eternity, and finally he came back with a box, and in that box he had some sacrament wafers. He said, "I don't know what you can do with them, but I'd like you to have them." And so he gave her the box, and she put it in the stroller and walked home. Somewhere along the way, somebody else stopped to talk to her. It was obvious she had been crying, and she told that person what had happened, and he said, "Wait just a minute." And he went into a store and came back with two pounds of powdered sugar. Mom just cried and cried, and she said, "The Lord has heard my prayer." So anyway, she had some money, and she gave that money to the person who had given her the powdered sugar, and she walked home faster and faster. She could hardly wait. When she got home, she opened the box and discovered the sacrament wafers. She took the powdered sugar and melted it with a little bit of milk, and then she took hundreds of those real thin sacrament wafers and put sugar between each one. That was our Christmas.

Toward the end of the war, the home of Annegret Reschke's grandparents was bombed out. She recalled the following:

> I remember going with Grandma to search through the debris of their apartment house the morning after the air raid. Although I had seen many bombed-out buildings, I was still stunned to see my grandparents' home reduced to a pile of rubble. Even though we had gone very early in the day, looters had been there even earlier. Nonetheless, we were elated when we found several of Grandma's leather-covered, velvet-lined boxes of silverware.[29]

Fig. 7. Anneke Reschke's grandmother rescued this silverware from the ruins of her home. (A. Reschke Rudolph)

Apparently not all members of the Hanover Branch were having positive spiritual experiences as the war neared its end. The minutes of June 26, 1944, include the names of five sisters who officially severed their ties to the Church. The minutes also suggest that branch president Karl Blombach was influenced by the spirit of National Socialism in this statement dated July 23, 1944: "At the beginning of our sacrament meeting, branch president [Karl] Blombach said a prayer thanking the Lord for saving our Führer [Adolf Hitler] from the cowardly assassination attempt carried out against him on July 20."[30]

By Christmas Eve 1944, Lilly Reschke and the three children had been living for two months a few miles west of Hanover, while Max Reschke stayed in town due to his employment.[31] As the sacred holiday approached, Brother Reschke picked up his family and took them to the big city. Annegret recalled the event:

> Finally the day arrived when my father came to take us home. The snow had fallen and had covered all the ugliness war brings. A true feeling

> of Christmas came over us as we rolled toward Hanover. My heart pumped a little faster the closer we came to our home. And, finally, there it was, straight and tall as ever. As we entered, it seemed as though the rooms were a bit darker than I had remembered them, but then it was snowing outside, I reasoned, and everything had a different color. However, after a while we realized that all the glass from the windows was missing. My father had replaced it with boards and cardboard. . . . We kept our warm coats on and huddled close together around the coal stove in the kitchen. . . . Finally, Christmas Eve was here. . . . We did not expect too much in the form of presents or even a Christmas tree, because we knew . . . those things would be out of reach until after the war. . . . At Christmas time the living room at our house was always converted into the Christmas room. Here Father and Mother helped Santa Claus on Christmas Eve.[32]

Life in the city of Hanover must have become nearly intolerable when the year 1945 arrived. On December 31, January 7, and January 14, no church meetings could be held due to constant air-raid alarms. Several members of the branch were among those residents whose homes were damaged or destroyed in the attacks. The minutes dated March 25 list the following families recently bombed out: Sieberling, Liebig, Schulz, Kuno, Fraatz, Wille, Wrobel, and Schmidt.[33]

Horst Reschke recalled one of the more humorous ways to collect items needed to support daily survival:

> During an air raid, . . . my mother and I came upon an elderly couple in the courtyard in the process of gathering propaganda leaflets, floating down from the sky. An American bomber had been kind enough to dump them on our property. The neighbors were aghast that we had caught them in a criminal activity.[34] They asked if we would turn them in. I told them no, if they would share the precious leaflets with us, not to enlighten us, but for a much more mundane purpose. Toilet tissues had long been unavailable for purchase. Instead, we let the daily newspaper serve dual purposes. But since the newspaper printing plant had been bombed out, the leaflets, measuring about 8 ½ × 11 inches, cut into four sections, could serve not only cerebral but also posterior functions, courtesy of the 8th U.S. Air Force.[35]

Fig. 8. Horst Reschke's Hitler Youth Group was housed in this building in Neuhaus/Solling during the war. (H. Reschke)

Horst mentioned some of the survival skills he learned as a young teenager—skills he hoped he would never need to apply again for as long as he lived: "I learned how to dodge bullets from a fighter plane while on a moving train, how to dig people out of a caved-in bomb shelter, and how to put out a fire caused by incendiary bombs. We learned to cope when the water and gas plants and the power stations were permanently eliminated."[36]

Only seven members of the branch attended the sacrament meeting held in the Grahn family home on April 8, 1945—just two days before the American army entered the city. Each of the attendees was asked or volunteered to pray: Brother Blombach, Brother Kubiak, Brother Grahn, Brother Thews, Sister Grundlach, Sister Heim, and Sister Sagebiel. It was likely too dangerous to take children through the streets of the devastated city on that Sunday. After the meeting, Brother Grahn was ordained a teacher in the Aaronic Priesthood by Karl Blombach.[37]

Annegret Reschke recalled the arrival of the

American tanks and soldiers on April 10. While across the street in the home of her best friend, Inge, she heard the roar of the tanks approaching and dared not cross the street to her home. Then her father darted across the street between tanks and took her back into the house. She continued to watch the proceedings from the window of their apartment, including an event that left her confused. Some soldiers built a fire in the gutter and boiled a bucket full of eggs. After several soldiers took and ate perhaps a dozen eggs, the rest of that rare commodity were dumped into the street and destroyed. Max Reschke then explained to his daughter the fact that invading soldiers were not to share food with the civilians.[38]

At the war's end, Doris Fraatz was very ill with scarlet fever, which might have been to her advantage. She was in a quarantine hospital out of town when the Allies entered Hanover and was thus quite safe—at least in some respects. While she was in the hospital, her father came to visit and brought the news that their apartment had been destroyed. The fires that burned the building to the ground had moved from the roof downward, leaving the family enough time to rescue their church books and several other important items. After finding a new apartment, they moved in with some of the furniture left to them by a grandmother who had recently passed away.

When Doris was well enough to travel, she was put on a bus and sent toward Hanover. Somewhere outside of town, the bus stopped and the very weakened seventeen-year-old was on her own to get through town on foot. Arriving at home after the curfew hour, she was fortunate to find a little girl who accepted her identification and let her into the new apartment house. The homecoming was a bit complicated, as she described in these words:

> I told my mother that I was not disinfected yet from the hospital because they did not take the time to wash us [when we left]. She took a bucket and put all of my clothing in it and put me into clean clothes. Although we took careful precautions, my sister still caught scarlet fever from me. She stayed home and was not taken to a hospital.

The clerk of the Hanover Branch dutifully made his notations through the end of the war and thereafter. Although he is not identified, he was probably one of four brethren mentioned as attending the meeting on April 8. He stated that the branch rooms at Volgersweg 54 had been destroyed but gave no date for that loss. On April 15, no meeting could be held because the American occupation forces had announced a curfew, but a meeting took place on the next Sunday, again in the Grahn home.[39]

Margaretha Bahe was still in Holtensen with her three little girls when the American army approached in April 1945. According to daughter Erika,

> We were scared when the American troops came in their jeeps. They sent in all the black troops first. We had never seen a black person. There were six or eight soldiers in the streets with their guns drawn. They came into the town, and that was scary. We had heard on the news that the war had ended. Now the Americans weren't angels either, of course. It was wartime. Their deeds were pretty monstrous. They would knock on doors. They came in, looked around for weapons and anything that could be used for war purposes or what not. And they would confiscate it. The little radio we had was gone. They took it. We had a camera that was my father's, and they took that, and of course that meant the world to us because it was Dad's. They did not hurt us. [But] when they came to the town, they had some large trucks, they gathered up anybody suspicious or German-looking (soldiers) and they lined them up behind the barn in single file and just shot them. We little kids saw that and will never forget it.

Erika's younger sister, Sylvia, did not recall being frightened but remembered instead the kindness the soldiers showed little children: "They got cans of fruitcake and stuff. If they didn't want the candies, they gave them to the little kids."

During the summer of 1945, Sister Bahe and her children were loaded onto a truck and returned to Hanover. According to Sylvia, "The city was destroyed. Everywhere you looked you saw rubble and bombed-out buildings." Erika recalled how her mother showed her the ruins of their apartment house. They looked for surviving items, but looters had already been there. Eventually, Hans Bahe also returned to Hanover, and life began anew for the family. They immediately sought out the Saints and joined in meetings in various apartments around town.

The war years were essentially the only life young Annegret Reschke could remember. It had seemed to her that the universal motto was "Wait until the war's over!" This applied to many of her requests but prominently to her baptism that finally took place in September 1945: "I was already nine years old by then, and, in my mind, it was high time for this very important event to take place."[40] This new religious phase of her life would coincide with new political and cultural phases in a Germany without Hitler and National Socialism.

Looking back on her experiences in Hanover during the war, Doris Fraatz commented, "My mother and my grandmother had strong testimonies of the Church. We did not doubt what Heavenly Father could do for us—that is when you really start having faith."

World War II had seriously (and in some cases tragically) interrupted the private lives of the Saints in the Hanover Branch, but they had worked diligently under constantly changing leadership to keep the branch alive and to worship their Father in Heaven on a consistent basis. Relatively few of them were still in the city when the war ended, but they eventually returned and gathered together again to worship and to revive their religious community.

Fig. 9. Many LDS women had non-LDS husbands who were killed in the war. Heinl Hirsch of Hanover was one of those casualties. (H. Hirsch)

In Memoriam

The following members of the Hanover Branch did not survive World War II:

Hans Heinrich Bahe b. Kreutzriehe, Hessen-Nassau, Preussen, 26 Apr 1878; son of Johann Friedrich Bahe and Engel Marie Voelker; bp. 20 Nov 1910; conf. 20 Nov 1910; m. Hannover, Hannover, 24 Sep 1905, Doretta Engelhardt; 2 m. Hannover 3 Jan 1909, Anna Henriette Louise Engelhardt; d. heart attack Hannover 14 Jan 1942 (Celle Branch general minutes, CHL LR 1519 11, 178; NFS)

Friedrich Heinrich Fraatz b. Hannover, Hannover, 22 Jul 1922; son of Heinrich Fraatz and Elise Lina Reichmann; bp. 26 Jan 1933; conf. 26 Jan 1933; ord. deacon 20 Sep 1936; ord. teacher 6 Nov 1938; ord. priest 23 Nov 1941; ord. elder 4 Jul 1943; d. lung disease 24 Nov 1943 (FHL microfilm 68809, no. 51)

Marie Dorothee Gehrke b. Nateln, Uelzen, Hannover, 22 Sep 1861; dau. of Joachim Friedrich Ludwig Gehrke and Dorothee Elizabeth Schulze; bp. 30 Oct 1927; conf. 30 Oct 1927; m. Rosche, Hannover, 8 or 28 Nov 1884, Johann Heinrich Wilhelm Maykus; 5 children; d. old age Schliekau, Hannover, 13 May 1940 (FHL microfilm 68799, no. 14; CHL CR 375 8 2439, no. 483; FHL microfilm 245228, 1930 and 1935 censuses)

Georg Heinrich Gleim b. Reichensachsen, Eschwege, Hessen-Nassau, 12 Apr 1861; son of Conrad Gleim and Elisabeth Otto; bp. 4 Dec 1925; conf. 4 Dec 1925; ord. deacon 3 Jul 1927; ord. teacher 3 Jun 1928; ord. priest 12 Apr 1936; ord. elder 7 May 1939; m. 26 Oct 1900, Anna Wilhelmine Vogt; d. stroke 10 Jul 1942 (FHL microfilm 68809, no. 57)

Kurt Arthur Helfer b. Hannover, Hannover, 25 Aug 1913; son of Kurt Franz Helfer and Erna Lehmann; bp. 27 Jan 1923; conf. 27 Jan 1923; missing (FHL microfilm 68809, no. 74)

Paul Willi Andreas Jochims b. Hannover, Hannover, 21 Aug 1915; son of Andreas Friedrich Paul Franz Jochims and Minna Marie Henriette Julie Schlein; bp. 5 Jun 1931; conf. 5 Jun 1931; d. frostbite and kidney failure, military hospital Krakow, Poland, 16 Jul 1942 (FHL microfilm 68809, no. 208)

Emma Anna Olga Marie Martha Jürges b. Braunschweig, Braunschweig, 11 Jul 1895; dau. of Carl Jürges and Marie H. Everding; bp. 25 Mar 1907; conf. 25 Mar 1907; m. Albert Paul Klug 26 May 1917; d. pancreatitis 23 Oct or 20 Nov 1939 (FHL microfilm 68809, no. 266)

Marie Karger b. Poditau, Schlesien, 15 or 25 Feb 1867; dau. of Franz Karger and Louise Neumann; bp.

13 May 1923; conf. 13 May 1923; m. Habelschwerdt or Altweistvitz, Schlesien, 10 Sep 1888, August Jüschke; 15 children; d. old age Visselhövede, Hannover, 6 Feb 1945, bur. Visselhövede 10 Feb 1945 (FHL microfilm 68799, no. 4; CHL CR 375 8 2439, no. 593)

Eva Marie Margreta Klug b. Braunschweig, Braunschweig, 14 Oct 1923; dau. of Albert Paul Klug and Marie Martha Jürges; bp. 10 Jul 1932; conf. 10 Jul 1932; k. air raid 10 Apr 1944 (FHL microfilm 68809, no. 268)

Elsbeth Anna Krix b. Braunschweig, Braunschweig, 12 Feb 1909; dau. of Kurt Krix and Else Seyer; bp. 5 Sep 1936; conf. 5 Sep 1936; m. Friedrich Wilhelm Liebig 25 Jul 1936; d. tuberculosis 13 Jul 1941 (FHL microfilm 68809, no. 283)

Lina Marie Frieda Kreth b. Hannover, Hannover, 28 Jul 1884; dau. of Wilhelm Kreth and Karoline Dill; bp. 12 Oct 1922; conf. 12 Oct 1922; m. Wilhelm Schlüter (div.); d. stroke 12 Aug 1944 (FHL microfilm no. 68809, no. 163)

Amalia Auguste Johanna Kruhl b. Görlitz, Schlesien, 2 May 1852; dau. of Karl Kruhl and Johanna Kotz; bp. 27 Jan 1923; conf. 27 Jan 1923; m. —— Richter; d. old age 11 Mar 1944 (FHL microfilm 68809, no. 144)

August Heinrich Wilhelm Küthmann b. Barsinghausen, Hannover, Hannover, 14 Jun 1874; son of Friedrich Küthmann and Wilhelmine Adening; bp. 2 Sep 1916; conf. 3 Sep 1916; ord. deacon 16 Feb 1919; ord. teacher 10 Apr 1924; ord. priest 5 Oct 1924; ord. elder 11 Mar 1932; m. 12 Jan 1900, Maria Ebers; d. diabetes 28 Jan or 20 Feb 1940 (FHL microfilm 68809, no. 96)

Auguste Hermine Lübke b. Argesdorf, Kloster Wennigsen, Hannover, 26 Dec 1864; dau. of Christian Friedrich Lübke and Dorothea Fündling; bp. 5 Jul 1914; conf. 5 Jul 1914; m. 21 Apr 1887, Wilhelm Heinrich Gleue; d. old age 30 Jul 1944 (FHL microfilm 68809, no. 60)

Marie Auguste Henriette Sophie Lüders b. Barneberg, Neuhaldensleben, Sachsen, 20 Feb 1871; dau. of Christian Lüders and Ernstine Hase; bp. 7 Jul 1918; m. Friedrich Reichmann 9 May 1896; d. heart attack 28 Dec 1942 (FHL microfilm 68809, no. 138; Doris Fraatz Mentzel)

Minna Friederike Ernstine Lüders b. Sommerschenburg, Neuhaldensleben, Sachsen, 20 Feb 1876; dau. of Heinrich Andreas Ernst Lüders and Ernstine Hase; bp. 13 Jul 1916; conf. 13 Jul 1916; m. 15 Apr 1895, Gustav Hermann Reuter; d. stroke 1940 (FHL microfilm 68809, no. 143)

Wilhelm Karl Markmann b. Schora, Jericho, Sachsen, 11 Aug 1867; son of Christian Markmann and Sophie Fritze; bp. 9 Aug 1919; conf. 9 Aug 1919; ord. teach. 6 Jun 1920; ord. priest 6 Sep 1925; ord. elder 15 Sep 1930; d. old age 27 Jan 1942 (FHL microfilm 68809, no. 103)

Wilhelm Plinke b. Barsinghausen, Hannover, Hannover, 19 Feb 1895; son of Georg Plinke and Dorette Vogel; bp. 4 Jun 1926; conf. 4 Jun 1926; m. 6 Dec 1919, Martha Amalie Sophia Gatzenmeyer; d. lung disease 30 Nov 1942 (FHL microfilm 68809, no. 127)

Auguste Pötzold b. Kalk, Köln, Rheinprovinz, 7 Jun 1874; dau. of August Pötzold and Johanna Pöhl; bp. 15 Sep 1914; conf. 15 Sep 1914; m. Ferdinand Klages 6 May 1894; d. arteriosclerosis 2 May 1941 (FHL microfilm 68809, no. 279)

Willi Wilhelm Dietrich Schlüter b. Döhren, Hannover, Hannover, 2 Dec 1909; son of Wilhelm Schlüter and Lina Marie Frieda Kreth; bp. 29 May 1923; conf. 29 May 1923; ord. deacon 8 Sep 1929; m. 22 Jul 1933, Auguste M. W. Dohmeyer; d. injury from air raid 15 Jul 1941 (FHL microfilm 68809, no. 162)

Willhelm Johannes Schrader b. Hannover, Hannover, 22 Sep 1864; son of Carl Friedrich Wilhelm Schrader and Anna Staufenbach; bp. 17 Jun 1930; conf. 17 Jun 1930; ord. deacon 7 Jun 1931; ord. priest 19 Jun 1932; m. Gudrun Sophia Leyers; d. old age 29 Jan 1944 (FHL microfilm 68809, no. 169)

Elsa Julia Johanna Schröder b. Grevesmühlen, Mecklenburg-Schwerin, 28 May 1895; dau. of Anna Schröder; bp. 2 Feb 1930; conf. 2 Feb 1930; m. Otto Brachert 27 Oct 1923; m. 15 Oct 1937, Karl Scharnickow; d. consumption 16 Jun 1942 (FHL microfilm 68799, no. 40)

Emilie Ida Alwine Thile b. Klein Bülten, Peine, Hannover, 24 Oct 1871; dau. of Heinrich Thile and Sophie Leinemann; bp. 26 Oct 1920; conf. 26 Oct 1920; m. Karl Heinrich Wilhelm Wehrspohn 9 Aug 1894; d. heart disease 15 Dec 1941 (FHL microfilm 68809, no. 185)

Karl Borwin Warnke b. Hannover, Hannover, 14 Oct 1914; son of Gustav Warnke and Johanne Oppermann; bp. 6 Nov 1923; conf. 6 Nov 1923; d. poor circulation Groß Rosen Concentration Camp, Schlesien, 26 Apr 1942; cremated (FHL microfilm 68809, no. 182)

Christa Karola Klara Wille b. Hannover, Hannover, 2 Dec 1940; dau. of Wilhelm Heinrich Karl Wille and Elisabeth Alma Bahe; d. pneumonia 13 Dec 1940 (FHL microfilm 68809, no. 313)

Ida Henriette Rutha Wolter b. Freienwalde, Pommern, 15 May 1861; dau. of Karl Wolter and Ulrike Schulz; bp. 16 Aug 1903; conf. 16 Aug 1903; k. air raid 9 Oct 1943 (FHL microfilm 68809, no. 204)

Louise Auguste Johanne Wolter b. Freienwalde, Pommern, 31 Dec 1859; dau. of Karl Wolter and Ulrike Schulz; bp. 4 May 1912; conf. 4 May 1912; m. 15 Nov

1899, Julius Kulling; d. old age Hannover, Hannover, 15 Jun 1942 (FHL microfilm 68809 no. 95)

Heidi Wrobel b. Hannover, Hannover, 19 Jan 1942; dau. of Kurt Waldemar Wrobel and Malfriede Friederike Sophie Wille; d. measles 4 Feb 1943 (FHL microfilm 68809, no. 317)

NOTES

1. Hanover city archive.
2. Doris Fraatz Menzel, interview by the author in German, Salt Lake City, March 21, 2009; summarized in English by Judith Sartowski.
3. Presiding Bishopric, "Financial, Statistical, and Historical Reports of Wards, Stakes, and Missions, 1884–1955," 257, CHL CR 4 12.
4. West German Mission manuscript history, CHL MS 1004 2.
5. Doris recalled a very rare situation: "My mother had a cousin who belonged to the Reorganized Church of Jesus Christ of Latter-day Saints. In fact, I even knew two members of that organization. I remember that when they came to visit us once, they started arguing a little about what we all believed in. One of the cousins had three sons who were ready to be ordained to the priesthood in their church. They also met in their branch in Hanover."
6. Hanover Branch general minutes, CHL LR 3594 11, 87.
7. Ibid., 88.
8. Annegret Reschke Rudolph, telephone interview with the author, April 1, 2009.
9. Horst Reschke, interview by Marion Wolfert, Riverton, UT, March 27, 2006.
10. Hanover Branch general minutes, 117.
11. Ibid., 120.
12. Ibid., 120.
13. Annegret Reschke Rudolph, personal history (unpublished); private collection.
14. Ibid.
15. Hanover Branch general minutes, 122.
16. Ibid., 131.
17. Ibid., 135.
18. Ibid., 148.
19. Ibid., 151.
20. Sylvia Bahe Schwemmer, interview by the author, Salt Lake City, August 21, 2009.
21. Hanover general minutes, 153. He kept his word and was baptized on December 19 in Celle "because all of the bathhouses in Hanover have been destroyed in the air raids," according to the branch clerk.
22. Ibid., 153.
23. Ibid., 160. It appears that Elder Pohlsander was a conscientious correspondent and that letters could still be sent to such countries as Denmark and Switzerland from Germany.
24. Erika Bahe Runnels, telephone interview with the author, March 12, 2009.
25. Horst Reschke, "When the War Came We Were Not Prepared" (unpublished manuscript); private collection.
26. Sawdust was a common ingredient in bread in many European countries in those days.
27. Annegret Reschke Rudolph, interview.
28. Annegret Reschke Rudolph, personal history.
29. In most German cities, the crime of looting was punishable by death. Nevertheless, when the damage was so widespread, it was impossible for police to enforce the laws. In addition, it was not always easy to determine the difference between a resident and a looter. Annegret eventually inherited the silverware.
30. Hanover Branch general minutes, 166. Count Claus Schenk von Stauffenberg had left a briefcase with a bomb in the conference room of Hitler's Eastern Front headquarters at Rastenburg, East Prussia. The explosion killed four men but only superficially injured Hitler. All of Germany was shocked by the event, and von Stauffenberg and hundreds of other conspirators were executed. It is not clear precisely when Karl Blombach became the branch president, but he is listed as conducting sacrament meeting on many occasions beginning in August 1943, and the name Richard Krafft is seen in the minutes only on rare occasions after that date.
31. Lilly was the second wife of Max Reschke; they had married in 1942, according to his daughter, Annegret.
32. Annegret Reschke Rudolph, personal history. In those days, it was still the custom in most of Germany that all gifts were given on December 24. Late that afternoon, the parents closed off the living room, set up the tree, and brought out the gifts. When all was prepared, the room was opened to the children and the gifts that the Christ child or Santa Claus had brought were handed out.
33. Hanover general minutes, 175.
34. The leaflets were printed with anti-Nazi messages, and German citizens could be fined for even having such papers in their possession. Toward the end of the war, the leaflets announced the arrival of Allied forces and even included maps showing how the territory of Germany was to be divided up among the conquering armies.
35. Reschke, "When the War Came."
36. Hanover Branch general minutes, 175.
37. Ibid., 176.
38. Annegret Reschke Rudolph, personal history.
39. Hanover Branch general minutes, 176.
40. Annegret Reschke Rudolph, personal history.

Kassel Branch

The northernmost major city of the historical province of Hessen-Nassau, Kassel, lies about one hundred miles south of the city of Hanover. As World War II approached, the city had 211,624 residents, only sixty-five of whom were members of The Church of Jesus Christ of Latter-day Saints.[1]

The church meetings were held in rented rooms on the third floor of an apartment building at a very fine location in town—Frankfurterstrasse 7.[2] A very traditional schedule was maintained, with Sunday School at 10:00 a.m. and sacrament meeting at 7:00 p.m. The Primary and the Relief Society met on Mondays at 5:00 p.m. and 8:00 p.m., respectively. MIA meetings were held on Tuesdays at 8:00 p.m. Leadership meetings were held for the branch presidency, the Sunday School, and priesthood brethren. A genealogy class was held twice each month in connection with the MIA meetings, and choir practice took place on Tuesdays at 9:15 p.m. As in so many branches of the Church in Gemany, the members of the Kassel Branch participated in meetings and activities several times each week.

Whereas the branch was dominated by women over the age of twelve, there were also fifteen priesthood holders among the membership. Only five children were included on the branch roster at the time. American missionary Howard Lyman was the branch president one month before the war, with Albert O. Baum as first counselor. It appears from branch records that Wilhelm K. Schade became the branch president when the American missionaries were required to leave for Denmark on August 25, 1939. The president of the Sunday School was Harry A. Niebuhr, and the Primary president was Marie Schade, while Albert O. Baum led the YMMIA, Inge Baum the YWMIA, and Barbara Kerseten Sr. the Relief Society.

Kassel Branch[3]	**1939**
Elders	4
Priests	1
Teachers	4
Deacons	6
Other Adult Males	4
Adult Females	41
Male Children	4
Female Children	1
Total	65

Fig. 1. The Ernst family home in 1938. (J. Ernst)

Justus Ernst (born 1928) described the branch leaders in these terms: "Brother Diederich was a book-binder, Brother Schade an upholsterer, Brother Baum a painter, and Brother Göttig worked for the railroad. None of them really in any way could be considered wealthy or middle class."[4] Eleven years old at the time, Justus recalled that the meeting facility consisted of one larger room for the general meetings and two or three other small rooms for classes. There was a pump organ in the main room, but the only décor he could remember was a picture of Joseph Smith. Average attendance in those days may have been as many as forty persons.

Young Justus had been baptized in the Fulda River in Kassel in 1936 and inducted with his schoolmates into the Jungvolk in 1938. As he recalled:

> I think they usually planned their meetings right at the same time as we had church meetings. I was also in the Hitler Youth at age fourteen. . . . There was some indoctrination about race and stuff like that, but I wouldn't call it heavy duty indoctrination. . . . We had some training with weapons—some shooting. As a matter of fact, my father had been in World War I and was very much convinced of the need to be able to shoot right. There was a course taught in a restaurant, and they had just air guns and small funny ones to shoot. And [my father] was interested in seeing that we could shoot.[5]

As part of his Hitler Youth service, Justus was assigned to help whitewash the attic spaces of downtown houses in order to retard fires that might be caused by incendiary bombs such as those already dropped on other German cities.[6]

Fig. 2. The Diederich family of the Kassel Branch in 1940. From left: Anna, Elfriede, Hugo, Margaret, Wilford and Fritz. (J. Ernst)

Hermann Ernst (born 1927) was ordained a deacon in 1941. In those days, teenage boys were not given the Aaronic Priesthood until the branch president identified a need for service in the branch. Hermann was prepared for that service, as he described in his journal: "I had been quite active. I remember participating in carrying out programs, for example in plays performed by the Primary Association."[7] He was also the second counselor to the Sunday School superintendant. Over the next two years, he made several comments in his journal about his willingness to serve and to be entrusted with more responsibilities in the Kassel Branch. During those years, he was working as a carpenter's apprentice in the shops of the national railroad system.

An unnamed clerk kept good records of the branch meetings and special events beginning in 1942. (It is not clear whether previous records were lost or not written at all.)[8] The following entries provide interesting details about branch life:

> August 6, 1942: Five brethren attended priesthood meeting. The branch president is Wilhelm K. Schade.
>
> August 20, 1942: Nine sisters attended Relief Society.
>
> August 30, 1942: District conference was held in Hanover.
>
> August 1942: Average sacrament meeting attendance for the month was twenty persons.
>
> September 20, 1942: The Relief Society meeting was attended by visitors from the mission office: Sister Louise Heck and her daughters Annaliese and Hannelore, and Sister Hildegard Waibel, mission Relief Society president. Sister [Deininger] from the mission office was also here.
>
> November 15, 1942: We had a visit by soldier Brother Kleinert from the Freiberg/Sachsen Branch [East German Mission]; he was asked to speak.[9]

The following entry was made in the general branch minutes in late 1942:

> From November 29 to December 27, 1942 we were not allowed to meet due to an order issued by the city police. The main reason was a report submitted by the neighbors. The mission leaders intervened and the matter was resolved. We were allowed to begin holding meetings again on December 27, 1942.[10]

Fig. 3. Relief Society sisters of the Kassel Branch celebrated the society's centennial in 1942 with a poster reading "Die Liebe höret nimmer auf!" (Charity never faileth!) (J. Ernst)

The general minutes of the Kassel Branch include the following comments in the fourth year of the war:

> February 28, 1943: Wilhelm K. Schade said good-bye; he was drafted and stationed in Frankfurt/Main.
>
> April 11, 1943: District conference in Hanover.
>
> April 18, 1943: Sister Dielmann nee Krauss died of pneumonia and heart disease; she was buried in Helsa by Kassel on April 18.
>
> July 18, 1943: District president Walther Pohlsander visited our meetings. He released Brother Schade as branch president due to his draft notice. A new presidency was called: Fritz Diederich, Albert Baum, Franz Ludwig Erich Niemann, with Konrad Göttig as secretary.
>
> August 14, 1943: Miss Magdalena Spangenberg and Hugo Diederich were baptized.
>
> August 15, 1943: Brother [Hermann] Schade Jr. is off to the Reichsarbeitsdienst.
>
> August 29, 1943: Fall district conference was held in Hanover.[11]

The average attendance at sacrament meeting in 1943 was eighteen persons, with seven attending priesthood meeting.

Hermann Ernst wrote in his journal about a trip to Munich with Elder A. O. Baum in July 1943. The two made the long journey by rail and attended church with the Munich Branch. As beautiful as the Bavarian capital city was, Hermann was apparently concentrating on matters of religion rather than culture and history: "The city of Munich didn't impress us too much without its monuments. But we were favorably impressed by the Munich Branch. We even had to talk in the sacrament meeting," he wrote. The two then traveled into the Alps just south of Munich. The mountains left a lasting impression of the power of God. His assessment of the entire experience reads thus: "Fully satisfied and [with] a stronger testimony of the truth we returned to our home."

The question of religion and church apparently was more than just a passing fancy to Hermann Ernst. On September 2, 1943, then sixteen years old, he went to city hall and asked to have his name removed from the records of the Lutheran Church in which he had been baptized as an infant. He made no other comments in his journal about this question, allowing the assumption that his request was granted. Just days later, he was ordained to the office of teacher in the Aaronic Priesthood.

In October 1943, the war came home to Kassel in a terrible way. There had been a dozen or so minor attacks from the air before that time, but nothing in comparison to the blows dealt the city in that month. The branch clerk made the following sad comments in his record:

> October 3–4, 1943: Air-raid attack on Kassel; the Schade and Diederich families lost their homes and some church property; other members lost their windows and doors. A bomb hit the church rooms. October 22, 1943: Another attack on Kassel. Church rooms at Frankfurterstrasse 7 II and all church property were totally destroyed. The apartments of many members were damaged or totally destroyed and the following were killed:
>
> Auguste Mülverstedt, born 12 Sep 1880 in Kassel
>
> Frieda Mülverstedt born 19 March 1904 in Kassel
>
> Katharine Wittrock born 7 Dec 1871 in Eschwege
>
> Sophie-Marie Elisabeth Diederich Sr. born 16 Feb 1886 in Hofgeismar
>
> Sophie Elisabeth Diederich Jr. born 13 April 1914 in Kassel
>
> We are told that the last two were singing "Nearer, My God, to Thee" just before they died.

The attack on Kassel on October 22 left nearly the entire downtown in ruins. The Ernst family lived across the river to the east in the Bettenhausen suburb and were spared the devastation that occurred just a mile away. Nevertheless, Justus was soon exposed to the real horrors of the war, and he recounted what happened the next morning:

> The streetcars didn't go, so I just started walking, and as I came to the inner part of the town there were hundreds of corpses laying on the street. And it was just really something. I had never seen a dead person in my whole life. And all of a sudden there were hundreds of them laying there, women and children and older men, not too many soldiers. The reason for their dying was actually that the fire was so intense, where they had been in the cellars and these shelters, that it had eaten up all the oxygen and they actually suffocated.[12]

According to branch records, the members began to be dispersed. In November 1943, branch president Fritz Diederich lost his home and moved to Vockerode to find new employment; he asked to be released and was replaced by Franz Niemann. Attempts were then made to locate branch members through the city's missing persons office and a newsletter (written by Hermann Ernst) was sent to several families who had left the city.[13]

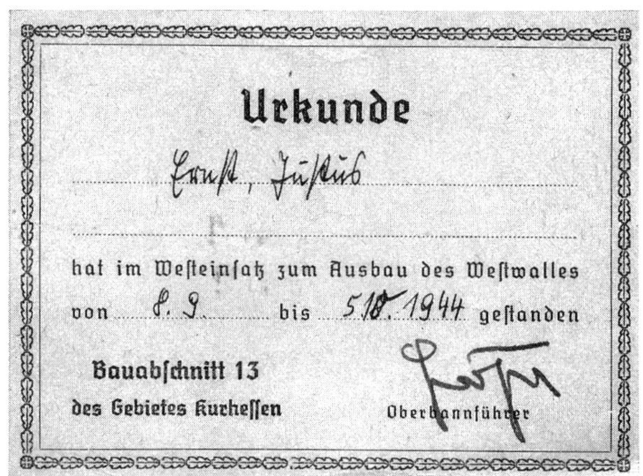

Urkunde

Ernst, Justus

hat im Westeinsatz zum Ausbau des Westwalles von 8. 9. bis 5.10. 1944 gestanden

Bauabschnitt 13
des Gebietes Kurhessen

Oberbannführer

Fig. 4. Justus Ernst was awarded this certificate after working on the Westwall defense system in France in 1944. (J. Ernst)

In early 1944, the Saints began to meet in the homes of the few member families still in Kassel. The names Schade and Ernst occur frequently in the branch records in this regard. All the while, a search was conducted for a new meeting place somewhere in town. In February, the branch was allowed to rent space in the Adventists Hall at Querallee 11. Hermann Ernst, the elder brother of Justus, spent a good deal of time helping this come about and reaped the praises of the branch president. The next few entries in the branch records are instructive:

> February 20, 1944: Sacrament meeting was held despite air raid alarms. In order to attend the meeting, Sister Baum and Brother Diederich had to get up at 4 a.m. The members are determined to do their duty.
>
> March 5, 1944: District conference in Hannover. Brother Niemann is set apart as branch president. Five sisters and four brethren went. All had to overcome major obstacles.
>
> March 19, 1944: Unfortunately, Hermann Ernst has been transferred to Graudenz. I [the branch president?] will lose a very capable and willing helper. . . . Sister Schade has asked me to locate the graves of our members who were killed on October 22–23 so that the graves can be dedicated and decorated with flowers.
>
> April 20, 1944: Konrad Göttig has been drafted. Because his family is living in Cologne, he asked me to have their records transferred to the Cologne Branch.
>
> April 21, 1944: Branch President Ludwig has been transferred to Westphalia. Brother Pohlsander gave him permission to make Gustav Ernst the temporary branch leader.[14]

It is not clear when Ludwig became the branch president, but this is a clear indication that the leadership of the Kassel Branch was changing almost as frequently as the meeting location. Gustav Ernst was not yet a priesthood holder at the time.

> May 28, 1944: Sacrament meeting began at 3 p.m. during an air raid alarm.
>
> June 18, 1944: Gustav Ernst is ordained to the Aaronic Priesthood and set apart as branch president.
>
> June 25, 1944: A celebration of the anniversary of the death of Joseph Smith was held. A resident of the building had just celebrated a wedding with lots of flowers, so the branch hall was already decorated for the Joseph Smith event. Eight members were in attendance.[15]

The typical apprenticeship in Germany ended with an examination, and Hermann Ernst passed his in carpentry with excellent marks in March 1944. At seventeen, he was a prime candidate for service to his country, and this began officially with his call to the national labor service. From June 7 to September 9, 1944, he worked in small towns in Lithuania and East Prussia. The literary talents that had inspired him to begin a newsletter for the Kassel Branch a few months earlier sought expression that summer, so he wrote two articles for a local newspaper. The titles were "Workmen on the East River" and "Send out the Watchmen." He was also a budding poet.

In the summer of 1944, Justus Ernst was sent to the Western Front to work on fortifications. The West Wall was designed to defend Germany against an anticipated invasion by the Allies. He recalled the following about his service as a sixteen-year-old: "I remember working at piling up ammunition. They had lots of piles, big piles of ammunition for good-sized artillery pieces. They were right in the forest and unprotected. They were just stacked up there; I don't know what they did with them."

Back in Kassel, it was becoming increasingly difficult to hold Church meetings. On December 24, 1944, the meeting had to be postponed from 2:00 to 4:00 p.m. due to air-raid alarms. Apparently the Querallee rooms were not available when the year 1945 arrived, because the Sunday meetings were held in the Ernst home in Bettenhausen in January and February.

Gustav and Martha Ernst were deeply concerned when their son, Hermann, was drafted into the Wehrmacht in November 1944. Just before receiving that call, Hermann wrote what could be called a summary of his young life:

> Thus, I look back on the years of being a citizen on this earth. I came into this world as a child of industrious, honest and god-fearing parents I grew up in common simplicity. I had a hard time

> to learn in school. I enjoyed history, geography and similar classes. Nevertheless, I passed all of my classes. Through an incident, brought about by God, I came into the Church of Jesus Christ. My parents and my brother also became members of the same. There I was very teachable. Very soon I was able to participate in plays and programs. I have proved my ability through constant effort and faithfulness to the Church. During my apprenticeship I excelled because of the strength of my character. I was always one of the best at the trade school. My character and my ability were also recognized in the pre-military training camp. The railway gave me a free tuition to be a student at the state school in Graudenz. A high recognition. Thus, I am now a student. I made much progress in the Church. From second counselor in the Sunday School to first counselor in the branch presidency within three years. . . . Thus, my life has been a life of success and work and may it continue to be so. The Lord may be my protector and my shield; my comforter in all my distress. Amen.

This young man with the successful past and hopes for an equally successful future had in reality very little time left on earth. He was killed near Guben, Germany, on February 23, 1945. The Red Army had just launched its attack on the German capital by crossing the Oder and Neisse Rivers southeast of Berlin. Justus recalled what his father had told him about hearing the news of Hermann's death: "Two guys from the [Nazi] party came to tell my parents that he had been killed. Then they offered [my father] 250 Marks to express their sympathy, I suppose. My father told them to keep that money. His son was worth more than 250 Marks."[16]

In a final war-time entry in the branch records, we read the following: "On March 14, 1945, our rooms at Querallee 11 were destroyed in an attack. No other damage [loss of life?] was suffered." For the rest of the war and several months thereafter, the Kassel Branch members had no official home for their meetings.

Following his service in the national labor force (January to March 1945), Justus considered volunteering for the Waffen SS—the elite combat troops commanded by Heinrich Himmler. Because many of his friends were being drafted from the Reichsarbeitsdienst directly into the Wehrmacht, Justus calculated that if he signed up with the Waffen SS he could go home for a while before being called up. "The basic training was supposed to take place in the Netherlands, and I thought that was a nice place to spend time." Fortunately for him, the call never came, and he was still home when the war ended. He described the entry of the American army on April 4–5, 1945:

> My parents were in the air-raid bunker—a big old cement box. And I was home, and I would cook some meals for my parents, like potatoes and spinach—just simple stuff, a little meat. And I put it in a bucket and took it down to the bunker. On the way there, I saw some retreating German troops. And it's interesting. The very same street (the Leipzigerstrasse) where the Germans came back from Poland after having a big [victory] parade in 1939, here was the very same street, but a very different army going the other way.[17]

That "very different army" consisted at the time mostly of disjointed units bereft of ammunition and food. They moved slowly back, away from the enemy, hoping to avoid combat that would result in death just days before what appeared to be certain defeat and the end of the war.

According to Justus, the conquering Americans were anything but well-disciplined.

> They were really drunk. I can still see it. They had loudspeakers mounted on their tanks, and they played jazz music. One lady must have been very happy to see the Americans, but she was a little disappointed that same night when she was raped by ten different soldiers. My mother went over there to see her, got her out of her house and brought her to ours. She saw a picture of Jesus, and she said, "I've suffered more than he suffered." The first thing the Americans did was come into our apartment—two guys. And they pointed at our radio and said, "Bring it." So, I carried the radio to their quarters. They were living in the next building. They had evacuated the whole next block, and they wanted to show me where they were going to put the radio so I could pick it up when they were leaving. I didn't realize that. My parents were scared stiff to see them take me away. They didn't care about me; they cared about the radio.[18]

Like so many German boys his age, Justus had not known any Germany other than the Third Reich. As he recalled, "I really couldn't compare it to anything else. When all this broke down in 1945, it was really quite a blow to me. I felt quite lost." He confided to his diary the fact that the war and the government's antichurch attitude actually had caused him to lose interest in the Church for a while.[19]

Figs. 5 and 6. Hermann Ernst (in the uniforms of the Hitler Youth and the Wehrmacht) was killed in February 1945 when the Red Army crossed the Neisse River near Guben. (J. Ernst)

The city of Kassel lost approximately eleven thousand citizens in the military service away from home and in the forty bombing attacks that occurred in the last two years of the war. The entire downtown was destroyed as well as approximately 80 percent of the rest of the city.

Regarding the LDS branch in Kassel, district president Hermann Walter Pohlsander submitted the following report to the mission office in Frankfurt in August 1945:

> The branch in Kassel suffered heavy losses. Seven [eight] members among them four [five] faithful sisters were killed. All [sic] the homes of members have been completely destroyed and the members had to find new homes. In spite of this the Saints are trying to return to this completely destroyed city to keep the branch alive. Brother Gustav Ernst, a priest who is 65 years old, is in charge of the branch consisting of 58 members. Of these about 60% have stayed true to the church. There has been no contact with the Kassel Branch since February 1945, since Kassel is located in the American [Occupation] Zone. The meeting hall, including all the inventory, has been destroyed. The damage has been reported to the city damage office in Kassel [for compensation].[20]

Fig. 7. Survivors of the Kassel Branch in July 1945. (J. Ernst)

Franz Niemann was released from a British POW camp and returned to Kassel on August 25, 1945. District president Walter Pohlsander released Gustav Ernst as the branch leader and called Brother Niemann to preside again.[21] Little by little, the dispersed surviving members of the Kassel Branch began to return to rebuild both their city and their church.

In Memoriam

The following members of the Kassel Branch did not survive World War II:

Sophie Elisabeth Dietrich b. Kassel, Hessen-Nassau, 13 Apr 1914; dau. of Karl Friedrich Dietrich and Sophie Marie Elisabeth Schuhmacher; bp. 22 May 1937; conf. 22 May 1937; k. in air raid 22 Oct 1943 (FHL microfilm 68809, no. 120; IGI)

Hermann Karl Georg Ernst b. Kassel, Hessen-Nassau, 26 May 1927; son of Gustav Hermann Ernst and Martha Elisabeth Ruppel; bp. 17 Jun 1935; conf. 17 Jun

1935; ord. deacon 16 Nov 1941; ord. teacher 12 Sep 1943; private; k. in battle Guben, Brandenburg, 23 Feb 1945 (CHL CR 375 8 2439, no. 592; FHL microfilm no. 25762, 1930 and 1935 censuses; www.volksbund.de)

Auguste Hahn b. Kassel, Hessen-Nassau, 12 Sep 1880; dau. of Johannes Hahn and Katharina Zeug; bp. 22 May 1937; conf. 22 May 1937; m. —— Mülverstedt; k. in air raid 22 Oct 1943 (FHL microfilm 68809, no. 117)

Sophie Koch b. Kassel, Hessen-Nassau, 1 Nov 1861; dau. of Justus Koch and Christiana Rudelbach; bp. 2 Nov 1901; conf. 2 Nov. 1901; m. —— Laum (div.); 2m. Heinrich Marks 24 Feb 1916; d. old age 19 Mar 1942 (FHL microfilm 68809, no. 26; FHL microfilm no. 245226, 1930 and 1935 censuses)

Margarethe Gertrude Mosebach b. Stolberg, Hannover, 7 Apr 1925; dau. of Max Mosebach and Marie Friedrichs; bp. 28 Dec 1937; conf. 4 Jan 1938; k. in air raid Kassel, Hessen-Nassau, 22 Oct 1943 (CHL CR 375 8 2439, no. 634; IGI)

Katharine Müller b. Eschwege, Hessen-Nassau, 7 Dec 1871; dau. of Friedrich Müller and Elise Grundherodt; bp. 23 Feb 1930; conf. 23 Feb 1930; m. 28 Jul 1900, Gustav Wittrock; k. in air raid Kassel, Hessen-Nassau, 22 Oct 1943 (FHL microfilm 68809, no. 81)

Frieda Mülverstedt b. Kirchditmold, Hessen-Nassau, 19 Mar 1904; dau. of Max Mülverstedt and Auguste Hahn; bp. 22 May 1937; conf. 22 May 1937; k. in air raid Kassel, Hessen-Nassau, 22 Oct 1943 (FHL microfilm 68809, no. 118; IGI)

Heinrich Ludwig Persch b. Kassel, Hessen-Nassau, 1 May 1879; son of Johann Georg Persch and Theodora Helm; bp. 4 Aug 1932; conf. 4 Aug 1932; d. 12 Oct 1944 (FHL microfilm 68791, no. 388; Frankfurt District book II; IGI)

Sophie Marie Elisabeth Schuhmacher b. Hofgeismar, Hessen-Nassau, 16 Feb 1886; dau. of Johann Christoph Schuhmacher and Marie Sophie Engelbert; bp. 22 May 1937; conf. 22 May 1937; m. —— Dietrich; k. air raid Kassel, Hessen-Nassau, 22 Oct 1943 (FHL microfilm 68809, no. 119; IGI)

Katharina S. Stuppi b. Pfeffelbach, Sankt Wendel, Rheinprovinz, 29 Sep 1867; dau. of Jakob Stuppi and Magdalena Spaniol; bp. 11 Apr 1902; conf. 11 Apr 1902; m. Joseph Webank; d. heart attack 1 Sep 1940 (FHL microfilm 68809, no. 124; IGI)

NOTES

1. Kassel City Archive.
2. West German Mission branch directory, 1939, CHL LR 10045 11.
3. Presiding Bishopric, "Financial, Statistical, and Historical Reports of Wards, Stakes, and Missions, 1884–1955," 257, CR 4 12.
4. Justus Ernst, oral history, 1985, CHL OH 728.
5. Justus Ernst, interview by the author, Salt Lake City, January 23, 2009.
6. Justus Ernst, interview.
7. Hermann Ernst, autobiography, unpublished.
8. Kassel Branch general minutes, CHL LR 4336 11.
9. Ibid.
10. Ibid.
11. Ibid.
12. Justus Ernst, interview.
13. Kassel Branch general minutes.
14. Ibid.
15. Ibid.
16. Justus Ernst, interview. At the time, 250 Marks was the equivalent of about $60 (not counting the deflation of the Reichsmark in the last year of the war).
17. Ibid.
18. Ibid.
19. Ibid.
20. Velzen Branch manuscript histort and historical papers, 1921–1973, CHL LR 9489 2.
21. Kassel Branch general minutes.

UELZEN BRANCH

Located sixty miles northeast of the city of Hanover, the branch in Uelzen was small and somewhat isolated. According to records kept in the mission office, there was only one elder in the branch as World War II approached. No page is found for Uelzen in the mission directory, and no eyewitnesses can be found as of this writing.

In August 1945 Hermann Walter Pohlsander, surviving president of the Hanover District, wrote the following paragraph to describe the condition of the Uelzen Branch:

> The branch has 21 members of whom 7 have proved to be faithful. All the priesthood apostatized already before the war. Living in Uelzen is Sister Marie Warnecke who is well known to all the missionaries and now is quite old. The faithful Sister Marie Hoppe, 72 years old, lives in Borg close to Uelzen. In Lüneburg is the residence of Sister Marie Hoppe and her children. These Saints are cared for spiritually by the Saints in Celle. A small amount of Church property is still there, but is of not much value. Bad

travel conditions make it impossible to visit these Saints at the present time.[1]

Uelzen Branch[2]	**1939**
Elders	1
Priests	1
Teachers	2
Deacons	2
Other Adult Males	3
Adult Females	16
Male Children	2
Female Children	1
Total	28

In Memoriam

The following members of the Uelzen Branch did not survive World War II:

Agnes Jüschke b. Habelschwerdt, Breslau, Schlesien, 3 Mar 1889; dau. of August Jüschke and Marie Karger; bp. 25 Jan 1923; conf. 25 Jan 1923; m. Eisleben, Sachsen, 4 Dec 1921, Friedrich Paul Horn; 1 child; d. pneumonia Uelzen, Hannover, 28 Aug 1941 (FHL microfilm 68799, no. 2; IGI)

Hermann Friedrich Wilhelm Schmitz b. Uelzen, Hannover, 15 Jul 1916; son of Josef Schmitz and Alwine Dorothee Elisa Wolter; bp. 12 Mar 1927; conf. 12 Mar 1927; m. 16 Nov 1940, Elfriede Eickelmann; rifleman; d. wounds Szuchimitschi or Suchinitschi, Russia, 9 Jan 1942 (FHL microfilm 68799, no. 26; www.volksbund.de; CHL CR 375 8 2439, no. 934)

Otto Erich Schmitz b. Uelzen, Hannover, 17 Jul 1920; son of Josef Schmitz and Alwine Dorothee Elisa Wolter; bp. 6 Oct 1928; conf. 6 Oct 1928; d. pleurisy 10 May 1942 (FHL microfilm 68799, no. 27; IGI)

Notes

1. Uelzen Branch manuscript history, CHL LR 9489 2.
2. Presiding Bishopric, "Financial, Statistical, and Historical Reports of Wards, Stakes, and Missions, 1884–1955," 257, CR 4 12.

Civil defense law required residents of large apartment houses to break openings into each adjacent building as emergency escape routes. This opening was sealed up after the war. It is about three feet tall and two feet wide. (R. Minert 2010)

This sign has hung on the wall since at least 1940. It points to two exit tunnels in the basement of a Berlin apartment house. (R. Minert 2010

KARLSRUHE DISTRICT

West German Mission

In the summer of 1939, the Karlsruhe District consisted of the entire historic territory of Baden (a former grand duchy), the Palatinate (a district of Bavaria west of the Rhine River), and the city of Worms on the left bank of the Rhine. The adjacent Church districts were Frankfurt to the north, Nuremberg to the northeast, Stuttgart to the east, and Strasbourg (German-occupied France as of 1940) to the southeast.

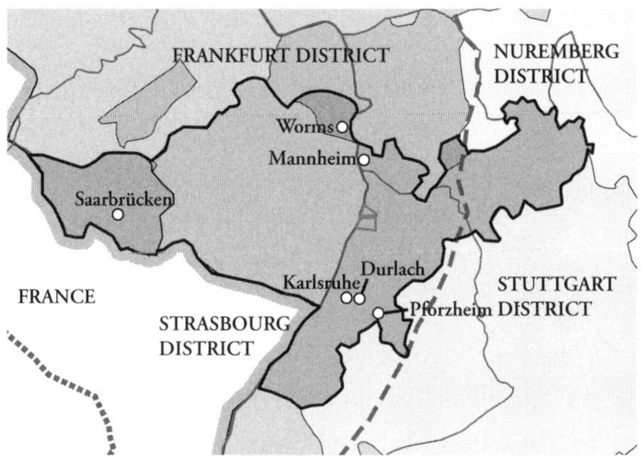

Fig. 1. The Karlsruhe District territory included large areas where no Latter-day Saints lived.

While the district was named after the city of Karlsruhe, in 1939 it was administered from the city of Mannheim, forty-five miles to the north. Other branches were located in Saarbrücken (seventy miles west of Mannheim) and Worms (twelve miles north of Mannheim). To the south, there were branches in Durlach (a suburb of Karlsruhe), Pforzheim (fifteen miles southeast of Karlsruhe), and Bühl (twenty-two miles southwest of Karlsruhe). A group of Saints lived in Freiburg/Breisgau, seventy-five miles south of Karlsruhe toward the Swiss border.

Karlsruhe District[1]	**1939**
Elders	28
Priests	19
Teachers	11
Deacons	21
Other Adult Males	97
Adult Females	265
Male Children	30
Female Children	22
Total	493

Eugen Hechtle (born 1906) was the district president when World War II began. From his home in Mannheim, he traveled to the various branches on a regular basis.[2] The district auxiliary leaders (all of whom served without counselors) represented various branches: George Stehle, Sunday School president and YMMIA leader (Pforzheim),

Hedwig Stapperfend, YWMIA leader (Pforzheim), Johanna Block, Primary president (Durlach), Berta Stapperfend, Relief Society president (Pforzheim), and Karl J. Fetsch, genealogical specialist (Bühl).

After the German conquest of France in June 1940, the provinces of Alsace and Lorraine (just across the Rhine River from Karlsruhe) were added to the territory of the Karlsruhe District. The branches of Saints meeting in the cities of Strasbourg and Mühlhausen (French: Mulhouse) were then added to the district. In 1943, a new district was created consisting of the Alsace-Lorraine territory, the Bühl Branch, and the few Saints (principally the Becker family) in Freiburg.

Only one report sent by President Hechtle to the mission office is preserved in the archives of The Church of Jesus Christ of Latter-day Saints in Salt Lake City:

> Saturday–Sunday, 22–23 April 1939
> District conference of Karlsruhe in Karlsruhe branch hall. Pres. Eugen Hechtle. Total attendance was 643. The attendance was not as large as it [was] last conference because of the number of Saints having to attend the mission conference in Frankfurt in May.[3]

Apparently, some of the Saints in the Karlsruhe District lacked the time or the money to attend both conferences and chose the mission conference over the district conference.[4]

The following details regarding activities in the Karlsruhe District are found in the general minutes of the Bühl Branch:[5]

> November 26, 1939: several members attended the district conference in Stuttgart.[6]
>
> November 1940: district fall conference in Karlsruhe. 289 attendees included four priests and five members of our branch.[7]
>
> March 9, 1941: district conference in Karlsruhe; ten of our members and one friend attended.[8]

Eugen Hechtle was activated from the reserve police force of the city of Mannheim the day the war began. He was one of the replacements for the regular police who were sent to war. He wrote this description of his duties: "Only old policemen were still there; and we, mostly businessmen, were put into the reserve police. We had to do city work, and when the air raids started, then slowly we had to watch what was going on, where there was damage, and where there was a fire that we had to call in."[9]

Fig. 2. District president Eugen Hechtle and his family in about 1940. (R. Hechtle)

President Hechtle was allowed eight days of vacation in 1941, and he planned it carefully, making arrangements for eight specific days. However, when his authorization papers were issued, he found that the dates were off by two days. His complaint was ignored. He took his vacation and, upon returning, learned that during the last two days of his absence (when he had originally planned to be home again) the Mannheim police had to take the Jewish people out of their homes and put them in trucks and take them away. "And terrible stories my colleagues told me of what they experienced. I know that the Lord had heard my prayers and prevented that I should be involved in this terrible business. . . . I [had been] praying every day that the Lord might help and protect me, that I would not have my hands in anything that was directed against the Jewish people. I knew that the police would have to do the dirty work . . . against the Jews."[10]

In early 1942, one of the first air raids against the city of Mannheim could have ended tragically for Eugen Hechtle. He was in a basement hallway of the police building downtown when bombs began to fall very close by. At one point, an officer called, came by, and requested that he go to a different room. Arriving there, he found that nobody needed him or understood why he had been summoned. At that moment, the building shook violently and he was showered with dust. He later discovered that a huge bomb had crashed through the building and landed where he had previously been sitting and that "all of the people that were in that hallway were buried."[11]

In the summer of 1942, Eugen Hechtle was sent to the Eastern Front and became a regular infantry soldier. As he recalled, "I had my scriptures with me. I was reading when I could, and I was keeping the Word of Wisdom all the way." His combat experience ended with a serious wound on January 11, 1943, when an artillery shell landed close enough to him to shatter his left heel. His foot was amputated in a field hospital, and later surgeons removed his leg at about five inches below the knee. As he later concluded, "This was the only way I could come back [from the war alive]. Still my mission was not fulfilled."

His route back to Mannheim was a long one that featured stops in hospitals in Kharkov, Ukraine, in Krakow, Poland, and in Brünn and Prague, Czechoslovakia. In the last two cities, he was successful in contacting local Latter-day Saints, who were equally pleased to meet him. He was even able to contact the leaders of the East German Mission in Berlin, who were allowed to travel to those Czech cities and visit the members there.[12]

Eugen Hechtle did not see Mannheim again until October 1943 but instead was sent to a hospital in the town of Schriesheim, ten miles east of Mannheim. There he was fitted with an artificial limb and assigned to keep records for physicians. He was still there when the war ended with the arrival of American soldiers in April 1945.

In January 1944, Paul Prison of the Saarbrücken Branch replaced Elder Hechtle as the president of the Karlsruhe District.[13] Elder Prison was able to continue district conferences throughout the war, apparently in the city of Karlsruhe. Again, the indications of this are found in the records of the Bühl Branch:

> April 11–12, 1942: spring district conference in Karlsruhe; 5 members attended.[14]
>
> October 17–18, 1942: district conference in Karlsruhe; eight members and 1 friend attended.[15]
>
> March 27–28, 1943: district conference in Karlsruhe; 8 members went.[16]
>
> April 23, 1944: district conference in Karlsruhe; 12 of us went; all meetings were conducted in good order, but there was one interruption when an air raid siren (impending danger!) was sounded. All attendees were able to leave for their homes in time, filled with the spirit to continue the fight against sin.[17]

The first time Eugen Hechtle had any contact with mission leaders after Germany's surrender occurred in the summer of 1945. He had finally come home to his family who had moved to the suburb of Feudenheim after their apartment was destroyed in 1943. Anton Huck, mission supervisor, came with an American army officer in a jeep, and they drove Elder Hechtle to a district conference in Karlsruhe.[18] The war was over and most of the cities severely damaged, but meetings in all branches of the Karlsruhe District were still being held.

Notes

1. Presiding Bishopric, "Financial, Statistical, and Historical Reports of Wards, Stakes, and Missions, 1884–1955," 257, CHL CR 4 12.
2. West German Mission manuscript history, CHL MS 1004 2.
3. West German Mission quarterly reports, 1939, no. 15, CHL LR 10045 2.
4. See the West German Mission chapter for details on that most ambitious conference that lasted for three days and involved hundreds of Saints from all over the mission.
5. Bühl Branch general minutes, CHL LR 1180 11.
6. Ibid., 55.
7. Ibid., 82.
8. Ibid., 96.
9. Eugen Hechtle, *Recollections of My Life* (unpublished autobiography, 2001), 20.
10. Hechtle, *Recollections*, 20, 21–22.

11. Hechtle, *Recollections*, 20, 22–23.
12. Roger P. Minert, *In Harm's Way: East German Latter-day Saints in World War II* (Provo, UT: Religious Studies Center, Brigham Young University, 2009), 30n32.
13. Mannheim Branch general minutes, CHL LR 5244 21.
14. Bühl Branch general minutes, 121.
15. Ibid., 132.
16. Ibid., 142.
17. Ibid., 167.
18. Hechtle, *Recollections*, 28–29.

DURLACH BRANCH

The German-language publication of The Church of Jesus Christ of Latter-day Saints, *Der Stern*, included the following announcement dated Monday, May 1, 1939:

> The Durlach Branch of the Karlsruhe District, that had been dissolved some time ago, was again organized. A beautiful, small meeting hall, well decorated, is available to the few members and the many friends of the branch and the blessing of holding meetings is again made available.[1]

Durlach Branch[2]	**1939**
Elders	1
Priests	1
Teachers	0
Deacons	1
Other Adult Males	7
Adult Females	19
Male Children	3
Female Children	2
Total	34

The town of Durlach is located just a mile east of Karlsruhe and is now a suburb of that major city. In 1939, the population of the city (18,658) included only thirty-four members of the Church. American missionary George Blake was serving in Durlach when the branch was organized and recalled the setting of the meetings:

> When the war started they were meeting in [rented rooms] at Adolf Hitler Strasse 34. It was right on the main street, in the backrooms of a beer hall. We had two rooms and put a sign out front, and we went around the back through an alley to get in. We built a podium in the Durlach chapel. The owner of the building had a swastika in the room and we didn't fight it; that would have been more hassle than it was worth.[3]

Establishing a new branch of the Church can be a substantial challenge, and Elder Blake described the assignment in these words:

> This was a very small group, but we worked it up to as many as thirty-two members and a few friends. Many of them were inactive because they didn't want to travel to Karlsruhe, and it was our job to reactivate them. So we got a local place, and they came out in greater numbers. One brother and his sister said they wouldn't come if the other was going to be there. We smoothed that over and called them to repentance; even though they had been living in the same town, they hadn't spoken in 16 years. . . . I don't know how long they [remained active].

Fig. 1. American missionaries built a rostrum for the new rooms of the Durlach Branch in the summer of 1939. From left: Paul Nichols, George Blake, Myron Seamons, and John Wesche. (G. Blake)

The members of the new Durlach Branch had some very pleasant characteristics, as Elder Blake described in his diary on Thursday, August 3, 1939:

> These Durlacher Fraus are good [to the missionaries]. We are fed practically every day of the week, and then are given large sweet bread loaves, gooseberries, plums, jam etc. for between times. We really almost have too much, but to refuse it is an insult so we have to take it and be tickled over it. . . . We seldom buy anything at the store for we have breakfast with the rent, dinner invitations about every day, and coffee in the afternoons which leaves no room for supper. In the last fourteen days I have spent around 7,00 RM for meals—around $1.50.[4]

A few days later, Elder Blake was transferred to the mission office in Frankfurt. The directory of the West German Mission showed Elder Whitney D. Hammond as the branch president on August 18, 1939—just two weeks before the war started. He and his companion, Myron Seamons, were evacuated from Germany on August 25, and it is not known whom they designated as the leader of the small branch. As of this writing, there are no records of the branch to be consulted, and no eyewitnesses can be found.

Fig. 2. Elder Blake recalled that baptisms were performed in this creek at a location known as Hagsfeld, near Durlach. (G. Blake)

In Memoriam

The following members of the Durlach Branch did not survive World War II:

Maria Ederer b. Weißenburg, Mittelfranken, Bayern, 2 Feb 1876; dau. of Franz Ederer and Franziska Gebhardt; bp. 13 Oct 1929; conf. 13 Oct 1929; m. 24 Oct 1875 [*sic*], Karl Bauer; d. 1944 (FHL microfilm 68788, no. 1; IGI)

Maria Kistler b. Schussenried, Donaukreis, Württemberg, 15 Jul 1879; dau. of Anton Kistler and Karolina Maier; bp. 23 Sep 1930; conf. 23 Sep 1930; m. —— Knodel; d. asthma 5 Feb 1945 (FHL microfilm 68797, no. 423; FHL microfilm 271380, 1930 and 1935 censuses; IGI)

Wilhelm Heinrich Sauter b. Aue Durlach, Karlsruhe, Baden, 29 Jan 1921; son of Georg H. Sauter and Luise Schäfer; bp. 23 Sep 1930; conf. 23 Sep 1930; noncommissioned officer; d. in field hospital 28 Nov 1944; bur. Cernjachovsk, Russia (FHL microfilm 68788, no. 22; www.volksbund.de; IGI)

Notes

1. *Der Stern*, May 1, 1939, 145.
2. Presiding Bishopric, "Financial, Statistical, and Historical Reports of Wards, Stakes, and Missions, 1884–1955," 257, CHL CR 4 12.
3. George R. Blake, interview by the author, Provo, UT, April 1, 2009.
4. George R. Blake, journal, CHL MS 17781. The coffee mentioned was malt coffee, such as Pero in the United States, and thus did not represent a departure from the Church's standards of health. Such drinks were common among the Saints all over Germany at the time.

Karlsruhe Branch

The city of Karlsruhe was laid out in a beautifully symmetrical way, such that the streets of the downtown ran from the city palace to the south like rays from the sun. The city was home to 184,489 people in 1939 and hosted a substantial branch of The Church of Jesus Christ of Latter-day Saints.

Although the record shows that the Karlsruhe Branch had eight elders in June 1939, an American missionary, Robert Kunkel, was serving as the branch president. His counselors were Johann Fauth and Eugen G. Bauer. Another missionary, John Wesche, was the leader of the YMMIA, but all other callings in the branch were entrusted to local branch members; Max Klotz was the president of the Sunday School, Johanne Block the leader of the YWMIA, Adleheid Schulz the president of the Primary, and Dorothea Bauer the president of the Relief Society.[1]

The branch meeting rooms were rented in a building at Waldhornstrasse 18, very close to the palace. Sunday School began at 10:00 and sacrament meeting at 3:00 p.m. The Primary met on Mondays at 6:00, the Relief Society on Wednesdays at 7:00 p.m., and Mutual an hour later.

Karlsruhe Branch[2]	**1939**
Elders	8
Priests	3
Teachers	2
Deacons	2
Other Adult Males	21
Adult Females	69
Male Children	5
Female Children	2
Total	112

The facility at Waldhornstrasse 18 had been secured by the branch in 1936. The following description is taken from the branch history:

> The branch moved into the building that belonged to a fraternity and was located near the corner of Kaiserstrasse. The peaceful location and a garden in front gave the building a dignified appearance. From a broad foyer the stairs led up to a large, bright hall with a painted ceiling. Three additional broad and spacious rooms had large windows. The main floor of the building housed the studio of an artist named Heil.[3]

Heini-Werner Seith (born 1930) described the meeting rooms in these words:

> The rooms were very comfortable and could easily fit about 120 people. We had a podium in the front where the branch presidency could sit. Three other rooms next to the large one were used for Primary, MIA, and Sunday School. We had decorations on the wall because the art students had left them there. We did not have to share the rooms during the week because the fraternity was not allowed anymore after Hitler came to power. . . . We had a pump organ. (The first one we owned, we still had to pump with our feet.) There was no sign at the door saying that we met there. During the war years, there were about forty people who attended regularly. . . . In the main room, we had single chairs so that we could move them around as needed. A room next to the large room also had a sliding wall, which made it possible for us to make the smaller rooms bigger. That was fantastic even back then. We could fit up to sixty people in the small rooms then. We never really celebrated anything in the "chapel" (the large room) but used the smaller rooms for those occasions. We also had a piano in the large room.[4]

Heini-Werner was only eight years old when he saw action taken against the Jewish community in Karlsruhe:

> On the day of the crystal night [November 9, 1938], I looked out of the restroom window in the branch building and saw the synagogue burning just one street over. My family was very connected to Jewish people because they were our customers in our store. Doctors and professors often came to us, and I went to see them a lot also. One family told us that they would have to leave for Israel in order to be safer.

Heinrich and Elsa Seith operated a delicatessen store and owned a small car as part of the business—"an Opel Super 6. It was a very nice car!" according to son Rolf (born 1932).[5] However, that car was not used to transport the family to church. Sister Seith and her sons took the streetcar or walked. According to Rolf, his mother sometimes did not go along but gave the boys money for the streetcar. They soon discovered that if they walked fast or ran to church, they could save the money and use it for the movie theater.

At the age of nine years, Heini-Werner had two experiences in the fall of 1939 that would remain clear in his recollection many decades later. The first was the departure of the American missionaries from Germany on August 26, 1939: "Elder [Robert] Kunkel left me a bicycle, which I never used because I was afraid that I would break it. It was so special to me. . . . After they found out that they had to leave, they came to us, took the most important things with them, and my father took them to the Karlsruhe West railroad station."

The second memorable experience took place just weeks after the missionaries departed. He described it in these words:

> About one hundred meters away from our home was a large army post. Karlsruhe was known for that, since we are located so close to France. We stood next to the post with flowers in our hands and put those flowers on the jackets of the soldiers as they left for duty. That is how we said good-bye to them. The soldiers then told us that they would be home in a month.

Fearing bombardment or invasion from the French just across the Rhine River, authorities in Karlsruhe ordered the evacuation of women and children. Sister Seith took her sons to the town of Sinsheim, near Heidelberg. Both boys recalled sleeping with other evacuees in a barn, but the conditions were not bad. The property owner was a Catholic priest who invited the newcomers to attend Mass; when all of them declined the offer, they were politely asked to leave. With nowhere to go, Elsa called her husband, and he picked them up in his car. He first smuggled them back into Karlsruhe, then drove them to a town in faraway Bavaria. Schaftlach was twenty miles south of Munich, and the three family members lived there under comfortable circumstances until the end of 1940. By then, the French had capitulated, and it was safe for them to return to Karlsruhe.

As a trained technical designer, Johann Albert Dahl (born 1912) had already worked for important industries such as Maybach and BMW when his draft notice arrived in December 1940. A veteran of the Swiss-German Mission, he spoke excellent English and was married to Betty Baer of the Nuremberg Branch. They both left Karlsruhe in December—he to Halle for training and she with their daughter Helga to stay with her parents in Nuremberg. Johann's assignment had its advantages, as he soon learned:

> Once you went through [the] Halle [training program], you were almost certain not to be called to the fighting front line. As a matter of fact we had a special paragraph in our military pass that no soldier of [our unit] FNR 601 could be transferred into any other unit of the German army. While in Halle, I had the opportunity to go and be active in my LDS Church each Sunday.[6]

Johann's service took him from Halle to Cologne, Brussels, and Paris, where he enjoyed three weeks of spring air and the pleasures of the French capital. Back in Brussels, he worked with telecommunications until May 1941, when his unit was transferred to Suwalki, on the Polish-Soviet border. By June, he was in Vilnius, Lithuania. It was there that he encountered something about the German occupation that shocked him: a Jewish man offered him and his comrades a great deal of money to drive him to a secret place in Lithuania. Johann's account reads as follows:

> We all felt sorry for this man, but we could not help him. . . . The risk for him and us to loose [*sic*] our lives was too high. He was sadly disappointed, and so were we. The next morning, a security man dressed in a green uniform, came to the hotel, telling us that last night they, the security service, had again killed 4000 Jews somewhere outside of Vilnius. They buried them in a mass grave. We were so upset that we asked him to leave us alone. This was the first time in my life that I learned firsthand about the final solution or extermination plan against the Jews and other ethnic groups.

In 1942, Rolf Seith was inducted automatically into the Jungvolk. He had this to say about the experience:

> I both liked it and disliked it. There are nice memories of things I learned during that time that I enjoyed—for example, first aid or how to

> make a fire when camping. We also played games that I would call military exercises. We had to go to an abandoned railroad track to learn how to guard it. We had to hide, and the goal was to not be seen. Another group had to try to put a barrel on the tracks. If they succeeded, we lost since the barrel represented a bomb. We were also trained in using hand grenades and small-bore rifles. These were all things that I liked doing. Except for the plays since they always ended up in huge fights until somebody won. Sometimes we could not determine a winner so we had to get in a line and the more people of the 70–80 people in one group got beaten down lost.

The Jungvolk experience went sour when the boys began fighting. Rolf was not interested in knocking others down, so he chose to skip the meetings. Soon a letter came to his home promising penalties if he did not return. Fortunately, he was able to discuss the matter with a reasonable leader who helped him transfer to a music group in the Jungvolk organization. "My new group was known for the plays they performed," Rolf recalled. "We learned songs and even recorded them. Those songs were then heard on the radio on most Sundays. I liked that much better; I didn't have to hit anybody, and I liked singing. I was still able to attend all church meetings even though I was in the Jungvolk."

During his years on the Eastern Front, Johann Dahl did indeed avoid spending time in a combat zone. He was even privileged to use the communications network he serviced to make infrequent calls home to his wife in Karlsruhe (although such calls were not allowed). His lifestyle was so unlike that of a combat soldier in the same area that he apologized somewhat in his autobiography: "While all this sounds more like a vacation, it was not. We were separated from our loved ones, had no chance to attend church, and most of the time were very lonesome . . . especially those of us with families at home . . . with their lives endangered by a terrible air war."

While in Saparzje, Russia, Johann was hospitalized with malaria for six weeks. He had just passed an advanced training course with excellent marks and was designated for a promotion, but the promotion was blocked: it turned out that officials had learned of his membership in an American church and suspected him of being a spy for the United States. He recalled, "Even though I did not care much about the promotion, yet I felt very much humiliated because I was on top of the class and the advancement would have meant more money for me and my family at home." An officer later chastised him for even mentioning his association with the Church, saying that Johann would have been promoted at least to corporal if the army had not known about his religion.

Religious instruction was standard in most German schools of the era, but classes were only available for Catholics and Lutherans. Heini-Werner Seith recalled his interaction with other religions as a schoolboy:

> Our neighbors in the Goethestrasse knew about us being members of the Church. It did not matter much to us because we lived in accordance with the eleventh article of faith.[7] We accepted them and they accepted us. I even attended the religion course at school until my teacher got really nervous because I already knew so much. I had gone to Primary and [Sunday School] classes and used all my knowledge in school. The teacher then told my mother that it would be better if I did not attend religion class anymore so somebody else would get the chance to learn.

Both of the Seith boys recalled air raids and alarms that disturbed the life of the inhabitants of Karlsruhe. They told of single airplanes that flew around over the city and generally harassed the people. Quite often, the planes did no damage, but on other occasions they dropped a bomb here and there or even swooped low over the streets and fired at vehicles and pedestrians. Sometimes the boys would watch the airplanes from the attic rooms of their apartment building. If the planes flew low, it meant a probable attack, and the youngsters raced for the basement shelter. As Rolf recalled, "Then we nearly jumped down all the stairs to the basement. It was like flying because we had to hurry so fast. It didn't take us more than twenty seconds to get to the basement from the seventh floor." As was the practice all over Germany, a nighttime air raid meant that school would begin one or two hours later the following morning.

Johann Dahl's four years at the Eastern Front included time in the city of Odessa on the Black Sea, where he enjoyed sightseeing, the opera, and purchasing rare items on the black market. However, most of his time was mundane, and the terrible cold of the winters provided sufficient opportunities for suffering. The ravages of war were also very depressing, as he noted while describing a transfer trip by rail:

> The [route] to the depot was filled with destroyed tanks and black burned house ruins. As mute witnesses of a senseless war they offered a cruel picture of destruction. The train crossed, slowly rumbling, over a squeaking emergency bridge destroyed by the Russians and reconstructed by German engineer troops just recently. Looking down into the frozen river made me dizzy. It revealed a picture of dead life and living death. I could have cried with heaven!

Eventually, the war came home to Karlsruhe in all its ferocity, as Heini-Werner recalled: "On September 27, 1944, we were bombed out for the first time. I will never forget that day. It was a nighttime air raid by the British." His family got out of the building in time but lost most of their possessions. A worse fate befell their relatives. "One of my aunts owned birds which she wasn't allowed to take into the shelter with her. She loved those birds a lot so [she and her children] decided to stay in their basement. A bomb hit the house, and my aunt was killed instantly; her daughter was badly burned, but her son was not injured."

Rolf's recollections were more detailed: he described how the building burned for several days and attempts were made to save both the structure and its contents. The residents were able to carry out many pieces of furniture, but the building inevitably fell victim to the flames. "It was not possible to take out the piano from the first floor. But then again, we did not need it in order to survive." When the fires died out, the basement was intact, and it was there that the Seith family took up residence again. According to Heini-Werner, "We lived in our basement for five years after that. Whenever it rained, there was so much water on the floor that our slippers would just float away."

Another attack struck the neighborhood of the Waldhornstrasse. Rolf described an experience that happened just a week before that attack:

> I found a cabinet in one of the smaller [meeting] rooms. I opened it and found the utensils for the sacrament. I opened the upper drawer and only found paper rolls. I took one out. In that moment, I heard my mother look for me and say my name. She had seen that I walked into that room. I put the small roll into my pocket, closed the drawer, and walked home with her. At home, I opened the paper roll and found three sacrament glasses in it. I hadn't meant to take those home. A week later, the meeting rooms were destroyed, and the only thing that was preserved were those three little glasses.[8]

Although all furnishings in the church meeting rooms were destroyed, the members still had their scripture books and hymnals, which were usually kept in the home. The branch membership records also survived the destruction, because those were kept in the home of the clerk or a member of the branch presidency.

According to the branch history,

> It was not possible to rent another place to meet after our rooms were destroyed, but a temporary solution was found: Sister Rosine Dahl, a widow and long-time member of the Church, invited us into her living room on the fourth floor of the apartment house at Tulla Strasse 74 in the eastern part of the city. It was a crowded situation but an offer we appreciated very much.[9]

Sister Dahl's son, Johann, was pleased to spend a week with his family in Karlsruhe in 1944. When informed of his orders to return to the Eastern Front, he told his commanding officer that he wanted a transfer to Munich instead. When asked for a justification, he explained that he had friends in Munich and that his wife was expecting their second child.

He recalled making this bold proclamation: "I explained to him that I did spend nearly four years in Russia and that I had enough of it and would not go [back]." Against all logic, he was assigned to go to Munich the next morning and recognized that his prayer had been answered.

Upon arriving in Munich, Johann Dahl immediately contacted district president Johannes Thaller. He asked if President Thaller could take him in along with his pregnant wife and their daughter, Helga. President Thaller did indeed have room, having evacuated his own wife and children to Haag am Hausruck in Austria. Brother Dahl found that, in many respects, life went on in Munich, the capital of Bavaria and a center of history and culture. "We went to church as we did before the war, even on the Sunday afternoon when Munich was taken at the end of the war," he explained. His wife returned to Karlsruhe, where their son, Rainer, was born on August 11, 1944.

Heini-Werner Seith had been in the Jungvolk since he was ten and advanced into the Hitler Youth at the age of fourteen. It was a mixed bag of positive and negative experiences in the last year of the war, as he explained:

> I was interested in vehicles and everything that I could drive, so I joined a motorized Hitler Youth unit. We were trained to drive and operate tanks. They did not tell us where they were taking us for the training, but we knew that it would be a camp somewhere. I was transported to Alsace-Lorraine near Strasbourg and I knew that I was now in a combat zone. Our task was to clean all the trenches although there were air raids constantly. It seemed like we were always on the move to a safer location. This eventually led to us to come back to Germany after all.

Heini-Werner was fortunate that his Hitler Youth experience never evolved into a Wehrmacht experience. His father was equally fortunate, mostly because he was diabetic and not fit for duty. For a short time, he served in a communications unit, then was sent home and assigned to be a neighborhood watchman. His duty consisted of making sure that no looting took place among the ruins of bombed-out apartment buildings and stores. The members of the Seith family all survived the war unscathed, but they lost several relatives, according to Heini-Werner: "I had three cousins who died while serving in Russia."

The people of Karlsruhe saw both French and American invaders in the spring of 1945. Whereas the Americans treated the populace humanely, the French were awarded the province of Baden as their occupation zone, and their behavior was far less kind, as Heini-Werner recalled: "When the French came, a lot of things changed. They raped women and did not treat us well. Even though the town square wasn't [previously] damaged, they burned it down and filmed it in order to show their families and friends at home how they had fought to take over the city."

The day after the American army entered Munich (encountering no resistance), Johann Dahl's commanding officer dismissed the unit, instructing them to find civilian clothing if possible. Johann did so and thus avoided being taken prisoner. Soon he was confronted by GIs who were surprised to learn that he spoke excellent English. Immediately, he was employed by the American occupation forces and paid well. In September 1945, Johann was able to find a way home to Karlsruhe. His wife had arrived there after spending four months in a small town hear Nuremberg as a refugee. They were pleased to be home in Karlsruhe, safe and sound; his mother, Rosina Dahl, had also survived the war in her apartment.

Heini-Werner had become so accustomed to good treatment at the hands of the Americans that he was shocked by the actions of one GI: "An American officer attended church with us once [after the war], and he mentioned that he was happy and laughed when he saw Karlsruhe burning. This statement hurt us very much. He was a member of the Church, and we really did not expect that from him."

Looking back on his experiences as a member of the Karlsruhe Branch during World War II,

Heini-Werner summarized his impressions in these words:

> Back then, all we had was church. We weren't involved in any sports activities and people didn't go on vacations as much. The church was the place we always went. We met very often together as Church members. We held little conferences, had dances, or met for cake in the afternoon. The Primary organized carnivals and we had Christmas parties in December. It seemed like we were in church a lot during the week. We were one big family. We also all lived relatively close to each other, which made it easier for us to get together and strengthen one another.

Shortly after the war ended, the branch leaders were able to rent space in the music hall of the Munz Conservatory on Waldstrasse. The facility was large enough for sacrament meetings and district conferences. The Relief Society continued to meet in Sister Dahl's apartment, and the youth met in the home of the Böhringer family, but "only Mother Nature had room enough for the Sunday School meetings."[10]

In Memoriam

The following members of the Karlsruhe Branch did not survive World War II.

Eugen Gottlob Bauer b. Möttlingen, Schwarzwaldkreis, Württemberg, 3 Jan 1884; son of Friedrich Nikolaus Bauer and Christine Dorothea Gackenheimer; bp. 6 Oct 1923; conf. 6 Oct 1923; ord. deacon 1 Jun 1924; ord. teacher 6 May 1928; ord. priest 30 Sep 1930; ord. elder 11 Oct 1931; m. Heimsheim, Calw, Schwarzwaldkreis, Württemberg, 25 Mar 1912, Dorothea Walz; 4 children; d. multiple sclerosis Baden 18 Oct 1944 (FHL microfilm 68797, no. 152; CHL CR 275 8 2441, no. 152; FHL microfilm 25719, 1930 and 1935 censuses; IGI)

Juliane Eicher b. Bühl, Baden, 2 Oct 1903; dau. of Adolf Eicher and Magdalene Schleif; bp. 19 Jun 1939; conf. 20 Jun 1939; m. 6 Aug 1935, Ignaz Gerber; missing as of 20 Dec 1946 (FHL microfilm 68797, no. 627)

Lina Katharina Gehreg b. Mannheim, Baden, 29 Jan 1886; dau. of Karl Gehreg and Katharina Baur; bp. 13 Oct 1929; conf. 13 Oct 1929; m. —— Deininger; d. kidney disease 23 Nov 1941 (FHL microfilm 68797, no. 339)

Christiana Grimmer b. Lippoldsweiler, Neckarkreis, Württemberg, 29 Aug 1864; dau. of Johannes Grimmer and Christiana Waibel; bp. 12 Oct or Dec 1894; conf. 12 Oct 1894 or Dec 1894; m. 29 Nov 1894, Ludwig Eckert; d. old age 2 Jan 1943 (FHL microfilm 68797, no. 139; CHL CR 275 8 2441, no. 139; FHL microfilm 25759, 1930 and 1935 censuses; IGI)

Marie Magdalena Heck b. Kippenheimweiler, Freiburg, Baden, 21 Aug 1866; dau. of Michael Heck and Katharina Zipf; bp. 29 Jun 1901; conf. 29 Jun 1901; m. 29 Apr 1893, —— Deser; d. heart attack 26 Mar 1944 (FHL microfilm 68797, no. 88; FHL microfilm 25754, 1930 and 1935 censuses; IGI)

Friederika Hirschbühl b. Hornberg, Wolfach, Karlsruhe, Baden, 31 Mar 1876; dau. of Karl Hirschbühl and Christine Haas; bp. 19 Jan 1914; conf. 19 Jan 1914; m. Hornberg 28 Dec 1901, Gottfried Moser; 1 child; d. tuberculosis Karlsruhe, Karlsruhe, Baden, 12 Oct 1940 (FHL microfilm 68797, no. 117; CHL CR 275 8 2441, no. 117; FHL microfilm 245238, 1930 and 1935 censuses; IGI)

August Kary b. Dumersheim, Baden 9 Sep 1874; son of Joseph Kary and Josephine Abath; bp. 8 May 1928; m. Louise Knappschneider; 1 child; d. 31 Mar 1946 (FHL microfilm no. 271376, 1930 and 1935 censuses; IGI)

Christina Klebsattel b. Spiegelberg, Neckarkreis, Württemberg, 29 Dec 1864; dau. of Jacob Klebsattel and Elisabeth Andres; bp. 6 Aug 1903; conf. 6 Aug 1903; d. old age 15 Jan 1940 (FHL microfilm 68797, no. 155, CHL CR 275 8 2441, no. 155; FHL microfilm 271380, 1930 and 1935 censuses; IGI)

Ernst Max Klotz b. Pforzheim, Karlsruhe, Baden, 16 Mar 1912; son of Friedrich Ernst Klotz and Emma Bonnet; bp. 8 Apr 1934; conf. 15 Apr 1934; ord. deacon 7 Jun 1934; ord. teacher 7 Aug 1938; m. 20 Oct. 1939, Dorothea Bauer; k. in battle 5 Apr 1944 (FHL microfilm 68797, no. 467; CHL CR 275 8 2441, no. 573; IGI)

Maria Magdalene Kraus b. Karlsruhe, Baden, 27 Feb 1875; dau. of Jakob Kraus and Maria Magdalena Neuweiler; bp. 2 Feb 1904; conf. 4 Feb 1904; m. Karlsruhe 12 Feb 1898, Phillipp Schmieder; 5 children; d. lung cancer Karlsruhe 28 Feb 1941 (FHL microfilm 68797, no. 161; CHL CR 275 8 2441, no. 161; IGI; AF)

Georg Johann Leyer b. Mannheim, Baden, 3 Jan 1918; son of Georg Johann Leyer and Anna Hess; bp. 1 Feb 1931; conf. 1 Feb 1931; m. 16 Mar 1940, Antonie Margarethe Wenzel; d. lung ailment 14 Dec 1942 (FHL microfilm 68797, no. 458; CHL CR 275 8 2441, no. 458)

Ernst Lichtenberg b. Herrensohr, Rheinprovinz, 3 Mar 1864; son of Georg Friedrich Lichtenberg and Louise Rosental; bp. 22 Nov 1901; conf. 22 Nov 1901; ord. priest 30 Aug 1903; ord. elder 11 Oct 1931; m. Kassel, Hessen-Nassau, 23 Mar 1889, Philippine Geldmacher; 4 children; d. heart attack and senility Karlsruhe, Baden,

11 Apr 1941 (FHL microfilm 68797, no. 92; CHL CR 275 8 2441, no. 92; FHL microfilm no. 271387, 1930 and 1935 censuses; IGI)

Anna Long b. Beihingen, Neckarkreis, Württemberg, 6 Dec 1877; dau. of Adam Long and Friederike Bötzner; bp. 1 Aug 1909; conf. 1 Aug 1909; m. 7 Jul 1900, Karl August Nagel; d. heart condition 18 Mar 1941 (FHL microfilm 68797, no. 97; CHL CR 275 8 2441, no. 97; IGI)

Lydia Lund b. Kappeln, Schleswig-Holstein, 29 Dec 1899; dau. of Johann August Lund and Anna Agnes Hampkens; bp. 20 May 1938; conf. 20 May 1938; m. Aug 1919, —— Halit; missing as of 20 May 1941 (FHL microfilm 68797, no. 661; CHL CR 275 8 2441, no. 661)

Karl Paul Müller b. Merseburg, Bitterfeld, Sachsen, 4 Jul 1869; son of Karl Ludwig Theodor Müller and Johanne Friedrike Pauline Meyer; bp 15 Mar 1913; conf. 15 Mar 1913; ord. deacon 25 Jan 1925; ord. teacher 17 Apr 1927; ord. priest 4 Jan 1931; ord. elder 11 Oct 1931; m. 4 Oct 1894, Emilie Steffen; k. in air raid 25 Apr 1944; bur. Karlsruhe, Karlsruhe, Baden (FHL microfilm 68797, no. 110; www.volksbund.de; CHL CR 275 8 2441, no. 110; IGI)

Luise Müller b. Ettlingen, Karlsruhe, Baden, 1 Oct 1905; dau. of Wunibald Müller and Josefine Lachner; bp. 13 Jun 1939; conf. 13 Jun 1939; k. in air raid 25 Apr 1944 (FHL microfilm 68797, no. 681; CHL CR 275 8 2441, no. 681; IGI)

Christiana Ott b. Oberniebelsbach, Schwarzwaldkreis, Württemberg, 15 Mar 1874; dau. of Gottlieb Ott and Barbara König; bp. 3 Oct 1909; conf. 3 Oct 1909; m. 27 Aug 1898, Karl Deuchler; d. dropsy and heart attack 9 Jan 1941 (FHL microfilm 68797, no. 99; IGI)

Edgar Schmieder b. Lauda, Mosbach, Baden, 26 Dec 1917; son of Phillip Schmieder and Maria Magdalene Kraus; d. 2 Aug 1942 (FHL microfilm 68797)

Gerald Fritz Schmieder b. Karlsruhe, Baden, 1 Feb 1924; son of Friedrich Philipp Schmieder and Sophie Elisabeth Clemens; bp. 16 Jun 1933; conf. 16 Jun 1933; ord. deacon 5 Sep 1937; k. in battle Kaukasus, Russia, 11 Nov 1942 (FHL microfilm 68797, no. 278)

Anna Maria Schwartz b. Machern, Elsaß-Lothringen, 25 Dec 1858; dau. of Michael Jean Schwartz and Elisabeth Lux; bp. 15 Jun 1909; conf. 15 Jun 1909; d. old age Oct 1939 (FHL microfilm 68797, no. 48; CHL CR 275 8 2441, no. 48; FHL microfilm no. 245260, 1930 and 1935 census; IGI)

Karl Emil Zapf b. Mannheim, Baden, 26 Aug 1878; son of Johann Casper Zapf and Katharina Hasslinger; bp. 13 Feb 1927; conf. 13 Feb 1927; ord. priest 16 Oct 1929; ord. elder 11 Oct 1931; m. Mannheim, Baden, 15 Sep 1900, Anna Maria Schott; d. heart attack Mannheim 10 Jan 1942 (FHL microfilm 68797, no. 343)

Notes

1. West German Mission branch directory 1939, CHL LR 10045 11.
2. Presiding Bishopric, "Financial, Statistical, and Historical Reports of Wards, Stakes, and Missions, 1884–1955," 257, CR 4 12.
3. *Chronik der Gemeinde Karlsruhe* (Karlsruhe, Germany: Karlsruhe Ward, 1997), 328.
4. Heini-Werner Seith, telephone interview with the author in German, May 5, 2009; unless otherwise noted, summarized in English by Judith Sartowski.
5. Rolf Seith, telephone interview with the author in German, May 19, 2009.
6. Johann Albert Dahl, "Vier Jahre im Verhassten Feldgrau" (unpublished autobiography).
7. "We claim the privilege of worshiping Almighty God according to the dictates of our own conscience, and allow all men the same privilege, let them worship how, where, or what they may." Articles of Faith 1:11.
8. The fact that Rolf took the paper home should not be considered theft. In those days, paper was a rarity, and he likely thought that any paper found in the cabinet could be put to better use. The implements used in the sacrament in Germany during the war were in fact small glass cups. Neither paper nor plastic was available for that purpose until many years after the war.
9. *Chronik der Gemeinde Karlsruhe*, 330.
10. Ibid.

Mannheim Branch

The city of Mannheim is situated on the east bank of the Rhine River at the northern extent of the old province of Baden. The Neckar River flows along the city's northern border into the Rhine. The city was home to 280,365 people in the summer of 1939, only 121 of whom were members of The Church of Jesus Christ of Latter-day Saints. In fact, the percentage of Church members among the city's residents was even smaller because some members of the Mannheim Branch lived across the river in Ludwigshafen, a city half the size of Mannheim. Ludwigshafen had enjoyed its own branch in the 1920s, but emigration had caused its demise. The members living there rode the streetcar across the Rhine to Mannheim to participate in meetings and branch activities.

Fig. 1. Youth of the Mannheim Branch in 1939. (L. Deininger Harrer)

Mannheim Branch[1]	**1939**
Elders	5
Priests	6
Teachers	4
Deacons	2
Other Adult Males	33
Adult Females	55
Male Children	7
Female Children	9
Total	121

The status of the leaders of the Mannheim Branch in the summer of 1939 is somewhat unclear. Reed Oldroyd, a missionary from the United States, was serving as the branch president. Despite the fact that the mission statistics show five elders and twelve Aaronic Priesthood holders as members of the branch, none are listed as counselors or secretaries to Elder Oldroyd.[2] Johann Martin Scholl, who had been the branch president for decades beginning in 1902, was still present and serving as the leader of the Sunday School. With the departure of the American missionaries on August 26, 1939, Brother Scholl likely was called to preside over the branch.

When the war broke out on September 1, 1939, the Mannheim Branch was meeting in rented rooms at D2–5. In the unique numbering system used in Mannheim, this notation means building number 5 on block D2, just a few hundred yards from the city's center.[3] The branch rented rooms in a Hinterhaus at that location. According to Elfriede Deininger (born 1921), "It was a large room connected to three smaller rooms on the side. There were about sixty members [attending]."[4] The meeting schedule included Sunday School at 10:00 a.m. and sacrament meeting at 4:00 p.m. Mutual was held on Tuesdays at 8:00 p.m., and the Primary and Relief Society meetings were held on Wednesdays at 3:30 and 8:00 p.m. respectively.

Gottfried Leyer (born 1927) recalled making the long trek from his home in a suburb of Mannheim north of the Neckar River downtown to church. "It took about an hour to walk to church and it was too far to go home for lunch and back for sacrament meeting, so we stayed in the church rooms or went with friends to their homes between meetings."[5]

Walter E. Scoville of the United States had served in the West German Mission before the war and kept up his correspondence with several families of the Karlsruhe District. He received the following letter from Elfriede Deininger of the Mannheim Branch dated March 6, 1940:

> It was such a nice time while you were here [in 1939]. Things have changed since then. It's really lonely around here. The men are all in the army and we women and children have lots of work. We are still holding meetings, but for how long? And our dear Father Scholl died [29 Feb 1940, age 78]. We held his funeral yesterday. This is a terrible loss for each of us, for the entire branch. The only men left are Brother Dönig, Brother Ziegler, and Andreas Leyer (but he is leaving soon). . . . Helene, Kläre, and I will also be leaving in the fall. We have to serve our "duty year" and this year they are calling up the girls born in 1920–1921 so the three of us have to be ready to leave. We are looking forward to this time when we too can serve Germany. The day before he died, Brother Scholl said to us, "Hitler will lead Germany to a marvelous and lasting peace and victory, even if it takes years. Every German is of this opinion nowadays. Actually, it is not an opinion but a sincere belief. We believe that God is with him, or else he would not have been able to accomplish such great things in the past and the present. And we know that God will be with our Führer in the future as well. The greater the pressure from foreign nations, the tighter the bond between our Führer and the people. No power on earth can break that bond, not even the English. Conditions in the branch are still very good, but we are short on priesthood holders.[6]

Spirits were high in Germany at the time. The Polish campaign had lasted less than a month, and Germany's enemies had not yet attacked. It appeared indeed as if Germany would be victorious. Although Elfriede's letter suggests that all of the members of the Mannheim Branch were convinced of Hitler's good standing with God, this certainly cannot be said about the German Latter-day Saints in general, as is clear from many eyewitness reports. The letter was written two months before the German army invaded France and before air raids on German cities became frequent and deadly.

Elfriede Deininger was a young woman dedicated to the Church. She later wrote of the problems in the branch after the priesthood holders left: "It was a lonely feeling to have no priesthood holders in our midst. But even with our men gone we could still have a prayer."[7] In her personal life, things were looking up in 1940 when she began dating Horst Prison, a soldier from the Saarbrücken Branch. He wrote her often from the Eastern Front, where he went through very difficult trials for the next three years.

Manfred Zapf (born 1930) was inducted into the Jungvolk through his school when he turned ten years of age:

> We had uniforms, and I attended the meetings. In a way, it was just like the Boy Scouts, so we enjoyed it. We played little games, like war games, and for Christmas we made toys for other children. We also marched around and did service projects. But really we were just kids and enjoyed being together. Sometimes my father would write an excuse because I had to help in the garden, but I never got into trouble [for missing meetings].[8]

"The first bombing of Mannheim was in about September 1941," recalled Gottfried Leyer. "Mannheim had a big airfield for fighter planes. When the first bomb came down on this one Sunday, all the people living nearby went out to see [where it landed]. I can picture it there, between houses, right in the garden, a big crater. That was probably the first bomb that fell on Mannheim."

Regarding the air-raid shelters available to city residents, Manfred Hechtle (born 1928) provided this description:

> The basements were made in such a way that they had a large room there where people could gather. And then, since apartment houses have one common firewall between them, it was required that

> they be broken through in the basement from one to another so that if something happened on one side, people could go through and to the [adjacent] basement. It could go for a whole block that way. But they bricked it back up. The bricks were set sideways, so then a sledgehammer was set next to it so it could easily be broken through.

Ludwig Harrer married Lina Deininger and was drafted soon after the war started. In February 1942, he came home on leave and told his sister-in-law Elfriede that he had disobeyed an order and was being punished; he had captured two black French soldiers and was commanded to execute them rather than to guard them as prisoners of war with the usual rights. He had refused to carry out the order and was punished with a transfer to the Eastern Front. He told Elfriede that he would soon join her deceased mother. Two weeks later he was killed in Russia.[9]

Fig. 2. The family of Ludwig and Lina Harrer in 1941. (L. Deininger Harrer)

Manfred Hechtle had been a member of the Jungvolk since the age of ten and advanced to the Hitler Youth when he became fourteen. He recalled that although his participation was required, he was given the choice of various kinds of activities, and he chose the air force training program: "I started out learning how to fly a glider. We practiced with the glider on the ground, learning how to keep it level and land it straight. We did this on a grassy meadow."[10]

As air raids caused increasing destruction in the city, the situation with schools became more challenging, as Manfred recalled:

> The school that I went to was only a block away from where I lived. In those days, of course, half of the school was for girls and half for boys. And they were physically separated in the building. My school was hit one night by [incendiary] bombs; the fourth [top] floor was actually eliminated. It was not in use anymore, but they put a roof over fast enough to continue school, so we were only off or transferred for a few weeks and then went back in.

According to Gottfried Leyer, "They had to combine classes; sometimes we had three classes combined as one. We didn't learn much." Manfred Hechtle indicated that younger teachers were replaced by older ones as the war dragged on and the amount of National Socialist propaganda preached by the teachers diminished.

Although air raids were frightful experiences, life went on afterward (as long as one's home was intact), and children found ways to entertain themselves. Gottfried recounted how he and his friends went out right after the all-clear siren to search for metal fragments lying in the streets. The larger ones were from enemy bombs and the small pieces from local antiaircraft fire. "Once I found one that was still hot because we went outside right away."

"I was an adventuresome kind of person," Ralf Hechtle (born 1929) explained:

> To me, an air raid was a great adventure where everybody ran to the shelters. I had to stand outside and watch. . . . In fact, once I saw an airplane that was shot down and barely missed hitting a house. It was coming down, and the sad thing was this: as it crossed the Neckar River I guess all the guys tried to jump out, but because the plane was so low they couldn't use their parachutes and they all ended up dead on the beach on the other side. I didn't actually see it crash, but I went right over there and saw it right after and saw the dead soldiers laying there. It was a big bomber.[11]

Manfred Hechtle recalled having regular youth activities in and around Mannheim until the

Fig. 3. The youth of the Mannheim Branch in 1942. (R. Hechtle)

middle of the war: "We met with young people from around the mission in the forests once or twice a year. Sometimes we went to a castle nearby. But as the war progressed, it became practically impossible to have any gatherings out of town. People were too nervous." Much of his free time was spent with his younger brother, Ralph, and his LDS friends, Gottfried Leyer and Manfred Zapf, "until about 1943 when things went topsy-turvy."

The program of evacuating children from high-risk cities was popular in Mannheim, as Manfred Zapf recalled:

> We went to the countryside just as everybody else did. My parents had to stay in the city while my brother and I were sent away. We got little cards with our names on them that we hung around our necks [indicating our destination] and we were sent to Kenzingen, near Switzerland. We stayed with a very nice family; the father was the chief surgeon in the Kenzingen hospital. We stayed in the building in which his maids also stayed. It was close to the actual home, though. We didn't know that family at all before we got there. [The government] just sent us there. I was very happy there because we had so many wonderful opportunities. I felt like a little king. My brother returned to Mannheim early because he had to attend high school, which was not available in Kenzingen.

Life in Mannheim in 1943 was becoming increasingly challenging for Elfriede Deininger, who described the situation in these words:

> I was working all day for a company, assembling small electrical motors, and at the same time I was a firefighter. As soon as we heard the alarm we had to change clothes and be ready to go out. We never knew which direction the air raids would come from. We would hear the sound of the falling bombs, then the building would shake and smoke would fill the air. We found whole housing blocks on fire. Some houses would remain standing, so we had to spray the water on the burning places of those houses. The people in the basements, can you imagine? They died when the scalding water came down on them. As buildings collapsed, people were crushed. . . .

> The constant bombing frazzled our nerves, our spirits, and left us exhausted.[12]

Ralf Hechtle remembered that the frequency of air-raid alarms without attacks was so great that it became a burden to go downstairs to the shelter. He was simply too tired to get out of bed each time (even though a friend had been killed in the basement of the building just across the street). "I think my mother got gray hair worrying about me during alarms. . . . One time in particular I remember I got to the top of the stairs in the cellar, where you go [down] to the cellar and a bomb hit just in the next block. And it just lifted me up and threw me all the way down the stairs, and I hit a chair at the bottom."

Fig. 4. Mannheim Latter-day Saints during the war.

Horst Prison was granted leave in January 1944, and he went to Mannheim to marry Elfriede Deininger. As she explained, "In preparation for our wedding day my sisters Paula and Helen obtained extra food stamps and were able to cook a nice dinner and make a cake. That evening the sirens went off, and we had to go to a bomb shelter."[13] The next day, they made the trip to Saarbrücken where mission leader Anton Huck performed a wedding ceremony and ordained Horst an elder. Within days, he returned to duty on the Eastern Front.

As pleased as Elfriede was to be married, her trials soon became much worse. She saw Horst in France a few months later and had the premonition that they would not be together again for a long time. She was pregnant, but after the day in August when she received word that Horst was missing in action, she did not feel the baby moving any more. A woman doctor confirmed her suspicion that the baby had died, and the discussion that followed became intense, as Elfriede recalled:

> The doctor was insolent: "There is no hospital open for you, but there is a midwife nearby who has a private clinic, and in an emergency I will come down, but you will have to pay in advance, for I doubt you will pull through." I was furious. I screamed at her, "If I have to die like an animal, so be it, but you dirty pig, you will not get my money!"[14]

The child was delivered stillborn two days later—a boy weighing six and one-half pounds. "During my recovery it was hard for me to watch the new mothers as they nursed their babies," Elfriede recalled. A crisis of faith ensued, but a friend from church explained an important principle to the heartbroken mother, who was wondering why God would let her child die: "Elfriede, that little word 'why' is the biggest tool in the devil's workshop. God loves you and will comfort you if you will let him. He knows 'why' and all about your heartache, but it is best for you. Someday you will understand."[15]

Manfred Zapf was still only fourteen years old and a member of the Hitler Youth when he came very close to the war in 1944, as he recalled:

> I was sent to France to help out with the military—for example [servicing] tanks. I remember that I stayed there for a little over a year and that we had to sleep on concrete with just a bit of straw underneath and it was the middle of winter. The regular soldiers didn't like us and wanted us to leave. We were too young for them and they had to watch us on top of everything else. Some of us were injured and that placed a greater burden on the soldiers. Some of my friends even got killed while we were there. It was a dangerous place to be. We eventually walked home from France—all the way back to Kenzingen.[16] We were able to travel in a vehicle only part of the way home.

The Hechtle family lost their apartment twice. The first one was located at Augartenstrasse 39 (east of the downtown) and the second on block S6. "There we had an underground bunker across the street," Manfred Hechtle explained. Not every bomb that fell on an apartment house during the war meant destruction. Manfred recalled how the Hitler Youth boys were trained to nullify the effect of an incendiary bomb. "We had to keep a bucket of water and sand in the attic so that we could [smother] the bomb. We actually did that once when we found an incendiary bomb stuck between the attic and the top floor [of the building]. It had just barely ignited. We always had somebody there standing guard."

Fig. 5. The ruins of the Hechtle apartment in 1943. (R. Hechtle)

On the day when the second Hechtle apartment building was struck by incendiary bombs, Ralf had an unforgettable experience. He had delayed seeking shelter when the attack began, and it nearly cost him his life:

> I looked up and saw countless airplanes up in the sky. And so I figured I'd better run to the shelter, because I was closer to the shelter than I was to my house. And so I ran, . . . and I could hear the bombs coming down, whistling like crazy. And [the air pressure] knocked me down and something hit me across the back, and I thought, "I'm gonna die here." And I looked up and I saw all these buildings collapsing around and fires starting, and I realized that I was hit by a branch of the tree which was lying by me. Through experience, I knew that the firebombs would [be dropped] after the big explosive bombs would come down. Because they're lighter, they take longer to come down. [The enemy] just dropped them like matchsticks. And I knew I had to get out of there, because they'd just drop everywhere. And people had been hit by those things and burned to death. So I ran to the entrance of the shelter, and of course, they wouldn't open the shelter during an attack. So I was standing there in the front of the door, and I watched all these firebombs drop. And as I looked across the street, I saw our house on fire.

After finishing public school, Ralf began an apprenticeship in a pastry shop. His work had interesting but unsettling aspects to it:

> My boss owned the building, and our shop was in the basement. Every time there was an attack, the shingles got destroyed on top of the roof, and he sent me up to reshingle—on top of a six-story building. I was fourteen years old. Well, I couldn't go up there and look down or I'd fall off. At first it didn't seem to bother me, but I got kind of disgusted with him after a while, and I said, "I'm here to learn the trade, and I don't want to be a roofer!"

In Gottfried Leyer's neighborhood on the outskirts of town, the situation was different. They lived in a two-family home that did not have indoor plumbing. "We kept four or five buckets of water lined up by the pump." One night an incendiary bomb struck the house and began to burn. Emerging from their hiding place in the basement, family members were able to extinguish the flames before too much damage was done.

Fig. 6. Andreas Leyer died of wounds suffered in Lithuania in August 1944. (G. Leyer)

Gottfried was drafted into the Wehrmacht at the age of sixteen. There was no longer time for service in the Reichsarbeitsdienst in those days; the army needed soldiers. Trained to serve at an antiaircraft battery, he was stationed near several cities in Germany and even in France for a few months. He was fortunate never to carry a gun or be involved in combat on the ground. When the Allies invaded Germany, Gottfried was in no real danger.

When Manfred Hechtle was still sixteen, he began training to become a pilot in the Luftwaffe and was sent to a small town northwest of Frankfurt. His training did not include flying, because airplanes were a rarity in Germany in the last year of the war. "We had more pilots than airplanes. They would draw lots to see who would fly. You can imagine what happened. They would go up and shoot down three planes and then be shot down themselves. A lot of them didn't come back." Eventually there was no fuel to fly the few airplanes left. Manfred was just barely tall enough to qualify for pilot training, but he never left the ground. Eventually, he was sent home, and the war ended before he could be given another assignment.

The general minutes of the Mannheim Branch illustrate the challenges faced by the members in the last eighteen months of the war:[17]

> January 30, 1944: Karl Josef Fetsch [of Bühl, currently working in Ludwigshafen] was sustained as the branch president. Paul Prison [of Saarbrücken] was called as district president.
>
> March 1, 1944: Air raids destroyed the home of the branch president and the branch meeting rooms; all church property and all records were destroyed. A new minutes book was started by Elder Karl Josef Fetsch. All possible records will be restored in this book. Meetings were held in the home of Sister Lina Harrer on Kappelerstrasse. Her home was also destroyed, so no meetings were held for a while. Then meetings began again in the home of Sister Luise Vokt at Ludwig Jolly Strasse 67.
>
> March 12, 1944: Georg Dönig, officially branch president, returned from the war severely wounded and decided to go to his wife's home in Grossgartach, Württemberg and thus joined the branch in Heilbronn.
>
> April 22–23, 1944: Ten Saints from Mannheim attended the district conference in Karlsruhe.
>
> December 10, 1944: Meetings were canceled due to air-raid alarms. Two weeks later, meetings were again canceled.
>
> January 6, 1945: Attacks damaged the downtown severely; no members were killed but some have slight property damage.
>
> January 14, 1945: Meetings were canceled again.
>
> January 21, 1945: More attacks, but no major damage among members. Meetings were canceled.
>
> February 18, 1945: The two worst attacks of the war happened today. Again the members suffered little damage and none were killed. Again the Lord has preserved their lives. Average attendance on recent Sundays is twelve.
>
> March 1, 1945: The worst attack of the war hits Mannheim and Ludwigshafen. The entire city is on fire. The Hechtles lose their home for the second time, but a few days later the Lord provides them a nice new place to live in Feudenheim at Talstrasse 67. The rest of the Saints (as far as we know) do not suffer any substantial damage.
>
> March 4, 1945: Meetings are canceled.
>
> March 22–29, 1945: There is fighting in Mannheim; American troops occupied the city. Those members who stayed in the city survived the fighting.
>
> April 15, 1945: Today we were able to hold the first meetings again.

In March 1945, Elfriede Deininger Prison was living with her parents-in-law in a town near Stuttgart. One day, they noticed enemy troops coming toward the house. "They wore gray-green corduroy coats, a hood, and turbans on their heads. . . . We retreated from the windows, too frightened to say anything. We told the children to quietly pray for the Lord's protection." The soldiers were either Algerians or Moroccans serving under French command and were feared by German civilians. Elfriede had already heard stories about atrocities committed by those troops in neighboring villages.

The next day, an enemy soldier entered the Prisons' house, and the situation was instantly tense. Fortunately, he was not searching for victims but rather for somebody to wash his clothes. Without speaking German, he made it clear that the women of that house were to feed his men and wash for them. Soon, he brought them food, and he and his four Moroccan comrades ate their meals with the household. His name was Rachau, and Elfriede's family was safe with him around.[18]

Fig. 7. The city of Ludwigshafen was included within the Mannheim Branch. Because of its critical chemical industry (BASF), the city was under attack at least 125 times. Huge bunkers such as these were constructed to protect the citizens, but more than 1,800 people (including several Saints) were killed.[19] (R. Minert, 1971)

When American tanks rolled into what was left of Mannheim, they fired a few shots, but little resistance was offered, and it was soon calm. The Hechtles had managed to find an apartment in a suburb of Mannheim called Feudenheim. When American soldiers came looking for housing, the Hechtles and many of their neighbors were evicted and not allowed to take anything with them. They spent the next two days at a lumberyard owned by their landlady. As Ralf recalled, the landlady—a beautiful young woman—was able to "charm" the Americans into letting the Hechtles return to their apartment.

According to Manfred, "[the GIs] liked to make friends and stand around talking, but in the evenings we weren't allowed to look out the window or we would be shot." As in all other occupied areas of Germany, curfew regulations were strictly enforced in Mannheim.

Just before the Americans arrived in Mannheim, Manfred Zapf and his mother had decided to go to Epfenbach (about twenty miles to the east and far from large cities).

> We had a little cottage in that town from which my father came. While we were on our way, it was just our luck that an air raid would happen. There were no German soldiers around anymore and nothing else to shoot at, so the [pilots] used us as target practice. Two fighter planes were chasing us around a big oak tree, and the tree was so thick that the bullets did not go through it. They were also in each other's way and had to be really careful not to fly into each other.

Manfred and his mother returned to Mannheim soon after this incident. Despite the fact that their home in the suburb of Käfertal was very close to several large industries, the building had suffered no more damage than a few broken windows during several attacks on those factories.

The end of the war for Ralf Hechtle was certainly enough to satisfy this adventuresome boy. Shortly before the Americans arrived at the end of March, he had been persuaded by a friend to see what items local German antiaircraft crews had left behind when they abandoned their positions.

> So we went to the outskirts of town. And we took our wagons and found all kinds of stuff in those antiaircraft batteries—typewriters, phonographs, rifles, hand grenades—and we loaded our wagons. As teenagers we thought that was pretty cool. . . . We put a blanket over the wagon and pulled it home. Just as I got to the corner near where we lived, I saw a tank coming up the street. I didn't pay that close attention, thinking, "Well, they're Germans." And pretty soon some soldiers came up with their ambulance, and they weren't Germans! I looked a little closer, and there was a [white] star on the tank, and I said, "Uh-oh." So [a GI] told me to stop, and he wanted to know what I had in my wagon. Well, he threw the blanket off, and there was all this stuff. He started throwing the things into an empty lot next to us. So I thought I'd help him. I picked up a hand grenade, and when he turned

> around and saw me, I thought he was going to shoot me right then. I was just thinking I'd help him unload the wagon.

Fig. 8. It is hard to imagine that in 1945 Ralf Hechtle looked old enough to be mistaken for a soldier. (R. Hechtle)

The next thing he knew, Ralf was a prisoner of war, pushed onto a truck with German soldiers headed west. For three days, the truck wandered around with no apparent goal, and during that time the men were given nothing to eat. Finally, they were unloaded at what appeared to be a construction site near the city of Kaiserslautern. They had no roof overhead, and it was cold and wet, but at least they were given some K-rations to eat. It was there that Ralf met a boy who was sixteen and also should not have been treated as a POW. The two were young but understood that they might be handed over to the French; that could only be a bad development, so they devised a plan to escape. At one end of the compound was a brick wall separating the camp from another camp that housed civilians. The boys scaled the wall, mingled among the civilians, and then found a way out of the camp. Unfortunately, they were caught that evening—not knowing about the new curfew regulations. This time they were not treated as soldiers but rather as civilians who had violated curfew. Locked up in the police station, Ralf finally had a decent place to sleep—on a bench. The next day he was interrogated, and his future looked a bit brighter, as he recalled:

> The American officer asked me if I knew the Boy Scout Oath. I recited it to him, and he said: "I'll give you a pass that's good for twenty-four hours. You'll have to make it home in twenty-four hours." And he gave me a package of gum and a little candy bar and sent me on my way. I was in my aunt's riding boots that had high heels. I had twenty miles to walk in twenty-four hours, because there was absolutely no transportation. And he told me, "American vehicles will not pick you up; they're not permitted to pick up anybody."

Along the way, Ralf spent a short night in a barn, and then moved on toward the Rhine. French soldiers detained him for a while, suggesting that his papers were not valid, but finally allowed him to pass. When he reached the Rhine, the only way to cross was on a pontoon bridge constructed by the Americans, but they refused to let him do so.

> I retreated a little ways and looked across the river. I said to myself, "Well, it's too cold to swim that river." (I'd done it before, but it was too cold at this time of year). And so I was praying and praying, and all of a sudden I was moved to walk. And I walked, and then a truck went across the bridge, and I walked behind that truck and nobody saw me—it was like I was invisible. Nobody said anything.

A few minutes later, he reached his home—barely within the time limit. His mother was thrilled to see him, having had no idea of his whereabouts.

When the war ended, Gottfried Leyer avoided becoming a POW. He was only seventeen and looked young for his age. Before the invaders arrived, he found some civilian clothing and volunteered to work for a farmer. The enemy soldiers moving farther into Germany paid him no mind. He remained on the farm for several months and then began working his way back toward Mannheim. "We would stop in at a farm and offer to work for a while, sleep there, and get something to eat. Then we would move on again. That's how we worked our way home." He was back in Mannheim toward the end of the summer of 1945.

For Elfriede Deininger Prison, the war would not truly end until Horst came home, but she returned to Mannheim in the summer of 1945. She described the conditions there in these words:

> The city had nearly been destroyed, but I found my sisters alive and well. It took considerable time, but slowly life began to return to normal. Our branch was reorganized, and some of our brethren returned, so we had the priesthood in our midst again. Some of the men had been killed in the war. All those bitter years brought us closer together.[20]

One Sunday, an American soldier knocked on the door of Sister Vokt's apartment, where the Saints had gathered. He had been a missionary in Mannheim before the war and wanted to determine the condition of the branch members there. The reunion was a joyous one, and a spirit of love and peace prevailed. According to Elfriede, "My anger at the Americans for bombing us disappeared in that meeting."[21]

The general minutes of the branch read as follows on June 4, 1945:

> Elder Eugen Hechtle [again district president] met with Major Warner, the representative of the [American] military government for church and educational affairs, and was treated very correctly. He was given two signs to be posted at the homes of Sister Vokt and the Hechtle family (where meetings are held), reading "Off limits to military personnel by order of the commanding general." Major Warner promised us all possible assistance and expressed his hope that the church may soon conduct all of its activities again. Because we have no contact with the mission office, he promised to establish contact for us there. He also requested that we report to him every month regarding our activities, our progress and our finances.[22]

Former missionary Walter E. Scoville worked hard to establish contact with Latter-day Saints in Germany after the war. He received this response to a letter to Helene Deininger of the Mannheim Branch on January 30, 1947; she offered a summary of the war's effect on the branch:

Fig. 9. Max Ziegler (shown here as a civilian in 1942) was one of several young men of the Mannheim Branch to die as soldiers.

> In the beginning, it was terrible for us to think about being at war, and we hoped that it would end soon. But we learned little by little to deal with it and to be patient. . . . Before he died in 1941, I used to pick up old Brother Scholl and walk with him to church and back. He had a little lantern and it was too dangerous for him to go alone during blackouts. . . . My own dear mother died a year after him. . . . She had a terrible kidney disease and wished to be relieved of her sufferings through death. . . . But she comforted us and encouraged us to remain faithful to the Church. . . . I would like to tell you about our experiences during the war. I would like to avoid the very sad things, but I really can't do that, because there were sad events. My sister, [Lina] Harrer, lost her husband and her home. I lived with her at the time. Elfriede [Deininger] married and her husband was missing in action in Russia for two years. Last year we were thrilled when she finally heard from him. They have been writing each other often and she hopes that he will return soon. . . . Paula has been waiting for five years for her fiancé to return. . . . After the first few air raids, we lost our beautiful meeting rooms at D4 [sic]. The sisters in the branch had to leave town with their little children and the brethren had to serve in the military. We could only meet on Sundays. There were only a few of us. We first met in the home of Sister Harrer, but she was bombed out so we met in Sister Vokt's home. . . . Life was hard but we enjoyed our church meetings. We often had to walk there because the streetcars were not running. . . . It took about 1½ hours each way. We really miss dear Brother Ziegler. We last heard from him just before the war ended. I still believe that he is alive and I always pray for him. Of all of the brethren, he stayed home the longest. After every air raid, he went out looking for the branch members. That was very encouraging for us. . . . Brother Andreas

> Leyer was killed in battle. He did a lot of work in the branch and was a great man. Brother Dönig died with a strong testimony of the truth. We lost track of him three years ago. Among the few items we could rescue are the holy scriptures you gave us. Shortly after Mother died, I worked in the mission office until I was called to a Pflichtjahr for ten months in 1942. My sister [Lina] and I took those books with us.[23]

Perhaps the last soldier of the West German Mission to return from a POW camp after World War II was Horst Prison, who arrived in Saarbrücken on December 31, 1949. His wife, Elfriede, had been living with his parents for some time and vividly recalled their reunion:

> I was at the market with my mother-in-law one day, and I had heard on the radio that [Horst] was on his way home. Everybody else thought I was crazy because I was still waiting for him to come home. The next morning at 2 a.m., I got a telegram telling me that I should pick him up at the Saarbrücken railroad station the next day. See, I was not crazy! But when I saw him, I realized that he was no longer the man I had married. The war had changed him. For a while, it was very difficult [to be with him]. He only said yes and no—nothing else. He did not want to see anybody. After quite a long time, he got back into our routine. I needed a lot of patience.

Fig. 10. Surviving Mannheim Branch members in 1945. (R. Hechle)

Elfriede offered this summary of her spiritual status after so many challenging experiences: "My testimony was strengthened through prayer. I found peace because I prayed. I have to say that all these things, although they might have been terrible and difficult to bear, made me a stronger person. There were so many instances in which I felt the help of my Heavenly Father. I knew he protected me—absolutely."[24]

Fig. 11. The ruins of downtown Mannheim in 1945. (R. Hechtle)

During the war, the members of the Mannheim Branch had been scattered to the four winds and suffered heavy losses in many respects, but the testimonies of survivors were strong and the future of the branch among the ruins of Hitler's Third Reich was promising.

In Memoriam

The following members of the Mannheim Branch did not survive World War II:

Susi Maria Bentz b. Mannheim, Baden, 29 Jul 1910; dau. of Theodor Bentz and Eva Pfeiffer; bp. 19 Dec 1926; conf. 19 Dec 1926; m. —— Braun; missing as of 20 Mar 1946 (FHL microfilm 68799, no. 37; CHL CR 275 8 2441, no. 386)

Johann Billian b. Mannheim, Baden, 25 Jun 1894; son of Johann Billian and Therese Weigert or Weigart; bp. 27 Jun 1908; conf. 25 Jul 1908; missing as of 20 Mar 1946 (FHL microfilm 68799, no. 1; CHL CR 275 8 2441, no. 345)

Katharina Burkart b. Hagenbach, Pfalz, Bayern, 25 Jan 1872; dau. of Franz Burkart and Katharine Gehrlein; bp. 13 Feb 1927; conf. 13 Feb 1927; m. 18 Jul 1927, —— Mai; missing as of 20 Mar 1946 (FHL microfilm 68799, no. 44; FHL microfilm 245225; IGI)

Elsa Frieda Fink b. Ludwigshafen, Pfalz, Bayern, 2 Nov 1917; dau. of Johann Fink and Frieda Emma Scharpf; bp. 22 Nov 1925; conf. 22 Nov 1925; missing as of 20 Mar 1946 (FHL microfilm 68799, no. 4; CHL CR 275 8 2441, no. 7; FHL microfilm 25766)

Eugenie Elisa Fink b. Rheinau, Mannheim, Baden, 12 Jun 1912; dau. of Johann Fink and Frieda Emma Scharpf; bp. 24 Sep 1921; conf. 24 Sep 1921; missing as of 20 Mar 1946 (FHL microfilm 68799, no. 3; CHL CR 275 8 2441, no. 5; FHL microfilm 25766)

Karoline Fresch b. Vellberg, Württemberg, 28 Sep 1879; dau. of Georg Fresch and Margarethe Wolpert; bp. 2 Apr 1920; conf. 4 Apr 1920; m. Otto Bruno Hätscher; missing as of 10 Dec 1944 (FHL microfilm 68797, no. 350; CHL CR 275 8 2441, no. 350; FHL microfilm 68799, no. 7)

Friedrich Hätscher b. Mannheim, Mannheim, Baden, 14 Feb 1913; son of Otto Bruno Hätscher and Karolina Fresch; bp. 1 Oct 1921; conf. 2 Oct 1921; missing as of 10 Dec 1944 (FHL microfilm 68799, no. 9; CHL CR 275 8 2441, no. 351)

Otto Bruno Hätscher b. Lissa, Posen, Preussen, 20 Mar 1876; son of Otto Hätscher and Ann Schwank; bp. 21 Aug 1920; conf. 22 Aug 1920; missing as of 10 Dec 1944 (FHL microfilm 68799, no. 6; CHL CR 275 8 2441, no. 349)

Ludwig Wilhelm Harrer; b. Mannheim, Mannheim, Baden, 13 Sep 1912; son of Wilhelm Christian Harrer and Elisabeth Eck; m. Mannheim, Mannheim, Baden, 27 Oct 1934, Lina Deininger; Waffen-SS sergeant; k. Kutilicka, near Wassiljewschtschina, Russia, 22 Feb 1942 (Prison; www.volksbund.de, IGI)

Gustav Wilhelm Emil Herzog b. Mannheim, Mannheim, Baden, 23 Jan 1922; son of Jakob Herzog and Maria Eva Schulz; bp. 1 Feb 1931; conf. 1 Feb 1931; missing as of 20 Mar 1946 (FHL microfilm 68799, no. 66; CHL CR 275 8 2441, no. 456; FHL microfilm 162782, 1930 and 1935 censuses)

Heinrich August Herzog b. Mannheim 6 Dec 1926; son of Jakob Herzog and Maria Eva Schulz; bp. 8 Sep 1935; conf. 8 Sep 1935; missing as of 20 Mar 1946 (FHL microfilm 68797, no. 598; FHL microfilm no. 162782, 1930 and 1935 censuses)

Ludwig Daniel Höflich b. Ludwigshafen, Pfalz, Bayern, 4 May or Sep 1909; son of Ludwig Höflich and Philippine Kratz; bp. 24 Sep 1921; conf. 25 Sep 1921; m.; missing 10 Dec 1944 (FHL microfilm 68799, no. 11; CHL CR 275 8 2441, no. 355)

Ludwig Höflich b. Ludwigshafen, Konstanz, Baden, 2 Aug 1881; son of Wilhelm Höflich and Charlotte Hassel; bp. Ludwigshafen, Pfalz, Bayern, 11 Feb 1930; conf. 11 Feb 1930; m. Philippine Kratz; 1 child; k. air raid 1943 (FHL microfilm 68797, no. 402; CHL CR 275 8 2441, no. 402; IGI)

Wilhelm Martin Rupprecht Höflich b. Mannheim, Mannheim, Baden, 13 Mar 1915; son of Ludwig Höflich and Philippine Kratz; bp. 26 May 1923; k. air raid 10 Dec 1943 or 1944 (FHL microfilm 68799, no. 12; FHL microfilm 68797, no. 356; FHL microfilm 162786, 1935 census)

Karl Josef Hoffmann b. Sinsheim, Heidelberg, Baden, 2 Jan 1886; bp. 16 May 1919; conf. 16 May 1919; d. 1943 (FHL microfilm 68799, no. 39; IGI)

Andreas Johann Leyer b. Mannheim, Mannheim, Baden, 14 Jul 1920; son of Johann Georg Leyer and Anna Hess; bp. 1 Feb 1931; conf. 1 Feb 1931; ord. deacon 3 Feb 1935; ord. teacher 30 Oct 1938; lance corporal; d. of wounds Akmene, Lithuania, 18 Aug 1944 (G. Leyer; CHL CR 275 8 2441, no. 460; FHL microfilm 68799, no. 65; www.volksbund.de; IGI)

Johann Georg Leyer b. Mannheim, Mannheim, Baden, 3 Jan 1918; son of Johann Georg Leyer and Anna Hess; bp. 1 Feb 1931; conf. 1 Feb 1931; home guard; d. tuberculosis Mannheim (G. Leyer; FHL microfilm 68799, no. 62)

Georg Müller b. Altleiningen, Pfalz, Bayern, 2 Aug 1870; son of Johann Müller and Juliana Alebrand; bp. 8 Aug 1927; conf. 8 Aug 1927; missing as of 20 Mar 1946 (FHL microfilm 68799, no. 47; CHL CR 275 8 2441, no. 5)

Gertrud Scharf b. Mannheim, Baden, 26 Oct 1914; dau. of Alois Scharf and Martha Wolf; bp. 21 Jun 1931; conf. 21 Jul 1931; m. —— Kohl; missing as of 20 Mar 1946 (FHL microfilm 68799, no. 68; CR 275 8 2441, no. 460)

Wilhelm August Heinrich Scharrer b. Karlsruhe, Karlsruhe, Baden, 31 Aug 1900; son of August Scharrer and Emilie Wolf; bp. 21 Jun 1916; conf. 21 Jun 1916; ord. priest 22 Jan 1918; missing as of 20 Mar 1946 (CHL CR 275 8 2441, no. 330; FHL microfilm 245258, 1930 and 1935 censuses)

Johann Martin Scholl b. Fränkisch Crumbach, Hessen, 12 Jan 1862; son of Johann Jakob Scholl and Margaretha Elisabeth Klinger; bp. 18 Feb 1899; conf. 19 Feb 1899; ord. elder 17 Sep 1916; m. Mannheim, Mannheim, Baden, 7 Jul 1888, Elisabeth Ültzhöfer; 4 children; d. cancer or heart ailment Mannheim, Baden, 29 Feb 1940; bur. Mannheim 4 Mar 1940 (Prison; Stern 1940, nos. 5–6, pg. 95; CHL CR 275 8 2441, no. 361; IGI, AF)

Karl Friedrich Scholl b. Mannheim, Mannheim, Baden, 25 Mar 1895; son of Johann Martin Scholl and Elisabeth Ülzhöfer; bp. 25 Nov 1906; conf. 25 Nov 1906; m. 4 Dec 1921 or 1927, Maria Berta Littic; d. insanity 30 or 31 Jan 1943 (FHL microfilm 68799, no. 15; CHL CR 275 8 2441, no. 362; IGI)

Emil Hermann Schulz b. Frankenthal, Pfalz, Bayern, 1 Jan 1911; son of Emil Friedrich Herm Schulz and Anna Maria Maltry; bp. 4 Dec 1921; conf. 4 Dec

1921; k. in battle 1942 or MIA 10 Dec 1944 (FHL microfilm 68799, no. 19; CHL CR 275 8 2441, no. 367; IGI)

Peter Schulz b. Mannheim, Mannheim, Baden, 24 Dec 1912; son of Emil Friedrich Hermann Schulz and Maria Maltry; bp. 4 Dec 1921; conf. 4 Dec 1921; ord. priest 10 Feb 1935; missing as of 20 Nov 1945 (CR 375 8 2451, no. 683; FHL microfilm no. 245260, 1925 and 1935 censuses)

Wilhelm Peter Schulz b. Frankenthal, Pfalz, Bayern, 7 Jan 1905; son of Emil Friedrich Hermann Schulz and Anna Maria Maltry; bp. 25 Oct 1922; conf. 25 Oct 1922; missing as of 20 Mar 1946 (FHL microfilm 68799, no. 18)

Friedrich Süss b. Ludwigshafen, Pfalz, Bayern, 21 Dec 1876; son of Johann Süss and Anna Maria Sophia Moritz; bp. 7 Aug 1891; conf. 7 Aug 1891; missing as of 20 Mar 1946 (FHL microfilm 68799, no. 13)

Minna Wagner b. Neuenburg, Württemberg, 22 Aug 1880; dau. of Karl Wagner and Karolin Rörk; bp. 13 Feb 1927; conf. 13 Feb 1927; m. —— Hofbauer; missing as of 20 Mar 1946 (FHL microfilm 68799, no. 43)

Franziska Viktoria Weber b. Raschlovke or Raschlovko, Preussen, 15 Dec 1873; dau. of Christian Weber and Olga Goschalandschie; bp. 30 Aug 1925; conf. 30 Aug 1925; m. —— Max Vogelmann; missing as of 20 Mar 1946 (FHL microfilm 68799, no. 31; CHL CR 275 8 2441, no. 10)

Else Wessa b. Ludwigshafen, Pfalz, Bayern, 10 Nov 1907; dau. of Georg Wessa and Anna Klara Bissantz; missing 20 Mar 1946 (FHL microfilm 68799, no. 48)

Anton Ziegler b. Mannheim, Mannheim, Baden, 19 Mar 1905; son of Markus Ziegler and Anna Müller; bp. 17 Nov 1929; m. 17 Aug 1929; d. as a soldier crossing a river in Russia 1943 or 15 Feb 1945 or MIA Ostpreußen 1 Jan 1945 (Prison; www.volksbund.de; IGI)

Notes

1. Presiding Bishopric, "Financial, Statistical, and Historical Reports of Wards, Stakes, and Missions, 1884–1955," 257, CR 4 12.
2. West German Mission branch directory 1939, CHL LR 10045 11.
3. The map of the city's interior shows approximately 150 blocks within a huge half circle. The house numbers on each block run consecutively around the block in a clockwise direction. Before the war, there were essentially no street names in that part of the city. The landlord to whom the branch paid rent was Albert Speer, at that time Hitler's personal architect and a rising star in Nazi Germany. He later became the minister of war production and was sentenced to twenty years in prison at the trial of the major war criminals in Nuremberg in 1945–46. His address on Schloss Wolfsbrunnenweg in Heidelberg in 1939 was the same location where the author interviewed Speer in October 1975.
4. Horst Peter Prison and Elfriede Deininger Prison, telephone interview with Jennifer Heckmann in German, October 24, 2008; summarized in English by Judith Sartowski.
5. Gottfried Leyer, interview by the author, Hyrum, UT, July 29, 2008.
6. Walter E. Scoville, papers, CHL MS 18613; translated by the author. Scoville's ambitious correspondence with German friends was interrupted when the United States entered the war on December 8, 1941.
7. Paul H. Kelly and Lin H. Johnson, *Courage in a Season of War* (2002), 264.
8. Manfred Zapf, telephone interview with the author in German, April 7, 2009.
9. Kelly and Johnson, *Courage in a Season of War*, 268–69.
10. Manfred Hechtle, interview by the author, Hyrum, UT, July 29, 2008.
11. Ralf (Ralph) Hechtle, interview by the author, Brigham City, UT, October 21, 2006.
12. Kelly and Johnson, *Courage in a Season of War*, 266.
13. Ibid., 266–67.
14. Ibid., 268.
15. Ibid., 268
16. He had been living in Kenzingen (south of Karlsruhe) for some time after being evacuated from Mannheim.
17. Mannheim Branch general minutes, CHL LR 5344 21.
18. Kelly and Johnson, *Courage in a Season of War*, 270–71.
19. Ludwigshafen city archive.
20. Ibid., 271–72.
21. Ibid., 272.
22. Mannheim Branch general minutes.
23. Walter E. Scoville, papers.
24. Kelly and Johnson, *Courage in a Season of War*, 272.

Pforzheim Branch

Famous for its jewelry industry, the city of Pforzheim had 78,320 inhabitants in 1939.[1] The branch of the LDS Church in that city numbered seventy persons, more than two-thirds of whom were females twelve years and older. There were only two elders in the branch at the time, but ten men or young men held the Aaronic Priesthood. Pforzheim is only fifteen miles from Karlsruhe, and the cities were connected by rail in those days, so it was a simple matter for Pforzheim Saints to attend district conferences in Karlsruhe.

Pforzheim Branch[2]	1939
Elders	2
Priests	3
Teachers	2
Deacons	5
Other Adult Males	9
Adult Females	49
Male Children	0
Female Children	0
Total	70

The branch rented meeting rooms at Nagoldstrasse 3, on the left bank of the Nagold River and only a few blocks from the center of town.[3] As the war approached, the branch was holding its Sunday School meeting at 10:00 a.m. and sacrament meeting at 7:00 p.m. The Primary organization met on Mondays at 5:30 p.m., the Relief Society on Wednesdays at 8:00 p.m., and the MIA on Thursdays at 8:00 p.m.[4] A genealogical course was given every third Thursday of the month.

Fig. 1. The Pforzheim Branch Primary children in 1936. (Der Stern)

During the weeks before World War II began, the branch president in Pforzheim was an American missionary, Sylvan Burgi. The mission directory of July 22, 1939, shows no counselors, but George Stehle led the Sunday School and Fritz Hermann the YMMIA.

Marianne Kappenstein (born 1928) describing the meeting rooms: "We had several rooms on the ground floor of an apartment building where we held the meetings. When you first came in, there were coat hangers all around the first room where you hung up your coats. And then you went to the back where there were chairs set up. . . . We had a piano in the room. There were not very many people in attendance."[5] The setting was so unimpressive that she was hesitant to tell her friends where the church met. After all, just a few houses down the street was a beautiful Lutheran church ("You could almost call it a cathedral").

Fig. 2. The Pforzheim Branch held its meetings in house no. 3 on Nagoldstrasse, the white four-story building to the left of the Lutheran church. (H.-P. Metzner)

At the age of ten, Marianne had been inducted into the Jungvolk, and she recalled participating in a number of very worthy activities. For example, at Christmas time she and her friends "would cut out wooden dwarfs or dolls and paint them as gifts for needy children." Regarding the question of political training, she claimed, "I cannot say that we were mistreated or brainwashed; we were never indoctrinated or involved in unwholesome activities."

According to young Marianne, several prominent

Fig. 3. Missionary George Blake took this photograph of Pforzheim Branch members on an outing in the forest in 1939. (G. Blake)

families comprised the majority of attendees at church meetings in the Pforzheim Branch. One of those families was named Frei. One Sunday morning, Elsa Frei and her two children, Doreanne and Karl Heinz, came to church very upset; they had just learned that Karl Gustav Frei (not a member of the Church) had passed away after being consigned to an asylum due to some kind of mental illness. "They didn't say it in so many words, but they let on that *they* had done away with him," according to Marianne Kappenstein. "We could guess who *they* were." Apparently Sister Frei believed that her husband had become a victim of the infamous Nazi euthanasia program.

Ursula Mussler and her mother, Frieda, were bombed out in Frankfurt in 1943 and moved to the town of Mühlacker, ten miles east of Pforzheim. Ursula said:

> There were about forty people in attendance in the Pforzheim branch. I always felt welcome in whatever branch I was on Sundays. We tried to attend the meetings as much as we could. Usually, we went every two weeks and whenever there was a conference. Those were held in Karlsruhe, so we went there by train. We always had enough priesthood holders to preside in sacrament meetings.[6]

The only information found regarding the leadership of this branch during World War II comes from the general minutes of the Bühl Branch (also in the Karlsruhe District): on February 26, 1944, the funeral of Maria Kappenstein took place under the direction of Friedrich Hermann, the branch president in Pforzheim.[7] Marianne and her sisters were then orphans, having lost their father the previous year.

As had happened in quite a few major cities in Germany during the war, the Allies mounted one massive attack to destroy Pforzheim in April 1945. Marianne Kappenstein recalled with clarity the event. She had already lost both parents and was under the guardianship of her elder sister, Ella. Early on that fateful day, Marianne watched Allied airplanes flying very low over the city, back and forth, following the course of the three rivers that flowed through the town. However, the planes dropped no bombs, and the all-clear was sounded. Marianne then left town and walked to a small factory outside of town. At sixteen, she was considered capable of watching out for bombs at the factory after a raid and either trying to put out fires or reporting them to the authorities. She and friend sat around for a while, but then the sirens sounded again just before dusk. They hurried into a cave dug in the mountainside to serve as a shelter. A terrible air raid was unleashed, and when Marianne emerged from the cave, "the city was totally destroyed and everything was burning."

Somehow, Marianne was able to ride a streetcar toward the city, but they could not get into the interior of Pforzheim. She then began a desperate search for her sisters. "Everybody was looking for everybody." At about four in the morning, somebody tapped her on the back, and it was Ella. She had attempted to save some of the family's property by carrying it down to the basement, but the fires destroyed the entire apartment house, and they lost everything. Fortunately, another sister had gone to the suburb of Wurm and was thus safe during the attack.

Following the catastrophic raid on Pforzheim, Marianne found herself with nothing but her sisters and the clothes on her back. In fact, she was wearing her old shoes, thinking it unwise to wear her good shoes to go to the factory the day before. Now she had no home, no church (the rooms at Nagoldstrasse 3 were likewise burned out), and no parents.

"When the war came to an end, we were staying in Mühlacker," explained Ursula Mussler. "The British came into our area first, later also the Americans. [Eventually] we moved to Bad Homburg near Frankfurt." Soon, Ursula's brother Hans joined them, and they looked forward to happier times. Ursula had this to say regarding the spirit of the Latter-day Saints during the war, based on her membership in the Frankfurt and Pforzheim Branches:

> The members helped each other out a lot during the entire war. We got along well and were striving for the same goal. We were grateful for the clothes that were shared and for the members who were there in difficult situations. My faith kept me going during the war. And also the fact that we attended Church whenever it was possible for us helped us very much.

Stan Clift, an American Latter-day Saint soldier, was stationed in a small town just south of Pforzheim in July 1945 and went in search of the members of the Church there. He wrote this account of meetings held in the home of the Stahl family:

> Nelly Stahl lived at [Hirsauerstrasse] 135 with her elderly parents. I would guess that the father was in his 70s. The church service was held in a home along side of the road through town, just a short walk north of the school building where I was bunked. There were about ten women, perhaps two or three small children and I vaguely recall one very elderly man. The women were in their 50s or so for the most part. Nelly was in her 30s I think. . . . She and one other lady spoke English. At the first service another LDS soldier and I blessed the sacrament and passed it to those present. We were asked to speak, which we did briefly, with our thoughts being translated into German by Nelly. They were appreciative of being able to partake of the sacrament. . . . After the service Nelly told me that they would like us to come back next Sunday and bless the sacrament in German. She volunteered to teach me how to pronounce the words. . . . Nelly indicated that the men in the church had been taken into the German army and were not back home yet.[8]

Whereas it is clear from Brother Clift's report that the Pforzheim Branch had survived the war, it is not known precisely when local priesthood holders were finally present to direct the activities of that branch.

Just before the war ended, the Kappenstein sisters had fled Pforzheim for Kassel, a city in northern Germany. As Marianne recalled, it took some railroad travel and lots of hitchhiking to get there. After returning to Pforzheim during the summer, she was finally baptized on October 20, 1945, by Johann Albert Dahl (of Karlsruhe) along with her younger sister.

The Pforzheim City Archive estimates that 17,600 people were killed during twenty attacks on the city. The entire downtown was destroyed as well as approximately 70–80 percent of the rest of the city. There was truly very little left when the French army entered the city in April 1945. On July 8, the French left the city, and it became part of the American occupation zone.[9]

In Memoriam

The following members of the Pforzheim Branch did not survive World War II:

Alois Arnegger b. Stuttgart, Stuttgart, Württemberg, 6 Jul 1915; dau. of Luise Arnegger; bp. 2 Aug 1924; conf. 2 Aug 1924; missing as of 20 Nov 1945 (CR 375 8 2451, no. 684; FHL microfilm 25713, 1930 census)

Elise Blombach b. Barmen, Rheinprovinz, 28 May 1900; dau. of August Karl Blombach and Amalie Lina Pauline Weinreich; bp. 20 Jan 1913; conf. 20 Jan 1913; m. Pforzheim, Karlsruhe, Baden, 2 Jan 1920, Eduard Sittel; k. air raid Karlsruhe, Karlsruhe, Baden, 22 or 23 Feb 1945 (CHL microfilm 2458, form 42 FP, pt. 37, all-mission list 1938–45, district list 250–51; CR 275 8 2441, no. 529; FHL microfilm 245266, 1935 census; IGI, AF)

Marie Gayde b. Pinache, Neckarkreis, Württemberg, 16 Aug 1888; dau. of Wilhelm Gayde and Rosine Pauline Huppenbauer; bp. 5 Aug 1932; conf. 5 Aug 1932; m. Pinache 9 Aug 1917, Karl Heinrich Kappenstein; 5 children; d. heart and kidney diseases Pforzheim, Karlsruhe, Baden, 24 Feb 1944 (FHL microfilm 68797, no. 519; IGI)

Elsa Paula Girrbach b. Dillweißenstein, Karlsruhe, Baden, 31 Jan 1912; dau. of Johann Georg Girrbach and Emma Mayer; bp. 15 Feb 1924; conf. 15 Feb 1924; m. 9 Dec 1933, Otto Renz; k. air raid Karlsruhe, Karlsruhe, Baden, 24 Dec 1944 (CHL microfilm 2458, form 42 FP, pt. 37, all-mission list 1938–45, district list 250–51; CHL CR 275 8 2441, no. 238; FHL microfilm 271401, 1935 census; IGI)

Willy Georg Girrbach b. Niefern, Karlsruhe, Baden, 27 Nov 1907; son of Johann Georg Girrbach and Emma Mayer; bp. 15 Feb 1924; k. Auray, Morbihan, France, 7 Aug 1944; bur. Mont-de-Huisnes, France (CHL microfilm 2458, form 42 FP, pt. 37, 1949 list 2:444–45; CHL CR 375 8 2458; www.volksbund.de; FHL microfilm 25774, 1930 and 1935 censuses; IGI)

Charlotte Ihle b. Pforzheim, Karlsruhe, Baden, 13 Jun 1925; dau. of Herman Heinrich Braun and Maria Theresia Ille; bp. 8 Apr 1934; conf. 22 Apr 1934; m. 1943, Walter Adolf Ratzenberger; m. —— Schmiedt; k. air raid Pforzheim 23 Feb 1945 (CHL microfilm 2458, form 42 FP, pt. 37, all-mission list 1938–45, district list 250–51; CHL CR 275 8 2441, no. 572; FHL microfilm 271364, 1935 census; IGI, AF)

Lina Maria Knodel b. Neuenbürg, Calw, Württemberg, 10 Dec 1874; dau. of Ernst Theodor Knodel and Elisabeth Friederike Burkhardt; bp. 25 Mar 1917; conf. 25 Mar 1917; m. Pforzheim, Karlsruhe, Baden, 25 Aug 1906, Leopold Christian Maleck; 4 children; d. dropsy Pforzheim 29 or 30 Jan 1940; bur. Pforzheim 1 Feb 1940 (*Stern* 1940, nos. 5–6, 95; CHL CR 275 8 2441, no. 247; IGI)

Bertha Elisabeth Maleck b. Pforzheim, Karlsruhe, Baden, 2 Apr 1909; dau. of Leopold Christian Maleck and Lina Maria Knodel; bp. 22 Jul 1919; conf. 22 Jul 1919; d. brain disease 11 Jun 1940 (FHL microfilm 68797, no. 250; CHL CR 275 8 2441, no. 250; FHL microfilm 245225, 1930 and 1935 censuses; IGI)

Emma Girrbach Mayer b. Elfringen, Bilfingen, Karlsruhe, Baden, 24 Mar 1887; dau. of Meinrad Mayer and Katharina Preschler; bp. 15 Feb 1924; conf. 15 Feb 1924; m. 26 Feb 1927, Jacob Mangold; k. air raid Karlsruhe 24 Dec 1944 (CHL microfilm 2458, form 42 FP, pt. 37, all-mission list, 1938–45; district list, 250–51; CHL CR 275 8 2441, no. 235; FHL microfilm 245225, 1935 census; IGI)

Amalie Johanna Schwarz b. Gonsenheim, Mainz, Hessen, 3 Nov 1914; dau. of Phillipp Schwarz and Frieda Stahl; bp. 15 Feb 1924; conf. 15 Feb 1924; m. 30 or 31 Mar 1934, Otto Friedrich Elfner; k. air raid Karlsruhe 24 Dec 1944 (CHL microfilm 2458, form 42 FP, pt. 37, all-mission list, 1938–45, district list, 250–51; CHL CR 275 8 2441, no. 264; IGI)

Frieda Stahl b. Pforzheim, Karlsruhe, Baden, 18 Feb 1892; dau. of Ludwig Stahl and Friedericke Zeeb; bp. 28 Aug 1920; conf. 28 Aug 1920; m. 14 Nov 1914, Phillipp Schwarz; 1 child; d. heart ailment 13 Dec 1943 (FHL microfilm 68797, no. 263; CHL CR 275 8 2441, no. 263; FHL microfilm 245260; IGI)

Notes

1. Pforzheim city archive.
2. Presiding Bishopric, "Financial, Statistical, and Historical Reports of Wards, Stakes, and Missions, 1884–1955," 257, CHL CR 4 12.

3. West German Mission branch directory 1939, CHL LR 10045 11.
4. With no children listed among the members at the time, one wonders if the Primary was not meeting then or if non-LDS children were being taught.
5. Marianne Kappenstein Gubler, telephone interview with Jennifer Heckmann, October 3, 2008.
6. Ursula Mussler Schmitt, telephone interview with Jennifer Heckmann in German, March 31, 2009; summarized in English by Judith Sartowski.
7. Bühl Branch general minutes, CHL LR 1180 11.
8. Stan Clift to the author, July 11, 2007.
9. Pforzheim city archive.

Saarbrücken Branch

The city of Saarbrücken lies astride the Saar River, which forms part of the boundary between Germany and France. Located in the middle of an important iron-ore region, the city's value to Germany caused it to be contested in several wars over the centuries. In 1939, the city had 131,000 inhabitants.[1] The local LDS branch was truly a frontier outpost, because the nearest branches to the west were deep inside Belgium and France.

With twenty-two priesthood holders among its 111 members, this branch was in very good condition as World War II approached. The branch president was Paul Prison. His family and several others lived in the town of Dudweiler, two miles east of Saarbrucken. According to the directory of the West German Mission, most Church programs were operating in this branch in July 1939.[2] Meetings were held in rented rooms at Kronprinzenstrasse 9 in Saarbrücken. As was true all over the mission, Sunday School began at 10 a.m. Sacrament meeting was held at 3:00 p.m., preceded on the last Sunday of the month by a genealogical meeting. The Relief Society met on Tuesdays at 6:30 p.m. and the MIA at 8:00 p.m. No Primary meetings were being held at the time, despite the fact that the branch membership included eighteen children.

Saarbrücken Branch[3]	**1939**
Elders	8
Priests	4
Teachers	3
Deacons	7
Other Adult Males	21
Adult Females	50
Male Children	10
Female Children	8
Total	111

Fig. 1. The wedding of Elisabeth Klein and Hans Reger in 1937 was celebrated in the chapel of the Saarbrücken Branch. Note the pictures of Joseph Smith (left) and Christ in Gethsemane (right). (H. Reger)

In August 1937, Elisabeth Klein married a fine non-LDS man, Hans Reger. A year later, she was the mother of a baby girl and he was away from home in the service of his country. Elisabeth lived in an apartment at Metzerstrasse 25 and continued to enjoy her association with the Saints in Saarbrücken. As she recalled, "We branch members were all friends. We didn't have any friends elsewhere. The Church was all of our activity. About forty or fifty people came to church in those days."[4]

Paul Prison (born 1925) described the building in which the branch met:

> The room was about thirty feet long and thirteen feet wide. It was kind of a Hinterhaus with an empty garage in front and a big door where we parked our bicycles. And then there were two steps to go into it and there was kind of a potbelly stove that we heated in the wintertime. There was a sign with the church's name on it, maybe three by four feet out where everybody could see it. Our building was across the street from a big Catholic church with a tall steeple. We had a pump organ and behind that was a door and there was a little room where the children went and we had another room on the right side (they took that away during the war because they needed room for the people to live there). There were four chairs on the left side and three on the right side of each row, maybe ten to twelve rows. I don't think we had more than thirty-five to forty people in there because some lived very far away.[5]

Paul recalled going with his father (branch president Paul Prison) to visit members who lived many miles from town. "They didn't come to church very often. I would say we had about fifteen to eighteen people out of town [as far as fifty miles away]."

Branch president Paul Prison was a coal miner. By the time the war was well under way, he was required to work seven days a week. However, according to his son, Paul, there were ways to avoid that in order to attend church. "My father told his boss that he was sick on Sunday. When they asked for a note from his doctor, he told them that the doctor's office was closed on Sunday. If you were productive (and my father was) and they needed you, you were safe. Wherever he worked, there was never a cave-in."

Even before the war began, a member of the Saarbrücken Branch became a victim of the Nazi regime. Harald Ludwig Adam (born 1931) was taken from the family when he was six years old. According

Fig. 2. This prewar photograph of members of the Saarbrücken Branch includes American missionaries. (G. Blake)

to his elder brother Max (born 1927), Harald was mentally handicapped and could not learn,

> but his body was in perfect shape. . . . When school time came and he was six years old, two devils came to my parents and told them of a wonderful hospital which was created by Hitler for people like my brother, and they would help him. He was taken to the hospital just north of Frankfurt. Idstein is the name of the town. . . . My parents always got a letter every two months that he was doing well and was happy. They said that we could not see him because if we saw him it would destroy what he had learned. Then we got a telegram that he passed away; it said that he died of the flu and a heart condition. But there is no [history of] heart condition in our family at all so I always wondered what happened. Mother in her heart knew what had happened.[6]

Harald was one of tens of thousands of victims of the government's infamous euthanasia program.[7]

Fig. 3. Youth of the Saarbrücken Branch with missionaries in 1938. (C. Hillam)

When France and Germany issued mutual declarations of war in September 1939, Elisabeth Klein Reger and her daughter were evacuated from Saarbrücken under the assumption that the border city would soon be under attack by the French. While living in Landstuhl, Elisabeth gave birth to another daughter. After the surrender of France in June 1940, Sister Reger and her two daughters (Isolde, born 1938, and Ingrid, born 1940) were allowed to return to Saarbrücken, where she lived in her widowed mother's apartment.

Young Paul Prison avoided associating with the Hitler Youth and somehow got by without punishment. However, the war inflicted pain on this fifteen-year-old early on when a bomb hit the home of a friend across the street from the Prison home in Dudweiler:

> My friend died in 1940, my good friend. He lived just kitty-corner across the street from us. He was my age. It was about 9 or 10 p.m. and I heard an airplane flying around and around very low, and then I heard a big explosion. That big explosion threw me right out of my bed, and I looked out the window, and my best friend's house was on fire. I got my clothes on and went there, and the house was completely collapsed, and there were already several people. We took our shovels and started digging people out. Eight people lived in that house, and my friend was the first one we could see, but he had a big beam right on top of him, and he was still alive. We couldn't get it off of him, so somebody went and got a big saw, and we had to saw it in three places. By the time we lifted the beam off, he was dead. Then we got the others out; we got his mother out, but she had no head anymore. Then we got his father out, and he was dead. Then we got the others out. Eight people, we laid them all out across the street on the grass. And while we were shoveling them out, the airplane came around several times and shot at us with machine guns.

At the age of ten, Max Adam had been inducted into the Jungvolk with his classmates at school. At fourteen, he was advanced into the Hitler Youth and the Sunday meetings of that organization conflicted with the branch meeting schedule. Max's father, master cabinetmaker Max G. Adam (not a member of the Church but a kind supporter of his wife and

Fig. 4. Max Adam in the uniform of the National Labor Service in 1942. (M. Adam)

sons), came up with a fine plan to allow young Max to miss the Hitler Youth meetings. One of the organization's programs collected gifts for children each Christmas. The leaders fell for Max's idea: if the boy could produce fifty toys for Christmas, he would be exempt from attending meetings. This allowed Max to continue to attend church meetings on Sundays.

At the age of fifteen, Max was assigned to work on a farm for a year. The farm was located several hundred miles from Saarbrücken, so Max was unable to visit his family at all during this year of service. Living with other boys in a camp, he participated in a flag-raising ceremony every morning before walking to the farm to which he was assigned. He was totally isolated from the Church while there. Back at home in 1942, he found that Saarbrücken was harassed by air-raid alarms quite often. Allied bombers rarely attacked, but every time they flew to other cities and passed within a certain number of miles of Saarbrücken, the alarms sounded and another night's rest was disturbed.

One night, the airplanes that had so often passed Saarbrücken on their way to other targets unloaded their bombs there. Within minutes, apartment houses were burning in the neighborhood of the Adam home. Max recalled being part of a bucket brigade as local residents worked feverishly to prevent a fire on the top floor of the building from spreading downward and to adjacent structures. In that same attack, the top floor of the Adams' apartment building was damaged, but the family's apartment was still inhabitable. They replaced broken windows with cardboard and were grateful to still have a place to live.

Horst Prison (born 1920) was drafted in 1940 and sent to nearby France. By June 1941, he was on the Eastern Front and participating in the invasion of the Soviet Union. His experiences there were extremely challenging, beginning with a bout of frostbite. The doctors wanted to amputate his feet, but he prayed intensely to his Father in Heaven, and within a few days he was able to walk again.[8] By the end of the first winter, he had received the combat infantry medal, which denoted three occasions of close-quarters combat with the enemy.

Paul Prison was called into the national labor force in 1942 and assigned to work on a farm in Bavaria. Back home, he was working as a payroll clerk in a small construction company when he received a notice to report for military service on January 3, 1943. Assigned to an artillery unit, he was trained as a radio man and learned Morse code. A few months later, he was stationed in France. In June 1944, he was a forward observer on the coast of Normandy.

Hans Reger was wounded in Russia in 1942 and spent a year in hospitals recuperating. Then he was sent home and resumed a somewhat normal life as a printer working for the post office. His presence was appreciated by his wife and two daughters, especially when a terrifying air raid took place over Saarbrücken in September 1944. As Sister Reger ran down the stairs with her husband and her elder daughter, Isolde, she was worried about her younger daughter, Ingrid, who was staying with her grandmother just two houses down the street. Fortunately, Ingrid and her grandmother were also able to reach the air-raid shelter, where the five were united. Signal flares were coming down around them, and some structures were already ablaze. When they emerged from the shelter, the scene was totally different; some structures had been destroyed and their own apartment house was burning. In the aftermath of the attack, they learned that they had lost everything but the clothes on their backs. About 90 percent of the city had been destroyed. Hans Reger's place of employment was also gone, and the family took up temporary residence on the outskirts of town in a building owned by another Church member. Soon they were given permission to move to a town not far from Saarbrücken, where they spent the remainder of the war in the home of Elisabeth's aunt. They were safe there but totally out of contact with the Church.

"It's funny—the things you remember," said Dieter Jung (born 1937). "Since my dad was a

Latter-day Saint he didn't smoke, so he would trade his cigarette rations for candy bars. When he was at the front, he would send the candy bars back home."[9] Richard Jung, a tailor, was a social democrat when Hitler came to power, but that political party had a short life under the National Socialist government. He had joined the Church in 1936 and was a priest when he volunteered for service in the Wehrmacht. According to young Dieter, "He volunteered so that Hitler wouldn't have the satisfaction of drafting him."

Dieter Jung was only six when he saw his father for the last time. Richard Jung had been sent home after suffering from frostbite on the Eastern Front. Soon after returning to his unit, he was killed. Back at home, his wife, Elfriede, had a premonition that he had been killed and was thus not shocked when two men knocked at her door with the sad news. They presented her with Richard's personal effects. According to Dieter, "They were sorry that my father had been killed, but on the other hand, he had died for the fatherland, and that's supposed to be an honor."

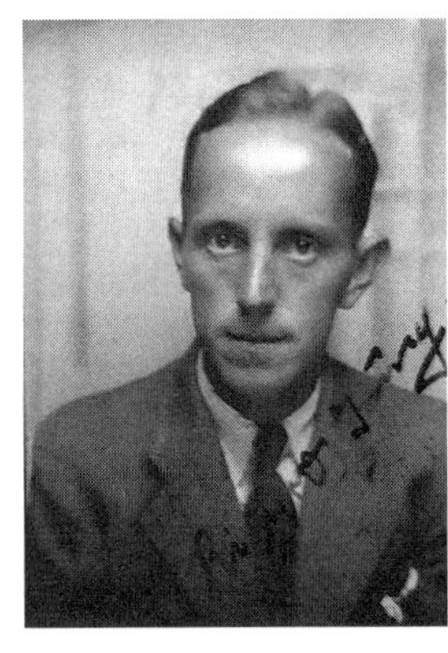

Fig. 5. Richard Jung had a wife and two sons when he was killed in the Soviet Union in 1943. (D. Jung)

In 1943, a draft notice arrived for Max Adam. Because both father and son used that name, the family at first feared that the father would be required to serve. However, the call was directed to sixteen-year-old Max, who had been agonizing about serving in the army of an empire he did not support. He described the situation:

> I knew that Hitler was bad, period. The Church teaches you one thing and [the Nazis] teach you another. I had a hard time going to war. How could I fight for such a man? I can't do that! I talked to the [branch president] and he said, "Max, you've just got to go!" I said, "But I can't!" So I was brave enough to go. . . . I prayed for a month about that. Then I got a distinct answer: "Go. You will come home safe."

Horst Prison was shot cleanly through the calf in Russia in 1943, but he escaped a potentially lethal bullet shortly thereafter despite what he later admitted was a reluctance to listen to the Holy Ghost. He was on guard duty, and somebody told him to take cover. He looked around and could not see anybody. Again he was told to take cover but did not heed the warning. The third time somebody literally pushed him down a hill. At that very moment, a bullet struck his shoulder but did not penetrate his uniform. Had he remained standing, the bullet might have pierced his heart. He never determined who pushed him down that hill, because there was nobody close enough to do so. However, from that time on, he always listened to what others said and listened to the Spirit. That dangerous incident was not his last in Russia. A tank once drove over him while he lay in a trench. After a comrade helped dig him out from beneath the mammoth vehicle, Horst determined that only his watch was broken.

When the Allied forces stormed the beaches of Normandy on June 6, 1944, Paul Prison was atop the slopes overlooking Utah Beach attempting to send radio messages back to his commander.[10] "I couldn't send the message [at first] because the airwaves were jammed [by music]. Finally, I used Morse Code to send the message. I told them that the invasion had started and they said it was just a bluff." He and his surviving comrades retreated from the fighting early on because they had quickly run out of ammunition. On August 17, Paul was wounded in three places by mortar fragments—one each in his abdomen, his thigh, and his arm. He made his way to an aid station and was sent to a monastery in Liege, Belgium. He could have died from loss of blood, but an observant elderly physician came to his aid and moved him from the floor onto a bed. After several months in German hospitals, he recovered and returned to his unit in time to celebrate Christmas not far from the area where the Battle of the Bulge was raging.

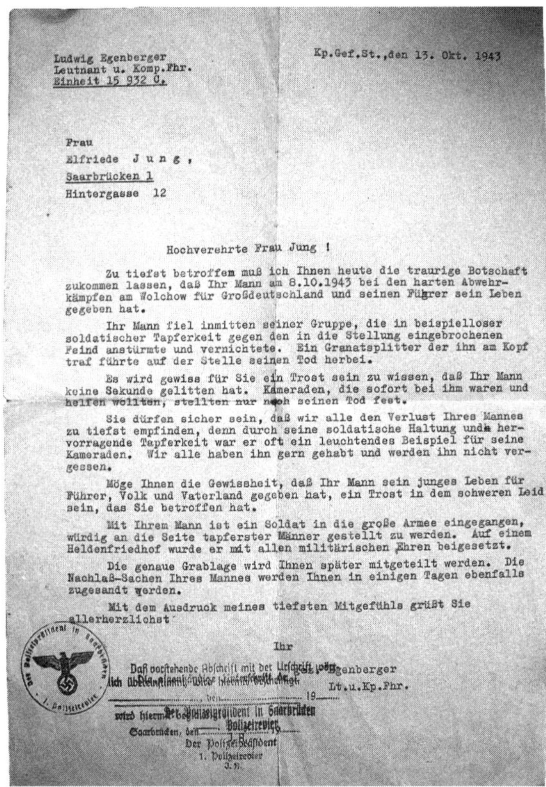

Ludwig Egenberger
Leutnant u. Komp.Fhr.
Einheit 15 932 C.

Kp.Gef.St.,den 13. Okt. 1943

Frau
Elfriede J u n g ,
Saarbrücken 1
Hintergasse 12

Hochverehrte Frau Jung !

Zu tiefst betroffen muß ich Ihnen heute die traurige Botschaft zukommen lassen, daß Ihr Mann am 8.10.1943 bei den harten Abwehrkämpfen am Wolchow für Großdeutschland und seinen Führer sein Leben gegeben hat.

Ihr Mann fiel inmitten seiner Gruppe, die in beispielloser soldatischer Tapferkeit gegen den in die Stellung eingebrochenen Feind anstürmte und vernichtete. Ein Granatsplitter der ihn am Kopf traf führte auf der Stelle seinen Tod herbei.

Es wird gewiss für Sie ein Trost sein zu wissen, daß Ihr Mann keine Sekunde gelitten hat. Kameraden, die sofort bei ihm waren und helfen wollten, stellten nur noch seinen Tod fest.

Sie dürfen sicher sein, daß wir alle den Verlust Ihres Mannes zu tiefst empfinden, denn durch seine soldatische Haltung und hervorragende Tapferkeit war er oft ein leuchtendes Beispiel für seine Kameraden. Wir alle haben ihn gern gehabt und werden ihn nicht vergessen.

Möge Ihnen die Gewissheit, daß Ihr Mann sein junges Leben für Führer, Volk und Vaterland gegeben hat, ein Trost in dem schweren Leid sein, das Sie betroffen hat.

Mit Ihrem Mann ist ein Soldat in die große Armee eingegangen, würdig an die Seite tapferster Männer gestellt zu werden. Auf einem Heldenfriedhof wurde er mit allen militärischen Ehren beigesetzt.

Die genaue Grablage wird Ihnen später mitgeteilt werden. Die Nachlaß-Sachen Ihres Mannes werden Ihnen in einigen Tagen ebenfalls zugesandt werden.

Mit dem Ausdruck meines tiefsten Mitgefühls grüßt Sie allerherzlichst

Ihr

gez. Egenberger
Lt.u.Kp.Fhr.

Der Polizeipräsident in Saarbrücken
Polizeirevier
Der Polizeipräsident
1. Polizeirevier

Fig. 6. This letter announced the death of Richard Jung to his wife and their two sons. "You may be comforted by the fact that your husband did not suffer even one second. Comrades who were at his side determined within moments that he died instantly." (D. Jung)

Elfriede Jung, now a war widow with two little boys, eventually lost her home in an air raid over Saarbrücken. Dieter, by then seven years old, recalled that the three of them had often gone to the air-raid shelter with their pillows and a few other items. Their apartment house "was totally destroyed—right down to the ground." His younger brother, Herbert (born 1939), also recalled air-raid experiences: "We went to this big mountain with a cave [as a shelter]. When the bombs hit the mountain, the lights went out. I put my pillow over my head because I thought that would protect me. A couple of days later, we came back out."[11]

Both boys recalled staying in various towns after their apartment in Saarbrücken was destroyed. For the rest of the war, Sister Jung and her sons were veritable refugees, eventually finding a place to stay in a small Bavarian town near the Austrian border. Herbert recalled how the local residents resented taking in refugees: "Nobody wants to have refugees [in their homes], so it was kind of tough." Dieter recalled being hungry and was therefore quite pleased one day when a farmer gave them a dozen eggs. Unfortunately, a Russian soldier took those eggs and ate them raw. "He was really reprimanded by an officer," Dieter recalled. While in that town hundreds of miles from Saarbrücken, the Jungs watched the American army come through in a peaceful takeover of the area in the last weeks of the war.

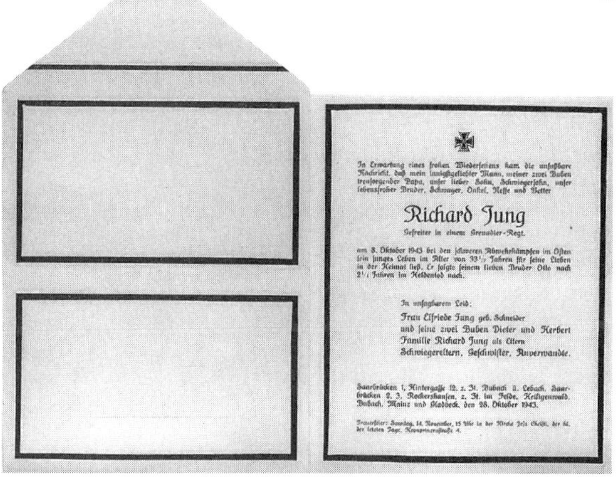

In Erwartung eines frohen Wiedersehens kam die unfaßbare Nachricht, daß mein innigstgeliebter Mann, meiner zwei Buben treusorgender Papa, unser lieber Sohn, Schwiegersohn, unser lebensfroher Bruder, Schwager, Onkel, Neffe und Vetter

Richard Jung

Gefreiter in einem Grenadier-Regt.

am 8. Oktober 1943 bei den schweren Abwehrkämpfen im Osten sein junges Leben im Alter von 33 1/2 Jahren für seine Lieben in der Heimat ließ. Er folgte seinem lieben Bruder Otto nach 2 1/4 Jahren im Heldentod nach.

In unsagbarem Leid:
Frau Elfriede Jung geb. Schneider
und seine zwei Buben Dieter und Herbert
Familie Richard Jung als Eltern
Schwiegereltern, Geschwister, Anverwandte.

Saarbrücken 1, Hintergasse 12, z. Zt. Dubach u. Lebach, Saarbrücken 2, 3, Rockershausen, z. Zt. im Felde, Heiligenwald, Dubach, Mainz und Gladbeck, den 28. Oktober 1943.

Trauerfeier: Sonntag, 14. November, 15 Uhr in der Kirche Jesu Christi der Hl. der letzten Tage, Kronprinzenstraße 4.

Fig. 7. The standard format for a death notice was still in use in Germany in 1943. A single sheet bore the message and was folded into an envelope. This one was sent by Elfriede Jung to family and friends to inform them of the death of her husband, Richard. The recipient knew by the black border that the contents of the letter would be tragic. (D. Jung)

Herbert Jung had the following recollections:

> I remember well when the Americans came. They came with their tanks and their trucks and all that. They liked the fresh fruit; they liked their chicken cakes, and they gave us canned goods. So basically that kind of took us away from [our dependency on] the farmers. They liked the fresh stuff; they didn't like the canned goods. And they gave us chocolates and gum. . . . And then of course we had never seen black people before. Oh, they were something else. We

> couldn't believe it. There were no black people in those days in Germany. So that was a big deal for us when we saw those black people.

In January 1945, Paul Prison and his friend Martin were riding on a truck just a few feet apart when an artillery round exploded nearby. Paul was not hurt, but Martin was struck by shrapnel just below his left armpit. Paul caught him as he fell from the truck. "I couldn't stop the bleeding," recalled Paul.

> A horse cart came along and we put him in it and took him to the first aid station. By four o'clock the next morning he was dead. Even if he had been on the operating table we couldn't have saved him. . . . Martin was a very fine person. I always said he was a better person than I am. He was always calm, and he was an altar boy at the Catholic Church, and he really believed in his church and was one of the best men I ever met.

In March 1945, the American army moved through Germany. Elisabeth Klein Reger recalled that there was no fighting when they reached her town and that the conquerors treated the locals with respect. The family soon returned to Saarbrücken, where the French had replaced the Americans as the military occupation force. The Regers were able to rejoin their LDS friends and bring the Saarbrücken Branch back to life. Before long, Hans Reger (who had attended church meetings on many occasions) became the newest member of the Church in Saarbrücken.

In the last months of the war, Max Adam was serving with an antiaircraft battery near the city of Leipzig. As a member of a five-man crew, Max was responsible for setting the vertical angle of the barrel of an 88 mm howitzer as directed. A second crew member moved the barrel left and right. Two other crew members loaded the shells and removed the casings while the fifth member gave the orders. In Max's recollection, "the men who carried the shells were muscle-men. We had 500 rounds at each station, 250 on the one side and 250 on the other side. We could fire a round in thirty seconds or less. Our duty lasted for two hours, then another crew took over." No kind of ear protection was used. The howitzer was situated in an area about thirty feet square surrounded by a thick wall of earth.

Fig. 8. The Reger girls, Isolde and Ingrid, in the ruins of the building in which the Saarbrücken Branch held its meetings before September 1944. (H. Reger)

Max was nearly killed one night while he and his four comrades were off duty. Sitting just a few feet from the howitzer during their two-hour break, they were stunned when an enemy artillery shell landed about ten feet from them. Although there was no barrier between the bomb and Max, he was not hurt but was knocked out. He regained consciousness to find another soldier shaking him and yelling that they had to get out of the area at once; the ammunition supply was on fire. He and his friends were already outside of the enclosure when approximately 125 unused rounds began to explode. "The fire in the air was unbelievable!" he recalled. "That was the first big experience when I was protected."

Fig. 9. The building on Kronprinzenstrasse where the Saarbrücken Branch had held its meetings was still a ruin a few years after the war. (H. Reger)

In March 1945, Max Adam was captured by the Americans and was a prisoner of war for three months. "I was in three different camps in three months, and I could not stand it! We sat there all day long with absolutely nothing to do. The soldiers picked fleas out of each other's hair. That was all we had to do. And wait for a small bowl of watery soup. That's all we had to eat."

Paul Prison's unit retreated slowly through central Germany before the advancing American army. In April 1945, he was captured and transported to a camp by Remagen on the Rhine River. There he lived in squalid conditions that he described as "worse than a concentration camp." He and his comrades drank filthy water from the river and a dozen men died every day. When they were given small quantities of clean water, they were forced to drink it all at one time, and any remaining water was poured onto the ground by their American guards. For about one week, the prisoners were forced to run up and down hills while being yelled at and beaten by guards. Toward the end of June, Paul was released and transported home to Saarbrücken.

A priest in the Aaronic Priesthood, Paul Prison never met another LDS soldier while away from home. He had lived for three years without reading Church literature, taking the sacrament, or praying with other Latter-day Saints, but he had a testimony and prayed daily. His weight dropped from 152 pounds to 97, but he maintained his allegiance to God and the Church. "We have our own agency; we can have our own testimony and can lose it; that is up to us. I chose to keep it many times. And I wondered why I was still alive; I think it was the hand of God that kept me alive."

One of the dubious honors accorded Horst Prison as a POW in the Soviet Union was the opportunity to march with thousands of German soldiers through Moscow as the Red Army celebrated its victory over Nazi Germany. The prisoners were starved and mocked as losers in a long and terrible war as they were paraded through the Soviet capital. At the same time, he was likely aware of the sufferings of the Soviet people that had led them to punish German soldiers and civilians long after the war was over.

In June 1945, Max Adam was lining up with other POWs to be released when he realized that the guards might have lied to the prisoners. Instead of being sent home, they might be sent to Belgium or the Netherlands for a year to clean up war damages. Not interested in any such extension of his POW term, he devised a plot to escape. After he successfully sneaked behind the latrines, he managed to scale a ten-foot chain link fence and join a group of POWs who had already been released. When guards checked his papers, he carefully placed his thumb over the area where the release stamp should have been and thus safely exited the camp.

Not far from the camp where Max had made his escape, his parents were living with relatives near the city of Halberstadt. Still just eighteen, he did not expect to see them and was simply walking down the road in the direction of Saarbrücken (hundreds of miles away) when he heard a familiar voice. It was his father yelling to him from a passing truck. Max G. Adam had recognized his son and told the truck driver to stop. As the young soldier recalled, "He jumped [off of the truck] and ran towards me. It was my father. It was a happy reunion, and I had a ride now. We went back to the evacuation town to pick up his suitcases, and then we headed home." They arrived in Saarbrücken in late May 1945. The first church meeting they attended was held in a school.

Elfriede Jung and her sons returned to Saarbrücken in June 1945. The city was under French military occupation at the time. Dieter recalled a clear distinction between the French soldiers in his hometown and the Americans he had seen in Bavaria: "The French soldiers didn't have much more than we had as far as food was concerned. American soldiers would treat the kids very nice, give them candy bars and stuff like that. It seemed like they were throwing things away and we were picking them up and eating them."

Until December 31, 1949, Horst Prison suffered many trials as a POW in the Soviet Union. During his more than nine years of military service and imprisonment, he had never had contact with Latter-day Saints except when on leave, which was rare. He had been ordained an elder in connection with his wedding in 1944 and carried his scriptures with him whenever possible, but he never participated in any Church meetings while he was away from home. Nevertheless, he maintained his testimony and his loyalty to God and the Church.

The members of the Saarbrücken Branch had been bombed out and scattered far and wide during the long years of the war and its aftermath, and at least ten of them did not survive the conflict. Little by little, the survivors returned to the city and reconstructed their branch. Peacetime would try them severely as they waited for years to find out whether the province of Saarland would remain in Germany, but their Latter-day Saint lives continued with optimism.[12]

Fig. 10. A German officer ponders his future among the ruins of Saarbrücken in May 1945. (Wikimedia)

In Memoriam

The following members of the Saarbrücken Branch did not survive World War II:

Harald Ludwig Adam b. Saarbrücken, Rheinland, 27 Jul 1931; son of Max Gabriel Adam and Ella Sophie Adam; d. euthanasia Idstein, Hessen-Nassau, 4 Apr 1939; bur. Saarbrücken 1939 (M. Adam; IGI)

Wilhelmine Biehl b. Saarbrücken, Rheinprovinz, 29 Jun 1875; dau. of Heinrich Biehl and Katharina Greis; bp. 9 Jul 1939; conf. 9 Jul 1939; m. Saarbrücken 12 Sep 1896, Heinrich Paul; d. during the evacuation of Saarbrücken in the Allied invasion 1945 (CHL microfilm 2458, form 42 FP, pt. 37, district list, 250–51; CHL CR 275 8 2441, no. 682; IGI)

Erich Debschütz b. Breslau, Schlesien, 7 Aug 1903; son of Olga Debschütz; bp. 25 May 1920; conf. 25 May 1920; missing as of 1946 (FHL microfilm 68797, no. 523; CHL CR 275 8 2441, no. 523; FHL microfilm no. 25753; 1930 and 1935 censuses)

Peter Ferdinand Flach b. Ebringen, Freiburg, Baden, 2 Jun 1882; son of Peter Flach and Katherina Graff; bp. 7 Jul 1908; conf. 7 Jul 1908; m. Louise Bach; d. 2 Jan 1941 (FHL microfilm 68797, no. 521; CR 275 8 2441, no. 521; FHL microfilm no. 25767; 1930 and 1935 censuses; IGI)

Richard Jung b. Saarbrücken, Rheinprovinz, 22 Apr 1910; son of Richard Jung and Elise Georg; bp. 10 or 20 Apr 1934; conf. 10 or 20 Apr 1934; ord. deacon 25 Nov 1934; ord. teacher 16 Feb 1936; ord. priest 3 May 1938; m. 5 May 1934, Elfriede Schneider; 2 children; corporal; k. in battle 3 km east of Dubowik 8 Oct 1943; bur. Sologubowka, St. Petersburg, Russia (Jung; FHL microfilm 68797, no. 575; www.volksbund.de; IGI)

Phillippine Knapp b. Frankfurt, Hessen-Nassau, or Mainz, Hessen, 9 Nov 1866; dau. of Margarethe Knapp;

bp. 10 Jul 1901; conf. 19 Jul 1901; m. 30 Mar 1887, Ludwig Neuenschwander; 1 child; d. old age 30 Dec 1940 (FHL microfilm 68797, no. 38; CHL CR 275 8 2441, FHL microfilm no. 245241; 1930 and 1935 censuses; no. 38)

Valentin Krämer b. Herrensohr, Rheinland, 15 Jul 1924; son of Valentin Krämer and Elisabeth Lina Rasskopf; bp. 15 May 1933; k. in battle 15 Jan 1943 (IGI)

Richard Friedrich Krämer b. Herrensohr, Rheinland, 31 Dec 1926; son of Valentin Krämer and Elisabeth Lina Rasskopf; bp. 13 Jun 1935; d. 1945 (IGI)

Peter Prison b. Dudweiler, Rheinprovinz, 3 Oct 1867; son of Jakob Prison and Maria Katharina Linnenbach; bp. 7 May 1922; conf. 7 May 1922; ord. deacon 19 Sep 1922; ord. teacher 20 Jan 1924; ord. priest 1 Jan 1934; ord. elder 1 Nov 1936; m. 20 Sep 1890, Theresia Trockle; 8 children; d. pneumonia Dudweiler 19 Dec 1943 (FHL microfilm 68797, no. 42; CHL CR 275 8 2441, no. 42; IGI)

Johannes Zimmer b. Karlsruhe, Baden, 16 Jul 1921; son of Albert Zimmer and Maria Magdalena Stahl; bp. 28 Aug 1930; conf. 28 Aug 1930; corporal; d. Orleans, France, 15 Jun or 23 Jul 1943; bur. Fort de Malmaison, France (CHL microfilm 2458, form 42 FP, pt. 37, district list, 250–51; FHL microfilm 68797, no. 59; FHL microfilm no. 245307; 1925 and 1935 censuses; www.volksbund.de)

Notes

1. Saarbrücken city archive.
2. West German Mission branch directory, 1939, CHL LR 10045 11.
3. Presiding Bishopric, "Financial, Statistical, and Historical Reports of Wards, Stakes, and Missions, 1884–1955," 257, CHL CR 4 12.
4. Elisabeth Klein Reger, interview by the author, Salt Lake City, July 19, 2007.
5. Paul Prison, interview by the author, Richmond, UT, November 22, 2008.
6. Max Adam, interview by the author, Bountiful, UT, April 18, 2007.
7. Harold died in the Kalmenhof Hospital in Idstein (as recorded in the margin of his official birth record in Saarbrücken). The book *Euthanasie im Nationalsozialismus* by Dorothea Sick (Frankfurt: Fachhochschule, 1983) shows that well over seven hundred persons of all ages were murdered in that hospital and buried nearby. Most murders were done by the injection of lethal drugs, but death was usually not instantaneous.
8. Horst Peter Prison and Elfriede Deininger Prison, telephone interview with Jennifer Heckmann in German, April 13, 2009; summarized in English by Judith Sartowski.
9. Dieter Jung, interview by the author, West Valley City, UT, June 20, 2006.
10. He did not know the name of the landing site until he lived in Utah years later. He and a neighbor (a GI and Normandy veteran) compared descriptions of the area and determined that they had been at the same location, serving in opposing armies.
11. Herbert Jung, interview by Michael Corley, Salt Lake City, October 30, 2008.
12. It was not until 1957 that the question of nationality for the Saarland was resolved and France gave up its claims to the valuable territory.

Worms Branch

The small branch of Latter-day Saints who called Worms their home strove in 1939 to maintain the programs of the Church. Of the thirty-three members of record, eighteen (55 percent) were females over twelve years of age and only four men and boys held the priesthood. The solitary elder was Friedrich Tisch, and his wife, Karoline, was the Relief Society president. The only other surname listed on the branch directory of June 1939 was Hammerle (Ellen, the leader of the YWMIA).[1]

Worms Branch[2]	1939
Elders	1
Priests	0
Teachers	0
Deacons	3
Other Adult Males	6
Adult Females	18
Male Children	5
Female Children	0
Total	33

In the fall of 1939, the Worms Branch held meetings in rented rooms at Renzstrasse 5. Sunday School began at 10:00 a.m. and sacrament meeting at 8:00 p.m. MIA was held on Thursdays at 8:00 p.m., and the Relief Society met on Tuesdays at the same hour.

As of this writing, the only surviving member of the wartime Worms Branch is Renate Tisch (born 1924). Her family lived at Gaustrasse 64 in the northern Worms suburb of Neuhausen. Friedrich Tisch was an employee of the Reichsbank and had moved his family to the city in 1926. Renate recalled the meeting location and the members:

> Before we moved in, another religious group had used the rooms. We met in the back. There was one small room and a nice, big room. We were able to hold all our meetings there but had to be careful about what we taught and said and what hymns we sang. Our branch wasn't very big—it consisted of my family, Sister Müller's family, and the Spengler family. I would say that we were about fifteen people in attendance. We did not have any pictures or special decorations on the wall or in the room. But there was a sign at the street that indicated that we met in those rooms. We didn't have any Primary class because there were no children.[3]

Upon completing her schooling at age fourteen, Renate was called to work for one year on the Spindler farm, only about twenty minutes from her home, and she was allowed to go to church on Sundays. Her pay was only 5 Reichsmark (about $1.50) per month.

American missionary Walter Scoville had served in Worms just before the war and maintained correspondence with the Tisch family before the United States entered the war in December 1941. He received an encouraging letter written by Friedrich Tisch on March 4, 1940, that included these lines:

> Brother Scoville, you needn't worry about us. We are not in need in any way. We have enough to eat and drink, more than we need. After all, we can't do more than eat until we're full every day. . . . More news: Sister Hammerle had a baby boy on September 21 last year. . . . And Sister Müller had a baby boy just before Christmas to keep the family name alive. Other than that, nothing is different. We still hold our meetings as always. . . . We still have the clothes we washed for [Elders] Kuhn and Oldroyd [when they left the country in August 1939]. We could not send it to them in Holland because there wasn't enough time, . . . and they haven't written to us. We will keep the clothes here until the missionaries come back.[4]

Fig. 1. The building at Renzstrasse 5 as it appears today. (P. W. Ehl)

Young Renate Tisch was destined to serve her country in several capacities away from home during the war, but she was still in Worms when an air raid left the branch meeting rooms in rubble. In her recollection, "We went to church every Sunday, and when we went that one day our building was gone. Everything was lost that we had in our meeting rooms. But we kept our songbooks at home. Since we weren't many people in the first place, we organized meetings in our living room." For the duration of the war, worship services in the Worms Branch took place in the homes of the members, usually the Tisch family's apartment.

"We covered our windows with something similar to black blankets in the evening," Renate explained:

> If there was a light, the [air-raid wardens] would come after us. We would always go into the air-raid shelter together, and I would make sure that I sat next to my family. If we died together, it would be all right. We had light in the air-raid shelters and took our flashlights. We also took a suitcase with us, with maybe a dress and underwear in it. My dad had important papers in his suitcase. When the alarm came, we grabbed our belongings and went. Our home was damaged during air raids, but we were still able to live in it.

At age eighteen, Renate answered the call of the Reichsarbeitsdienst and was sent south to the town of Zell, in the Wiesenthal valley in Baden. She described the situation in these words:

> That was quite a long ways away from home for me. [Our leaders] taught us everything we should know about the Allies. They told us from which side each country would come and how we could conquer America. I lived in a brand-new house during that time. It was built just for us girls. Upstairs it had five big rooms and downstairs, we had other rooms. By 10:00 a.m. we had to go out to work for the farmers or families with many children where the husband was serving in the military. During the year I was there, I did not have the opportunity to attend chrch. But I was able to go home for a couple of weeks once.

Renate had been fortunate to meet a fine young LDS man at a mission conference. She recalled that Anton Huck carried photographs of young people in the mission. ("It seemed that he wanted us to fall in love.") Paul Eysser was a member of the Nuremberg Branch and was serving in the military near Worms. This allowed him to attend church meetings in the home of the Tisch family. "I got to see him quite a lot for a few weeks, and he wrote letters too," recalled Renate.

Renate and Paul were married at city hall in Worms on October 9, 1943, and then traveled to Nuremberg where the branch (the second largest in the mission) celebrated with them. Renate recalled:

> All the branch members were there, and it was a big feast. My parents supplied geese, rabbits, and chickens. We also had dumplings and vegetables. At least forty people were there.
>
> We found somebody to take the pictures and to bring some flowers. We had about one week together before Paul had to go back to his military duty.

With her husband gone again so soon, Renate went back to work. Her next assignment was as a civilian in an army office in Bensheim, only ten miles east of Worms. For a while, she was able to commute to work on the train, but eventually Allied bombers destroyed the bridge over the Rhine River, and Renate could not often make the longer trip south to Mannheim, across the river to Ludwigshafen and north to Worms. She spent the nights in Bensheim. All the while, her father (who was too old to be drafted) was conducting church meetings in his home, trying to keep the branch intact despite increasing absenteeism among the branch members.

"I worked in the payroll office. Soldiers weren't paid much, but it was more than the 2,40 Reichsmark [60 cents] I was paid each month, along with room and board," Renate explained. During the final months of the war, she was sent to Munich in Bavaria; her office was transferred there to stay out of the way of the invading Allied troops. She located a cousin in the Bavarian capital and was able to live in her apartment. "Munich was bombed terribly, and we spent a lot of time in the basement shelters," she recalled.

Renate Tisch Eysser was still in Munich when the American army entered the city and the war ended. "There were many black soldiers who we had never seen before. I turned to my coworker and said: 'My goodness! Look at that!' But I wasn't afraid of them. They were nice to us." Shortly after the war ended, Renate looked for a way to return to Worms. That way was by rail in a coal car. She made it as far as Mannheim, where the American forces occupied the city. The French controlled the area across the river and initially made matters difficult for the young woman. Fortunately, she ran into Anton Huck, who directed her to the home of Eugen

Hechtle, the district president, where she spent the night. The next day, Renate convinced the French guards to allow her to cross the river and proceed to her home in Worms.

Paul Eysser had been taken prisoner by the Americans at the end of 1944 and was sent to Missouri as a POW. He was released in 1946 and made his way first to Nuremberg and then to Worms, where he was reunited with his wife, as she recalled: "He came home in April 1946. Nobody knew that he was alive. No messages could be sent through the Red Cross. Not even his parents knew where he was. The last thing that I had heard from him was that he was headed for Russia."

Renate had the following summary comments about some of the spiritual trials that occur in wartime: "My mother always used to tell us that we have to have faith. That stuck with me. We had to believe that Heavenly Father would be with us. We prayed a lot. When we went into the air-raid shelters, the neighbors would feel relief and be happy that we were there. They believed that we brought some kind of peace and that made them less afraid of the situation to come."

On December 26, 1946, President Tisch wrote a letter to his missionary friend, Walter Scoville, in the United States. The war had been over for eighteen months, and Brother Tisch was finally able to offer some good news about the conditions in Worms:

> We have survived this terrible war, though there were several occasions when we were close to being killed. We lost our meeting rooms and were forced to hold meetings in our apartment. . . . The members of the Worms Branch were able to stay in their homes for the most part. Sister Mink lives in a different part of Worms, but was able to rescue her property. Our beautiful city became a victim of the air raids. . . . You know how close our home is to the railroad station. There are 22 bomb craters in the gardens around our home. But our home still stands and the damage it suffered has already been repaired. We have gone through very painful times, and every day we are still moving rubble out of our way. . . . We want to live as faithful Latter-day Saints and be prepared to bear testimony of the truth of the Restoration. . . . By the way, our daughter Renate married an elder [Eysser] from the Nuremberg Branch back in October 1943. He was a POW in Missouri for a year and just returned in April [1946].[5]

The Worms Branch had survived World War II and the members were looking forward to gathering together to worship in peacetime.

No members of the Worms Branch are known to have died during World War II.

Notes

1. West German Mission branch directory, 1939, CHL LR 10045 11.
2. Presiding Bishopric, "Financial, Statistical, and Historical Reports of Wards, Stakes, and Missions, 1884–1955," 257, CHL CR 4 12.
3. Renate Tisch Eysser, interview by the author, North Salt Lake, UT, May 20, 2009.
4. Walter E. Scoville, papers, CHL MS 18613.
5. Ibid.

MUNICH DISTRICT

West German Mission

The southern half of the historic kingdom of Bavaria was the territory of the Munich District of the West German Mission in early 1938. Essentially all of southeastern Germany from Austria north to the Danube River was included in this district. It consisted at the time of only two branches: Munich with 228 members and Augsburg with 57 members. The traditional dominance of the Catholic Church may have been one reason for the scarcity of Latter-day Saints in the region.

After the annexation of Austria by Germany in March 1938, it became so difficult for American missionaries to travel from Austria to Switzerland that work in the Swiss-Austrian Mission was hindered. Therefore it was decided that Austria should be included within the boundaries of the West German Mission. This change went into effect on November 1, 1938, and the small branches in Salzburg, Haag am Hausruck, and Frankenburg were added to the West German Mission. They became part of the Munich District because it was easier at the time for the Saints in those three towns to travel to district conferences in Munich than to Vienna, the capital of Austria. With the expansion of the Munich District, the southern border extended south to Switzerland on the west, Italy on the southwest and Yugoslavia on the southeast. Most of the district territory was mountainous and sparsely populated.

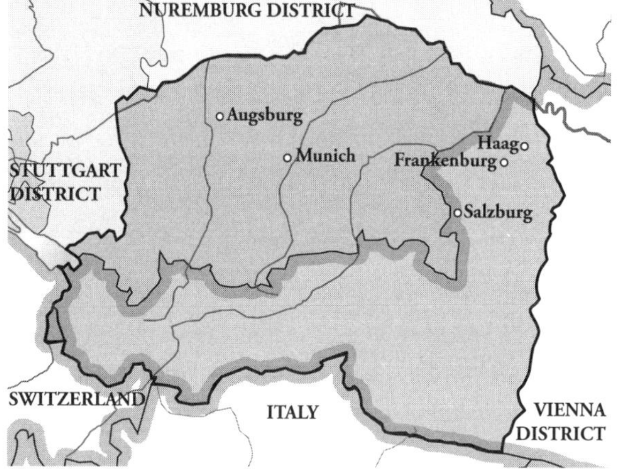

Fig. 1. The Munich District included all of western Austria since November 1938.

Munich District[1]	**1939**
Elders	22
Priests	22
Teachers	21
Deacons	22
Other Adult Males	62
Adult Females	207
Male Children	25
Female Children	24
Total	405

The leadership of the Munich District was in the very capable hands of Johann Thaller (born 1907), who lived in Solln, a southern suburb of Munich. His work afforded him the convenience of a company automobile and a delivery van that he was allowed to use for private purposes as well. He eagerly seized the opportunity to travel to the five branches in the district as well as to conferences in Nuremberg, Frankfurt, and Stuttgart. According to his son, Edwin (born 1938), "He had his own company and represented another company operating within the state of Bavaria. One was a Lebkuchen company based in Nuremberg, and the other was a soup company based in Frankfurt."[2]

The report of the 1939 spring conference of the Munich District indicates the vitality of the Saints in southern Bavaria. The following is recorded under May 6–7: "All meetings [were] held in the Munich Branch hall that was filled to capacity. Sister Wood [wife of mission president M. Douglas Wood] conducted a dress rehearsal for the [choir] performance of the Munich members in the upcoming mission conference in Frankfurt."[3] At least fifty members of the district made the long journey by rail to Frankfurt in late May to participate in what was probably the largest mission conference held to date.

Members and missionaries alike would later tell of being transported from place to place in one of Elder Thaller's vehicles. Such transportation was indeed a rare facet of life among the Latter-day Saints in Germany in 1939. According to his son Werner (born 1939), "My dad used to have a delivery truck. I imagine that it was an Opel, and he used to haul people around all the time. He used to put people in the back and put a couple wooden benches in, and people would sit facing each other just like you're riding in an old train with wooden benches."

Fig. 2. District president Johann Thaller in the uniform of a medic. (W. Thaller)

Werner described his father's personality traits in these words:

> Many times he would roll the carpet back in the house and put a record on, and [he and Mom] would dance. He had a good sense of humor. I don't know of anyone who didn't like Dad. He made friends easily. He loved his kids and his wife. He loved to work. He loved the gospel. He would read the scriptures on a regular basis. He knew the gospel well. He loved the Lord. He had daily prayers with his family—family prayer, individual prayers. [He was] always active in the Church and did whatever he could to further the kingdom.

Johann Thaller was in many respects a remarkable man. As a traveling businessman, he sought opportunities to visit the Saints everywhere he went. His name shows up in the general minutes of the Haag and Frankenburg Branches and at conferences in the mission home. He enjoyed the confidence of the mission leadership, as is evident from the fact that he was asked in 1943 to perform the duties of first counselor to mission supervisor Anton Huck.

Elder Thaller was drafted into the German army and served on reserve duty in the Munich area. He was trained as a medic to work with doctors at an army hospital and was never required to report for active duty in the Wehrmacht. Toward the end of the war, he was assigned to medic duties in downtown Munich. According to his son Werner, he received a draft notice in the last months of the war, but a compassionate soldier volunteered to serve in his stead. That would have been a rare occurrence in Germany during the war. The volunteer was not seen again.

Thanks to Josef Grob, President Thaller was not alone in directing the affairs of the Munich District. Elder Grob was an employee of the national railway system and was stationed for several years in Innsbruck, Austria. He was able to take the train north to Munich on Sundays to attend church meetings. By the same means, he assisted President Thaller in visiting the distant branches of Haag, Frankenburg, and Linz (in the Vienna District) as well as individuals and families living near Wels, Austria.[4]

Fig. 3. Johann Thaller (left) served after the war in the North German Mission. He is shown here with young Otto Förster of Frankfurt, also a husband and father. (O. Förster)

The stress of serving as a district president in the Church would be difficult for any man in any country, but Johann Thaller carried out his duties in addition to representing two large food companies. His son Edwin described the situation in these words: "My father was very busy taking care of the two businesses in [his sales territory] and on top of that being the district president and having to visit six or seven branches regularly. He was gone during the week for business and gone on weekends for church [visits]. We rarely saw him."

Shortly after the war ended, Johann Thaller was called to leave his wife and his five children and serve on a full-time basis in the North German Mission. As those who knew him would expect, he answered that call and served an honorable mission.

Notes

1. Presiding Bishopric, "Financial, Statistical, and Historical Reports of Wards, Stakes, and Missions, 1884–1955," 257, CHL CR 4 12.
2. Edwin Thaller, telephone interview with the author, February 10, 2009.
3. West German Mission quarterly reports, 1939, no. 19, CHL LR 10045 2.
4. Helga Seeber, "Werden und Wirken der Mormonen in München" (unpublished, 1977).

Augsburg Branch

Augsburg is located just twenty-five miles west of Munich. Situated on the banks of the Lech River, it was an important Protestant city in an intensely Catholic region of the former kingdom of Bavaria. As World War II approached an unwitting populace in the late summer of 1939, the city had 180,039 inhabitants, of whom fifty-seven were members of the LDS Church. They met in rooms rented at Liebig Platz next to the Emelka Theater, according to the mission directory.[1] The meeting schedule was similar to other LDS branches in Germany, with Sunday School beginning at 10:00 a.m. and sacrament meeting at 7:00 p.m. The auxiliary organizations that existed held their meetings on Wednesday evenings—MIA at 7:45 and Relief Society at 9:00. The priesthood holders met at the same time as the Relief Society, as well as on the first Sunday of each month at 11:30 a.m. With only three children of record, there was no Primary organization at the time.

The leader of the Augsburg Branch in July 1939 was an American missionary, Stanford Poulson. His first counselor was a local member, Otto Wintermayr. Elder Poulson's mission companion at the time was Erich W. Bauer, apparently a native of Germany, who was serving as the second counselor. It is not known as of this writing whether Brother Wintermayr was designated as branch president when Elder Poulson left Germany on August 26 or whether Elder Bauer left Augsburg as well.

Augsburg Branch[2]	**1939**
Elders	1
Priests	3
Teachers	2
Deacons	4
Other Adult Males	14
Adult Females	30
Male Children	2
Female Children	1
Total	57

The city of Augsburg attracted the attention of the Allied air forces. At least 1,499 persons are known to have lost their lives in attacks on the city, while an additional 9,500 Augsburg men perished in fighting away from home. On April 28, 1945, the US Seventh Army entered the city with no resistance. The conquerors found that at least 25 percent of the city's dwellings had been destroyed. Experts evaluated the losses at 155,000,000 Reichsmark.[3] Several members of the Augsburg Branch disappeared during the air raids and were never seen again.

As of this writing, no eyewitness testimonies or reports could be located to describe the life of the Latter-day Saints in Augsburg from 1939 to 1945. It is known only that the branch was still functioning when the war ended, though a substantial percentage of the membership had died or were killed by 1945.

In Memoriam

The following members of the Augsburg Branch did not survive World War II:

August Anhalt b. Wittislingen, Schwaben, Bayern, 9 Sep 1923; adopted son of Friedrich Josef Anhalt and Sofie Ackermann; bp. 3 Aug 1935; conf. 3 Aug 1935; navy; corporal; k. in battle 21 or 26 Dec 1942 or 1943 (CR Augsburg Branch, FHL microfilm 68783, no. 3; CHL CR 375 8 2445, no. 725; www.volksbund.de; IGI)

Erich Willy Bauer b. Zschornewitz, Bitterfeld, Sachsen, 24 Jun 1919; son of Robert Alfred Bauer and Marie Sofie Wassmuss; bp. 30 Jun 1927; conf. 3 Jul 1927; ord. deacon 26 Aug 1934; ord. priest 27 Mar 1938; ord. elder 19 Mar 1939; m. 21 Aug 1943, Adina Blechschmidt; corporal; d. wounds field hospital at Brest-Litowsk, Belarus, 23 or 28 Oct 1943 (no. 61; CHL CR 375 8 2445, no. 926; FHL microfilm 25719, 1925 and 1930 censuses; www.volksbund.de; IGI)

Lydia Heck b. Hohengehren, Jagstkreis, Württemberg, 30 Jan 1892; dau. of Christian Heck and Karoline Wolf; bp. 23 Jan 1925; conf. 23 Jan 1925; m. Friedrich Alwin Queitsch; missing as of 20 Jul 1946 (CHL CR 375 8 2445, no. 347; FHL microfilm 271398, 1925 and 1935 censuses)

Herbert Heinhaus b. Barmen, Jülich, Rheinprovinz, 5 Aug 1914; son of Walter Heinhaus and Klara Gutjahr; bp. 14 May 1938; conf. 14 May 1938; ord. deacon 18 Dec 1938; m. 7 Sep 1939 Anni Wein; k. in battle Ukraine 14 Sep 1941 (no. 55; CHL CR 375 8 2445, no. 765; IGI)

Helga Elisabeth Heinhaus b. Augsburg, Augsburg, Bayern, 23 Aug 1941; dau. of Herbert Heinhaus and Anni Wein; missing as of 20 Jul 1946 (CHL CR 375 8 2445, no. 955)

Wolfgang Herbert Heinhaus b. Augsburg, Augsburg, Bayern, 13 Mar 1940; son of Herbert Heinhaus and Anni Wein; missing as of 20 Jul 1946 (CHL CR 375 8 2445, no. 932)

Xaver Franz Klughammer b. Göggingen, Augsburg, Bayern, 11 Nov 1905; son of Anselm Männer or Menner and Philomina Häring; bp. 6 Apr 1928; conf. 6 Apr 1928; d. neurological disease 7 Feb 1945 (no. 11; CHL CR 375 8 2445, no. 517; FHL microfilm 271380, 1930 and 1935 censuses)

Ludwig Josef Lang b. München, München, Bayern, 4 Jun 1917; son of Ludwig Janner and Rosa Marie Theresia Lang; bp. 25 Sep 1930; conf. 25 Sep 1930; ord. deacon 2 Oct 1932; m. 3 or 6 or 10 Feb 1940, Kreszentia Senkmajer; corporal; k. in battle Jabokrok, Russia, 21 Apr 1944; bur. Potelitsch, Ukraine (no. 13; KGF; CHL CR 375 8 2445, no. 654; www.volksbund.de; IGI)

Franz Xaver Lutz b. Augsburg, Augsburg, Bayern, 20 Oct 1926; son of Georg Lutz and Kreszentia Hehl/Kehl; bp. 22 Jun 1937; conf. 22 Jun 1937; missing as of 20 Jul 1946 (CHL CR 375 8 2445, no. 750)

Erich Queitsch b. Esslingen, Württemberg, 2 Jan 1915; son of Friedrich Queitsch and Karoline Leiss; bp. 23 Jan 1925; conf. 23 Jan 1925; missing as of 20 Jul 1946 (CHL CR 375 8 2445, no. 343; FHL microfilm 271398, 1925 and 1935 censuses)

Friedrich Alwin Queitsch b. Filtan, Sachsen, 3 Mar 1883; son of August Karl Queitsch and Pauline Kirsten; bp. 23 Jan 1925; conf. 23 Jan 1925; missing as of 20 Jul 1946 (CHL CR 375 8 2445, no. 344; FHL microfilm 271398, 1925 and 1935 censuses)

Fritz Queitsch b. Esslingen, Neckarkreis, Württemberg, 28 Dec 1909; son of Friedrich Queitsch and Karoline Leiss; bp. 23 Jan 1925; conf. 23 Jan 1925; missing as of 20 Jul 1946 (CHL CR 375 8 2445, no. 345; FHL microfilm 271398, 1925 and 1935 censuses)

Otto Karl Queitsch b. Esslingen, Neckarkreis, Württemberg, 6 Aug 1911; son of Friedrich Queitsch and Karoline Leiss; bp. 23 Jan 1925; conf. 23 Jan 1925; missing as of 20 Jul 1946 (CHL CR 375 8 2445, no. 348; FHL microfilm 271398, 1925 and 1935 censuses)

Willy Paul Queitsch b. Esslingen, Neckarkreis, Württemberg, 4 May 1913; son of Friedrich Queitsch and Karoline Leiss; bp. 23 Jan 1925; conf. 23 Jan 1925; missing as of 20 Jul 1946 (CHL CR 375 8 2445, no. 350; FHL microfilm 271398, 1925 and 1935 censuses)

Mina Richter b. Augsburg, Augsburg, Bayern, 2 Sep 1876; dau. of August Richter and Pauline Östreicher; bp. 1 Aug 1937; conf. 1 Aug 1937; m. Johann Seidel; d. 3 Mar 1944 (no. 36)

Christine Schramm b. Augsburg, Augsburg, Bayern, 5 Aug 1890; dau. of Matthias Schramm and Walburga Vaumann; bp. 1 Nov 1930; conf. 1 Nov 1930; m. —— Braun; d. lung ailment 22 Sep 1940 (CHL CR 375 8 2445, no. 644; IGI)

Elise Emilie Schreitmüller b. Bertenbreit, Kaishaim, Bayern, 15 Jun 1923; dau. of Johann Schreitmüller and Emilie Wörnle; bp. 5 Nov 1933; conf. 5 Nov 1933; d. stomach operation 9 Aug 1940 (CHL microfilm 2447, pt. 26, no. 652; FHL microfilm 245258, 1930 census; IGI)

Beno Senkmayer b. Augsburg, Augsburg, Bayern, 11 Jun 1913; son of Emilian Senkmayer and Kreszintia Hoermann; bp. 1 Sep 1929; conf. 1 Sep 1929; m. 1 Jun 1940, Maria Durner; MIA near Iwan See or Naswa Fluss or Pakalowo or Tschernosem 1 Jun 1944 (CHL CR 375 8 2445, no. 623; FHL microfilm 245261, 1935 census; www.volksbund.de)

Joseph Spendler b. München, München, Bayern, 1 May 1900; son of Maria Spendler; bp. 3 Mar 1914; conf. 3 May 1914; m. 5 Sep 1931, Karolina ——; missing as of 20 Jul 1946 (CHL CR 375 8 2445, no. 711; FHL microfilm 245272, 1935 census)

Kreszenzia Wolf b. Augsburg, Ausgburg, Bayern, 12 Apr 1913; dau. of Josef Wolf and Viktoria Mayer; bp. 20 Jan 1929; conf. 20 Jan 1929; m. Nov 1934, Artur Hatmann; missing as of 20 May 1943 (CHL CR 375 8 2445, no. 588)

Elisabeth Agatha Zoller b. Augsburg, Augsburg, Bayern, 12 May 1943; dau. of Hans Zoller and Sophie Kerner; bl. 6 Jun 1943; d. croup 18 Aug 1943 (no. 73; CHL CR 375 8 2445, no. 982; IGI)

Notes

1. West German Mission branch directory, 1939, CHL LR 10045 11.
2. Presiding Bishopric, "Financial, Statistical, and Historical Reports of Wards, Stakes, and Missions, 1884–1955," 257, CHL CR 4 12.
3. Augsburg city archive.

Frankenburg Branch

The town of Frankenburg is located deep in the hills of the state of Upper Austria—as the crow flies, twelve miles southwest of Haag am Hausruck and thirty miles northeast of Salzburg. With a population of less than a thousand inhabitants when World War II approached, it was an unexpected venue for a branch of The Church of Jesus Christ of Latter-day Saints.

The mission directory for the branch in Frankenburg shows only a few offices assigned. Mathias Steindl was the branch president when the war began. The only other surnames that appear in the branch directory in 1939 are Altmann and Brückl. The meetings at the time were held in the Steindl apartment in house no. 61. According to branch meeting minutes of the war years, other members of the branch belonged to the Limberger and Schachl families.

The faithful Saints in Frankenburg were physically isolated but by no means forgotten. The branch meeting minutes show a great number of visitors coming and going from 1938 to 1940 when the records end. West German Mission president M. Douglas Wood and his wife were there in 1938, as was Vienna District president Georg Schick. After the branch was transferred to the Munich District, president Johann Thaller came for visits on at least five occasions. Presidents Franz Rosner and Rudolf Niedermair of the Haag and Linz Branches (respectively) also came, as did Georg Mühlbacher, president of the branch in Salzburg. Those visits were not made without sacrifice, however, because public transportation from the major cities to Frankenburg was not at all convenient. One of the last reported visits was by Anton Huck, first counselor to the mission supervisor in Frankfurt.[1]

Frankenburg Branch[2]	**1939**
Elders	0
Priests	1
Teachers	1
Deacons	0
Other Adult Males	2
Adult Females	9
Male Children	1
Female Children	1
Total	15

Because the branch was in a rural setting, communications were slightly slower. Thus American missionaries Nephi Henry Duersch and Robert J. Gillespie were probably the last to hear of the evacuation of foreign missionaries from all of Germany and Austria one week before the war began. Returning to their apartment in Frankenburg from a lengthy bicycle tour in Haag and towns along the route, they found the telegram instructing them to leave on August 25. It was already September 2. They immediately left, taking a train first to Germany and then crossing the border south into neutral Switzerland.[3]

Fig. 1. Church leaders attending the dedication of the branch meeting rooms in 1938. Left to right: Joseph Grob, Georg Schick, Thomas E. McKay, Horace G. Moser, and Rao K. Parker. (G. Koerbler Greenmun)

"They gave me a bicycle," recalled Auguste (Gusti) Steindl (born 1928), "It was sad because we were very close to the missionaries. We didn't have much [money] before the war, but we invited them for dinner. . . . It was a very nice time."[4] Gusti had the following to say about her father, the branch president: "We read the Bible and the Book of Mormon, and my father was very strict about the Sabbath day. Oh my, I remember one time, my cousins came from the city, and they wanted to take me to a movie [one Sunday]. Oh, no! Those cousins didn't talk to him for a long time after that."

When the war broke out in September 1939, the branch in Frankenburg felt its effects immediately. President Steindl was drafted but for a time was close enough to home to remain the leader of the congregation. In September, he purchased house no. 62 and moved his family in. Following "tremendous work" by the members, a storage room in the house became the meeting place. Soon thereafter, Brother Steindl was quoted as stating that "the branch has endured [difficulties] since 1937, but that the Lord has helped us to overcome all of those difficulties."[5] Branch records show a total attendance at meetings during 1939 as 2,624, yielding an average attendance of fifteen persons at the 174 meetings.[6]

During the first month of the war, the sacrament meeting time was changed to 4:00 p.m. to accommodate the blackout regulations. The clerk kept very detailed records in those days, noting the names of speakers and their topics. The minutes of the Sunday School include the term *Klassentrennung*, meaning that the Saints separated into at least two groups for instruction.

The Frankenburg Branch was increased in size substantially by the arrival of the family of Franz Dittrich from nearby Haag in 1940. Margaretha Dittrich (born 1931) recalled the following about her father's employment: "When we moved to Frankenburg in 1940, my father started working as a streetworker. He cleaned the streets, and that was difficult for him to do that work because he knew that he could do better. He never found work as a baker again."[7] She also described the branch meeting rooms in Frankenburg:

> We met in house no. 61 near the market square. We only had one room on the first floor. The Steindl family had their apartment in the same building. During the week, we also held Primary. We had benches and a pump organ. There were also pictures that we hung up. One of them was a picture of Jesus Christ on his knees praying in the Garden of Gethsemane. It was quite large. All of our neighbors knew that we were members of the Church and it did not matter to them.

Young Hildegard Dittrich (born 1927) was naturally worried about changing schools and leaving her dear friends in the Haag Branch.[8] She finished her public school experience in 1941 and was soon called upon to serve her Pflichtjahr on a farm in support of the national war effort. This service interfered with her plans to become a secretary.

After communications between the Saints in Europe and Church headquarters in Salt Lake City were interrupted in December 1941, the office of the West German Mission in Frankfurt was hard pressed to supply the branches with instruction manuals for Church programs. Hildegard recalled that her father "had to copy lessons for Sunday School out of very old Church books or Church magazines." This did not last for long, however, because in the spring of 1942, Franz Dittrich (a veteran of World War I) was drafted into the Wehrmacht and assigned to work as a radio operator in the police office in Linz, forty miles to the east. He would remain there until the end of the war.

The records of the branch for the years 1940–41 include a discouraging note: apparently one of the women accused another of endangering her marriage. The accused demanded a retraction of the charge. The unidentified branch clerk added a note to the effect that he and his wife did not feel the Spirit of the Lord when entering the second sister's house. The negative feelings were mentioned again on April 24, 1940. Months later, in January 1941, Anton Schindler (born 1873), a veteran member of the Church from Munich, came with Franz Rosner of Haag "to help resolve differences in the branch . . . but left town without having achieved success in the conflict." By May 3, 1941, the matter was resolved and a "nice spirit" prevailed.[9]

Following her Pflichtjahr, Hildegard Dittrich was pleased to find employment in the post office in Frankenburg. After work and on weekends, she was very busy with Church callings. Despite her age (she was only sixteen at the time), she served simultaneously as a Primary teacher, chorister or organist (on a pump organ), and Relief Society secretary and treasurer.

Hildegard later wrote that even though her father was away from home, the family had just enough to eat during the war years, but food was by no means easy to come by:

> Every day very, very early in the morning, my sister Grete would go to the store and bakery and stand in line for a few hours so she could buy a loaf of bread for us or some sugar or flour or anything edible. Most of the time the bread in the store was already gone before she got to the counter, and so it was with everything else, and that went on for lots of days.

Along with her schoolmates, Margaretha Dittrich was inducted into the Jungvolk in 1941 at age ten. She described the experience in these words:

> We had to attend the meetings, if we wanted or not, but we did not believe in it. We had church on Sunday mornings, so I did not go to the Jungvolk meetings. The leaders were angry and asked me at school where I had been. My parents were cautious and did not say anything about it. I had to justify why I missed the meetings. But I was always the black sheep anyway because of my religion, so it did not really matter. Later, I was a member of the League of German Girls. We got a brown jacket and had to know how to tie the knot a certain way. I burnt it after the war was over.

Fig. 2. The family of Franz and Margaretha Dittrich was baptized in late 1939. As Margaretha recalled, "It took place in Haag in the public pool. After the meeting on Sunday, we walked to the pool. But we had told the owner of the pool that we would come, so he let us be there alone. I was not the only one being baptized that day."[10]

For young Margaretha, the political situation under Hitler's Third Reich was not particularly impressive: "There were some members of the party in our branch but we did not talk about [politics] in church. And I never heard anybody pray for Hitler, but we prayed for the safety of all the soldiers."

Although at first it seemed to Hildegard and her family that Germany would win the war, conditions changed, and it was clear that Hitler's Third Reich was in trouble. In the last years of the war, Allied bombers came within range of Austrian cities, and they were bombed despite Austria's status as a conquered nation. The Dittrich family covered their windows in response to blackout regulations and wondered if the many airplanes flying overhead would drop their bombs on the village of Frankenburg; fortunately, that never happened. Regarding their survival under the increasingly difficult conditions, Hildegard wrote, "We could do nothing but keep on working and doing our jobs in the branch and at work as good as we could. We prayed every day very hard to our Heavenly Father for His protection. We knew that He will bless us if we keep His commandments."[11]

In a small town far from the war, life was a bit easier than in more critical locations. According to Gusti Steindl, it was still possible to be a teenager and have fun: "We went to dances sponsored by the Catholic Church. We still had parties, games, dates. Things just sort of went on as before. We were fortunate to be in such a quiet area."

When all of the local priesthood holders were absent from Frankenburg, Heinz Jankowsky was assigned to visit the Frankenburg Branch and to administer the sacrament there. There was no cessation of worship services in the small branch during the war. The branch meeting minutes continued without interruption through the end of the war as if nothing out of the ordinary were happening. It is clear that the Saints were doing all that they could to maintain the Church in Frankenburg. The Relief Society records were also duly kept from 1940 to 1945 and state at the end of 1943, "The sisters set a goal to carry out their duties with greater dedication in the coming year." Sunday School attendance was often less than ten persons, but the Primary reported attendance of from seven to thirteen children during the years 1940–41.[12]

According to Margaretha Dittrich, there was little danger to the residents of Frankenburg during the war: "We had some low flying planes [toward the end] but they didn't damage anything. A real attack never happened in Frankenburg. But whenever we heard an alarm, we did go into a basement near our home to make sure we were safe."

For Gusti Steindl, those fighter planes (*Tiefflieger* in German) represented a real danger: "[My mother] used to go in the morning to the farmers and collect the eggs. And one time when she was coming home, there was some airplanes flying over, and they started shooting at her. But that was the only time. Otherwise, I don't remember anything really dangerous happening."

By some quirk of fate, Franz Dittrich was able to negotiate the forty miles from the city offices of Linz to his home in Frankenburg amid the confusion of the last days of the war. The enemy did not take him prisoner. According to Margaretha, "My father was already home when [the invaders] came."

Fig. 3. Franz Dittrich (left) served as a radio operator in Linz for the last few years of the war.

In April 1945, the American army moved through Upper Austria. The invaders met little or no opposition and found no reason to disturb the residents, but they did use Frankenburg schools for their housing. As in many areas of western Germany and Austria, the residents saw black men for the first time. As Margaretha recalled, "When we saw the black people for the first time, we were scared. . . . But then we were told that they were good people, and then we trusted them. We got chocolate from them."

"We didn't hang out a [white] flag; everybody welcomed [the conquerors]," recalled Gusti Steindl. "We even had three or four soldiers in our home and they were very nice. My mother gave up the bedroom and the living room. . . . But some people were beaten by the Americans. I remember there was an old lady in a big restaurant, and they really whipped her. But one [soldier] protected us [from searches and drunkards]. And he brought us food—meat and sugar and stuff like that."

By the end of the summer, all of Austria had been organized into four military occupation zones under American, British, French, and Soviet forces. During the transition, Hildegard Dittrich lost her job in Frankenburg and was sent to the post office in Salzburg. Afraid of the many soldiers in that big city, she asked to be released from her employment and was allowed to return home, where she found her father safe and sound. He had avoided becoming a POW, returned home safely, and had been assigned to lead the branch.

Among the occupying forces were several members of the LDS Church who soon located the branch meeting rooms and joined the local Saints in their meetings. They also brought food to share with their new friends. With peace restored, the branch in Frankenburg had survived, and the future looked difficult but bright.

No members of the Frankenburg Branch are known to have died during World War II.

Notes

1. Frankenburg Branch general minutes, CHL LR 11253 11.
2. Presiding Bishopric, "Financial, Statistical, and Historical Reports of Wards, Stakes, and Missions, 1884–1955," 721, CR 4 12.
3. Terry Bohle Mantague, *Mine Angels Round About*, 2nd ed. (Orem, UT: Granite, 2000), 101–02.
4. Auguste Steindl Rosner, interview by the author, South Jordan, Utah, March 2, 2007.
5. Frankenburg Branch general minutes, 78.
6. Ibid., 90.
7. Margaretha Dittrich Schauperl, interview by the author in German, Frankenburg, Austria, August 7, 2008; summarized in English by Judith Sartowski.
8. Hildegard Dittrich Cziep, autobiography (unpublished); private collection.
9. Frankenburg Branch general minutes, 128–29, 139, 158.
10. Margaretha Dittrich Schauperl, interview by the author in German in Frankenburg, Austria, on August 7, 2008; summarized in English by Judith Sartowski. Cziep, autobiography.
11. Cziep, autobiography.
12. Frankenburg Branch Primary Association minutes and records.

Haag am Hausruck Branch

In the history of The Church of Jesus Christ of Latter-day Saints in Austria, the branch in the small town of Haag am Hausruck plays a unique and significant role. Founded largely upon the missionary efforts of Johann Huber just after the turn of the century, the branch grew steadily to become the second largest in Austria when the momentous events of 1938 and 1939 occurred.

Haag am Hausruck Branch[1]	**1939**
Elders	3
Priests	2
Teachers	1
Deacons	3
Other Adult Males	6
Adult Females	27
Male Children	5
Female Children	7
Total	54

According to his granddaughter Theresia Rosner (born 1923), Johann Huber was converted through a friend who had immigrated to the United States.[2] The friend became acquainted with the Church there and then returned to Austria and showed some Church literature to Johann Huber. Brother Huber was baptized in Munich on April 27, 1900, and soon returned to Haag to share the message of the gospel with his family and friends.[3] It is said that he led thirteen families into the Church in the vicinity of Haag.

The Huber farm (German: *Hof Huber* or *Huberhof*) is located just outside of the village of Rottenbach, two miles northeast of Haag, and is still owned by the descendants of Johann Huber. The farm played an important role in the lives of many Huber descendants and other members of the Church in Austria and Germany.

Fig. 1. In the Rosner home in March 1938. From left: Theresia Rosner, Theresia Huber Rosner, Franz Rosner, missionaries Clark Hillam and George Gould. (C. Hillam)

Fig. 2. The charming main street of Haag am Hausruck as it looked during the war. (E. Cziep Collette)

The family of branch president Franz Rosner lived in a building along the main highway leading into Haag from the north. Their address was Kirchegasse 6. Brother Rosner later purchased house no. 7 next door and constructed a room to be used as the branch chapel. Daughter Theresia recalled that the room could accommodate forty persons. "We often had visitors from other branches, too," she stated. The meeting room was outfitted with a pump organ but was otherwise quite spartan in its appearance. Sunday School was held in the morning and sacrament meeting in the evening, with auxiliary meetings taking place during the week. Margaretha Dittrich (born 1931) recalled:

> There was also a small podium in the room. We had a picture of Joseph Smith behind the podium. There must have been about twenty people who attended the meetings. Sunday School started at 9 a.m. and at 5 p.m.; we all came back to hold sacrament meeting. . . . We did not have a sign at the side of the building saying that we met there. There were too many Catholics in our area, and if they had known, they would have [persecuted] us more than they already did.[4]

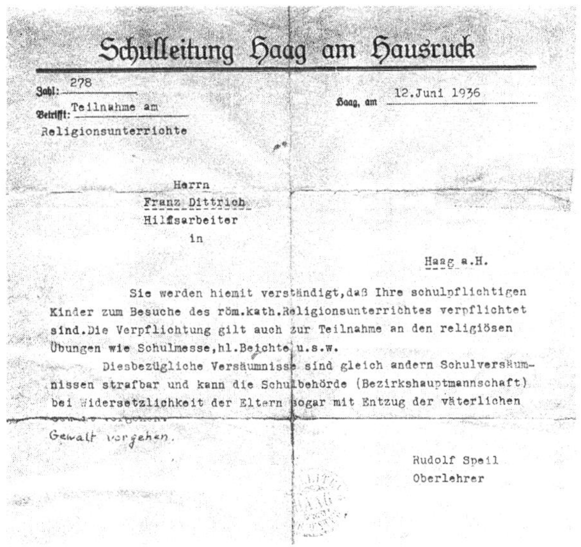

Schulleitung Haag am Hausruck

Zahl: 278
Betrifft: Teilnahme am Religionsunterrichte

Haag, am 12.Juni 1936

Herrn
Franz Dittrich
Hilfsarbeiter
in
Haag a.H.

Sie werden hiemit verständigt, daß Ihre schulpflichtigen Kinder zum Besuche des röm.kath.Religionsunterrichtes verpflichtet sind. Die Verpflichtung gilt auch zur Teilnahme an den religiösen Übungen wie Schulmesse, hl.Beichte u.s.w.

Diesbezügliche Versäumnisse sind gleich andern Schulversäumnissen strafbar und kann die Schulbehörde (Bezirkshauptmannschaft) bei Widersetzlichkeit der Eltern sogar mit Entzug der väterlichen Gewalt vorgehen.

Rudolf Speil
Oberlehrer

Fig. 3. Franz Dittrich received this stern warning from the principal of the local school regarding the required participation of his children in Catholic instruction. (H. Rosner)

Branch member Theresia Rosner said, "Our branch had a very wonderful climate; we knew each other very well, and support was always needed and given." Perhaps the need for support was a result of the fact that those few Saints were living in an otherwise entirely Catholic rural community of 1,819 residents.[5] Before the war, Brother Rosner was accused of keeping his children from attending Catholic religion classes in school but was able to defend himself in court against that charge. Neighbors were not very tolerant when it came to having a "sect" holding meetings in a local residential structure such as Kirchgasse 7, and they sought ways to make the Rosner family's life difficult.[6]

Fig. 4. The sisters of the Haag and Frankenburg branches enjoy a bicycle tour. (T. Rosner Thill)

Immediately after joining the Church in 1935, Franz Dittrich had difficulties similar to those of Franz Rosner. One year later, Brother Dittrich received a letter from the local school authority reminding him that the law required him to send his children to Catholic instruction in school, as well as to the Catholic Church for school-related events. The letter threatened that his children could be taken from their home in the case of noncompliance. Soon after this dispute, Franz Dittrich lost his employment as a master baker.

After the Anschluss (Austrian annexation) in March 1938, life under Germany's swastika flag changed very quickly for the Dittrich family. Young Hildegard was substantially underweight and thus sent off to Germany to a children's convalescent home for six weeks. She did not gain weight there. Four months after returning home, she was sent away again, this time to the Heinisch family in Westphalia for one month. As she recalled, "I had a great time with that family, lots of food and fun. [But] they belonged to the Lutheran Church and I had to go with them to their church. . . . My parents were glad to see me come home and I was glad to be home with my family and that I could go to church and Primary again."[7]

Fig. 5. The Rosner house at Kirchgasse 6 as seen from behind in about 1942. (T. Thill)

Fig. 6. A festive dinner in the Haag branch. (T. Thill)

Unfortunately, the Dittrich family suffered two tragedies in less than a year: daughter Ernstine died in November 1939 and her brother, Franz Xaver, followed in July 1940. According to Hildegard, "My parents were very glad and thankful that they had the gospel which gave them the strength to overcome all these trying times." By October 1939, Franz Dittrich had found new employment in Frankenburg, and the family moved to that small town the next year.[8]

Despite the problems of being LDS in a Catholic town, Theresia Rosner felt very much at home in her Hitler Youth group, the meetings of which did not interfere with her attendance at church meetings. At the age of seventeen, she was assigned to work in the home of a family in Munich under the Pflichtjahr program. She was already acquainted somewhat with the city and the branch there, having taken the long bus ride with her family on several occasions to attend district conferences there.

Fig. 7. Members of the Haag Branch next to the meetinghouse in 1943. (T. Thill)

While in Munich, Theresia was given time off to attend meetings of the Munich Branch at Kapuzinerstrasse 18. The Weiss family of that branch saw to it that she had a way to church. At the completion of her year, she returned home and sought work nearby. The employment office found her a position with a family in the town of Ried, only ten miles west of her home in Haag. While in Ried, Theresia received word that her grandpa Huber had passed away in late November 1941. Just a few weeks later, her brother, Wilhelm, died of meningitis at the age of nine. Franz Rosner then asked his daughter to come home to fill the void in the family, and she did.

Fig. 8. These members of the Haag Branch traveled to Munich for a district conference. (T. Thill)

The condition of the branch during the war was described by the former branch president Franz Rosner and his wife, Leopoldine, in an interview in 1974: "We had about fifty to sixty members at the time. All of the young men were gone [in the military], but there were older priesthood holders at home the whole time. There were no Nazi Party members in our branch that [we] can recall. We were very fortunate in that none of our branch members died [as a result of] the war."[9]

There were no air raids over Haag, and no battles took place when the Americans moved through the area in April 1945, but Theresia recalled enemy fighter planes cruising by at very low levels to shoot at people in the area. No members of the Church lost their homes. "We had no interruptions in our branch meetings all through the war. As for me, my life was never in danger," she recalled.

In wartime, the Huberhof continued to be a gathering place for family members and other Latter-day Saints. In 1941, Albert Göckeritz, president of the Chemnitz District of the East German Mission, spent ten days with the Rosner family for a much-needed vacation.[10] At the end of the war, Gertrud Hoppe, widow of the Breslau District president, sought refuge at the Huberhof with her children and stayed for four years.[11]

Fig. 9. Even in wartime, children knew how to amuse themselves. (T. Thill)

After the war ended, the absent members of the branch in Haag am Hausruck gradually returned to their homes and carried on their lives as Latter-day Saints, anxiously awaiting the day when they would have their own church building and real freedom from religious persecution.

One of the first postwar events in the Haag Branch was the baptism of a convert from Breslau, Silesia (East German Mission)—former Wehrmacht soldier Paul Gildner. He and Hanni Goetzeberger were driven by an American soldier in a jeep from Salzburg to Haag for their baptism. The driver was stopped en route at an American checkpoint and asked the identity of the Germans he was transporting. He answered that they were "Nazi swine" whom he was taking in for questioning. They were allowed to pass and reached Haag safely.[12]

In Memoriam

The following members of the Haag Branch did not survive World War II:

Ernestine Dietrich b. Ebensee, Oberösterreich, Austria, 1922; d. disease Haag Am Hausruck, Wels,

Oberösterreich, Austria, 7 Nov 1939 (Dietrich-Cziep; *Der Stern* 1 Jan 1940, no. 1, 15)

Franz Xaver Sebastian Dittrich b. Ebensee, Gmund, Oberbayern, Bayern, 25 Sep 1925; son of Franz Xaver Dittrich and Maria Gaigg; bp. 19 Nov 1939; conf. 19 Nov 1939; d. tuberculosis Haag am Hausruck, Oberösterreich, Austria 6 July 1940 (Dietrich-Cziep; CHL CR 375 8 2445, no. 920; IGI)

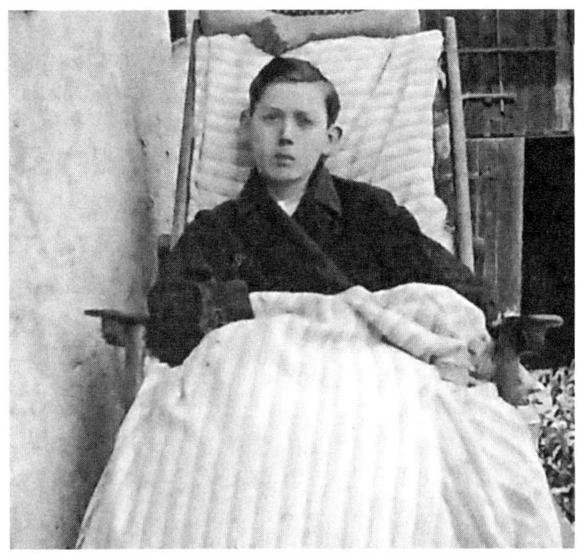

Fig. 10. Franz Xaver Sebastian Dittrich in 1939.

Maria Gransgruber b. Haag am Hausruck, Grieskirchen, 21 Jan 1878; dau. of Karl Gransgruber and Aloisa Schnitzinger; bp. 6 Aug 1939; conf. 6 Aug 1939; m. 24 Apr 1928, Johann Haslinger; d. heart ailment 3 Jan 1945 (CHL CR 375 8 2445, no. 912)

Johann Huber b. Rottenbach, Grieskirchen, Oberösterreich, Austria, 4 Mar 1861; son of Peter Huber and Franziska Polz; m. Rottenbach 11 Nov 1890, Theresia Mayer; 12 children; 2 m. Rottenbach 4 Aug 1910, Anna Bertha Köhler; 2 children; d. diphtheria Rottenbach 30 Sep or Nov 1941 (K. Hirschmann; FHL microfilm 162791, 1925 and 1935 censuses; PRF, AF)

Jörg Jankowsky b. Haag am Hausruck, Oberösterreich, Austria, 16 Apr 1942; son of Heinz Jankowsky and Maria Anna Kroiss; d. lung ailment 5 Sep 1942 (CHL CR 375 8 2445, no. 971; AF)

Ferdinand Kussberger b. Haag am Hausruck, Oberösterreich, Austria, 8 Sep 1870; son of Jakob Kussberger and Theresia Klingseis; bp. 21 Feb 1922; conf. 21 Feb 1922; ord. deacon 17 Feb 1924; d. 21 Feb or 13 Dec 1941 (CHL CR 375 8 2445, no. 825; FHL microfilm 271382, 1935 census; IGI)

Wilhelm Franz Rosner b. Haag am Hausruck, Oberösterreich, Austria, 7 Jun 1932; son of Franz Rosner and Theresia Huber; bp. 29 Jun 1940; conf. 29 Jun 1940; d. meningitis 10 Dec 1941 (CHL CR 375 8 2445, no. 837; IGI)

Johann Stuhl b. Frankenburg, Oberösterreich, Austria, 1 Dec 1913; son of Johann Stuhl and Julia or Juliane Pixner; bp. 13 Mar 1938; conf. 13 Mar 1938; m. 18 Apr 1942; k. air raid Wels, Oberösterreich, Austria, 30 May 1944 (CHL CR 375 8 2445, no. 798; IGI)

Notes

1. Presiding Bishopric, "Financial, Statistical, and Historical Reports of Wards, Stakes, and Missions, 1884–1955," 721, CHL CR 4 12.
2. Theresia Rosner Thill, interview by the author in German, Haag am Hausruck, Austria, August 7, 2008; unless otherwise noted, summarized in English by Judith Sartowski.
3. Details of the story were published in the *Deseret News* on August 5, 1978, under the title "Stalwart John Huber," by William G. Hartley.
4. Margaretha Dittrich Schauperl, interview by the author in German, Frankenburg, Austria, August 7, 2008.
5. Haag am Hausruck city archive.
6. Hartley, "Stalwart John Huber."
7. Hildegard Dittrich Cziep, autobiography (unpublished); private collection.
8. See the Frankenburg Branch section for more on the Dittrich family.
9. Franz and Leopoldine Rosner, interviewed by Douglas F. Tobler, Haag am Hausruck, Austria, March 16, 1974, 16–17, CHL MS 1882.
10. Karl Göckeritz, diary (unpublished, 1909–43); private collection.
11. Roger P. Minert, *In Harm's Way: East German Latter-day Saints in World War II* (Provo, UT: Religious Studies Center, Brigham Young University, 2009), 141.
12. Arthur Gustav Paul Gildner, autobiography (unpublished); private collection; used with the kind permission of Ingeborg Neugebauer Gildner of Munich, Germany.

Munich Branch

Titles such as "the Venice of the North" and "the northernmost Italian city" have been applied to Munich because of its architectural beauty and rich cultural heritage. The city has been the capital of Bavaria for hundreds of years. Tracing its beginnings to the end of the nineteenth century, the Church's branch in Munich was large and vibrant at the start of the war, but Saints were rare in this city of 815,212 people. The branch had fifty-nine priesthood holders, and the president, Anton Schindler, had already served in that capacity for more than thirty years.[1]

In 1928, the Munich Branch had found nice rooms to rent for their meetings at Kapuzinerstrasse 18, located about one and one-half miles southwest of the city's center.[2] The building was a Hinterhaus with only one floor, a former workshop. Elisabeth Grill (born 1914) described the setting:

> The rooms were very simple with a small heater in the middle of the main room. One brother always had to come earlier to heat up the rooms and make sure that the smoke would be mostly gone out of the rooms. There was one larger room and a smaller one without a window. It always looked dark. I used that smaller room to teach classes. We had another small classroom. The adult Sunday School class took place in the large room. The rooms were in the back of a building. They always told us to be quiet, to not say anything and to walk quickly and not linger anywhere. The people in the front building did not want to be disturbed by us.[3]

Munich Branch[4]	**1939**
Elders	16
Priests	13
Teachers	16
Deacons	14
Other Adult Males	29
Adult Females	114
Male Children	13
Female Children	13
Total	228

Elisabeth recalled a sign indicating the presence of the Church in that building. She estimated the size of the congregation at sixty to seventy persons on

Fig. 1. Members of the Munich Branch a few years before the war. (M. Behrens)

a typical Sunday. Berta Wolperdinger (born 1922) recalled the green curtains that hung on the rostrum behind the podium as well as a banner with letters cut from gold paper that read in German, "Prove all things; hold fast that which is good."[5] That was later replaced by a rhyming motto reminding the Saints to come to church on time: "*Fünf Minuten vor der Zeit ist des Mormonen Pünktlichkeit*" (Five minutes early is Mormon punctuality). "The children usually sat in the front rows. It was a wonderful atmosphere," Berta recalled. "We had pictures of the prophets on the walls, and the chairs could be moved to the sides of the room for other activities."[6]

Berna Probst (born 1926) recalled that a Brother Mathes changed the sayings on the wall now and then. One of the sayings he displayed was "The Glory of God Is Intelligence." She also remembered that a Brother Westermaier was in charge of the cloak room; with his wooden leg (a reminder of the Great War), he was always in a hurry to keep up with the members as they arrived and handed him their coats.[7]

Fig. 2. American missionaries visiting the Nussbaumer family in late 1938. (C. Hillam)

The counselors to Anton Schindler when the war began were Ludwig Vikari and August Burkart (who also served as Sunday School president). Anton Vikari was the president of the YMMIA and Paula Leypold the president of the YWMIA. Marie Lerchenfeld led the Primary organization and Anna Wienhausen the Relief Society. Rudolf Netting served as the branch genealogical consultant and the Stern subscription coordinator.

Fig. 3. Anton Schindler served for decades as the president of the Munich Branch. (M. Behrens)

As was the case in nearly all German branches, the Sunday School in Munich began at 10:00 a.m. Sacrament meeting began at 7:00 p.m.[8] The Primary met on Mondays at 3:00 p.m., and the Relief Society met that evening at 7:30 p.m. MIA meetings took place on Wednesdays at 8:00 p.m., and the genealogical class met after Sunday School on the first Sunday of the month.

"My parents and I were all baptized on August 20, 1939, in the suburb of Unterhaching in a public pool," recalled Berta Wolperdinger. "We had to pay a fee to enter. The ceremony started at 6:00 a.m. before the public was admitted to the facilities. We were also confirmed that day at the same place." This baptism story reflects conditions all over the West German Mission at the time, since only three branches had a baptismal font in their meetinghouses.

American missionaries participated in that baptismal ceremony, but just six days later, they were gone—evacuated from Germany. Berta recalled that the atmosphere was uneasy even before the missionaries left Munich. "We felt that war was inevitable in 1939, and some bomb shelters had already been prepared."

The Habermann family of the Munich Branch traveled to Sunday church meetings in much the same way as LDS families all over Germany did.

Fig. 4. Berta Wolperdinger (front row, third from left in the overcoat) was baptized just twelve days before the war began. (B. Wolperdinger)

Gustav Habermann (born 1922) provided this description:

> We lived in the Nussbaumstrasse 12. It took us about twenty minutes to walk to church. There was no other transportation available. We got dressed early in the morning and always went to church with our widowed mother. After Sunday School, we walked home and went back later for sacrament meeting. Our neighbors knew that we went to church. It was normal to go to church on Sundays for all of us—Catholics, Protestants, Mormons.[9]

Erna Probst recalled that her parents, Johann and Thekla Probst, were not at all enthusiastic about the Nazi regime under which they lived. She had no interest in the League of German Girls, and her parents supported her in avoiding involvement with the group. The Probsts were concerned that their three sons would become victims of the war. Sister Probst was even bold enough to make negative statements about Hitler in public, but her husband constantly reminded her of the dangers of such talk.

As soon as Thekla Probst heard that war had been declared, she sent her daughter Erna to the store to buy anything she could find. According to Erna:

> She explained that we couldn't know how long the situation would last so we needed to prepare. I then went and got sugar and flour and whatever I thought we would need. It was interesting for me because I didn't understand at all what it meant to be in a war, or why my brothers had to leave to serve in the war and why I, in the end, had to leave also.

Just after the Polish campaign ended victoriously on September 21, 1939, Gustav Habermann decided to join the army. He recalled:

> Before I volunteered for the service, I thought about how I didn't like hearing that whatever Adolf Hitler said, everybody had to obey (*Führer*

befiehlt, wir folgen!). I knew that I would be drafted when I turned twenty-one and I wanted to choose for myself where I was assigned. My goal was to serve in the paratroopers, but I ended up in the air force. I received my basic training in a period of three months and then worked as a technician for airplanes. The basic training was in Flensburg.

Fig. 5. Branch president Anton Schindler lost his dear wife in 1940. In the final war years, resources for such formal death announcements were no longer available. (M. Behrens)

The family of Josef and Philomena Hörner had gone through severe trials even before the war started. A veteran of the Great War, Brother Hörner was a political malcontent and had gained many enemies in high places by the time Hitler came to power. During the Nazi era, the police were constantly on his trail, hoping to find a crime for which he could be tried and imprisoned. To add to his woes, he had an extramarital affair and was excommunicated from the Church.[10] During the 1930s, his family was not seen in church very often, but by the time the war began, Josef was attending meetings again. His son, Georg (born 1926), recalled the pressure his father's activities put on the family, especially Georg's mother:

> When the police came to get him, he would hide in the bushes or in the forest. Then my mother would send my older sister to him with some food. He often came home during the night and we heard our parents talking. But at around 2 a.m., the police would come in and my father had to hide. They would have killed him before our very eyes if they could have. When the police asked us during the night where our father was, we didn't say anything. . . . Often, my father would climb out the window when the police came in, and they would look for him but couldn't find anything. When they were gone, my mother would open the window or knock, and my father was able to come back in again. . . . For us children it was a horrible time seeing our father like that.[11]

In the fall of 1940, Josef Hörner "was tired and in such a bad condition that he no longer cared what happened," according to Georg. He was caught in his home and thrown down the stairs while neighbors watched. Not long thereafter, he was sent to the Mauthausen Concentration Camp near Linz, Austria. Georg's account of his father's demise continued:

> It didn't take long before a letter came saying that my father had died of pneumonia. They also said that if we wanted his ashes, they would send us the urn. We did, but we knew even then that the ashes could have been from many different people. We buried the urn by the grave of my brother Joseph, who had died while a member of the Reichsarbeitsdienst before the war.

The German government believed it necessary to thoroughly indoctrinate every boy and girl, including Rudolf Strebel (born 1931). He had this recollection of the program:

Fig. 6. This Munich Branch photograph was taken at the rear of the main meeting hall. (E. Probst Höhner)

> When I was ten years old, our class was drafted into the Jungvolk. We got the uniform and participated in the activities. We saw it as part of normal schooling but we didn't necessarily like it. We had to run a lot. For me, it wasn't much fun. We marched in the parades but never did anything like camping. They did teach us about Hitler and the National Socialist ideals, but that happened in a non-compulsory manner. We made the commitment right at the beginning that we would never miss a church meeting because of a Jungvolk activity. Sunday was my church day. All other days, I would be available. I never got into trouble because of it.[12]

The meeting rooms at Kapuzinerstrasse 18 were lost relatively early in the war. An air raid in 1941 totally destroyed the building, and the Saints were compelled to seek other meeting venues.[13] Elisabeth Grill recalled meeting for a while on Hebelstrasse and also on Reisingerstrasse. In each location, only one room was available. According to Berta Wolperdinger, "We would find out each Sunday where the meetings would be held the next week."

Elisabeth Grill was an employee of an insurance company that had offices at Goetheplatz in Munich. As the only Latter-day Saint in that office, she was often asked about her faith. The other employees were Catholic and complained about the church tax they paid.[14] They wondered how she could afford to pay tithing on her meager salary. As she recalled:

> They tried to get me to drink coffee and would say that just one drink would not make any difference. But I told them that one drink would also not benefit me at all. Then they quit trying. When we celebrated something like Christmas or birthdays, they were very considerate and would offer me a glass of juice instead of champagne or wine.

Erna Probst recalled what her family knew about the situation of the Jews in Hitler's Germany:

> My father worked at the local railroad station so we always lived close to it. The trains that took people to the concentration camp in Dachau always passed our house. The prisoners had to work in Munich and wore striped suits and hats. My mother would often say that she had to go shopping and would cut some bread and take it with her. She passed the trains and would give the bread to the prisoners. My father was so scared that she would get caught.

Fig. 7. The rostrum at the end of the main meeting room was used on many occasions for theatrical performances. (E. Probst Höhner)

Alfred Gerer (born 1934) was the youngest child of the family of Josef and Barbara Gerer; he watched as his older brothers left for military service. He recalled how his widowed father learned of the death of his son Lorenz at Stalingrad, Russia, in December 1942, when the German Sixth Army was encircled and destroyed:

> A man came to our home with a telegram. My father knew that a telegram could only mean one thing. And that's what it was. It said that my brother Lorenz died in Stalingrad and that his body would remain there. It also told us that they could not send anything back except his medals. The message hit my father very hard. We held a funeral service in the branch with his picture displayed.[15]

As the war dragged on, the building in which Elisabeth Grill's insurance office was housed was damaged and working conditions became challenging: "We also didn't have stairs anymore, but we used a simple ladder to get to the second floor. To heat the rooms, we used a small oven. The broken windows were covered with simple cloths. It was difficult and not very pleasant to work under those circumstances."

Air raids experienced at home were not pleasant either. Elisabeth Grill explained that the public shelter was too far away from the family's apartment and would likely have been full by the time they arrived, so the residents of her building simply went downstairs into their basement. The building suffered damage to windows and doors, but the damage was minor compared to the house across the street, which was totally demolished. "If our building had suffered a direct hit, we wouldn't have survived," she concluded.

Berta Wolperdinger also experienced most air raids in the basement of her home. Her father had built a small house in the suburb of Taufkirchen, six miles south of Munich. Just a few yards from the local railroad station, the house was in danger of being bombed every time the trains were attacked.

"I remember that when our windows burst, we had glass all over our beds," Berta explained.

Political speeches over the radio were daily fare in Germany during the war. Georg Hörner recalled how he watched police officers clear the sidewalks just before a broadcast, so that nobody had an excuse for missing a speech: "Whenever Hitler spoke, we got time off of work and we were required to listen to the radio." Before his arrest, Georg's father had listened to such broadcasts; he had even told Georg that Hitler was not such a bad man but that there were "lots of little Hitlers" around who were bad.

Alfred Gerer of the Munich Branch was certainly not the only boy who did not fully understand why wars are fought, as he recollected: "When the war started, I didn't understand much of it. But for a boy my age, it also had an adventurous aspect." His story continued:

> My father was responsible for all the people in our house during an air raid. He had to make sure that all of us were in the basement or a shelter. He didn't manage to do that with me. I went back outside all the time to watch the American planes drop their "Christmas trees" [illumination flares used to mark bombing targets]. Very close to our home was a factory that produced all kinds of tires [Metzler Gummiwerke]. I knew that the Americans wanted to get that factory. For me, it looked like the finest fireworks. When my father found me, he grabbed me by the ear and dragged me downstairs again.

Alfred was caught between religious loyalties when his widowed father married a Catholic woman. She had no children of her own and did not wish to go to Mass by herself, so she added a few cents to Alfred's allowance to persuade him to go along with her. He wanted the money, and she enjoyed showing off a boy who appeared to be her son.

The family of Anton and Ursula Roggermeier lived in the eastern Munich suburb of Berg am Laim. The area was quite rural in those days and their son, Herbert (born 1936), enjoyed the fact that his mother's parents owned a dairy just a short distance from his home. He went there on his way home from school each day to spend time with his grandparents and a variety of animals. "I came home late sometimes, but my mother always knew where I was," he recalled.[16] Herbert saw very little of his father, who was drafted in 1939. As an artist and interior decorator, Anton Roggermeier was not well suited for combat. Perhaps the Wehrmacht recruiters recognized this, because he was assigned to serve as a fireman at airfields. His son recalled that Anton was stationed in Munich, Vienna, Romania, and France. Fortunately, he was never wounded or otherwise damaged by the experience of military service.

Fig. 8. The Thaller home in the Munich suburb of Solln in about 1940. (W. Thaller)

District president Johann Thaller purchased a home for his family in the southern Munich suburb of Solln. His son Edwin (born 1938) described the setting:

> My father bought a house just outside of Munich in a wealthy area in 1939. (It wasn't a new house.) He hired a maid. The house was large enough to

> have all the members of his family live in it. We also had a double-car garage with a sliding door. We were able to keep our own chickens on a one-half-acre piece of land adjacent to the house. The house was a single family home with four bedrooms and one and one-half bathrooms. We had a living room, a kitchen, a family room, and an office. We had very comfortable living standards as far as everything goes—we had a refrigerator, a telephone, and an electric stove.[17]

Testimonies of eyewitnesses allow the assumption that Elder Thaller was pleased to share his resources and talents with Church members and nonmembers alike. In 1942, he moved his family to the Austrian town of Haag am Hausruck. The LDS branch president there, Franz Rosner, found them a place to stay in the building in which the branch held its meetings. Life in Munich had become very uncertain, and thousands of people were leaving the city. The Thallers moved back into their home in Solln in the last year of the war.

By the middle of 1943, Georg Hörner had left home for northern France. "After that, I didn't have any contact with the Church until after the war." As a Hitler Youth member, he had been trained to use a rifle, but he was not required to use weapons during the war. He spent his first months of service in France, and things were quiet there, but such peaceful conditions would not last long.

According to Rudolf Strebel's recollection:

> We had constant air raids from 1943 to 1945. The Siemens electrical factory was located just about two blocks away from us, which meant that we lived in a targeted area. When an air raid happened, we went downstairs into the basement. It was fortified with the ceiling having extra supports. We also had break-out sections in the walls just in case we needed to climb through into the building next to ours. I remember that a bomb hit the hill in front of our apartment house once and part of the roof came off. But nothing happened on our side of the building, which was on the opposite side. During that attack, we had all of our windows open and nothing happened to them. But the people who had theirs closed came home to broken windows.

Fig. 9. Max Grill of the Munich Branch was one of the hundreds of German Latter-day Saint men who were killed before they could become husbands and fathers. (E. Grill)

Due to the increased danger of living in Munich, Rudolf Strebel was evacuated with his entire school class of boys to the Alpine town of Bad Reichenhall. As part of the Kinderlandverschickung program, he stayed there for eighteen months, with infrequent visits from his mother. Rudolf had the following to say about his time away from home:

> Every three to four months, I was able to go home. I was very homesick during that time—I was still so young! It took us about two hours to reach home when we used the train. [In Bad Reichenhall] we could often see the [American] bombers flying towards Munich. We also heard some pounding in the far, far distance. [Munich] was about 100 miles away. There weren't any other larger targets around us, so we knew they wanted to attack Munich.

On a few Sundays, Rudolf took the train to Salzburg, just seven miles distant. "I wasn't totally isolated from the Church. I couldn't go that often, but if I had the chance, I would. That was maybe once a month or so. The members were so kind and took me in for dinner. [But] they didn't come to Bad Reichenhall to visit me."

Gustav Habermann's military service took him to stations all over Europe. After being trained in engineering in Bernburg, Germany, he learned to fly in Danzig, Germany, but never flew in combat. While in Danzig, he met the girl he eventually married. (She was a Lutheran, which did not please Gustav's mother back in Munich.)[18] Although there was a large and active branch of the Church in Danzig at the time, Gustav did not attend meetings there. He explained the situation in these words:

> I didn't think about the Church at all during that time. I was not yet a priesthood holder and did not carry scriptures with me. While being isolated from the Church during my military service, I didn't have a testimony of the Church yet. I didn't pray and even doubted that there was a God. I drank alcohol as a soldier, and I also started smoking but stopped when I got home after the war.

Unfortunately, in Danzig, Gustav made the mistake of refusing to get out of bed one day. "I told the officer I didn't want to get up, so they took me to a court-martial, and I was given a punishment of six weeks at the front." After surviving that experience, he was trained in the Netherlands to drive a tank and from there was transferred to Italy and finally to the Eastern Front. By 1944, he was engaged to be married.

A young adult during the war years, Berta Wolperdinger admitted that life offered very little entertainment in those days: "There was no opportunity for us to go out and have fun. It was dangerous to go out during the evening. If we went downtown with the streetcar, we didn't feel very safe. Everything was dark. All my friends lived in other villages, and we were all scattered." The daily chores also left little time for amusement: "We went grocery shopping with the food ration cards. We also owned some property on which we could grow things, and that helped get us through the war. It was nothing much, but we always had fruit and vegetables. We still had our problems, but it wasn't as severe as if we had had to live on the ration cards."

By the time Herbert Roggermeier was old enough to attend school, the war in Europe was well under way. Regarding the possibilities of enjoying life as a boy at such times, Herbert had the following comments:

> During the war, I played with my school friends a lot; we liked to play soccer. But we could never play very long because we had to go home very quickly when an alarm went off. Also, the school was next to a huge antiaircraft battery. If there was an alarm while we were in that area, we ran home immediately; we knew what we had to do. . . . There was no situation in the war when I thought that I would die. I was a child, and children don't take things like that too seriously. But I had to sit in a shelter and realized that bombs were being dropped on my city.

On June 8, 1944, Erna Probst was inducted into the national labor service and sent to the town of St. Stefan in southern Austria. Because her leaders thought her physically frail, they assigned her to work in a storage area rather than on the farm. She stayed there until the harvest was finished in October and then was transferred to Vienna. In Austria's capital city, Erna was assigned to be a night watchperson. During the day, her unit was to monitor enemy air traffic and report on the number and types of planes flying over. She was also fortunate to attend church with the Vienna Branch on one occasion. She recalled:

> I liked my time there because we girls were a fun group, but I didn't like the fact that we had to stay there over Christmas. Near the end of the war, we heard that the Russians were coming closer. We were then trained in marching during the day and night and even got special boots for that. Then, we heard that we had to leave Vienna and we walked [120 miles west] to Linz.

In the last years of the war, life became increasingly difficult, as Elisabeth Grill described: "Sometimes the electricity wouldn't work, or it would be turned off. It was the same with gas and water. We began to store water in case it was turned off. We were often very cold because there wasn't enough wood or coal. We couldn't even go out and get wood anywhere. I collected pine cones from the ground around trees."

The lives of Munich residents were not just in peril when air-raid sirens were wailing. As Elisabeth recalled, one could be killed just walking through town. On one occasion, she was crossing a long railroad bridge when enemy dive-bombers flew over. Fortunately, they did not return to drop bombs on the trains rolling along below the bridge. "I was very scared, but I didn't feel as if I was going to die," she recalled. "I had many spiritual experiences during the war, and those kept me in the Church."

After the Allied landing on the coast of Normandy in June 1944, Georg Hörner's unit of the national labor service was moved slowly away from the advancing battlefront. As the enemy pushed eastward, Georg marched through northern France to the Netherlands and on to Cologne on the Rhine. From there he was transferred to central Germany near Halle and Leipzig. When the city of Dresden was destroyed in the terrible firebombing of February 13–14, 1945, Georg was just a dozen miles away, working at the Leuna factory. Because he was never officially drafted into the Wehrmacht, he was not required to confront the enemy invaders and was not classified as a prisoner of war at the conclusion of the conflict.

Trying to stem the tide of invasion from the east was essentially impossible for the Wehrmacht in the spring of 1945. Gustav Habermann was stationed near the Baltic Sea and—like thousands of his comrades in the German army—he wanted nothing other than to make his way west before the Soviets could capture him.

> I decided to take a ship, but it was harder to get on the boat than I thought. I saw a soldier who was severely wounded, and I took him with me on a small boat so that we could reach the larger ship. They allowed us to board and we sailed to Stettin. I got off of the ship in Stettin wearing a jacket with the word *Flak* [antiaircraft] on it. They had told us that men with that assignment were allowed to leave the ship first, and that's what I wanted. When a ship is full of soldiers, nobody really knows where anybody belongs. From Stettin, I made my way to Berlin.

A few months before the end of the war, Dorothea Strebel went to Bad Reichenhall to pick up her son. The Hitler Youth leaders did not wish to let him go, but she exercised her rights as a parent and took him home to Munich. Rudolf recalled that after his return home, the branch held meetings in the German Museum. "On our way to church after air raids, we saw many areas destroyed. But we took our bicycles anyway and went to the meetings."

Returning from Austria to Solln, the Thaller family had to deal with the increasing frequency of air raids in their suburb. An antiaircraft battery had been set up just a few hundred yards from their house and the guns relentlessly fired at enemy aircraft. On one occasion, an airplane was shot down and landed not far from the house. According to young Werner, the plane's motor was detached and struck the ground next to the house; the impact cracked or broke every window. "It was so close that I could touch the house with one hand and touch the motor with the other hand," he recalled.[19]

Werner's brother, Edwin, had similar memories:

> One night after an air raid, we picked fifty [incendiary] bombs out of our yard and our house.[20] One went through our tile roof into my mother's bedroom and closet. It started burning there [but we extinguished it]. They were similar to phosphorus bombs—you couldn't put them out with water but had to use your hands or blankets. One also hit our car, and it burned out. Luckily, our second car was still intact.

The Thallers were typical Germans in that they were always on the lookout for neighbors who needed help during air raids. Werner described the conditions in these words:

> There's no way you could call a fire department or anything because it just wasn't available. Once we saw flames coming out of our neighbor's roof, so we went over to alert them and found them huddled down in their basement. But because we were alert, awake enough to see, we were able to save them and their house and get the fire put out. The house on the other side of them was a small wooden house and it got hit, but it burned before we could do anything to stop it.

Erna Probst arrived home from Vienna in early March 1945. She already knew that their apartment building had been damaged extensively in an air raid, but her parents had managed to find rooms to live in next door. She remained in hiding for the next few weeks, because she was officially required to report for duty again but had no desire to do so. Fortunately, her neighbors did not report her disobedience, and her father burned her Arbeitsdienst uniform.

Fig. 10. The family of Johann Probst when the war began. (E. Probst Hörner)

"Our home was destroyed in the last attack on Munich," recalled Alfred Gerer. The event was almost tragic for his family, as he explained it:

> I was sitting in the basement next to my father and his wife. First, we heard the sounds, but then it was like everything moved in slow motion. Some cracks appeared in the walls, and then everything fell apart. Everybody was running towards the hole in the wall [to the adjacent building], which was too small for everybody at once. All the people made it through the opening except for my father's wife. She was a bit larger than everybody else, and she was stuck in the ruins of our basement. We all got shovels and got her out of there. We also poured water over her, which was in buckets everywhere [to prevent burns]. When she regained consciousness, her first words were: "The meatloaf is still in the oven." My father told her that she did not have to worry about that anymore. She was not seriously hurt.

When the fires died out, Alfred returned to the ruins to search for a personal treasure: "I was the only boy in the neighborhood who had a film projector, and I was looking desperately in the ruins. It was very dear to me. I never found it. We had lost everything in the ruins."

On March 20, 1945, the American army entered Munich under peaceful conditions. The surviving Saints wondered what kind of treatment they would experience at the hands of the conquerors. According to Berta Wolperdinger:

> It was not always a nice situation. They occupied whatever rooms they wanted. We could not sleep very well anymore because it was such an uncomfortable situation. The first night they were there, they came into our house. We were all so tired, and we didn't think that they would take things away from us. But they did. I guess other soldiers did the same. . . . I always carried my watch with me because it was a keepsake. That night, I put it on the nightstand and they stole it. But they kept everything else in order and didn't destroy anything. They also didn't molest us.

"The Americans came down our street and stopped to have lunch," recalled Rudolf Strebel. "Then they moved on. There wasn't any fighting; the German troops had already left. . . . We hung out white sheets, but in reality it wasn't even necessary. Two or three days later, they looked through our homes for weapons or soldiers, but that was all."

The Gerer family moved to the suburb of Allach in northwestern Munich after they lost their home. The Dachau concentration camp was just a few miles to the north, and conditions in the area became very insecure when inmates of that camp were released at the end of the war. According to Alfred, "They came into our house and took our jewelry. I was scared of the prisoners since they had a feeling of revenge inside, but I was not scared of the American soldiers." For the duration of the war and for some time thereafter, the family took the train to downtown Munich on the way to church. Josef Gerer was a railroad employee, so they rode for free. Church meetings were still being held every Sunday.

Fig. 11. Herbert Roggermeier of the Munich Branch was baptized in 1944 in this idyllic stream in Taufkirchen, a suburb six miles south of the downtown.[21] *(R. Minert, 2008)*

Herbert Roggermeier remembered the day the Americans entered the suburb of Berg am Laim:

> We children thought it was cool that they came in Jeeps. We ran towards them. They gave us Hershey's chocolate and bubble gum. There were both black and white American soldiers. I didn't know . . . even how to eat a banana. I would have eaten it with the skin.

Next to Herbert's grandparents' home was a prison, and his grandmother often threw bread or other food over the fence to the prisoners. After the war was over, the former prisoners found some guns and, according to Herbert, "stood in front of the dairy and made sure that nobody came to do any harm to it. The prisoners were from Eastern Europe—Ukraine and other countries."

The war was over, but new challenges and adventures presented themselves. Young Werner Thaller recalled one that is common in many cultures:

> There was an instance when one of us kids picked up a pack of cigarettes; we saw [American] soldiers driving or walking by and smoking, so we thought that's the thing to do. We got us a match and sat down out behind our house. As a group of neighborhood kids, we passed the cigarettes around and lit them up. And of course, Mom found out and she got upset and took them away. She told Dad, and he took us into a room. Back in those days, the punishment was always a belt or a wooden spoon or something. So before Dad even began to spank us, we started crying. So mom came in and said something to Dad. I don't know what she said, what she whispered in his ear, but Dad all of a sudden put the wooden stick down and he knelt down with us and we had a word of prayer.

The Probst family had previously discussed possible outcomes of the war. Erna's father, Johann, had indicated that conditions in Germany would be worse if Hitler were victorious and that he wanted to take his family to Ukraine if that happened. According to Erna, "We were not scared of the Americans and they didn't do anything at all to us." All three of Erna's brothers had been drafted, and her parents were delighted when they came home. Ernst and Ludwig returned soon after the war's end, but Sebastian did not come home until 1947. Suffering from a serious lung ailment, he needed surgery and a long hospitalization period before he could recover.

By May 1945, Gustav Habermann was serving with a tank unit in Czechoslovakia. When the men heard that Hitler was dead and the war over, they were told to head for home any way they could. Gustav's crew loaded a tank with food and planned to drive it to Germany but soon decided it was better to split up. "On my way [to Berlin], none of the Russians bothered me. All they took away from me was a ring and my watch. They left me my engagement ring. I saw a jacket on a scarecrow and took it so that I would look different. I tried to make them think I was an Italian. I was on my way to Berlin because I had heard that if I went to Munich the Americans would make me a prisoner of war." Arriving in Berlin on May 20, he located his fiancée, and they were married in the Soviet occupation zone in June.

At the end of the war, the branch members still alive and still in town gathered for meetings in rooms of the Deutsches Museum on the Museum Island in the Isar River in downtown Munich. Few members of the Munich Branch were still in the city by then. As Berta Wolperdinger explained, "When the war began, our branch was very close and we saw each other very often. But as the war continued, we felt more and more torn apart." By the spring of 1945, many families were still living as evacuees in rural communities, and more than sixty of the members had been killed or had died of other causes.

Fig. 12. The building in which the Munich Branch met during the first years of the war stood adjacent to the Hinterhaus seen at the left in this picture. No structure has been built at that location since the war. (R. Minert, 2008)

In May 1945, Rudolf Strebel had never known any government but the Hitler regime. However, he understood that some aspects of life in Nazi Germany had not been good:

> We were glad when the system broke down. We were free again. There had always been a certain pressure on us—what we were allowed to say or do. I knew of one family where the woman was lying on the floor, crying her heart out, because what she had believed in wasn't there anymore. She was really a fanatic national socialist.

The once beautiful city of Munich lay in ruins. At least six thousand people had been killed in seventy-three air raids, and fifteen thousand more had been injured. Twenty percent of the city was totally destroyed, including more than seventy-six thousand apartments.[22] In addition to the sufferings of the populace, thousands of refugees from eastern Germany had come to Munich and were competing for housing and food.

Fig. 13. In the last days of the war, the Munich Branch was meeting in a lecture hall of the Deutsches Museum in Munich. (R. Minert, 1973)

The Munich Branch had been scattered to the four winds, and the losses of property and life among the members were among the worst in the West German Mission. Nevertheless, eyewitnesses insist that meetings were held somehow at whatever locations became available and that the spirit of the gospel did not diminish through those challenging and often sorrow-filled years.

Erna Probst summed up her church experiences during the war in these words:

> We had a wonderful branch before, during, and after the war. I always loved going to church, and I liked the talks and the music. We had a

wonderful choir, also. When somebody died in the war, the funeral services were extraordinary. There was a large picture of that person on a table on the podium surrounded by flowers. And then we held a sacrament meeting in that person's behalf. I know we did that for Ludwig Lang, Edwin Thaller, and Otto Scharmbeck.

In Memoriam

The following members of the Munich Branch did not survive World War II:

Richard Amerseder b. München, München, Bayern, 4 Aug 1927; son of Karl Amerseder and Amalie Hubauer; bp. 28 Sep 1940; conf. 28 Sep 1940; ord. deacon 6 Jun 1943; k. in battle Romania or d. dysentery in a field hospital Focsani, Romania, 13 Aug 1945; bur. Focsani, Romania (FHL microfilm 68801, no. 305; CHL microfilm 2458, form 42 FP, pt. 37, all-mission list, 1943–46, 186–87; CHL 2445, no. 10; CHL CR 375 8 2445, no. 943; www.volksbund.de; IGI)

Georg Bader b. Altfreimann(?), München, Bayern, 30 Jan 1900; son of Georg Bader and Anna Walter; bp. 25 Jan 1930; conf. 25 Jan 1930; ord. deacon 14 Dec 1930; ord. teacher 24 Jan 1932; ord. priest 26 May 1935; ord. elder 10 May 1937; m. 2 May 1931, Magdalene Rietzl; d. stroke 7 Jun 1943 (FHL microfilm 68801, no. 13; CHL CR 375 8 2445, no. 634; IGI)

Alma Peter Bartl b. München, München, Bayern, 19 Feb 1912; son of Andreas Bartl and Walburga Adler; bp. 28 Feb 1920; conf. 28 Feb 1920; ord. deacon 2 Oct 1932; ord. teacher 12 Nov 1933; m. 3 Jun 1933, Magdalena Pitrak; missing as of 20 Aug 1946 (CHL CR 375 8 2445, no. 16)

Elisabeth Bausch b. Eningen, Schwarzwaldkreis, Württemberg, 17 Aug 1866; son of Johann Bausch and Regina Eitel; bp. 5 Jul 1924; conf. 5 Jul 1924; m. 21 Feb 1916, Josef Krempl; missing as of 21 Aug 1946 (CHL CR 375 8 2445, no. 154; FHL microfilm 271381, 1935 census; IGI)

Theresia Bitter b. Donauwörth, Schwaben, Bayern, 22 Jul 1893; dau. of Hans Bitter and Anna Ziegler; bp. 15 Jun 1926; conf. 20 Jun 1926; m. —— Egensberger; missing as of 20 Aug 1946 (CHL CR 375 8 2445, no. 50; CHL CR 375 8 2445, no. 5; FHL microfilm 25760, 1925 and 1930 censuses)

Babette Boeher or Bocher b. München, München, Bayern, 12 Jun 1879; dau. of Christian Boeher or Bocher and Maria Satzinger; bp. 5 Apr 1936; conf. 5 Apr 1936; m. —— Drezer or Dreher; d. heart condition 13 Jun 1941 (FHL microfilm 68801, no. 245; CHL CR 375 8 2445, no. 49; CHL CR 375 8 2445, no. 734; IGI)

Auguste Anna Bösmüller b. München, München, Bayern, 20 Oct 1868; dau. of Rudolf Egidi Georg Bösmüller and Auguste Carolina Simbeck; bp. 10 Mar 1937; conf. 10 Mar 1937; m. 23 Nov 1893, E. Morald Ehe; 2m. 12 Aug 1895, Anton Bauer; missing as of 20 Aug 1946 (CHL CR 375 8 2445, no. 19; IGI)

Anna Breitsameter b. München, München, Bayern, 19 Dec 1881; dau. of Franz Xaver Breitsameter and Anna Sturm; bp. 11 Feb 1903; conf. 11 Feb 1903; m. München 25 May 1920, Anton Pichler; 1 child; d. stroke München 3 or 9 May 1944 (FHL microfilm 68801, no. 120; CHL CR 375 8 2445, no. 335; IGI)

Agathe Brem b. Kirchdorf, Freising, Bayern, 23 Mar 1871; dau. of Aurel Brem and Anna Maria Meyer; bp. 29 May 1920; conf. 29 May 1920; m. Kirchdorf 27 Feb 1907, Otto Spichtinger; 3 children; d. stroke München, München, Bayern, 21 Jun 1940 (FHL microfilm 68801, no. 158 CHL CR 375 8 2445, no. 389; IGI)

Heinz Horst Harry Engelhardt b. Königsberg, Ostpreußen, 23 Nov 1912; son of Ernst Paul Engelhardt and Elise Berta Klein; bp. 2 May 1925; conf. 2 May 1925; d. 27 Oct 1942 (FHL microfilm 68801, no. 284; CHL CR 375 8 2445, no. 896)

Willibald Fendl b. München, München, Bayern, 15 Oct 1899; son of Josef Fendl and Katharina Sandl; bp. 20 Jan 1909; conf. 20 Jan 1909; missing as of 20 Feb 1944 (FHL microfilm 68801, no. 55; CHL CR 375 8 2445, no. 158)

Lorenz Gerer b. München, München, Bayern, 2 Apr 1919; son of Josef Gerer and Barbara Rottler; bp. 2 Apr 1927; conf. 2 Apr 1927; ord. deacon 2 Oct 1932; ord. teacher 10 May 1936; ord. priest 30 May 1937; k. in battle Stalingrad, Russia, 12 Dec 1942 (FHL microfilm 68801, no. 48; CHL, CR 375 8 2445, no. 84; CHL CR 375 8 2445, no. 48; A. Gerer; IGI)

Theresia Greimel b. Reinting, Hohenpolding, Bayern, 29 Aug 1862; dau. of Josef Greimel and Therese Schreff; bp. 2 Jul 1927; conf. 2 Jul 1927; m. Taufkirchen, Oberbayern, Bayern, 5 May 1884, Lorenz Nonimacher; 1 child; m. 24 Mar 1900, Johann Burkhardt; d. old age München, München, Bayern, 4 Aug 1944 (FHL microfilm 68801, no. 30; CHL CR 375 8 2445, no. 74; IGI)

Max Grill b. München, München, Bayern, 11 Apr 1917; son of Josef Grill and Maria Sandl; bp. München 23 May 1925; conf. 23 May 1925; ord. deacon 26 May 1935; corporal; k. in battle Italy 15 or 20 Apr or 20 Jul 1945; bur. Futa-Pass, Italy (E. Grill; www.volksbund.de; FHL microfilm 68801, no. 53; CHL microfilm 2458, form 42 FP, pt. 37, 463–64; CHL CR 375 8 2445, no. 208; IGI)

Andreas Jakob Gröber b. München, München, Bayern, 4 Jul 1904; son of Andreas Gröber and Magdalena Hagn; bp. 16 Jun 1923; conf. 16 Jun 1923; missing (FHL microfilm 68801, no. 96)

Gottfried Hartmaier b. Steinen, Lörrach, Baden, 29 Jan 1911; son of Gottfried Hartmaier and Maria Schneider; bp. 13 Jun 1926; conf. 13 Jun 1926; missing as of 20 Mar 1944 (CHL CR 375 8 2445, no. 855; FHL microfilm 162777)

Maximilian Hierboeck b. Weihmörting, Weihmörting, Bayern, 25 Sep 1864; son of Georg Hierboeck and Elisabeth Unterbuchberger; bp. 20 Feb 1909; conf. 20 Feb 1909; ord. deacon 14 Nov 1915; ord. teacher 3 Nov 1916; ord. priest 4 Feb 1917; ord. elder 1 Dec 1920; m. München, München, Bayern, 11 Apr 1891, Anna Kislinger; 7 children; k. air raid München 13 Jul 1944; bur. München (FHL microfilm 68801, no. 68; CHL CR 375 8 2445, no. 240; www.volksbund.de; IGI)

Josef Hörner b. München, München, Bayern, 27 Apr 1898; son of Georg Hörner and Anna Angermaier; bp. 17 Oct 1956; m. München 17 or 27 Aug 1919, Philomena Ficklscherer; 6 children; d. in concentration camp Hartheim, Linz, Oberösterreich, Austria, 9 Nov 1940 (Hörner; IGI)

Joseph Hörner b. München, München, Bayern, 3 Apr 1918; son of Josef Hörner and Philomena Ficklscherer; bp. 12 May 1928; d. asphyxiation München 16 or 21 Jun 1939; state funeral (G. Hörner; *Der Stern* no. 24, Christmas 1939, 387)

Franz Xaver Mathias Huber b. Pfaffenhofen, Ilm, Bayern, 19 Feb 1870; son of Josef Huber and Karolina Eufronia Wunner; bp. 15 Jun 1926; conf. 20 Jun 1926; ord. deacon 27 Jan 1932; ord. teacher 3 Jul 1938; m. 16 Oct 1906 or 1916, Franziska Müller; d. lung disease 22 or 23 May 1944 (FHL microfilm 68801, no. 78; CHL CR 375 8 2445, no. 7; IGI)

Karolina Jordan b. Zwerchstraß, Schwaben, Bayern, 11 Sep 1873; dau. of Georg Jordan and Fanny Hammel; bp. 4 Jul 1914; conf. 4 Jul 1914; m. Georg Wiesent; missing as of 20 Aug 1946 (CHL CR 375 8 2445, no. 354; CHL CR 375 8 2445, no. 500)

Friedrich Karl b. München, München, Bayern, 6 Jun 1915; son of Johann Karl and Therese Vollmer; bp. 30 Nov 1935; conf. 30 Nov 1935; missing as of 4 Apr 1945 (FHL microfilm 68801, no. 242; CHL CR 375 8 2445, no. 731)

Helene Gertrud Rosa Kirschning b. Braunschweig, Braunschweig, 1 Apr 1909; dau. of Friedrich Kirschning and Gertrud Moller; bp. 7 Sep 1918; conf. 7 Sep 1918; m. 9 Sep 1938, Heinrich Hartmann; missing as of 5 Apr 1945 (FHL microfilm 68801, no. 281; CHL CR 375 8 2445, no. 778)

Anna Kislinger b. Adlkofen, Landshut, Bayern, 13 Dec 1870; dau. of Anton Kislinger and Anna Maria Strohhofer; bp. 20 Feb 1909; conf. 20 Feb 1909; m. München, München, Bayern, 11 Apr 1891, Maximilian Hierboeck; 7 children; k. air raid München 13 Jul 1944 (FHL microfilm 68801, no. 67; IGI)

Elisabeth Kowald b. Köln, Rheinprovinz, 4 Jun 1904; dau. of Andreas Kowald and Emma Forstmann; bp. 5 Jul 1921; conf. 5 Jul 1921; m. 3 Dec 1928, Karl Zimmermann; missing as of 20 Feb 1940 (FHL microfilm 68801, no. 269; CHL CR 375 8 2445, no. 763)

Josef Krempl b. Karlshuld, Schwaben, Bayern, 9 Sep 1859; son of Michael Krempl and Kreszenz Rai; bp. 2 Aug 1924; conf. 2 Aug 1924; m. 21 Feb 1916, Elisabeth Bausch; missing as of 20 Aug 1946 (CHL CR 375 8 2445, no. 155; CHL CR 375 8 2445, no. 2811; IGI)

Maria Lög b. München, München, Bayern, 22 Sep 1858; dau. of Georg and Kreszens Türk; bp. 19 Jun 1908; conf. 19 Jun 1908; m. —— Riss; d. old age 19 Jun 1942 (FHL microfilm 68801, no. 147; CHL CR 375 8 2445, no. 359; IGI)

Georg Merkel b. München, München, Bayern, 18 Nov 1926; son of Adalbert Merkel and Margarete Weininger; bp. 16 Jun 1940; conf. 16 Jun 1940; private; d. mobile field hospital 681 1 Feb 1945; bur. Kaliningrad, Russia, (FHL microfilm 68801, no. 304; CHL CR 375 8 2445, no. 934; www.volksbund.de; IGI)

Oskar Meyer b. Schrobenhausen, Oberbayern, Bayern, 20 Oct 1917; son of Wilhelm Meyer and Josepha Huiss; bp. 5 Apr 1932; conf. 5 Apr 1932; k. in battle 12 Sep 1944; bur. Wesel, Wesel, Rheinland (FHL microfilm 68801, no. 110; CR 375 8 2445, no. 677; www.volksbund.de; FHL microfilm 245232 1935 census; IGI)

Philippine Meyer b. Schrobenhausen, Oberbayern, Bayern, 17 Apr 1916; dau. of Wilhelm Meyer and Josepha Huiss; bp. 5 Apr 1932; conf. 5 Apr 1932; missing as of 20 Aug 1946 (CHL CR 375 8 2445, no. 200; CHL CR 375 8 2445, no. 676; FHL microfilm 245232; 1935 census)

Rudolf Gottlieb Netting b. München, München, Bayern, 26 Apr 1884; son of Karl Gottlieb Netting and Agathe Kober; bp. 7 Jun 1924; conf. 7 Jun 1924; ord. deacon 18 Mar 1925; ord. teacher 15 May 1927; ord. priest 11 Nov 1930; ord. elder 12 May 1935; m. 7 Oct 1918, Therese Knoll (div.); 2 children; 2m. 2 Jan 1929, Elisabeth Maria Liebler or Liebl (div.); 3m. 3 Apr 1937, Veronika Ligmanovski or Lygenanovek or Lygenanowek; d. stomach cancer München 8 Mar 1940 (FHL microfilm 68801, no. 115; CHL CR 375 8 2445, no. 60; FHL microfilm 245241, 1925 and 1935 censuses; IGI)

Anna Babette Oberseither b. Winterhausen, Unterfranken, Bayern, 24 Jan 1873; dau. of Emanuel Decker and Sofie Dorothea Oberseither; bp. 30 Aug 1898; conf. 30 Aug 1898; m. München, München, Bayern 23 Feb 1897, Anton Schindler; 7 children; d. heart condition München 16 Dec 1940 (FHL microfilm 68801, no. 164; CHL CR 375 8 2445, no. 297; IGI, PRF)

Franz Ewald Walter Polier b. Liegnitz, Liegnitz, Schlesien, 27 Jul 1912; son of Franz Albert Joseph Polier and Anna Ernestine Pauline Friedrich; bp. 14 Sep 1929; conf. 14 Sep 1929; ord. deacon 6 Sep 1931; lieutenant; k. in battle Gusaki, Brysgalowo, Russia, 20 Aug 1942 (FHL microfilm 68801, no. 243; CHL CR 375 8 2445, no. 230; CHL CR 375 8 2445, no. 729; www.volksbund.de; IGI)

Sigmund Popp b. München, Bayern, 20 Apr 1905; son of Eduard Popp and Katharina Weinsinger; bp. 11 Jul 1914; conf. 11 Jul 1914; missing as of 20 Jul 1944 (FHL microfilm 68801, no. 125; CHL CR 375 8 2445, no. 229; CHL CR 375 8 2445, no. 338)

Antonie Katharina Redle b. München, München, Bayern, 10 Oct 1925; dau. of Katharina Hütterer; bp. 5 Jun 1938; conf. 5 Jun 1938; missing as of 20 Aug 1946 (CHL CR 375 8 2445, no. 771)

Maximilian Redle b. Freising, Freising, Bayern, 26 Sep 1897; son of Maximilian Redle and Maria Hollmeder; bp. 5 Jun 1938; conf. 5 Jun 1938; m 14 Aug 1931, Maria Hollmeder or Hutterer; k. in battle Russia 18 Oct 1944 (FHL microfilm 68801, no. 271, no. 273; CHL CR 375 8 2445, no. 770; IGI)

Franziska Ring b. Kelheim, Niederbayern, Bayern, 14 Feb 1866; dau. of Johann Ring and Maria Seebauer; bp. 13 Jun 1911; conf. 13 Jun 1911; m. 6 May 1893, Anton Amann; d. stroke 29 Nov 1943 (FHL microfilm 68801, no. 6; CHL CR 375 8 2445, no. 83; IGI)

Johann Sandl b. München, München, Bayern, 3 Aug 1893; son of Therese Sandl; bp. 20 Jan 1909; conf. 20 Jan 1909; ord. teacher 6 Sep 1914; missing as of 20 Feb 1944 (CHL CR 375 8 2445, no. 385; FHL microfilm 245257, 1935 census)

Katharina Sandl b. Sünching, Bayern, 18 Nov 1870; dau. of Josef Sandl and Anna Behner; bp. München, München, Bayern, 20 Jan 1909; conf. 20 Jan 1909; m. Josef Fendl; d. stroke 1 Apr or Jul 1943 (FHL microfilm 68801, no. 32; CHL CR 375 8 2445, no. 54; CHL CR 375 8 2445, no. 159)

Dina Christina Schäfer b. Frankfurt/Main, Hessen-Nassau, 13 Feb 1915; dau. of Friedrich Christian Schäfer and Christina Bausch; bp. 28 Feb 1925; conf. 28 Feb 1925; m. 7 Nov 1938, Wilhelm Allmann; missing as of 20 Aug 1946 (CHL CR 375 8 2445, no. 305; CHL CR 375 8 2445, no. 762)

Otto Schamböck b. München, München, Bayern, 16 Apr 1922; son of Otto Schamböck and Rosa Lang; bp. 25 Sep 1930; conf. 25 Sep 1930; ord. deacon 2 Jul 1939; k. in battle Eastern Front 17 Sep 1943 (Hörner; FHL microfilm 68801, no. 161; CHL CR 375 8 2445, no. 652; IGI)

Anna Schenkel b. Neuschwetzingen, Untermarfeld, Bayern, 3 Jan 1883; dau. of Johann Schenkel and Anna Babette Koch; bp. 7 Jun 1924; conf. 7 Jun 1924; m. Triefing, Oberbayern, Bayern, 11 Oct 1904, Friedrich Burkhard; 7 children; 2m. Ingolstadt, Oberbayern, Bayern, 29 May 1916, Benedikt Bachmann; 2 children; 3m. 22 Apr 1940, Josef Mathias Ertl; d. heart attack München, München, Bayern, 8 Sep 1941 (FHL microfilm 68801, no. 9; CHL CR 375 8 2445, no. 142; FHL microfilm 25715, 1930 census; IGI)

Rosine Schenkel b. Neuschwetzingen, Neuburg/Donau, Schwaben, Bayern, 20 Jul 1875; dau. of Johann Schenkel and Anna Babette Koch; bp. 5 Jul 1941; conf. 6 Jul 1941; m. Neuschwetzingen 3 or 5 Aug 1903, Nikolaus Selzer; d. lung disease Neuburg/Donau 22 Jan 1947 (CHL CR 375 8 2445, no. 947; IGI)

Rudolf Ludwig Schulz b. Neusalz/Oder, Brandenburg, 18 Jan 1898; son of Rudolf Schulz and Anna Wolf; bp. 16 Jul 1925; conf. 16 Jul 1925; ord. elder 6 Dec 1931; m. Frankfurt/Main, Hessen-Nassau 15 Jul 1925, Christina Bauch or Bausch (div); 3 children; missing as of 20 Nov 1939 (FHL microfilm 68801, no. 260; CHL CR 375 8 2445, no. 311; IGI)

Franz Schuster b. München, München, Bayern, 26 Aug 1918; son of Jakob Schuster and Maria Anna Schalch; bp. 23 Jun 1928; conf. 23 Jun 1928; ord. deacon 2 Oct 1932; missing as of 5 April 1945 (FHL microfilm 68801, no. 315; CHL CR 375 8 2445, no. 526)

Sophie Seidl b. Langenfeld, Neustadt, Oberbayern, Bayern, 24 May 1886; dau. of Johann Georg Seidl and Salwina Hagner ; bp. 22 Jun 1929; conf. 22 Jun 1929; m. Karl Bindewald; d. old age 9 Oct 1939 (FHL microfilm 68801, no. 22; CHL CR 375 8 2445, no. 607; FHL microfilm 25723, 1930 census; IGI)

Anton Wilhelm Spaehn b. Reutin, Bayern, 10 Nov 1899; son of Xaver Spaehn and Karolina Demptle; bp. 15 Jun 1926; conf. 20 Jun 1926; missing as of 20 Aug 1946 (CHL CR 375 8 2445, no. 275; CHL CR 375 8 2445, no. 6)

Elisabeth Maria Steinseder b. Hirten, Altötting, Oberbayern, Bayern, 19 Nov 1891; dau. of Georg Schukbeck and Maria Steinseder; bp. 22 Dec 1928; conf. 22 Dec 1928; m. 2 Jan 1929, Rudolf Netting; 2m. 18 May 1936, Jakob Schmid; missing as of 20 Aug 1946 (CHL CR 375 8 2445, no. 317; IGI)

Erwin Julius Thaller b. Nürnberg, Mittelfranken, Bayern, 7 Jan 1915; son of Georg Thaller and Regina Böhm; bp. 26 Apr 1924; conf. 26 Apr 1924; ord. deacon 29 Nov 1931; ord. teacher 4 Nov 1934; m. 16 Dec 1939, Anna Reithmeier; constable; d. on the Feodosia-Kertsch branch of the Koy Asan railway 26 Feb 1942; bur. Sewastopol, Ukraine (W. Thaller; www.volksbund.de; FHL microfilm 68801, no. 178; CHL CR 375 8 2445, no. 331; CHL CR 375 8 2445, no. 451; FHL microfilm 245283, 1925 and 1935 censuses)

Eugen Theobald Thaller b. Nürnberg, Mittelfranken, Bayern, 12 or 13 Nov 1912; son of Georg Thaller and

Regina Böhm; bp. 26 Apr 1924; conf. 26 Apr 1924; ord. deacon 2 Oct 1932; m. 6 Feb 1939, Rosa Pestenhofer; k. in battle Isle of Grado, Italy 27 Jun 1944; bur. Costermano, Italy (W. Thaller; FHL microfilm 68801, no. 179; CHL CR 375 8 2445, no. 452; www.volksbund.de; FHL microfilm 245283, 1925 and 1935 censuses; IGI)

Werner Gerhard Vikari b. München, München, Bayern, 5 Feb 1945; son of Anton Vikari and Hildegard Plötz; d. 20 Apr 1945 (FHL microfilm 68801, no. 338; CHL CR 375 8 2445, no. 2; IGI)

Christian Voigt b. Zwickau, Zwickau, Sachsen, 18 Sep 1909; son of Kurt Alfred Voigt and Melanie Beleman; bp. 10 May 1929; missing (Membership Records LDS C 189)

Karolina Wiesent b. München, München, Bayern, 25 May 1911; dau. of Georg Wiesent and Karolina Jordan; bp. 29 Sep 1923; conf. 29 Sep 1923; missing as of 20 Feb 1944 (FHL microfilm 68801, no. 218; CHL CR 375 8 2445, no. 502)

Katharina Wiesinger b. München, Bayern, 28 Apr 1877; dau. of Jakob Wiesinger and Marie Barbara Steinbeiser; bp. 1 Apr 1913; conf. 1 Apr 1913; m. Josef Wiendl; missing as of 20 Aug 1946 (CHL CR 375 8 2445, no. 501; FHL microfilm 245299 1925 and 1935 censuses)

Anton Wimmer b. Altenburg, Landshut, Niederbayern, Bayern, 12 June 1880; son of Peter Wimmer and Anna Nitzel; bp. 4 Oct 1924; conf. 5 Oct 1924; ord. deacon 29 Jan 1928; ord. teacher 18 Apr 1932; ord. priest 30 May 1937; m. München, München, Bayern, 27 Jul 1908, Katharina Kraus; 7 children; d. heart and circulation München 9 Feb 1941 (FHL microfilm 68801, no. 196; CHL CR 375 8 2445, no. 344; CHL CR 375 8 2445, no. 506; IGI)

Notes

1. Munich city archive.
2. Helga Seeber, "Werden und Wirken der Mormonen in München" (unpublished history, 1977).
3. Elisabeth Grill, interview by the author in German, Munich, Germany, August 10, 2006; unless otherwise noted, summarized in English by Judith Sartowski.
4. Presiding Bishopric, "Financial, Statistical, and Historical Reports of Wards, Stakes, and Missions, 1884–1955," CR 4 12, 257.
5. 1 Thessalonians 5:21.
6. Berta Wolperdinger, interview by the author in German, Munich, Germany, August 22, 2008.
7. Erna Thekla Probst Lankes Hörner, interview by the author in German, Ramerberg, Germany, August 10, 2006.
8. West German Mission branch directory, 1939, CHL LR 10045 11.
9. Gustav Adolf Habermann, interview by the author in German, Munich, Germany, August 22, 2008.
10. After the war, Georg Hörner wrote to President David O. McKay to explain the circumstances of his father's excommunication. President McKay then restored the membership status of Josef Hörner.
11. Georg Hörner, interview by the author in German, Ramerberg, Germany, August 10, 2006.
12. Rudolf Strebel, interview by the author, Bountiful, UT, April 10, 2009.
13. Eyewitnesses disagree about the date. Several indicate that the building stood until 1944. No branch records exist to resolve the question.
14. The Church tax consisted of less than one percent of an employee's income that was automatically deducted by the government tax office from the employee's pay. The only way to avoid paying that very small tax was to officially withdraw from the Church. Both the Catholic and the Lutheran churches collected the tax in those days and still do.
15. Alfred Gerer, interview by the author in German, Tutzing, Germany, August 21, 2008.
16. Herbert Roggermeier, interview by the author in German, Taufkirchen, Germany, August 22, 2008.
17. Edwin Thaller, telephone interview with the author, February 10, 2009.
18. Gustav actually found the opportunity to take his fiancée to Munich to meet his mother. Sister Habermann was inactive at the time and was reportedly told by one branch member that if she did not attend church, her sons would not survive the war. Several of them were already in uniform.
19. Werner Thaller, telephone interview with the author, February 5, 2009.
20. Many eyewitnesses told of extinguishing incendiaries and recalled that a great many of that type of bomb did not ignite at all.
21. When the author visited Roggermeier in 2008 and asked about his baptism, he responded, "Come out on the balcony [of the eighth story apartment] and I'll show you where I was baptized." He then pointed to the tree by the creek about six hundred yards away.
22. Munich city archive.

Salzburg Branch

The western outskirts of Salzburg form the border of Austria and Germany. This beautiful city on the Salzach River had not joined Austria until 1815 and had 77,172 inhabitants when German troops marched in on March 12, 1938.[1] The small branch of Latter-day Saints had existed in the city for only a few years at the time, and the branch president was traditionally a young missionary from the United States. Clark Hillam of Brigham City, Utah, was one such branch president. He recalled that the members he met in January 1939 were "pretty solid." However, "compared to Munich it was a small branch."[2] When the American missionaries were evacuated from the continent in August 1939, Josef Duschl became the branch president.

Salzburg Branch[3]	1939
Elders	2
Priests	3
Teachers	1
Deacons	1
Other Adult Males	11
Adult Females	27
Male Children	4
Female Children	2
Total	51

Like so many LDS branches in Germany and Austria, the branch in Salzburg was characterized by a large number of adult women, many of whom were the only members of the Church in their homes. Sunday School began at 10:00 a.m. and sacrament meeting at 8:00 p.m. MIA and Relief Society meetings were held on Wednesday evenings at 7:30 and 8:30 respectively, and the Primary association met on Tuesdays at 4:00 p.m.

The annexation of Austria by Germany had an immediate impact on the LDS missionary work: all five Austrian branches were transferred from the Swiss-Austrian Mission to the West German Mission. The records of the mission office in Frankfurt include the following report dated December 2, 1938:

> President and Sister M. Douglas Wood and Private Secretary Richard E. J. Frandsen, visited the second meeting of the series of these gatherings which were held on this trip into the newly acquired branches in Austria, now belonging to the West German Mission. In Salzburg, there were fifteen members, six friends and ten missionaries, present. Other visitors present were: district Presidents Ludwig Weiss from Nuremberg and Johann Thaller from Munich; Fred. W. Babbel, Nuremberg; Grant Baker, Augsburg; and John G. Teasdale, Munich. It was a thrill for these Saints to meet President and Sister Wood for the first time and to enjoy the fine spirit of the meeting which was held there.[4]

As the war approached in the late summer of 1939, the Salzburg Branch was holding its meetings in a small residential structure just a few yards from the Salzach in the northern part of the city; the address was Jahnstrasse 2. Rudolph Weissenburger (born 1913) joined the Church in 1934 and recalled that the branch moved into the building shortly after his baptism. "There was a small room and a large room that we used. Brother Nestlinger helped a great deal to [find] a meeting hall."[5] No other details of the rooms are available.

Fig. 1. The building at Jahnstrasse 2 in Salzburg where the branch held its meetings during the war. (R. Minert, 2008)

With so few priesthood holders among the members in Salzburg, it must have been difficult to watch the young men be drafted and leave the area. Rudolph Weissenburger donned the uniform of the Wehrmacht in 1940 and began an odyssey that took him all around Europe and as far as the Mediterranean Sea. From Salzburg, he went first to Innsbruck and Graz (two of Austria's largest cities), then to Nienburg in northern Germany, where he was trained as an engineer. He spent a few months in France, Poland, and Russia. "We marched almost the entire distance," he recalled. "In one day we marched 75 kilometers [47 miles]." By then it was 1941, and the German army had moved deep into the Soviet Union.[6]

Brother Weissenburger was one of the many German LDS soldiers who struggled with the problem of what to do if he was in a position to shoot at enemy soldiers. "When I was drafted, I fasted for a day and prayed that I would not be forced to shoot anyone during the war. This was my prayer." In Russia, he operated a machine gun, and on two consecutive days was close enough to Red Army soldiers to be in great danger. In each case, he did not fire, and the soldiers hastily retreated.[7]

Rudolph's time in Russia was relatively short because he fell victim to frostbite in February 1942. "My fingers were frozen and they turned black. . . . The flesh fell off. It didn't hit the bones. Had the frost hit the bones, there would have been a need for amputation. The same with the feet. Then I returned to Tapiano in East Prussia." After recuperating in various hospitals, he was sent back to Austria, where he volunteered to serve in Africa. "'It's not too cold there,' I said to myself."[8]

Like his counterparts in other LDS branches all over Germany, the clerk of the Salzburg Sunday School kept regular records of the meetings. However, the great detail common in the records before the war declined during the war, and the entries featured only the numbers of attendees and the names of Sunday School officers. The attendance for 1941 and 1942 vacillated from ten to twenty-six persons. Forty-three members and friends attended the Christmas program.[9]

Herbert Schreiter (born 1901) had been the president of the Chemnitz Center Branch before being drafted into the Wehrmacht. Everywhere he went as a soldier, he sought a connection with the Church. His first opportunity came when he was transferred to Salzburg in January 1943 to work as a gunsmith. He recalled:

> Of course, I immediately went looking for the branch. The branch president was Brother Duschl and he was 82 years old. The other brethren had all been drafted and the branch consisted almost entirely of sisters. So I arrived and was [soon] called to be the Sunday School president. . . . I sat up front in my uniform, and I brought a few other soldiers along because they were bored.[10]

Herbert's arrival in Salzburg was most timely, for Josef Duschl was too weak to carry on, and Herbert found himself the only priesthood holder left in the Salzburg Branch. Brother Duschl's wife, Elisabeth, passed away about that time, and Herbert borrowed a suit in order to conduct her funeral. At the last minute, Munich District president Johann Thaller arrived and dedicated the grave.

Herbert enjoyed his time in the Salzburg Branch very much, where the Sunday meetings were often followed by group walks amid the local hills. He was disappointed when he had to leave in mid-1944, although the transfer took him back to his native Chemnitz.

The dedication of the remaining Latter-day Saints in Salzburg must have been exemplary, because despite the lack of priesthood holders, the attendance at Sunday School in 1943 and 1944 remained consistent. The numbers swung from thirteen to twenty-seven in 1943 and were as high as forty-six in 1944. Surnames frequently seen in the minutes are Leitner, Herbert, Schreiter, Mayr, Mühlbacher, Schauperl, Standl, Götzenberger, Duschl, Rauch, and Hingshammer.[11]

Rudolph Weissenburger's next assignment in late 1942 took him from Austria to the island of Crete in the Mediterranean. There was little to do both in Crete and in his next location, Greece. Back on Crete when the war ended, Rudolph and his comrades surrendered themselves to British forces on June 8, 1945. As prisoners of war, they were sent to a camp near Great Bitter Lake in Egypt. He was released there just in time to return to Salzburg by Christmas 1946.[12] The branch was still holding meetings, and several American soldiers had joined them by that time.

The Saints in Salzburg were fortunate that nearly all of them lived in homes and apartments that survived the war. The city was bombed fifteen times by the US Army Air Corps, and 47 percent of the structures were damaged or destroyed and 482 persons killed. At least 65 of the sons of this city died in military service. American soldiers entered Salzburg in April 1945, and the city surrendered without a fight.

In Memoriam

The following members of the Salzburg Branch did not survive World War II:

Adolf Duschl b. Guigl, Salzburg, Austria, 17 Jun 1911; son of Josef Duschl and Elisabeth Stockinger; bp. 2 Nov 1921; ord. teacher; m. Cottbus, Brandenburg, 4 Apr 1938, Minna Berta Galow; d. Teodorowka, Russia, USSR, 17 Sep 1944 (FHL microfilm 25758, 1935 census; IGI; AF)

Maria Lindt Gaigg b. Ebensee, Oberösterreich, 11 January 1880; dau. of Johann Loidl and Anna Stueger or Anna Maria Vogl; bp. Bern Switzerland Temple 25 February 1959; conf. 25 February 1959; m. Ebensee 18 November 1900 or 1903, Sebastian Gaigg; d. Ebensee 11 January 1937 (NFS)

Johann Mayr b. Mitterbreitsach, Eberschwang, Oberösterreich, Austria, 11 Jun 1909; son of Johann Mayr and Maria Katzboeok; bp. 27 Jul 1923; conf. 27 Jul 1923; ord. deacon 4 Aug 1929; ord. teacher 15 Apr 1934; ord. priest 3 Feb 1935; m. 1 Oct 1934, Adele Przybyla; 4 children; corporal; k. in battle at Malowa Gora, Poland, 28 Jul 1944 (Dozekal-Vazulik; CHL CR 375 8 2445, no. 864; www.volksbund.de)

Josef Mühlbacher b. Molln, Oberösterreich, Austria, 23 Jul 1923; son of Michael Mühlbacher and Katharina Gurtner; bp. 13 May 1934; conf. 13 May 1934; ord. deacon 15 Mar 1936; d. wounds 10 Aug 1944; bur. Mont-de-Huisnes, France (Dozekal-Vazulikl; CHL CR 375 8 2445, no. 873; www.volksbund.de)

Elisabeth Stockinger b. Geboltskirchen, Oberösterreich, Austria, 21 Oct 1875; dau. of Sebastian Stockinger and Elisabeth Arminger; bp. 2 Nov 1921; conf. 2 Nov 1921; m. Guigl, Salzburg, 7 Oct 1909, Josef Duschl; 3 children; d. heart ailment Guigl, Salzburg, Austria, 24 Apr 1944 (CHL CR 375 8 2445, no. 853; FHL microfilm 25758, 1935 census; IGI; AF)

Antonia Tibisch b. Molln, Oberösterreich, Austria, 9 Jan 1871; dau. of Vinzenz Tibisch and Antonia Thaler; bp. 18 Aug 1928; conf. 19 Aug 1928; d. stroke 2 Apr 1941 (CHL CR 375 8 2445, no. 889; FHL microfilm 245285, 1930 and 1935 censuses)

Notes

1. Salzburg city archive.
2. Clark Hillam, interview by the author, Brigham City, Utah, August 20, 2006.
3. Presiding Bishopric, "Financial, Statistical, and Historical Reports of Wards, Stakes, and Missions, 1884–1955," 721, CHL CR 4 12.
4. West German Mission quarterly reports, 1938, no. 45, CHL LR 10045 2.
5. Rudolph Weissenburger, interview by Justus Ernst, April 30, 1986, Salt Lake City, 4, 14, CHL MS 9260; trans. the author.
6. Weissenburger, interview, 11.
7. Ibid., 13.
8. Ibid., 11.
9. Salzburg Branch, Sunday School minutes, CHL LR 7846 15.
10. Herbert Schreiter, interview by Matthew K. Heiss, Leipzig, Germany, October 11, 1991, CHL; trans. the author.
11. Salzburg Branch, Sunday School minutes.
12. Weissenburger, interview, 4–5.

NURUREMBERG DISTRICT

West German Mission

Comprising the northern half of the former kingdom of Bavaria, the Nuremberg District had possibly the lowest proportion of Latter-day Saints within the indigenous population of any Church district in Germany in 1939. The district consisted of only three branches—two in Nuremberg and Fürth (essentially the Nuremberg metropolitan area) and one in Coburg (sixty miles north of Nuremberg). The territory of the district was bordered on the north by Saxony (in the East German Mission) and Thuringia, on the east by Czechoslovakia, on the south by the Danube River, on the west by the Stuttgart District, and on the northwest by the Frankfurt District. The district territory was sparsely populated, and Latter-day Saints were few and far between outside of the city of Nuremberg.

A report sent to the mission office in Frankfurt in March 1939 may be indicative of activities in the Nuremberg District in the months just before World War II:

> Saturday to Monday, March 25–27, 1939
>
> Conference of the Nuremberg District in the Nuremberg Branch hall. Total attendance 863 members and 110 friends. Because of overfilled halls, etc. there was quite some disturbance at these meetings but everyone was happy with the messages that were presented.[1]

Nuremberg District[2]	1939
Elders	25
Priests	15
Teachers	16
Deacons	24
Other Adult Males	43
Adult Females	192
Male Children	20
Female Children	23
Total	358

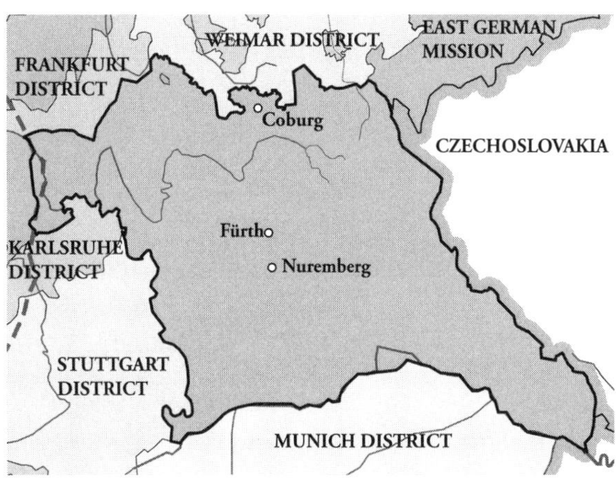

Fig. 1. The Nuremberg District consisted essentially of northern Bavaria. Vast portions of the territory had no Latter-day Saint residents.

The meeting rooms of the Nuremberg Branch were located at the time at Hirschelgasse 26, a building that did not have large rooms. The attendance of 973 included persons who attended all meetings (possibly six) held on those three days.

The president of the Nuremberg District was Ludwig Weiss. Little is known about him, but he was apparently dedicated to the work of the Church, because his name is seen frequently in the records of branch, district, and mission conferences in Munich, Austria, and Frankfurt.

Daughter Waltraud Weiss (born 1930) recalled that as part of the district conferences, "we also held *bunte Abende* [musical or theatrical programs]. Once, we had an opera night. Many other members of the district attended. The rooms at Untere Talgasse were large enough to hold those conferences. All of our free time was connected with Church activities."[3]

Waltraud also recalled that her father often sneaked out the back door of their apartment house on Sundays to go to church, trying to hide his activities from a neighbor who was an ardent Nazi. The man was always on the lookout for some reason to report Ludwig Weiss to the police. The informer was also unhappy about the fact that Sister Bertha Weiss was not employed, preferring to stay at home with her daughter Hertha, who suffered all of her life from a kidney disease. Despite her ailments, Hertha was required to serve a duty year away from home. Her labor assignment (maintaining aircraft) may have contributed to a decline in her health; she died in 1946 at twenty-two.

President Weiss was a veteran of the Great War and was too old to serve in the German army, but he was inducted into the home guard in the last year of the war. Fortunately, a friend helped him avoid Volkssturm service on Sundays so that he could attend to his church duties. The friend warned President Weiss when other members of the group inquired about his absence. Thus Ludwig Weiss was able to spend the entire war at home in Nuremberg, where he could serve the Saints. Waltraud recalled how he went in search of the members of the Church following air raids in order to determine their status and needs. In the recollection of Lorie Baer, Weiss also served as the branch president in Nuremberg after Paul Eysser was drafted.[4]

Several eyewitnesses recalled Ludwig Weiss as a strict man, though not unfriendly. Young Helga Mördelmeyer remembered him visiting her family one evening. "He reminded us that our curtains weren't closed enough [for blackout regulations] and that too much light would come through at night. He wasn't pleased and made us fix it."[5] President Weiss was, of course, concerned primarily about the family's safety in the absence of Helga's father, who was away in the Wehrmacht.

Fig. 2. Georg and Elisabeth Gentner moved from Nuremberg to Bamberg during the war. They are seen here in about 1939 with their children and Elisabeth's mother, Kunigunde Schöpf. (G. Gentner Kammerer)

In 1943, the Gentner family moved from Nuremberg to Bamberg. Within a few months, they learned that other Latter-day Saints had come to that city, namely the Ostertag family. A Brother Hansen from Kiel in northern Germany also had moved to Bamberg with his wife and two sons. He was asked to lead the group of Saints there, and they began to hold meetings at Urbanstrasse 6. According to Gerda Gentner, they continued to hold meetings there until after the war.[6]

Survivors recounted that all three branches of the Nuremberg District were still functioning at the end of the war, though the Saints in that part of Germany had suffered greatly from the loss of housing. Deaths among Church members in the district were also quite high in number.

Notes

1. West German Mission quarterly report, 1939, no. 12, CHL LR 10045 2.
2. Presiding Bishopric, "Financial, Statistical, and Historical Reports of Wards, Stakes, and Missions, 1884–1955," 257, CHL CR 4 12.
3. Waltraud Weiss Burger, interview by the author in German, Fürth, Germany, May 27, 2007; unless otherwise noted, summarized in English by Judith Sartowski.
4. Lorie Baer Bonds, interview by Michael Corley, Provo, UT, March 6, 2008.
5. Helga Mördelmeyer Campbell, interview by the author, Provo, UT, May 28, 2009.
6. Gerda Gentner Kammerer, interview by the author in German, Bamberg, Germany, August 13.

Coburg Branch

At the far northern extent of the former kingdom of Bavaria, the city of Coburg was about as far as it could be from any other German city in which a branch of Latter-day Saints was found in 1939. About ninety minutes by train from Nuremberg, the city was otherwise not located along any major transportation routes. The members of the Coburg Branch were very isolated in that location and also few in number.

The records of the West German Mission show a branch population of only twenty-nine persons, none of whom were Melchizedek priesthood holders. The branch president when the war began was Johann Schmidt, who traveled to Coburg from his home in Nuremberg to direct the activities of the branch. According to the mission directory, there were no Sunday School, Primary, or MIA programs operating in the branch at the time. The Relief Society was led by a local woman, Alma Bauer, and she enjoyed the services of a secretary, Metha Franke.[1]

The formal address of the Coburg Branch in 1939 was Kalenderweg 5, the house in which Sister Franke lived. It is not known whether she invited the branch members into her home each Sunday, or whether other rooms in the building were used. The mission directory offers a little additional information with the statement, "A small room is rented whenever larger sacrament meetings are held."[2]

Coburg Branch[3]	1939
Elders	0
Priests	1
Teachers	2
Deacons	1
Other Adult Males	4
Adult Females	19
Male Children	1
Female Children	1
Total	29

Fig. 1. The home at Kalenderweg 5 in which the Coburg Branch held meetings in 1939. (W. Kohlase)

Two meetings were held on Sundays in August 1939: a sacrament meeting at 3:00 p.m. and a cottage meeting at 8:00 p.m. The only other meeting scheduled at the time was Relief Society on Wednesdays at 8:00 p.m.

Due to a lack of eyewitness testimony and branch records as of this writing, nothing else is known about the Coburg Branch during World War II.

In Memoriam

The following members of the Coburg Branch did not survive World War II:

Albert Christian Beck b. Frankenheim, Mittelfranken, Bayern, 29 Aug 1884; son of Johannes Beck and Karoline Guttmann; bp. 6 Sep 1933; conf. 6 Sep 1933; k. in battle Dec 1939 (FHL microfilm 68802, no. 453)

Flora Maria Becker b. Coburg, Bayern, 8 Jun 1914; dau. of August Wilhelm Becker and Johanna Karoline Luise Menke; bp. 5 Nov 1932; conf. 6 Nov 1932; m. 21 May 1938, Alfred Bernhard; d. heart failure 15 Aug 1940 (FHL microfilm 68786, no. 37; FHL microfilm 68802, no. 439; IGI)

Rudolf W. Bosseckert b. Kleinhennersdorf, Dresden, Sachsen, 8 Jun 1917; son of Walter Bosseckert and Elsa or Ella Binczik or Bincyik; bp. 27 Jun 1934; conf. 27 Jun 1934; ord. deacon 4 Nov 1934; ord. priest 5 Apr 1936; corporal; k. in battle Flanders, Belgium, 27 May 1940; bur. Lommel, Belgium (FHL microfilm 68786, no. 44; FHL microfilm 68802, no. 470; www.volksbund.de; IGI)

Margot Hanst b. Bald Wildungen, Bayern, 7 Mar 1925; dau. of Johannes Hanst and Ella Richter; bp. 11 Jun 1934; conf. 11 Jun 1934; d. suicide 16 Mar 1943 (CHL CR 275 8 2458, 107; FHL microfilm 68802, no. 467)

Paul Jakob Naumann b. Mittwitz, Bayern, 14 Feb 1910; son of Alwin Gundermann and Christina Margaretha Jakob; bp. 4 May 1920; conf. 4 May 1920; d. meningitis 8 Oct 1940 (FHL microfilm 68786, no. 35; FHL microfilm 68802, no. 300; IGI)

Notes

1. West German Mission branch directory, 1939, CHL LR 10045 11.
2. West German Mission branch directory, 1939.
3. Presiding Bishopric, "Financial, Statistical, and Historical Reports of Wards, Stakes, and Missions, 1884–1955," 257, CHL CR 4 12.

Fürth Branch

Located just six miles northwest of the Nuremberg city center, Fürth was a city of 78,838 people when World War II began. The branch of The Church of Jesus Christ of Latter-day Saints had existed there for not quite one year at the time, as we read in the records of the West German Mission:

> Sunday, September 11, 1938: The newly organized Fürth Branch held a special sacrament meeting with Pres. [M. Douglas] and Sister [Evelyn] Wood in attendance.[1]

Fürth Branch[2]	**1939**
Elders	2
Priests	5
Teachers	3
Deacons	3
Other Adult Males	13
Adult Females	34
Male Children	5
Female Children	4
Total	69

Although less than a year old, the Fürth Branch had a stable unit, with thirteen men and boys holding the priesthood. As was the case in so many branches in Germany in those days, the number of women over twelve years of age dominated the Fürth Branch population at 49 percent. The smallest portion of the branch consisted of the children.

The branch president in July 1939 was Johann Schmidt. A resident of Nuremberg, he may have been chosen for the assignment as an expatriate of Fürth.[3] According to the branch directory, President Schmidt could be reached by telephone at his office in a Nuremberg insurance company from 8:00 a.m. to 4:00 p.m. His wife, Frieda, was the leader of the YWMIA. President Schmidt's counselors were Heinrich Beck and Georg Beck. Georg Völker was the leader of the YMMIA, and Anna Beck was the president of the Relief Society. Robert Beck was the superintendent of the Sunday School and the instructor of the genealogical research group.

The Fürth Branch met in rooms on the third floor of a Hinterhaus at Pfisterstrasse 16. Sunday School began at 10:00 a.m. and sacrament meeting at 7:00 p.m. MIA met on Tuesday evenings at 8:00

p.m., and the Relief Society met on the second and fourth Tuesdays at 7:00 p.m. The choir rehearsed on the third Sunday, and the genealogical study group met on the fourth Sunday.

In the absence of any eyewitnesses or surviving branch reports, nothing more is known about the Fürth Branch during the years 1939 to 1945. Several eyewitnesses from the Nuremberg Branch indicated that they attended church meetings on an infrequent basis in Fürth after their own branch rooms were destroyed on January 2–3, 1945. The city of Fürth was the object of fifteen air raids that damaged 11 percent of the city's structures.[4]

In Memoriam

The following members of the Fürth Branch did not survive World War II:

Johann Beck b. Fürth, Nürnberg, Bayern, 26 Jan 1883; son of Georg Beck and Elisabetha Ernsberger; bp. 3 Oct 1922; conf. 3 Oct 1922; m. Fürth 17 Aug 1907, Pauline Louise Seidel; 8 children; d. stomach cancer Fürth 28 Sep 1942 (FHL microfilm 68802, no. 5; CHL CR 375 8 2458; FHL microfilm no. 25720 1925 and 1935 censuses; IGI)

Kunigunda Ernsberger b. Siegelsdorf, Bayern, 26 Feb 1858; dau. of Johann Christof Strattner and Elisabetha Ernsberger; bp. 9 Mar 1891; conf. 9 Mar 1891; m. Burgfarrnbach, Fürth, Bayern, 25 Nov 1888, Georg Konrad Pfund; d. old age 15 Apr 1944 (FHL microfilm 68802, no. 10; CHL CR 375 8 2458; FHL microfilm no. 271393; 1925 and 1935 censuses; IGI)

Margarethe Ott b. Geißengrund, Bayern, 4 Jun 1883; dau. of Magdalina Ott; bp. 22 Sep 1923; conf. 22 Sep 1923; m. Georg Mangold; d. 31 Oct 1944 (FHL microfilm 68802, no. 25; FHL microfilm no. 245225; 1930 census)

Joseph Rothmeier b. Fürth, Nürnberg, Bayern, 8 Aug 1911; son of Anton Rothmeier and Franziska Bierl, bp. 2 Mar 1924; conf. 2 Mar 1924; ord. deacon 17 Feb 1931; k. in battle Russia 30 Dec 1943 (FHL microfilm 68802, no. 41; CHL CR 375 8 2458)

Christian Völker b. Fürth, Nürnberg, Bayern, 27 Jul 1917; son of Georg Völker and Elise Feiertag; bp. 12 Oct 1930; conf. 12 Oct 1930; sergeant; d. field hospital in Bos. Novi/Croatia 11 Sep 1944 (CHL microfilm 2458, form 42 FP, pt. 37, 10–11; FHL microfilm 68802, no. 368; www.volksbund.de)

Konrad Völker b. Nürnberg, Nürnberg, Bayern, 26 Sep 1914; son of Georg Völker and Elise Feiertag; bp. 1 Sep 1923; MIA near Bjelgorod or Bolchowetz or Dnjeprodsershinssk or Melechowo or Kaminowatka or Nikolajewka 1 Aug 1943 (CHL microfilm 2458, form 42 FP, pt. 37, 10–11; www.volksbund.de)

Margarete Zuckermandel b. Schweighausen, Bayern, 27 Oct 1898; dau. of Michael Zuckermandel and Margarete Wörlein or Schwarz; bp. 8 Oct 1939; conf. 8 Oct 1939; m. 30 Dec 1940, Friedrich Eckert; d. spinal infection 31 Oct 1942 (FHL microfilm 68802, no. 546; CHL CR 375 8 2458; IGI)

Notes

1. West German Mission quarterly report, 1938, no. 33, CHL LR 10045 2.
2. Presiding Bishopric, "Financial, Statistical, and Historical Reports of Wards, Stakes, and Missions, 1884–1955," 257, CHL CR 4 12.
3. Brother Schmidt was simultaneously serving as the president of the Coburg Branch.
4. Fürth city archive.

Nuremberg Branch

The Nuremberg Branch, the second largest branch in the West German Mission and one of the ten largest in all of Germany in 1939, had 259 members of record. It was a vibrant group of Saints when the war approached. The list of branch leaders compiled in July of that year shows that all Church organizations and programs were functioning, with the exception of the Primary organization ("because there are currently too few children").[1]

Nuremberg Branch[2]	1939
Elders	23
Priests	9
Teachers	11
Deacons	20
Other Adult Males	26
Adult Females	139
Male Children	13
Female Children	18
Total	259

Otto Baer was the president of the branch and was assisted by counselors Georg Strecker and Richard Schöpf. The former also served as the leader of the YMMIA and the latter as the president of the Sunday School. Berta Engel was the president of the Relief Society, Alma Klein the leader of the YWMIA, and Albert Frenzel supervised genealogical research in the branch.

When the war began in September 1939, the Nuremberg Branch was holding meetings at Hirschelgasse 26. That small street is located in the northern part of the downtown, not far from the castle and the historic home of Albrecht Dürer, one of Germany's most famous artists. Hirschelgasse was part of the core of the city that was still surrounded by a massive city wall when the war began. The neighborhood featured some of the finest structures of the Middle Ages crowded around several squares and along narrow streets. Perhaps one-fourth of the city's 420,349 residents lived in that part of the city.[3]

The first Sunday meeting was sacrament meeting at 9:00 a.m., and Sunday School followed at 10:50. The genealogical research group met every other Sunday at 7:00 p.m. Relief Society meetings took place on Mondays at 8:00 p.m., and MIA met on Wednesday evenings at 8:00.

The records of the West German Mission include no reports submitted by the Nuremberg Branch for the years 1939 to 1945, but this notice from the Church's German-language magazine, *Der Stern*, dated October 22, 1939, is of interest:

> The Nuremberg Branch moved from its rooms on Hirschelgasse (where they had met for eleven years) to rooms at Untere Talgasse 20. The city ordered the move due to the implementation of a new sanitation program. The dedication of the new rooms was attended by Otto Baer (branch president), Ludwig Weiss (president of the Nuremberg District), Johann Schmidt (president of the Fürth Branch), and Johann Thaller (president of the Munich District).[4]

According to Wilhelm (Willy) Eysser (born 1924), the rooms at Untere Talgasse 20 were better than those at Hirschelgasse. "We met on the third floor, and some branch members lived on the fourth floor. There were about 125 people in attendance at the time."[5] Two families who were members of the Church lived in the same building—the Gentners and the Geudters, according to Gerda Gentner (born 1934).[6]

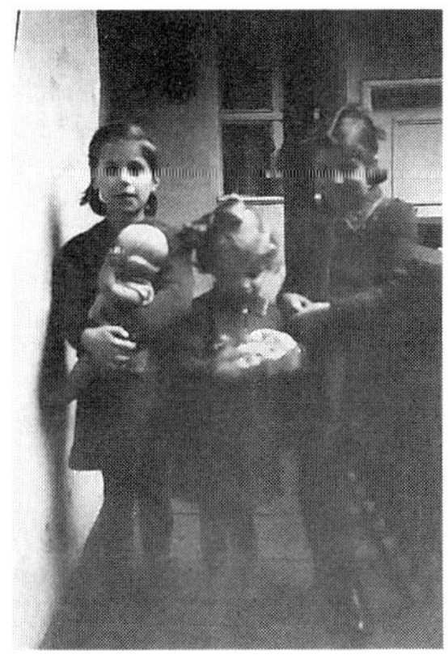

Fig. 1. Gerda Gentner (left) with her sisters Helga and Else in about 1941. (G. Gentner Kammerer)

Fig. 2. The Gentner family celebrating Christmas Eve in about 1938. (G. Gentner Kammerer)

Waltraud Weiss (born 1930), a daughter of the district president, provided more detail about the new meeting rooms:

> The owner of the building had attended Sunday School as a boy (but had not joined the Church) and helped us any way he could. The rooms were tall and had very ornate ceilings. We removed one wall to make the main meeting room larger. We heated the rooms with coal. There was a patio behind the building with a backyard that was open to everybody.[7]

The family of Ludwig Weiss lived in the suburb of Lauf am Holz. From that location, they walked about thirty minutes to reach the streetcar that took them to church. Between Sunday meetings, they usually did not go home again but rather stayed in town with other branch members.

Helmut Schwemmer (born 1933) recalled two significant prewar events with remarkable clarity. The first was the Reichskristallnacht (Night of Broken Glass) of November 9, 1938:

> Our whole family was awakened by this terrible noise of breaking glass and screaming. My dad told us that it was the Nazi SA men (Hitler's special bodyguards) on a rampage in the neighborhood. The next morning we found our favorite bakery across the street completely demolished, and the owners were nowhere to be found.[8]

He learned years later that this violence meant the end of many of the Jews who had not yet left Germany.

The second prewar event of great significance in the life of young Helmut Schwemmer was the Nuremberg Party Rally. An annual spectacle, the rally brought tens of thousands of soldiers, Nazi Party members, and civilians to the city. Helmut recalled watching workers erect viewing stands along the route from the main station to the party rally grounds at Luitpoldhain, passing within a block of Helmut's apartment house. He later wrote:

> As a six year old I was awed by the never ending columns of soldiers, tanks, cannons, bands and other army equipment. The highlight of the parade was of course when all participants were in the stadium and Hitler and his cronies made their speeches which lasted for hours. . . . This same show was repeated every day for a week. . . . The Hitler Youth choir I belonged to marched in the parade on one of the days during the week dedicated to the Hitler Youth of Germany. Although I could not see much of what was going on, . . . three things transpired which are permanently etched into my memory: (1) the booming voices of the speakers—especially Hitler, . . . (2) the deafening and seemingly endless cheers of *Sieg Heil,* . . . (3) the lighting of thousand of torches in the evening.[9]

When the American missionaries were evacuated from Germany on August 25, 1939, many of the local Saints were sad and concerned about the future. Those emotions may not have been obvious to young Lorie Baer (born 1933), but she did recall vividly that "the American missionaries knocked on the door in the middle of the night and said, 'Brother Baer, we are called home!' They gave my father all the materials they used in their missionary work such as books."[10]

Walter Schwemmer (born 1931) was baptized in the Pegnitz River in Nuremberg just weeks after the war began. He recalled:

> We went there late at night. We didn't really want anybody who was not a member of the Church to see what was happening. My uncle, Christian Schwemmer, baptized me. We had our pajamas on, and it was cold outside. After the baptism, my dad took us home on his bicycle while we were still wet. After all, it was October.[11]

Elisabetha Baier (born 1906) had married Georg Strecker (born 1906) in 1932, and they had two daughters by the time war broke out in 1939. Georg worked at the Mann munitions factory, and Elisabetha had a sewing job at home. Because Georg was a member of the branch presidency, the police came to the Strecker home twice during the war to search for Church books. According to Elisabetha, "The police felt the Mormon Church was an American church so they were suspicious of us."[12] Nothing ever came of the investigation.

Branch president Otto Baer owned and operated a health food store not far from the main station in Nuremberg. His daughter, Lorie, recalled how the Nazi Party compelled her father to join in order to maintain his business. She claimed that her home was one of the first to be destroyed in Nuremberg when enemy planes targeted the main railway station nearby. It was a most frightening experience for which the family was not at all prepared:

> We were in the shelter, and when the attack was over, my mother ran upstairs and grabbed a suitcase. . . . We also grabbed a bottle of mineral water and a handkerchief for everybody and made sure that we held the wet handkerchief over our mouths. The street in which we lived had about sixteen large apartment buildings. Of

those, only three were not hit that night. By the time we got out of our basement and grabbed our things, everything on the street was burning. We stood at the end of the street and looked back—everything was gone. We could only take what we had on, and that was it. This was in the middle of the night. My mother looked at me and said that we have to leave. She had a very close friend with whom we could stay. I called her Aunt Käthe because we ended up staying with her for three years. We knocked on her door in the middle of the night, and she let us in and gave us a safe place to stay. The next morning, my mother went back to our home to see if there was still something there, but everything was gone.

Fig. 3. Otto and Ella Baer with their daughter, Lorie, in the doorway to their health food store Kräuter-Handlung Baer in 1938. (L. Baer Bonds)

Shortly after the war began, branch president Otto Baer was drafted. He spent most of the next six years away from home in such places as Poland, France, Romania, and Russia. Initially, he was succeeded by Paul Eysser, who in turn was drafted and replaced by Ludwig Weiss, who was still serving as the district president.[13]

Waltraud Weiss was inducted automatically into the Jungvolk program in her school at the age of ten. She recalled, "I had piano lessons on Wednesdays after school and couldn't participate in the meetings. On Fridays, my mother had a sewing class, so I couldn't attend on those days either. But I made sure to attend a few times, just to stay out of trouble."

"When you were a woman [during the war], you had to be in the work force, and your children

Fig. 4. Hans Eysser (far right) as a new recruit at a Wehrmacht post in Ansbach, Bavaria. An elder in the Nuremberg Branch, Hans was killed in Russia in 1942. (W. Eysser)

were left alone throughout the day," recalled Marie Strecker Mördelmeyer (born 1912).[14] She had married in 1935 and had two daughters, Annemarie and Helga, before the war started. "When the sirens would sound an attack, the children had to flee to the bomb shelter alone, and I never knew in what part of town they were. My husband was a soldier, away from home from the years 1939 to 1945." The burden on mothers raising their children alone during the war was extremely heavy in many respects.

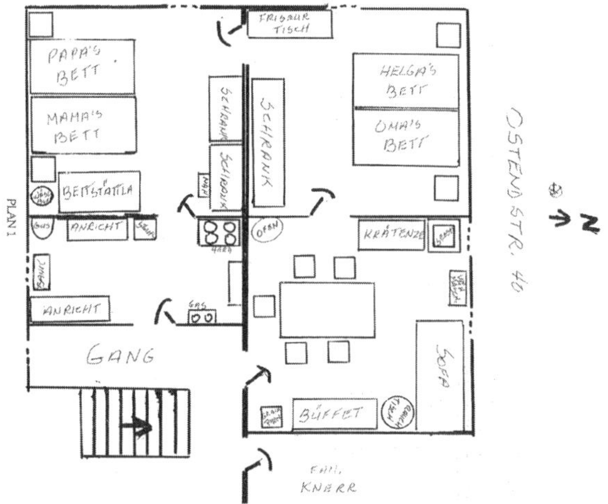

Fig. 5. The floor plan of the Mördelmeyer apartment at Ostendstrasse 40 in Nuremberg. The family lived there from 1935 to 1944. Tisch = *table,* Bettstättla = *bedstand,* Schrank = *closet,* Gang = *hall,* Anricht = *cupboard,* Sessel = *overstuffed chair,* Stuhl = *chair. (H. Mördelmeyer Strauber)*

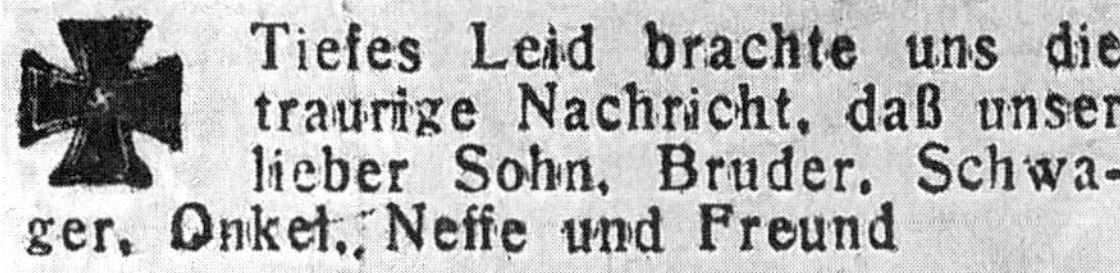
Tiefes Leid brachte uns die traurige Nachricht, daß unser lieber Sohn, Bruder, Schwager, Onkel, Neffe und Freund

Hans Eysser

Soldat in einem Infanterie-Rgt.

sein junges Leben im Alter von 23 Jahren im Osten für sein geliebtes Vaterland opferte.

Nürnberg-Süd (Linnéstr. 20).

In tiefer Trauer: Familie Wilhelm Eysser, Eltern, und Geschwister; Fam. Wendler, Geuder u. Pfeiffer

Fig. 6. This notice was printed in a Nuremberg newspaper in April 1942. It reads in part, "It is with deep sadness that we received the news that our dear son, brother, brother-in-law, uncle, nephew and friend, Hans Eysser, a soldier in an infantry regiment, sacrificed his life on the Eastern Front for his beloved fatherland at the age of twenty-three years." (W. Eysser)

"When I was ten years old, I was inducted into the Jungvolk," recalled Walter Schwemmer. His story continued:

> Actually, it was not mandatory, but they put so much pressure on the parents that they eventually decided to send their children to the activities. I was a part of the Hitler Youth later on [age fourteen] too, and I attended the meetings. They never interfered with Church, though. I can't actually remember what we did exactly, but I know that it had to do with sports. I liked those activities. We also marched.

Lorie Baer was sent to live with her aunt in 1941. Her mother felt that the little girl would be safer in a small town and could attend school without constant interruptions. Lorie lived with her aunt for an entire year, sleeping in a storage room and eating with a different family. It was an unhappy time, as she recalled:

> As soon as classes were over on Friday afternoon, I would take a train back home to Nuremberg. I was seven years old at the time, and it was scary. I wanted to spend the weekend with my mother. I even had to change trains in the middle, and I waited for forty-five minutes for the next train to come. Every Sunday afternoon for a year, I cried and cried because I had to leave my mother again. . . . After a year I was so homesick for my mother that I said to her that if she got killed, I wanted to be also, and I stayed home with her.

Back in Nuremberg, Lorie lived with her mother again in the apartment house the government had since rebuilt for them and their neighbors.

Little Helga Mördelmeyer recalled how her father was assigned as a dog handler in the army. During training sessions conducted in a nearby town, he taught his German shepherd to sniff out partisans on the Eastern Front. "He would come home on weekends, but he was not allowed to bring his dog. He later told us that his dog had often saved his life during difficult times. When it was a cold night in Russia, the dog would lie down right next to my father and keep him warm. . . . The dog protected him."[15]

Schoolteachers in Nazi Germany were state employees and were required to belong to the National Socialist Party. Although not all were believers in the Nazi philosophy, one of Waltraud Weiss's teachers apparently was. She explained: "When I was in sixth grade, I had a teacher who was politically involved and wanted to teach us those things. The first thing he did every morning was to read aloud from the newspaper the accomplishments of the government. We were actually supposed to learn many other things, but for him, it was more important that we know about current events and politics."

"You always had to salute and say 'Heil Hitler!' when you entered a store," recalled Oswald Schwemmer (born 1935), "or they would question you." Oswald's father, Christian Schwemmer, was a tailor who operated his own business on the main floor of an apartment building on Angerstrasse, just south of the main railroad station in Nuremberg. The Schwemmers joined their neighbors in the basement when the air-raid sirens wailed. During one attack, a bomb fell close by, and the vibration caused the door to the furnace ash removal chamber to fly open. As Oswald recalled, "Everybody looked black as Negroes from the soot."[16]

Oswald soon learned that air raids were not bad in every regard; there were advantages for little children. Besides having fun collecting pieces of metal from bombs and antiaircraft shells, the children found other treasures to gather: "There was a toy factory nearby. We had the time of our lives going through the rubble [of the factory] finding toys and stuff."

Waltraud Weiss described being sent home from school when the first air-raid alarm sounded: "When I rode the train home [to our suburb], it would not stop but would roll slowly through the station, and we had to jump off." At home, her parents listened to forbidden radio broadcasts from the Allies in order to receive advance warnings about air raids. Waltraud's account continued: "Hearing the sounds of the planes and seeing the 'Christmas trees' [flares dropped by the attackers to mark the bombing targets] made me scared, but at least we knew where the bombs would fall."

In 1942, at the age of ten, Hermann Baer (born 1932) was inducted into the Jungvolk. As he recalled:

> I didn't want to go, so they came to my home and told my parents that if they didn't send me to the Hitler Youth, they would be arrested. So I had to go in order to protect my parents. It was like being in the Boy Scouts, but the indoctrination was different. They trained you to believe what they told you to believe.[17]

Ella Paula Baer traveled to Schweinfurt on one occasion with her daughter, Lorie, to visit relatives. Just as they boarded the train for home, enemy planes attacked the railroad station, and chaos broke out. A bomb hit the car they were in, and Lorie was suddenly surrounded by dead travelers. Her story continued:

> My mother had fainted, and I thought she was also dead. I dragged my mother out of the train, being eight years old. The minute I got her out of there, another bomb hit the train. After that, everybody was dead. I think it was only my mother and I and maybe one other person who survived that attack. My mother then went to look for our luggage while I stayed where she left me. While looking for our things, my mother stepped on a mine, and it exploded. All that happened to her was that she lost a heel of her shoe. That was all. But the people around her got hurt.

Helga Mördelmeyer started school in 1942. Because she was neither Catholic nor Lutheran, she had to sit around and "do nothing for an hour during the religion class. The teachers didn't make fun of [my sister and me], and the other pupils didn't care much." In the fall, Helga contracted pneumonia and was hospitalized. In her recollection, "during air raids they put all of the children in the halls, far away from the windows. When I came home, I saw that two buildings in our neighborhood had been bombed."

The year 1942 was tragic for the Schwemmer family. In October, Heinrich Schwemmer was killed in Russia. His son Walter recalled that two Nazi Party men in uniform knocked at the family's door one evening and informed Sister Schwemmer that her husband had given his life for his country. Later, she learned that Heinrich was killed trying to save his lieutenant, who had been wounded by a land mine. The man wanted to shoot himself, but Brother Schwemmer was able to convince him that his pregnant wife needed him back home. The lieutenant surrendered his pistol to Heinrich, who also stepped on a mine and sustained wounds from which he bled to death. The lieutenant made it home to Germany and wrote to Sister Schwemmer to explain the circumstances of Heinrich's death.

Just eleven days before he was killed, Heinrich Schwemmer had written home to his mother:

> Tine has probably told you that I have been wounded three times already. I hope that there will not be another time and that I can come home as I am now [healthy]. The first time was on June 6 (three pieces of shrapnel), the second on August 18 when we were attacked by a dive-bomber (three bomb fragments), and the third on September 5 (two more pieces of shrapnel from heavy artillery while we were clearing land mines). . . . I still have five pieces of metal in me; they can be taken out after the war if they are

> causing me trouble. . . . My dear mother, you didn't raise any cowards, but rather seven men who can find their place in the world. . . . I can look death calmly in the eye, if it absolutely must be so. . . . May you be privileged to see your seven soldiers return from the front in good health.[18]

It is not clear whether the letter Heinrich wrote on October 4 arrived in Nuremberg before the news that Heinrich had been killed.

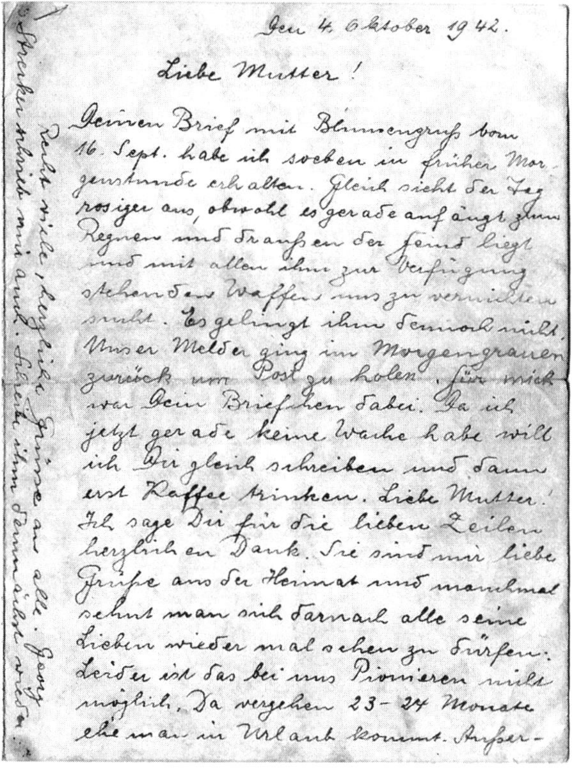

Den 4. Oktober 1942.

Liebe Mutter!

Deinen Brief mit Blumengruß vom
16. Sept. habe ich soeben in früher Mor-
genstunde erhalten. Gleich sieht der Tag
rosiger aus, obwohl es gerade anfängt zum
Regnen und draußen der Feind liegt
und mit allen ihm zur Verfügung
stehenden Waffen uns zu vernichten
sucht. Es gelingt ihm dennoch nicht.
Unser Melder ging im Morgengrauen
zurück um Post zu holen. Für mich
war Dein Briefchen dabei. Da ich
jetzt gerade keine Wache habe will
ich Dir gleich schreiben und dann
erst Kaffee trinken. Liebe Mutter!
Ich sage Dir für die lieben Zeilen
herzlichen Dank. Sie sind mir liebe
Grüße aus der Heimat und manchmal
sehnt man sich darnach alle seine
Lieben wieder mal sehen zu dürfen.
Leider ist das bei uns Pionieren nicht
möglich. Da vergehen 23–24 Monate
ehe man in Urlaub kommt. Außer-

Fig. 7. Letter written by Heinrich Schwemmer to his mother just eleven days before he was killed in Russia. (W. Schwemmer)

Later that year, Walter Schwemmer was evacuated to a place near Leitmeritz, Czechoslovakia, along with his entire class of boys and their teacher. He described his new setting in these words:

> We lived in the residence of a bishop of the Catholic Church. We had to wear our Hitler Youth uniforms very often and had to take care of them and wash them ourselves. We even ironed them. . . . We stayed there for two and one-half years—totally isolated from the Church. It was difficult being so far away from home. I think I was the only Mormon in that group. We attended the religion class at school, and I chose to attend the Protestant class.

"I was drafted by the Wehrmacht in December 1942, but I didn't want to go," recalled Willy Eysser. Of course, there was no other option but prison for refusing to serve in the military, so Willy and his brethren in the Nuremberg Branch reported for duty when called. His religious experience as a soldier over the next few years was typical of German LDS men: "I was a teacher in the Aaronic Priesthood at the time. I never saw another member of the Church who was also a soldier. I couldn't attend any meetings while I was in the military. . . . I couldn't partake of the sacrament the entire time, and I also didn't have my scriptures with me." Nevertheless, he attended church meetings on the few occasions when he came home on leave.

One particular air-raid experience remained clear in the memory of Elisabetha Strecker years later:

> One August [1943] night the siren warnings went off. . . . Usually when the sirens went off we had ten to fifteen minutes to get to the bunkers before the bombs started falling. But that night there was no [first] warning. As George, myself, and Brigitte left our apartment we walked out on the street and the upper street had already been bombed and was in flames. We ran as fast as we could, and George and I literally had to drag Birgitte to the bomb shelter. . . . I think it was the worst night I ever experienced.[19]

In October, the Strecker apartment was damaged, and the family lived with a woman in the branch named Sister Paulus for the next three months.

Waltraud Weiss recalled the efforts expended by her father to repair their apartment after it was damaged in an air raid in August 1943:

> My father tried his best to rebuild everything so that we could at least live in the house again. We received permission to use the materials in the ruins of the neighbor's house to repair our own. In March 1944, phosphorus bombs landed on our property but were stuck in the wrought iron and didn't get inside the house. My uncle was close enough to the bomb to have his hair singed.

Fig. 8. Members of the Nuremberg Branch on their way home after Sunday School. (L. Baer Bonds)

Marie Mördelmeyer lived with her two daughters in an apartment at Gugelstrasse 102. Like most residents of large cities in Germany, they usually sought shelter in their basement during air raids. One night, a bomb hit the adjacent building. She recalled, "I believe there were 42 persons dead. They burned to death. In that night I took my two kids under my arms and my prayer was, if it should hit us also that our Heavenly Father will make it quick. But our lives were spared. . . . We lost all that night." She was able to find a single room for her four-member family in the apartment building in which her parents lived. The family stayed there until November 1945.[20]

Young Annemarie Mördelmeyer (born 1935) explained that going to church meetings was a real challenge.[21] Her family had to be on constant lookout for a shelter to hide in if the air-raid sirens went off. In her recollection, church meetings were rarely interrupted once they started, but sirens were heard many times on their way home—a walk that took about a half hour. Little children were often left home during the evening meetings because travel was complicated and their sleep patterns needed to be maintained if possible.

"The government wanted to send my sister and me away in the Kinderlandverschickung program," recalled Annemarie:

> My mother would only let us go if she was given permission to come with us and leave her work at the munitions factory. She was told that they wanted to save the lives of the youth, not the lives of the old. My mother then explained that we would all stay together right where we were. They told her that she would have to go to a concentration camp. My grandmother then explained that she would also take care of us. Then we were able to stay home.

Fig. 9. Willy Eysser's military service record, like that of millions of German soldiers, airmen, and sailors. It measured 4 inches by 5¾ inches. (W. Eysser)

Friedrich Frenzel was an employee of the national postal system but an outspoken opponent of the Nazi Party. His son, Benjamin (born 1936), was aware of his father's attitude, and that apparently was clear to his schoolteacher. Fortunately, she took steps to prevent any trouble, as Benjamin recalled:

> When the Gestapo came [to school], she had the feeling that she should do something to protect me. I sat in the very front row, in front of her desk. The day the Gestapo came to visit, she put me at the very back on the left side of the classroom. As soon as the Gestapo entered, the children would have to raise their arms in order to say "Heil Hitler," and she was very much aware of the fact that I never did that. . . . The Gestapo did not ask any questions. My teacher was even a member of the Nazi Party but only because the law required her to be.[22]

Fig. 10. The Eysser family during the war. (W. Eysser)

Many Germans took pity on foreign prisoners of war and workers from other countries. Benjamin's mother, Katharine Frenzel, was one such sympathetic German. Benjamin recalled an odd incident that happened one day when they entered their garden space in a public garden district:

> My mother went in, and we were still waiting at the gate. Suddenly she started screaming, turned to us, and told us that we had to leave. The woman in the garden next to us wanted to know why my mother suddenly wanted to leave. My mother lied and said that a rat had run across her feet. Instead, there was a [foreign] prisoner of war hiding among the bushes. The authorities had divided the garden area into two parts and made a prison camp out of one half. Mother gave the man the sandwiches that she had brought for us and left him there, telling nobody that she had seen him. If somebody had found out that she lied, she could have been punished for treason.

The childhood memories of Helmut Schwemmer constitute a collage of life in wartime:

> Days and days without having to go to school because of the nightly air raids; sitting in the cellar on Mom's lap listening to the bombs explode all around and being very scared; the putrid smell of houses on fire and bombed out old buildings; windows covered with black cloth and inspected from the outside every night for the slightest amount of light shining through . . . ; collecting and trading bomb fragments; Hitler Youth boys choir; . . . collecting pencil lead–like

"fire sticks" from partially burned firebombs and making firecrackers with them; one of my friends lost half of his face and an arm when a firebomb he was trying to dismantle blew up in his face.[23]

Walter Schwemmer recalled an occasion when he nearly lost his life to a dive-bomber. "We were in our garden house at the time, and I told everybody to duck down when the plane approached. The bullets went right through our house, and I remember one flying right over somebody's head. We were glad that he didn't stand up [right then]."

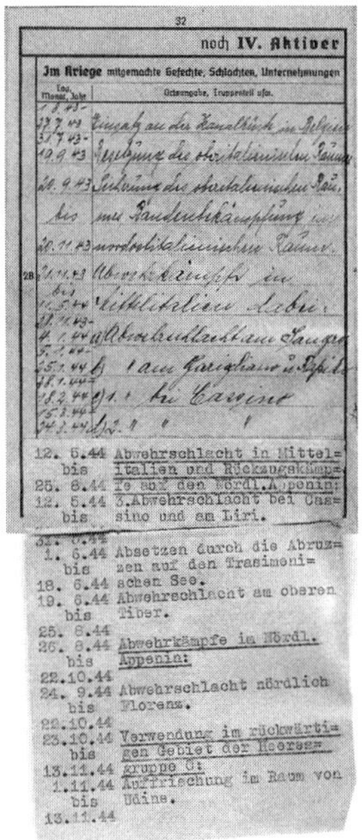
32

noch IV. Aktiver

Im Kriege mitgemachte Gefechte, Schlachten, Unternehmungen

Tag, Monat, Jahr	Ortsangabe, Truppenteil usw.
12. 5.44 bis 25. 8.44	Abwehrschlacht in Mittelitalien und Rückzugskämpfe auf den Nördl. Apenin:
12. 5.44 bis 31. 5.44	3. Abwehrschlacht bei Cassino und am Liri.
1. 6.44 bis 18. 6.44	Absetzen durch die Abruzzen auf den Trasimenischen See.
19. 6.44 bis 25. 6.44	Abwehrschlacht am oberen Tiber.
26. 8.44 bis 22.10.44	Abwehrkämpfe im Nördl. Appenin:
24. 9.44 bis 22.10.44	Abwehrschlacht nördlich Florenz.
23.10.44 bis 13.11.44	Verwendung im rückwärtigen Gebiet der Heeresgruppe C:
1.11.44 bis 13.11.44	Auffrischung im Raum von Udine.

Fig. 11. *Willy Eysser's military service record did not have enough space to record all of his combat experience, so a sheet was attached. (W. Eysser)*

Willy Eysser described one combat experience in Hungary:

> On May 7, 1944, I was wounded. I was hit in the left leg, and it hit a nerve, so I was not able to move my leg for a while. They took me to a field hospital in the middle of nowhere. They put me in the back of a room and laid me on my stomach, so I wasn't able to drink or eat anything because I couldn't keep it down. It was a while before I was able to walk again."

Following his recuperation, he was allowed to go home for a rare visit.

While Christian Schwemmer was away at war and his tailor business was discontinued, his wife, Babette, took their children away from the big city to the farming community of Ehlheim, twenty-five miles to the southwest. There they lived in total isolation from the Church, but Babette's son Oswald recalled how she "taught us the principles [of the gospel] and prayed with us." She read to her children from the scriptures and taught them through example, but it would be several years before they would attend church meetings in Nuremberg again.

According to Oswald, the town of Ehlheim consisted of about seventeen farmers and their families. To attend school, he had to walk two miles to Dittenheim: "This was OK in the summertime, but in the winter or rain, it was terrible. The road was not asphalt, and it was very muddy when it rained, and in the winter it got very cold, and the snow was very high." To young Oswald, the distance to school seemed twice as far as it really was.

It was not uncommon in those days for parents to attend sacrament meetings on Sunday evenings while their children stayed at home. Such was the case one Sunday in the George Strecker home. Two daughters, Wanda (born 1935) and Brigitte (born 1938), stayed at home, and for their safety, their parents locked the apartment door from the outside with a large key. During the sacrament meeting, the air-raid sirens sounded, and the little girls could not leave the apartment for the basement shelter. Brigitte explained what happened next:

> My sister and I pulled out a chair, and we knelt down and said a prayer. My sister said a beautiful prayer, and she was [nine] at that time. I think I was only [six]. And so, about fifteen or twenty minutes later, my parents came. But you know, we knew what to do as children. We knew that Heavenly Father would watch over us, and he touched us, and we knew that. And when they came we were so happy, of course, to see them, and nothing happened to us, and they came home as quickly as they could.[24]

Young Benjamin Frenzel experienced enough air raid alarms and attacks to recall the alarm sequence vividly: "The first alarm meant that there was a possibility that the enemy would come. The second alarm meant that we had to get ready for sure and head to the shelter. When the third alarm sounded, we knew that the enemy would only need five to seven more minutes to attack." On one occasion, a Gestapo agent was checking the identification papers of people entering the bomb shelter. "My father did not have his with him. He then went up to the castle, where he found another shelter. My mother and all of my siblings at that time stayed close to our home."[25]

Friedrich Frenzel attempted to construct a radio that could receive broadcasts from stations beyond the German borders—something the common German radio could not do. The activity was also strictly forbidden. According to his son, Benjamin, local merchants became aware of Brother Frenzel's designs:

> One day, the Gestapo came to our door, and we could hear those boots in the hallway. It just so happened that my father was home. My father put his fingers to his lips to indicate that we needed to be extremely quiet. We obeyed. He waited, and they knocked and knocked again. He did not open the door. We heard them walk away, and we wanted to jump up again to play, but my father put his fingers to his lips again. It seemed like we sat there for twenty minutes doing absolutely nothing. We then heard some more boots in the hallway walking away. My father had known that there were at least five men standing outside the door. Even fifty minutes after the initial knocking, we still heard them walk away. We were then allowed to get up again to play.

In the summer of 1944, Helga Mödelmeyer turned eight and was baptized. "I think that Brother Schwemmer baptized me and my uncle confirmed me. That took place at the indoor swimming pool. We waited until everybody was out of the pool. Two or three others were baptized that night, too. I think Oswald Schwemmer was one of them."

Ferdinand Schwemmer (born 1934) recalled a frightening experience his mother had on a shopping expedition late in the war:

> Our mother went into town once in order to find food for us. She was at the main town square when an air raid started, and she went into the big public bunker. When the attack was over, she had the feeling that she needed to get out of the bunker as soon as possible. The [wardens] didn't want to let her out yet, but she forced her way out anyway. As she hurried toward our house, the attackers came again. They dropped aerial mines, and one hit the city square where my mother had just barely left the bunker. All the people in the bunker were killed. My mother was so lucky that she left. She explained that she just had this feeling, and she knew she had to follow through with it.[26]

Ferdinand also recalled that his parents had a little house just north of the city prison near the railroad yards.[27] The small home could not have withstood a bomb, so Sister Schwemmer was compelled to take her children to the nearest public shelter, at least fifteen minutes away on Layerstrasse. According to Ferdinand, "We were late getting to the bunker many times, and bombs would be falling before we got there. We hid in a ditch and prayed that we would get out of the situation alive. My mother [crouched] over us to cover us, and we waited until the attack was over. We heard people screaming, and it was really scary."

The new year 1945 began in a most tragic way for the city of Nuremberg. Allied airplanes flew over on January 2 and dropped more bombs that night than during all previous attacks combined. The core of the city was almost totally destroyed, and countless architectural, historical, and artistic treasures were lost forever. Several thousand residents died in the attack, and tens of thousands were rendered homeless. According to Waltraud Weiss, the branch meeting rooms at Untere Talgasse 20 were destroyed that night.

Annemarie Mördelmeyer recalled clearly the night of January 2:

> The night before, all of Nuremberg looked like it had layers of sugar everywhere because it had snowed. It looked beautiful with the full moon. It was so peaceful, and no alarm destroyed that peace. On January 2, we sat on benches in the basement, which was not larger than twenty square meters. My mother always sat in the middle and put her arms around us to make us feel safe. We heard the bombs falling; the noise was unbearable, and we knew exactly what it meant for us. Afterwards, there was no snow anymore—we experienced a [fire-]storm that night, with lots of wind pulling us toward the burning

> buildings. It was horrible. I would say that every third house was in flames that night. I saw the bodies of the people who used to live in the neighboring house. As children, we wanted to see it because it was something we had never seen before. But our mother didn't want us to look. The bodies were so much smaller than we would have ever thought. The smell wasn't pleasant.

Her sister, Helga, also had vivid memories of that night: "There was a young woman in our apartment building who had gotten married on Christmas Day. She died during that horrible air raid. I watched the entire city burn the next day. We didn't really go to school after that because there weren't any buildings available or teachers, for that matter."

Fig. 12. The Mördelmeyer family lived in this house on Ostendstrasse when the American army arrived in April 1945. (H. Mördelmeyer Campbell)

Although not quite five years old at the time, little Zenos Frenzel (born 1940) saw things that night that he could never forget:

> When we came out of the shelter, the city was burning brightly. We had to get out of the city somewhere, which was the only solution. And while we were walking, the walls of the houses we passed collapsed next to us, which could have hurt us very badly. It was a weird feeling because the city was so hot although it was in the middle of winter. When we arrived at the outskirts of the city, it was suddenly colder again. There was snow that winter and also that night. We had only the clothes we were wearing, and my mother had her purse. In this one night, we had lost all of our earthly possessions.[28]

The Frenzels found a place to stay in Heroldsberg, where Brother Frenzel's employer had erected some temporary barracks. According to Zenos, "the temporary structure consisted of two rooms, one about eighteen by eighteen and the other about eighteen by sixteen. We had no light, no water, no gas, no telephone, no toilet (just an outhouse), and no stove." For the Frenzels, "temporary" became five years, but when so many people had lost their homes, their shack was a veritable blessing. The secret to their survival in the immediate aftermath of the war was the food supply that Hans Albert Frenzel had stored for his family at the home of his brother in Burgthann, some fifteen miles from Heroldsberg. Hans Albert made many trips there to retrieve some of the food for his family of six. They were all glad that Brother Frenzel had heeded the advice of the Church leaders to set aside food for bad times.

Willy Eysser recalled hearing that the Schröpf family (residents of the top floor of the building at Untere Talgasse 20 and members of the branch) were killed in their basement shelter on January 2. Apparently the bombs burst wine bottles and barrels of vinegar stored there, and the occupants of the shelter drowned in the ensuing chaos.

Following the destruction of the branch rooms, there was no building available to the branch until well after the war. Eyewitnesses still in the city in the spring of 1945 recall meeting in a school and in the apartments of surviving members, usually in groups of ten to twenty persons. Waltraud Weiss said that on several occasions, her father traveled across the city from their home in the eastern suburbs to visit the Fürth Branch to the west—a distance of six miles that took about two hours to negotiate.

Hermann Baer recalled seeing the ruins of the church building: "It was all burned out. The only thing left standing were the bare walls. There was nothing saved. After that, we met in a school for a while." He had recalled seeing pictures of Jesus Christ and President Heber J. Grant on the walls of the meeting rooms before the building was destroyed, but it would be some time before such was the case again in the Nuremberg Branch.

Walter Schwemmer's evacuated school class included boys who wanted nothing more than to go home in January 1945. The group had been away from Nuremberg for more than two years—first in Czechoslovakia and then in Rothenburg, Bavaria. Soon, several boys simply took off for home and actually made it safely there. Finally, the leaders relented and sent all of the boys home to Nuremberg.

In February 1945, Georg Strecker was drafted into the Wehrmacht. By war's end, he was a POW, and his wife did not know his whereabouts for two years. He was in Marseilles, France, but Elisabetha's letters to him through the French government were never delivered (nor were his to her). Finally, he decided to write to a friend in the United States, who wrote to his mother in Nuremberg. She was able to contact Elisabetha Strecker with the news that her husband was alive. She had left Nuremberg when her husband was drafted—following the recommendation of the government that she take her children to a safer location. She stayed on a farm near Hohenstadt until October of that year.[29]

"The war ended with the Americans coming in," according to Walter Schwemmer:

> We saw the tanks coming in and the soldiers walking down the street. They waved at us kids and threw candy. We weren't afraid. . . . Those were the first Americans we had ever seen. There was no fighting. I remember learning in the Hitler Youth that they were our enemies. . . .We heard that the black soldiers would come and kill us, would cut our heads off or would do other terrible things to us. But in reality, they were the nicest ones to us. They were the ones to throw the candy and to smile and wave.

"As the Americans marched into our city, one can say that they were very humane," recalled Marie Mördelmeyer. Her husband had returned to Nuremberg in May 1945 and soon found work with the occupation forces. Marie explained that "he worked at the 'SS' barracks [now occupied by the US troops] fixing the bathtubs and toilets and all the other things that were ruined during the war and during the takeover of the city. And it continued to get better."[30] The Mördelmeyer family was indeed fortunate in many respects during the summer of 1945.

The invading Americans stopped long enough in the northern suburbs of Nuremberg to set up artillery near the Baer home. Young Hermann recalled how the GIs took possession of his home. The Baers moved into another apartment for the next two weeks, but Hermann was allowed to return to the house several times in order to retrieve food and other needed items. He was not happy with what he saw, recalling, "They would put their feet up on the dining room table, and I went in there and put a table cloth on it and told them not to put their feet up there. They did a little bit of damage but not that much." However, what began as a relatively harmless situation nearly took a tragic turn. Some neighborhood boys informed the GIs that there were girls nearby, including Hermann's sister. As he recalled:

> One soldier came at night, and he brought us chocolate and stuff and then he wanted to take my sister up in the bedroom and rape her. He had a pistol. He set it down, and I picked it up and threatened him and said, "You're not going upstairs." My sister took off up the stairs, and my older sister stood in front of the door. [The GI] could speak a little German, and I told him, "If you're going to push my sister around, I'm going to shoot you." Then my mother went outside and yelled for an MP, and the GI got scared and left. . . . I think I would have shot him if he physically attacked my older sister.

Fig. 13. Survivors of the Nuremberg Branch in 1947. (L. Baer Bonds)

When the fighting stopped in Czechoslovakia in the spring of 1945, Willy Eysser and his comrades found themselves trapped between the Americans advancing from the west and the Soviets from the east. Their captain instructed the men to load a vehicle with supplies and prepare to move toward the American lines. When a general came by and learned of the plan, he drew his pistol and threatened to shoot the men for desertion. Fortunately, the captain came by in time to convince the general of the wisdom of the plan. The men did indeed surrender to the Americans and became some of the twenty-four thousand German soldiers who became POWs under the Allied invaders at that location.

Fearing that they would be turned over to the Soviets, Willy Eysser was greatly relieved when he and a few thousand other POWs were told by their American captors in July 1945 "to hurry home, but watch out for the curfew restrictions," as Willy recalled. He wasted no time in making his way home to Nuremberg, where an uncle informed him of the whereabouts of his parents. They had been bombed out of their home and were living on a farm a few miles from the city. Willy was able to find a place to stay amid the ruins of Nuremberg before the summer was out, and he joined perhaps twenty-five persons for church meetings there.

"When the war was over, we received a letter stating that my father had served as a fine soldier but that he was missing in action," recalled Lorie Baer. "My mother nearly fainted and knew that if they wrote that, he was [most likely] dead somewhere. As soon as we got over the news, I remembered that my father had said that he was not going to go back to his unit, and I told my mother that." As it turned out, Otto Baer had gone into hiding in Austria rather than to his unit on the Eastern Front. On his way home after the war ended, he was confronted by GIs who demanded to see his papers. He showed them his little book with the names and addresses of Americans with whom he had served as a missionary in the early 1930s. The GIs were impressed and sent him on toward Nuremberg, rather than take him prisoner.

"When the war was over, we could see practically from one end of Nuremberg to the other," claimed Ferdinand Schwemmer. "That's how bad the destruction in the city was." Indeed, contemporary photographs show very few structures still standing within the old city walls.

Elisabeth Gentner had been living in Bamberg with her children since 1943. She had lost her husband in Russia in 1944 and was hoping for a calmer life by leaving Nuremberg. She and her children were told to stay in the basement when the American army approached Bamberg in April 1945. She recalled her first encounter with the invaders:

> We woke up the next morning not expecting anything, opened up the trap door [from the basement], and walked into our living room. American soldiers were sitting everywhere, and it was the first time for me that I saw a black person. We were not scared. [Some of] the first soldiers who entered our home were Mormons. They were very nice to us, and they started talking to us. We asked them where they were from, and when they answered that they were from Utah, we said that we had relatives living there. Then we found out that we were all members of the Church. We could all speak a little bit of each other's languages.

The Gentners therefore had several reasons to be relieved that the war was over. Their conquerors were good people, and the violence of the past few years had finally ceased.

Brunhilde Baer, daughter of Ferdinand Baer and niece of Otto Baer, was born one week before the war began—just in time to experience the worst years of the twentieth century in Germany. "I remember wearing the same clothes every single day. They were washed on Fridays, and then we would wear them again for the rest of the week."[31] Her family was bombed out and found a place to stay in the town of Markt Erlbach, fifteen miles west of Nuremberg.

At first, it must have seemed nice to have a room in a farmhouse far from the ruins of her hometown, but Brunhilde recalled that the invading American soldiers moved into that room and relegated the Baers to the cellar:

> The cellar was filled with potatoes and other food, and it was cold and wet. We lived down there for an entire year. It was so cold in the cellar, and there was no way to heat it—no stove or oven. We had lanterns down there because we didn't have electricity. The Americans lived upstairs. They didn't steal or take any of our property. But they didn't respect our home either—they were pretty rough.

Brunhilde also recalled begging for food from local farmers. Her story is typical of the times:

> One time, we didn't have anything to eat, and I remember that we cried ourselves to sleep that night. Our stomachs hurt so much. We knelt down and said a prayer. Another member of the Church was also living in our town, and the next morning we found a basket with potatoes and mushrooms in front of our door. That was the moment in which I gained my testimony of prayer.

Fig. 14. Friedrich and Maria Mördelmeyer with their daughters Helga and Annemarie. (H. Mördelmeyer Campbell)

On April 17, 1948, Georg Strecker came home from his POW experience in France. Arriving in Nuremberg, he first hugged and kissed his sister-in-law, thinking that she was the wife he had not seen for three years.[32] His daughter Brigitte, by then ten years old, did not know at first what to call her father, "because he was gone so long. Everybody was an uncle to me. I called them uncle this and uncle that, even though they were strangers. So I said, 'Should I call him "uncle" or "dad" or what?' and they said, 'Well, he's your papa, so you call him "Papa."' I said, 'Okay.'"[33] In all likelihood, a higher percentage of members of the Nuremberg Branch lost their homes and were forced to leave town than any other branch in Germany. They had been scattered all over the continent, and it would take literally years before the survivors could return. Neverthess, the few who were still in the city when World War II ended never ceased to hold meetings whenever or wherever possible. Their losses were great, but they did not attribute those losses to God. On the contrary, they believed that it was God who had preserved the survivors and the branch.

In Memoriam

The following members of the Nuremberg Branch did not survive World War II:

Ferdinand Johannes Bär b. Nürnberg, Nürnberg, Bayern, 21 Oct 1908; son of Johannes Bär and Luise Pauline Weigand; bp. 18 Jun 1921; m. 1 Dec 1937; 4 children; k. in battle Russia 11 Aug 1943 or 1944 (Eysser Weiss-Burger; IGI)

Hildegard Ottilie Bär b. Nürnberg, Nürnberg, Bayern, 7 Jul 1938; dau. of Ferdinand Johannes Bär and Ottilie Grill; d. diphtheria 31 Jul 1941 (CHL CR 375 8 2458; IGI)

Michael Baumgärtner b. Erlingshofen, Eichstädt, Mittelfranken, Bayern, 12 Sep 1873; son of Johannes Baumgärtner and Johanna Schwäbel; bp. 22 Jul 1907; conf. 22 Jul 1907; ord. teacher 31 Jul 1921; m. Nürnberg, Nürnberg, Bayern, 25 Oct 1897, Nanette Anna Barbara Specht; 1 child; 2m. Nürnberg 4 Aug 1924, Margarete König; d. stomach cancer Nürnberg 4 Oct 1942; bur. 7 Oct 1942 (FHL microfilm 68802, no. 64; CHL CR 375 8 2458; IGI)

Johann Beierlein b. Rosenbach, Oberfranken, Bayern, 20 May 1870; son of Heinrich Beierlein and Anna Katharina Reusch; bp. 1 Jan 1909; conf. 3 Jan 1909; ord. teacher 1 Oct 1922; ord. priest 29 Jul 1928; ord. elder 10 Apr 1932; m. 8 Aug 1900, Marie Kathrina Glaser; 2 children; d. old age 21 Nov 1944 (FHL microfilm 68802, no. 65; CHL CR 375 8 2458; FHL microfilm 25721, 1925 and 1930 censuses; IGI)

August Blum b. Ruppichteroth, Rheinland, 18 Mar 1860; son of Karl and Wilhelmine Blum; bp. 18 Jun 1921; conf. 18 Jun 1921; ord. deacon 7 May 1922; ord. teacher 30 Nov 1924; ord. priest 2 Jun 1929; ord. elder 24 Oct 1937; m. Friedrika-Karolina Gerner; d. old age 29 Oct or Nov 1940 (FHL Microfilm 68802, no. 76; CHL CR 375 8 2458; FHL microfilm 25725, 1925 and 1930 censuses; IGI)

Babette Senft or Brohmann b. Herbolzheim, Mittelfranken, Bayern, 10 Apr 1885; dau. of Anton Brohmann and Barbara Senft; bp. 8 Apr 1913; conf. 8 Apr 1913; m. 6 Jan 1906, Johann Weiss; d. diabetes 4 Jul 1944 (FHL microfilm 68802, no. 171; CHL CR 375 8 2458; IGI)

Max Denerlein b. Nürnberg, Nürnberg, Bayern, 27 Dec 1886; son of Johann Matthias Denerlein and Anna Babette Eder; bp. 26 Apr 1942; conf. 26 Apr 1942; ord. deacon 28 Feb 1943; m. 18 Sep 1920, Katherina Stengel; d. uraemia 25 Sep 1943 (FHL microfilm 68802, no. 569; CHL CR 375 8 2458; IGI)

Johann Eysser b. Nürnberg, Nürnberg, Bayern, 1 Jan 1919; son of Johann Wilhelm Eysser and Anna Kathrine Pfeiffer; bp. 3 Jun 1928; conf. 3 Jun 1928; ord. deacon 25 Mar 1934; ord. teacher 5 Apr 1937; ord. priest 10 Mar 1940; ord. elder 10 Nov 1941; infantry; k. in battle Fomino (possibly near Zwetowka), Russia, 12 Apr 1942 (Eysser; www.volksbund.de; IGI; FHL microfilm 68802, no. 277; CHL microfilm 2458, form 42 FP, pt. 37, 10–12; FHL microfilm no. 25763, 1930 and 1935 censuses; www.volksbund.de)

Fig. 15. Hans Eysser. (W. Eysser)

Maria Fetzer b. Nürnberg, Nürnberg, Bayern, 11 Nov 1881; dau. of Johann Jobst Fetzer and Margarete Brehm or Mauser; bp. 30 Dec 1923; conf. 30 Dec 1923; d. suicide 28 Mar or 20 Apr 1943 (CHL CR 375 8 2458; FHL microfilm 68802, no. 211; IGI)

Josua Helaman Albert Frenzel b. Nürnberg, Nürnberg, Bayern, 12 Aug 1938; son of Hans Albert Frenzel and Frieda Babette Burkhardt; d. of diarrhea and sickness 17 Dec 1939 (FHL microfilm 68802, no. 527; FHL microfilm 25769, 1935 census)

Friederika Gentner b. Regensburg, Oberpfalz, Bayern, 16 Jan 1891; dau. of Johann Gentner and Eva Hermann; bp. 30 Dec 1923; conf. 30 Dec 1923; m. Hermann Guck; 2 children; d. heart disease 8 Feb 1945 (FHL microfilm 68802, no. 215; FHL microfilm 25779, 1930 and 1935 censuses; IGI)

Georg Friedrich Gentner b. Nürnberg, Nürnberg, Bayern, 24 Jan 1909; son of Hermann Guck and Frieda or Friederika Gentner; ord. deacon; m. Elisabeth Charlotte Schöpf; 3 children; noncommisioned officer; d. in Russia 1944 (Gentner; FHL microfilm 25773, 1935 census)

Margarete Gentner b. Regensburg, Mittelfranken, Bayern, 18 Oct 1892; dau. of Johann Georg Gentner and Eva Herrmann; bp. 30 Dec 1923; conf. 30 Dec 1923; m. 25 May 1929, Andreas Mehringer; missing (FHL microfilm 68802, no. 216; FHL microfilm 245231, 1930 census; IGI)

Otto Gentner b. Nürnberg, Nürnberg, Bayern, 3 Jun 1910; son of Hermann Guck and Friederika Gentner; bp. 30 Dec 1923; conf. 30 Dec 1923; m. 19 Nov 1935; sergeant; k. in air raid Paris, France, 29 Mar 1944; bur. Champigny-St. Andre, France (CHL microfilm 2458, form 42 FP, pt. 37, 10–11; FHL microfilm 68802, no. 214; FHL microfilm 25773, 1930 census; www.volksbund.de; IGI)

Hermann Hermann b. Weinau, Ebersdorf, Bautzen, Sachsen 10 Oct 1870; son of Joseph Hermann and Agnes Köhler; bp. 19 Sep 1905; conf. 19 Sep 1905; ord. priest 28 Feb 1915; ord. elder 30 Mar 1931; d. cardiac insufficiency 24 Jan 1940 (FHL microfilm 68802, no. 101; FHL microfilm 162782, 1930 and 35 censuses; IGI)

Elisabeth Höhne b. Nürnberg, Nürnberg, Bayern, 14 Oct 1866; dau. of Rudolf Höhne and Katharina Pabst; bp. 15 Sep 1901; m. —— Hirner; d. old age 10 Jul 1940 (FHL microfilm 68802, no. 97)

Konrad Hofmann b. Birkenreuth, Oberfranken, Bayern, 8 Feb 1869; son of Johann Hofmann and Anna Modschiedler; bp. 10 Jun 1894; conf. 10 Jun 1894; ord. priest 3 May 1903; ord. elder 2 Apr 1933; d. old age 13 Mar 1944 (FHL microfilm 68802, no. 98; CHL CR 375 8 2458; IGI)

Sophie Katherina Hofmann b. Nürnberg, Nürnberg, Bayern, 28 Mar 1917; dau. of Karl Bernhardt Joseph Hofmann and Katherina Schmidt; d. bone disease 3 Mar 1942 (CHL CR 375 8 2458; IGI)

Kunigunde Horn b. Bayreuth, Oberfranken, Bayern, 23 Jan 1886; dau. of Wolfgang Horn and Katharina Hoffmann; bp. 25 May 1924; conf. 25 May 1924; m. Plauen, Zwickau, Sachsen, 18 May 1907, Richard Schöpf; 5 children; k. in air raid Nürnberg, Nürnberg, Bayern, 2 Jan 1945 (Gentner; CHL microfilm 2458, form 42 FP, pt. 37, 10–11; FHL microfilm 68802, no. 241; IGI)

Kurt Peter Josef Kormann b. Nürnberg, Nürnberg, Bayern, 22 Feb 1925; son of Ernst Baptist Kormann and Maria Magdalena Baier; bp. 22 Jul 1933; conf. 22 Jul 1933; d. blood disease Nürnberg 10 Sep 1939 (FHL microfilm 68802, no. 377; FHL microfilm 271381, 1935 census; IGI; PRF)

Anna Marie Lang b. Marktbergel, Unterfranken, Bayern, 3 Aug 1868, dau. of Leonhard Christoph Lang and Regina Barbara Reichert; bp. 31 Jul 1923; conf. 31 Jul 1923; m. 23 Feb 1891, Lorenz Gottlieb Hofmann; 5 children; d. stomach cancer Nürnberg, Nürnberg, Bayern, 27 May 1942 (FHL microfilm 68802, no. 196; CHL CR 375 8 2458; IGI, AF, PRF)

Karl Morgenroth b. Bamberg, Oberfranken, Bayern, 3 Apr 1923; son of Ludwig or Joseph Morgenroth and Marie Loerber or Lorber; bp. 20 Sep 1943; conf. 20 Sep 1943; m. Bamberg, Bayern, 15 or 19 Apr 1944, Barbara Melber; k. in battle Latvia 30 Oct 1944 (CHL microfilm 2458, form 42 FP, pt. 37, 10–11; FHL microfilm 68802, no. 579; IGI)

Babette Popp b. Fürth, Nürnberg, Bayern, 12 Oct 1879; dau. of Michael Popp and Margaretha Eder; bp. 29 Oct 1889; conf. 29 Oct 1889; m. 24 Dec 1900, Alexander Köstel; d. chronic rheumatism Bürnberg, Bayern, 20 Feb or 10 Jun 1945 (FHL microfilm 68802, no. 239; FHL microfilm 271381, 1935 census; IGI)

Georg Alfred Popp b. Nürnberg, Nürnberg, Bayern, 19 Dec 1924; son of Georg Popp and Anna Elisabeth Ulmer; bp. 4 Jan 1936; conf. 5 Jan 1936; ord. deacon 2 Apr 1939; corporal; d. of wounds Dnjepropetrowsk, Russia, 16 Sep 1943 (CHL microfilm 2458, form 42 FP, pt. 37, 10–11; FHL microfilm 68802, no. 496; FHL microfilm 245255, 1935 census; www.volksbund.de; IGI)

Ellen Elsa Precht b. Bamberg, Oberfranken, Bayern, 15 Jul 1913; dau. of Johann Barnabas Sieghärtner and Gertraud Precht; bp. 15 Jul 1928; conf. 15 Jul 1928; m. Nürnberg, Mittelfranken, Bayern, 3 Nov 1936, Andreas Bundle; d. accident or endocarditis Nürnberg, Nürnberg, Bayern, 1942 (FHL microfilm 68802, no. 282; CHL CR 375 8 2458; IGI)

Joseph Rothmeyer b. Fürth, Nürnberg, Bayern, 8 Sep 1911; son of Anton Rothmeier and Franziska Bierl; d. of wounds Russia 20 Dec 1943 (CHL microfilm 2458, form 42 FP, pt. 37, 10–11)

Margarete Sandhofer b. Neustadt, Mittelfranken, Bayern, 24 Jun 1861; dau. of —— Witt and Margarete Sandhofer; bp. 19 or 20 Sep 1905; m. Franz Sandhofer;

1 child; d. old age 5 Dec 1941 (CHL CR 375 8 2458; FHL microfilm 245257, 1935 census; IGI)

Johann Georg Schmidt b. Nürnberg, Nürnberg, Bayern, 13 Sep 1888; son of Johann Schmidt and Anna Nannette Barbara Specht; bp. 27 Nov 1905; conf. 27 Nov 1905; ord. elder 17 Jul 1920; m. 10 Jun 1916, Frieda Katharina Sauer; 1 child; d. lung ailment Nürnberg 23 Jan 1942 (FHL microfilm 68802, no. 131; CHL CR 375 8 2458; IGI; AF)

Kuno Schönstein b. Nürnberg, Nürnberg, Bayern, 15 Oct 1912; son of Johann Schönstein and Margarete Amalie Mahr; bp. 30 Dec 1923; conf. 30 Dec 1923; ord. deacon 6 Jan 1929; m. Nürnberg 9 Apr 1936, Anna Katharina Reher; private; k. in battle Lyk, Ostpreußen, 19 Apr 1943; bur. Bartosze, Poland (CHL microfilm 2458, form 42 FP, pt. 37, 10–11; FHL microfilm 68802, no. 220; FHL microfilm 245258, 1925 census; www.volksbund.de; IGI)

Richard Schöpf b. Hirschberg/Saale, Thüringen, 6 Oct 1882; son of Karl Otto Wilhelm Alexander Schöpf and Karolina Friederika Dietlein; bp. 25 May 1924; conf. 25 May 1924; ord. deacon 12 Jul 1925; ord. teacher 19 Jun 1927; ord. priest 2 Dec 1928; ord. elder 22 Sep 1930; m. Plauen, Zwickau, Sachsen, 18 May 1907, Kunigunde Horn; 5 children; k. in air raid Nürnberg, Nürnberg, Bayern, 2 Jan 1945 (Gentner; B. Frenkel; IGI; CHL microfilm 2458, form 42 FP, pt. 37, 10–11; FHL microfilm 68802, no. 240)

Heinrich Schwemmer b. Nürnberg, Nürnberg, Bayern, 29 Mar 1908; son of Johann Konrad Schwemmer and Elisabeth Scheitler; bp. 18 Nov 1918; conf. 18 Nov 1918; ord. deacon 10 Apr 1932; ord. teacher 25 Mar 1934; ord. priest 25 Dec 1938; m. 4 Apr 1930; 4 children; corporal; k. in battle H. V. Pl. Gaiduk (probably near Noworossijsk, Russia) 15 Oct 1942 (Eysser; www.volksbund.de; IGI; FHL microfilm 68802, no. 409; CHL microfilm 2458, form 42 FP, pt. 37, 10–11)

Konrad Schwemmer b. Nürnberg, Nürnberg, Bayern, 10 Apr 1917; son of Johann Konrad Schwemmer and Elisabeth Scheitler; bp. 24 Apr 1925; ord. deacon 11 Oct 1931; ord. teacher 4 Apr 1937; m. Olga Maria Weigand; private; d. in POW camp near Daugawpils, Latvia, 16 Jun 1945; bur. Daugavpils, Latvia (Eysser; CHL CR 275 8 2458, 446; FHL microfilm 68802, no. 152; FHL microfilm 245259, 1935 census; www.volksbund.de)

Elisabeth Walter b. Gottmannsdorf, Heilsbronn, Mittelfranken, Bayern, 21 Jun 1912; dau. of Georg Leonhard Walter and Anna Elise Dürsch; bp. 3 Oct 1922; conf. 3 Oct 1922; m. 6 Jul 1935, Wilhelm Nicklas; d. lung disease 4 Oct 1940 (FHL microfilm 68802, no. 181; FHL microfilm 245293, 1930 and 1935 censuses)

Fig. 16. Kunigunde and Richard Schöpf with their grandchildren in about 1939. The Schöpfs were killed on January 2, 1945, in the air raid that destroyed the church rooms at Untere Talstrasse 20 and most of the downtown Nuremberg. (G. Gentner Kammerer)

Pauline Weigand b. Nordheim, Neckarkreis, Württemberg, 17 Jun 1869; dau. of Otto Weigand and Luise Stoll; bp. 5 Jul 1902; conf. 5 Jul 1902; m. —— Bär; 3 children; d. old age 30 May 1943 (FHL microfilm 68802, no. 61; CHL CR 375 8 2458; FHL microfilm 25715; IGI)

Anna Wendler b. Lauf, Entmersberg, Mittelfranken, Bayern, 25 Mar 1854; dau. of Andreas Wendler and Katherina Wittmann; bp. 31 Jul 1919; conf. 31 Jul 1919; d. old age 3 Mar 1945 (FHL microfilm 68802, no. 162; FHL microfilm 245296, 1930 and 1935 census; IGI)

Karoline Betty Willeitner b. Nürnberg, Nürnberg, Bayern, 18 Feb 1928; dau. of Ludwig Willeitner and Agnes Barbara Lindner; bp. 23 May 1936; conf. 23 May 1936; d. heart ailment 5 Oct 1944 (FHL microfilm 68802, no. 274; CHL CR 375 8 2458; IGI)

Notes

1. West German Mission branch directory, 1939, CHL LR 10045 11.
2. Presiding Bishopric, "Financial, Statistical, and Historical Reports of Wards, Stakes, and Missions, 1884–1955," 257, CR 4 12.
3. Nuremberg city archive.
4. *Der Stern*, 1939, 386.
5. Wilhelm Eysser, interview by the author in German, Salt Lake City, March 10, 2006; unless otherwise noted, summarized in English by Judith Sartowski.
6. Gerda Gentner Kammerer, interview by the author in German, Bamberg, Germany, August 13, 2006.
7. Waltraud Weiss Burger, interview by the author in German, Erlangen, Germany, May 27, 2007.
8. Helmut Schwemmer, "Memories and Reminiscences, vol. I" (unpublished manuscript, 1998), 7.
9. Schwemmer, "Memories," 7.
10. Lorie Baer Bonds, interview by Michael Corley, Provo, UT, March 6, 2008.

11. Walter Schwemmer, interview by the author, Salt Lake City, August 21, 2009.
12. Elisabetha Eva Baier Strecker, autobiography (unpublished, 1992), 6.
13. For more about Paul Eysser, see the story of the Worms Branch in the Karlsruhe District.
14. Marie Strecker Mördelmeyer, "My Life Story" (unpublished autobiography, 1978), 3.
15. Helga Mördelmeyer Campbell, interview by the author, Provo, UT, May 28, 2009.
16. Oswald Schwemmer, interview by the author, Salt Lake City, July 10, 2009.
17. Hermann Baer, telephone interview with the author, August 6, 2009.
18. Heinrich Schwemmer to Elisabeth Scheitler Schwemmer, October 4, 1942. Used with the kind permission of Walter Schwemmer. Heinrich's younger brother, Konrad, died as a POW in June 1945.
19. Baier Strecker, autobiography, 6.
20. Strecker Mördelmeyer, autobiography, 5.
21. Annamarie Mördelmeyer Stauber, telephone interview with the author in German, August 6, 2009.
22. Benjamin Frenzel, telephone interview with the author, April 6, 2009.
23. Schwemmer, "Memories," 2.
24. Brigitte Strecker Burns, interview by the author, Park City, UT, June 25, 2009.
25. During the final years of the war, air-raid wardens in some cities refused to allow Jews and foreign workers (and other "undesirables") to take refuge in public shelters. Experts estimate that only about 20 percent of the residents of cities could be accommodated in concrete bunkers. In rural communities, such shelters were unknown.
26. Ferdinand Schwemmer, interview by the author, Salt Lake City, August 21, 2009.
27. The city prison is located on Fürtherstrasse and served as the venue for the Trial of German Major War Criminals, or the Nuremberg Trials, in 1945–46.
28. Zenos Frenzel, interview by the author in German, Bountiful, UT, June 25, 2009.
29. Baier Strecker, autobiography, 7.
30. Strecker Mördelmeyer, autobiography, 3.
31. Brunhilde Baer Schwemmer, interview by the author, Salt Lake City, August 21, 2009.
32. Baier Strecker, 7.
33. The term *Onkel* is still used in German today (mostly by little children) to denote not only an actual uncle but also any adult male who is a good friend of the family. Brigitte's confusion on that occasion was predictable.

Many bunkers designed to protect civilians during air raids were built so well that they are essentially impossible to remove. This one is a permanent feature of Hamburg's skyline. (R. Minert, 1975)

RUHR DISTRICT

West German Mission

In 1939, the Ruhr River region of northwest Germany was home to a great concentration of branches and members of The Church of Jesus Christ of Latter-day Saints. In that area, rich in mining and industry, more cities had populations of higher than one hundred thousand than anywhere else in Hitler's Germany. In many respects, that area was convenient for missionary work, primarily because the distance from city to city was only a few miles.

Ruhr District[1]	**1939**
Elders	69
Priests	23
Teachers	24
Deacons	47
Other Adult Males	135
Adult Females	407
Male Children	52
Female Children	39
Total	796

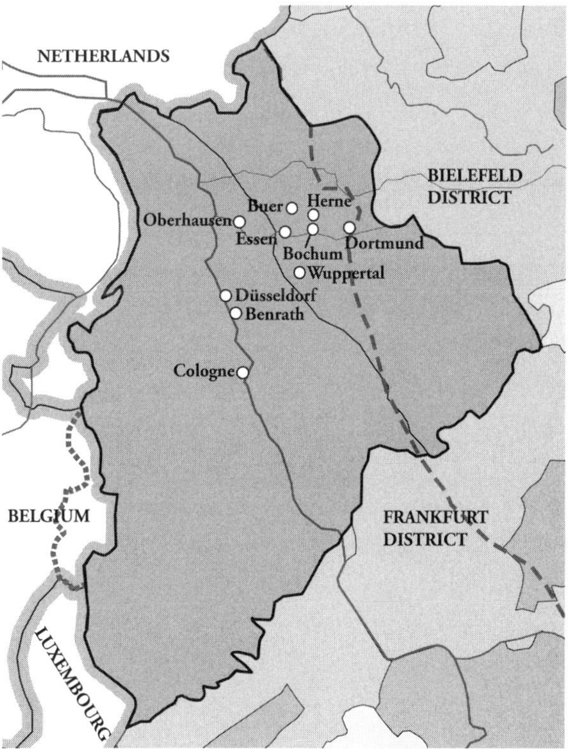

Fig. 1. The ten branches of the Ruhr District were closely grouped among the large cities of this industrial region.

The center of the district was the city of Essen, which had a very strong branch. From there, the distance to the other ten cities in the mission was never more than thirty-five miles. To the north was Buer (nine miles); to the northeast, Herne (thirteen miles); to the east, Bochum (sixteen miles) and Dortmund (thirty-six miles), to the south, Wuppertal (fourteen miles), to the southwest, Düsseldorf (eighteen miles), Benrath (twenty miles), and Cologne (thirty-three miles), and to the west, Oberhausen (six miles). The population of the Church in the Ruhr District was 796, making it the second largest district in the West German Mission.

Church administrative areas surrounding the Ruhr Districts were the Bielefeld District to the north, the Hannover District to the east, the Frankfurt District to the south, and the Netherlands Mission to the west.

In the summer of 1939, the president of the Ruhr District was Friedrich Ludwig Biehl of the Essen Branch. Raised in a large family steeped in LDS tradition, President Biehl was a veteran of the Swiss-German Mission and, at twenty-six, possibly the youngest German district leader in all of Germany.[2] When the American missionaries were evacuated from Germany in August 1939, mission president M. Douglas Wood selected President Biehl to lead the entire mission. By October 1939, he had moved to the mission office in Frankfurt and was replaced by Wilhelm Nitz Sr., who served as the district president throughout the war. His name is mentioned frequently as a visitor in branch meetings, as are those of his counselors.

Other district leaders were Carl Schlingmann of Essen (YMMIA), Grete Keller of Düsseldorf (YWMIA), Heinrich Ludwig of Essen (Sunday School), Luise Schwiermann of Essen (Primary), and Johanna Neumann of Essen (Relief Society).[3] Jakob Kirchhausen of Essen was the genealogical expert and Gustav Mellin of Herne the president of the elders quorum.[4]

Georg Hübner and Johann Friedrich Biehl served in the last few war years as traveling elders. Their names appear in the minutes of branch meetings during that time. The names Gustav Melling and Heinrich Ludwig also appear frequently, indicating that those men were apparently willing and able to travel to neighboring branch meeting places throughout the war years.

District conferences were very popular events in the Ruhr District. Because of the short traveling distances, it was relatively easy for the Saints to gather. They usually met in Essen but also met on several occasions in Herne. From the records of various branches, it is evident that those conferences were held at least through the fall of 1944.

Because of the concentration of mining operations and heavy industry in the Ruhr region, the cities there were constantly under attack by Allied air forces. More than one thousand air raids were carried out in the region, and the cities were extensively damaged. More than two-thirds of the Saints in the Ruhr District were bombed out. A great number of families in the branches were split up when the mothers took their infant children to safer localities and when schoolchildren were sent away under the Kinderlandvershickung program. In March and April 1945, the region was surrounded by invading Allied forces and besieged in what was called the *Ruhrkessel* (Ruhr cauldron). That meant additional damage through artillery fire and combat. When the conquest of the enclave was complete, the damage in the cities often exceeded 70 percent. Nevertheless, most of the branches in the district were still holding sacrament meetings, and all still had at least cottage meetings in the intact apartments of members still in the region.

Notes

1. Presiding Bishopric, "Financial, Statistical, and Historical Reports of Wards, Stakes, and Missions, 1884–1955," 257, CHL CR 4 12.
2. For more about the life of Friedrich Biehl, see the West German Mission chapter.
3. West German Mission branch directory, 1939, CHL 10045 11.
4. The geographical extent of the elders quorum is not known. There may have been two elders quorums in Germany overall or in the West German Mission in 1939. No specific references in the mission records can be found regarding this organization.

Benrath Branch

The town of Benrath is located five miles southwest of the city of Düsseldorf. The branch of The Church of Jesus Christ of Latter-day Saints in that town had only thirty-one registered members when World War II began. Peter Ernst was the branch president and Johann Zimmer his first counselor, but many of the other leadership positions were vacant. Jakob Schumacher was the superintendant of the Sunday School, and Maria Ernst was the president of the Relief Society.[1]

The Ernst family lived in the suburb of Reisholz, about one mile north of Benrath. Peter Ernst set up one room for the branch in their single-family home at Rotdornweg 33. According to his youngest daughter, Erna (born 1926), there were about twenty chairs for the branch members and their friends. The average attendance was fifteen persons in the early war years, before members were called away to military service or lost their homes and moved out of Benrath.[2]

Alfred Koch (born 1937) recalled the names of several member families in the branch: "There were the Ernsts, the Riedels, two Zimmer families, a single sister Jochheim, my family and my grandmother, and a few others."[3] Alfred's family lived in a suburb of Düsseldorf near Hilden and traveled a few miles to church each Sunday.

Benrath Branch[4]	**1939**
Elders	4
Priests	0
Teachers	1
Deacons	2
Other Adult Males	3
Adult Females	15
Male Children	4
Female Children	2
Total	31

Sunday School was held at 10:00 a.m. and was followed at 11:15 a.m. by sacrament meeting. The priesthood and Relief Society meetings both took place beginning at 4:00 p.m. on Thursday afternoons. No other meetings were listed on the branch directory of July 1939. The meetings were not interrupted during the war because Brother Ernst, a veteran of the Great War, was not required to join the Wehrmacht and was always in Benrath.

Although no official Primary organization existed in the Benrath Branch during the war, Alfred recalled that "Sister Ernst [tried] to get a Primary going. Our instruction took place when the adults would go in Sunday School, although I don't think that it ever was called Primary; but to us it was Primary."

The branch history includes minutes for all sacrament meetings from the early 1930s to the postwar era. The minutes were likely kept by Peter Ernst, the branch president, and were done with great consistency during the war years. The following is a typical entry:

> June 6, 1942: Sacrament meeting. Brother Peter Ernst conducted. Hymn no. 37. Invocation Sister Erna Jochheim. First talk by Brother Jakob Schumacher. Second talk by Brother Peter Ernst. Closing hymn no. 6. Benediction by Sister Irmgard Schulz. In attendance: 2 elders, 5 members, 5 visitors, 2 friends; total 14 persons.[5]

Erna Ernst was inducted into the Jungvolk at age ten but attended the meetings only for a short while. Regarding the activities, she recalled:

> We would meet at the school, outside on the yard, and then they made us march. And sometimes they would make us stand there in rows and our leaders went into the building and we were outside in the cold, and some of us got sick. And so my mother told them I wasn't coming anymore.

The war was a frightening concept for young Erna: "They started teaching us first aid in school, and they gave us a gas mask. You get scared as a child." When the bombs began to fall on both military and civilian targets in the area, the Ernst family was very fortunate; the only damage their home suffered occurred when an incendiary bomb buried itself in the outside wall. According to Erna, her father removed it without difficulty. "He had been in World War I, so he was never afraid." A high-explosive bomb once landed behind the neighbor's house, but it was a dud, and experts removed it.

"My dad [Walter Koch] was not pro-Hitler, but he was in favor of the economic [upswing] because he had gone through World War I—when his father was killed—and the hard times and hyperinflation that followed," recalled Alfred Koch. He continued:

> My dad would not join the Nazi Party, and we never had a swastika flag at our home. Right across the street lived a guy who was a member of the Nazi Party—some kind of bureaucrat. He would go to work on a bicycle in his Nazi uniform, a brown uniform with a swastika armband and his brown cap. I can remember him coming over—and it must have been in 1941 or something like that—and was talking to my dad, berating him. He had never talked to my dad before, although he lived right across the street. In 1942, I believe, there was a swastika flag on our house.

In 1942, Walter Koch was drafted by the Wehrmacht. He was gone for the duration of the war and was eventually captured by Red Army soldiers. Marie Koch continued to go to church with her sons and her mother as often as circumstances permitted. From their home near Zuringen, they could often see the red skies over Düsseldorf and other large cities as they burned following air raids. According to Alfred, "It was very scary for us kids. Mother was worried, which we automatically sensed. Huddling in the basement you could hear the bombers flying overhead. The only time any bombs fell close to us they landed in fields nearby." "Nearby" was close enough to damage the Koch home; the windows burst and several cracks appeared in the walls, but the house remained inhabitable. "After that," Alfred explained, "we played in the bomb craters in the field."

There was little opportunity for entertainment for young people during the war, but this did not bother Erna. She had trained as a beautician and was quite busy during the day. For fun she depended on her family: "There were many things we couldn't do because of a lack of money. You just got close with your family. We would sing and play games, other than that there wasn't much to do. I never felt that life was unfair because my parents were always so good to us; they did many things to keep us happy."

Alfred Koch began school in the fall of 1944. He was the only Latter-day Saint and recalled that it was difficult to stand and announce his religious affiliation as being anything other than the usual Catholic or Lutheran. At school and in the neighborhood, "we were looked at as being a bit different. Everybody in the neighborhood knew that we were *Mormonen*. We had to live our religion despite the fact that nobody was really concerned what we were."

Toward the end of the war, survival became more of a challenge for the members of the Benrath Branch. The prime concern was physical safety, something that could not be taken for granted even by a teenage girl who rode her bicycle a mile to work and back every day. As Erna Ernst recalled, dive-bombers were a constant threat to civilians:

> They would shoot the farmers in the fields, and that was terrible. I can remember I was on my bicycle riding home, and the plane was going around, and I looked up and the plane had a ring [symbol] and so I knew it was British, and so the plane went around. I was riding along a cemetery wall, and he came down and he started shooting, and I jumped off my bicycle and stood against the wall. When he had to turn again is when I ran. At the end of the wall there was a farmer's house, so I ran to the farmer's house and ran inside to wait till the plane was gone. I don't know if they did that for fun, or if they really wanted to [hurt people].

Branch meetings were interrupted in October 1944. The branch history describes conditions at the time:

> 8 October 1944: Beginning on this date, the war made life terribly difficult for us. Our branch members sought refuge in places far from here and we could no longer hold meetings. Brother Peter Ernst remained in his home with his youngest daughter. There was a tremendous amount of

> unrest. Bombs and artillery shells rained down around our homes. We hid in our basements for protection, and we slept there. Those were the conditions when we experienced the invasion of enemy soldiers and collapse of our nation that had celebrated sin and godlessness. Nobody harmed us because the hand of God was over us. All of the brothers and sisters and their children returned to their homes. Five brethren were taken prisoner by the Russians, but all returned.[6]

Another danger for the civilians was disease. With shortages of food and the interruption or destruction of utilities, illnesses were constant and could be fatal. Erna described the government's ongoing attempts to keep people healthy in these words: "We got so many shots, all kinds of shots! They shot us to death during the war!"

In the last month of the war, it became almost impossible to find food. Fortunately for the Ernst family, one of their daughters was assigned to work in a soup kitchen. She was allowed to take packages of soup home to her family, but eventually even those ran out. Erna recalled a different source of nourishment that came in handy: "We went along the sides of the roads in the ditches to pick dandelions and stinging nettles, and my mother would cook sauce or make salads out of them." According to her, even though they still had ration cards, there was often nothing left to buy in the grocery stores.

The invading American army approached the Koch home from the east. Alfred recalled that day vividly:

> I can remember climbing up a streetcar pole in front of our house, and looking down the road to see if the Americans were there. Sure enough, there was a tank standing in the middle of the road, and it seemed to me that the barrel was a foot across, although the tank was about three hundred to four hundred meters down the road. Then I climbed down and back up to hang out our bed sheet, and then we waited. And I was worried, really worried, because Mother was in town, which was in the opposite direction. What are they going to do when they find my mother? Finally the troops moved in, and my brother and I huddled behind a window. There was some noise outside, and I looked up, and about a foot or two outside our window an American soldier walked by. He didn't see me, but I ducked right behind the window again. They were checking behind houses to see if there were pockets of resistance. And then my mother came home. All of a sudden, the war was over.

As was common all over western Germany, the invaders gave candy and gum to the children. Alfred recalled that as well:

> I can remember once or twice receiving a cigarette, which I took to my mother, which was like gold. You could get anything for a cigarette. And although I knew that we were not supposed to have cigarettes, that was something that Mother could trade in for coal or something else. So to us it was harmless. It was actually kind of a relief. If anything, if I can say that as a child, it was relief to have the war over. But we didn't know where Dad was.

As it turned out, Walter Koch was a POW in Russia and his whereabouts would remain a mystery until July 1946, when a card he had written the previous December was finally delivered to his wife.

In May 1945, the war ended and branch life began anew. The following was written by the clerk on May 6th: "Today was Sunday and we held our first Sunday School and sacrament meeting since October 8, 1944. The conditions of war made it impossible to meet in the interim."[7] This was followed by a concise report of the proceedings of the sacrament meeting in precisely the same style as they had been reported in during the previous eight years. No other comments were made relating to the war or the conclusion thereof.

Although neither Alfred Koch nor Erna Ernst could recall any branch members leaving the Church because of a loss of faith, they recalled that times were very difficult. Alfred summed up his feelings in these words:

> The certain amount of peace and comfort and assurance we had despite the hell that was going on all around us was because of the gospel that we had. . . . The Church was really an anchor

> in this turmoil, in this time of deprivation, of uncertainty of life. . . . Because of the faith of our mother and because of our prayers, we knew that things would be okay.

Things were indeed all right in September 1949 when Walter Koch returned from his tenure as a POW in Russia, having been separated from his family for seven years. He returned to a small but vibrant Benrath Branch that had been "held together by Brother Ernst," according to young Alfred.

No members of the Benrath Branch are known to have died during World War II.

NOTES

1. West German Mission branch directory, 1939, CHL 10045 11.
2. Erna Ernst Fiedler, interview by the author, Sandy, UT, February 17, 2006.
3. Alfred Koch, interview by Sarah Gibby Peris, Preston, ID, November 24, 2006.
4. Presiding Bishopric, "Financial, Statistical, and Historical Reports of Wards, Stakes, and Missions, 1884–1955," 257, CHL CR 4 12.
5. Benrath Branch history, 134, CHL LR 67111 11.
6. Ibid., 153. Because this entry was made by a different scribe and contains information not available at the time, it was likely written a few years after the war.
7. Ibid., 154.

BOCHUM BRANCH

The city of Bochum had nearly 305,469 inhabitants in 1939, but the LDS branch in that city numbered only forty-eight persons. Most were active and acquainted with the members of other branches in the Ruhr District. Essen was just six miles from Bochum, and Herne was just four.

In the late summer of 1939, the Bochum Branch met in rented rooms at Rathausplatz 9 downtown. The only members of the branch listed on the branch directory were President Max Hackbarth and Sunday School superintendent Anton Bühler. The only meetings listed were Sunday School at 10:00 a.m., priesthood meeting at noon, and sacrament meeting at 7:00 p.m.[1]

Bochum Branch[2]	**1939**
Elders	4
Priests	0
Teachers	2
Deacons	3
Other Adult Males	13
Adult Females	26
Male Children	0
Female Children	0
Total	48

George Blake, a missionary from Vineyard, Utah, was assigned to work in Bochum from late 1937 to May 1938. He described the setting at Rathausplatz 9 in these words:

> We had two small rented rooms in the building, which was a business building that fronted on the town square. On the wall next to the entry [outside], there was a small plaque about a foot square with the name of the church on it. The rooms were on the ground floor with a pump organ in them, which was common in those years, and a few chairs, and that's about all the furniture there was. I don't remember any decor on the walls. We moved the chairs off to the side for the Christmas Party. Thirty people would have filled the room; normally we had twelve to twenty people [in attendance]. . . . The principle population of the branch was very much blue collar, the working class. . . . The branch was small and not well attended. On our books we maybe had fifty people, but we only had about fifteen at our services, so most of our work as missionaries was trying to activate members.[3]

Just a few months prior to the war, another Utah missionary, Erma Rosenhan, recorded the following in her diary: "Sunday, April 9, 1939: Visited the Bochum Branch with district president [Friedrich] Biehl. The branch in Bochum is small and the

Fig. 1. Christmas 1937 with Saints of the Bochum Branch. (G. Blake)

larger branches help it along. There were only nine people there altogether."[4] Apparently, the branch in Bochum was losing strength. The following surnames appear more than once in the branch meeting minutes of the summer of 1939: Hackbarth, Bauer, Kaminski, Bühler, Heiden, Mietze, Kegelmann, Melter, Preuss, Klamma, Leithäuser, and Kossowski.[5]

On November 20, 1939, just a few months after the war began, a meeting was held for the branch and district leaders. According to the minutes of that meeting, two agents of the Gestapo were present. Nothing noteworthy happened, possibly because branch president Hackbarth was a member of the Nazi Party (Elder Blake recalled seeing him wearing a party membership pin on his suit coat).[6]

The following statement is found in the branch minutes written in November 1939:

> Due to the war conditions our sacrament meetings have been held on a very irregular basis. In September and October, only two meetings took place, namely on September 28 and October 5.

Fig. 2. A group of Saints in Bochum in 1938. District president Friedrich Biehl is standing at left. His brother Walter is third from the right. (G. Blake)

> . . . Meetings were not held on the other Sundays because the members' work schedules did not permit them to attend. The fall [branch] conference that was scheduled for October 22, 1939 could not take place; the [city government] forbid it because we did not have a suitable bomb shelter.[7]

Two sad reports are found at the conclusion of the Bochum Branch meeting minutes. The first is dated December 10, 1939, and reads as follows:

> It was announced that the Bochum Branch was being closed temporarily and the members transferred to the Herne Branch as of today. The speakers today were Brothers Bühler and Ludwig, both of whom reminded the members to remain true to the Church. All branch property was transferred to Herne with the exception of eight chairs, one clock, one mailbox and some firewood, which were sold for a total of 12 RM. The branch funds totaling 4,52 RM went to Herne, except for bus money (1,80) that was necessary due to bad weather. After cleaning costs were deducted, the Herne Branch received 0,60 RM. The Relief Society funds of 41,65 RM were sent to the mission office in Frankfurt/Main.[8]

The branch president added this statement a month later:

> The Bochum Branch and its rooms at Rathausplatz 9 have been closed due to insufficient attendance. Too many of the branch members are not available to serve in callings. There were forty-eight registered members but they are scattered among various neighborhoods and could not attend the meetings. All sincere members hope that the branch can be reestablished after the war. Max Hackbarth, branch president in Bochum, January 1940.[9]

It is not known whether any of the members of the Bochum Branch did indeed attend meetings in Herne or elsewhere. It is likely that at least some were hindered by the problem of transportation or the challenges of wartime life and discontinued their association with the Church.

Located near the middle of the Ruhr region with its critical war industries, the city of Bochum suffered severely during the war. Before the American army entered the city on April 10, 1945, there had been more than one thousand air raid alarms for at least 147 actual attacks, twelve of which were considered "heavy attacks." At least 4,095 persons were killed, 5,000 more were injured, and "countless residents were left homeless."[10] Of the city's living space, 22 percent was totally destroyed and another 74 percent badly damaged. Of the many Bochum men who served in the military, 7,048 died. As late as 1948, there were 8,089 residents reported missing or still prisoners of war. Life in Bochum was clearly fraught with hazards; therefore it is remarkable that no Latter-day Saints in Bochum became casualties of the war.

In Memoriam

Only one member of the Bochum Branch is known to have died in World War II:

Marianna Hildegard Uhlig b. Chemnitz, Chemnitz, Sachsen, 24 Oct 1902; dau. of Oskar Uhlig and Auguste Hilde Wittig; bp. 1 Aug 1913; conf. 1 Aug 1913; m. 3 Jun 1922, Kurt Walter Müller; 2m. Chemnitz 19 Oct 1928; d. 20 Sep 1939 (FHL microfilm 68784; CHL microfilm 2447 pt. 26 no. 231; FHL microfilm no. 245239 1925 and 1930 censuses; IGI)

Notes

1. West German Mission branch directory, 1939, CHL 10045 11.
2. Presiding Bishopric, "Financial, Statistical, and Historical Reports of Wards, Stakes, and Missions, 1884–1955," CR 4 12, 257.
3. George Blake, interview by the author, Provo, UT, April 1, 2009.
4. Erma Rosenhan, papers, MS 16190, Church History Library.
5. Bochum Branch general minutes, CHL LR 804 11; trans. the author.
6. Ibid., 215.
7. Ibid., 227.
8. Ibid., 229–30.
9. Ibid., 229–30.
10. Monika Wiborni, *Bochum im Bombenkrieg: 4. November 1944* (Bochum, Germany: Wartberg, 2004), 46.

Buer Branch

The smallest branch in the Ruhr District was in the community of Buer, nestled between several large cities in the region. Only ten miles north of Essen, the Latter-day Saints in Buer would have faced no great obstacles in attending district conferences in Essen. Thirty-one residents of this town were recorded as members of the LDS branch.

Buer Branch[1]	**1939**
Elders	2
Priests	2
Teachers	0
Deacons	1
Other Adult Males	0
Adult Females	11
Male Children	15
Female Children	0
Total	31

The dominant character in the Buer Branch in 1939 was Johann Nowotczin. Little is known about him, but he filled several positions in branch leadership: branch president and clerk, Sunday School president and clerk, YMMIA superintendant and secretary, and *Der Stern* magazine agent. His wife, Johanna, served as the president and secretary of the Primary organization, which had fifteen male children at the time. Their daughter Agnes served in two roles—Sunday School secretary and Primary secretary. The only person in leadership who did not belong to the Nowitczin family was Adolf Kerstan, Brother Nowitczin's first counselor.[2]

The branch meetings were held in rented rooms at Horsterstrasse in Buer. Nothing is known about the building. Sunday School began at 10:00 a.m. and sacrament meeting at 3:00 p.m. The Primary met on Tuesdays at 5:00 p.m., and MIA met two hours later.

As of this writing, no eyewitnesses from the Buer Branch can be found, and no records from that branch exist in the Church History Library.

No members of the Buer Branch are known to have died during World War II.

Notes

1. Presiding Bishopric, "Financial, Statistical, and Historical Reports of Wards, Stakes, and Missions, 1884–1955," 257, CHL CR 4 12.
2. West German Mission branch directory, 1939, CHL LR 10045 11.

Cologne Branch

In 1939, the city of Cologne was the fourth largest in the Reich with 767,222 inhabitants. Situated on the left bank of the Rhine River, it had been founded by the Romans nearly two thousand years earlier and featured the tallest twin-tower cathedral in the world.

Cologne Branch[1]	**1939**
Elders	9
Priests	3
Teachers	3
Deacons	5
Other Adult Males	29
Adult Females	78
Male Children	3
Female Children	13
Total	143

At the far south extent of the Ruhr District (forty miles southwest of Essen), the Cologne Branch was, by population, large enough to sustain itself; but for some reason no functioning YWMIA, Relief Society, or Primary organization existed in 1939. (It is especially curious that a branch with so many adult women had no official Relief Society leadership.) The branch president was Gerhard Geller, and his counselors were Hugo Romboy and Albert Bauske. The Sunday School was led by Johannes Sachon and the YMMIA by Hubert Ernst. The only woman listed was Maria Ernst, who represented *Der Stern* magazine.[2]

The meeting rooms were rented in a building at Mozartstrasse 11. The only available description is provided by missionary George Blake of Vineyard, Utah:

> They had a large room and two small rooms. There was a picture of Christ at Gethsemane and a picture of the First Vision on the left wall, and a board to post the numbers of the hymns on the right wall. Typical attendance [in December 1938] was more than thirty persons. The Romboys played a major role in the branch because there were so many of them.[3]

When the war began in September 1939, only three meetings were scheduled for the Cologne Branch: Sunday School at 10:00 a.m., sacrament meeting at 7:00 p.m., and Mutual on Tuesdays at 8:00 p.m.

"I remember that my dad [Paul Romboy] was drafted in 1941," explained Ursula Romboy (born 1939). In addition to her memories of being alone with her mother, Grete, during the war, she recalled the air raids that severely damaged the city in the later years of the war:

Fig. 1. Paul Romboy as a Wehrmacht soldier around 1942. (U. Romboy Gamble)

> We went into our cellar a lot of times during the heavy bombing in 1943 and 1944. There were bunk beds, and my mother took snacks, and so I never

> remember being afraid. I was excited to see the planes fly overhead in our street, and my mother would grab me and rush me down to the cellar. Our house was not damaged, but there were bomb holes in the street, and the top of the house next to us was destroyed.[4]

In the summer of 1944, Paul Romboy was struck in the leg by several pieces of shrapnel and eventually arrived at a hospital in Lüneburg. He was pleased to have his wife and his daughter come from Cologne to visit him there—a rare privilege for a German soldier. From Lüneburg, he returned to the Western Front, and his family traveled back to Cologne.

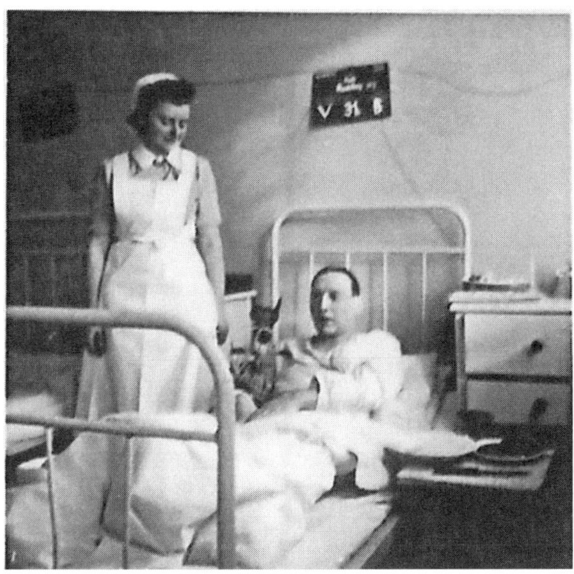

Fig. 2. Paul Romboy in a Lüneburg hospital after shrapnel was removed from his leg in 1944. (U. Romboy Gamble)

Fig. 3. The Romboy brothers of the Cologne Branch. From left: Karl, Paul, Hugo, and Gustav. (U. Romboy Gamble)

In January 1945, life in the smoldering city of Cologne was becoming intolerable. Grete Romboy was evacuated with her daughter to the town of Seeben near Halle in central Germany. Grete's sister-in-law, Gertrude Romboy, was also there with her four sons. In February, Grete gave birth to a son she named Roderick. The two Romboy families survived the invasion of the Red Army and the end of the war at that location.

In the summer of 1945, the time came for Grete Romboy to take her family home to Cologne. Ursula recalled riding in cattle cars for several days, sitting on straw: "When the train stopped [along the way], maybe we could get some milk or something to eat. When we arrived in Cologne, the bridge [over the Rhine] was totally collapsed. We walked from the station to our home in the center of the city, and we found total destruction with bomb craters as big as houses."

Postwar life in a big city had many challenges, but Ursula recalled that her mother was quite resourceful: "She could make something out of nothing. She once took the curtains down and made us clothes. We used everything, and we didn't waste scraps." Sister Romboy needed to be efficient because her husband was a POW and might not be coming home soon.

Fig. 4. Grete Romboy with her children Ursula (seven) and Roderick (one) in 1946. (U. Romboy Gamble)

Paul Romboy was captured by the Americans and incarcerated in France after the war. As a typical POW, he wanted more than anything to go home to his family. From March 1946 to July 1947, he wrote at least eighty letters to his wife in Cologne. Those letters have survived and offer important insights into Paul's physical and mental condition during his time in France. The primary topic was his concern for the welfare of his family. The secondary message was that his own health was good. The third most popular theme was his desire to return to them. Other topics commonly mentioned were the food in the camps, the work he was required to do, and the frequent transfers to other camps.

Because the French censors were always prepared to delete negative statements from the letters written by German POWs, Paul had to be careful to avoid condemning his captors, but enough statements slipped through to let his wife know that he did not trust the French.

The following are comments taken from the letters written by Paul Romboy in France:[5]

> April 12, 1946: I started as a welder, then as a tailor, . . . then three weeks as a laborer, then I did embroidery, [and I] last worked with the U.S. Army film exchange as a laborer.

> April 17, 1946: I hope and strongly believe that the good and the bad in life will balance out, although it seems at the moment injustice is taking the upper hand. . . . Most of all through all this disaster of war we are still alive and our home is mostly intact and then during the worst time of the war the real eternal happiness never left us.

Fig. 5. German POWs in Marseilles, France. Paul Romboy is in the front row at left with the white tie. (U. Romboy Gamble)

> May 12, 1946: The world is one of destitution and of the devil, one must really pass through devil's gate to gain freedom once more.

> July 27, 1946: Every additional day that I spend here makes the reality of captivity more real and twice as hard. This no shaft of light, sometimes I feel like an alien, no promise of home, no mail, no friends and a religion that no one wants to know of and can't understand.

> August 2, 1946: The Lord had me come here and he always hears my prayers. He will bring me peace and let me return home soon.

> September 9, 1946: How often have I thought and wondered how the Cologne Branch is doing, what Mutti is doing and if Roderick has already been blessed in Church. But as long as the branch has not been reactivated he can't be blessed. . . . Fast Sunday is past but I can still fast next Sunday.

> October 18, 1946: Everything comes in due time, such as the food provisions from America. . . . It is good that Church headquarters has not forgotten the members in Germany.[6]

> October 27, 1946: I'm really happy I received the *Family Home Evening Manual* [in English].

Fig. 6. LDS chaplain Howard Badger (left) wth German POW Paul Romboy in France in 1946. (U. Romboy Gamble)

> November 3, 1946: At times I feel that there is no decency left here. The best thing is to stay away and keep to myself. The day will come when I can talk to my wife, who thinks and speaks my language. Right now all seems very dim, one could just despair.

> November 20, 1946: I am a priest and an elder in the Mormon Church and I am desperately needed at home.

> December 1, 1946: I can work as a craftsman, a saddler, a locksmith, etc.

> December 25, 1946: At 11 p.m. the Catholic priest came from the village and celebrated a Christmas program in a little chapel. I attended it although I was not necessarily spiritually uplifted. But all in all everything was really nice. Then one more thing: the International Red Cross gave all the prisoners a Christmas card and 5 cigarettes.

January 6, 1947: Again I want to stress the fact how the Lord hears and answers my prayers.

February 16, 1947: We are always told not to get too friendly with the French or make any kind of advances toward them.

Fig. 7. Paul Romboy as a German POW in France. (U. Romboy Gamble)

February 28, 1947: For some strange reason they have taken our stoves from us and also additional lights. This has occurred in every room large or small. Then for some reason salt will now be rationed or none at all. They feed us pea soup at noon and night. So now we sit here in the cold and all that wood is stacked outside . . . They seem to get pleasure out of annoying us.

April 20, 1947: All prisoners over the age of 45 years have now left the prison camp for home. Now the rest of us are awaiting our turn, but when?

May 11, 1947: I will not forget to thank my God for all that has been given to me and that I always have something additional to eat.[7]

It was 1948 before Paul Romboy returned home to his family and took up his church and business activities in Cologne again.

The fate of the Latter-day Saints in wartime Cologne was reported in letters written by branch members after the war. Walter E. Scoville, an American missionary who served in the branch before the war, worked hard to establish contacts with members after the war. The following are extracts from letters he received:

Gerda Romboy (Cologne, February 4, 1947):

We have been through terrible times. We lost our home four times and my husband (Brother Hugo Romboy) came back from a POW camp very ill. His brothers, Karl-Paul and Gustav, have not yet returned. My son Helmut was officially listed as missing in action two years ago. . . . Our branch meeting rooms were totally destroyed. . . . You would not recognize our beautiful city of Cologne if you came back. . . . Most of the members survived the war, only Helma Webank was killed in an air raid.[8]

Auguste Bauske (Cologne, early 1947 through British censor):

Brothers Gustaf Priefler and Sachon were killed in battle. Brothers Hubert Ernst, Karl Romboy and Paul Romboy are still POWs. My husband [Albert Bauske] did not have to serve and survived the war well. . . . Köln [Cologne] is 80% destroyed and no longer a beautiful city. The rooms at Bremerstrasse 24 were totally destroyed in an air raid.[9]

G. [Maria] Geller (Engelskirchen, Rheinland on March 4, 1947):

What we went through in the war years was the most terrible experience of our earthly lives, but we felt God's hand protecting us. He saved us from death and suffering. We lost everything but thank heavens our boys Hans and Bub are home, as is Richmund's husband. And Mäusgen's husband will come home soon from his POW camp. Hans suffered much during the war but he is still alive and we are so happy. Brother Geller is still the leader of the branch. He had to go through a lot of hard experiences and the members were so grateful that one man was at home to lead us. . . . Brothers Gustav Priefler and Hans Sachon were killed in battle. . . . We accepted the will of the Lord and said with Job, "The Lord giveth, the Lord taketh away."[10]

Elisabeth Schmidting (May 29, 1947):

[My daughter and I] were evacuated to Thuringia in terrible cold; we starved and froze. We had two suitcases with our valuables and the Russians stole it all. "Seek ye first for the kingdom of heaven" "Sammelt himmlische Schätze" (lay up treasures in heaven) is what we had learned. When I came back [to Cologne] on December 20, 1945 to [the suburb of] Bruesk, Klausenberg 76, I was without my daughter. I had lost her. My apartment was occupied and my furniture was rented out. I was deathly ill and the godless people living there didn't even take me in for one night. They had stolen lots of our stuff. I had to spend two weeks sleeping out in the open in the most bitter

> cold. Nobody would take me in. Nurses found me in the streets and put me in a hospital. Then I was in a sanitorium for seven months and was bedridden for 17 months with a lung disease. Now I am among the mentally ill.[11]

Most members of the branch fared better than Sister Schmidting, but many lost relatives and homes. Many spent part of the war away from home. The branch dwindled in the last war years. As the survivors returned, there was reason to hope that the branch and the grand city of Cologne would revive and prosper.

In Memoriam

The following members of the Cologne Branch did not survive World War II:

Peter Bell b. Köln, Rheinprovinz, 1 Sep 1911; son of Simon Bell and Anna Marie Klaukert; bp. 20 Jul 1921; conf. 20 Jul 1921; d. stroke 14 Mar 1944 (FHL microfilm 68786, no. 13; FHL microfilm 25721, 1930 census; IGI)

Michael Borkowski b. Burdungen, Ostpreußen, 13 Nov 1878; son of Christoph Borkowski and Katharine Nasienski; bp. 30 Nov 1923; conf. 30 Nov 1923; ord. deacon 14 Sept 1924; ord. teacher 12 Apr 1932; ord. priest 3 Oct 1937; m. 6 Sep 1901, Marie Kerstan; d. heart attack Gelsenkirchen, Bür, Westfalen, 20 Nov 1944 (CHL microfilm 2447, pt. 26, no. 39; FHL microfilm 25726, 1925 and 1930 censuses; IGI; PRF)

Karoline Wilhelmine Hassel b. Niederhausen, Sieg, Westerwald, Rheinprovinz, 23 May 1875; dau. of Johann Heinrich Hassel and Karoline Wilhelmine Schmidt; bp. 5 Jul 1905; conf. 5 Jul 1905; m. Hamm, Sieg, Westerwald, Rheinprovinz, 22 May 1895, Gustav Hugo Theodor Romboy; 8 children; d. Klosterseelte, Hoya, Hannover, 16 Jun 1945 (FHL microfilm 68786, no. 7; FHL microfilm 271406, 1930 and 1935 censuses; IGI)

Günther Hermann Keller b. Köln, Rheinland, 27 Sep 1923; son of Hermann Keller and Henriette Nadrowski; bp. 1 Jul 1932; m.; d. MIA Russia 1 Aug 1944 (FHL microfilm 271377, 1925 and 1935 censuses; IGI; www.volksbund.de)

Paul Klein b. Elberfeld, Rheinprovinz, 28 Jan 1895; son of Robert August Klein and Lydia Böhmer or Döhmer; bp. 23 Aug 1907; conf. 23 Aug 1907; m. Grete Frosholt; d. amentia 26 Apr 1945 (FHL microfilm 68786, no. 670; FHL microfilm 271380, 1930 and 1935 censuses)

Josef Karl Körtgen b. Köln, Rheinland, 24 Apr 1921; son of Franz Körtgen and Christine Weissbarth; bp. 8 Jun 1929; conf. 9 Jun 1929; private; k. in battle in forest southwest of Teremez, near Chlewischtschi, Russia, 30 May 1942 (FHL microfilm no. 68786, no.74; CHL microfilm 2458, form 42 FP, pt. 37; district list 1947, 330–31; district list 1943–47, 430–31; FHL microfilm 271381; 1925 and 1935 censuses; www.volksbund.de; IGI)

Sophie Charlotte Katharina Lichtenberg b. Herrensohr, Saarbrücken, Saarland, 4 Dec 1858; dau of Georg Friedrich Lichtenberg and Christiana Luise Henrietta Rosenthal; bp. 27 Sep 1901; conf. 27 Sep 1901; m. August Schmidt or Schmid; 1 child; m. —— Schäfer; d. Monbachtal, Neuhausen, Würtemberg, 26 Jan 1945 (CHL CR 275 8 2441, no. 282; FHL microfilm 245258; 1930 and 1935 censuses; IGI, AF, PRF)

Elisabeth Mank b. Hellersdorf, Köln, Rheinprovinz, 9 Aug 1870; dau. of Simon Mank and Katharina Wimel; bp. 17 Jun 1924; conf. 17 Jun 1924; m. Josef Prager; d. heart attack Apr 1943 (FHL microfilm 68786, no. 102)

Josef Prager Sr. b. Koblenz, Rheinprovinz, 6 May 1870; son of Franz Josef Prager and Anna Lobenthal; bp. 17 Jun 1924; conf. 17 Jun 1924; d. war causes Köln 1943 (FHL microfilm no. 68786, no. 101; CHL microfilm 2458, form 42 FP, pt. 37; all mission list, 1943–46, 186–87; district list, 202–3; FHL microfilm 271395; 1920 and 1935 censuses; IGI)

Gustav Adolf Priefler b. Köln, Rheinprovinz, 12 Jul 1906; son of Gustav Priefler and Emma Auguste Speiser; bp. 19 Sep 1923; conf. 29 Sep 1923; ord. deacon 28 May 1924; ord. teacher 3 Dec 1928; ord. priest 12 Jan 1930; ord. elder 1 Nov 1931; noncommissioned officer; k. in battle west of Baranowiczy (Baranowitschi), Belarus 6 Jul 1944 (FHL microfilm 68786, no. 98; www.volksbund.de; CHL microfilm 2458, form 42 FP, pt. 37, 430–31; IGI)

Gustav Hugo Theodor Romboy b. Mühlheim an der Ruhr, Rheinprovinz, 21 Dec 1868; son of Bernhard Josef Romboy and Sophie Frentzen; bp. 28 Dec 1905; conf. 28 Dec 1905; ord. deacon 3 Dec 1928; ord. teacher 7 Sep 1930; ord. priest 1 Nov 1931; ord. elder 3 Oct 1937; m. Hamm, Sieg, Westerwald, Rheinprovinz, 22 May 1895, Karoline Wilhelmine Hassel; 8 children; d. hemorrhage Köln, Rheinland, 22 Jul 1944 (FHL microfilm 68786, no. 104; FHL microfilm 271406, 1930 and 1935 censuses; IGI)

Helmut Hugo Romboy b. Köln, Rheinland, 14 Aug 1927; son of Hugo Emil Romboy and Gertrud Widdenhoefer; bp. 10 Jun 1936; private; k. in battle between 18 and 22 Jan 1945; bur. Heinsberg, Germany (CHL CR 375 8 2460, 728–29; FHL microfilm 271406, 1930 and 1935 censuses; www.volksbund.de; IGI)

Hans Heinrich Sachon b. Holthausen, Herne, Westfalen, 2 May 1920; son of Johannes Heinrich

Fig. 8. Helmut Hugo Romboy. (U. Romboy Gamble)

Sachon and Klara Emilie Hinz; bp. 1 Jun 1929; conf. 1 Jun 1929; ord. deacon 6 Jun 1933; private first class; k. in battle Italy 6 Dec 1943; bur. Cassino, Italy (CHL microfilm 2447, pt. 26, no. 496; FHL microfilm 68803, no. 496; FHL microfilm no. 245256, 1935 census; IGI; www.volksbund.de)

Johannes Karl Schumer b. Leipzig, Sachsen, 17 Oct 1918; bp. 15 Jul 1927; d. 1942.

Karl Hans Schumer b. Leipzig, Sachsen, 10 Apr 1882; son of Johann Heinrich Schumer and Augusta H. A. or Christiane Lohse; bp. 19 Apr 1909 or 10 Apr 1911; conf. 19 Apr 1909; ord. elder 2 Apr 1933; m. Leipzig, Sachsen, 23 Oct 1915, Helene Martha Vogel; three children; d. pneumonia Köln, Rheinland, 27 Sep 1939 (FHL microfilm 68803, no. 838; FHL microfilm 245260, 1930 and 1935 censuses; IGI)

Helma Maria Erna Webank b. Köln, Rheinland, 4 Oct 1930; dau. of Hermann Josef Webank and Berta Emillie Erna Stüber; k. air raid 27 Sep 1944 (FHL microfilm 245295, 1930 and 1935 censuses; IGI)

Margarete Weibel b. Köln, Rheinland, 23 Feb 1920; dau. of Magdalene Schminnes; bp. 8 Jun 1929; conf. 9 Jun 1929; k. air raid Köln 29 Jun 1943 (FHL microfilm 68786, no. 133; CHL microfilm 2458, form 42 FP, pt. 37; 1948 list, 1524–25; IGI)

Notes

1. Presiding Bishopric, "Financial, Statistical, and Historical Reports of Wards, Stakes, and Missions, 1884–1955," 257, CHL CR 4 12.
2. West German Mission branch directory, 1939, CHL LR 10045 11.
3. George Blake, interview by the author, Provo, UT, April 1, 2009.
4. Ursula Romboy Gamble, interview by Marion Wolfert, Salt Lake City, March 16, 2006.
5. Paul Romboy letters to Grete Romboy, private collection, used with permission of Ursula Romboy Gamble.
6. Elder Ezra Taft Benson toured war-ravaged Europe in 1945 and 1946 and arranged for relief supplies to be shipped from Salt Lake City to starving Saints in numerous locations in Germany and other countries.
7. Additional money was earned by prisoners for overtime projects; articles produced were often sold to guards or local French citizens by prisoners who were allowed to leave the camps during the day.
8. Walter E. Scoville, papers, CHL MS 18613.
9. Ibid.
10. Ibid.
11. Ibid.

Dortmund Branch

One of the largest cities in the Ruhr region of northwest Germany, Dortmund had 546,000 inhabitants in 1939. Eighteen miles east of Essen, Dortmund was an important industrial and transportation hub and therefore critical to Germany's war effort.

The Church of Jesus Christ of Latter-day Saints existed in Dortmund in the form of one branch with eighty-two members. Eighteen of those members held the priesthood, forty members were women over twelve, and eight were children when World War II approached in the late summer of 1939. The branch president at the time was W. Georg Gould, a missionary from the United States. His counselors were local members Franz Willkomm and Felix Kiltz. Other branch leaders were August Kiltz (Sunday School), August Bernhardt (YMMIA), Melitta Matuszewski (YWMIA), Antonin Kiltz (Relief Society), and Ernst Proll (genealogy).[1]

Dortmund Branch[2]	1939
Elders	6
Priests	1
Teachers	3
Deacons	8
Other Adult Males	16
Adult Females	40
Male Children	4
Female Children	4
Total	82

At the time, the Dortmund Branch met in rented rooms on the second floor of a building at Auf dem Berge 27. Erich Bernhardt (born 1920) had this recollection of the setting:

> Those were the first meeting rooms that we really liked. They were really nice rooms. It was a commercial building that was used for piano recitals [during the day]. About one hundred people could comfortably sit there and listen to the concerts. There were also a few smaller rooms on the sides. We used those to hold our Sunday School and MIA meetings. The large room could be divided into two smaller areas. The branch had about one hundred members on record, but forty to fifty were regularly in attendance in Sunday School or sacrament meetings.[3]

The meeting schedule was as follows: Sunday School at 10:00 a.m. and sacrament meeting at 7:00 p.m. MIA met on Tuesdays at 7:30 p.m. and the Relief Society met on Wednesdays at the same time. A genealogy class took place on the third Sunday of the month at 5:30 p.m.

Fig. 1. Herbert Kiltz in Russia wrote this letter to his family in Germany in February 1944. He was reported missing in action four months later. (R. Asisi-Bonini)

A dedicated branch clerk (who never mentioned himself by name) compiled a detailed history for the years 1939 to 1946. He made this comment on August 26, 1939: "A decisive event in the history of our branch occurred on August 26 when the missionaries were called away. W. George Gould left as our branch president along with John Wells due to the fact that war was anticipated. This was a painful loss to us to no longer have missionaries in our midst. The missionaries transferred their authority to Brother August Kiltz."[4]

Young Paul Todebusch (born 1928) recalled the departure of the missionaries: "Before they left, they said good-bye to us. I remember that one of them was sitting on his suitcase, totally devastated that they had to leave."[5]

The following is found in the branch history and provides evidence that a number of branch members were willing and able to make the short trip to Essen:

> November 26, 1939: A branch conference was held and twenty-five persons attended.
>
> December 15, 1939: Thirty-four branch members attended the district conference in Essen.

"I volunteered for the military because I really wanted to work for the aircraft maintenance department," explained Erich Bernhardt. "I got in, and that was such a big blessing for me. I was in the Deutsche Luftwaffe, and trained to be an aircraft mechanic." Little did Erich know that an even greater blessing came in the form of a miscommunication. He was sent to Norway in the place of another man but was kept there for five years because he had the required skills. In Norway, he had an opportunity rare for German LDS soldiers:

> When I arrived in Norway in 1940, I sent a letter to my father asking him to provide me with the mission office address in Oslo because I wanted to make contact with the Church there. He sent me the address and I made contact with the mission office. They received me very nicely and I felt at home there. They treated me like a returned missionary although we, as the [German] soldiers, were occupying the country. We were not liked much by the Norwegians. But the membership made me a brother in the Church. And for the Saints there, that was the only vital thing to talk about. I kept contact with the Church in Oslo, Trondheim, Stavanger, and Narvik. It

was a great blessing to be able to be a part of the Church, even in Norway.

Paul Todebusch was first a member of the Jungvolk and then of the Hitler Youth. He recalled his feelings about the experience:

> I didn't like to go and had a strong opinion against it. I didn't like what they taught us and what they did in general. Once, we had to meet and stand in rows as the Jungvolk and the Hitler Youth together. We stood parallel to each other. All of sudden, everybody was fighting and somebody was stabbed to death. That incident truly made a difference in how I thought about the war.

We read again from the branch history:

> February 2, 1941: Bernhard Willkomm and Melitta Matuszewski were married.
>
> August 31, 1941: Annaliese Frölke was baptized during a district conference.
>
> March 1942: The first great event of the year 1942 was the centennial celebration of the Relief Society on March 22. A fine program was presented in Essen and several members of our branch participated. It was a very spiritual event.
>
> April 19, 1942: Elsa Dreger was baptized in Essen by Elder Gustav Dreger.
>
> August 30, 1942. Nineteen persons attended a genealogical conference.

In the fall of 1942, Herbert Bergmann (born 1936) started school. Regarding the training of school children in the Third Reich years, he recalled the following: "We sang the national anthem every morning. We had to hold up our arms [in the Hitler salute] during the entire song, which was quite a challenge."[6]

Herbert also recalled activities relating to the frequent air raids over Dortmund:

> After every air raid, we would go out and collect all the shrapnel. We took a little box and even compared them in school to see who found the best pieces. In the beginning of the war, it was also more like a game still. We would see the planes and the Christbäume [flares] and would think it was fun. When we realized that the anti-aircraft was gone, war became more of a reality. It was a total nightmare. You sit in your basement, and you hear the bombs coming down with that shrill noise, and you know how close they are. Some sounded like they were right above us. Others were farther away. That is what we learned to distinguish. There were moments when I thought I would not survive. We were all crowded in the basement together—all six families of the house together. I remember one lady who went totally nuts. She started screaming, and they had to hold her down and put something over her mouth. She was never normal again.

Fig. 2. Herbert Bergmann with the traditional cone full of treats on his first day of school. (H. Bergmann)

Erich Bernhardt played a crucial role in the life of a young Norwegian Latter-day Saint in 1942, as Erich recalled:

> The auditorium of the University of Oslo was burned down by students, some of whom were Nazi sympathizers. The branch president's son was a student at that university but not a supporter of what had been done. Every student of the school was picked up by the police and taken to a concentration camp—so was he. The members of the family approached me and asked if I could help the police understand that the boy had had nothing to do with the incident and that he was not politically involved. I went to the German administration building in Oslo and talked to one of the leading officers. I explained

> that the boy's family was religious and in no way harmful or politically active. About two weeks later, that student was called out of a large group of other students and told that he could go home. His name was Per Strand, a son of Einar A. Strand, who was the branch president.

One of the most vivid memories Eugen Bergmann (born 1934) had of wartime Dortmund was a confusing and sad one. He recounted:

> My mother and I walked to Church one Sunday morning in Dortmund. The streetcars weren't working anymore, so we had to walk the whole way. We had to cross a square, and we were just about in the middle of it when soldiers came and shot at the windows of the houses and yelled and commanded that everybody should leave the square immediately. I personally saw that day how the soldiers pulled Jewish people out of their homes and how they put the star [of David] on them. It was an awful sight for me. It got worse when I heard the soldiers call the Jews pigs. By that time, I had learned who Jewish people were. We had learned about them in school, and people in our neighborhood talked about them too. Especially some of the older students in my school talked about the Jews. I didn't like that.[7]

Eugen's father was a machinist in a steel factory. In 1942, he was transferred to a factory in Lebenstedt by Salzgitter (about 150 miles east of Dortmund). His wife and their baby followed him to Lebenstedt, but Eugen and his younger brother, Herbert, were sent to towns in the Black Forest in southern Germany. As two of the hundreds of thousands of children sent away from home under the program called Kinderlandverschickung, the boys had distinctly different experiences. Eugen told this story:

> The families picked us up from the train station. I stayed with the Volz family [in Bad Sulzburg]. They had nine children—two girls and seven boys. The last one was drafted into the war, being seventeen years old, when I arrived. All of the children were gone. They didn't own a farm—just a house with a yard. The father was working at a mill in a different town. I had a really good time there. We didn't feel much of the war happening down there. I had to take care of some cows and about sixty rabbits. I also chopped wood, but I still had time to make friends with the locals. I went horseback riding. It was a pleasant time. In the beginning, I was very homesick. I missed my mother and my brothers. I was totally cut off from the Church. While I was away from home, I participated in a Lutheran religion class. I was also helping the bell ringer at church. But nobody gave me a hard time because of my religion. The family I lived with were North German Lutherans. I was in that town for about thirteen months.

Herbert Bergmann was not so fortunate when it came to his assignment with a family in the farming community of Grunern:

> I lived in the Black Forest for that year, and I had to go to the Catholic Church, which was no fun at all—I hated it. We had Polish workers there; there was only supposed to be one but we had two for some reason. The second guy made great whiskey, and in the mornings I would go into the orchards to pick up all the fruit that was lying on the ground. I would take it to him, and he would make great whiskey from it. Other people from the town would also bring their fruit to him. It was such a small town—everybody knew everybody. One Polish worker did the regular farmwork—the other made whiskey.

Grete Bergmann rescued her son Herbert in early 1944, and Eugen's father picked him up later that year. They all went to their new home in Lebenstedt where the boys could see their father every day for the first time in three years. As Eugen recalled, "We all came together again in a new house. It was a row house with a basement, first floor, and second floor. It was wall to wall with the neighbors. We had indoor plumbing but there was still no refrigerator or ice box. We were in that location when the war ended."

The branch history includes the following report:

> In the night of May 4–5, 1943, our branch meeting rooms on the second floor at Auf dem Berge 27 were destroyed in an air raid. All branch property was lost. Therefore we were not able to hold any meetings on May 9 and 16, because we had a lot of adjustments to make. . . .

Fig. 3. Members of the Dortmund Branch. (H. Bergmann)

> The Relief Society was also unable to hold any meetings. The Relief Society funds were distributed among needy members with the permission of district president Wilhelm Nitz and district Relief Society president Johanna Neumann. The first meeting after the destruction of our meeting rooms was held on May 23, 1943, in the apartment of Brother Scharf.

Eugen Bergmann recalled seeing the aftermath of the attack and specifically the remains of the church building at Auf dem Berge 27: "The whole front façade had collapsed to the ground. The pump organ was even hanging out over the edge of the destroyed building. We had a prayer meeting after that."

The same attack that destroyed the branch's meeting rooms destroyed the home of the Frölke family. According to their son Hans (born 1927), the war did not affect them much until 1943: "We were bombed out twice in two weeks. The first time, we lived in a large apartment building, and we were on the main floor; the house burned from the top to the bottom, and all the people from upstairs tried to take as many things outside as possible [while the fires burned]. Because we lived on the ground floor, my father broke the window with an ax, and we could carry lots of things out [before the fire burned down to our level]."[8]

The Frölke family then moved into the apartment of Hans's paternal grandparents in a suburb of Dortmund. On May 23, that apartment was hit and Hans was nearly killed. He explained:

> I always slept on the couch in the living room, and I rarely got up when there was an alarm, only when I heard bombs falling—then I got up. That particular night was the same. I waited until I heard [the airplanes] dropping bombs, and then I got up, left the room, and closed the door. I was standing at the front door when I heard a noise in the room that I was sleeping in—the entire room was burning.

That same night, Paul Todebusch's father (who was not a member of the Church) was killed. He was in the official air-raid shelter at a local school. Fortunately, Paul and his mother were away visiting relatives. Soon after the attack, Sister Proll of the branch found Paul's mother and informed her of the tragedy. As Paul later learned, his uncle had identified the body based on the fact that Paul's father always wore brown shoes. Paul's reaction to the loss of his father was predictable:

> I was fifteen years old when my father died. We were very close—one heart and soul. Every night when my father came home, he would eat the dinner that my mother had prepared for him, wearing the slippers that we put by the door. He would read the newspaper and smoke his cigarette. He was a happy man. And he wasn't against the church. He allowed my mother to go to church any time she wanted and to pay tithing.

The branch history offers these details about problems caused by the Gestapo:

> Brother August Bernhardt went to the Gestapo after our rooms were destroyed and asked for permission to hold home meetings. His request was denied. . . . Later, Brother August Kiltz went to the Gestapo with the same request and was given permission to hold home meetings. Our first meeting was held on September 26, 1943.

Paul Todebusch recalled hearing his uncle describe the visit with the Gestapo:

> My uncle [August Kiltz] had been blind since he was eighteen years old. He was invited to the office of the Gestapo with the Bible, the Book of Mormon, and the hymnbook and had to explain. All the members were nervous about what might happen. He went there, and they looked at everything he had brought. They then told him that we were not allowed to sing the hymns that used the word "Zion." After that, we did not have any problems with the Gestapo anymore. We do not know who told the Gestapo about us.

More interesting details about the activities of the Dortmund Branch are these from the branch history:

> October 10, 1943: August and Anna Grywatz were baptized along with Sister Schneider of Wuppertal; the baptism was performed by Bernhard Willkomm (a priest) in the city bathhouse in Hamm.
>
> During the year 1943, several of our members were bombed out of their homes and had to be evacuated. Eight persons were evacuated. Despite these fateful developments, our members remained loyal to God and to the kingdom.
>
> March 26, 1944: Branch president August Bernhardt was drafted by the Wehrmacht. . . . His successor is August Kiltz.

In February 1944, Herbert Kiltz of the Dortmund Branch wrote a letter to his family, who had been evacuated from Dortmund to southern Germany. He thanked them for sending Christmas packages, of which he had received no fewer than fifteen. In his opinion, he was eating better in Russia ("great meals!") than was his family at home. He was in good health and looking forward to a furlough in March. Whether he ever actually left the combat zone for that furlough is not known. He was reported missing in action in Russia on June 7, 1944, and was declared dead by a court decree after the war.[9]

The hardships of living in an apartment that had been damaged by air raids was something Paul Todebusch could not forget:

> Our home was not destroyed during the war, but our balcony was burned, and our windows burst. Our rooms were mostly intact, though. We put blankets and paper over the windows so it would not be so cold during the night. The electricity also didn't work anymore. We fetched water a little farther away from the home. We had to carry it. I think it was more than one hundred meters away. We were allowed to get water twice a day.

In 1944, Hans Frölke and his schoolmates were assigned to operate antiaircraft batteries on the outskirts of Dortmund. By then, his mother and his sisters had been evacuated from the city and were living in Diersheim near Strasbourg, France. Following the "flak" assignment, all of the boys but

Fig. 4. Members of the Dortmund Branch during the war. At far right is the blind branch president August Kilz. (H. Bergmann)

Hans were drafted into the Reichsarbeitsdienst. Hans was sent to a premilitary conditioning camp for six weeks, where he had "a most wonderful time and learned a lot."

Just a little girl, Rita Böhmbeck (born 1940) recalled a terrible experience that happened during an air raid over Dortmund in 1944:

> We were trapped for the longest time in the bomb shelter in the Kesselstrasse. There was no food or drink for us. We knocked, but it took them so long to get us out. The door was made out of iron. It was actually a normal basement with a stronger door. It was so dark, and the people knocked on the stones that connected our basement with the neighboring one. The oxygen started to run out. People screamed and prayed and were scared. People in the neighboring house heard the screaming and got out us out through a small hole. I was just four years old. I remember everything. The sight I saw when I left the shelter was horrible. My mother put everything that she thought we would need in a crisis situation into a box and built wheels and attached those to the box. It was filled with silverware and plates. She also wrapped her accordion in blankets and my doll also. That night, we had to sleep on the street.[10]

The branch history provides this information about the disturbances caused by the war for members of the Dortmund Branch:

> October 15, 1944: Due to the confusion caused by the huge air raid over Dortmund on October 6, we could not hold any meetings today. We had to rearrange our affairs totally. We could not hold our fast and testimony meeting on October 1, so we moved it to October 15.

Back at home for Christmas, Hans Frölke was alone with his father. Brother Frölke sent Hans to bring his mother and his sisters home because the American army was approaching the area. It was no longer safe to stay there. From Diersheim, the group traveled to Erfurt, in central Germany, to stay with friends. Shortly thereafter, they returned to Dortmund, where an order awaited Hans: he was to report immediately for service with the Reichsarbeitsdienst. The date was January 1945.

Hans Frölke seemed to live a charmed life. Following six weeks of service in Schwerte (barely four miles from home), he was instructed to return to Dortmund and report for his next military assignment. While Hans was speaking to the officer who would have made that assignment, an air-raid siren and attack interrupted them, and no decision was made. After the attack, Hans's father told him to take advantage of the confusion and join his mother in Erfurt. From there, he wrote to his father in Dortmund, but that turned out to be a mistake. The postal officials informed the military office in Dortmund of Hans's location, and he received a notice to return immediately. As Hans recalled, "The Americans came to where we were the next day and freed me from having to report for duty." Hans had avoided military duty at a time when young men were dying in great numbers in the hopeless attempt to keep Germany's enemies from her gates.

The branch secretary explained some of the problems encountered by the Saints as the war drew to a close:

> Despite the fact that the war's disturbance has reached its zenith, we have tried to hold sacrament meetings. Nevertheless, we had to stop our meeting after the sacrament on March 11 because the alarms sounded and an attack followed. Some of the members were not able to attend the meeting. Constant alarms and attacks on March 18 prevented the members of the Dortmund Branch from attending the district conference, nor could we hold our own meetings on that day. The same was true on March 25, April 1, and April 8. Peace was restored in our city after the arrival of the American troops, and we were able to conduct a sacrament meeting without disturbance on April 15, 1945. On May 6, 1945, the Sunday School started again, having not met since October 15, 1944, due to the increasing dangerous conditions.

At the end of the war, Paul Todebusch was sixteen. He had already done a short stint with the Reichsarbeitsdienst and was actually drafted at the last minute by the Wehrmacht. Fortunately, he did not see any action and was at home in Dortmund when the American conquerors arrived. For some reason, his uncle suggested that Paul surrender to the Americans as a German soldier, even though he had already divested himself of his uniform. Dutifully, young Paul reported to a police officer: "He asked me if I was crazy and told me to go home. I went home and told this to my uncle, who sent me back. The second time, the police kept me, and after a while the Americans took me, put me on a truck, and sent me to a camp. I was a POW for about two months."

As the war neared its conclusion, Herbert Bergmann was nine years old and able to understand some of the military action he witnessed. For example, he noticed that enemy airplanes did not attack the factory where his father worked, but instead tried to destroy the antiaircraft batteries that guarded that factory. "This went on for two days. The enemy sent five planes each time and they were all shot down. They shot down at least twenty-five planes. The factory functioned until the end of the war, and my father was never in danger."

In Lebenstedt, the Bergmann boys watched as the American soldiers entered the town. In the confusion of the takeover, Eugen joined with other boys in collecting goods from destroyed stores in town. He later recalled finding a large box of cinnamon and a pair of boots. At the last minute, several fighter planes made another pass over the neighborhood; their machine guns left several holes in the walls of the Bergmann home. Eugen also remembered how the local mayor had wanted to surrender the town and therefore had raised a white flag above a bunker. A fanatic Hitler Youth boy then shot the mayor for committing treason.

When the war was finally over and Germany defeated, Herbert realized that his dream of joining the Hitler Youth would never be realized. "I wanted so badly to be in the Hitler Youth. All I had ever known in my young life was Hitler's Germany."

Erich Bernhardt was taken prisoner a few days after the war ended on May 8, 1945, and was kept in Stavanger, Norway, for about three months. As he recalled:

> An American unit took us prisoner, and we were very well treated. A British unit occupied the air base that I was working in, and I worked for them during that time. I spoke a little English and was fluent in Norwegian by then, which allowed them to give me different assignments. I was very well liked. They even wanted to keep me from returning back to Germany in August of that year.

Fortunately, he was released that month and returned to Dortmund. A few weeks later, his father came home from a Soviet POW camp; he had been drafted in midwar. The family's apartment had been damaged but was still inhabitable.

Erich Bernhardt assessed his wartime experiences in these words:

> I had a very good experience in Norway. I was never in combat and never wounded. I had contact with other [German] LDS soldiers while I was there. They usually attended the meetings in the branches I was visiting so we met there. I was able to translate their testimonies into Norwegian. We talked about our experiences in the war, and they were all as well received in the branches as I was. Being in Norway taught me that the Church is the same everywhere in the world and that even in a war situation the Saints focus on what is most important and don't let themselves become too influenced by politics.

Eugen Bergmann had the following to say about his mother, Grete, who had tried to raise her children without the help of their absent father:

> My mother went through a challenging time, with four young children at home, her husband gone, but she always stayed faithful in the gospel. My mother always taught us from the scriptures that we took with us everywhere. She taught us Primary songs. She kept the gospel alive in our home although we couldn't attend church [in Lebenstedt].

The city of Dortmund recorded 6,341 official deaths in air raids, but historians believe that the actual total was substantially higher. Ninety-nine percent of the city center was destroyed. The city was taken by the American army on April 13, 1945.[11]

In Memoriam

The following members of the Dortmund Branch did not survive World War II:

Gustav Ernst Dietrich b. Uderwangen, Ostpreußen, 28 Nov 1897; son of Hermann Dietrich and Rosine Neufang; bp. 4 Aug 1929; conf. 4 Aug 1929; m. Louise Wilhelmine Jeckstadt; 2 m. 5 May 1934, Anna Warbruck; d. industrial accident 24 Nov 1943 (FHL microfilm 68787, no. 3; CHL microfilm 2447, pt. 26, no. 512; FHL microfilm 68803, no. 512; IGI)

Margarete Hertel b. Althaidhof, Haidhof, Oberfranken, Bayern, 7 Jun 1884; dau. of Matheus Hertel and Katharina Hoffmann; bp. 6 Sep 1931; conf. 6 Sep 1931; d. heart attack 9 Apr 1941 (FHL microfilm 68787, no. 72; CHL microfilm 2447, pt. 26, no. 598; FHL microfilm 68803, no. 598; FHL microfilm 162782, 1935 census; IGI)

Herbert Felix Kiltz b. Elberfeld, Rheinprovinz, 4 Jan 1913; son of Felix Kiltz and Anna Paulina Lemmens; single; 1 child; bp. 17 Jan 1924; MIA Russia 7 Jun 1944; declared dead 31 Dec 1945 or 20 Mar 1954 (Deppe; FHL microfilm 271378, 1930 and 1935 censuses; IGI)

Anna Amalie Elisabeth Kreimeyer b. Höxter, Westfalen, 11 Dec 1897; dau. of Karl Heinrich Kreimeyer and Maria Elisabeth Schimpf; bp. 26 Aug 1925; conf. 26 Aug 1925; m. Dortmund, Westfalen 13 May 1921, Friedrich Julius Franz Todebusch; 2 children; d. heart disease Dortmund 3 Sep 1943; bur. Dortmund 7 Sep 1943 (FHL microfilm 68787, no. 46; CHL microfilm 2447, pt. 26, no. 374; FHL microfilm 68803, no. 374; Dortmund Branch history; IGI)

Joseph Sammler b. Wongrowitz, Bromberg, Posen, 18 Mar 1891; son of Adelbert Zbierski and Katharine Pazdzierska; bp. 14 Sep 1930; conf. 14 Sep 1930; m. 8 Jul 1921, Elfriede Kroll; d. stroke 20 Mar 1940 (FHL microfilm 68787, no. 36; CHL microfilm 2447, pt. 26, no. 560; IGI)

Friedrich Julius Franz Todebusch b. Duisburg, Rheinprovinz, 5 Jul 1895; son of Wilhelm Todebusch and Gertrud Heier; d. Dortmund, Westfalen, 24 May 1943.

Eugen Erwin Trenkle b. Dorndorf, Donaukreis, Württemberg, 15 Nov 1910; son of Eugen Trenkle and Louise Friedricke Deck; bp. 28 Jul 1920; conf. 28 Jul

1920; m. Anna Wösterfeld; k. in battle Eastern Front 15 Jan 1944 (FHL microfilm 68787, no. 51; CHL microfilm 2447, pt. 26, 379; IGI)

Gerda Christine Wegener b. Dortmund, Westfalen, 13 Jun 1916; dau. of Gottlieb Otto Wegener and Auguste Ida Schönhoff; bp. 26 May 1929; conf. 26 May 1929; MIA 20 May 1943 (CHL microfilm 2447, pt. 26, no. 498; FHL microfilm no. 245296, 1930 and 1935 censuses)

Gustav Wiemer b. Volmarstein, Westfalen, 17 Apr 1885; son of Gustav Wiemer and Liselotte Diekermann or Dieckertmann; bp. 30 Jul 1933; conf. 30 Jul 1933; ord. deacon 22 Aug 1937; d. 12 Jun 1944 (FHL microfilm 68787, no. 121; CHL microfilm 2447, pt. 26, no. 648; IGI)

Edmund Heinrich Willkomm b. Dortmund, Westfalen, Preussen, 10 Jul 1917; son of Franz Willkomm and Wladislawa Maria Tabaczynski; bp. 6 Sep 1931; conf. 6 Sep 1931; ord. deacon 30 Nov 1932; ord. teacher 31 Oct 1933; ord. priest 1 Dec 1935; k. in battle France 23 Mar 1940 (FHL microfilm 68787, no. 69; CHL microfilm 2447, pt. 26, no. 596; IGI)

Johann Willkomm b. Dortmund, Westfalen, Preussen, 2 Aug 1920; son of Franz Willkomm and Wladislawa Maria Tabaczynski; bp. 6 Sep 1931; conf. 6 Sep 1931; ord. deacon 30 Nov 1932; d. lung disease contracted while in the army Dortmund 20 Dec 1946 (FHL microfilm 68787, no. 71; FHL microfilm 68803, no. 594; CHL microfilm 2458, form 42 FP, pt. 37, all-mission list 1943–46, 186–87; IGI)

Notes

1. West German Mission branch directory 1939, CHL 10045 11.
2. Presiding Bishopric, "Financial, Statistical, and Historical Reports of Wards, Stakes, and Missions, 1884–1955," 257, CHL CR 4 12.
3. Erich Bernhardt, telephone interview with Jennifer Heckmann in German, March 31, 2009; unless otherwise noted, summarized in English by Judith Sartowski.
4. Dortmund Branch history, 1939–46, 2, CHL LR 2296 22.
5. Paul Erwin Todebusch, interview by the author in German, Dortmund, Germany, August 7, 2006.
6. Herbert Bergmann, interview by the author, Provo, UT, April 2, 2009.
7. Eugen Bergmann, telephone interview with the author, April 8, 2009.
8. Hans Erwin Froelke, interview by Marion Wolfert, Salt Lake City, February 2006.
9. Herbert Kiltz to his family, February 1944; used with the kind permission of Rita Assisi-Bonini.
10. Rita Böhmbeck Assisi-Bonini, interview by the author in German, Dortmund, Germany, August 7, 2006.
11. Dortmund city archive.

Düsseldorf Branch

Düsseldorf is one of the principal industrial cities along the Rhine River in northern Germany. With 535,753 inhabitants in 1939, it was also one of the largest cities in the Ruhr River area.[1] The branch of the LDS Church in that city was relatively small, having only sixty members and fourteen priesthood holders as World War II approached.

Missionary Clark Hillam of Brigham City, Utah, was serving as branch president at the time, and the branch directory shows that he had no counselors.[2] Paul Schmidt was the Sunday School superintendant, Manfred Knabe the leader of the YMMIA, Margarete Keller the leader of the YWMIA, and Hedwig Klesper the president of the Relief Society, but no organized Primary existed at the time. Paul Doktor Sr. was the genealogical instructor.

Duesseldorf Branch[3]	**1939**
Elders	4
Priests	4
Teachers	3
Deacons	3
Other Adult Males	13
Adult Females	28
Male Children	5
Female Children	0
Total	60

The meeting schedule for the Düsseldorf Branch shows Sunday School starting at 10:00 a.m. and sacrament meeting at 7:00 p.m. The only other meetings held in July 1939 were on Wednesdays: MIA at 8:00 p.m. and Relief Society at 9:00 p.m.

Branch meetings were held in rented rooms at Worringerstrasse 112. Kurt Fiedler (born 1926) described the rooms as being on the second floor of the building at that address. "It was a business building. We set up chairs [each week] in the main meeting room, and there was another smaller room as well. There might have been thirty people in church on a typical Sunday."[4]

"It was a very small group, but a good branch," recalled Clark Hillam regarding the Saints in Düsseldorf. He was sad when the telegram came on August 25, 1939, instructing him to leave the country immediately. The telegram also told him to appoint a successor as branch president. He described the situation:

Fig. 1. Elders Welti (standing left) and Hillam in the home of the Schmidt family. (C. Hillam)

> After we got our evacuation notice, I still had enough time to go to Brother [Paul] Schmidt to tell him that he would be the new branch president. I handed all the records over to him, and he knew that he would be on his own. They were all very sad when they heard that all the missionaries had to be evacuated. They knew that if the missionaries had to leave, that problems were not far away. They believed in the fact that they would be safer if missionaries were around them.[5]

Kurt Fiedler was one of six children in a family who lived in the eastern suburb of Grafenberg, about three miles from downtown Düsseldorf. His mother, Elli, was the secretary of the Relief Society, and his father (though not a member of the Church) "was always active in the branch as either the drama director or the entertainment director. He really loved that," Kurt recalled.

Just prior to the war, Kurt was a member of the local Hitler Youth group. He remembered the following: "We were trained in survival and camping. I never saw a gun in the Hitler Youth. We did a lot of marching because they mainly taught us discipline. We didn't have political lessons, but we wore our uniforms for meetings, and that was in itself a political lesson."

Manfred Knabe (born 1930) provided a fine description of the conditions in wartime Düsseldorf:

> We lived under a blackout. All windows had to be totally darkened with black material so that no light could be seen outside. Wardens monitored that very closely and fines were given to people who did not comply. There was an air raid warden in each apartment house. My mother had that duty in our building. She had to see to it that there were buckets of sand and water on each landing in the staircases. And there had to be a broom with a bag over the end to be used to beat out the flames. Every basement was outfitted to serve as an air raid shelter. Thick logs were used to fortify the ceiling joists and bunk beds were installed. A hole was made in each wall to an adjacent building, about one meter in diameter, then the bricks were replaced loosely. If we needed to escape our basement, we could kick the bricks out of the opening and escape.[6]

Preparations for survival during air raids were serious activities, but collecting shrapnel and bomb fragments on the mornings after the raids was a favorite pastime for city children. Manfred recalled that the brass cases from antiaircraft rounds were especially valuable pieces of his collection.

As the war progressed and Düsseldorf became a frequent target of Allied bombers, Kurt Fiedler was called to perform a most unpleasant duty:

> I was assigned to what you would call the home defense. After air raids, we had to dig up the dead or rescue the living who were trapped under rubble—the clean-up after the air raids. It was not very pleasant because, especially when they bombed apartment homes, we had to go down [into the basements]. We were only fifteen and sixteen years old then. We had to remove the bodies of those who were killed. When we found a group of survivors, we felt very successful; that was a good feeling. [But the memory of finding bodies] stays with you for a while.

According to the city historian, Düsseldorf suffered nine heavy air raids and 234 raids resulting in medium damage.[7] During one of those many raids, the branch meeting rooms were bombed out. According to Kurt, meetings thereafter were held first in schools; when that was no longer possible, the Latter-day Saints met in the apartments of member families. Some of the branch members living in the southern neighborhoods of the city also attended meetings with the branch in Benrath, just a few miles south of Düsseldorf.

In January 1943, Manfred Knabe and his classmates were sent off to eastern Germany as part of the Kinderlandverschickung program. They were housed in a very nice dormitory in the small town of Döntschen and supervised by their teacher and by a Hitler Youth leader. Manfred described the daily life of the thirty-six boys in these words:

> We had our classes in the mornings. After lunch, we had quiet time, that is, we had to lie on our beds. Then we did our homework, of course under the watchful eye of our teacher. Then we had our afternoon coffee and our Hitler Youth drills. Then came sports, marching, and war games. We usually had a great time in those activities because our Hitler Youth leader did his job very well. Then several boys were sent off to do small tasks such as fetching milk and mail, peeling potatoes, etc. That kept us in good shape socially. All in all, it was a good experience—except for the homesickness!

Manfred was allowed to go home in November 1943, but he arrived precisely at the conclusion of a terrible air raid. Passing burning buildings on their way home, his mother suggested that he might be better off back at Döntschen. In a subsequent attack, their home burned to the ground, and the family saved only what they could carry. By January 1944, Manfred was back with his schoolmates in eastern Germany, but in a different town. They had been moved to Seiffen, a town famous for its toy manufacturing. Manfred was hosted by the family of a wood carver, and he enjoyed helping the artisan in his shop. Winter sports such as skiing were also a great activity for a big city boy from Germany's flatlands.

Not far from Seiffen was the town of Rechenberg-Bienenmühle, where a small LDS branch held Sunday School. Manfred learned of their meetings and received permission from his teacher to walk there on several Sundays. As he recalled, "My mother had told me where they met, and I was so happy. I walked to Brother Fischer's house with my hymnal; he was the Sunday School president. They even had a pump organ, but nobody could play it, so I did it as well as I could—usually with two fingers."

The family of branch president Paul Schmidt lived at Lorettostrasse 51 in Düsseldorf. According to his son, Siegfried (born 1939), they walked perhaps twenty minutes to church. Unfortunately, Brother Schmidt's term as the branch leader ended in 1943 when his apartment was destroyed. Although only four at the time, Siegfried recalled clearly the night his home was hit by Allied bombs. With the building above them in flames and the exit from the basement blocked, he and his mother had to leave through a hole in the basement wall into the next building. Emerging onto the street, they saw that their building would not survive the flames. He described what happened next:

> All I could see was fire everywhere. Seeing us walking down the street, a woman stopped and asked us if we had lost our home. When we told her that we had, she invited us to come to her house so we would have a safe place to stay. Soon, my father came home [from Leipzig] and stood in front of a house that seemed to be unfamiliar—he could still see our kitchen. My mother had taken a board and written where he could find us in case he came home and hung the board on the front door. My father later told us that he said a prayer the moment he realized that we were alive, giving thanks to his Heavenly Father.[8]

Paul Schmidt was a construction engineer for the Rheinmetall Co., a manufacturer that had been compelled to move its operations into the interior of Germany a few months earlier. When he found an apartment near Leipzig, Brother Schmidt moved his family out of Düsseldorf, hoping to take them a bit farther away from the dangers of the war.

The Schmidt family's new apartment was in Zehmen, a few miles from Leipzig. Siegfried recalled walking more than an hour to the outskirts of town on Sunday mornings, then taking a streetcar to church. Because it was too far for them to go home between meetings, they stayed at the home of Siegfried's aunt in Leipzig in the afternoons, then returned to the rooms of the Leipzig West Branch for sacrament meeting.

In 1943, Kurt Fiedler was drafted into the national labor force and sent off to help build air fields. He did that for three months. Back at home in November 1943, he knew that a call to the Wehrmacht would arrive soon, so he volunteered in order to choose his branch of the service. He selected the navy and was sent to the Netherlands, where he was assigned to a submarine unit. Fortunately, he was not sent to sea but rather was trained as a torpedo specialist and sent to an arsenal at a French port city. The closest he came to actual service at sea was an overnight voyage in a submarine that was short of crew members.

Fig. 2. Celebrating "the spirit of the pioneers" in 1939. (C. Hillam)

By the summer of 1944, the Allied forces that landed at Normandy were moving toward the interior of France, and Kurt Fiedler's unit was sent eastward. "We had lost too many submarines by then, and they didn't need us for that duty anymore," he explained. "They sent us in small groups because the French underground were looking for us. One of our small groups was totally wiped out. Eventually, a train picked us up and took us eastward—past Berlin and all the way to Kolberg [near the Baltic Sea]."

Arriving in Kolberg three days behind schedule, the young soldiers were first threatened with court martial due to their tardiness; they managed to convince their officers that constant bombings had delayed their transportation. Kurt and his comrades then received an assignment to work on the assembly of the V-2 rocket bomb. They remained at that factory until early 1945. Bombed out of work at the factory, they were sent to Cuxhaven on the North Sea coast, where they were assigned to a ship that never came. They simply waited there until the British invaders surrounded the harbor.

When it appeared to the people of Seiffen that the war was lost and the Soviets would be in their town soon, they entered the forest and buried any items bearing swastikas, such as uniforms and books. On May 8, a Soviet officer came to town and ordered the people to remove antitank barriers. After doing that, the boys and their leaders began a long hike toward home, having no desire to wait until the Red Army arrived. After walking more than one hundred and fifty miles westward through the Erzgebirge Hills in about nineteen days, they arrived in the city of Eisenach. Their leaders were able to find four trucks to take them westward toward home. A few days later, Manfred arrived at the home of his parents in a devastated Düsseldorf. His family had lost their home and most of their possessions, but fourteen-year-old Manfred (from whom nothing had been heard for several months) had come home safe and sound.

Siegfried Schmidt recalled experiencing the end of the war as a six-year-old:

> A large group of [German] antiaircraft crew members went marching by under American guards. Each prisoner had his hands behind his head. That was the first thing I could recall about peacetime. When the Americans came into our town, they gave me a bar of chocolate and a pat on the back. I knew that they were looking for German soldiers in our houses, but there was nothing wrong with that.

Things worked out for POW Kurt Fiedler everywhere he turned. His British captors did not work their prisoners very hard, and before long Kurt found himself working in the kitchen. "I had all the food I could eat." In August 1945, the camp commandant asked Kurt if he wanted a leave to go home for ten days. "He said that if I could either enroll in school or find a job; he would give me my final release when I returned to the camp." He was even allowed to use British transportation on his way home to Düsseldorf. After a successful ten days, he returned to the camp only long enough to get the release papers. The British even loaded his duffel bag with food and other valuables that he could take home to his family.

During his two years away from home as a soldier and a POW, Kurt Fiedler never saw combat action. He also never saw the inside of an LDS church, met another LDS soldier, or took the sacrament. His only contact with any church came when the POWs were required to attend a service in the local Lutheran church. As he explained, "We had to go to church on Sunday. If we didn't or couldn't, they would make us do KP duty or clean toilets. Of course, nobody wanted to do that."

The Fiedler home in Grafenberg was fortunate to survive the war without a scratch, although Kurt recalled coming home to the sight of buildings down the street that were damaged to some degree. Most of the Latter-day Saints in Düsseldorf were still alive in 1945, but four of Kurt's non-LDS friends had lost their lives in the service of their country. "It was a bit lonely when I came home," he explained, "but soon I fell in love with a young lady from the Benrath Branch who eventually became my wife."

The loss of Kurt's brother Herbert Eduard, known as Eddy, was especially difficult to understand. At the end of the war, Herbert was only fourteen but was not normal as defined by Nazi health standards. Kurt described his younger brother in these words: "He was an autistic child who had trouble learning. He was a good kid, a great kid. He was smart." During the war, a doctor required the boy to be sent to an institution. On one occasion, Kurt visited Eddy at a town somewhere in the Rhineland. Toward the end of the war, the family received notice that Eddy had died of pneumonia. They were certain that he had become a victim of the heinous euthanasia program. Kurt recalled the following:

> They did experiments with kids [like Eddy]. We learned later on from a nurse who worked there. She contacted my mother, and she said they worked with those kids, and they experimented with them and killed them. That was in a place called Rupert. I visited him there once; he was in bad shape. I could see that already. It was not Eddy anymore, he was a different person. That was shortly before they announced that he died of pneumonia.

The metropolis of Düsseldorf appeared to be a hopeless landscape in the summer of 1945. More than nine thousand people had perished during the destruction of the city, and it would be years before there would be enough housing for the survivors.[9] Like their neighbors, the Latter-day Saints of the Düsseldorf Branch would return over the next few years from countless locations in Germany, Europe, and elsewhere to begin a new life.

In Memoriam

The following members of the Düsseldorf Branch did not survive World War II:

Herbert Eduard Fiedler b. Düsseldorf Stadt, Rheinland, 18 Jun 1930; son of Alexander Ferdinand Valentin Fiedler and Minna Ella Hecker; d. euthanasia, hospital in Rheinland 1944 or 30 May 1945 (Karl Fiedler; IGI)

Eduard Oskar Huettenrauch b. Kunitz, Jena, Sachsen-Weimar-Eisenach, 16 Oct 1866; son of Eduard Huettenrauch and Auguste Heuslar or Heussler; bp. 3 Sep 1931; conf. 3 Sep 1931; ord. deacon 19 Jun 1932; d. heart disease 11 Jan 1941 (CHL CR 375 8 2430, no. 949; FHL microfilm 162792, 1935 census; IGI)

Heinrich Laux b. Straßburg, Elsaß-Lothringen, 21 May 1886; son of Georg Laux and Alwine Weimar; bp. 1 Jul 1932; conf. 1 Jul 1932; d. 4 Jul 1943 (FHL microfilm 68788, no. 53; CHL CR 375 8 2430, no. 973; IGI)

Hubertine Reiner b. Baal, Rheinprovinz, 10 Feb 1871; dau. of Otto Reiner and Anna Maria Porten or Perten; bp. 12 Sep 1924; conf. 12 Sep 1924; m. Oct 1898, Wilhelm Heinrich Hermann Schnell; d. heart attack 1 May 1943 (FHL microfilm 68788, no. 43; FHL microfilm 68786, no. 162; FHL microfilm 245258, 1925, 1930, and 1935 censuses)

Lena Eliese Grete Wachsmuth b. Haspe, Westfalen, 2 Mar 1901; dau. of Friedrich Georg Hubert Wachsmuth and Selma Alma Clauder; bp. 8 Feb 1925; conf. 8 Feb 1925; d. 7 Dec 1938 (FHL microfilm 68788, no. 44; IGI)

Franz Josef Wolters b. Dorsten, Westfalen, 10 Nov 1857; son of Josef Johannes Clemens Wolters and Anna

Maria Bernhardine Schulte; bp. 16 Oct 1920; conf. 16 Oct 1920; ord. priest 15 Dec 1935; ord. elder 15 Dec 1935 or 21 May 1939; m. Essen, Rheinprovinz, 21 May 1889, Friederike Francisca Brücker; 7 children; d. old age 23 Jan 1944 (FHL microfilm 68788, no. 73; CHL microfilm 2447, pt. 26, no. 690; FHL microfilm 68803, no. 690; FHL microfilm 245303, 1935 census; IGI)

Wilhelmine Marie Clara Rosa Zacher b. Erfurt, Sachsen, 29 Jul 1884; dau. of Wilhelm Zacher and Anna Louise Wilhelmine Amanda Müller; bp. 6 Dec 1901; conf. 6 Dec 1901; m. 26 Apr 1914, August Weber; d. blood poisoning 25 Jul 1944 (FHL microfilm 68788, no. 45; FHL microfilm 68786, no. 114; IGI)

Notes

1. Düsseldorf city archive.
2. West German Mission branch directory, 1939, CHL LR 10045 11.
3. Presiding Bishopric, "Financial, Statistical, and Historical Reports of Wards, Stakes, and Missions, 1884–1955," 257, CHL CR 4 12.
4. Kurt Fiedler, interview by the author, Sandy, UT, February 17, 2006.
5. Clark Hillam, interview by the author, Brigham City, UT, August 20, 2006.
6. Manfred Knabe, autobiography (unpublished); private collection.
7. Düsseldorf city archive.
8. Siegfried Helmut Schmidt, telephone interview with Judith Sartowski in German, February 25, 2008; summarized in English by Judith Sartowski.
9. Düsseldorf city archive.

Essen Branch

Located essentially in the center of the Ruhr industrial district in northwest Germany, the city of Essen was long famous for the gigantic Krupp Stahlwerke. The company had produced military equipment for decades before the start of World War II in September 1939. Essen is located on the north bank of the Ruhr River and had 664,523 inhabitants at the time.[1]

The largest branch in the Ruhr District of the West German Mission, the Essen Branch had 162 registered members. With so many members, the branch leadership directory dated June 27, 1939, shows all callings occupied.[2] The branch president at the time was Walter Biehl, a member of one of the largest and most faithful families of Latter-day Saints in Germany. Walter's brother, Friedrich, was at that time the president of the Ruhr District and was called in September to lead the entire mission.

Essen Branch[3]	**1939**
Elders	16
Priests	6
Teachers	8
Deacons	12
Other Adult Males	28
Adult Females	82
Male Children	5
Female Children	5
Total	162

The branch directory was filled out by Walter Biehl and shows his beautiful handwriting, a re-creation of the Fraktur style used mostly in printing. The list shows first counselor Aloys Müller and second counselor Jakob Kirchhausen. Other leading men were Heinrich Schmitz (Sunday School), Carl Schlingmann (YMMIA), Paul Müller (*Der Stern* representative), and Walter's father, Friedrich Biehl Sr. (genealogy). Leading women in the branch were Berta Kirchhausen (Relief Society), Luise Schwiermann (Primary), and Ella Schmitz (YWMIA).

When the war began, the branch was holding its meetings in rooms rented since the 1920s in a Hinterhaus behind the building at Krefelderstrasse 27. Karl Müller (born 1922) provided this description:

> The building looked like a barrack. We walked up some wooden stairs, and then we entered the meeting room. The classrooms were located on

> the main floor. We also had a podium. There must have been about thirty people in attendance each Sunday. We sat on chairs, not on benches. When I was the Sunday School secretary, I had my own table at the front of the room.[4]

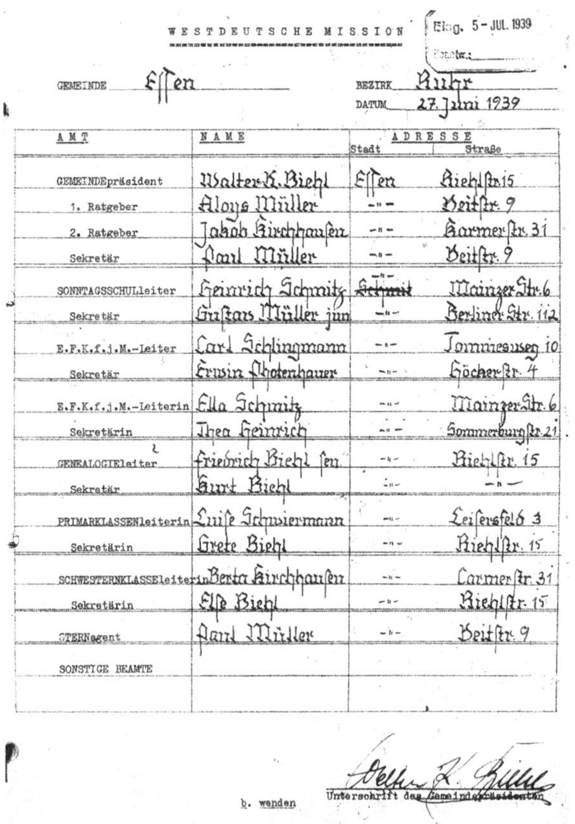

WESTDEUTSCHE MISSION

Eing. 5-JUL. 1939

GEMEINDE Essen

BEZIRK Ruhr

DATUM 27. Juni 1939

AMT	NAME	ADRESSE Stadt	Straße
GEMEINDEpräsident	Walter K. Biehl	Essen	Biehlstr. 15
1. Ratgeber	Aloys Müller	-"-	Veitstr. 9
2. Ratgeber	Jakob Kirchhausen	-"-	Karmerstr. 31
Sekretär	Paul Müller	-"-	Veitstr. 9
SONNTAGSSCHULleiter	Heinrich Schmitz	-"- ~~Schmit~~	Mainzer Str. 6
Sekretär	Gustav Müller jun	-"-	Berliner Str. 112
E.F.K.f.j.M.-Leiter	Carl Schlingmann	-"-	Tommiesweg 10
Sekretär	Erwin Photenhauer	-"-	Höcherstr. 4
E.F.K.f.j.M.-Leiterin	Ella Schmitz	-"-	Mainzer Str. 6
Sekretärin	Thea Heinrich	-"-	Sommerburgstr. 21
GENEALOGIEleiter	Friedrich Biehl sen.	-"-	Biehlstr. 15
Sekretär	Kurt Biehl	-"-	-"-
PRIMARKLASSENleiterin	Luise Schwiermann	-"-	Leisersfeld 3
Sekretärin	Grete Biehl	-"-	Biehlstr. 15
SCHWESTERNKLASSEleiterin	Berta Kirchhausen	-"-	Carmerstr. 31
Sekretärin	Else Biehl	-"-	Biehlstr. 15
STERNagent	Paul Müller	-"-	Veitstr. 9
SONSTIGE BEAMTE			

b. wenden

Walter K. Biehl
Unterschrift des Gemeindepräsidenten

Fig. 1. Front page of the branch directory showing Walter Biehl's artistic handwriting. (Church History Library)

Artur Schwiermann (born 1927) recalled that the words "The Glory of God Is Intelligence" were painted on the wall behind the podium. Among those who attended Sunday School were several children whose families did not belong to the Church (which was the case in most branches in Germany). He explained the presence of those children in Primary as well: "Everybody in the neighborhood knew we were members of the Church. The children would say, 'Frau Schwiermann, when can we go to Primary?' There were six or seven whom she took along to Primary."[5]

The Essen Branch enjoyed a most rare feature in their meeting rooms—one of only three baptismal fonts in the entire mission. The Essen Branch history gives the following description:

> There was even a baptismal font located next to the Relief Society room. For each baptismal ceremony the water had to be heated in large tin containers. Cold water was added by means of a hose. However, there was no way to drain the basin. . . . The sisters scooped the water out after each ceremony, using various containers. In the years prior to the construction of the font, baptisms had been carried out in the Ruhr River or in the Friedrich Bathhouse.[6]

Missionary Erma Rosenhan from Salt Lake City observed a baptism in Essen on Sunday, March 19, 1939, and recorded the event in her diary:

> Up at 6 a.m. . . . By 7:15 I was in the Branch to see the baptisms. There were quite a few people there. There was a regular program given. The water was heated by stoves and there were pine needle boughs all around the font to make it look nice. There were 3 children and one adult (man) baptized.[7]

Willi Ochsenhirt (born 1928) was also baptized in that font. In addition, he recalled a picture of Christ's baptism showing the Holy Ghost descending in the form of a dove. That picture hung on the wall behind the podium. There was enough room on the rostrum for a large choir. "I remember once that we had a choir competition with the Herne Branch," Willi explained. "They won because they had a spectacular soloist."[8]

Branch members had several opportunities each week to go to church. Sunday School began at 10:00 a.m. and sacrament meeting at 6:00 p.m. The genealogy class met on the second and fourth Sundays of the month at 8:45 a.m. On Tuesdays, Primary began its meeting at 5:30 p.m., and that was followed by MIA at 7:30 p.m. The Relief Society sisters and the priesthood holders gathered on Wednesdays at 7:30 p.m. in separate rooms.

Sister Rosenhan's comments about the Essen Branch include this comical assessment of the Primary children: "Sunday, August 13, 1939: Had to teach the [Primary] 'B' class again this morning. They were little 'devils' and certainly angered me."

Other comments reflect the fear of approaching war: "Wednesday, August 23, 1939: Relief Society and choir practice. Because of having to darken [blackout] everything we couldn't have choir practice last night."

Fig. 2. The Biehl family in Essen. Branch president Walter Biehl is in the back row, far right. Mission supervisor Friedrich is seated next to his father. (M. Biehl Haurand)

Fig. 3. The Essen Branch meeting rooms were large but modest. Note the photograph of Church President Heber J. Grant. (G. Blake)

One of the saddest events in the life of the Essen Saints was the departure of Sister Rosenhan on August 25, 1939 (her mission companion, Sister Heibel, was a German citizen who remained in Essen). Sister Rosenhan was assisted by president Walter Biehl in transporting her trunk to the railroad station for the trip to Amsterdam. As they went back and forth across the city in response to contradictory instructions from harried railroad officials, they stopped at Walter's home to say good-bye to his family. Sister Rosenhan wrote this description of the situation:

> Sister Biehl was crying. While [her husband] was helping me get away. He had received his military summons and had to report that very day. Pres. Biehl slumped back in the taxi and said he would not go to work that day. I gave him most of the money I had. . . . I can still see the faces of my companion and Pres. Biehl as the train left. We all cried. . . . Pres. Biehl called [the mission home in] Frankfurt to tell them that I had left.

Fig. 4. Members of the Essen Branch in 1939. (M. Biehl Haurand)

Friedrich Ludwig Biehl was released as the supervisor of the West German Mission and was succeeded by Christian Heck of Frankfurt on December 31, 1939. Elder Biehl's personal history is very short from the day he entered the military and reads as follows:

> I was drafted into the army on 14 December 1939 so I could no longer function as the mission leader, but I kept the calling [for two more weeks]. I came to the infantry in Bromberg [Posen]. During the month of March I went to Kleve, West Germany. Then I was in the campaign in Holland, Belgium, and France. In April 1941, I was back in Germany. From Marienburg, West Prussia, we marched to the Eastern border and then with the beginning of the Eastern campaign we went to Lithuania, Estonia and Russia. We started combat with the Russians on 23 [22] July 1941. It would be too difficult to write about the afflictions, sufferings and distress that I experienced from these [campaigns].[9]

Walter Konrad Biehl (born 1914) was a copy editor and had married just three months before the war began. In his detailed autobiography, he reported being stationed in many locations on the Western Front: in the Netherlands, in Belgium, in Luxembourg, in France near the Maginot Line, and in several towns in western Germany not far from his own home. He traveled on furloughs to Tilset in East Prussia, the home of his wife, Gertude. He rejoiced in every opportunity to see his daughter, Angelika, who was born on April 10, 1940. Whenever and wherever possible, he attended church meetings.

Margaretha Biehl (born 1927) recalled the pressure put on her by the leaders of the League of German Girls. They instructed her to report on Sundays for activities or assignments. "They would give us a permission form to take to our parents. So I came home and I showed it to my father and he said, 'Sunday I take my children to church and nothing else. You cannot go.' And I prayed every day, because I knew that the government could put my father in a concentration camp if he interfered with something like this. And I just didn't know what to do."[10]

Margaretha also recalled the propaganda films she and her classmates were required to watch. They all went to the movie theater on Mondays to see films showing how Hitler's government had made everything better. One of the films showed the people in the Netherlands welcoming the German invaders as liberators. "I can still see that in my mind," she said.

"We lived right on a plaza across from an entrance to a park in a very visible location," recalled Johannes Biehl (born 1929), "so my dad was assigned to display a large swastika flag. But he often forgot and wasn't very conscientious about it. He was visited once by a representative of the Gestapo who told him, 'Sir, if you forget again to display the flag, you will be in trouble.' And of course, now we know what he meant by trouble."[11]

Johannes recalled other aspects of life in Nazi Germany:

> The [Hitler Youth and League of German Girls] collected money quite frequently, sometimes on national holidays. They used metal containers and rattled them and begged people going by to donate. I remember that my Dad always responded by saying that he had already given to the church. They even came into the apartment building to collect, but my father never gave them any money.

Regarding political matters in the branch, Johannes recalled:

> In our sacrament meetings we had a bit of turmoil. I remember one brother who was a Nazi at heart and prayed once in a while that Germany would be victorious. Eventually, he was not asked to pray anymore. On the other hand, there was a brother who prayed that the church would be victorious—not necessarily that Hitler would get out of the way, but it was clear that he was opposed to Hitler's government.

Some of the earliest members of the Essen Branch were the family of Friedrich and Emilie Ochsenhirt. They had arrived in the city from Darmstadt, Hesse, during World War I when Friedrich was assigned to work as a blast furnace stoker at Krupp. When Willi was born in 1928, the family was complete with twelve children. It was a serious challenge for Brother Ochsenhirt to provide for his family, and he did many odd jobs on weekends and holidays. When the war began, Friedrich was over seventy years of age, and several of his children were still living at home.[12]

"Three weeks before finishing my apprenticeship as a carpenter, I was drafted into the Reichsarbeitsdienst," recalled Karl Müller, "I worked on sewage systems and drained fields in Silesia." Upon his return to Essen, he was drafted by the Wehrmacht and sent to Norway. Following a period of training as a radio man, he was assigned to a very remote outpost near the Arctic Circle. While there for three and a half years, he dealt with isolation and did not know much about what was happening elsewhere in the war. Regarding his circumstances, he recalled: "I did not feel sad or depressed [in isolation]. I tried to make the best out of the situation. I did not have my scriptures with me while I was up there." Like so many other German LDS soldiers, he was totally isolated from the Church and the Saints while away from home.

Artur Schwiermann was first a member of the Jungvolk and was then advanced to the Hitler Youth. Under the motto *Jugend führt Jugend* (youth lead youth), he was given charge of a group of younger boys. "We marched, sang and shot. We had air rifles and would go camping, which I always thought was fun." On occasion, the meetings interfered with Sunday School, but Artur then was all the more determined to attend sacrament meeting that evening.

Fig. 5. Willy Ludwig as a Jungvolk boy in April 1939.

Many German civilians came into contact with prisoners of war or forced laborers from conquered countries, but fraternization was strictly prohibited. Nevertheless, Artur recalled watching his mother hand apples or potatoes to Russians they passed one day. "Somebody asked my mother if she wasn't ashamed for giving food to the enemy and I joined in with 'Yeah, Mom, you shouldn't do that.' She looked at me and replied, 'Remember one thing: They are all children of our Heavenly Father.' My mother was a saint."

Fig. 6. Gertrude, Angelika, and Walter Biehl in September 1942. (A.Biehl Bremer)

During the last months of 1942 and the first months of 1943, Walter Biehl received training at what he called a "war school" near Prague, Czechoslovakia. He described it as an unpleasant experience but was pleased to be promoted to sergeant major. Following another furlough at home with his family, he was transferred to the Eastern Front in April 1943.

To escape the increasing danger in Essen, Johannes Biehl and his classmates were sent away in early 1943. He recalled the setting:

> My class was sent to Austria to the Zillertal along with a teacher or two teachers in those days. They taught every subject that students needed to be taught in school, and an adult Hitler Youth Leader was also there. [We were put up in] a small hotel. We had to march in line to our meals, and instead of having a blessing on the food, we would have to stand up and raise our arms and say, "Heil Hitler!" and the same at the beginning of the school class and at other gatherings. It was always "Heil Hitler!"

On March 3, 1943, former mission supervisor Friedrich Biehl was killed in an accidental fire in Russia. The letter written to his father by the company commander dated March 4 provides a description of the event:

> In a temporary company barrack a fire suddenly broke out that rapidly spread to two adjacent barracks. A strong wind fanned the fire and in no time the entire structure was in flames. Although his other comrades were able to escape the conflagration, the company later determined that your dear son was not to be found and was probably consumed by the flames. Along with the entire company, I express my deepest sympathies.[13]

Walter Biehl soon wrote to the company commander to inquire about the tragic event. His letter reads in part as follows: "Allow me to ask most respectfully: Was any trace of my brother found after the fire? From your letter, Herr Leutnant, it is not clear whether my brother actually perished in the flames." The response was equally respectful, but negative: "I can report only that two days after I wrote my letter, the men searched the ruins of the barrack for any possible evidence that would allow the definite conclusion that your brother did indeed perish in the flames. Nothing could be found."

It would seem that the lack of clarity about Friedrich Biehl's fate was somehow recorded in Wehrmacht records. After the war, the German Commission for the Preservation of War Graves expressed the theory that his remains—as those of an unknown soldier—had been buried at a German war cemetery in Korpowo, Russia.[14]

Friedrich's death was a terrible blow to Walter. He wrote this assessment of his brother in the following months:

> Fritz was always a good example for me in everything. I will always have a respectful memory of him. I thank my Creator for the knowledge, that I will see my beloved brother and my other beloved ones after this life on earth. From the time of this death I have felt a deeper duty to the work of the Lord. Fritz left to me many good and noble thoughts, which I will use, so far as it is in my power. I wish the time were soon at hand that I could work again in the Church of Jesus Christ.

The following postscript was written by his father, Friedrich Johannes Biehl: "So far and to this point the writings of my son Walter. 'Man thinks, but the Lord directs.' So it was decided by the Lord to take our dear Walter to him on September 1, 1943." The family received the following letter informing them of Walter's death in combat:

> Dear Mrs. Biehl:
>
> As the successor of the killed company leader of your husband, I perform the sad duty of informing you that your husband lost his life on 1.9.43 . . . as the head of his platoon.
>
> . . . He was always an excellent comrade and, in hours of peril, a brave leader.
>
> In heartfelt memory of a hero, who gave in the war his life for his homeland and family, I salute you with a Heil Hitler,
>
> Yours
> Rolf Kuhn
> Lieutenant and Comp-Leader

Following the death of two sons, Friedrich Biehl was predictably angry, blaming Hitler's government for the family's tragedies. His daughter, Margaretha, recalled how he came home from work for lunch one day and stated that he was going to "tell them." Understanding that any complaints in public could lead to imprisonment and other penalties, Sister Biehl begged her husband not to make any protests to anybody. According to Margaretha, "I can still see my mother holding on to him and begging him to not say anything. [After that] maybe he just talked about it to people he trusted."

In Austria, young Johannes Biehl found that letters he wrote to his brother Friedrich were returned. Soon after his father informed him of Friedrich's death, another brother, Alfred, came for a visit along with his wife. Johannes was very discouraged, and Alfred reported that to their father. When Walter was killed, Brother Biehl felt that Johannes should not have to go through another such tragedy alone, so he traveled to Austria and told the authorities that he was taking his son home to Essen. Because most schools in Essen had been rendered useless, Johannes was sent to Wommen in Hesse to live with an uncle and to attend school.

The branch meeting rooms at Krefelderstrasse 27 were destroyed early in the war, after which meetings were held first in the Krupp Realschule, and then in the apartments of various families, including the Biehls. That ended when the building in which the Biehls lived was gutted by bombs and flames. None of the family members were harmed; some were in the basement, others in public shelters, and Margaretha was visiting relatives in Wommen, Hesse. When she returned to Essen, she found her family living in her uncle's apartment.

It seemed to Margaretha Biehl that the Allied air forces specifically planned to miss the huge Krupp factories when they dropped their bombs on Essen. According to her recollection, "They didn't hit Krupp until the end of the war, but they hit most of the residential areas of the city." In fact, official reports show that 90 percent of the city's industrial area was destroyed and 60 percent of the entire city. Of the 664,523 residents in 1939, at least 30,746 were killed in the attacks and 1,356 prisoners of war were also victims. A total of 242 attacks were made on the city, of which 30 were considered "severe."[15]

A remarkable incident occurred during an air raid that began during a church meeting on Sunday. Margaretha recalled that the Saints in attendance hurried to the shelter:

> We were meeting at the Küppers on that Sunday. And then the sirens went off. And so we all went to an old high school (where we later held meetings) because they had a nice air-raid shelter underneath. There were other people in the shelter, and we [LDS] were in one corner—about twenty of us. And then we all knelt down to pray, and Brother Müller said the prayer. And he said, "And Heavenly Father, watch over these our brethren in the airplanes that they would return home safely." He called them our brothers. And we had to be careful that the others didn't hear.

Fig. 8. The Biehl family lived on the second floor of this apartment building until it was bombed and burned out. (M. Biehl Haurand)

Artur Schwiermann was inducted into the national labor force in 1943 at the age of sixteen. He served on an antiaircraft crew in Steinfeld and Villach, Austria. "I was only there for a few months, but I saw a lot of action. The Americans flew over and it was my job to shoot them down. I was trained on the 88 mm howitzer and learned how to use a radio." While in the Reichsarbeitsdienst, Artur made the mistake of failing to salute a Gauleiter (regional leader of the Nazi Party).[16] In order to avoid a court-martial, he volunteered to join the Wehrmacht and was in the air force in early 1944.

The Ochsenhirt family also experienced tragedies during the war. The worst took place on October 25, 1944, according to daughter Berta (born 1909):

> Our good mother and [our sister] Thekla got killed in an air raid. Myself, I was in Upper Hesse when that happened. . . . I traveled back [to Essen] partly by train, partly walking by foot, and sometimes riding in a farmer's wagon. After two and a half days, I arrived in Essen because everything was destroyed. . . . People took me home but I don't know who. There my father sat alone. He cried like a child. The next day was the funeral on the terrace cemetery. My father had a nervous breakdown.

For the next few months, Berta struggled to care for her distraught father. She eventually moved him into an asylum in Giessen, then to another in Mockstadt, and then back to Essen. During air raids in the last years of the war, she had to seek refuge with him in the same shelter in which his wife and his daughter had died.[17]

Berta's brother, Willi Ochsenhirt, had been moved with his schoolmates and his teacher to a town in Czechoslovakia in 1942. It was there that he heard about the air raid that had killed so many people in Essen. In 1944, he was surprised to see his mother come to visit him. He was still in that town when she was killed in October. Soon after the air raid, Willi and his friends were told that the attack on Essen had taken the lives of many people, but Willi did not know if any of his family members were among the victims. Nevertheless, when permission was given for some of the boys to go to Bratislava and from there to Germany, he was one of those who left. On the way to Bratislava (approximately twenty miles), he met a man he would call his good Samaritan.

> I was walking along in my Hitler Youth uniform trying to get passing German trucks to give me a ride, but nobody would. Then a Slovakian truck came by and a man asked if I needed help. I told him what I needed [a ride to Bratislava], and he took me right to the railroad station there. My own people would not help, but he did, even though the Slovaks hated us and the [Hitler Youth] uniform I was wearing.

Willi traveled to Vienna, where he found his sister. The two then made their way home to Essen and arrived in November to find that their mother and their sister had indeed been killed. According to Willi, his mother was fortunate to be buried in a coffin at a time when most of the dead were simply wrapped up and placed in mass graves. A few months later, boys of Willi's age were required to report for an army physical. Being very small (still not even five feet tall), he was told by the army physician, "You're too little. Go back home to your mama." Some of Willi's friends were drafted, and some were killed in the final months of the war.

Fig. 9. Air-raid damage done to the apartment house in which the Schwiermanns lived. (A. H. Schwiermann)

Shortly before the war ended, Karl Müller's unit was moved from Norway to southern Germany to escape the advancing Soviet army. In Germany, Karl was taken prisoner by the Americans and later handed over to the French. As POWs in France, Germans learned the dangers of working with two kinds of mines—the coal mines whose terrible conditions cost many young men their health, and the land mines that had to be removed from fields and forests where German attackers and defenders had laid them. Because he was not robust, Karl was put on the land mine removal detail. He described the work in these words:

> We received training on how to remove the mines safely. I did think about the fact that I could die when I was a prisoner removing those mines. But for some reason, I always had the feeling that nothing would happen to me although I saw people dying because of this every day. My clothing was often ripped apart but my skin was never hurt. One never knew if there was a mine with every step that was taken.

A combat veteran by the end of the war, Artur had seen many of his friends killed, mostly in Poland and eastern Germany as the Soviet army moved inexorably into Germany. Along the way he had several opportunities to take the life of an enemy, but he never did so. He described one such situation in these words:

> One time, we had orders to take prisoners. Three Russians came, out and I knew that if I turned them in, that they would be shot. I shot at them but missed them on purpose by quite a ways. They got the message and took off. It is possible to have a good heart even though one is a soldier. My dad always told me that if somebody surrendered, you give them all the courtesy you can. Because he could have killed you and he didn't. My father knew that from spending four years in the trenches in World War I.

Artur's unit eventually moved through Czechoslovakia and surrendered to the Americans coming from the west toward Dresden. Unfortunately for Artur, the Americans turned him over to the Soviets (a German soldier's worst nightmare), and he began a term of four and a half years as a POW. "They didn't give us enough to eat, and I went from 185 pounds to 95 pounds in the first six months. I kept going for the next four years. I stole a lot and tried to survive that way—whatever I could get my hands on."

Johannes Biehl experienced the end of the war at his uncle's home in Wommen. Just a few miles from Eisenach, Johannes had been able to visit the Wartburg Castle, where Martin Luther had translated the New Testament into German. In that location, Johannes came into contact with both American and Soviet invaders in April 1945, because the border of the two occupation zones ran between Wommen and Eisenach. He recalled that when the Americans came through Wommen, a black soldier saw his watch: "He said, 'Beautiful!' and then he ripped the watch off my wrist." Fortunately, that incident was the worst thing that happened to Johannes Biehl in Wommen. A few months later, he was home in Essen.

The following text from the branch history reflects the difficulties experienced by Latter-day Saints still in the city of Essen after their meeting rooms at Krefelderstrasse 27 were destroyed:

> The members were once again left up to their own devices and had to improvise. The Paul Küpper, Schwiermann and Naujock families allowed the Saints to meet in their homes. The Küpper family provided space in their basement. The Naujocks family had a single family dwelling on Lepsiusweg in the suburb of Frohnhausen and the Schwiermann family had a large apartment. The meetings were thus held alternately at those locations. . . . Eyewitnesses . . . testify that they could truly feel the spirit of the Lord under those humble circumstances, despite all of the problems they had to contend with on a daily basis.[18]

By the time the war ended, Willi Ochsenhirt had left Essen and joined two of his sisters in a small ancestral town north of Frankfurt. It was there that he experienced the arrival of the American army. As he recalled, "I had a knife with a handle made of deer bone. I went up to a soldier and gave it to him (I had learned to speak English in school). They were checking everybody to see if we had weapons, so I just gave it to him." Like most boys his age (sixteen at the time), Willi was always ready for a new adventure. So it was that he and some friends found an American tank abandoned in the mud, and they climbed inside. There they found cigarettes and food "and stuff." Later, they discovered a German *Panzerfaust* (bazooka); having been shown previously how to operate the weapon, they successfully fired it at a tree.

In 1947 and 1948, Karl Müller received a more merciful assignment as a POW in France. No longer did he have to remove land mines, but rather he worked with electronics and repaired watches. Regarding his time away from home, he said the following:

> During the seven years I was away from home, I never met another member of the Church or had any contact with the Church. My parents received a letter stating that I was missing in action and they did not know where I was or if I was still alive for some time. And then my grandmother (who was not a member of the Church but a very good woman) had a dream that I had visited her to tell her that I was in French captivity and that I was doing well. I also gave her the name of the place where I was. She then went and looked for that place and found it on a map. She told my parents where I was and that I was safe.

Returning to Essen in 1948, Karl learned that his parents had been bombed out of their home but had survived and were well, living in a suburb of Essen. He concluded his story with this statement: "My testimony was not shaken because of the war. I did not worry about the idea that God would let things like this happen. I knew that his ways were not our ways."

During his years as a POW in the Soviet Union, Artur Schwiermann endured harrowing conditions but eventually regained much of his weight. Part of the suffering was emotional, caused by the overseers' practice of promising that a prisoner would be sent home soon, only to postpone the move time and time again. Regarding his spiritual condition during those times, he offered the following summary:

> I was in the service for seven years and never had the opportunity to attend a meeting, meet a member of the Church, or read the scriptures. I had a testimony of the Church before I went away in the army. I held my own Sunday Schools on Sundays alone and because I remembered some of the songs, I just listened to them in my mind. I promised the Lord that if he would get me out of this hell, I would never miss a church meeting again. While I was gone in the service, I could have answered correctly all of the questions asked in a temple recommend interview.

Several members of the Essen Branch were killed in the air raids that reduced the city to rubble. Several others were among the 18,864 men of the city who died in the service of their country. The few Saints who were still in Essen when the American army arrived on April 11, 1945, were still holding meetings and looking forward to the time when their loved ones would return.

In Memoriam

The following members of the Essen Branch did not survive World War II:

Elisabeth Helene Bernicke b. Essen, Rheinprovinz, 31 Mar 1904; dau. of Heinrich Bernicke and Auguste Kutz; bp. 6 Oct 1921; conf. 6 Oct 1921; d. rib infection 20 May 1945 (FHL microfilm 68789, no. 1; CHL microfilm 2447, pt. 26, no. 16; FHL microfilm 25722; 1930 census; IGI)

Friedrich Ludwig Biehl b. Essen, Rheinprovinz, 26 Feb 1913; son of Friedrich Johannes Biehl and Marie Nölker; bp. 14 Dec 1924; conf. 14 Dec 1924; ord. deacon 14 Apr 1929; ord. teacher 25 Jan 1931; ord. priest 13 Dec 1932; ord. elder 4 May 1934; German-Swiss Mission 7 Mar 1934 to 1 Nov 1936; supervisor West German Mission 1 Sep to 31 Dec 1939; private; company clerk; d. in fire Buregi, Ilmensee 3 Mar 1943 (M. Biehl Haurand; FHL microfilm 68789, no. 4; CHL microfilm 2447, pt. 26, no. 20; www.volksbund.de)

Walter Konrad Biehl b. Essen, Rheinprovinz, 11 Jul 1914; son of Friedrich Johannes Biehl and Marie Nölker; bp. 14 Dec 1924; conf. 14 Dec 1924; ord. deacon 14 Apr 1929; ord. teacher 17 Apr 1932; ord. priest 3 Oct 1937; ord. elder 13 Jan 1938; West German Mission 12 Jan 1938 to 6 Jan 1939; m. 27 May 1939, Gertrud Lotte Mamat; 1 child; lieutenant; k. in battle Russia 1 Sep 1943 (FHL microfilm 68789, no. 5; CHL microfilm 2447, pt. 26, no. 24; M. Biehl Haurand; H. Haurand; IGI)

Bendix Christian Karl Breitenstein b. Herbede, Westfalen, 5 Mar 1907; son of Heinrich Gottfried Breitenstein and Elisabeth H. Mintrup; bp. 16 Apr 1921; conf. 16 Apr 1921; m. Feb 1929, Anna Zaremba; police constable; k. in battle Trojana Pass, Balkans, 23 Aug 1944 (FHL microfilm 68789, no. 19; CHL microfilm 2458, form 42 FP, pt. 37, 202–3; CHL microfilm 2447, pt. 26, no. 43; FHL microfilm 25728, 1925 and 1930 censuses; www.volksbund.de; IGI)

Ernst Johann Heinrich Gallep b. Kettwig, Werden, Rheinprovinz, 24 Jul 1914; son of Heinrich Gallep and Martha Eumann; bp. 9 Jun 1928; conf. 10 Jun 1928; ord. deacon 1 Sep 1929; ord. teacher 13 Dec 1932; ord. priest 27 Feb 1933; ord. elder 4 Jul 1934; missionary 28 Dec 1932; m. 17 Dec 1938, Liesbeth Böttcher or Boettger; k. in battle Mal Skabino, Russia, 25 Jan 1944 (FHL microfilm 68789, no. 27; CHL microfilm 2447, pt. 26, no. 431; IGI)

Elisabeth Marie Luise Heckmann b. Kirchheimbolanden, Rheinprovinz 14 Sep 1861; dau. of Peter Heckmann and Karoline Hofmann; bp. 20 Mar 1923; conf. 20 Mar 1923; m. 15 Jun 1885, Wilhelm Karl Fahrbach; d. old age 4 Feb 1943 (FHL microfilm 68789, no. 190; CHL microfilm 2447, pt. 26, no. 813; IGI)

Leo Karbacher b. Klein Tarpen, Graudenz, Westpreußen or Essen, Rheinprovinz 29 Dec 1899; son of Leo Karpinski and Pauline Stankewitz; bp. 22 Aug 1925; conf. 22 Aug 1925; m. 16 Aug 1924, Therese Anna Horn; k. bomb explosion 25 Oct 1944; bur. Terassenfriedhof, Essen, Rheinprovinz (FHL microfilm 68789, no. 51; CHL microfilm 2447, pt. 26, no. 160; FHL microfilm 271376; 1925, 1930, and 1935 censuses; www.volksbund.de; IGI)

Ernst Lehnert b. Niklasberg, Böhmen, Austria, 16 Oct 1879; son of Johann Lehnert and Anna Krause; bp. 28 Oct 1928; conf. 28 Oct 1928; ord. deacon 1 Sep 1929; ord. teacher 1 Feb 1931; ord. priest 17 Apr 1932; ord. elder 6 Mar 1937; m. 5 Jun 1910, Auguste Emilie Minna Luthin; d. lung disease 29 Apr 1945 (FHL microfilm 68789, no. 65; CHL microfilm 2447, pt. 26, no. 446; FHL microfilm 271386, 1930 and 1935 censuses)

Hermann Benjamin Mantwill b. Mulk, Ostpreußen, 6 Jan 1876; son of Karl Ludwig Mantwill and Auguste Dorothea Schmidt; bp. 3 Apr 1920; conf. 3 Apr 1920; ord. deacon 24 Jul 1921; ord. teacher 14 Jun 1925; ord. priest 14 Apr 1929; ord. elder 12 Jul 1936; m. 26 Apr 1905, Johanna Louise Gärtner; 3 children; d. gastric ulcer Essen, Rheinprovinz, 9 Aug 1941 (FHL microfilm 68789, no. 73; IGI)

Karl Gustav Müller Jr. b. Ellrich, Grafschaft Hohenstein, Sachsen (province), 22 Sep 1888; son of Johann Philipp Karl Müller and Hennriette Karoline Dorothea Schoenemann; bp. 22 Aug 1925; conf. 22 Aug 1925; ord. deacon 14 Sep 1926; ord. teacher 14 Apr 1929; ord. priest 1 Feb 1931; ord. elder 6 Mar 1937; m. Ellrich 8 Apr 1912, Friederike Emilie Fuchs or Krone; 2m. 11 Oct 1921, Katharina Elise Somm; 1 child; d. pneumonia Essen, Rheinprovinz, 31 Jan 1945 (FHL microfilm 68789, no. 82; IGI)

Heinz Erwin Emil Naujoks b. Hamborn, Rheinprovinz, 9 May 1915; son of Emil Naujoks and Berta Marta Eschrich; noncommissioned officer; d. Chemin-des-Dames, France 8 Jun 1940; bur. Ford-de-Malmaison, France (IGI; www.volksbund.de)

Emilie Ochsenhirt dau. of Thekla Ochsenhirt (M. Biehl Haurand)

Friedrich Ochsenhirt b. Darmstadt, Hessen, 4 Jul 1912; son of Friedrich Ochsenhirt and Emilie Schwarzhaupt; bp. 11 Sep 1920; conf. 11 Sep 1920; m. Hessen 10 Nov 1935, Elise Gottschalk; d. MIA Stalingrad, Russia, 1942; bur. Rossoschka, Wolgograd, Russia (W. Ochsenhirt; www.volksbund.de)

Thekla Ochsenhirt b. Ranstadt, Hessen, 15 Dec 1906; dau. of Friedrich Ochsenhirt and Emilie Schwarzhaupt; bp. 23 Aug 1919; conf. 23 Aug 1919; k. air raid

25 Oct 1944 (FHL microfilm 68789, no. 100; CHL microfilm 2447, pt. 26, no. 2530)

Erwin Pfotenhauer b. Essen, Rheinprovinz, Preussen, 25 Sep 1921; son of Waldemar Wilhelm Pfotenhauer and Christine Kohl; bp. 28 Feb 1931; conf. 1 Mar 1931; ord. deacon 3 Jan 1937; lance corporal; k. air raid Liebau, Latvia, 22 Nov 1944 (FHL microfilm 68789, no. 152; Jansen, KGF; CHL microfilm 2458, form 42 FP, pt. 37, 186–87; CHL microfilm 2447, pt. 26, no. 575; FHL microfilm 271393; 1925, 1930, and 1935 censuses; IGI; www.volksbund.de)

Werner Hermann Pfotenhauer b. Essen, Rheinprovinz, 24 Nov 1917; son of Waldemar Wilhelm Pfotenhauer and Christine Kohl; bp. 22 May 1926; conf. 22 May 1926; ord. deacon 7 Aug 1932; m. 20 Apr 1940, Anneliese Brosch; lance corporal; d. in POW camp 99 Spasskij Sawod, Ural, Russia, Jun or Jul or Sep 1941 (FHL microfilm 68789, no. 113; Jansen; www.volksbund.de; CHL microfilm 2458, form 42 FP, pt. 37, 1949 list, 764–65; FHL microfilm 271393, 1925, 1930, and 1935 censuses; IGI)

Hermann Rehkopf b. Niedernjesa, Göttingen, 7 Jun 1898; corporal; k. Dunquerque, France, 25 Feb 1945; bur. Bourdon, France (www.volksbund.de)

Friedrich Schäl b. Gottesberg, Schlesien, 9 Feb 1889; son of —— Schäl and Ernestine Heinzel; bp. 18 Sep 1926; conf. 18 Sep 1926; ord. deacon 31 Oct 1933; ord. teacher 10 Jan 1937; ord. priest 9 Oct 1938; m. 26 Dec 1912, Klara Ida Ludwig; at least 3 children; k. air raid 27 Apr 1944; bur. Essen, Rheinprovinz (FHL microfilm 68803, no. 338; FHL microfilm 245258; 1930 and 1935 censuses; www.volksbund.de; IGI)

Paul Erich Schäl b. Essen, Rheinprovinz, 20 Nov 1916 or 22 Nov 1916; son of Friedrich Schäl and Klara Ida Ludwig; bp. 10 Jul 1925; conf. 10 Jul 1925; lance corporal; k. in battle Kutowaya, Russia, 30 Jun 1941; bur. Petschenga-Parkkina, Russia (FHL microfilm 68789, no. 136; CHL microfilm 2447, pt. 26, no. 342; FHL microfilm 245258; 1925, 1930, and 1935 censuses; www.volksbund.de; IGI)

Emilie Schwarzhaupt b. Ranstadt, Oberhessen, Hessen, 20 Oct 1885; dau. of Konrad Schwarzhaupt and Minna Westerweller; bp. 7 May 1910; conf. 7 May 1910; m. Ranstadt 17 Aug 1902, Friedrich Ochsenhirt; k. air raid 25 Oct 1944 (FHL microfilm 68789, no. 99; CHL microfilm 2447, pt. 26, no. 252; IGI)

Auguste Wilhelmine Stadie b. Groß Jegersdorf, Insterburg, Ostpreuß, 3 May 1873; dau. of Christoph Stadie and Dorothea Braemer; bp. 14 Dec 1924; conf. 14 Dec 1924; m. Norkitten, Ostpreußen, 16 Jan 1895, Ferdinand Wilhelm Schmude; d. old age Roxheim, Hessen, 22 Apr 1943 (FHL microfilm 68789, no. 137; CHL microfilm 2447, pt. 26, no. 356; FHL microfilm 245258, 1925, 1930, and 1935 censuses; IGI; AF)

Augusta Szillat b. Ossingken, Ostpreußen, 14 Feb 1870; dau. of Daniel or David Szillat and Marie Szebang or Szebauy; bp. 12 Feb 1932; conf. 12 Feb 1932 (div.); d. heart attack 27 Jan 1945 (FHL microfilm 68789, no. 189; CHL microfilm 2447, pt. 26, no. 812; FHL microfilm 245279, 1935 census; IGI)

Notes

1. Essen city archive.
2. West German Mission branch directory, 1939, CHL LR 10045 11.
3. Presiding Bishopric, "Financial, Statistical, and Historical Reports of Wards, Stakes, and Missions, 1884–1955," 257, CHL CR 4 12.
4. Karl Gustav Müller, interview by the author in German, Breitenbach, Germany, August 18, 2008; unless otherwise noted, summarized in English by Judith Sartowski.
5. Artur Heinz Schwiermann, telephone interview with the author in German, November 30, 2009.
6. Essen branch history, 29. For some reason, the branch history gives the house number as 29, whereas the branch directory and eyewitnesses agree that the number was 27.
7. Erma Rosenhan, papers, CHL MS 16190.
8. Willi Ochsenhirt, interview by the author, Riverton, UT, April 6, 2007.
9. Friedrich Ludwig Biehl, "Life Story" (unpublished autobiography), chapter 7; private collection.
10. Margaretha Biehl Haurand, interview by the author, Bountiful, UT, April 6, 2007.
11. John A. Biehl, telephone interview with the author, August 6, 2009.
12. Berta Ochsenhirt Hommes, "The Ochsenhirt Family History" (unpublished manuscript); private collection.
13. Original in the collection of Margaretha Biehl Howard, Bountiful, UT.
14. See the commission's website at www.volksbund.de. The commission is understandably very reluctant to provide any but exact details regarding the whereabouts of missing German soldiers.
15. Essen city archive.
16. He defended himself with the derogatory statement, "I don't see a reason to salute every streetcar conductor" (a dangerous reference to Nazi Party officials as being nonmilitary and thus superfluous).
17. Friedrich Ochsenhirt never recovered from the shock of his wife's death. Eventually, Berta took him to Upper Hesse, near his birthplace, where he died in 1950.
18. Essen Branch history, 31.

HERNE BRANCH

The Herne Branch was located in a city that lies between Essen and Dortmund. The 129 members of the branch were distributed throughout a city that numbered nearly one hundred thousand inhabitants when World War II broke out. In general, the Herne Latter-day Saint represented in their socioeconomic status the local society, dominated by blue-collar workers in industry and mining.

The branch met in rented rooms at Schäferstrasse 28. Helga Gärtner (born 1929) described the setting:

> The Schäferstrasse was a little outside of the city center and we did not have to meet anywhere else during the war. The rooms were in the Hinterhaus. We entered the building in the back door and were then standing in a small room. From that small room, one could enter the large room in which we held our meetings. The bathroom was located upstairs and could be reached by a small staircase. Everything was kept very simple. We held all of our meetings in that large room since we did not have smaller ones to use. . . . It was all so simple but we were so happy. There were about twenty to thirty people in attendance on a good Sunday. . . . We even celebrated Christmas in those rooms.[1]

A missionary in Herne in 1938, George Blake of Vineyard, Utah, described the branch as "one of the strongest branches I worked with in Germany." He recalled several members who were educated and strengthened the branch. With the departure of the American missionaries in August 1939, Franz Rybak was asked to lead the branch, which he did for the next nine years. According to the branch history, he was initially assisted by counselors Eugen Kalwies and Hermann Heider.[2] Other leaders of the branch in 1939 were Gustav Mellin (genealogy), Alma Domina (Primary), Fritz Gassner (music), and Augusta Ryback (Relief Society).[3]

Herne Branch[4]	**1939**
Elders	13
Priests	2
Teachers	1
Deacons	6
Other Adult Males	21
Adult Females	63
Male Children	12
Female Children	11
Total	129

Fig. 1. A baptism in the canal by Herne in 1933. (H. Uhlstein)

According to the branch directory, the first meeting on Sunday was a teacher training class at 8:30 a.m., with Sunday School at 10:00 a.m. and sacrament meeting at 7:00 p.m. Tuesday was a busy day in the branch, with the Relief Society meeting at 5:00 p.m. and a Bible study class (apparently replacing MIA) at 7:00. The genealogy class met every fourth Tuesday at 7:00 p.m. The Primary met on Thursdays at 4:00 p.m., and an entertainment activity was scheduled for each Friday evening at 7:00 p.m.

Edith Kalwies (born 1931) recalled being baptized in connection with a district conference in Essen:

> Whenever there was a district conference there, people would be baptized because they had a baptismal font. All the children who had birthdays were baptized that day. It was December 17, 1939. My father was away in the service so I was baptized by Brother Ryback. We were confirmed by Brother [Christian] Heck, the [mission supervisor].[5]

When the war began, Helga Gärtner was a new member of the Jungvolk. She had these recollections of the organization:

> For us it was a wonderful program, similar to the Boy and Girl Scout program of today. Once a week, we would go to home evening. We were taught world history, of course with the emphasis on Hitler's agenda. We were told to read his book, *Mein Kampf*, but I never did. I found it too boring. All I was interested in was the fun that was offered. . . . Once in a while they would take us to classic films. The best were the Shirley Temple films. She was our idol. The whole troupe would go downtown to a real theater as a group with our leader. After one year, we were given uniforms to wear. I loved going there for the fun and the friendships I made.[6]

In the midst of a crucial mining region, the city of Herne was subjected to constant bombardment from the air. Early in the war, Andreas Gärtner was drafted. Soon thereafter, his wife and their two children lost their apartment. Helga recalled that terrible night:

> We had fled to the bunkers again one night. When my mother, my grandmother, my brother and I emerged the next morning, we all turned to look at our mother in shock. The sheer terror of the bombing and the realization that our home had received a direct hit and was gone, had paralyzed the left half of my mother's face. She never regained any sensation to that half of her face to the end of her life.[7]

With her home in ruins, Emma Gärtner allowed her children to be sent away from Herne. Fortunately, both Helga and Reinhard (born 1933) were placed in homes in the small town of Urloffen, near Kehl in Baden. Helga described the experience in these words:

> Reinhard and I were able to see each other during the school hours. My brother was so homesick and I was desperately sad for him. He missed our mother so much. We didn't have an easy life either. After school we were required to earn our keep and do chores around the farm. In this little farming community, there was a trade school for nurses and we would serve as models of critically injured patients for them to practice on.[8]

Edith Kalwies and her siblings were likewise sent away from Herne. For nine months, they lived with various families in a small town near Weimar in Thuringia. Back home, it was decided that they should again be evacuated. The second time saw them in a hotel commandeered for their use in a town near Berchtesgaden in Bavaria. While there, an unusual event occurred—Adolf Hitler came to town. She recounted:

> One day, somebody came running and said that Hitler was in the village. And they wanted all the youth groups there to put on our [Jungvolk] uniforms they had given us. Black skirt, white blouse, and a black kerchief. We were to assemble ourselves and walk down to the village where Hitler supposedly was visiting. I think he was paying a condolence call to a widow whose husband was a military officer who had been killed. There was a staff car and bodyguards, and there were quite a few of us, and we were half-circled around the house, and they told us to chant for him until he finally came out. He shook hands with a few who were right in the front and then waved his hand and said good-bye and took off in his car. I had actually seen Hitler with my own little eyes!

Fig. 2. The Herne Branch in 1939. (H. Ulstein)

Andreas Gärtner was not happy when he learned that his children were separated from their mother. When the term of her Bavarian stay ended, Edith's classmates all headed west for Herne, while little Edith boarded a train east to the home of relatives. Her journey took her hundreds of miles to East Prussia to a town near the city of Tilsit. It must have been a daunting expedition for such a little girl. "I had my little suitcase and a little sign around my neck with my name and my destination. They told the stationmaster to look out for me and call ahead to the stationmaster where I was supposed to go and let him know that a little girl was coming and to look out for me." The destination was the farm of Brother Gärtner's uncle, and Martha Kalwies was welcomed there with her children. On several Sundays, the Kalwieses were able to attend church meetings with the Tilsit Branch. It was a long walk that they sometimes made on Saturday evening in order to be on time the next morning. A single lady in the branch often took them in.

It was about 1942 when the Fritz Gassner family lost their home for the first time. They were living on Schäferstrasse not far from the branch rooms. Daughter Ingrid (born 1932) recalled the sight when she, her mother, and her brother emerged from their basement shelter when the all-clear sounded: "We looked up and the rooms above us were destroyed. We saw a woman who was severely injured by a piece of metal. My mother was able to get us out of there. It was scary."[9] They found another apartment and were bombed out again. Finally, they returned to the Schäferstrasse and lived in the same building as the church rooms; that building survived the war.

Herbert Uhlstein (born 1934) had about as many exciting experiences as any boy could want—and several that were definitely unwanted. The first may have been the destruction of the apartment building in which his family lived. When a bomb struck the side of the building near the third floor, the inhabitants in the basement shelter could hear the structure begin to collapse. As was required all over Germany, a hole had been opened into the adjacent basement and closed again temporarily. Herbert recalled how it took only seconds to open the hole and move the fourteen persons (including his mother, his baby cousin, and himself) through a series of basements before emerging onto the street. He described what happened next in the commotion:

> My mother was trying to hold her hands over my mouth [to keep the dust out] when the building collapsed. Our house and the house next to it were burning. I was carrying my baby cousin, and I ran right into a bomb crater in the street. A bomb had hit there and broken the water pipes, so it was already full of water, and I fell into it. Thank goodness there was a gentleman right behind us; he jumped in and got us out.[10]

The aftermath of the air raids was a shared experience in wartime Germany. Herbert recalled being loaded onto trucks with other youth and taken to areas of the city where the youths were required to help rescue people trapped in basements and to recover bodies of the victims. "I found a man just standing there in a bombed-out building. He looked perfectly alive, and I hollered at him to come and get out of there. He fell over, and his whole back was burned from top to bottom. He was already dead."

Herbert learned how to survive in wartime, but he had a hard time understanding certain political concepts, such as the Nazi treatment of the Jews: "My best friend was Jewish. I played with him and grew up with him. One afternoon we were playing together, and the next day they took him away.

I couldn't understand why he hadn't said good-bye. I asked my mother why and a lot of questions. She tried to explain it to me."

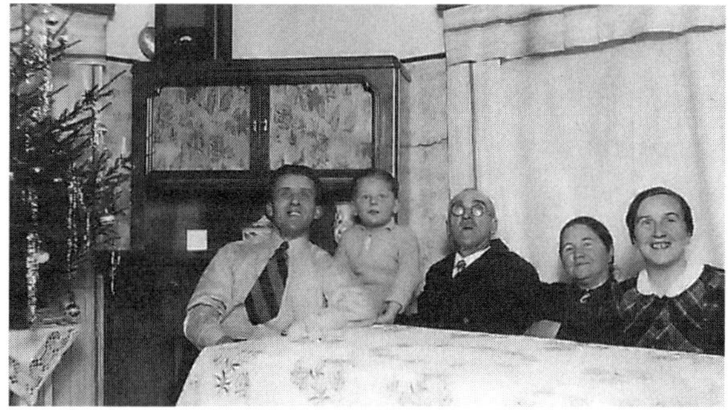

Fig. 3. Left to right: Heinrich Uhlstein, Herbert Uhlstein, Andreas and Sara Gärtner (parents of Sara Uhlstein), and Sara Gärtner Uhlstein. (H. Uhlstein)

Heinrich Uhlstein was already in uniform at the time and therefore could not help his wife and son find another place to live. Fortunately the family of Gustav Mellin (also members of the branch) took them in for the next few weeks. About a year later, the government wanted to send Herbert to Hungary as part of the Kinderlandverschickung program, but Sister Uhlstein resisted. The Uhlsteins may have escaped some of the unpleasant aspects of life in Nazi Germany, but another threatened them in 1944: Herbert turned ten and was to be inducted into the Jungvolk program. His parents were distinctly anti-Hitler and would gladly have kept Herbert away from that influence. He recounted the story:

> First we got letters and then I had to do a lot of fibbing. I wasn't going to tell them the truth because my mother would be in trouble. Then two Nazi soldiers came and took me away to be interrogated. They had me in that room for quite a while. I was really scared. I told them that my mother didn't want me to go [to Jungvolk activities] because I was skinny and frail. After that, we took off and went to Erfurt.

Sister Uhlstein took Herbert to the home of relatives near Erfurt in central Germany, where they stayed for about ten months. She had already received notice that her husband was missing in action, and she must have felt very lonely and discouraged. In any case, they had escaped the Jungvolk leaders and were safe in a relatively peaceful part of Germany.

Helga and Reinhard Gärtner stayed in Urloffen for three years, and though they were visited only once by their mother, they wrote many letters. Back in Herne, Emma Gärtner and her mother had moved into a small cabin on a garden property at the outskirts of town. In 1944, the children were finally allowed to return home and were taken in at the garden property. Helga viewed the devastation of her home town but was pleasantly surprised by one thing:

> The Schäferstrasse was still intact and the meeting rooms were not damaged. It was astonishing, but we still met regularly on Sundays and everything seemed to be just the same. The only change we noticed was that the attendance declined during the war years, but that was something we knew would happen. I am not sure if we always had enough priesthood holders during the war [because I was gone] but I know that some elderly brethren and sisters were still there.

Ingrid Gassner joined the throngs of children being evacuated from Herne in 1944. The destination for her class was near Bratislava in Czechoslovakia. Gone for nearly three years in all, she was also housed in locations near Prague and in Passau, Bavaria. Because Fritz Gassner suffered from a kidney ailment, he was not drafted. He and his wife were even able to visit their daughter on one occasion. The government's youth programs were in full swing where Ingrid was, as she explained:

> The Jungmädel program taught us cleanliness and exercise and good manners. We knew we had to keep our rooms in order. . . . Our leaders taught us the basic way of life. I wasn't really homesick while I was gone because we had our teacher with us and we knew our classmates. But I was isolated from the Church and never had an opportunity to attend meetings.

Ingrid and her company were moved farther west as the war drew to a close and the Soviet army approached from the east. By the time the end of the war came, they were in territory conquered by the Americans. Somehow, they found rail transportation and made their way safely home.

When the Red Army invaded East Prussia in the fall of 1944, Martha Kalwies realized that she needed to take her children and head west. She made a small backpack for each child and filled it with clothing, shoes, and a favorite toy. As Edith recalled, "The German troops were retreating column by column, and most of the populace was on the road. We heard that the Russians had already broken through." Sister Kalwies was most fortunate to rescue her children from that dangerous situation. By the end of the war, they were back in Herne. Andreas Kalwies was reported missing in action, but it was eventually reported that he was a POW of the Americans. The family had lost their apartment and nearly all of their earthly possessions, but when Brother Kalwies returned several years after the war, they were at least all together and healthy.

Like Sister Kalwies, Sara Uhlstein had no desire to be in the path of the invading Soviet soldiers. She took Herbert one day and began the trek west to Herne, nearly two hundred miles away. They walked with thousands of refugees. When it was clear that they did not know which way to go, Sister Uhlstein took her son into the forest, where they knelt and prayed for guidance. Then she announced that she knew which way to go. They soon crossed over railroad tracks, and she told her son that they were to follow the tracks. "When I saw that the tracks were unused and the weeds two feet high, I told her, 'Mother, no train is coming down this track. It hasn't been used for a very long time!" Nevertheless, they went where she directed, and eventually a train did come. It was a military transport that had been rerouted due to a damaged main line. The two jumped aboard and rode with the soldiers until enemy planes attacked the train. Later, they found a ride on some trucks, did a lot of walking, and arrived safely in Herne.

Their return was safe, but being in Herne again was fraught with danger. In the last months of the war, Herbert Uhlstein and his mother spent more and more time standing in line to get food from stores with ever-decreasing supplies. On one such day, Herbert was in one line and his mother in a second when a potentially disastrous incident occurred, as he recalled:

> It was right before the end of the war when the enemy was shelling the town with artillery. They hit the house across the street from where my mother was in line. The shrapnel came flying and hit her right on the side of her hip where she carried her canister with a gas mask in it. It hit that steel canister and flattened it. Those canisters were really well built. The blow knocked her down, and she was sore for a long time. She had a big bruise, but nothing was broken.

When the British occupied Herne in 1945, Franz Ryback's apartment was searched and the branch funds were confiscated. Soon after that incident, he appeared in the office of the British commandant in the Herne city hall and informed the officer that The Church of Jesus Christ of Latter-day Saints enjoyed protected status under the Americans and that the confiscation of the branch funds was illegal. The commandant ordered that the funds be returned, and the branch was allowed to develop without restriction.[11]

With the war over, Helga Gärtner and many other Germans had to deal with the fact that Hitler had caused unspeakable things to be done. She recalled being told during the war that the Jews were Germany's ruin and were simply being deported from Germany; she and other German youth believed those claims. When the truth about the murder of the Jews was uncovered after the war, she said, "We didn't believe this at first because our leader always spoke of honor, goodness, and kindness and love of our fellowman."[12]

The incessant bombings by the Allies killed only one member of the Herne Branch but drove many others from the city for years at a time. At least six men died in combat. It would have been easy at the end of the war to give in to despair, but the Latter-day Saints in that battered city did not. Their meetinghouse still stood, and they gathered in increasing numbers as the dust of war settled.

Fig. 4. Members of the Herne Branch during World War II. (H. Ulstein)

In Memoriam

The following members of the Herne Branch did not survive World War II:

Auguste Bweski b. Pierlafkin, Ostpreußen, 19 May 1885; dau. of Martin Bweski and Gottliebe Librida; bp. 12 May 1909; conf. 12 May 1909; m. Adolf Starbatti; k. air raid 11 Nov 1944 (FHL microfilm 68796, no. 114; CHL microfilm 2447, pt. 26, no. 362; FHL microfilm 245273; 1930 and 1935 censuses; IGI)

Julie Auguste Dobrzinski b. Barloschken-Neidenburg, Ostpreußen, 1 Dec 1885; dau. of Frieda Dobrzinski; bp. 4 Sep 1927; conf. 4 Sep 1927; m. 19 Nov 1905, August Jedamski; d. stomach cancer 2 May 1943 (FHL microfilm 68796, no. 166)

Egon Drawe b. Herne, Westfalen, 10 May 1939; son of Wilhelm Gottlieb Drawe and Marie Anna Müller; d. lung sickness or lung operation 6 Mar 1940 (FHL microfilm 68796, no. 147; CHL microfilm 2447, pt. 26, no. 840; IGI)

Wilhelm Gottlieb Drawe b. Herne, Westfalen, 11 Aug 1900; son of Heinrich Christoph Christian Drawe and Karoline Justine Kijewski; bp. 14 Nov 1937; conf. 14 Nov 1937; m. Herne 19 Oct 1928, Marie Anna Müller; 7 children; d. stomach surgery Castrop-Rauxel, Westfalen, 15 Jul 1940; bur. Herne 18 Jul 1940 (FHL microfilm 68796, no. 32; CHL microfilm 2447, pt. 26, no. 777; FHL microfilm 25757, 1935 census; IGI, PRF)

Elfriede Berta Heider b. Husen-Kurl, Westfalen, 10 Jan 1913; dau. of Hermann Karl Heider and Paulina Anna Schwabe; bp. 12 Jul 1921; conf. 12 Jul 1921; m. 9 Aug 1932, Otto Hellmich; d. stroke 21 Sep 1940 (FHL microfilm 68796, no. 61; CHL microfilm 2447, pt. 26, no. 505; FHL microfilm 68803, no. 505; FHL microfilm 162780; 1930 and 1935 censuses; IGI)

Hermann Karl Heider b. Ober Peilau, Schlesien, 4 Nov 1873; son of Pauline Anna Heider; bp. 28 Jul 1920; conf. 28 Jul 1920; ord. deacon 10 Sep 1922; ord. teacher 1 or 2 Mar 1925; ord. priest 31 Jan 1926; ord. elder 6 Jun 1933; m. 3 Nov 1895, Pauline Anna Schwabe; d. stroke 5 Nov 1941 (FHL microfilm 68796, no. 52; CHL microfilm 2447, pt. 26, no. 110; FHL microfilm 162780; 1925, 1930, and 1935 censuses; IGI)

Gerlinde Waltraut Hoffmann b. Herne, Westfalen, abt 1941; dau. of Emil Hoffmann and Klara Franziska Mixan; d. abt 1941 (FHL microfilm 68796, no. 198; IGI)

Eugen Walter Kalwies b. Herne, Westfalen, 24 Feb 1934; son of Eugen Kahlwies and Martha Maria Rasavski; bp. 19 Apr 1942; conf. 19 Apr 1942; d. Argenfelde, Tilsit, Ostpreußen, 20 Sep 1943 (FHL microfilm 68803, no. 677; FHL microfilm 271376; 1930 and 1935 censuses)

Gerhard Günther Klein b. Herne, Westfalen, 17 Nov 1934; son of Karl Jakob Wilhelm Klein and Elfriede Sophie Waschke; d. spinal meningitis 30 March or 5 Apr 1940 (FHL microfilm 68796, no. 71; CHL microfilm 2447, pt. 26, no. 769; IGI; AF)

Maria Kruska b. Awayden, Sensburg, Ostpreußen, 30 Mar 1871; dau. of Karl Kruska and Marie Duda; bp. 25 Jan 1925; conf. 25 Jan 1925; m. Aweyden, Sensburg, Ostpreußen, abt 1892 or 22 Feb 1900, Michael Nadolny or Nadolmy; 3 children; d. stroke Awayden 1 Mar 1943 (FHL microfilm 68796, no. 99; CHL microfilm 2447, pt. 26, no. 234; IGI)

Kurt Walter Müller b. Kappel, Chemnitz, Sachsen, 12 Sep 1900; son of Robert Wendelin Müller and Anna Maria Boeckel; bp. 28 Jul 1926; conf. 28 Jul 1926; m. 3 Jun 1922 or 19 Oct 1928, Marianne Hildegard Uhlig; d. stomach cysts or tumors 14 Jul 1941 (FHL microfilm 68796, no. 174; CHL microfilm 2447, pt. 26, no. 230; FHL microfilm 68803, no. 230; IGI)

Egon Anton Rutrecht b. Börnig, Herne, Westfalen, 24 Nov 1920; son of Anton Rutrecht and Martha Marie Lau; bp. 1 Jun 1929; conf. 1 Jun 1929; ord. deacon 6 Jun 1933; stormtrooper; k. in battle Mischkino, south of Leningrad, Russia, 13 Feb 1943 (FHL microfilm 68796, no. 106; CHL microfilm 2447, pt. 26, no. 499; FHL microfilm 271408; 1925, 1930, and 1935 censuses; www.volksbund.de; IGI)

Karl Heinz Rybak b. Recklinghausen, Herne, Westfalen, 9 Nov 1919; son of Franz Rybak and Auguste

Konetzka; bp. 23 Jul 1928; conf. 23 Jul 1928; ord. deacon 6 Jun 1933; k. in battle 20 Dec 1941 (FHL microfilm 68796, no. 110; CHL microfilm 2447, pt. 26, no. 438; FHL microfilm 271408; 1925, 1930, and 1935 censuses; IGI)

Fritz Gustav Semrau b. Herne, Westfalen; or Nekla, Posen, 26 May 1920; son of Hermann Emil Semrau and Marie Martha Hildebrandt; bp. 14 Jun 1928; canoneer; d. field hospital 239 by Stadniza, 10 km south of Semljansk, Voronezh Woronesh, Russia, 24 Aug 1942 (Semmrau; FHL microfilm 245261; 1925, 1930, and 1935 censuses; www.volksbund.de; IGI)

Karl Theodor Spittank b. Sodingen, Herne, Westfalen, 6 Nov 1910; son of John Otto Spittank and Ida Wilke; bp. 27 Jun 1931; conf. 27 Jun 1931; m. 12 Feb 1934, Franziska Skrycak; corporal; k. in battle Babiza 27 Jan 1944; bur. Glubokoje, Belarus (FHL microfilm 68796, no. 181; www.volksbund.de; IGI)

Heinrich Herbert Uhlstein b. Herne, Westfalen, 15 Apr 1909; son of Christian Max Uhlstein and Johanna Karolina Weis; bp. 2 Nov 1924; m. Herne 24 Dec 1931, Sara Gärtner; d. Witebsk, Russia, 30 Jun 1944 (IGI; FHL microfilm 245289; 1935 census)

Karl Heinz Friedrich Vahrson b. Herne, Westfalen, 13 May 1916; son of Karl Heinrich Otto Vahrson and Anna Martha Maria Meier; bp. 8 Aug 1926; conf. 8 Aug 1926; k. in battle or d. Herne 12 Mar 1945 (FHL microfilm 68796, no. 126; CHL microfilm 2458, form 42 FP, pt. 37, all-mission list 1943–46, 186–87 and district list, 202–3; CHL microfilm 2447, pt. 26, no. 387; FHL microfilm 245289; 1925, 1930, and 1935 census; IGI)

Auguste Elfriede Liesette Wilke b. Langendreer, Westfalen, 15 May 1870; dau. of Andreas Wilke and Wilhelmine Menthof; bp. 19 May 1930; conf. 19 May 1930; m. 19 Sep 1903, Wilhelm Haarhaus; d. heart failure 15 Jun 1942 (FHL microfilm 68796, no. 157; CHL microfilm 2447 pt. 26 no. 550; IGI)

Julia Zẏwitz b. Schönwiese, Saalau; or Heilsberg, Ostpreußen, 15 Mar 1866; dau. of Johann Zẏwitz and Julia Schimitzki; bp. 18 Aug 1914; conf. 18 Aug 1914; m. 10 Mar 1917, Wilhelm Chmielewski; d. pyelitis 1 May 1944 (FHL microfilm 68796, no. 27; CHL microfilm 2447, pt. 26, no. 53; FHL microfilm 25739; 1925 and 1930 censuses; IGI)

NOTES

1. Helga Gärtner Recksiek, interview by Michael Corley in German, Salt Lake City, December 12, 2008; summarized in English by Judith Sartowski.
2. *Hundert Jahre Gemeinde Herne* (Herne Ward, 2001).
3. West German Mission branch directory, 1939, CHL LR 10045 11.
4. Presiding Bishopric, "Financial, Statistical, and Historical Reports of Wards, Stakes, and Missions, 1884–1955," 257, CHL CR 4 12.
5. Edith Kalwies Crandall, telephone interview with Judith Sartowski, May 6, 2008.
6. Helga Gärtner Recksiek, "My Book of Remembrance" (unpublished autobiography); private collection.
7. Ibid.
8. Ibid.
9. Ingrid Gassner Schwiermann, telephone interview with the author, November 30, 2009.
10. Herbert Uhlstein, interview by the author, Bountiful, UT, June 20, 2006.
11. *Hundert Jahre Gemeinde Herne.*
12. Helga Gärtner Recksiek, "Book of Remembrance."

OBERHAUSEN BRANCH

The thirty-one Latter-day Saints living among the nearly two hundred thousand inhabitants of the city of Oberhausen would have had reason to feel lonely, had there not been a close connection to the other branches of the Ruhr District. As World War II approached, this branch was so weak that only two leaders were shown on the branch directory submitted to the mission office in Frankfurt: Gustav Müller as branch president and Anton Pyta as Sunday School superintendant.[1] Because the address given for Brother Müller is in Essen, it can be assumed that district president Friedrich Biehl asked him to preside at the meetings in Oberhausen.

Documents in the mission office show that the Oberhausen Branch had been established less than a year before the war began: "December 18, 1938: the branch moved into a new hall in the little city of Oberhausen, because the members are closer to there than to Duisburg."[2] The meeting rooms were rented in a Hinterhaus at Rolandstrasse 43. No description of the setting is available.

American missionary Erma Rosenhan provided some detail regarding the Oberhausen Branch in her diary after a visit there in 1939: "Sunday, August 13, 1939: Went with Bro. Naujoks to Oberhausen. It is just a small branch of about 20 to 25 persons. Only 6 were present. I had to play the organ there too. Bro. Naujoks and I both talked. We sang a song too and I accompanied. Sunday School and [sacrament meeting] followed one another."[3]

Oberhausen Branch[4]	1939
Elders	3
Priests	2
Teachers	0
Deacons	1
Other Adult Males	3
Adult Females	22
Male Children	0
Female Children	0
Total	31

Nothing is known about the activities of the branch members during the war, but the list of losses indicates that they were not excluded from the sufferings of the inhabitants of this important industrial city.

In Memoriam

The following members of the Oberhausen Branch did not survive World War II:

Minette Borrmann b. Altenburg, Anhalt, 5 Jan 1870; bp. Oberhausen, Oberhausen, Rheinland, 26 Nov 1932; missing as of 15 Nov 1946 (FHL microfilm 68802, no. 2; IGI; AF; PRF) Friedrich "Fritz" Wilhelm Jakob Hemp b. Duisburg 3 Aug 1912; son of Friedrich Hemp and Helma Roemmert; bp. 21 May 1927; m.; missing as of 15 Nov 1946 (FHL microfilm 68802, no. 9; FHL microfilm 162781; 1930 and 35 censuses)

Frieda Minna Krohse b. Abau Schönwalde, Westpreußen, 24 Jan 1906; dau. of Ernst Krohse and Emilie A. O. Brauer; bp. 19 Oct 1930; conf. 19 Oct 1930; missing as of 15 Nov 1946 (FHL microfilm 68802, no. 10; CHL microfilm 2447, pt. 26, no. 557)

Josef Sattler b. Liege, Belgium, 12 Apr 1908; son of Jakob Sattler and Maria Katharina Schapperdoth; bp. Oberhausen, Oberhausen, Rheinland, 18 Sep 1926; k. in battle Western Front 5 Sep 1944 (CHL microfilm 2458, form 42 FP, pt. 37, all-mission list 1943–46, 186–87; IGI)

Elisabeth Spindler b. 25 May 1894; bp. 6 Feb 1913; missing as of 15 Nov 1946 (FHL microfilm 68802, no. 21)

Anna Temme b. 18 Oct 1895; bp. 11 Oct 1919; missing as of 15 Nov 1946 (FHL microfilm 68802, no. 22)

Frieda Theunissen b. 24 Apr 1907; bp. 25 Jun 1927; missing as of 15 Nov 1946 (FHL microfilm 68802, no. 24)

Notes

1. West German Mission branch directory, 1939, CHL LR 10045 11.
2. West German Mission quarterly report, 1938, no. 45, CHL LR 10045 2.
3. Erma Rosenhan, papers, CHL MS 16190.
4. Presiding Bishopric, "Financial, Statistical, and Historical Reports of Wards, Stakes, and Missions, 1884–1955," 257, CHL CR 4 12.

Wuppertal Branch

A week after the president of the West German Mission departed Frankfurt, he wrote from Copenhagen, Denmark, regarding the status of several small branches. Two of those were the Barmen and Elberfeld Branches of the incorporated city of Wuppertal. President Wood recommended that the two branches be joined into one in order to strengthen the Church's presence in that city.[1] It is not known precisely whether that happened or when. For purposes of describing the activities of individual Saints from Wuppertal, it will be assumed that the two branches were indeed combined.

The Wupper River runs west through a narrow valley toward the Rhine. On its way it links the historic towns of Barmen on the east and Elberfeld on the west. The city of Wuppertal was formed by combining those towns and several others. Beginning in 1903, the famous *Schwebebahn* (suspended monorail) allowed easy travel through the city as it glided suspended above the river. By the time World War II began, 405,000 people were living in Wuppertal.

Wuppertal-Barmen Branch[2]	1939
Elders	6
Priests	1
Teachers	0
Deacons	2
Other Adult Males	4
Adult Females	20
Male Children	1
Female Children	1
Total	35

Wuppertal-Elberfeld Branch[3]	1939
Elders	2
Priests	2
Teachers	3
Deacons	4
Other Adult Males	5
Adult Females	22
Male Children	3
Female Children	3
Total	44

Very little is known about the Wuppertal Branch during the war, and the available eyewitness testimonies do not mention the location of the meeting rooms or leadership of the branch. It is known only that in the summer of 1939, the Elberfeld Saints were meeting in rooms in the Hinterhaus at Uellendahlerstrasse 24, and their Barmen counterparts met at Unterdörnen 105. Neither branch had a functioning Relief Society, MIA, or Primary at the time.[4] One eyewitness identified Paul Schwarz as the branch president in 1943; he had been the president of the Barmen Branch in 1939.[5]

Rudolf Schwarz (born 1914) was the superintendant of the Sunday School in the Barmen Branch when the war began, but he was soon in uniform (for the third time). He married Charlotte Becker in 1938 and was a father to little Helga. When it came time for his unit to swear the oath of a German soldier, his staff sergeant refused to allow him and two other soldiers to participate, insisting that they were not Catholics or Protestants. (One was of the Baptist faith.) When the commanding officer learned the next day of the mistake, the three were ordered to report to the parade ground in dress uniform, and the ceremony was repeated for their sake. According to Rudolf, "This was a very interesting beginning in the German army."[6]

With his time and grade as a soldier, Rudolf was a top sergeant and adjutant by the end of 1941. By then, the German army had moved hundreds of miles into the Soviet Union and was experiencing the terrible Russian winter. On January 7, 1942, the Red Army broke through the German lines, and chaos threatened. The temperature dropped to thirty to forty degrees below zero, and the Germans were not as well dressed as their enemies. At a time when a determined commander was needed, Rudolf's captain had a nervous breakdown and was out of commission. Rudolf stated, "I felt it was my job to take over the command." He organized a scouting mission, learned that the enemy soldiers were only about one hundred feet away, and then positioned his men with their machine guns to repel the attack. They were successful, and Sergeant Schwarz accepted the surrender of about one hundred soldiers. Many were wounded, so he transferred them to a local village and asked the women there to care for the men. All this was done without any involvement of the captain, who afterwards was awarded the Knight's Cross (although Rudolf claimed that everybody gave him the credit for the victory).

A week later, Rudolf was in combat again and assisted in the destruction of Soviet tanks, for which he was awarded the Iron Cross First Class. Soon the enemy was not the Red Army but the terrible cold. Rudolf and his men were crossing a long stretch of ice and learned an important lesson in survival:

Fig. 1. Wuppertal-Elberfeld Branch in early 1939. (G. Blake)

> We walked about thirteen hours. We found out that the cold makes you mentally and physically very unstable. At some time you would like to lay down and forget all about it. If we saw somebody laying down or sitting down, we kicked them and told them to go on. Two of [the men] died. It was a great march, and nobody can imagine how painful it was to walk under that condition. Nothing to eat, nothing to drink. . . . Everybody had problems walking—like you had arthritis everywhere.

By March 1942, Rudolf Schwarz was a platoon commander and was soon on his way home on leave. He first visited his parents and attended church with the Wuppertal Branch, then headed south to Bavaria, where his wife and daughter were staying in the town of Unterelsbach (Upper Franconia). From there it was back to the Eastern Front, where Rudolf stepped on a land mine on July 7, 1942: "A terrible noise, and I was thrown up into the air and I turned around in the air and fell on the ground." His men carried him back to a field hospital, and he spent the next year in various hospitals. Surgery and orthopedic devices eventually allowed him to walk again, but he was released from active duty in 1943. While in the hospital in Deutsch Krone, Pomerania, he was visited by Lotte and Helga. His condition was worsened several times by infections and appendicitis, but he eventually recovered and was downgraded to reserve status.

Gerda Rode (born 1921) was surprised in 1942 when she received a letter from an LDS soldier of the Bad Homburg Branch, near Frankfurt. Hans Gerecht had been a missionary in Wuppertal in 1937–38 and recalled her as a "very blond girl." It was several months before she responded to his letters. He was already a Wehrmacht soldier and as such was not free to visit her. In April 1943, he was given leave to go home to Bad Homburg and asked her to join him there. Just after they parted, she received a telegram with the text: "Do you want to be my wife? Please let me know immediately. Hans." Her reply was one word in the affirmative.

In June 1943, Hans Gerecht was allowed to visit his fiancée in Wuppertal. He was there just in time to experience a horrific attack on the city. As they were huddled in a cellar, the building was hit; one man close to them was killed, and they ended up digging their way out of the rubble. After moving Gerda and her mother to a safe location, Hans returned to help rescue their neighbors. They soon learned of a comical situation involving a Brother Fischer from the branch. He was suffering from diarrhea and was sitting on the toilet when a bomb hit his apartment building. When the house collapsed, he dropped a full story—still seated on the toilet—but was not seriously injured.

Fig. 2. Missionary George Blake at the pump organ in Wuppertal. This model of organ could be seen in meeting rooms all over Germany during the war. (G. Blake)

Returning to their apartment house, Gerda, her mother, and Hans gazed upward into the open apartment; the building's façade had been blown away. They were able to go upstairs and rescue a very expensive mattress, after which they went to the Bühlers, another LDS family, and were given a place to sleep. Homeless, the three took the train to Bad Homburg. Hans was soon given another leave, and he and Gerda were married in Frankfurt on July 24, 1943. She recalled one important aspect of the event: "I had nothing to wear. A sister in Frankfurt gave me her long black dress and a white veil. This sister was so kind, she gave this dress to all the brides, and it fit them all. We were all undernourished and slim." After a few days together as man and wife, Hans was on his way back to the Eastern Front.

The news of the terrible attack on Wuppertal was communicated throughout the West German Mission, and a relief campaign was instituted. The following report was filed in Frankfurt regarding that campaign:[7]

> Jul 1943:
> According to general newsletter no. 2 of the West German Mission dated June 27, 1943, as well as by the request of the Hamburg District Presidency, a request is being made of all members to voluntarily donate anything they can—be it money, clothing, or other items—for the relief of the members of the Ruhr District, especially the branches in Barmen and Elberfeld, who have lost their homes in recent air raids. The following items were then collected and prepared for shipment to the district leaders in Hamburg:
>
> | | |
> |---|---|
> | Brother Louis Gellersen | 200 Marks |
> | Brother Christian Tiedemann | 20 Marks |
> | Emma Hagenah (non-member friend) | 5 Marks |
> | | 225 Marks total |
>
> The following items were donated by Sister Helene Gellersen of Stade:
> [coats, underwear, sweaters, pants, blankets, jackets, pens, paper, cutlery, soap, cups, etc.]
>
> Stade on July 9, 1943
> Louis Gellersen, branch president

Fig. 3. Sisters of the Wuppertal Branch. (G. Blake)

In March 1944, Gerda Rode Gerecht's mother passed away. Three months later, her brother Ernst was killed in the first fighting against the invading

Allies near Normandy, France. Just prior to her brother's death, she welcomed Hans home for a furlough. When it came time for him to report for duty again, he convinced her to ride the train to Vienna, Austria, with him so that they could spend more time together. He smuggled her onto a troop train; after they said good-bye in Vienna in May 1944, she returned to Bad Homburg.

During the last year of the war, Rudolf Schwarz was sent to a technical school in Nuremberg, not far from where his family was living in Unterelsbach. His course was not yet completed when Nuremberg was devastated in the attack of January 2, 1945, but he was at least prepared to work as a draftsman. Rudolf returned to Unterelsbach and found work in the nearby town of Bad Neustadt. With the American army approaching the area in March 1945, the local Nazi Party leader approached Rudolf and informed him that he was to lead the local Volkssturm (home guard); he was the best man for the job, based on his combat experience.

> My job was to get about 100 old men ready to fight in that very last battle. It was a joke, but I couldn't get out right away, so I started training and organizing in regulated time with these men which I hardly knew. . . . After a while the situation got real critical, as the front line came closer to our area. One day we could hear the artillery from the American army. I had to make a decision one way or the other what to do with that Volkssturm. . . . I [received] orders from the Party that I was in charge of the whole area. . . . Needless to say we didn't have any weapons. So I dissolved the Volkssturm as an organization. I told the men to go home and take care of their families.

Rudolf knew that he could be shot as a traitor, but the Americans were in town within hours, and he explained to them that no defense would be offered by the local men.

One day in April 1945, Gerda went to the home of Hans's parents. She recalled what happened there:

> I had a key. I waited for them and lay on the sofa. "Gerda," [Hans] called with a voice full of love and sadness. "Gerda," I heard my name the second time. I looked around; I didn't see him but felt his presence. Later I heard that this must have been the time that he was shot in the face. . . . He died at that very time. This was confirmed when I was notified . . . that he had given his life for the fatherland in heavy fighting.

One last tragedy awaited the young widow: Gerda's father, Heinrich Jakob Rode, was shot with several other men by the Gestapo in April. She made inquiries after the war and was told that seventy-two men were rounded up as traitors—apparently having refused to fight as Volkssturm—and executed by the Gestapo. She claimed to have found the mass grave in 1948 near Immigrath, about twenty miles south of Wuppertal. During her visit, she located a neighbor who confirmed that the atrocity had indeed occurred there. A monument marked the spot, but no names were engraved thereon.

The city of Wuppertal suffered substantial losses inflicted by 126 air raids. At least 8,363 people were killed, and 38 percent of the city was destroyed (including 64 percent of the dwellings). The American army entered the city on April 16, 1945.[8]

In the summer of 1945, Rudolf Schwarz was determined to take his family (which now included a son named Roman) back to Wuppertal. His wife had acquired some nice furniture during her four years in Unterelsbach, and they wanted very much to take it back with them. Rudolf was successful in arranging with a railroad agent for the shipment of the furniture in a box car to a point close to Wuppertal. After arriving there, local friends were enlisted to transport the valuable cargo to Wuppertal, where the Schwarz family prepared for life in a new Germany.

In Memoriam

The following members of the Wuppertal Barmen and Elberfeld Branches did not survive World War II:

Catharina Emilie Callies b. Elberfeld, Wupperthal, Rheinprovinz, 7 Feb 1869; dau. of Johann Ferdinand

Callies and Katharina Rau; bp. 20 Sep 1942; conf. 20 Sep 1942; m. 1 Oct 1890, Ernst Ewald Steffens; d. stroke 12 Nov 1944 (FHL microfilm 68808, no. 55; CHL microfilm 2447, pt. 26, no. 879; FHL microfilm 68803, no. 879; IGI)

Karl Adolf Harzen b. Elberfeld, Wuppertal, Rheinprovinz, 23 Nov 1890; son of Alexander Harzen and Auguste Druseberg; bp. 13 Nov 1932; conf. 13 Nov 1932; ord. teacher 26 Nov 1933; d. pleurisy 30 Jan 1941 (CHL CR 375 8 2430, no. 976; FHL microfilm 162777; 1935 census; IGI)

Richard Kühhirt b. Mühlhausen, Sachsen (province), 22 May 1896; son of Julius Kindhoff or Windhoff and Christine Kuhirt; bp. 27 Mar 1905; conf. 27 Mar 1905; m. 2 Jun 1915, Luise Emma Seyfarth; d. influenza and heart attack 25 Feb 1941 (FHL microfilm 68786, no. 35; FHL microfilm 271381; 1935 census; IGI)

Mathilde L. Oswald b. Mühlhausen 27 May 1872; dau. of Ludwig Oswald and Regine ——; bp. 29 Oct 1903; conf. 29 Oct 1903; m. Fritsch; d. old age 5 Jul 1943 (FHL microfilm 68803, no. 922; FHL microfilm 25770; 1930 and 1935 censuses)

Ernst Rode b. Elberfeld, Rheinprovinz, 22 Jun 1909; son of Heinrich Jakob Rode and Alwine Morenz; bp. 15 Apr 1923; conf. 15 Apr 1923; m. 14 or 16 Dec 1934, Hilde Metzer or Melzer; private first class; k. in battle France 12 Aug 1944; bur. La Cambe, France (SLCGW; FHL microfilm 68808, no. 51; FHL microfilm 68786, no. 568; www.volksbund.de; IGI)

Emilie J. E. Schrick b. Vohwinkel, Rheinprovinz, 18 Jan 1870; dau. of Wilhelm Schrick and Julie Hollhaus; bp. 6 Apr 1930; conf. 6 Apr 1930; m. 10 Feb 1890, Karl Amhäuser; d. asthma and old age 10 Feb 1941 (CHL CR 375 8 2430, no. 904; FHL microfilm no. 25710; 1930 census; IGI)

Heinrich Wagner b. Elberfeld, Rheinprovinz, 21 Nov 1856; son of Heinrich Wagner and Wilhelmine Meissner; bp. 28 Oct 1910; conf. 28 Oct 1910; ord. deacon 6 Jul 1913; ord. priest 21 Mar 1915; d. 25 Jun 1943; bur. Elberfeld, Wuppertal (FHL Microfilm 68786, no. 580; www.volksbund.de; FHL microfilm no. 245291; 1925 and 1935 censuses; IGI)

NOTES

1. M. Douglas Wood, papers, CHL MS 10817.
2. Presiding Bishopric, "Financial, Statistical, and Historical Reports of Wards, Stakes, and Missions, 1884–1955," 257, CHL CR 4 12.
3. Ibid.
4. West German Mission branch directory, 1939, CHL LR 10045 11.
5. Gerda Roda Gerecht, "My Marriage to Hans Gerecht," CHL MS 19186.
6. Rudolf Schwarz, unpublished autobiography; private collection.
7. Lübeck Branch history, 10, CHL LR 5093 21.
8. Wuppertal city archive.

SCHLESWIG-HOLSTEIN DISTRICT

West German Mission

At the far north extent of the West German Mission in 1939 was the district of Schleswig-Holstein. With the Danish Mission to the north and the Hamburg District to the south, this district consisted of a very small territory. The four branches were all located north of a line running essentially from the North Sea east to the Baltic Sea, through the city of Neumünster.

This district was administered from the city of Kiel on the Baltic. From there, the distances to the other three branches were not significant: forty-three miles north to Flensburg, twenty miles west to Rendsburg, and twenty miles farther to Friedrichstadt.

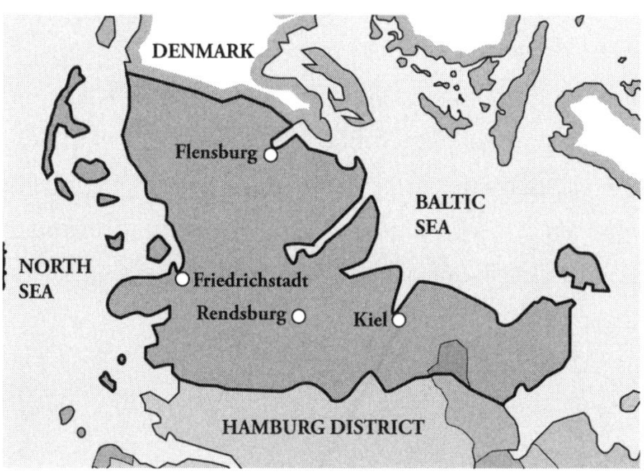

Fig. 1. The Schleswig-Holstein District was located among the flat lands of northern Germany.

The population of the district was very small, and most of the members (175 of them, 54 percent) belonged to the Kiel Branch. Indeed, it is difficult to envision missionaries even traveling to such small towns as Friedrichstadt and Rendsburg to seek out people to whom the gospel could be introduced.

Schleswig-Holstein District[1]	1939
Elders	26
Priests	8
Teachers	5
Deacons	26
Other Adult Males	51
Adult Females	193
Male Children	8
Female Children	10
Total	327

The mission directory page listing the leaders of the Schleswig-Holstein District in the summer of 1939 either was never received in the mission office or has not survived. All that is known about those leaders is taken from various reports found in the mission archives. For example, one reads the following entry dated Saturday–Sunday, April 15–16,

1939: "A district conference for Schleswig-Holstein was held in the Kiel Branch hall. Presiding was Robert Salopiata. A wonderful spirit prevailed among saints and friends."[2]

It appears that Elder Salopiata of the Flensburg Branch was inducted into the military at the onset of the war, because his availability to serve as the district president ended already in September 1939. The new supervisor of the West German Mission, Friedrich Biehl, wrote to former mission president M. Douglas Wood (then in Stockholm, Sweden) with this message on September 26, 1939: "Brother Kurt Müller of Kiel has agreed to serve as District President of Schleswig-Holstein. Brother Salopiata can now be released."[3]

It is believed from eyewitness reports that Elder Müller served in that office for the majority—if not the rest—of the war years. Nothing else is known about the men and women who assisted Elder Müller in directing the affairs of the four branches in that district.

According to the history of the Kiel Branch, the district conference held in Kiel on March 31, 1940, was attended by mission supervisor Christian Heck as well as Hamburg District president Alwin Brey. The attendance consisted of 255 members and 28 friends. In November of that year, another district conference was held, to which two hundred persons came.[4]

Fig. 2. Members of the League of German Girls in Kiel marching to an activity. (R. Radack)

Notes

1. Presiding Bishopric, "Financial, Statistical, and Historical Reports of Wards, Stakes, and Missions, 1884 1955," 257, CHL CR 4 12.
2. West German Mission quarterly report, 1939, CHL LR 10045 2 16.
3. M. Douglas Wood, papers, CHL MS 10817. The history of the Kiel Branch shows this change of leadership taking place on December 10, 1939.
4. Kiel Branch history; courtesy of Karl-Heinz Goldmund.

Flensburg Branch

The northern suburbs of the city of Flensburg reached almost to the border of Denmark in 1939. This port city on the Baltic Sea was thus the northernmost city of substantial size (68,042 inhabitants) in Hitler's Germany when World War II began. With its large port facilities and industry, it was a city crucial to the war efforts of the Third Reich.

The branch of The Church of Jesus Christ of Latter-day Saints met in rooms rented on the second floor of a building at Grossestrasse 48 in Flensburg. According to the branch history, the main meeting hall was complemented by four small classrooms.[1]

A small branch of fifty-four persons called that location home in the summer of 1939. The president of the branch was Max B. Müller, but he was called to be the district president by the end of September. It is not known who succeeded him then. When the war began in September 1939, Otto Schwan was the superintendant of the Sunday School, Friedrich Hansen the leader of the YMMIA, and Constanze Klindt the leader of the YWMIA. The Primary was directed by Elfriede Callesen, and the Relief Society by Margarete Salopiata (who also represented *Der Stern* magazine). Genealogical research was supervised by Max Müller.

The meeting schedule for the Flensburg Branch in 1939 was as follows: Sunday School at 10:00 a.m. and sacrament meeting at 7:00 p.m., entertainment

Fig. 1. The main meeting room of the Flensburg Branch in about 1940. (Church History Library)

(of unspecified variety) on Mondays at 7:30 p.m., Primary on Tuesdays at 4:00 p.m., MIA on Thursdays at 7:45 p.m., followed by priesthood and Relief Society meetings at 8:45, and genealogical study on the second and fourth Thursdays of the month at 6:00 p.m.

Flensburg Branch[2]	**1939**
Elders	6
Priests	1
Teachers	1
Deacons	4
Other Adult Males	11
Adult Females	30
Male Children	0
Female Children	1
Total	54

The surviving manuscript branch history only extends through the end of the year 1940 but includes several comments about life for the Latter-day Saints in the Flensburg Branch during those seventeen months:[3]

> August 22, 1939: A special meeting was held in the Kiel Branch hall with Joseph Fielding Smith as the speaker.

> August 27, 1939: Margo Karl Klindt and Albert Dittmer were drafted. Beginning on September 5, sacrament meeting was to begin at 6:00 p.m. due to blackout regulations.

> October 15, 1939: Sacrament meeting was to begin at 5:00 p.m. due to blackout regulations.

> December 24, 1939: A Christmas program was presented; twenty-five persons attended.

The average sacrament meeting attendance since the war began was eighteen persons.

> January 14, 1940: Relief Society meetings started again after a hiatus of four months. The Flensburg Sunday School was discontinued until further notice.

> March 30–31, 1940: Twelve members of the branch attended the district conference in Kiel.

> April 21, 1940: Max Müller and Elisabeth Bräuer [?] were married; "we gave the young couple a fine reception."

> April 20, 1940: Uwe Wischniewski died at the age of 21–22 months; he was buried on April 24 at the Friedenshügel cemetery; twenty-five persons attended the funeral.

> May 26, 1940: [Sunday] meeting times were changed: MIA at 10:30 [a.m.], sacrament meeting at 11:45, Relief Society and priesthood meetings at 12:30.

The average attendance at Sunday meetings in April 1940 was twelve to fourteen persons. It is clear from those entries that wartime conditions had interrupted and even temporarily curtailed branch activities. Nevertheless, it is equally clear that the members of the Flensburg Branch carried on as best they could.

Harry Christensen was born in Denmark in 1922 and baptized in the town of Sonderburg, just north of Flensburg in Denmark, in 1933. His father found work in Flensburg in April 1939 and moved his family south into the city to avoid the long bicycle ride to work. Harry, who was sixteen years old and finished with public schooling, recalled finding work for himself at the time as well:

> I started job training in a garden market when I lived in Flensburg but I didn't live at home. My boss had all of his trainees stay in his home. We worked every day from 6 a.m. to 6 p.m. I had one day off a month and that was usually a Sunday. This was the only time that I could go home and get my laundry done, so I didn't have many opportunities to attend church.[4]

As a citizen of Denmark, Harry could not be drafted into the military nor subjected to other involuntary programs under the National Socialist government. In other respects, Harry and his family found it important to assimilate themselves in Germany. For example, they spoke German at home. In fact, both of Harry's parents were born in Germany, but his father had since become a Danish citizen.

"The first British attack on Flensburg destroyed the branch meeting rooms," recalled Harry. "The young men were drafted, and mothers with their children left town for safer places." Even Danish citizens could not escape the dangers of war, and Harry's life would be interrupted several times by personal loss.

The Flensburg Branch history indicates that changes were made in the Relief Society on September 14, 1940. Margarete Salopiata was called as the new Relief Society leader again, and the following were released: president Paula Thomsen, first counselor Elfriede Callesen, and second counselor Alwine Dittmer. New Sunday School leaders were called: president Franz Luhmann, first counselor Albert Dittmer, and second counselor Thomas Thomsen.[5]

The branch clerk wrote an enlightening paragraph in his record at the conclusion of the year 1940:

> So ends the second year of the war. Under the circumstances, the meetings were held for the most part without interruption. All organizations are still functioning well. Sunday School takes place from 11:00 to 12:00, priesthood and Relief Society meetings from 2:00 to 3:00, and sacrament meeting from 3:00 to 4:00. There are 55 members of record: 9 priesthood holders, 11 other males, 29 females, 6 children.[6]

The branch population was constantly in flux, as is clear from an analysis of the above report. Beginning with fifty-four members in 1939, the membership had risen to fifty-five, despite the fact that two members died during 1940. Thus it can be assumed that three persons were baptized that year.

Harry Christensen moved to Kiel and met a nice Catholic girl there. They were married in the civil registry office in 1943 and moved into a modest apartment. In that huge port city, the Christensens were in for very frightening adventures because the city was targeted constantly by Allied bombers. As Harry recalled:

> We lost our home three times during the war and lost everything. But because we didn't have anything left, we were given coupons with which to buy the things we were missing. But even though we had the money, those things were not available to buy. I remember one time when my bike was destroyed by a bomb, I received a new one from France that looked really neat. . . . We had four different strollers for our son. We could not take one inside the air-raid shelter, so we left it outside, where it was destroyed.

During the last two years of the war, Harry was assigned duty as an air-raid warden. He recalled many occasions when he watched buildings burn after attacks and wondered about the reactions of residents: "During those times of stress, we often saw people doing things that were not rational. For example, people would throw their belongings out the windows of burning houses but did not think about the fact that the things would break [when they hit the ground]. All they could think about was how to save their property."

After a terrible raid on December 26, 1943, Harry's wife and their little boy were put on a bus and sent to an unspecified location at a safe distance from Kiel. They were eventually assigned a room in the town of Lütjenburg (eighteen miles to the east). The confusion of the times was such that several months passed before Harry found out where his family was and before they found out that he was still alive back in Kiel. Any hope of a normal life together must have seemed impossible to them under those conditions.

Harry joined his family in Lütjenburg before the British army arrived there on May 5, 1945, and the war ended. The takeover was peaceful, but local residents were subject to a strict curfew. Harry had to sneak around town at night to find a midwife to assist in the birth of his daughter.

Upon finally returning to Kiel in 1946, Harry Christensen established contact with the LDS branch there and met the branch president. "He kept everybody together," Harry explained.

Back in Flensburg, the branch members likely experienced similar losses as they too tried to survive in a port city. As of this writing, no information is available regarding the location or frequency of church meetings among the Latter-day Saints who remained in Flensburg.

In Memoriam

The following members of the Flensburg Branch did not survive World War II:

Hellmuth Hermann E. Ahrnes b. Toftlund, Schleswig-Holstein, 17 Jul 1912; son of Hermann Ahrnes and Margarethe Sören; bp. 17 Sep 1932; conf. 17 Sep 1932; rifleman; k. in battle Jewanowa, Russia, 2 Aug 1941; bur. Korostyn, Russia (CHL microfilm 2448, pt. 27, no. 413; www.volksbund.de; IGI)

Uwe Andersen b. Flensburg, Schleswig-Holstein, 4 Jan 1940; son of Albert Andersen and Elly Schröder; d. stroke 20 Apr 1940 (CHL microfilm 2448, pt. 27, no. 505)

Fritz Ludwig Beuermann b. Flensburg, Schleswig-Holstein, 18 May 1924; son of Ludwig Friedrich Diedrich Beuermann and Hedwig Luise Schwichtenberg; bp. 17 Sep 1932; conf. 17 Sep 1932; lance corporal; k. in battle north of Podujevo 2 Nov 1944 (CHL microfilm 2448, pt. 27, no. 360; www.volksbund.de)

Alfred August Dittmer b. Flensburg, Schleswig-Holstein, 30 Oct 1927; son of Albert August Dittmer and Wilhelmine Johnsen; bp. 1 Sep 1936; conf. 1 Sep 1936; grenadier; k. in battle 8 Jan 1945; bur. Recogne-Bastogne, Belgium (CHL microfilm 2458, form 42 FP, pt. 37, all mission list 1938–45, 137–38; CHL microfilm 2448, pt. 27, no. 359; www.volksbund.de)

Julius Heinrich Grell b. Hamburg 5 May 1874; son of Franz Grell and Emilie von Eitzen; d. 28 Jul 1944 (CHL CR 375 8 2458, 840–41)

Fritz Emil Hansen b. Flensburg, Schleswig-Holstein, 6 Aug 1921; son of Friedrich Peter Christian Hansen and Elsabe Wilhelmine Johanna Louise von Ehren; bp. 15 Aug 1929; conf. 15 Aug 1929; noncommissioned officer; k. in battle close to Jankapass Peijapolje-Pass-Pleolja, 25 Nov 1944 (CHL microfilm 2448, pt. 27, no. 317; www.volksbund.de; FHL microfilm 162773, 1930 and 1935 censuses; IGI)

Constanz Klindt b. Twedterfeld, Schleswig-Holstein, 22 Jun 1922; son of Hans Christensen Klindt and Constanze Amalie Lorenzen; bp. 16 Aug 1930; d. 10 Feb 1945 or 1 May 1947 (SLCGW; IGI)

Hans Bruno Klindt b. Twedterfeld, Schleswig-Holstein, 28 Jun 1919; son of Hans Christensen Klindt and Constanze Amalie Lorenzen; bp. 27 Aug 1928; MIA Forst 1 Apr 1945 (SLCGW; www.volksbund.de)

Walter Rolf Hans Christian Klindt b. Flensburg, Schleswig-Holstein, 4 Oct 1914; son of Hans Christensen Klindt and Constanze Amalie Lorenzen; MIA Stalingrad, Russia, 1 Jan 1943 (SLCGW; www.volksbund.de)

Otto Fritz Edward Siegmund b. Plön, Schleswig-Holstein, 11 Jan 1877 or 1887; son of Johann Heinrich Julius Siegmund and Sophia Dorothea Henriette Genske; bp. 10 Nov 1923; conf. 11 Nov 1923; ord. deacon 2 Jun 1929; ord. teacher 2 Nov 1930; ord. priest 27 Apr 1932; ord. elder 8 May 1934; d. suicide 18 or 19 Oct 1940 (CHL microfilm 2448, pt. 27, no. 227; FHL microfilm 245264; 1925, 1930, and 1935 censuses; IGI)

Uwe Wischniewski b. Flensburg, Schleswig-Holstein, 9 Feb 1940; son of Ernst-Walter Nikolaus Tollgaard and Gertraud Irmgard Christensen; d. Flensburg 20 Apr 1940; bur. Friedenshügel cemetery 24 Apr 1940 (CHL LR 2884 11, 230)

Notes

1. Flensburg Branch manuscript history, 230, CHL LR 2884 11.
2. Presiding Bishopric, "Financial, Statistical, and Historical Reports of Wards, Stakes, and Missions, 1884–1955," 257, CHL CR 4 12.
3. Flensburg Branch manuscript history, 232–44.
4. Harry Christian Wilhelm Christensen, interview by the author in German, Murray, UT, March 17, 2006; summarized in English by Judith Sartowski.
5. Flensburg Branch manuscript history, book 2, 10.
6. Ibid. 15.

FRIEDRICHSTADT BRANCH

The branch in Friedrichstadt was very isolated. The city was located just a few miles from the mouth of the Eider River at the North Sea, and Latter-day Saints there had to cross almost the entire breadth of Schleswig-Holstein (forty miles) to reach Kiel. The landscape around Friedrichstadt is extremely flat, some of the territory having been reclaimed from the North Sea since 1700 and protected ever since by a network of earthen dikes.

Friedrichstadt, a town of only 2,197 in 1939, had an LDS branch consisting of seventy-one souls, twelve of whom held the priesthood. Over two-thirds of the members were women over twelve years of age.[1] According to the list of branch officers, several members lived in towns and villages a few miles to the north, such as Husum and Mildstedt. Rail connections at the time were such that members who did not live in Friedrichstadt may have walked substantial distances to attend church meetings.

Friedrichstadt Branch[2]	**1939**
Elders	4
Priests	1
Teachers	1
Deacons	6
Other Adult Males	7
Adult Females	46
Male Children	1
Female Children	5
Total	71

Andreas D. Andresen was the president of the Friedrichstadt Branch in the summer of 1939. His counselors were Jakob H. Peters and a Brother Fuhrmann. The latter was also the superintendant of the Sunday School, while Brother Peters also directed the YMMIA. The leaders of the YWMIA and the Relief Society were respectively Johanne Danklefsen and Emma Micheelsen, while Friederike Peters was the local genealogical class instructor.

The branch meetings were held in the apartment of a Sister Vogt—in a single room, according to Dora Micheelsen (born 1923).[3] "The children often had to sit on the floor because the room was not large enough." The priesthood meeting began at 9:00 a.m. and was followed by Sunday School at 10:00 and sacrament meeting at 2:00 p.m. The Relief Society sisters convened on Wednesdays at 6:30 p.m. and the MIA members at 7:30. A genealogy class was held on the second Sunday of the month at 1:00 p.m.

Baptisms were conducted in the Treene River, which flows through Friedrichstadt into the Eider. There was no need to keep the ceremonies secret because relationships with people of other religions were quite unencumbered in those days, as Dora recalled: "I had a Jewish friend, and I took her to church, and I also went to the synagogue with her." Even though the branch members were instructed to avoid singing hymns with the words *Israel* and *Zion*, Dora stated that they did not observe the rule.

One of the few quiet corners of the war in Germany was certainly the area of Schleswig-Holstein around Friedrichstadt. The vicinity was not home to significant industrial or transportation installations and thus was not particularly attractive to Allied bombers. Although the residents there heard bombers overhead on their way to other locations in Germany, few bombs fell on Friedrichstadt. According to Dora, "All in all, I have to say that we got through the war pretty well. We didn't have much to complain about." While they were not bombed out or driven out of town, the residents of Friedrichstadt were called upon to house some of the millions of refugees from eastern Germany. Dora explained that her family took in nine refugees: "We all felt like we were engaged in a common cause." That cause, in the last year of the war, was simply survival.

Dora Micheelsen recalled that the Friedrichstadt Branch was never without a place to meet on a Sunday ("but there were difficulties now and then") and that there was always at least one priesthood holder to provide the required leadership and services. Her own mother died during the war, but Dora had younger siblings to care for and her family employment to keep her sufficiently busy. Regarding her well-being as a member of the Church, she had this to say in retrospect:

> During the war, my testimony grew and grew. With all the things we had to go through, our Heavenly Father protected us and helped us find a way. We used to say to each other, "It's so good that we have the Church in our lives!" Whatever happened, we seemed to think about the Church first and how it could help us. It was the first thing we turned to.

The little Friedrichstadt Branch in its rural setting survived the war in general, but two of the members died in the service of their country, two more disappeared and were not seen again, and two more died of illnesses not common in peacetime. There were enough members left in the summer of 1945 to carry on the activities of faithful Latter-day Saints.

In Memoriam

The following members of the Friedrichstadt Branch did not survive World War II:

Andreas Martin Albertsen b. Mildstedt, Husum, Schleswig-Holstein, 12 May 1909; son of Albert Bahne Albertsen and Anna Maria Petersen; bp. 10 Jul 1920; conf. 10 Jul 1920; lance corporal; k. in battle Ravienna or Russia 3 Mar 1944 (CHL CR 275 8, no. 1; www.volksbund.de; FHL microfilm 25708; 1925 and 1930 censuses; IGI)

Gottfried Ernst Bernhard Christiansen b. Mildstedt, Husum, Schleswig-Holstein, 2 Apr 1915; son of Johannes Wilhelm Friedrich Christiansen and Anna Sass or Christiansen; bp. 16 Jul 1924; conf. 16 Jul 1924; sergeant; k. near Goldberg, Schlesien, 8 Mar 1945 (CHL microfilm 2448, pt. 27, no. 78; www.volksbund.de; IGI)

Gertrud Rosa Degen b. Elmshorn, Schleswig-Holstein, 23 Oct 1912; dau. of Willy Degen and Maria Kohn; bp. 17 Jul 1921; conf. 17 Jul 1921; missing as of 20 Feb 1942 (CHL microfilm 2448, pt. 27, no. 91; FHL microfilm 25753; 1925, 1930, and 1935 censuses)

Henning Detlef Franzen b. Hude, Husum, Schleswig-Holstein, 21 Mar 1870; son of Henning Detlef Franzen and Anna Dorothea Olm or Ohm; bp. 5 Jun 1921; conf. 5 Jun 1921; ord. deacon 18 Jun 1922; ord. priest 1924; m. 11 Jun 1909; d. lung disease 19 Nov 1940 (CHL microfilm 2448, pt. 27, no. 95; FHL microfilm 25769; 1935 census; IGI)

Peter Franzen b. Hude, Husum, Schleswig-Holstein, 14 Apr 1911; son of Henning Detlef Franzen and Helene Margarethe Spiecker; bp. 5 Jun 1921; conf. 5 Jun 1921; ord. deacon 28 Mar 1927; m. 20 Aug 1939, Kaethe Kroger; d. typhus 30 Apr 1944 (CHL CR 275 8, no. 1; CHL microfilm 2448, pt. 27, no. 97; IGI)

Emma Catharina Peters b. Moordorf, Steinburg, Schleswig-Holstein, 7 Oct 1893; dau. of Claus Peters and Anna Catharine Kunstmann or Kuntzmann; bp. 5 Jun 1921; conf. 5 Jun 1921; m. Breitenberg, Schleswig-Holstein, 28 Jan 1915, Karl August Brassat; 1 child; 2m. Friedrichstadt, Schleswig-Holstein, 11 Mar 1922, Claus Christian Bernhard Micheelsen; 4 children; d. stomach cancer Tönning, Schleswig-Holstein, 2 Aug 1944 (CHL microfilm 2448, pt. 27, no. 185; FHL microfilm 245233; 1930, 1935 censuses; IGI; AF; PRF)

Karl Rehder b. Flensburg, Schleswig-Holstein, 14 Sep 1905; son of Karl Rehder and Bertha Mölln; bp. 31 Aug 1929; conf. 31 Aug 1929; missing as of 20 Jan 1940 (CHL microfilm 2448, pt. 27, no. 321; FHL microfilm 271400; 1930 and 1935 censuses)

Erna Theede b. Drage, Friedrichstadt, Schleswig-Holstein, 17 Oct 1912; dau. of Jürgen Theede and Katharina Kirchner; bp. 18 Jun 1922; conf. 18 Jun 1922; d. tuberculosis 24 Aug 1944 (CHL microfilm 2448, pt. 27, no. 254; FHL microfilm 245283; 1925, 1930, and 1935 censuses; IGI)

Margarethe Theede b. Hohn, Rendsburg, Schleswig-Holstein, 17 Oct 1901; dau. of Jürgen Theede and Katharina Kirchner; bp. 18 Jun 1922; conf. 18 Jun 1922; d. typhus 10 April 1944 (CHL microfilm 2448, pt. 27, no. 422; FHL microfilm 245283; 1925, 1930, and 1935 censuses)

Notes

1. West German Mission branch directory, 1939, CHL LR 10045 11.
2. Presiding Bishopric, "Financial, Statistical, and Historical Reports of Wards, Stakes, and Missions, 1884–1955," 257, CHL CR 4 12.
3. Dora Micheelsen Zentner, telephone interview with Jennifer Heckmann in German, March 6, 2009; summarized in English by Judith Sartowski.

Kiel Branch

The port city of Kiel is located on a fjord of the Baltic Sea near the eastern end of the canal that joins the Baltic to the North Sea. The capital of the province of Schleswig-Holstein for many years, the city had 261,298 inhabitants when World War II began. As a crucial venue for maritime operations, the city's workforce was primarily occupied in the construction and maintenance of ships of war.

Kiel Branch[1]	**1939**
Elders	13
Priests	6
Teachers	3
Deacons	14
Other Adult Males	28
Adult Females	101
Male Children	6
Female Children	4
Total	175

The branch of The Church of Jesus Christ of Latter-day Saints in Kiel was relatively strong, with 175 members, among whom were thirty-six priesthood holders. Since May 4, 1936, the branch meetings had been held in rented rooms in the old Hotel Kronprinz at Hafenstrasse 13–15.[2] The branch president at the time was Kurt Müller, and it was his honor to greet Elder Joseph Fielding Smith in Kiel for a conference on August 22, 1939. Elder Smith and his wife, Jessie Evans Smith, were traveling with mission president M. Douglas and Evelyn Wood through northern Germany. Saints from other branches in the district were among the 108 persons who attended the event. Little did anyone know that the visitors and American missionaries in Germany would be instructed to leave the country just three days later.[3]

Fig. 1. Else Mueller and her infant son Lothar in 1940. (L. Mueller)

The branch directory for the late summer of 1939 shows leaders in all organizations except for the Primary. Wilhelm Metelmann and Heinz Kuhr were the counselors to Kurt Müller; Felix Schmidt, the superintendent of the Sunday School; and Gustav Girnus, the leader of the YMMIA. Eva Behrendt led the YWMIA, and Fanny Metelmann was the president of the Relief Society. Brother Metelmann was also the genealogy expert, and *Der Stern* magazine was promoted by Johann Ceglowski.[4]

Ursula Leschke (born 1930) was baptized by the American missionaries on the beach by the Kiel harbor just before the war began. Her father was not a member of the Church, but her mother was dedicated to the gospel and took Ursula along as she made visits to sisters of the Relief Society. The family lived in the suburbs east of the harbor. Ursula recalled making the long walk to the harbor, then taking a ferry across to the city center, then walking about fifteen minutes to the Hafenstrasse address.[5]

The location of the branch rooms was nice (very close to the city center), but Ursula recalled some negative aspects of the facility: "It was an old beer hall, and we had to clean it up every week before we could use it. I believe that it was just one large room with a small podium."

The war that began in September 1939 was not the only challenge Brother Müller had to deal with in those days. According to the branch history, high water from the Kiel Fjord reached the old Hotel Kronprinz on October 29, and church meetings were canceled.[6] The same problem occurred on January 21, 1940, and on November 2, 1941.

Changes happened quickly in the LDS Church in the first months of the war, principally because many of the brethren were drafted into the army and had to be replaced in their callings. So it was that Kurt Müller was called to be the president of the Schleswig-Holstein District on December 10, 1939. His successor as branch president was Wilhelm Metelmann.

Fig. 2. The Kiel Branch met in rooms in the old Hotel Kronprinz at Hafenstrasse 13–15 (on the right side). This photograph was used for a postcard in the 1920s. (K. Goldmund)

Karla Radack (born 1930) was sent away from her home in Kiel three times as part of the Kinderlandverschickung program, each time for about nine months. "I was first in Göhren on the island of Rügen, where we used to go to the beach and pick sea grass. The second time, I went to [the state of] Thuringia. The third time was in Frankenstein in Saxony. Our teacher and our [League of German Girls] leader always came along. I was able to go home between all those trips, but I had no contact with the Church when I was away from home."[7]

Fig. 3. The Radack home on Langenbergstrasse in Kiel. (K. Radack Siebach)

On one of those trips, Karla saw something she could hardly have comprehended at her age. "In Thuringia we were transported by train. Another train passed us on the other side, and it was full of Jewish people being transported to concentration camps. A lot of German people had water in their hands, and they walked up and gave it to them. That was one of my first recollections of those happenings." She had no way of knowing the fate of those Jews under a government determined to rid the country of the race.

At the age of sixteen, Ehrenfried Radack (born 1926) was already an active participant in the war. He was drafted along with his schoolmates to operate an antiaircraft battery at the outskirts of Kiel. He was frightened to shoot at airplanes cruising overhead on their way to attack Kiel. As he recalled, "We had seen them destroy our city piece by piece. . . . We had our classes right there [at] the battery, and we continued our education while we were serving our country."[8]

One of the favorite activities of German LDS branches was the baptismal ceremony that happened perhaps once or twice a year. The Kiel Branch history lists only three such occasions during the war years. On two of those occasions, a leader of the West German Mission (Christian Heck or Anton Huck) presided and participated. Baptisms in the Kiel Branch took place on a beach or in a bathhouse.

Verwendung als Führer — Leiter erfolgte:

Von 15.7.42 bis

als Kameradschaftsführer

Marine-HJ-Gefolgschaft 5/184

Kiel Karl Stein

Unterschrift des vorgesetzten Führers.

Von ... bis ...

als ...

Unterschrift des vorgesetzten Führers.

Von ... bis ...

als ...

Unterschrift des vorgesetzten Führers.

Verwendung als Führer — Leiter erfolgte:

Von ... bis ...

als ...

Unterschrift des vorgesetzten Führers.

Von ... bis ...

als ...

Unterschrift des ... Führers.

Von ... bis ...

als ...

Unterschrift des vorgesetzten Führers.

Führerausweis

der

Hitler-Jugend

Figs. 4 and 5. Like almost all children in Hitler's Germany, Ehrenfried Radack was inducted into the Jungvolk at age ten. (R. Radack)

Ursula Leschke's father worked as a naval engineer designing submarines. At one point in the war, his office was moved to a place near Hanover, away from the threat of air raids. At home, Ursula's mother, Ellie, failed to fly the swastika flag from her window at the expected times. One day, she found a note pushed through the mail slot by her door—likely by a patriotic neighbor—reminding her of her duty. Her mother also did not greet people with the customary "Heil Hitler!" and one day was challenged by a loyal schoolteacher to explain her actions. According to Ursula, her mother offered a brave reply:

> My mother said, "I don't believe in it. I don't think he is a righteous man or that he's doing the right things." Afterwards my mother went home, and she was just scared to death because Fräulein Müller, my teacher, could have easily denounced her to the authorities and my mother would have ended up in a concentration camp. She told me that she went home and she really prayed that Heavenly Father might protect her that she might not be turned in.

All over Germany, LDS men were answering the call to arms, but at least one member of the Church declined to do so. Karla Radack recalled the situation with her uncle:

Fig. 6. Members of the Kiel Branch in 1944 on an outing in a local forest. (M. Radack Kramer)

> My uncle Helmut Radack was picked up because he did not want to join the army. One early morning, soon after he had decided against it, he was picked up and put in a concentration camp. He passed away in that camp. They sent the ashes to my grandmother, but my parents later found out that those weren't his ashes after all. They were probably just scooped up and sent to them in an urn. It was very sad for them.[9]

It is interesting to note that while building materials were scarce all over Germany during the war, the branch was able to secure what they needed to renovate the rooms at Hafenstrasse 13–15. Perhaps the challenge of finding the needed materials contributed to the long term of renovation that lasted from October 18, 1942, to March 7, 1943. No details regarding the work done are available.

Sometime during the intermediate war years, Ursula Leschke was sent to Bansin on the Baltic Sea island of Usedom as part of the Kinderlandverschickung program. Later, her group was transferred to the city of Bromberg in occupied Poland. In the late summer of 1944, that area was in the path of the invading Red Army, so Ursula and her classmates were sent home to Kiel. Back at home, she learned that her school had been destroyed, so she was required to live in Neumünster (twenty miles to the south), where a school was available. However, Allied airplanes soon attacked that city, and the school there was destroyed too. She returned to Kiel to stay and to experience the end of the war. "By then, the harbor ferry was destroyed and we had to walk all the way around [the south end of] the harbor to attend church meetings."

Even in Kiel, one of the prime targets for Allied bombers, it was possible for children to have some fun during the war. Karla Radack had this recollection:

> To have fun as kids and teenagers, we went out and looked for shells from bombs. I had a little cigar box that I got from a store. My friends and I liked to collect the outside copper shell cases of antiaircraft ammunition. Those were the best pieces, which we would trade. But we also found toys that blew up when you touched them.[10] We used to go to roller-skate, play ball and games. We also went to the beach quite often.

A traditional thrill for German children (and often their parents as well) was a visit by Adolf Hitler. Karla recalled how they heard that the Führer was supposed to come to the harbor in Kiel one day: "My father and I went down there. He bought a little folding chair because the vendor was yelling, '*Wer den Führer heut' will sehen, muss auf einem Klappstuhl stehen*' [If you want to see our leader, you'll need a folding chair.] I sat on his shoulders and was able to see the Führer."

Fig. 7. Karla Radack in a dress made out of her father's old army coat. (K. Radack Siebach)

After finishing public school, Karla was called upon to serve her Pflichtjahr (duty year). She and a friend were assigned to a family with little children in a town not far from Kiel. Unfortunately, the host family did not treat Karla and her friend very well at all. On one occasion, the girls simply went home to Kiel, but the leaders of the Pflichtjahr program forced them to return. Finally, Karla's mother went to pick up the girls and rescue them from the ill treatment.

In January 1944, Ehrenfried Radack was drafted and classified as an officer candidate. Following five months of training in Oldenburg, he was sent to Saarlautern, near the French border. While there, he learned of the assassination attempt on Adolf Hitler on July 20. His company commander assembled the men, informed them of the abortive attempt, and instructed them that from that time forward they were to use the Hitler salute (the straight, raised right arm) rather than the traditional military salute. As Ehrenfried recalled, "Our commander did not seem to be happy about [the new salute]."[11]

In Saarlautern, Ehrenfried somehow contracted diphtheria and was hospitalized for six weeks. When he asked to return to his unit, the physician ordered him to remain for several more weeks. By the time he returned to the Western Front, the Allies were making steady advances through France and Belgium toward Germany. Soon, Ehrenfried developed an infection in his foot and was again hospitalized, despite the assertion of his sergeant that he was only trying to avoid combat duty. He later realized that his medical problems were blessings in disguise: "How lucky I was; while I was in the hospital, our unit had to fight around Aachen with heavy losses. As I was told later, only one of our group survived." When he was subsequently transferred from town to town within Germany, he realized that "everything went like it was foreseen [predestined] for me." He never saw combat on the Western Front but should have on at least two occasions.[12]

The city of Kiel and its harbor were bombed many times during the war, but the air raid of July 24, 1944, was especially tragic for the Latter-day Saints. The old Hotel Kronprinz was destroyed, and somewhere in Kiel, Wilhelm Metelmann was killed. One week later, a sad branch welcomed

Fig. 8. Members of the Kiel Branch in 1944. (M. Radack Kramer)

Edwin Küchler as their new leader. Gustav Girnus and Walter Köcher continued to serve as the counselors.

"Brother Metelmann had done a lot of genealogy," recalled Ursula Leschke. She recalled hearing that the branch president was not killed in an air-raid shelter but had died during the firestorm that followed the bombing.

With the destruction of the branch rooms and the apparent lack of suitable rooms elsewhere in the city, the branch began to hold meetings in the homes of members. The history lists the names of six families who hosted Sunday services from October 1944 to March 1945: Girnus, Starkjohann, Leschke, Metelmann, Heimann, and Radack. It is likely that the attendance by that time had been substantially reduced by calls to military service and the departure of mothers with small children to safer places. The remaining Saints could indeed be accommodated in the largest room of a typical apartment.

Karla Radack was in Kiel for the last year of the war and thus experienced many of the worst air raids against that port city. The shelters constructed for the residents were enormous and solid, but she recalled the lack of sufficient ventilation and the air that was almost too thin to support life. People were sitting almost on top of each other, and anxiety was always high, she explained.

> Toward the end of the war, we went to bed with our clothes on and with a suitcase ready. I remember one time when the sirens went off, my father came to help me get dressed. But I didn't want to wake up and was still half asleep. I remember that was the only time that he hit me. The people were running in the streets, and everything was so crowded. Parents had their babies in little

> baskets and carried them on each side. A voice from the loudspeaker told us to hurry up because the Allied planes were nearly over Kiel.

Young Marlies Radack (born 1940) could recall little more than air raids during her first five years of life: "That was a nightly thing. We slept in our clothes. There was nothing we could do about it, and it happened every night. You take it day by day. And if you don't know anything different, it's pretty normal."[13] Marlies explained that she and her mother usually sat in the basement of their apartment building during the attacks unless there was time to run to the closest public bunker. "One night, a bomb hit really close to the house. And then there was one that was by our door and it didn't explode. They had to call somebody to defuse it. The glass in our windows was all broken. If that bomb had gone off, we wouldn't have [survived]."

In early December 1944, Corporal Ehrenfried Radack left Germany on a train headed for Wiener Neustadt, a city south of Vienna, Austria. He was to complete officer candidate training there. In March he and his comrades were informed that if they completed the final examination, they would be promoted to second lieutenant on April 20, Hitler's birthday. Ehrenfried was indeed one of those who passed the test, but before he could enjoy his new status, it was learned that the Soviet army had broken through the German lines near the border of Austria and Hungary, just a few miles to the east. There followed a most confusing confrontation with the invaders, and Ehrenfried and his friends were sent with small arms to fight against the feared Soviet T-34 tank.

Fig. 9. Ehrenfried Radack in the uniform of an officer candidate. (R. Radack)

In the battle that ensued, Ehrenfried watched as his friends were killed, and he was the only survivor. Captured, he was nearly executed several times within one hour. Fortunately, a Soviet officer recognized his rank and singled him out for better treatment. On their way away from the fighting, an odd incident occurred. Ehrenfried wrote this account:

> [The Soviet officer and I] approached a trench dug across the road. At this time, when we got ready to jump over, something made me push the Russian officer into the trench with me following him, when [an artillery round] fired by the German artillery hit and exploded at the very spot where we had been standing. He looked at me realizing what had happened, and while we were still in the trench, he shared with me his ration of food. When we finally got up to proceed a few minutes later, he turned me over to a Russian soldier giving him strict orders to take me safely to the battalion commander. He then went away as suddenly as he had appeared to save my life.[14]

Lieutenant Radack had survived his first and only combat experience, but he would later describe the adventure that began that day as "the beginning of a long tragedy." With a thousand other German POWs, he was marched through Austria, Hungary, and other countries on their way to the Black Sea. By the early summer of 1945, he was in the city of Krapotkin, Russia, where his first job was to help rebuild a sunflower factory.[15]

Fig. 10. Edeltraud Radack sending Morse code messages in Husum. (K. Radack Siebach)

Fig. 11. Edeltraud Radack at the beach sitting on a defused sea mine. (K. Radack Siebach)

Karla Radack's last wartime assignment required her to work in a submarine construction facility where she was given drafting projects for four months. That work ended when the facility was bombed out of commission in early 1945.

The branch history does not list any meeting dates between March 11, 1945, and August 19, 1945. It is possible that the events of the last months of the war and the first months of the British military occupation did not facilitate gatherings. On September 12, 1945, Gustav Girnus was installed as the branch president. It would be largely his charge to rebuild the Kiel Branch from the ruins of that large but devastated port city.

The span of Ehrenfried Radack's military service during the war (just sixteen months) was very short compared to his time as a POW in the Soviet Union. Year after year dragged by for the young man as he battled to stay healthy, all the while longing for home. Two letters written to his family in Kiel reflect his thinking in the last months of his incarceration:

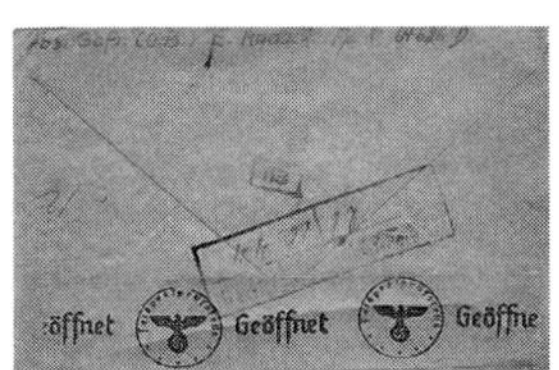

Fig. 12. The envelope carrying Ehrenfried Radack's letter home to his parents was opened by censors. The stamp (geöffnet, *"opened") attests to the process.* (R. Radack)

> February 15, 1949:
>
> My beloved ones, next month it will be four years since my last farewell to you. I remember it so well. Who would have realized then that our reunion would be so far away and still not even know when the time will come. . . . It is difficult to preserve the spiritual and moral strengths, but if I didn't have any faith and all you have taught me, I would have turned out to be like everybody else. . . . Here I have to live the life how it is in reality but still preserve my own dignity.[16]
>
> June, 1949:
>
> I look forward to be together with you again. Many things will have changed at home in the four years I was gone. . . . I, too, have changed, more matured by the hard and true face of life. It has pulled me away from the dream world of my youth for life into an unmerciful period of time. But this has given me strength and knowledge and faith and the desire to always choose the right. . . . I know our Father in Heaven will hold his protecting arm around me until we meet again.[17]

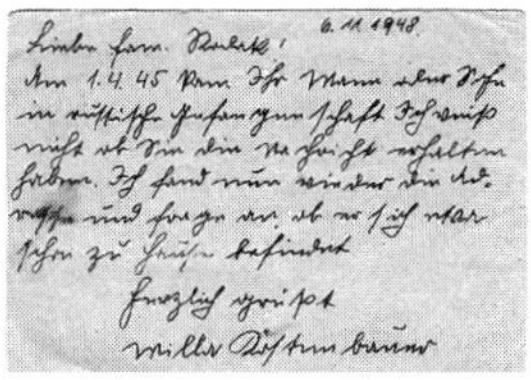

Fig. 13. This card was sent by German POW Milla Köstenbauer to the Radack family in Kiel in 1948: "I don't know if you have been informed that your son was taken prisoner by the Russians. Or is he already home again?" (R. Radack)

In August 1949, still in only his twenty-fourth year, he was released from captivity in the Soviet Union and returned to his family in Kiel. He was one of the last Latter-day Saints of the West German Mission to come home after the war, but he had seen enough death in the camps to know that many other German soldiers would never come home.

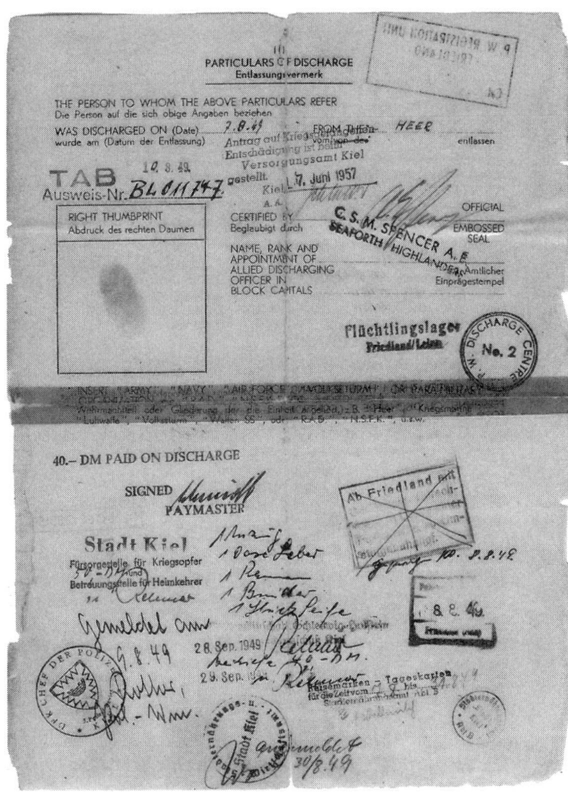

PARTICULARS OF DISCHARGE
Entlassungsvermerk

THE PERSON TO WHOM THE ABOVE PARTICULARS REFER
Die Person auf die sich obige Angaben beziehen
WAS DISCHARGED ON (Date) 7.8.49 FROM THE HEER
wurde am (Datum der Entlassung) entlassen

TAB 10. 8. 49.
Ausweis-Nr. BL 011747
Antrag auf Kriegsgefangenen-Entschädigung ist beim Versorgungsamt Kiel gestellt. Kiel 17. Juni 1957

RIGHT THUMBPRINT
Abdruck des rechten Daumen

CERTIFIED BY
Begleubigt durch
NAME, RANK AND APPOINTMENT OF ALLIED DISCHARGING OFFICER IN BLOCK CAPITALS
C. S. M. SPENCER A. E.
SEAFORTH HIGHLANDERS

OFFICIAL EMBOSSED SEAL
Amtlicher Einprägestempel

Flüchtlingslager Friedland/Leine

DISCHARGE CENTRE No. 2

40.– DM PAID ON DISCHARGE

SIGNED
PAYMASTER

Ab Friedland

Stadt Kiel
Fürsorgestelle für Kriegsopfer und Betreuungsstelle für Heimkehrer

8. 8. 49.

28. Sep. 1949
29. Sep. 1949

30/8.49

Fig. 14. The release papers for POW Ehrenfried Radack in 1949. (R. Radack)

In Memoriam

The following members of the Kiel Branch did not survive World War II:

Walter Erich Baron b. Breslau, Schlesien, 15 May 1919; son of Alfred Fritz Baron and Meta Klara Cäcilie Kosalek; bp. 17 Dec 1935; conf. 17 Dec 1935; k. in battle (CHL microfilm 2458, Form 42 FP, pt. 37, all-mission list 1945–46, 170–71; CHL microfilm 2448, pt. 27, no. 489; IGI)

Paula Johanna Christine Anna Dibbert b. Regensburg, Oberpfalz, Bayern, 4 Jul 1888; dau. of Johannes Peter Detlef Dibbert and Johanna Christine M. Dibbert; bp. 24 Jul 1929; conf. 24 Jul 1929; m. —— Kol; d. nerve condition 17 May 1941 (CHL microfilm 2448, pt. 27, no. 314; IGI)

Max Wilhelm Friedrich Drews b. Trassenheide, Usedom, Pommern, 6 Sep 1884; son of Johann Karl Friedrich Drews and Marie Wilhelmine Friederike Lewerentz; bp. 23 Dec 1922; conf. 23 Dec 1922; m. Kiel, Schleswig-Holstein 17 Nov 1906, Emma Ottilie Emilie Schmalz; 4 children; d. heart condition Pahlhude, Dittmarschen, Schleswig-Holstein, 29 July 1945 (CHL microfilm 2448, pt. 27, no. 86; FHL microfilm no. 25757, 1925, 1930, 1935 censuses; IGI; AF)

Rudolph Paul Heinz Otto Haak b. Kiel, Schleswig-Holstein, 15 Mar 1924; son of Konrad Friedrich Heinrich Haak and Marie Louise Niehus; bp. 4 Jun 1932; conf. 5 Jun 1932; ord. deacon 9 Apr 1939; navy lieutenant; k. in battle near Essel, Hannover, 12 Apr 1945; bur. Essel, Germany (CHL microfilm 2458, form 42 FP, pt. 37, all-mission list 1938–45, 137–38; CHL microfilm 2448, pt. 27, no. 118; www.volksbund.de; IGI)

Anni Sophie Katharina Hutzfeldt b. Kiel, Schleswig-Holstein, 2 Feb 1913; dau. of Waldemar Ludwig Hutzfeldt and Emma Eliese Dorothea Schlueter; bp. 10 Nov 1923; conf. 11 Nov 1923; m. 9 Mar 1935, Waldemar Claussen; k. air raid Kiel (CHL microfilm 2458, form 42 FP, pt. 37, all-mission list, 1945–46, 170–71; CHL microfilm 2448, pt. 27, no. 132; IGI)

Hermann Gustav Jahn b. Landsberg/Warthe, Brandenburg, 5 Dec 1916; son of Gustav Jahn and Anna Nowakowsky; bp. 13 Dec 1931; conf. 13 Dec 1931; ord. deacon 1 Jul 1934; noncommissioned officer; k. on air force bombing mission 24 Nov 1940; bur. Norderney, Hannover (CHL microfilm 2458, form 42 FP, pt. 37, 1949 list, 1490–91; www.volksbund.de; IGI)

Dorothea Henriette Friedericke Japp b. Altona, Schleswig-Holstein, 29 Jan 1866; dau. of Christian Heinrich Japp and Elisa Anna Marg Grammerstorf; bp. 16 Apr. 1920; conf. 16 Apr 1920; m. 17 Oct 1885, Ludwig Jürgens; d. old age 15 Sep 1943 or 15 Dec 1944 (CHL microfilm 2448, pt. 27, no. 147; FHL microfilm 271375; 1930 census; IGI; AF; PRF)

Hans Krämer b. 3 March 1909; k. Russia July 1942 (Marlies Radack Krämer)

Wilhelmine Kroll b. Schmoditten, Pr. Eylau, Ostpreußen, 14 May 1864; dau. of Wilhelmine Kroll; bp. 13 Sep 1927; conf. 13 Sep 1927; m. August Simon; d. old age 28 Jul 1941 (CHL microfilm 2448, pt. 27, no. 281; FHL microfilm 245265; 1935 census)

Herbert Fritz Karl Kuhr b. Kiel, Schleswig-Holstein, 16 Mar 1914; son of Heinrich Wilhelm Kuhr and Betty Emilie Jansen; bp. 5 Jun 1923; conf. 5 Jun 1923; ord. deacon 1 Jun 1930; lance corporal; k. in battle by Wesel, Rheinland, 26 Mar 1945; bur. Mönchengladbach-Haardt, Germany (CHL microfilm 2448, pt. 27, no. 154; FHL microfilm 271381; 1925, 1930, and 1935 censuses; www.volksbund.de; IGI, AF, PRF)

Heinrich Friedrich Wilhelm Metelmann b. Diepholz, Hannover, 22 Sep 1874; son of Johann Heinrich Hans Asmus Metelmann and Sophie Marie Elisabeth Dohse or Fahse; bp. 7 Jun 1930; conf. 8 Jun 1930; ord. deacon 19 Oct 1931; ord. teacher 2 Oct 1932; ord. priest 2 Dec 1934; ord. elder 17 May 1936; m. 17 Oct 1899, Fanny Wilhelmine Butenschön; k. air raid 24 Jul 1944 (CHL microfilm 2448, pt. 27, no. 334; FHL microfilm 245232; 1930 and 1935 censuses; IGI)

Helmut Evan Reinhold Radack b. Kiel, Schleswig-Holstein, 28 Apr 1912; son of Friedrich Wilhelm Gustav Ernst Radack and Rosa Christine Larsen Winter; bp. 21 Dec 1924; conf. 21 Dec 1924; d. 15 May 1941 (CHL microfilm 2448, pt. 27, no. 216; FHL microfilm 271398; 1925, 1930, and 1935 censuses; IGI)

Wilhelm Rosenkranz b. Kiel, Schleswig-Holstein, 24 Oct 1915; son of Johannes Heinrich Rosenkranz and Ema Sophia Antoinette Schaar; bp. Kiel 8 Oct 1932; conf. 8 Oct 1932; ord. deacon 1 Oct 1933; ord. teacher 10 Nov 1935; corporal; k. in battle near Wichotwice or Leczyca, Poland, 9 Sep 1939; bur. prob. Siemianowice, Poland (*Der Stern*, Oct 1939, 372; www.volksbund.de; CHL microfilm 2448, pt. 27, no. 418; IGI)

Therese Auguste Mathilde Sakolowski b. Elisabethsthal, Bütow, Köslin, Pommern, 14 Feb 1876; dau. of Wilhelm Erdmann Sakolowski and Karoline Wilhelmine Albrecht; bp. 10 Nov 1923; conf. 10 Nov 1923; m. 4 Nov 1899, Julius Kretschmann (div.); 2m. Kiel, Schleswig-Holstein, 2 Mar 1918, Wilhelm Heinrich Martin Geist; 3 children; d. lung and heart problems Kiel 12 Jan 1943 (CHL microfilm 2448, pt. 27, no. 105; FHL microfilm 25773; 1925, 1930, 1935 censuses; IGI, AF)

Marie Dorothea Sievers b. Jevenstedt, Rendsburg, Schleswig-Holstein, 2 Jul or Sep 1865; dau. of Claus Sievers and Magdalena Nickels; bp. 25 Jun 1927; conf.

25 Jun 1927; m. —— Clausen; d. old age 5 Apr 1942 (CHL microfilm 2448, pt. 27, no. 34; IGI)

Johann August Weiss b. Dirschau, Westpreußen, 15 Aug 1894; son of Henrietta Jantczel; bp. 20 Sep 1924; conf. 20 Sep 1924; m. Anna Wischnewski; d. stroke 29 Apr 1941 (CHL microfilm 2448, pt. 27, no. 269; FHL microfilm no. 245296; 1925, 1930, and 1935 censuses)

Rosa Christine Larsen Winter b. Haderslev, Haderslev, Denmark, 9 May 1865; dau. of Jens Larson Winter and Petruline Lund; bp. 8 or 9 May 1898; conf. 9 May 1898; m. Kiel, Schleswig-Holstein, 2 or 21 Aug 1893, Friedrich Wilhelm Gustav Ernst Radack; seven children; d. old age Kiel 8 Dec 1939 (CHL microfilm 2448, pt. 27, no. 215; FHL microfilm 271398; 1925, 1930, and 1935 censuses; IGI)

Notes

1. Presiding Bishopric, "Financial, Statistical, and Historical Reports of Wards, Stakes, and Missions, 1884–1955," 257, CHL CR 4 12.
2. Karl-Heinz Goldmund to the author, May 3, 2009. Goldmund located the date in a history of the Kiel Branch as well as on a postcard.
3. For details of the evacuation, see the West German Mission chapter.
4. West German Mission branch directory, 1939, CHL LR 10045 11.
5. Ursula Leschke, telephone interview with Jennifer Heckmann, October 24, 2008.
6. Kiel Branch History; copy courtesy of Karl-Heinz Goldmund.
7. Karla Radack Siebach, interview by Russell H. Michael and Judith Sartowski in German, Alpine, UT, February 20, 2010, summarized in English by Judith Sartowski.
8. Ehrenfried Radack, sacrament meeting talk, 4–5; private collection.
9. Helmut Radack was the only German LDS soldier to refuse to serve in the military.
10. Karla is one of several Church members who remembered enemy bombers dropping toys that were actually booby traps and that severely injured children who picked them up.
11. Ehrenfried Radack, "My Autobiography" (unpublished); private collection.
12. Ibid.
13. Marlies Radack Kramer, interview by Michael Corley, Sandy, UT, March 21, 2008.
14. Radack, "My Autobiography."
15. Radack, sacrament meeting talk, 9.
16. Ehrenfried Radack to Karl and Martha Radack, February 15, 1949; private collection.
17. Ehrenfried Radack to Karl and Martha Radack, June 1949; private collection.

Rendsburg Branch

Situated on the north bank of the Kiel Canal that connects the North and the Baltic Seas, the city of Rendsburg is in the middle of the German Schleswig-Holstein state. One of the smallest branches in Germany at the time, it nevertheless had enough members to fill Church auxiliary leadership positions in the months that preceded World War II. Thilo Hopf was the branch president, and he was assisted by one counselor, Wilhelm Nissen.[1] Those men were two of five priesthood holders among the Saints in Rendsburg.

Rendsburg Branch[2]	**1939**
Elders	3
Priests	0
Teachers	0
Deacons	2
Other Adult Males	5
Adult Females	16
Male Children	1
Female Children	0
Total	27

Other branch leaders were Marie Hopf (YWMIA) and Margarete Tank (Relief Society). These few Saints met in rented rooms at Altstätter Markt in downtown Rendsburg. Four of the weekly meetings were held on Sundays: Sunday School at 10:00, Mutual and the genealogy class at 6:00 p.m., and sacrament meeting at 7:00 p.m. The Relief Society sisters met on Tuesday evenings at 7:00 p.m.

The only information available regarding this small branch comes from the manuscript history in the collection of the Church History Library. The following entries are of interest for the war years:[3]

Tuesday, August 22, 1939: Joseph Fielding Smith spoke in Kiel. Nine members from Rendsburg attended.

Sunday, December 22, 1940: Due to illness, only seven persons attended the Christmas program.

Sunday, November 30, 1941: No meetings were held today; attendance is often only four persons nowadays.

Sunday, March 15, 1942: The centennial of the Relief Society was commemorated [the same program was presented a week later in Flensburg].

Sunday, May 3, 1942: The conference of the Schleswig-Holstein District was held in Flensburg; four persons from the Rendsburg Branch attended.

Sunday, May 2, 1943: The conference of the Schleswig-Holstein District was held in Kiel; several members from Rendsburg attend.

Sunday, September 26, 1943: The conference of the Schleswig-Holstein District was held in Kiel; three members from Rendsburg attended.

The records kept by the Rendsburg Branch clerk during the war years were very sparse. Nevertheless, attendance numbers were usually recorded and show that during the last months of the war (January–May 1945), the attendance at Sunday meetings fluctuated between three and five persons. Annual events in the branch included Mother's Day.

Due to a lack of other records and eyewitnesses, nothing more is known about the Rendsburg Branch during World War II. No members of the branch are known to have died during the war years or later as a result of the war.

Notes

1. West German Mission branch directory, 1939, CHL LR 10045 11.
2. Presiding Bishopric, "Financial, Statistical, and Historical Reports of Wards, Stakes, and Missions, 1884–1955," 257, CHL CR 4 12.
3. Rendsburg Branch manuscript history, CHL 7408 2. Page numbers of the entries quoted above are 142, 152, 158, 159, 162, 165, and 167.

STRASBOURG DISTRICT

West German Mission

At the outset of World War II, there were no organized branches in the province of Alsace-Lorraine, France. The territory was located on the west bank of the Rhine River and also bordered Germany's Palatinate and Rhineland provinces. The provinces changed hands between Germany and France several times and since 1918 had belonged to France. Most of the residents in the area spoke German, and both the Catholic Church and Protestant churches were well represented. In order to protect the region (and their entire nation, for that matter), the French had constructed a sophisticated line of defenses known as the Maginot Line. Located just a few miles from the German border, it was designed to stop any German attack. In May 1940, the German military disregarded the Maginot Line and simply moved around it, attacking France across the Belgian border to the west and conquering the Maginot Line from behind. The territory of Alsace-Lorraine was then placed under German military and political occupation authorities.

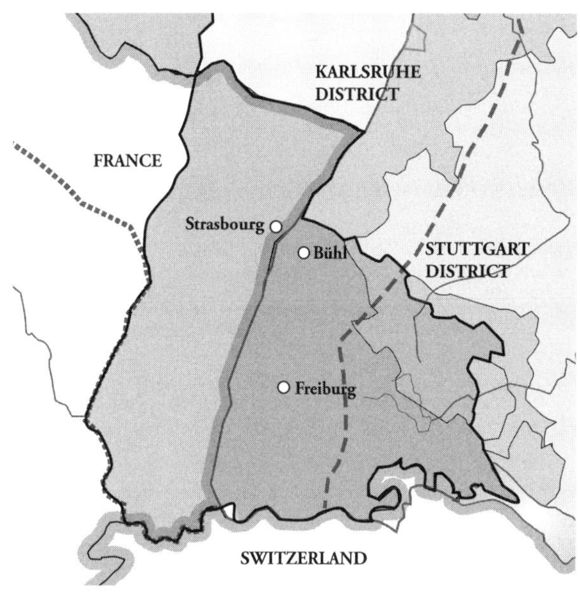

Fig. 1. The Strasbourg District consisted of Alsace-Lorraine in German-occupied France and a small portion of southwest Germany. It was the only district to be established in either German mission during the war.

During the first few years of the war, reports regarding branches in Alsace-Lorraine arrived in the mission office in Frankfurt. Mention was made of Latter-day Saints in the capital city of Strasbourg on the Rhine River and in Mülhausen (French: Mulhouse) to the south. The general minutes of the Bühl Branch (Karlsruhe District) report a number of activities undertaken by members in Bühl and across the Rhine in Strasbourg.[1] The first such report was dated March 3, 1942: Anton Huck (first counselor to the mission supervisor) conducted a funeral for a sister Maria Kuester in Strasbourg and two members of the Bühl Branch attended the service. On April 26, 1943, eleven Bühl Saints and eight from the Strasbourg Branch had a party at the home of the Paul Kaiser family in Grüneberg, near Strasbourg.

The arrival of Kurt and Charlotte Schneider in Strasbourg in 1940 was the decisive factor in making the Church better known in Alsace Lorraine. Brother Schneider had served a full-time mission in the Swiss-German Mission a few years earlier and was a devout Latter-day Saint who never tired of telling friends and acquaintances about his beliefs. It appears that he also enjoyed a close relationship with mission leaders at the time. It is very probable that the Schneiders used Kurt's company automobile (with a chauffeur) to facilitate religious and social interaction with the members of the Bühl Branch (just twenty-five miles northeast) and the Mülhausen Branch (fifty miles to the south) as well as with Latter-day Saints scattered among towns on both sides of the Rhine River. In every regard, Kurt Schneider was the right man to serve as the first (and only) district president.

The fact that Kurt was the director of the Thyssen Company's Strasbourg division did not mean that he was immune from suspicion under a government that kept close tabs on its citizens. Kurt had a radio hidden behind a secret panel in his company office and used the radio to listen illegally to enemy broadcasts. One day, he was prompted to change the dial to a German station just before turning it off. He recalled what happened next:

> About the time I was ready to leave my office again, two tall Nazi SS men in black uniforms with the swastika on their sleeves and guns in their belts entered my office. One leaned against the wall and touched the exact spot in the paneling which opened the secret compartment hiding the radio. They acted surprised, but I could tell that they had been tipped off. One of them reached over and turned on the radio, which began playing music from the German station in Stuttgart. Had the "Voice of America" still been on, they would have taken me away to be executed without further delay. . . . An answer to our prayers and exercises for protection? Yes![2]

In August 1943, a new meeting place for the Strasbourg Branch was dedicated under the leadership of Anton Huck. Eleven members of the Bühl Branch were in attendance, as were forty more members from the branches of Frankfurt, Saarbrücken, Karlsruhe, Mannheim, Pforzheim, and Freiburg. Paul Kaiser was the branch president in Strasbourg.

On December 12, 1943, Anton Huck presided over a meeting in which a new Strasbourg District was established, which included the neighboring branch in Bühl.[3] The only Alsace-Lorraine branches named in the record were those in Strasbourg and Mülhausen.[4] For the next year, several more activities involving Saints in occupied France and Bühl were reported in the Bühl Branch minutes.

In his company car, Kurt Schneider was able to visit the Saints in and around Strasbourg. His wife's diary notes excursions to such places as Mülhausen, Saarbrücken (in Germany), and Saarburg. Brother Schneider also used the car to drive to conferences in several cities in Germany, such as Frankfurt, Mannheim, and Karlsruhe. Due to the close relationship the Strasbourg Saints enjoyed with the members of the Bühl Branch, the Schneiders also traveled to that town and to Biberach and Lahr, where Bühl Branch members lived. They also visited isolated Church members in Zebelnheim and Freiburg in Germany.

On January 20, 1944, Kurt Schneider founded the newest branch of the Church in Germany in the city of Freiburg. The events of one week in February 1944 give a glimpse into the Church service rendered by Kurt Schneider and his family. On Tuesday, February 22, Anton Huck came from Frankfurt for a discussion with President Schneider.[5] On Thursday, the Schneiders drove their car north to Saarburg. According to Sister Schneider, "We were in the Schmidts' home this evening for dinner and for the night. We slept on the sofa because there was no bedding in the hotel. Late in the evening huge squadrons of airplanes flew over the city. I was scared because there were no shelters [close by]." The next night, enemy planes returned to Saarburg: "We sat in a shelter for awhile and heard bombs and saw illumination flares." Her diary entry the next day shows that they were already home again. The report was more encouraging: "We had a baptism today in the indoor swimming pool: Herr Dietlin and his wife. Then sacrament meeting; afterwards seven members from Mülhausen came to our apartment." It was a happy ending to a busy week.

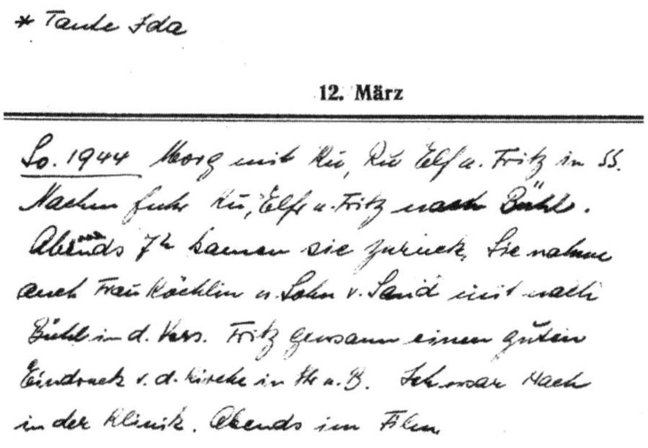

* Tante Ida

12. März

So. 1944 Morg. mit Kü, Rü Elf u. Fritz in SS. Nachm. fuhr Kü, Elf u. Fritz nach Bühl. Abends 7h kamen sie zurück. Sie nahmen auch Frau Röcklin u. Sohn v. Sand mit nach Bühl in d. Vers. Fritz gewann einen guten Eindruck v. d. Kirche in Str. u. B. Schwester Hach in der Klinik. Abends im Film.

Fig. 2. Charlotte Schneider made this entry on March 12, 1944: "This morning to Sunday School with Kurt, Ruth, Elfriede [Recksiek], and Fritz. Kurt drove Elfriede and Fritz to Bühl this afternoon. They returned at 7 p.m. They also took Mrs. Röcklitz and her son from Sand to the meetings in Bühl. Fritz was impressed by the Church in Strasbourg and Bühl. I went to the hospital [with Werner] and went to a movie this evening." (C. Bodon Schneider)

During the spring and summer of 1944, President Schneider visited several branches in both Germany and Alsace-Lorraine, sometimes accompanying Anton Huck, who by then was functioning as the mission supervisor. On the first weekend of June, the Schneiders hosted a two-day district conference. Charlotte did not indicate in her diary how many persons attended, but it appears that the conference was a success. Some Saints came from as far away as Stuttgart to participate in the event.

Kurt Schneider was a tireless worker whose influence spread over an ever-increasing area during the last year of the war. In July, Richard Ranglack (supervisor of the East German Mission) visited Strasbourg, and President Schneider soon reciprocated with a trip to Berlin. He met with the leaders of the East German Mission and attended meetings in several branches in the Reich's capital city. According to Charlotte, Kurt was very impressed with the Saints in the other German mission.

When the American army advanced toward Strasbourg in the late summer of 1944, Kurt Schneider received permission from his company to move his family to the town of Schönwald, in Germany's Black Forest. The move was not very far (forty-five miles), but it took them back into Germany and made it nearly impossible for him to maintain contact with members of the Church on the other side of the Rhine. The reconquest of Strasbourg by the Allies returned the provinces of Alsace-Lorraine to France and made Germans like Kurt Schneider unwelcome there.

The Schneiders arrived in Schönwald on August 26, 1944.[6] For the duration of the war, President Schneider devoted his efforts to his employer and to his family. Contact with the Saints became a rare event, but Kurt Schneider found many opportunities to discuss the gospel with people everywhere he went.

On November 6, Kurt received a telegram indicating that he was to report for military duty by November 8 "at the latest." Another telegram arrived on November 9 with instructions to report immediately. He disregarded both messages, but nobody inquired about his lack of obedience.[7] Two months later, he became quite ill and had to be admitted to the hospital in Triberg (three miles north of Schönwald). While there, he was visited by his wife and August Flad, of the Bühl Branch, who came to give him a priesthood blessing. Although seriously ill, Kurt was able to write a missionary tract, which his wife edited for him.

In early May, Kurt was arrested by French authorities and incarcerated for more than two weeks under (at times) harsh conditions. Once the French had collected sufficient evidence to determine that he was neither a soldier nor a dedicated National Socialist, he was released and sent home to his wife and his son in Schönwald.[8]

Of the three branches of the Strasbourg District, only the Bühl Branch in Germany was definitely holding meetings at the end of the war. It is not known whether the same was true of the Saints in Strasbourg or Mülhausen.

Notes

1. Bühl Branch general minutes, 144, CHL LR 1180 11.
2. Kurt Schneider, *Imagining Success* (Salt Lake City: Schneider, 1977), 276.
3. Bühl Branch general minutes, 150.
4. No reports have been found regarding the branch in Mülhausen.
5. Charlotte Bodon Schneider, diary (unpublished); used with permission.
6. Ibid.
7. Ibid.
8. See the details of his sixteen days as a prisoner of the French in the Strasbourg Branch chapter.

Bühl Branch

At the onset of World War II, the Bühl Branch was part of the Karlsruhe District. Located twenty-four miles southwest of Karlsruhe in the Rhine River Valley, Bühl was about the same distance from Strasbourg on the west side of the River. When the Strasbourg District was established in late 1943, the Bühl Branch and the Freiburg group of the Karlsruhe District were included under the leadership of Kurt Schneider of Strasbourg.

Bühl Branch[1]	**1939**
Elders	3
Priests	2
Teachers	0
Deacons	1
Other Adult Males	0
Adult Females	5
Male Children	0
Female Children	1
Total	12

The city of Bühl had about six thousand inhabitants in 1939. Only twelve of those were members of The Church of Jesus Christ of Latter-day Saints. A very rare characteristic of this branch was the fact that three (one-fourth) of those members were elders (Karl Josef Fetsch, August Friedrich Flad, and August Friedrich Haug) and three more (their sons) were holders of the Aaronic Priesthood. As it turned out, this branch enjoyed fine leadership and unity during the difficult years of the war.

The only other leader listed in the branch directory in the summer before the war began was Frieda Fetsch, president of the Relief Society.[2] The meetings were held in rented rooms at Grabenstrasse 5. Priesthood meeting began at 9:30 a.m., followed by Sunday School at 10:00. Sacrament meeting was scheduled for 7:00 p.m. The only other gatherings were MIA on Wednesdays at 7:30 p.m., Relief Society on Thursdays at 5:00 p.m., and a genealogical class on the first Wednesday of the month at 7:30 p.m.

Franz and Frieda Mussler lived in the spa city of Baden-Baden, just six miles from Bühl. Their children, Ursula (born 1929) and Hans Karl (born 1934), both recalled making the trip to Bühl on Sunday mornings to attend church. According to Ursula,

> The branch met at Grabenstrasse 5. The rooms were part of a one-family house. The Church rented five or six rooms. First, we held Sunday School in two separate groups—the adults and the children. Sacrament meeting followed. There weren't many of us in attendance (maybe twenty-five) but it was still enjoyable.[3]

Hans Karl Mussler described how they took the streetcar to the railroad station at Oos, then the train to Bühl, after which they took a short walk to the home of the Fetsch family. Simple chairs were the only seating, but a pump organ lent an air of formality to the setting. Hans Karl recalled a very small group of people meeting in the Fetsch home, "because there wouldn't have been enough room for very many people in their living room."[4]

This was an excellent example of a tiny branch functioning in all aspects of the gospel with only rare interruptions during the war. Karl Josef Fetsch was the branch president. In the absence of a branch clerk, he kept meticulous records of meetings, including contents of talks given. Those records show that most of the branch members gave a talk in one of the meetings each week. The minutes suggest that this was a close-knit group of Latter-day Saints.

On February 24, 1940, the letter sent to all branches in the West German Mission by Thomas E. McKay was read aloud in the Bühl sacrament meeting. The members knew that the mission leadership had been transferred to local Saints and that communications with Church leadership in the United States would be difficult if possible at all. Nevertheless, it is clear from the records that Karl Josef Fetsch was determined to sustain all of the programs of the Church in Bühl.

The minutes for the sacrament meeting on January 26, 1941, are typical of the years from 1939 to 1945:

> The branch president presided over the meeting which was conducted by his first counselor. The invocation was given by Brother August Friedrich Haug and the benediction by Sister Annamarie Haug. The sacrament was blessed by Brother August Friedrich Flad and passed by Brother Günther Flad. Speakers were as follows: 1 August Friedrich Flad and 2 Karl Josef Fetsch. Four priests and four members attended.[5]

Minutes were likewise kept for Relief Society meetings and genealogical classes (both were usually held monthly), as well as for special gatherings such as baptisms, weddings, funerals, or when members sought healing blessings. For example, on August 17, 1940, Irmgard Bühler of Biberach was baptized in the city swimming pool. Alice Fetsch was baptized by her father at the same location on August 3, 1941.

During the war, two weddings were celebrated in the branch meeting rooms (in each case following the official ceremony in the presence of the civil registrar at city hall). On March 30, 1941, Georg Schröder of Schierstein by Wiesbaden married Annamarie Haug. Eleven members and four friends attended the ceremony in the church. On September 15, 1942, Friedrich Heinrich Richard Haug (a sergeant in the Luftwaffe and only recently a Latter-day Saint) married Marianne Grüner (possibly from the nearby Strasbourg Branch). On the latter occasion, the church rooms were decorated. Anton Huck from the mission office in Frankfurt then ordained Brother Haug an elder. Alice Fetsch played the pump organ.

One of the highlights in the lives of these few members was the semiannual trip to Karlsruhe and other cities to participate in district conferences. For example, the 1940 fall conference was attended by "four priests and five members of our branch." Ten branch members and one friend attended the spring conference of 1941.

Sunday, July 13, 1941, must have been a very important day in the Bühl Branch: mission leader Christian Heck came from Frankfurt accompanied by Richard Ranglack and Paul Langheinrich (counselors to East German Mission supervisor Herbert Klopfer). All three attended Sunday School and spoke. Elder Heck visited the branch again on February 22, 1942, with his counselor Anton Huck.

The small Bühl Branch could hardly afford to lose any members, but such was the case when Rosa Maria Flad passed away on March 3, 1942. Anton Huck came from Frankfurt to preside at the funeral. On the other end of life's spectrum was the birth of a child in the Georg Jakob Schröder family in April 1942. Although the branch membership included only a few women, the Relief Society centennial was celebrated in 1942, as was the case all over the West German Mission.

Mission leaders in Frankfurt were aware of the small branch, as is clear from the meeting minutes. On September 9, 1942, Anton Huck presided over the baptism of Georg Jakob Schröder (a soldier) and Karl Fauth (of the Karlsruhe Branch) in Bühl. After the baptism, the participants "walked to a huge pear tree where Anton Huck gave a talk about baptism." Other noteworthy events of the year 1942 include the ordination of Karl Bühler of Biberach (in the Black Forest) to the office of elder. Christian Heck came to Bühl again on November 22 and sang a solo for the branch ("Noch Nicht Erfüllt"). The Christmas program that year was attended by six persons.

With the establishment of the Strasbourg District of the West German Mission in late 1943, interaction between the Saints in Alsace-Lorraine (German-occupied France) and Bühl increased in frequency. For example, an exchange outing took place on April 26, 1943, when eleven Saints from Bühl met with eight Saints from the Strasbourg branch at the Paul Kaiser family home in Grüneberg. When the Strasbourg Branch held a dedication of its meeting rooms on August 1, eleven members of the Bühl Branch made the short trip to Strasbourg. More than fifty persons came from other branches for that occasion, including Frankfurt, Saarbrücken, Karlsruhe, Mannheim, Pforzheim, and Freiburg.

The Bühl Branch minutes include the following entry dated March 15, 1944: "We travelled to Mülhausen [in Alsace-Lorraine] to meet with the new members there; they have no priesthood holders." Two weeks later, branch members traveled to Biberach (thirty miles to the south) to hold a meeting in the home of Karl Bühler. It is apparent that Bühl's location along the main north–south railway line (which connected Karlsruhe with Basel, Switzerland) was most advantageous to the Church.

Twelve members of the Bühl Branch attended the district conference in Karlsruhe on April 23, 1944. The branch minutes contain this comment: "All meetings were conducted in good order, but there was one interruption when an air raid siren (impending danger!) was sounded. All attendees were able to leave for their homes in time, filled with the spirit to continue the fight against sin."

Due to his political attitudes, in late 1944 Karl Josef Fetsch attracted the attention of the police, was taken into what was euphemistically referred to as "protective custody," and was removed from Bühl. According to the branch minutes, August Friedrich Flad, his substitute as branch president, responded to a request of Frieda Fetsch to find her husband; he traveled to Mannheim and Ludwigshafen to inquire as to the whereabouts of Brother Fetsch. No further details are available, but Brother Fetsch was home again by September 13, apparently unharmed by the experience.

Bühl was not a large or important city during the war, but every city in Germany was threatened by the Allies, who enjoyed superiority in the German skies during the final months of the conflict. It comes as no surprise when one reads that no church meetings could be held on October 4 and 10, 1944, due to air raid alarms. The same was reported on November 19 and December 6. The entry written on January 7, 1945, is interesting and reflects the fears of Church members as the invading Allied forces neared their city:

> Following a recommendation made by Brother Karl Josef Fetsch, all attendees of our fast and testimony meeting desired to receive a special blessing from the elders for special protection against the attacks from the air and the approaching enemy. We wished the blessings of the Lord in health and strength, and that we might continue to enjoy the Lord's continued blessings and have our lives and our property preserved. Friedrich August Haug blessed Karl Josef Fetsch, Klara Haug, and Gisela Hess; Karl Josef Fetsch blessed August Friedrich Flad, Friedrich August Haug, Frida Fetsch, and Alice Fetsch; August Friedrich Flad blessed Anna M. Haug, Emma Distelzwey, Rota Fauth, Erika Fauth, and Heinz Fauth.

The meetings were again interrupted by air raid alarms on February 11, 1945. Despite the many ways in which life was complicated in Bühl from 1939 to 1945, the attendance at branch meetings remained remarkably consistent. During the sporadic absences of branch president Karl Josef Fetsch, August Friedrich Flad functioned very dependably as the leader of this small group of faithful Saints.

The final entry of the war years in Bühl was written on April 15 and reads as follows:

> On the day after the entry of the French army into Bühl, there was still a very great deal of unrest. The entire population was held in check as everybody wondered what the conquerors would do. We brethren therefore decided that each family should hold their own sacrament meeting in their apartment and to see that talks were given. This was possible because there was an elder in each family. In our branch we are all thankful to our Creator and our Redeemer that all of the members are still alive and have suffered relatively little property damage.[6] Even Brother Günter Distelzwey has returned from military service in good health and is already back at his civilian employment. We members of the Bühl Branch have been so blessed that we can hardly consider ourselves worthy. We continue to hope for blessings if we can remain faithful, endure to the end, and use wisdom in all things.

The members of the Bühl Branch continued to hold church meetings as regularly as possible after the Third Reich collapsed. The following was written on June 20, 1945:

> Because our branch president, Brother Karl Josef Fetsch, will now be in Bühl on a permanent basis, he today assumed the official leadership of the branch in all respects. He thereby relieves Brother August Friedrich Flad, who since 1941 has been his substitute, which he will remain.

These few Saints had performed their church duties with great dedication during the challenging years of World War II. With so few losses in life (and apparently none in property), the branch membership had grown through births, convert baptisms, and marriages, and the future looked bright in the summer of 1945.

In Memoriam

The following members of the Bühl Branch did not survive World War II:

Friedrich Heinrich Richard Haug b. Bühl, Karlsruhe, Baden, 24 Apr 1918; son of August Friedrich Haug and Klara Koch; bp. 8 Aug 1927; conf. 8 Aug 1927; ord. deacon 4 Jan 1931; ord. teacher 18 Jun 1933; ord. priest 20 May 1934; ord. elder 15 Sep 1942; lance corporal; MIA 9 Jun 1943 (FHL microfilm 68785, no. 11; CHL CR 275 8 2441, no. 211; IGI)

Anna Maria Uber b. Freudenstadt, Schwarzwaldkreis, Württemberg, 17 Aug 1857; dau. of Lorenz Uber and Elisabeth Bohnet; bp. 17 Jul 1923; conf. 17 Jul 1923; m. Freudenstadt 11 Nov 1883, Jakob Friedrich Haug; 10 children; d. heart attack Bühl, Karlsruhe, Baden, 1 Oct 1942 (FHL microfilm 68785, no. 7; CHL CR 275 8 2441, no. 208; IGI; AF)

Notes

1. Presiding Bishopric, "Financial, Statistical, and Historical Reports of Wards, Stakes, and Missions, 1884–1955," 257, CHL CR 4 12.
2. West German Mission branch directory, 1939, CHL LR 10045 11.
3. Ursula Mussler Schmitt, telephone interview with Jennifer Heckmann in German, March 31, 2009; German summarized in English by Judith Sartowski.
4. Hans Karl Mussler, interview by the author, Preston, Idaho, November 22, 2008.
5. Bühl Branch general minutes, CHL LR 1180 11. All quotations from the branch history were taken from this source.
6. This statement does not reflect the fact that one elderly sister had passed away during the war and that soldier Friedrich Heinrich Richard Haug had been missing in action since June 1943 and would never return.

Freiburg Branch

An LDS branch had existed in the city of Freiburg in southwestern Germany from time to time since 1927. Karl Becker and his wife had watched the branch thrive and decline several times by 1939. In his short history of the early years of the branch, he wrote that "from 1936 to 1938 I [branch president Becker] with my wife and my daughter, Rosemarie, were the only members in Freiburg. I used this time to collect data for the redemption of the dead in my family."[1]

Even as the only LDS male in Freiburg, Karl Becker was not ashamed of the gospel of Christ. He spent a good deal of time with a Mr. Schuppiser, a printer who produced the Church's

German-language publication, *Der Stern*. The printer and his wife were converted and were baptized into the Church in Basel, Switzerland, on May 7, 1939. There were thus five Saints in Freiburg when the American missionaries left and the war began.

The city of Freiburg is located seventy-five miles south of Karlsruhe, but was closer to the office of the Swiss Mission in Basel (only thirty-five miles to the south). After 1943, the area of southern Baden was added to the newly established Strasbourg District under the leadership of Kurt Schneider.[2] President Schneider enjoyed the use of a company car and a chauffeur and was thus able to drive to Freiburg on several occasions to visit the Beckers.

Karl Becker listed these events in his history of the Freiburg Branch during the war years:[3]

> January 20, 1944: District president Kurt Schneider declares the Freiburg Branch to be an official unit of the Church.
>
> February 7, 1944: Cottage meeting in the Becker family home; Sister Stapperfend was our visitor.[4]
>
> March 23, 1944: The Beckers visited Mrs. Maria Huber, a widow, in her home.
>
> April 14 and 20, May 7 and 18, 1944: Cottage meetings in the Becker home.
>
> May 18, 1944: Elder August Flad of the Bühl Branch visited us.
>
> June 3–4 and June 10–11, 1944: We attended district meetings in Strasbourg.
>
> May 23, June 17, 20, 27, and 30, and July 11: Meetings in the Becker home.
>
> June 18 and 25, July 9: We attended the meetings of the Mühlhausen Branch.[5]
>
> July 25 and August 1: Meetings in our home.
>
> August 3, 1944: District president Schneider spoke in sacrament meeting.
>
> September–October: [Eight cottage meetings were held.]
>
> November: [War conditions prevented the holding of meetings.]

Fig. 1. Members and friends of the Freiburg Branch in about 1944. (C. Bodon Schneider)

The following lines describe the personal tragedy suffered by the Becker family on November 27, 1944:

> November 27, 1944 was a black day for Freiburg. During twenty minutes of brutal violence, large portions of our city were destroyed and thousands of people lost their lives. Among the innocent victims was my wife. My home was reduced to rubble. I believe that during the exploding of the bombs, the burning of the buildings, and the crash of structures collapsing that night, I went through the greatest trial of my faith that I ever had to endure. With a broken heart, I knelt before the wreckage of my home and prayed to my Father in Heaven to help me recover the body of my wife from the ruins intact. I wanted to find and identify her among the sixteen persons killed in that building. A great effort was made and my purpose achieved. Along with many others, she was buried in a mass grave at the Freiburg cemetery. From that time on, I have endeavored to preach the gospel with greater energy.[6]

On December 12, 1944, Brother Becker pronounced a dedication on the mass grave containing the body of his wife and those of 191 others. He recorded the prayer:

> We two brethren of the Church of Jesus Christ stand at this grave and beg for Thy blessing, that the earthly body of Sister Elisabeth Becker may be preserved from any damage and that no power [under] heaven will disturb her. We beg

> Thy blessing that this sister may continue to serve where she is now, as she had begun to serve on this earth. Please grant her the strength and ability to continue this work and to accomplish even greater tasks.[7]

The following entries are found in the branch history recorded by Karl Becker:

> November 27, 1944: Sister Elisabeth Becker was killed in an air raid.
>
> December 1944: [War conditions prevented the holding of meetings.]
>
> January 9, 1945: Elder Flad came for a visit.
>
> January 11–12, 1945: Sister Rosemarie Becker visited Brother Schneider in the hospital in Triberg.[8]
>
> January 14 and 21, 1945: Cottage meetings.
>
> January 28, 1945: Brother Schuppiser was ordained a deacon.
>
> February and March, 1945: [War conditions prevented the holding of meetings.]
>
> April 21, 1945: The city of Freiburg is occupied by Allied troops. The church records were kept hidden from April 19 to July 1, 1945.
>
> April 23, 1945: Brother Becker gave priesthood blessings to the Schuppisers.
>
> June 6, 1945: President Schneider received the first letter from Brother Becker and the answer was received on June 21; thus written communication was reestablished.
>
> July 22, 1945: Brother Schuppiser was ordained a teacher by President Schneider and Brother Becker. . . . The branch can be considered recreated as of this date.
>
> July 24, 1945: Elder Wilhelm Kenneth Firmage from New York visited us. He is a lieutenant in the U.S. Army. He brought greetings from the First Presidency and the prophet, seer, and revelator, Heber J. Grant.[9]

The LDS branch in Freiberg began the postwar period with four members. By 1948, there would be twenty-one baptisms as a strong branch emerged.

In Memoriam

Only one member of the Freiburg Branch did not survive World War II:

Maria Magdalena Elisabeth Gaebler b. Leipzig, Sachsen, 27 Jul 1893; dau. of Gottlieb Bernhard Gaebler and Luise Auguste B. Goldhorn; m. Karl Friedrich Becker; k. air raid Freiburg, Baden, 27 Nov 1944 (Karl Becker; NFS)

Notes

1. Karl Becker, *Gemeinde Geschichte der Gemeinde Freiburg/Brg* (unpublished), 1, CHL LR 3026 11.
2. See Strasbourg District chapter.
3. Becker, *Gemeinde Geschichte*, 2.
4. This was likely Berta Stapperfend of Pforzheim, the district Relief Society president.
5. The town of Mühlhausen was across the river in occupied France.
6. Becker, *Gemeinde Geschichte*, 1–2.
7. Ibid., 3.
8. It would seem that Rosemarie and her father were not with her mother in the basement of their apartment when Elisabeth Becker was killed. However, Brother Becker wrote that his wife "was praying aloud to God when she was killed and remained a loyal member of the Church to the very end."
9. Heber J. Grant died May 14, 1945.

Strasbourg Branch

Strasbourg, the capital city of the historic province of Alsace-Lorraine, had been a cultural center for centuries. When Kurt and Charlotte Schneider moved from Stuttgart, Germany, to Strasbourg, France, in 1940, the city had just been conquered as a result of the war. "My husband worked for a metal products company, Thyssen Rheinstahlwerke. He was the director of the new Strasbourg division of the company. They made pots and pans out of aluminum."[1] They had married just weeks after the war began and were looking forward to a happy life together.

The move to Strasbourg as the new director may not have taken place had Kurt not suffered a small accident in Stuttgart just after the war began. In the dark of the blackout, a German soldier running down the street hit Kurt and broke his ankle. When informed of the accident, Charlotte expressed delight rather than sorrow. She realized that the accident might well delay or prevent Kurt's call to the Wehrmacht. Indeed, his promotion to director soon came through, and his war-critical employment exempted him from military service during the entire war.[2]

Fig. 1. Members of the Strasbourg Branch gathered for this photograph in 1941. It appears that the branch was renting rooms in a nice downtown neighborhood at the time. Charlotte and Kurt Schneider are at the far left. (C. Bodon Schneider)

There had apparently been a small group of Latter-day Saints in the city for several years, and the Schneiders lost no time in seeking them out. Over the next four years, the diary of Charlotte Schneider includes hundreds of entries featuring the branch. The following names are prominent: the Georg Müller family, Sister Feister, the Kaiser family, the Hechleiter family, Sister Staperfend, and Brother Renk.[3] As she recalled, "The Saints spoke German but nearly everybody could speak French also. We met in rented rooms."

"We had such a beautiful apartment in Strasbourg," recalled Charlotte Schneider. Indeed, Kurt's company put the couple up in a fine apartment near the downtown area. This setting is consistent with his position as director in a large corporation. Charlotte (called "Lotte" by her family and friends) soon fell in love with that beautiful old city, and her diary reflects the attachment: they attended the theater and the cinema and became acquainted with the city's beautiful parks.

Kurt Schneider apparently became the leader of the Strasbourg Branch soon after his arrival, but the exact date of the call cannot be determined. Nothing is said about this in the mission records, and the branch records did not survive the war. However, Charlotte's diary includes many references to leadership functions, and the fact that Kurt was allowed to use his company automobile for church activities likely made him the primary traveler among the Saints on the west side of the Rhine.

The Schneiders became parents in November 1943 with the birth of their son Werner. As befitted an upper-class family of the era, they sent out a formal announcement beginning with the line, "We are thrilled to announce the birth of a strapping little boy."

That the Strasbourg Branch was still in its infancy in early 1944 is clear from the diary entries of Sister Schneider. The entry dated February 14 reads, "Founded the Relief Society today; the leaders are [Sisters] Abogast, Grob and Kaiser."[4] Discussions on the founding of that society in the Strasbourg Branch had begun earlier that year. There is no indication of when the meetings were held nor how many sisters attended. From various entries in the diary, we learn that Sunday School was held in the morning and sacrament meeting at 3:00 p.m. Primary meetings were held on Mondays.

Some entries from Charlotte's diary from 1944 are indicative of the ongoing activities of the branch and the family during a time when it was becoming increasingly clear that Hitler's armed forces were not sufficient to contend against enemies on several fronts. Her diary comment of June 6 (D-day) is interesting: "Great excitement! The Allies have succeeded in their invasion."[5] She shared the excitement of the people of Strasbourg, who were waiting to be liberated after years of life under German occupation.

Die glückliche Geburt eines strammen Jungen

zeigen hocherfreut an

Frau CHARLOTTE SCHNEIDER
geb. Bodon
z. Zt. Klinik Prof. Jakobi
Bürgerspital

und

KURT SCHNEIDER
Direktor
Steinring 17

STRASSBURG, den 11. November 1943

Fig. 2. The Schneiders announced the arrival of their first child with this card. (C. Bodon Schneider)

During the spring and early summer of 1944, little Werner Schneider became seriously ill and was hospitalized for weeks. In those days, parents were not allowed to stay with children in the hospital, and Charlotte's diary entries reflect her agony at having to leave the boy among strangers. His condition did not improve completely during the next year and was a constant subject in his mother's diaries.[6]

The branch still had nice rooms to meet in, as is apparent from Charlotte's diary entry dated Friday, August 11: "The fifteenth [air raid] today. The city center was hit. I took Werner to the doctor. The windows in our branch rooms were broken."[7]

In August 1944, the American army was approaching, bent on liberating the provinces of Alsace-Lorraine from their status as occupied territory. Kurt Schneider's company was soon forced to curtail operations in its facilities around Strasbourg. The family would have to give up the luxurious apartment in the city they had grown to love during the previous four years. Charlotte Schneider made several diary entries from August 15 to 25 expressing the difficulty of packing up their belongings in preparation for the move (as many other German citizens in Alsace-Lorraine were doing at the time).

Fig.3. The bedroom of the Schneiders' apartment in Strasbourg. (C. Bodon Schneider)

As sad as the Schneiders were to leave Strasbourg, Charlotte's diary reflects their happiness in Schönwald Baden, a very small town far from the war. However, she was aware that the war was nearing its end and the future was uncertain when she wrote this entry on September 5: "Great weather but a bit stormy. Had my hair done, and then sat out in the sun behind the house this afternoon. I am very worried about the future. We hear that there is already fighting in Saarbrücken." Her entry the next day was comforting: "I read all day long. We can survive up here [in Schönwald]."

Back in Strasbourg, conditions for the remaining Saints were deteriorating. A terrible attack against that city took place on September 25, but a Brother Eyer called the Schneiders to report that the branch members were spared.[8]

Elfriede Recksiek (born 1925) of the Bielefeld Branch had been living with the Schneider family for some time as a domestic servant. She decided to return to her parents in Bielefeld for the Christmas season and departed Strasbourg on December 24.[9] Charlotte wrote the following in her diary: "This morning Elfriede left for Bielefeld. I cooked a pork schnitzel. After our dinner I sat in the sun with Kurt behind the bath house. This evening we celebrated Christmas Eve with the Dold family. Werner saw the Christmas tree. We exchanged small gifts and played games until 11 [p.m.]."[10] Elfriede returned to Schönwald on January 2, 1945, to resume her duties in the Schneider household, but she left for good at the end of the month. She was fortunate to be at home in Bielefeld before the American army arrived there in March.

Life in the beautiful Black Forest would have been more pleasant for Charlotte during the winter months of January and February 1945, but Kurt was hospitalized, and their son, Werner, then fifteen months old, was constantly ill. Several times, Sister Schneider had to carry the little boy through the snow to the hospital in Triberg for treatments and shots. Amid the health trials, she was also asking herself serious questions about the German leaders. The following diary entries reflect this:

> Saturday, February 24: I heard Hitler speak today [on the radio]. He prophesied a German victory this year and said that history will take a turn for the better.
>
> Wednesday, February 28: [propaganda minister Josef] Goebbels spoke on the radio: we have to do more with less. There will be no new weapons.
>
> Tuesday, March 20: I am really unhappy about the current political situation. What the [German] people have to go through now is terrible![11]

By mid-April 1945, life in little Schönwald was becoming chaotic for the Schneider family. German troops were moving through town, retreating from the approaching French. Russian and Polish POWs were being moved out of the area. French artillery and German antiaircraft fire were making it too dangerous to be outside, and the Schneiders spent much of the time huddled in their basement. Military vehicles were moving through the streets in every direction. On Sunday, April 22, Charlotte wrote, "We got up early. Great excitement. We are surrounded. The traffic has come to a stop on the roads. We heard shooting and Kurt saw two vehicles that looked like tanks."[12] The French troops had conquered the area around Schönwald and were moving farther north and east.

Fig. 4. The cover of Charlotte Bodon Schneider's second diary. (C. Bodon Schneider)

With the fighting over and the war only a few days from its official conclusion, Kurt Schneider likely thought that the family's greatest troubles were behind them. However, this was not to be the case under the French military occupation forces, as the Schneiders learned firsthand. The events of the next sixteen days were recorded in great detail in a new post office savings account book Kurt somehow acquired. With paper almost impossible to come by at the time, Brother Schneider was fortunate to have anything to write on. The following are excerpts from that diary:[13]

> Wednesday, May 2: Arrested at 9:30 a.m. in front of my house. I didn't know that there was a curfew. We stood around in the snow in front of the church until 10:30. We were searched for weapons twice and they checked our papers. Then they took me and four others to the city hall. We were allowed to have somebody bring us something to eat. Searched again for weapons and papers at [4:30 p.m.], then loaded into

a truck. The major (a coward!) didn't do anything to help us. Somebody told Lotte what was happening and she came by just in time. I gave her some money and kept 65 Marks for myself. They drove us through Furtwangen to Villingen. During the trip each of us was given two crackers. The only thing we were allowed to keep were our personal ID and our wedding rings.

Friday, May 4: [Terrible sleeping conditions] Very concerned and sad.

Saturday, May 5: A very pleasant period began in the camp.

Sunday, May 6: They marched us on foot to Rottweil (13 miles). We had hardly anything to eat: 8 pieces of bread, margarine. Three rest stops. In Rottweil the civilians were separated [from the soldiers] and released immediately. They were loaded into trucks. Then they drove us back to Schwenningen and put us into the Gestapo prison. The cells were in the basement. . . . I tried to stay happy by thinking about being released.

Tuesday, May 8: Read a novel by Dora Holderich.

Saturday, May 12: My stomach couldn't tolerate a piece of bacon. I'm not accustomed to such food any more. . . . There is nobody here to represent us [in getting out]. . . . Spent an hour in the yard this afternoon. Had a conversation with a comrade about the gospel—a long, intense conversation.

Sunday, May 13: Very bad night. Hardly got any sleep. The snoring was intolerable. . . . Very worried about my family. In general very depressed. . . . Studied French this evening. Read a novel.

Monday, May 14: Wrote cards to inform Lotte of my status (to be passed along from person to person).

Wednesday, May 16: Had a very long discussion in our room about the gospel. I bore a powerful testimony. H. Warner had become acquainted with the Church in Zürich [Switzerland]. Hogwash! The usual stupid rumors. I was able to dispel them. About 10–12 persons in attendance.

Thursday, May 17: It is so sad to see how the people stand around waiting for a bite to eat. Like a zoo. It is shameful that when some food is brought around, they won't share with others. . . . Another interrogation: occupation, party affiliation, family status, what I plan to do now [for work]. Still very intense and exact. It's hard to remain positive. Finally I was released. . . . I preached the gospel to two comrades.

One day, Kurt and several other prisoners were loaded onto a train to be sent to France. He knew that such a move might mean that he would never return. Agonizing about how to escape despite the many guards surrounding the prisoners, he suddenly recalled two verses from the Bible: Joshua 1:9 and John 14:27. He knew what to do and recalled the situation in these words:

> The spirit commanded me to jump from the car. It was as if I were pushed by a higher power. Soldiers with machine guns came running from all directions. I stood straight and unafraid. Then I pushed them away. They lowered their guns, which had been pointed at me. My actions stupefied those grim-looking soldiers. The looks on their faces indicated fear and respect. I spoke English to them, I don't know where it came from: "I am in the service of America. I am on an important mission." One of the officers understood my English and called the station commander. I told him my story in a more forceful manner, with strong body language. He released me! Then I was escorted into the town where the French captain in charge was stationed. I related my story to him and I was set free immediately.[14]

The rest of the adventure is told in his diary:

> Friday, May 18: [On the way home] I wasn't used to walking so far anymore and my body was weakened. The sight of us caused quite a stir in the village. Mrs. Dold was in her garden and nearly stared herself blind when she saw us. . . . Lotte and Ruth were beside themselves with joy. Sometimes I can't believe it myself—that I'm free and my trials are over.

During Kurt's absence, Charlotte Schneider had been in perhaps a worse situation. With French soldiers on the prowl for loot and female victims, she had to hide herself while caring for two little boys. Even such simple tasks as hauling water from a local well could be very dangerous to her at the time.

Watching her husband be arrested and taken away for no apparent reason was painful to this young wife. She made the following entries in her diary during his absence:[15]

> Wednesday, May 2: Very unlucky day. Kurt went to the tailor. While he was gone an order was issued regarding curfew. On the way home he was caught by three French soldiers and hauled away. They first put him in the church and then in the city hall. Then they put him on a truck with three other men to be taken away. Where to? I saw him as they drove away and he was very discouraged.
>
> Thursday, May 3: Kurt is still gone. I think he is in Villingen. I fasted for him this evening.
>
> Friday, May 4: Kurt is still gone. I went to the city hall to ask where he is.
>
> Sunday, May 6: We heard today that there is a cease-fire [the war is over].
>
> Sunday, May 7: I asked Mr. Scherzinger if he would walk to Villingen with me [to search for Kurt] but he said no.
>
> Tuesday, May 8: Mr. Brucker came back from Villingen and said that Kurt is not there.
>
> Tuesday, May 15: I spoke with the [French] commandant and gave him a letter for Villingen. He will try to forward it.
>
> Friday, May 18: Kurt came back from his imprisonment at 7 p.m. He is in very good spirits and even took a bath. He talked about [his experiences] until midnight.

It can hardly come as a surprise that Sister Schneider was unable to find somebody who could penetrate the French POW system to rescue her husband. In the confusion that reigned during the last days of the war and the ensuing fragile peace, soldiers and civilians alike were incarcerated and interrogated by the invaders. Kurt Schneider was not a soldier, but as a member of the National Socialist Party he was automatically suspected of contributing to the misdeeds of the fatherland.

On July 23, 1945, Charlotte Schneider was walking to Triberg. Instead of taking the main road, she chose to walk a small path by some waterfalls. It was there that she was attacked by a Moroccan soldier. "I had seen dark-skinned people before, so I was not particularly scared. . . . [but this time] I was attacked by a Moroccan. I was scared to death and screamed for help." Fortunately, somebody came by in time to intervene on her behalf.

The Strasbourg Branch had never been particularly strong during the war, but in May 1945 the prominent family was miles away in Germany, and the prospects of a return to Strasbourg (again part of France) were bleak. As of this writing, there is no information regarding the members of this branch in the early postwar years.

No members of the Strasbourg (France) Branch of The Church of Jesus Christ of Latter-day Saints are known to have lost their lives in World War II.

NOTES

1. Charlotte Bodon Schneider, interview by the author, Salt Lake City, June 25, 2009.
2. Kurt Schneider, *Imagining Success* (Salt Lake City: Schneider, 1977), 130.
3. Charlotte Bodon Schneider, diary (unpublished); used with permission.
4. Charlotte Bodon Schneider, diary.
5. Ibid.
6. Ibid.
7. Ibid.
8. Ibid.
9. Elfriede Recksiek Doermann, interview by the author, Salt Lake City, May 4, 2009.
10. Ibid.
11. Ibid.
12. Ibid.
13. Kurt Schneider, diary (unpublished); used with the kind permission of Charlotte Bodon Schneider.
14. Schneider, *Imagining Success*, 140.
15. Charlotte Bodon Schneider, diary.

STUTTGART DISTRICT

West German Mission

The Stuttgart District boundaries were essentially those of the historical kingdom of Württemberg. Surrounded by the provinces of Baden and Bavaria in twentieth-century Germany, Württemberg has a proud history that is centered in its capital city, Stuttgart. The neighboring districts of the church in 1939 were Karlsruhe to the West, Nuremberg to the northeast, Munich to the southeast, Strasbourg to the southwest, and the Swiss Mission to the south.

Stuttgart District[1]	**1939**
Elders	41
Priests	9
Teachers	12
Deacons	26
Other Adult Males	69
Adult Females	264
Male Children	36
Female Children	27
Total	484

The population of the Stuttgart District was relatively small in 1939: 484 members distributed among six branches—approximately eighty members per branch. To attend district conferences in Stuttgart, the members of the outlying branches did not have far to travel. Heilbronn was twenty-five miles to the north, Feuerbach three miles north, Esslingen six miles east, Göppingen twenty miles east, and Reutlingen twenty miles southeast.

Fig. 1. The six branches of the Stuttgart District were clustered around the city of Stuttgart. Much of this territory had no LDS units.

Regarding the status of the district as the war approached, a solitary entry in the records of the West German Mission gives a good impression:

> Saturday–Sunday, April 22–23, 1939: the Stuttgart District conference [was held] in the Gustav Siegle House in Stuttgart. President Emil B. Fetzer [presided]. Two buses brought Saints from the Frankfurt District to sing Evan Stephens's "The Martyrs." The Stuttgart [District] choir and orchestra also performed.[2]

This report is a reminder that nearly all districts of the Church in Germany had organized choirs in those days. Rehearsals were taken very seriously, and performances were offered at district conferences, mission conferences, and on other occasions. Like district conferences all over Germany, the one held in Stuttgart in April 1939 was a two-day affair. (In some cases, events took place on three or even four consecutive days.)

KIRCHE JESU CHRISTI
DER HEILIGEN DER LETZTEN TAGE

Herzliche Einladung
zur
FRÜHJAHRS-KONFERENZ
des Stuttgarter und Karlsruher Distrikts
am 6. und 7. April 1940 in Stuttgart

Am 6. April im Gemeindesaal Hauptstätterstr. 96
Am 7. April im Mozartsaal der Liederhalle
zu erreichen mit der Straßenbahn Linie 7, 18 und 20

Anwesend sind Missionsleiter Christian Heck und Anton Huck
beide aus Frankfurt
sowie die übrige Missionsleitung
Westdeutscher Hauptsitz Frankfurt a. M., Schaumainkai 41 p

Eintritt frei *Keine Sammlung*

Fig. 2. The official program of the spring district conference of 1940.

By late July 1939, Elder Fetzer had been succeeded by missionary Norman Seibold of Idaho as the president of the district. Following the departure of the American missionaries a month later, the leadership of the Stuttgart District was vacant for three months. It is assumed that the following district leaders continued to serve during that time: Emil Geist (Heilbronn) as superintendant of the Sunday School, Kurt Schneider (Stuttgart) as the leader of the YMMIA, Elsa Hörger (Esslingen) as the leader of the YWMIA, Gretel K. Fingerle (Esslingen) as the president of the Primary organization, Maria Speidel (Stuttgart) as the president of the Relief Society, and Meinrad Greiner (Stuttgart) as the genealogical supervisor.

The district general minutes indicate that a new president of the Stuttgart District was called by mission supervisor Friedrich Biehl on November 26, 1939: Erwin Ruf was a good choice, having served the previous eight years as the president of the Stuttgart Branch. He in turn chose Karl Lutz and Heinrich Bodon as his counselors. As of that date, President Ruf began to keep the district general minutes, which had been neglected since 1926.[3]

With the same dedication exhibited by many district presidents in Germany, Elder Ruf scheduled a conference in Stuttgart on April 6–7, 1940. The program for the session held on Sunday at 10:00 a.m. in the Stuttgart Liederhalle is representative of this and other conference sessions:

> Mozart Auditorium
> Sunday School conference
> Presiding: Emil Geist
> Prelude: Wilhelm Ballweg
> Chorister: Kurt Kirsch
> Hymn: 132
> Prayer: Johann Knödler
> Hymn: 129
> 1. Sacrament prelude
> 2. Announcement of speakers: D. Rügner
> 3. Sacrament postlude
> 4. Talk: Gustav Wacker
> 5. Sustaining of the general authorities: Erwin Ruf
> 6. Teaching instruction: Sister Frey

7. Story: Anita Neff
8. Poem: Liesel Lutz
9. Choral number: Stuttgart Branch children's choir (Maria Ruf)
10. Prayer: Emil Geist
11. Choral number: district mothers' choir
12. The experience of prayer: Georg Stehle
13. Solo: Sister Bechtle
14. Mission leadership: Anton Huck

Hymn: 72
Prayer: Eugen Keller
Attendance: 250 persons

The final statement in the district general minutes about the conference reads as follows: "It is noteworthy that a fine spirit was felt in all sessions. The combined attendance at all sessions was more than 800 persons."[4]

President Ruf's record includes notes about visits he made to the six branches on a weekly (and at times even daily) basis. The short distances between cities made it possible for him to attend meetings in as many as three branches on a single day. In most cases, he indicated the topics of the talks he gave in those meetings. He also visited individual members and families living in towns outside of the branch cities.

Erwin and Anna Ruf had two daughters, Maria (born 1923) and Esther (born 1929). Esther recalled how her father always seemed to be traveling for church work: "It seemed like he was gone every weekend."[5] President Ruf worked in a factory for critical war products, and this employment kept him at home throughout the war. The family lived in the Gablenberg suburb of Stuttgart and needed about forty-five minutes to get to church. According to Esther, "There was a streetcar, but we were very conservative with our money, so we walked. After

Fig. 3. Members of the Feuerbach Branch after a district conference. (R. Rügner)

Sunday School, we walked home for dinner, then back to church in the late afternoon."

Young Helga Hock of the Heilbronn Branch had fine memories of President Ruf, whom she saw on many occasions. "He had curly white hair and a slight speech impediment. And he was very friendly and usually visited our family before he left town again."[6] Helga recalled taking the train to Stuttgart twice each year to attend the district conference. "That was always an exciting event for us children."

As was the custom in the West German Mission during the war, Ruf attended conferences of other districts. On October 12–13, 1940, he was in Nuremberg participating in the conference of the Nuremberg District. Mission leaders Christian Heck and Anton Huck were there, as was Johann Thaller, the president of the Munich District. In most district conferences, all visiting district and mission leaders were asked to speak.[7]

The district conference held in Stuttgart on November 9–10, 1940, took place in the concert hall of the city's Bürgermuseum. As was his tradition, Erwin Ruf recorded the names of all speakers and musicians. He also wrote regarding the Sunday meal, namely that "the [local] sisters provided lunch for more than 100 persons in the [Stuttgart] branch rooms." The afternoon session that Sunday was attended by enough people to "nearly fill the hall," which accommodated four hundred persons.[8]

In the spring of 1941, with the war in its second full year, another district conference was convened. This time, the meetings took place in the Stuttgart Branch rooms. It is possible that by that time, many of the Saints had been called away to military service or employment or had sought the safety of smaller towns. In any case, Erwin Ruf's comments were still enthusiastic: "There was a fine spirit in all meetings. The songs rendered by the various choirs were especially impressive. More than 200 persons attended the afternoon session."[9]

The district conference held on September 27–28, 1941, was likewise a success. Mission leaders Christian Heck and Anton Huck again came from Frankfurt to participate. It would appear from Ruf's record that all programs of the Church in this district were still functioning well at the time. Indeed his final comments for the year 1941 include these numbers: the district member population was 466, five children were born, six persons were baptized, eight were ordained to the priesthood, and eight had died during the year.[10]

The book in which Erwin Ruf kept the general minutes of the district in the early war years was full as of June 28, 1942, and the book in which he very probably continued his record has not been found. The last two major events described in the surviving book were the celebration of the Relief Society centennial on March 21, 1942 (130 attendees), and the spring district conference held on March 28–29 (210 attendees).[11]

The only change in the meetings of six branches of the Stuttgart District during the first three war years was introduced by Ruf in March 1942: he asked that the priesthood holders meet once a week on an evening with the Relief Society sisters. In the following weeks, he attended such meetings and was apparently pleased with the innovation.

The following information regarding the district conference held in Stuttgart on October 18, 1943, is found in the general minutes of the Göppingen Branch:

> Brother [Anton] Huck and his wife from Frankfurt attended. The rooms of the Stuttgart Branch were so badly damaged in the attack on October 7–8 that they can no longer be used. The roof of the meeting hall in Munich was also damaged. The afternoon and evening sessions [of this conference] were cancelled when the police confiscated the building for the housing of people who have lost their homes in the air raids. When Erwin Ruf delivered this message to the home of Brother Biebinger, the latter suffered a heart attack.[12]

Thanks to his employment in Stuttgart, Erwin Ruf served faithfully in the calling of district president throughout the war. He was not ashamed of the gospel or the church, as his daughter Esther recalled:

> When we went to the air raid shelter, he would always leave a copy of the *Improvement Era* (I think it was in English) on our table in case somebody came into our apartment. That way they would realize that we were Mormons, that our church was connected with the United States. He would also leave a copy of the Book of Mormon on the table.

Elder Ruf was in Stuttgart when the war ended and continued to visit the six branches of the Church in that district as they attempted to regroup. At least four of those branches were looking for new places to meet in the summer of 1945.

Notes

1. Presiding Bishopric, "Financial, Statistical, and Historical Reports of Wards, Stakes, and Missions, 1884–1955," 257, CHL CR 4 12.
2. West German Mission history quarterly report, 1939, no. 15, CHL LR 10045 2.
3. Stuttgart District history, 166, CHL CR 16982 11.
4. Ibid., 167.
5. Esther Ruf Robinson, telephone interview with the author, April 13, 2009.
6. Helga Hock Seeber, autobiographical report (unpublished); private collection.
7. Ibid., 173.
8. Ibid., 175–176.
9. Ibid., 181.
10. Ibid., 193.
11. Ibid., 195–196.
12. Göppingen Branch general minutes, vol. 15, 226, CHL LR 3235 11.

Esslingen Branch

The city of Esslingen had 48,732 inhabitants in the year 1939.[1] Six miles east of Stuttgart, it was the home of the second-largest LDS branch in the Stuttgart District at the time. Of the 117 members, twenty-seven were priesthood holders. Under branch president Karl Zügel, all programs of the Church were functioning as the war approached.

According to the branch directory, Brother Zügel's counselors were Kurt Kirsch and Gottlob Maier. Johann Knödler led the Sunday School, Albert Heinemann the YMMIA and Paula Krieger the YWMIA. Friederika Heinemann was the president of the Primary and Lina Kugler the president of the Relief Society. Brother Kirsch was *Der Stern* magazine representative and Brother Maier directed genealogical research among branch members.[2]

When the war began in September 1939, the branch was holding meetings in a house at Plochingerstrasse 4 in Esslingen. Sunday School began at 10:00 and sacrament meeting at 7:00 p.m. Mutual met on Tuesdays at 8:00 p.m. and the Primary on Wednesdays at 6:00 p.m., followed by Relief Society at 8:00. The genealogical study group met on the third Tuesday of the month at 8:00 p.m.

Esslingen Branch[3]	**1939**
Elders	9
Priests	6
Teachers	3
Deacons	9
Other Adult Males	22
Adult Females	58
Male Children	7
Female Children	3
Total	117

"I can remember the beginnings of the war very well," recalled Ilse Neff (born 1929):

> I was ten years old, and we lived in a street where everybody knew their neighbors very well. One night, we heard a loud noise outside, and we woke up. My parents went to see what was going on, and I was terribly scared. I saw a group of men knocking on everybody's door and windows. I asked my father what that meant, and he explained to me that those men were soldiers and that they were looking for men to draft for a possible war. That scared me. . . . One night, we

> came back from helping my mother's friend with her canning. Suddenly, we heard Hitler's voice on the radio saying that beginning at [4:45 a.m.] Germany was shooting back. I can still hear that in my mind today. That was September 1, 1939.[4]

Ilse recalled that the rooms at Plochingerstrasse were confiscated early in the war because the building had belonged to a Jewish family named Moses. Several homes became available for meetings during the war, but Ilse stated that there were no interruptions in the meetings when the locations changed.

Walter Tischhauser (born 1935) described the meeting rooms in the Moses building in these words: "It was quite a large building that was four or five stories high. The rooms were also large—a little bit like small halls. This building belonged to the Moses family, who were Jewish. We called the building the 'Moses house.'"[5]

Fig. 1. Anita Neff's father with his model of the Salt Lake Temple. (A. Neff Bauer)

The walk to church took forty-five minutes for Lina Tischhauser and her children. Her husband was not a member of the Church, but he did not oppose their desire to attend meetings. Daughter Elsbeth (born 1932) remembered walking home after Sunday School, then back again for sacrament meeting in the evening. That meant a total of three hours on the way. "I think there were about fifty people in the meetings in those days," she said.[6]

Fig. 2. The living room of the Oppermann home was one of several locations of branch meetings during the war. (Oppermann family)

The Stuttgart District general minutes written by president Erwin Ruf include reports of his many visits among the Saints in Esslingen. His record of January 23, 1940, indicated that the meetings that Sunday had to be cancelled due to a lack of coal to heat the room.[7] A few months later (June 3), he wrote the following: "Attended the Sunday School and the fast meeting of the Esslingen Branch. Today the members of the Feuerbach and Stuttgart Branches were fasting and praying that the Esslingen Branch would be successful in locating new rooms to meet in."[8] A month later, the meetings were still being held in the home of the Fingerle family while the search continued. It was not until December that a decision was made to designate the Fingerle home as the official venue for branch meetings: "[Erwin Ruf] visited the Esslingen Branch fast meeting and offered the dedicatory prayer on the rooms in the Fingerle home where meetings will be held."[9]

The hostess, Bertha Pauline Fingerle, was Walter Tischhauser's grandmother. He described the branch's new location as follows:

> On the main floor of her house, she emptied the living room in which up to twenty-five people could be accommodated. The classes for Sunday School were taught in smaller rooms in the house, for example the bedrooms. I remember sitting on the bed and being taught. This house

was located at Mellinger Strasse 12a. During this time, the branch was not larger than twenty-five people usually.

Early in the war, an incident occurred that convinced some Church members in Esslingen that Germany's government was willing to hurt its own citizens. Young Ilse Neff recalled her friendship with Helene Zügel, one of the ten children of the branch president. Helene was intellectually disabled but was not socially inept. Ilse told this story:

> The government ordered the family to send Helene to an institution, since they wanted to help her (or so they said). But one day, the family received a letter describing her sudden death. We all knew how she died and that it hadn't been a sudden death. She must have been about [eighteen] years older than me. She could communicate well and would sometimes come to visit us in our home. She liked talking to my mother, although she had to walk a long way to get to our home from where she lived. She knew so many things. One time, she even explained to me what the Millennium would be like. I was so impressed about the way she explained it to me. She also sang Church hymns with me.

Fig. 3. A prewar photograph of the Esslingen Branch. (A. Neff Bauer)

Helene was likely a victim of the heinous euthanasia program carried out by the government. The official cause of her death was given as "septic angina." She was twenty-nine years old.

The district general minutes mention the deaths of several Esslingen Saints, notably Erwin Riecker, who was killed in Russia in March 1942. A memorial service was held in the branch for him.[10] He was, of course, only one of several men of this branch to give their lives for Germany.

Fig. 4. Three of the eight Tischhauser children. (A. Neff Bauer)

Elsbeth Tischhauser recalled how the army put pressure on her brother Rudolf to join:

> Every month, people from the [Nazi] party came and told my parents that my brother would be the perfect soldier because he was so tall. And they also said that if we won the war, he would have the best life possible. After all these things, my mother eventually said to my brother Rudolf that he should go. For us, it was a horrible time when my brother left, and we had to realize that many of the soldiers were killed in battle.

Esslingen was spared great damage, despite the fact that the city is so close to Stuttgart and was home to a railroad repair facility. According to Ilse Neff, "We didn't have many air raids, but when we went to bed at night, we each had a chair next to the bed with our clothes on it to get dressed fast. We also had a small bag to carry with us to the basement. Sometimes, there was an hour between the first sirens going off and the all-clear signal." A girl of faith, Ilse was impressed when she heard that branch president Karl Zügel and his counselor Gottlob Maier had gone up the hill above the city to offer a prayer. They petitioned God to protect that city and the Saints who lived there.

In 1943, Walter Tischhauser was planning to be baptized, but a minor crisis of faith occurred when he turned eight, as he described it:

> My aunts (with last name Fingerle) were my teachers in the Church, and I loved them very much. When I was eight years old, I wanted to be baptized because that is what I had always been taught in Church. My mother wrote of my desires in a letter to my oldest brother, who was then serving in the Arbeitsdienst in the Rhineland. He wrote back wondering why I wanted to be baptized since he thought I always wanted to become a great Hitler boy. Then he explained that one could not be a good Mormon boy and at the same time be a good Hitler boy. That is when I decided to not get baptized. All of my family members who were in the Church were shocked, but I was convinced that I had made the right choice.

Walter did not turn his back on the Church for long, as he explained: "I was baptized when I was eleven years old in 1946. The war was over by then, so I could concentrate on becoming a good Mormon boy again."

Regarding the challenge of finding enough food to eat during the war, Walter made this comment:

> Although we were quite a large family, we never had to go without the basic food groups. I remember that I never had to be hungry. It was more difficult for us to find enough clothing—especially shoes. Those things we would only get with ration coupons. My brother had to serve in the military and sent the cigarette coupons home. Nobody in our family smoked, so we could exchange the smoking cards for something else.

Elsbeth Tischhauser recalled how the city government had ponds dug around town so that water for fighting fires after air raids would always be available. In about 1944, her father sent her to the local pond several times to remove waste with a bucket. On one such occasion, she was kneeling by the pond when she heard airplanes approaching:

> I was wondering why there was no alarm and thought that they must be German planes. But they started shooting right away. I kept on working. A window in the house next to me opened, and a woman shouted to me that I should get into her house as fast as possible. The planes aimed directly at me. I ran down into the basement, but when it was over, the people had a hard time getting me to come out again because I was shaking so much. If I didn't have a thousand angels next to me that day, I wouldn't have survived.

Entertainment for teenagers was a challenge, Ilse Neff recalled. "I remember one Heinz Rühmann movie that was in the theaters, and my mother allowed me to go. We had to go three different times until we could watch the entire movie because an air raid happened during the first two showings. We had to go into the basement of the movie theater when the alarm sounded."

Young Hans Fingerle (born 1940) was just old enough to recall being with his father for a short time before Ludwig Fingerle (born 1913) was drafted into the air force. In his father's absence, Hans had plenty of experiences to pass the time. He recalled this one aspect of life during the last years of the war when Germany was losing on many fronts:

> We had refugees stay with us in our apartment even during the war. One day, somebody from the housing office came and told us that we had too much room to spare and that they would send people to stay with us. We did not know any of them but they lived in one of the rooms of our apartment with four people. They spoke a different dialect, but I do not know if they were from the east. One of the boys in the family was my age, so we played a lot together.[11]

Fig. 5. Ludwig and Margarete Fingerle with their son Hans in about 1943. (H. Fingerle)

Hans's father, Ludwig (born 1913) had been drafted into the air force and, like so many other soldiers on both sides of the conflict, would rather have been home. One can sense the longing in these words written to his wife on February 11, 1945, from Ober Ursel, near Frankfurt:

> I hope you are all well and happy. How did you spend your birthday? I am still waiting for a letter from you. Your last letter was written on January 20. Since then, so much has happened that I don't know which of it would most interest you. One thing: the next few weeks will determine what will happen to our people and our country. May the Lord have mercy on us. We must pray that our enemies do not overcome us. Now I understand that in Joseph Smith's vision, he had to turn away his eyes when he saw the misery that would befall mankind. . . . May God protect you and all of our loved ones.[12]

The trials of a mother caring for her children during the absence of her soldier husband are reflected clearly in the letter written by Margarete Fingerle to Ludwig on April 8, 1945—just one month before the end of the war:

> You have probably heard that the front moves closer and closer to us. But we won't be discouraged or give up. We maintain the hope that we will stay healthy and see you again. How beautiful the world could be; the flowers are beginning to blossom around here and I am with you in my thoughts, my dear. . . . I am so glad that we had time together to travel and see some wonderful places. Will we ever be able to do that again? . . . I have to go now; it's 11 o'clock. How we all are awaiting the day when we will see you again.
>
> Hugs and kisses from your dear Gretel[13]

Sister Fingerle would have to wait until the next life to see her husband again. The letter was returned as undeliverable. The chaos that reigned around Berlin in the last days of the war made it impossible for army postal officials to find Ludwig Fingerle.

Soldier Rudolf Tischhauser was a member of the Church, but in one of his last letters written as the end of the war loomed, he told his mother that he would rather shoot himself than be taken prisoner by the Russians. Neither scenario was his fate; he was killed in an artillery barrage. By the time the war ended, Lina Tischhauser had lost two sons and two brothers, as her daughter Elsbeth explained:

> My brother Ludwig was killed in the war in December of 1944. Rudolf was later killed in April 1945. My uncle died around April 20, 1945. And my oldest brother Otto Fingerle died the day that the war was declared lost. He was shot by partisans. It was such a difficult time for all of us, especially for my mother.[14]

Ilse Neff recalled how the American invaders appeared one day in the spring of 1945 on the hills above Esslingen. When the city's mayor initially refused to surrender the city, the enemy threatened to bombard the town. Fortunately, several influential citizens conducted talks with both sides and were able to motivate the mayor to renounce his call for resistance. The city surrendered without a fight, and the people were spared. According to Ilse, the Americans were merciful to the populace, but the same could not be said of the French: "It was a different atmosphere. . . . We were a little scared of the Africans who served among the French troops. We had never before seen so many in one group. Especially the women were afraid." Fortunately, the Esslingen Branch members did not suffer much at the hands of the conquerors.

Little Hans Fingerle described an experience he had with the occupation forces:

> I was not afraid of the black soldiers I saw. One time, I was with a friend from kindergarten, and we saw a pickup truck with American soldiers. I thought it was funny that they had a broom on the side of their truck. When the truck passed us, I pointed to the broom, and we both laughed. All of sudden, somebody hit me in the rear, and when I turned around, I saw a black soldier standing there. He must have thought that I had laughed about him. That was my first encounter with a soldier that was not white.

Ludwig Fingerle was killed in the defense of Berlin on April 25, 1945, but his wife did not have proof of his fate until a letter written by a comrade arrived in August 1948. Horst von Glasenapp returned from a POW camp in the Soviet Union that summer and fulfilled his self-imposed duty of writing to Margarete Fingerle. He explained how his antiaircraft battery, which included Corporal Ludwig Fingerle, had moved in several directions through the capital city, trying to avoid a direct confrontation with the invading Red Army. Eventually, the men found themselves at the north edge of the Tiergarten (Berlin's equivalent to New York City's Central Park). Von Glasenapp's very detailed letter includes the following description of the events of evening of April 25:

> We expected to be attacked by the Russian night fighters at any moment. When we heard the motors of the planes and saw the illumination flares they dropped, I ordered my unit to stop and to take cover as fast as possible. We were across the street from Bellevue Palace. We sensed instinctively the impending danger, but the first bombs fell even before we had found safety in the trenches. At dawn the next day, April 26, we survivors buried our three comrades who were killed, including Ludwig Fingerle, under the trees of the Tiergarten, across the street from Bellevue Palace.[15]

Without the letter of this kind commanding officer, the fate of Ludwig Fingerle may well have remained a mystery.

Lina Tischhauser had raised her children in the faith before and during the war, but her husband was not a member of the Church and did not encourage his children to be baptized. However, some of his misgivings about religion were apparently resolved after Germany's catastrophic defeat, as his son Walter recalled:

> My father always believed very strongly in the [Hitler] regime and the system. When the war was over, my father basically broke down and had to reevaluate everything that he believed in. Especially because he found out what had really happened in connection with the Jews, for example. He stated that he felt so used and betrayed that he would never believe and trust anybody again. During the [Third Reich], he also never wanted to hear anything about the Church. But because there were so many children in our family, we always got extra support from the Church (food, clothing, etc.) after the war. The branch presidency then told my father that the Church had helped his family so much—now would be the time to be baptized. Even my mother testified that the blessings had been the biggest help getting through the war.

Richard Tischhauser was baptized in 1948.

The city of Esslingen was indeed fortunate to emerge from the war nearly unscathed. Official city records show that only forty-seven civilians and seventy military personnel from Esslingen lost their lives and that only 3 percent of the structures (all of them in suburbs) were destroyed. The war ended for the people of Esslingen when the French arrived in April 1945. The branch membership had been reduced significantly, but the meetings continued, and the Saints in that city looked forward to life in a peaceful Germany.

In Memoriam

The following members of the Esslingen Branch did not survive World War II:

Marie Kathrine Bäuerle b. Esslingen, Neckarkreis, Württemberg, 24 Aug 1863; dau. of Jacob Bäuerle and Sophie Karle; bp. 2 Mar 1910; conf. 2 Mar 1910; d. pneumonia 20 Oct 1944 (FHL microfilm 68807, book 2, no. 301; IGI)

Otto Alfred Brändle b. Marbach, Neckarkreis, Württemberg, 18 Mar 1918; son of Rudolf Brändle and Emma Walker; bp. 23 Dec 1928; conf. 23 Dec 1928; noncommissioned officer; k. in battle Orschiza, Ukraine, 20 Sep 1941 (FHL microfilm 68807, book 2, no. 471; FHL microfilm 25728, 1930 census; IGI; www.volksbund.de)

Lina Frida Rosa Brodbeck b. Esslingen, Neckarkreis, Württemberg, 9 Jun 1907; dau. of Paul Brodbeck and Frida Claus; bp. 6 Apr 1930; conf. 6 Apr 1930; m. Esslingen 24 Oct 1936, Eugen Vollmer; d. throat and lung ailment Esslingen 11 Aug 1944 (FHL microfilm 68807, book 2, no. 574)

Bernhard Johannes Fingerle b. Esslingen, Neckarkreis, Württemberg, 29 Jul 1914; son of Christian Johann Fingerle and Barbara Ulmer; bp. 9 Aug 1922; conf. 9 Aug 1922; ord. deacon 7 Dec 1930; ord. teacher 14 Jul 1935; ord. priest 19 Jul 1942; m. 7 Dec 1943; sergeant; k. in battle Michelbach, Alsace-Lorraine, France, 7 Dec 1944; bur. Cernay, France (FHL microfilm 68807, book 2, no. 252; FHL microfilm 25766; 1930 and 1935 censuses; IGI, AF; www.volksbund.de)

Ludwig Erwin Fingerle b. Esslingen, Neckar, Württemberg, 15 May 1913; son of Christian Johann Fingerle and Barbara Ulmer; bp. 14 Jul 1921; m. Esslingen 3 Jul 1937, Margarete Alma Kirsch; 2 children; k. in battle Berlin 25 Apr 1945; bur. Berlin 26 Apr 1945 (H. v. Glasenapp)

Otto Bernhard Jakob Fingerle b. Esslingen, Neckarkreis, Württemberg, 28 Nov 1901; son of Christian Johann Fingerle and Bertha Pauline Kiesel; bp. 30 Aug 1911; conf. 30 Aug 1911; ord. deacon 5 Aug 1923; m. Esslingen, Neckar abt 1921, Lina Ahles; k. in battle Berlin, 8 May 1945 (FHL microfilm 68807, book 1, no. 828; FHL microfilm 25766; 1930 and 1935 censuses; IGI, AF)

Albert Heinemann b. Jebenhausen, Donaukreis, Württemberg, 30 Oct 1906; son of Carl Heinemann and Julie Nothdürft; bp. 31 Oct 1924; conf. 31 Oct 1924; ord. deacon 7 Feb 1926; ord. teacher 15 Aug 1926; ord. priest 6 Dec 1936; m. 16 Feb 1929, Friederike Maier; at least three children; k. in battle Russia, 13 Feb 1944 (FHL microfilm 68807, book 2, no. 93; FHL microfilm 162780; 1930 and 1935 censuses; IGI)

Hans Heinemann b. Oberesslingen, Neckarkreis, Württemberg, 5 Oct 1917; son of Karl Heinemann and Julie Nothdürft; bp. 18 Jan 1926; conf. 18 Jan 1926; noncommissioned officer; k. in battle San. Kp. 1/178 H. V. Pl. Wyssokoje-West, near present-day Wysokoje, Orscha, Belarus, 11 Mar 1944 (FHL microfilm 68807, book 2, no. 177; FHL microfilm 162780; 1930 and 1935 censuses; IGI; www.volksbund.de)

Frida Klaus b. Wäldenbronn, Esslingen, Neckarkreis, Württemberg, 25 Jul 1879; dau. of Gottlieb Klaus and Christine Clauss; bp. 28 Aug 1943; conf. 28 Aug 1943; m. —— Brodbeck; d. dysentery 17 Sep 1944 (FHL microfilm 68807, book 2, no. 754; IGI)

Walter Knödler b. Stuttgart, Neckarkreis, Württemberg, 19 May 1921; son of Johann Knödler and Karoline Bauer; bp. 7 Sep 1929; conf. 7 Sep 1929; ord. deacon 6 Dec 1936; radio operator; k. in battle South Tunisia 23 or 28 Mar 1943; bur. Bordj-Cedria, Tunisia (FHL microfilm 68807, book 2, no. 392; FHL microfilm 271380; 1930 and 1935 censuses; IGI; www.volksbund.de)

Maria Theresia Merkt b. Spaichingen, Schwarzwaldkreis, Württemberg, 18 Aug 1866; dau. of Sylvester Merkt and Josephine Merkt; bp. 2 Jun 1924; conf. 2 Jun 1924; m. Wilhelm Friedrich Krötz; d. asthma 24 Dec 1940 (FHL microfilm 68807, book 2, no. 5; FHL microfilm 271381; 1930 and 1935 censuses; IGI)

Erwin Eugen Riecker b. Mettingen, Esslingen, Neckarkreis, Württemberg, 8 Dec 1917; son of Eugen Riecker and Ernestine Margarete Fingerle; bp. 23 Dec 1928; conf. 23 Dec 1928; ord. deacon 7 Jul 1935; lance corporal; k. in battle Ssokorowo, Russia, 27 Mar 1942 (FHL microfilm 68807, book 2, no. 8; FHL microfilm 271403; 1930 and 1935 censuses; IGI; www.volksbund.de)

Elise Sprenger b. Wetzikon, Zürich, Switzerland, 15 Oct 1868; dau. of Johannes Sprenger and Agnes Eugster; bp. 11 Apr 1924; conf. 11 Apr 1924; m. —— Kurle; missing as of 20 Nov 1946 (FHL microfilm 68807, book 1, no. 926; FHL microfilm 271382; 1930 and 1935 censuses; IGI)

Wilhelmine Stierle b. Stetten, Echterdingen, Neckarkreis, Württemberg, 2 May 1872; dau. of Andreas Wilhelm T. Stierle and Rosine K. Gehr; bp. 18 Jul 1914; conf. 18 Jul 1914; m. Stetten, 10 Dec 1893, Franz Smyzcek; 5 children; d. asthma Esslingen, 6 or 13 Oct 1941 (FHL microfilm 68807, book 2, no. 693; IGI, AF)

Walter Rudolf Tischhauser b. Stuttgart, Neckarkreis, Württemberg, 23 Aug 1926; son of Richard Karl Tischhauser and Lina Rosa Fingerle; bp. 23 Jul 1939; conf. 23 Jul 1939; infantry; k. in battle Kampenau near Gotenhafen, 5 Apr 1945 (CHL microfilm 2458, form 42 FP, pt. 37, all-mission list 1943–46, 186–87, district list 218–19; FHL microfilm 68807, book 2, no. 206; www.volksbund.de; E. Tischhauser Ertel, AF, PRF)

Helene Elsa Zügel b. Rudersberg, Jagstkreis, Württemberg, 21 Feb 1911; dau. of Karl Gottlob Zügel and Ernestine Wenninger; bp. 22 Jun 1919; conf. 22 Jun 1919; d. septic angina (suspected euthanasia) 16 Dec 1940 (FHL microfilm 68807, book 2, no. 306; FHL microfilm 245307, 1930 and 1935 censuses; IGI)

Walter Nephi Karl Zügel b. Esslingen, Neckarkreis, Württemberg, 9 May 1923; son of Karl Gottlob Zügel and Ernestine Wenninger; bp. 25 Jun 1931; conf. 25 Jun 1931; ord. deacon 21 May 1939; k. in battle near Metz, Alsace-Lorraine, France, 9 Nov 1944; bur. Andilly, France (FHL microfilm 68807, book 1, no. 814; FHL microfilm 245307; 1930 and 1935 censuses; IGI; www.volksbund.de)

Notes

1. Esslingen city archive.
2. West German Mission branch directory, 1939, CHL LR 10045 11.
3. Presiding Bishopric, "Financial, Statistical, and Historical Reports of Wards, Stakes, and Missions, 1884–1955," 257, CR 4 12.
4. Ilse Anita Neff Bauer, interview by Jennifer Heckmann in German, Esslingen, Germany, August 23, 2007; unless otherwise noted, summarized in English by Judith Sartowski.
5. Walter Richard Tischhauser, telephone interview with Jennifer Heckmann in German, January 20, 2009.
6. Elsbeth Tischhauser Ertel, interview by Jennifer Heckmann in German, Langen, Germany, August 14, 2006.
7. Stuttgart District general minutes, 162, CHL CR 16982 11.
8. Ibid., 169.
9. Ibid., 177.
10. Ibid., 199.
11. Hans Ludwig Fingerle, interview by the author in German, Hermannsweiler, Germany, August 20, 2008.
12. Ludwig Erwin Fingerle to Margarete Kirsch Fingerle, February 11, 1945; trans. the author; used with the permission of Hans Fingerle.
13. Margarete Kirsch Fingerle to Ludwig Erwin Fingerle, April 8, 1945; trans. the author; used with the permission of Hans Fingerle.
14. Lina also lost a half-brother. Four of the five men were members of the Church.
15. Horst von Glasenapp to Margarete Fingerle, August 11, 1948; trans. the author; used with the permission of Hans Fingerle.

Feuerbach Branch

"The branch meeting rooms were in a Hinterhaus on Elsenheimsstrasse," recalled Reinhold Rügner (born 1931). "We went through the main building at number 8, then across a courtyard and into the Hinterhaus. We had all of our meetings in one large room. There was room for forty to sixty people. We also used the foyer and the kitchen for classes. We didn't have restrooms."[1] Such was the setting of the Feuerbach Branch.

Hermann Mössner (born 1922) added the following details to his cousin's description:

> A family who belonged to the Apostolic Church owned the building. They were very religious people and strong members of their church. They allowed us to use their rooms but we weren't allowed to dance or have dance lessons, which the young members of our Church always liked. The rooms were located near a chicken coop and every time we went to meetings, the chickens were very loud. It wasn't a very inviting atmosphere for Church meetings, but we accepted it. On the inside, the rooms were kept very simple.[2]

Barely three miles north of the center of Stuttgart, Feuerbach was nearly a suburb of the provincial capital. The branch there had sixty-three members and was in good condition in the summer of 1939. Reinhold's father, Gottlob Rügner, was the branch president and was assisted by counselors Johann Buck and Hans Lang. Other branch leaders at the time were Hermann Mössner (YMMIA), Bretel Buck (YWMIA), and Maria Greiner (Relief Society). The branch president was also the genealogy instructor and Sister Greiner was *Der Stern* magazine representative. There was no Primary organization at the time.[3]

The meeting schedule shows several gatherings beginning at 8:00 p.m., such as the Relief Society on Mondays and the MIA on Tuesdays, which must have been slightly inconvenient for the branch members who lived in other towns around Feuerbach. The Sunday School began at 10:00 and was followed by priesthood meeting at 11:30, with sacrament meeting at 7:00 p.m.

Feuerbach Branch[4]	**1939**
Elders	7
Priests	1
Teachers	4
Deacons	2
Other Adult Males	7
Adult Females	36
Male Children	4
Female Children	2
Total	63

Brother Rügner's family walked about one hour to church from Weilimdorf. With eight children, there was not enough money to pay for a streetcar ride unless the weather was bad. According to Reinhold, "We walked there for Sunday School, then went home and came back later for sacrament meeting." That would have amounted to four hours of walking each Sunday. He added, "One got used to it."

Hermann Mössner recalled the beginnings of war in September 1939:

> I was seventeen years old when World War II started, and for me nothing changed that much. But I remember that some members of our branch became members of the National Socialist Party and even brought their flag into the branch rooms. I remember the exact day that the war started in September of 1939. I was in the third year of my work training as a plumber, and we were working on a project when we heard that Adolf Hitler had declared the war at midnight the night before. It was such an uncertain situation for all of us, and we didn't understand why there was a second war now [after Germany lost the Great War in 1918].

Fig. 1. The Jungvolk group to which Reinhold Rügner belonged in about 1942. (R. Rügner)

"I was baptized in either 1939 or 1940 in the Neckar River. It was summer and the water was warm. Karl Mössner baptized me, and he died as a soldier a little bit later [1941]," recalled Reinhold Rügner. By 1943, life in Weilimdorf was becoming difficult as attacks on Stuttgart threatened the towns nearby. Reinhold was evacuated with his class to the town of Kuchen, where the boys were taken in by local families. Reinhold lived with a widow from 1943 to 1944 and described the situation in these words:

> During that year, I was never allowed to go home. Kuchen is about forty miles away from our home. My mother was also not able to visit me during that time. We didn't have the financial means. My father was assigned to visit the Göppingen branch every month or so. On those Sundays, I took the train from Kuchen to Göppingen so that I could attend the meetings with him. I looked forward to those days because I could see a member of my family.

In 1944, Reinhold was sent to a higher-level school in Nürtingen near the Neckar River: "It was a school that was mostly run by the [Nazi] Party. They used it to train their future party members, but it was not official. We stayed in boarding schools. My plan was to finish the degree and then work in the government somewhere later on."

Hermann Mössner was old enough to be drafted by 1942, but his work in a munitions factory in Feuerbach allowed him an exemption. During those years, he often attended branch meetings in Stuttgart when he was off duty. In July 1944, he emerged from a shelter where he had spent many hours during what he called "the heaviest attack on Stuttgart" to find that the rooms of the Stuttgart Branch had been totally destroyed. Because his own apartment was also destroyed, he returned home to live with his parents. By September, he was in the uniform of the German Wehrmacht: "I left my wife with tears in my eyes. We were married for only a

Fig. 2. The Rügner family and other members of the Feuerbach Branch. (R. Rügner)

few weeks." After an abbreviated training period, he was sent off to the Western Front.

As a forward observer in lines opposing British troops, Hermann's responsibility was to report the movements of the enemy. He was so close to the action that while he and his comrades were sheltered in the basement of a house, a British tank ran over the building. Hermann was not harmed, but he was found by the enemy later that day and taken prisoner. It was November 18, 1944, near the city of Aachen, Germany. One month later, the fierce Battle of the Bulge would begin very close to that city; Hermann was safer as a POW. From the first camp in Belgium, he was moved to another in Leeds, England.

The Rügner family apartment was destroyed in an air raid in January 1945, and the family lost most of their property. All that remained were the things they had carried into the shelter and some items that had been stored in the basement. Reinhold was allowed to leave school for a few weeks to assist his father in the cleanup. About that time, the branch meeting rooms were damaged, but the broken windows were covered up, and life went on.

Reinhold recalled losing his brother Werner in the last year of the war: "He told us right before he left that he really did not want to leave [for war] anymore. My brother died in an airplane accident on June 6, 1944, in Czechoslovakia. He had been on leave until June 1 and had just reported back for duty. A telegram with the message of his death was handed to us by a city official."

Reinhold was sent home from the Nürtingen school in April 1945 and arrived in time to see the French invaders arrive. He told this story:

> To be honest, we had great respect for the French. It was a scary time. Many of the French soldiers had dark skin because they came from Morocco. That was the first time that I saw dark-skinned people. I knew that they existed, but it was a good experience to finally meet an African person. Often, they acted very uncivilized and would steal the chickens and rabbits that we raised for food. We also had a curfew and were not allowed to leave the house after four or five p.m.

Fig. 3. The Primary organization of the Feuerbach Branch. (R. Rügner)

Life under military occupation was an insecure existence at best. Gottlob Rügner once stood between his daughter and French soldiers with evil intent who threatened to shoot the branch president. He stood his ground, and the soldiers left. On another occasion, Reinhold and a sister climbed out of their window after curfew and ran two blocks to a house where a French officer was quartered to report soldiers threatening their family. The officer returned with them, "raised his gun, and walked into our home. He escorted the soldiers out just in the nick of time."

Fig. 4. Family members of Reinhold Rügner. (R. Rügner)

As a POW in England, Hermann Mössner was a very successful missionary for the Church. He told this story:

> I was the only Latter-day Saint [among the German POWs]. I taught the other soldiers who shared a room with me and they were ready to get baptized when it was time for us to go home. The baptism took place while we were still prisoners. The British Latter-day Saints came and picked us up and the entire camp noticed it. The Catholic priest, who was also a German, started to complain to the commandant of the camp. I was then invited to the office of the British major, and next to him stood a representative of the Church of England. He was the only one who spoke to me and it was not in a nice tone of voice. He asked me, "By what authority to do baptize your fellow prisoners?" He screamed that question. I, in contrast, answered him with a calm voice that we did it with the authority of the priesthood (I had been ordained an elder in 1943). He then yelled at me to get out of the room. By the end of the time in the camp, there were five of us members of the Church. They went home and even converted their families. I also carried my scriptures with me—even in the most dangerous situations at the front. I was so blessed through that. I lost my scriptures, which were given to me by my grandfather, when I was at the front one day. But when I was in England, I wrote a letter to the mission office in London, and they sent me Church literature to read.

Brother Mössner was allowed to conduct the baptisms of his friends in the Bradford/Leeds chapel.[5] On many Sundays, the POWs walked three miles from the camp to church, where they struggled with the English language but not with the communications of the Holy Spirit. Hermann was actually called to be the Sunday School president while a POW there. Unashamed of the gospel of Christ and not afraid of his captors, Hermann also worked to find a dignified place to meet in the camp with the converts. His story continues:

> The officers in the camp did not allow us to hold meetings in the chapel that was available. But I wrote to Salt Lake City and complained that we wanted a place to meet. Just a short time later, I was again asked to go into the commandant's office. He then allowed us to hold meetings in the chapel. Gordon B. Hinckley was the one who received my postcard and wrote a letter to the camp in which we were held. We conducted our meetings but we didn't have the sacrament during that time. We also had some investigators who attended our meetings. We were also allowed to leave the camp on Sundays, so six or more German prisoners of war walked to Leeds

City to find a branch to attend. People spit at us and laughed. The branch in Leeds was so welcoming, and they were happy to have us.[6]

Fig. 5. Hermann Mössner, a German elder and the men he introduced to the gospel (from left): Wolfgang Krüger, Willi Raschke, Hermann Mössner, Heinz Borchert, Erich Rühlike. (H. Mössner)

During his incarceration, Hermann was called to the camp office one day and introduced to Hugh B. Brown, then the president of the British Mission. President Brown had been conducting a district conference nearby and had heard of this young German Latter-day Saint. Hermann was moved by the compassion of that great leader.[7]

Hermann Mössner's remarkable story of religious dedication among German POWs had a happy ending:

> I was sent home in May 1948. My son was already three years old, and it was the first time that I was able to see him. Coming home was the most wonderful day of my life. The train stopped in the station, and the authorities told us that we had to wait until we were released the next day. We thought that because the train was already at its final destination, we would be able to walk those few miles home. That's what we did. The next morning, I walked back to the train and we were released. Everybody was so surprised to see me again.[8]

The Feuerbach Branch had suffered significant losses in families, homes, and property, but the survivors continued to hold meetings and regrouped in the summer of 1945. In retrospect, Hermann observed:

> The accounts of distress of individual families whose fathers and sons had died at the war front, and the losses among the members due to air raids were painful; yet it was the faith in our God and the firm hope of eternal life that gave us the strength to carry on.[9]

In Memoriam

The following members of the Feuerbach Branch did not survive World War II:

Karoline Friederike Bauer b. Neuenhaus, Nürtingen, Schwarzwaldkreis, Württemberg, 1 Nov 1887; dau. of Ernst Ludwig Bauer and Marie Katharine Schlecht; bp. 27 Sep 1928; conf. 27 Sep 1928; m. Ludwigsburg, Ludwigsburg, Württemberg, 14 Jan 1912 or 1913, Adolf Peukert; d. peritonitis, 11 Nov 1940 (FHL microfilm 68807, book 2, no. 325; FHL microfilm 245254; 1930 and 1935 censuses; IGI)

Emil Buck b. Stuttgart, Feuerbach, Neckarkreis, Württemberg, 13 Jul 1912; son of Johannes Buck and Sophie Löffler; bp. 11 Apr 1924; conf. 11 Apr 1924; corporal; d. H.V. Pl. Melnitschny/Kuban 10 Aug 1943; bur. Apscheronsk, Russia (FS; www.volksbund.de)

Frieda Patzsch Lehmann b. Triberg, Villingen, Baden, 16 Dec 1891; dau. of Lukas Lehmann and Kandide Schweer; bp. 30 May 1931; conf. 30 May 1931; m. Hermann Louis Patzsch; m. 18 Dec 1938, Gottfried Horrlacher; d. sickness 20 Sep or Oct 1939 (FHL microfilm 68790, no. 39; CHL CR 375 8, 2451, no. 499; IGI)

Hildegard Mössner b. Feuerbach, Neckarkreis, Württemberg, 13 Jan 1918; dau. of Karl Mössner and Rosine Wilhelmine Schönhardt; bp. 22 May 1927; conf. 22 May 1927; d. hemoptysis and tuberculosis 10 Feb 1940 (FHL microfilm 68790, no. 15; IGI; FHL microfilm 68807, book 1, no. 402; CHL CR 375 8, 2451, no. 402; FHL microfilm 245238; 1930 and 1935 censuses)

Karl Mössner Jr. b. Feuerbach, Neckarkreis, Württemberg, 11 Dec 1912; son of Karl Mössnerk Sr. and Rosine Wilhelmine Schönhardt; bp. 10 Feb 1924; conf. 10 Feb 1924; ord. deacon 15 Apr 1928; ord. teacher 23 Aug 1931; ord. priest 9 Feb 1935; ord. elder 25 Apr 1937, Swiss-German Mission; m. 15 Feb 1936, Else Kübler (div.); m. 29 Oct 1938, Olga Poers or Evers; rifleman; k. in battle near Karoli, Belarus, 18 Jul 1941 (FHL microfilm 68790, no. 13; www.volksbund.de; FHL microfilm 68807, book 1, no. 860; CHL CR 375 8, 2451, no. 860; IGI; AF)

Esther Rügner b. Feuerbach, Neckarkreis, Württemberg, 20 Apr 1919; dau. of Gottlob Rügner and Lina Dorothea Schonhardt; bp. 6 Jun 1928; conf. 6 Jun 1928; m. Stuttgart, Neckarkreis, Württemberg, 5 Feb 1938, Herbert Helmrich; d. Typhoid, Bad Diersdorf, Eulengeb., Sil., Preußen, 9 or 10 September 1935 (FS; Reinhold Rügner)

Werner Friedrich Rügner b. Stuttgart, Neckarkreis, Württemberg, 12 Jan 1923; son of Gottlob Rügner and Lina Dorothea Schönhardt; bp. 25 Jan 1931; conf. 25 Jan 1931; ord. deacon 20 Jun 1937; ord. teacher 2 Mar 1941; ord. priest 30 Mar or May 1944; lance corporal; k. airplane accident Wobora, 6 Jun 1944; bur. Plzen, Czechoslovakia (FHL microfilm 68790, no. 24; FHL microfilm 68807, book 1, no. 434; FHL microfilm no. 271407; 1930 and 1935 censuses; www.volksbund.de; IGI; AF)

Fig. 6. Werner Rügner as a Hitler Youth and as a soldier of the Luftwaffe. (R. Rügner)

Notes

1. Reinhold Rügner, interview by Michael Corley, Salt Lake City, December 5, 2008.
2. Hermann Mössner, interview by Jennifer Heckmann in German, Stuttgart, Germany, August 23, 2007; summarized in English by Judith Sartowski.
3. West German Mission branch directory, 1939, CHL LR 10045 11.
4. Presiding Bishopric, "Financial, Statistical, and Historical Reports of Wards, Stakes, and Missions, 1884–1955," 257, CHL CR 4 12.
5. Hermann Mössner, "Mormon Pioneers in Southern Germany" (unpublished manuscript).
6. Mössner, interview.
7. Mössner, "Mormon Pioneers."
8. Mössner, interview.
9. Mössner, "Mormon Pioneers."

Göppingen Branch

The city of Göppingen is located twenty miles east of Stuttgart on the main railway line to Munich. With 28,101 inhabitants in 1939, the city was in many respects representative of towns in the historic south German region of Swabia.[1]

Göppingen Branch[2]	**1939**
Elders	2
Priests	0
Teachers	0
Deacons	0
Other Adult Males	4
Adult Females	14
Male Children	3
Female Children	2
Total	25

The branch of the Latter-day Saints that met in rented rooms on the second floor of the building at Poststrasse 15 in Göppingen was one of the smallest in the West German Mission in 1939. Of the twenty-five members, only two (both elders) held the priesthood. The largest component of the membership were women over twelve years of age. The meeting schedule showed Sunday School beginning at 10:00 and sacrament meeting at 7:00 p.m. The Primary organization met on Wednesdays at 3:00 p.m. and the MIA on Wednesdays at 8:00 p.m.

The leader of this small branch throughout the war was Georg Schaaf. The other elder and the only other man listed among the branch leaders in July 1939 was Friedrich Weixler, who served at the time as the first counselor in the branch and as the superintendant of the Sunday School. The lone woman in the branch directory was Dorothea Weixler (the president of the Relief Society).[3]

Brother Schaaf kept detailed minutes of the meetings held in this small branch. Those minutes survived the war and give important insights into the status of the branch during the years 1939 to 1945. For the most part, only the activities of the meetings are given, with rare information about events elsewhere. For example, there is no mention of the departure of the American missionaries in August 1939 nor the outbreak of war a week later. Nothing is written about air raids over Göppingen or of the end of the war when the American army entered the town on Hitler's birthday, April 20, 1945.[4]

Ruth Schaaf (born 1930), a daughter of the branch president, recalled that there were two rooms used by the branch at Poststrasse 15. She did not recall specific furnishing or decorations but said that there was a pump organ that was moved to her family's apartment when the branch rooms were confiscated. "Some members from Ulm also came to our branch meetings because they didn't have a branch anywhere near them."[5] Werner Weixler (born 1932) recalled that Poststrasse 15 was an office or manufacturing building owned by the Stern family, who were Jewish. There was no sign on the building indicating the presence of the branch there.[6]

Friedrich Weixler (born 1909) was drafted into the German army in 1940. He had been employed as a department head in a leather factory but had attracted negative attention in at least one respect. One day the government suddenly discontinued paying child support to the Weixler family. When Brother Weixler inquired of the local Nazi Party boss, he was told that as long as he paid 10 percent of his income to the Church, he would not receive subsidies for his children.[7] "After my husband left for the service, we had just enough money to pay the rent but hardly any money for food or anything else," recalled Dorothea Weixler (born 1910).

Like most German schoolchildren, Ruth Schaaf was a member of the Jungvolk. She recalled the experience in these words:

> We mostly learned about the country's leaders, for example, where they were born, etc. I still remember when Hitler was born and where. We also learned how to do crafts. We also wore our uniforms (that was required)—a white blouse and a black skirt combined with a khaki jacket. Later on, we also had a black necktie and a special kind of knot in the front. We went and waved whenever there was a parade. We also stood at attention at a specific location whenever there was a radio broadcast with a speech by the Führer.

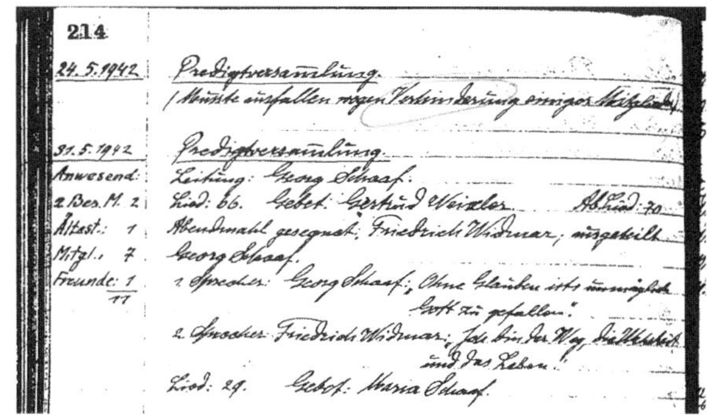

214

24.5.1942 Predigtversammlung.
(Musste ausfallen wegen Verhinderung einiger Mitglieder)

31.5.1942 Predigtversammlung.
Anwesend: Leitung: Georg Schaaf.
2 Bez.M. 2 Lied: 66. Gebet: Gertrud Weixler. Abl. Lied: 70
Ältest.: 1 Abendmahl gesegnet: Friedrich Widmar; ausgeteilt
Mitgl.: 7 Georg Schaaf.
Freunde: 1 1. Sprecher: Georg Schaaf: „Ohne Glauben ists unmöglich
11 Gott zu gefallen."
2. Sprecher: Friedrich Widmar: „Ich bin der Weg, die Wahrheit
und das Leben."
Lied: 29. Gebet: Maria Schaaf.

Fig. 1. An example of Göppingen branch minutes. (CHL)

The branch minutes feature prominently the names of three families: Schaaf, Weixler, and Ceol. These families clearly constituted the majority of the attendees at sacrament and fast meetings for at least the years 1939 through 1942. The average attendance in those days was twelve persons (very precisely counted). An example of a typical sacrament meeting record is as follows:

> May 31, 1942: Sacrament meeting
> Presiding: Georg Schaaf; hymn 66; invocation: Gertrud Weixler; sacrament hymn 70; sacrament blessed by Friedrich Widmar and passed by Georg Schaaf. First speaker: Georg Schaaf "Without faith it is impossible to please God;" second speaker: Friedrich Widmar "I am the way, the truth and the life;" hymn 29; benediction: Maria Schaaf. Attendance: two members from the district, one elder, seven members, one friend.[8]

The average attendance at meetings of the Göppingen Branch actually increased during the war thanks to an influx of visitors from the district and other branches. From twelve persons in 1942, the number rose to seventeen in 1943 and eighteen during the final year and a half of the war. On occasion, there were as many as twenty-three persons present, but there were likewise days when only nine persons came to church. On a regular basis, district president Erwin Ruf inspected the records and added his signature of approval.

As the president of the Relief Society in Göppingen, Dorothea Weixler once arranged to have a celebration in the banquet room of a local restaurant, as she recalled: "But when we got there, we were not alone. Somebody from the government came to see what we were doing. We had a good party—and he liked it too. He stayed with us the entire time."

Werner Weixler recalled the influence of the Nazi Party in his school. On political holidays, his teachers wore SA uniforms. He described some of his teachers:

> I clearly remember two of them. I was still friendly with one of them after the war; he was just misled. But the other one was a real fanatic: Herr Beck. He was our history teacher and he always brought the Bible with him. He really knew the Bible, but not because he was a good Christian—just the opposite. He loved to show us everything bad about the Jewish people and their literature.

Magdalena Ceol (born 1931) was the daughter of an Italian (Guiseppe Francisco Ceol) and a German (Renate Marie Maier). The Ceol family regularly attended branch meetings (where Brother Ceol's name was recorded as "Georg Franz"), but Magdalena recalled that social and political pressures were applied to her father because of his Italian heritage: "My whole family hated the German government because of this." In response, Brother Ceol decided to take his family to Italy in 1943. They lived in relative peace there, although two of the Ceol sons were drafted into the Italian army.[9]

Heinz Weixler turned ten in 1943 and was automatically inducted into the Jungvolk program. He gave the following description of the group's activities:

> For me, it was a lot of fun. Every Wednesday and Saturday, we had to appear at the meetings. On Wednesdays, we put on our uniforms. We had one for the summer and one for the winter. Our leaders were only two or three years older than we were. The oldest boy in the entire unit could have been eighteen or nineteen. We even had our own rooms to meet in. They taught us how the war was going and we played war games. We went to the forest and had little colored strings around our arms. Red meant that that you belonged to one group, and blue the other group. They encouraged fighting and wrestling. It was a lot of fun for most of us but not for everybody. It depended on whether you were athletically inclined or not. But if there was a boy that was not physically fit, he was made fun of.

District conferences held in Stuttgart were evidently important occasions for the Göppingen Saints who could make the trip in less than one hour by train. The branch minutes indicate that substantial numbers traveled to the capital city twice each year to participate. On October 18, 1943, sixteen members and five friends from Göppingen attended the conference and were informed that the Stuttgart Branch rooms had been damaged so severely in an air raid on October 7–8 that they could no longer be used.[10]

A close study of the branch minutes allows the inference that President Georg Schaaf was in poor health for much of the war. At least once a month, meetings were cancelled due to his illness or simply the fact that he was unable to attend. On occasion, a visiting elder presided over the meetings. By mid-1944, Gottlob Rügner, an elder from the Feuerbach Branch, had been asked to assist the branch in Göppingen.

A sad development was recorded in the minutes in August 1944: "On August 9, we were required to make our meeting rooms available for use by people bombed out of their homes. Until further notice, the meetings will take place in the branch president's apartment. The following items were left in the rooms: a stove, a table, two chairs, a lamp, and the blackout curtains."[11]

Ruth Schaaf recalled that her family lived in a very poor neighborhood. Her father had suffered a serious injury to his hand as a young man, which prevented him from becoming a craftsman. This impediment relegated the family to a low socioeconomic status. Werner Weixler recalled being a bit embarrassed at entering the Schaafs' neighborhood to attend branch meetings in the branch president's home: "It wasn't a great neighborhood, and I was embarrassed that when we were singing, the neighbors could hear us."

Werner recalled another situation at school. He was an excellent pupil and was tested for candidacy for an elite Nazi Party school in Rottweil. It was a great honor in Germany at the time, but Friedrich Weixler would not sign the admission papers for his son. As a social democrat before the war, Brother Weixler was still very much opposed to Hitler's party and the government.[12] Werner recalled being somewhat disappointed when one of the other boys chosen for that school came home on vacation: "I was jealous of him because he always had a sharp uniform. I could have been one of them."

"I never met another Mormon soldier while I was away from home," recalled Friedrich Weixler, "but I carried a Book of Mormon with me. I served in Russia, Hungary, Poland, Bulgaria, Albania, and France." Back in Göppingen, Sister Weixler firmly believed that her husband would come home some day: "I never thought anything else," she said. He came home on leave only two or three times during his five years of service and never wrote to say that he would be coming home soon.

By August 1944, Renate Ceol had returned from Italy to Göppingen with her daughter Magdalena, and the two experienced the air raids of the last few months of the war. During one of those attacks, the Ceols' apartment building was hit by incendiary bombs. Magdalena recalled that when she and her mother emerged from the basement shelter as the all-clear signal sounded, the upper floors of the building were already on fire.

In 1944, Ruth Schaaf was called upon to serve her Pflichtjahr, an experience that she described as follows:

> I served my duty year in the home of another family. I was allowed to choose between helping on a farm or living with a family who had many children. I helped a Mrs. Wendling, who had four little children. They also lived in Göppingen. At first, I still lived with my parents, but after a while I had to move in with the family. After I was done with my duty year [in February 1945], I worked for a wood company in Göppingen-Holzheim.

During one of the attacks on Göppingen, the Schaafs' apartment house was damaged. Ruth recalled, "I was on my way down to the basement when I stopped and wondered where my little sister Elfriede was. I turned around, went back up to the apartment and found her underneath all the shattered glass from the window. I grabbed her and carried her downstairs."

Elfriede Schaaf was only four years old when Göppingen was targeted by the Americans for bombings, but she clearly recalled being showered by glass that day. She explained that her parents usually took the children to a concrete bunker not far from their home but that they also took shelter in their own basement on occasion. "If I close my eyes the film starts: I can still see the bombs falling and my sister running out of the room. . . . I was only a child, but I already knew what war was about."[13]

On the other hand, war had its elements of adventure for little boys. Werner Weixler recalled looking out the attic window to see the American bombers going by. On one such occasion, however, the thrill of the spectacle nearly turned to tragedy: "They were almost right overhead. Suddenly we saw the bomb bays open and the bombs dropping. We were so shocked that we had barely crossed the room when the first bombs struck the ground just a little ways down the street. [Afterward] we went out and saw huge holes in the street and houses burning."

One day, Werner went to school to find out that his closest friend was not there; he had been killed in an air raid.

With the events of the war intensifying in the spring of 1945, meetings of the Göppingen Branch were frequently canceled. Such was the case on four consecutive Sundays beginning on March 18. The entry on April 15 includes two important and rare events in the branch: infant Siegfried Schaaf was blessed, and Magdalena Ceol was confirmed a member of the Church. Both ordinances were performed by visiting elder Meinrad Greiner during the Sunday School hour "for fear of an impending air raid alarm."[14] Just five days later, the American army arrived; the war was over for the people of Göppingen.

Little Elfriede Schaaf remembered interacting with the conquerors:

> American soldiers were very good to us children. They shared their food with us. We each picked one soldier and called him "my soldier." One time, while I was waiting for my soldier to come, I was trying to follow my siblings and friends when they climbed up onto something. But it was too high for me. A black soldier lifted me up and gave me a kiss on the cheek. I ran home that day thinking that I would turn black if I didn't wash my face. So I washed. I told my mother the story because she was already wondering why I was in such a panic. She laughed when she heard what had happened.

"When the Americans entered Göppingen, we were hiding in the basement. We heard the trucks and tanks driving by," recalled Heinz Weixler. "I was not scared when the Americans came to Göppingen," his mother explained, "but I had a funny feeling. It was so strange to see the enemy in our town." Like millions of Germans, they realized that they had lost the war and simply hoped for decent treatment at the hands of the victors.

Looking back on her youth during the war years, Ruth Schaaf offered this observation: "Even though it was a war situation, I was not afraid of getting hurt or dying. When the war was over, I was fifteen years old. So in a sense, playtime for me was already over anyway. But we found ways to entertain ourselves even despite the realization that there was a war being fought around us."

Friedrich Weixler served as a communications specialist, his principal duty being to lay telephone wires. Looking back on his time as a soldier, he explained: "I was a good Mormon. I didn't smoke or drink alcohol. I was a good soldier and didn't shoot people. It was important for me to not be guilty of that. The Lord protected me in every way." On one occasion, Friedrich was commanded to execute four civilians but was fortunate because even though he declined to shoot innocent civilians, he escaped punishment for refusing to obey an order. In May 1945, he was captured by the Americans in southern Germany. However, in the confusion of the immediate aftermath of the war, he managed to slip away and make his way home to Göppingen. He thus avoided what could have been years of imprisonment.

The city of Göppingen suffered four major air raids that cost at least 325 people their lives, and approximately two thousand of the town's men died for their country.[15] On May 6, 1945, Georg Schaaf made his first peacetime entry in the branch minutes, allowing the presumption that the Göppingen Latter-day Saints were determined to maintain the life of their branch in a ruined but renewed Germany. They had weathered a terrible war and remained faithful in their callings.

IN MEMORIAM

The following members of the Göppingen Branch did not survive World War II:

Erich Arthur Ceol b. Göppingen, Württemberg, 22 Apr 1919; son of Joseph Franz Ceol and Maria Renata Maier; bp. 10 Oct 1929; conf. 10 Oct 1929; missing as of 20 Mar 1944 (CHL CR 375 8 2445, no. 783; FHL microfilm no. 25738; 1930 and 1935 censuses; IGI; AF; PRF)

Wilhelm Rube b. Unterurbach, Jagstkreis, Württemberg, 25 Nov 1878; son of Johann Georg Rube and Sabine Zehnter or Zehender; bp. 13 Sep 1929; conf.

13 Sep 1929; m. 28 May 1910, Margarethe Katherina Stettner; 2 children; d. suicide, Göppingen, Donaukreis, Württemberg, 29 Jun 1946 (FHL microfilm 68807, book 2, no. 399; FHL microfilm no. 271407; 1930 and 1935 censuses; IGI)

Paulina Wittlinger b. Holzheim, Donaukreis, Württemberg, 6 Sep 1871; dau. of Johannes Wittlinger and Katharine Hörmann or Hermann; bp. 14 Jul 1929; conf. 14 Jul 1929; m. —— Lang; d. old age 7 Nov 1946 (FHL microfilm 68807, book 2, no. 381; FHL microfilm no. 271383; 1930 and 1935 censuses; IGI; PRF)

Notes

1. Göppingen city archive.
2. Presiding Bishopric, "Financial, Statistical, and Historical Reports of Wards, Stakes, and Missions, 1884–1955," 257, CR 4 12.
3. West German Mission branch directory, 1939, CHL LR 10045 11.
4. Göppingen Branch general minutes, vol. 15, CHL LR 3235 11.
5. Ruth Schaaf Baur, telephone interview with the author in German, April 13, 2009; unless otherwise noted, summarized in English by Judith Sartowski. The city of Ulm was thirty miles southwest of Göppingen.
6. Werner Weixler, interview by the author, Salt Lake City, March 23, 2007.
7. Friedrich, Dorothea Gertrud, and Heinz Weixler, interview by the author in German, Salt Lake City, March 16, 2007.
8. Göppingen Branch general minutes, 214.
9. Magdalena Ceol, telephone interview with the author in German, April 28, 2009.
10. Göppingen Branch general minutes, 226.
11. Ibid., 235.
12. Friedrich Weixler was one of many Germans who listened to BBC radio broadcasts, which was strictly illegal. Werner recalled how his mother scolded her husband for endangering himself and the family.
13. Elfriede Schaaf, telephone interview with the author in German, April 13, 2009.
14. Göppingen Branch general minutes, 240. Magdalena told of being baptized in an indoor pool in Stuttgart.
15. Göppingen city archive.

Heilbronn Branch

The city of Heilbronn on the Neckar River has been an important cultural center for centuries. Located twenty-five miles north of Stuttgart near the borders of the states of Baden and Hessen, the city once had a flourishing Jewish community and was the center of business for miles around.

Heilbronn Branch[1]	1939
Elders	3
Priests	2
Teachers	0
Deacons	3
Other Adult Males	7
Adult Females	30
Male Children	3
Female Children	6
Total	54

As war approached in Europe in the late summer of 1939, the branch of The Church of Jesus Christ of Latter-day Saints in Heilbronn numbered fifty-four persons. The great majority were twelve or older, and eight men and boys held the priesthood. Most branch leadership positions were filled in those days, with Emil Geist serving as the president. His only counselor at the time was Josef Schurr. President Geist was also the leader of the Sunday School, while Richard Geist guided the activities of the YMMIA and Rosa Christmann the YWMIA. Käthe Geist was the president of the Relief Society and Otto Christmann promoted *Der Stern* magazine subscriptions. There was no Primary president or genealogical instructor in the branch at that time.[2]

The Sunday School was held at 10:00 a.m. in 1939, and sacrament meeting convened in the evening at 7:00 p.m. The MIA members met on Tuesday evenings at 8:00 p.m., and the Relief Society on Fridays at 8:00 p.m. All meetings were held in rented rooms in a building at Goethestrasse 41. Heinz Mahler (born 1931) recalled the nice furnishings in the room in a Hinterhaus, including a rostrum, a pump organ, and a banner hanging over the podium with the words "The Glory of God Is

Intelligence." There were several classrooms and even a kitchen.[3] Heinz recalled walking a few miles to the meeting house; many other branch members also had a long walk there.

Helga Hock (born 1934) added the following detail:

> We met in the upper rooms of the Hinterhaus. There was one large room for sacrament meeting and several smaller rooms for Sunday School. We had pictures on the wall of Joseph Smith and other prophets of the Church. We also had a picture of the temple. . . . We sat on chairs in our rooms and took those with us [when we moved out of the building]. On a typical Sunday, there were about twenty-five to thirty members in attendance.[4]

Heinz Mahler recalled clearly the outbreak of war in 1939: "Soldiers marched through the town to the railroad station, and people walked with them; the kids walked along with them, they had flowers in their rifles. It was a big, spectacular parade." He also recalled the victory parade at the end of the campaign against France in June 1940: "There was a regiment of white horses from Heilbronn. We stood in the window of the city hall where my aunt worked, and we could see the big parade." Spirits were very high in Germany at the time.

According to the centennial history of the Heilbronn Branch, Emil Geist was too old to be drafted and thus was able to stay in town and direct the activities of the branch during the entire war. In 1941, the contract for the rental of the meeting rooms was canceled, and a new location needed to be found. Eveline Christmann Mohr described the situation:

> My father [Otto Christmann] was one of the first men to be drafted. We had moved into our new home with its art studio in the spring [of 1939] and he had to leave his 30-year-old wife and their three little children. So we rearranged the studio to make room for the branch meetings. There were [on average] about twenty people in attendance. Our house was spared the damage of the air raids.[5]

Eveline's brother, Alex (born 1932) recalled that the studio was a former garage, but once outfitted for meetings, "it looked like a real church building. We had one large room and two smaller rooms with a podium and chairs. It was a smaller branch, but we liked our group."[6]

Alex described wartime life and feelings in these words:

> During the first few years of the war, it seemed that our daily schedules were not interrupted very much. We went to school, did our homework, helped in the house, and played outside. During the last two years, it got more difficult because of the constant air raids. It was hard for me to realize that everything was being destroyed and people were dying. I became very angry at the people who caused so many to suffer. I was angry and disappointed at the British and the Americans for leaving so much chaos behind. But war is war—what else could I expect?

Fig. 1. The Christmann home on Viktor Scheffel Strasse in which branch meetings were held from 1941 through the end of the war. (100 Jahre Gemeinde Heilbronn)

Emil Geist was the brother of Martha Mahler and uncle of Heinz, who recalled how his uncle was once summoned to the police office along with the branch records. President Geist insisted that he was not allowed to show the records to anybody but Church officials, which made the police that much more suspicious. Then Heinz's father, Ludwig Mahler (a former longtime member of the Nazi Party's SA organization) went to the aid of his brother-in-law. He promised the police that Emil Geist was telling the truth and that the only information in the records books was that of donations made by members to the Church. President Geist was released without penalty.

Helga Hock explained that her father was quite opposed to National Socialist politics. She recalled the following:

> There were also some brethren who came to Church in their uniforms. It made my father very angry because he didn't understand what that had to do with the Church. Those brethren also made sure that we knew that they supported Hitler. They also prayed for the Führer. My father was not interested in politics at all. He had served in World War I and had lost all of his brothers in that war. He said that one war in his life was enough for him, and he knew that when Hitler became the chancellor, another war would be the result.

Little Gisela Mahler (born 1937) recalled the political forces influencing her young life: "We had to hang out a swastika flag from the window. And when we were out in public we had to raise our arms and say 'Heil Hitler.' And even in school we had to greet the teacher with 'Heil Hitler, teacher so-and-so.'"[7]

A huge air raid struck Heilbronn on September 10, 1944. According to Heinz Mahler, "Nobody was prepared for that. We didn't take it seriously because it hadn't happened before. Lots of people didn't even go to the shelters." The building in which the Mahlers lived was hit by incendiary bombs and began to burn. Down in the basement, the smoke was so thick that little Gisela (age seven) passed out. Heinz first thought that she was dead, but he lifted her up and carried her out of the basement. In escaping the building, he had to jump over a small pool of phosphorus that had not yet ignited. Still carrying his little sister, he was finally able to get out in the open. A soldier helped revive Gisela. Their father located them a few minutes later at a prearranged meeting place. Heinz then noticed that there were several holes burned in his clothing by cinders falling from the sky.

That air raid cost the family their earthly belongings, but they were all still alive. However, Heinz lost a dear friend, as he recalled:

> When I was about twelve or thirteen, I loved to build model ships. A neighbor girl would come over to the house and help me; she would cut out the pieces and I would glue them together. She was a good friend. I once gave her a string bracelet that she tied around her wrist. After the terrible air raid of September 10, 1944, I was worried about her, so I ran down the street toward her house, seeing lots of smoke in that direction. Apparently her neighborhood had been hit. When I got there, I saw a long row of bodies laid out on the sidewalk, covered up by tarps. At the end of the row I saw an arm uncovered, and I recognized the bracelet on the wrist. I was absolutely crushed when I realized that she had been killed.

Fig. 2. Members of the Heilbronn Branch in 1944. (100 Jahre Gemeinde Heilbronn)

Helga's grandfather was eighty-four years old and a bit feeble. One day when it came time to hurry to an air-raid shelter, he insisted on staying in the basement of his own apartment house. Other family members got out of the building after it was hit and began to burn, but the old man went the wrong direction; he left the basement through the back exit and found himself trapped by a fence. The next day his burned body could be identified only by the bones in his hand that had been fractured years earlier.

Toward the end of 1944, Helga Hock followed her mother to the town of Weinsberg, three miles east of Heilbronn and presumably a safer place to live. However, there were other dangers lurking, such as the fanaticism of die-hard Nazis. In 1945, Helga's brother was to be drafted into the Volkssturm as he turned sixteen that year. As Helga recalled: "My mother told him that we had paid enough for the war already and that nobody knew what was going to happen. She wouldn't let him go. So we hid him." Of course, such action was considered treason, and the penalty in those final days of the war was usually death. Fortunately, the boy was not discovered. Helga assumed his duties, such as fetching milk, because he could not show himself in public.

On December 4, 1944, the majority of Heilbronn's downtown was destroyed in a catastrophic air raid. The building at Goethestrasse 41, where the branch had met until 1941, was nothing but rubble. At least two branch members died in the attack, and others lost their apartments, but those who lived on the outskirts of town survived in good condition.[8] Helga Hock lost several of her relatives in that attack—her grandfather, her great-aunt Marie, Marie's daughter Rosa, and the wife of Helga's uncle Karl Christmann and five of their seven children.[9]

As a teenager, Alex Christmann wanted to see the air raids for himself. He recalled one occasion when he went upstairs to look out the attic window instead of going down into the basement shelter:

> The airplanes started flying over the city. We were in the northern part of the city then, and they attacked the southern part. . . . I saw the flames and the smoke in the sky. The attacks were about [three to four miles] distant, so it didn't harm us in any way. But what we could do was watch, and that was just as hurtful. We also had members of our branch who lived in that area, but as far as I know, nobody was directly affected. The city center was heavily destroyed, and even some areas outside the center were damaged. We lived right at the border of the city, and even that area was affected in part. But our street was kept safe for some reason. Nothing happened to us. About two hundred meters away from us, houses had been destroyed and burned out.

The Christmann grandparents died in one raid and several other relatives were killed during the war. Despite the fact that their home on Viktor Scheffel Strasse was not destroyed, Sister Christmann took her children away from Heilbronn. Her parents lived in Grossgartach, just five miles to the west, and the Christmanns lived with them there for perhaps the last year of the war.

Gisela Mahler remembered that her father moved the family out of Heilbronn after they were bombed out for the second time. They first lived in Renzen with their uncle Hermann Frank and his wife, Lydia. Later, Brother Mahler found an apartment in the town of Oberhöfen just a few miles away. The family remained in Oberhöfen for the ensuing five years. Just before the end of the war, Heinz and his little sister Inge had a serious scare, according to Gisela: "My brother had a little wooden wagon, and my sister was in it. Heinz saw an American airplane coming at them very low to the ground—so low that Heinz could see the pilot's face. And he got scared, so he grabbed Inge to protect her. Just then the pilot dipped his wings in a friendly gesture and then flew away."

Heilbronn was one of the few major cities in southern Germany that offered resistance to the invading Americans. The city history shows that defenders held the Americans at bay from April 3 to 12 before the fight came to an end. More than two-thirds of the city lay in ruins, and approximately 7,100 civilians had died in the air raids (officially twenty-seven attacks) and during the final battle. At least 2,741 Heilbronn men had died in the service of their country.

Out in Weinsberg, any hopes of the Hock family seeing the war end in peace were dashed when the town refused to surrender. Helga related the problems that followed:

> In Weinsberg, there was a Nazi Party group leader. The Americans told us that if Weinsberg would capitulate, they would not harm us. That group leader told us that we shouldn't capitulate. The people who had already hung out white flags were murdered that day. Then the American deadline passed, and because we didn't capitulate, the Americans came with four planes and completely destroyed the little town of Weinsberg.

Thinking back on the behavior of her parents during the war, Helga made the following comment:

> My parents had a strong testimony of the gospel. I know that during the war, all of the members came closer to their Heavenly Father—we prayed while waiting for the attacks to be over. For my father, it was always a testimony that the Lord protected us, even though we lost our home. Many of the situations were difficult, but we never lost our testimonies. We felt the Lord's protection.

According to Eveline Christmann, the American soldiers occupied all of the houses on their street with the exception of the Christmann house "because we had 'an American church' meeting there. I believe that we enjoyed very special protection there."[10] When Otto Christmann returned from the war at the end of 1945, he needed his studio again, so the branch meetings were hosted by Josef and Johanna Schurr in their apartment at Liststrasse 3.[11]

In Memoriam

The following members of the Heilbronn Branch did not survive World War II:

Marie Anna Braun b. Nordrach, Offenburg, Baden, 24 Mar 1870; dau. of Anton Braun and Magdalene Erdrich or Endrich; bp. 27 Aug 1902; conf. 27 Aug 1902; m. 9 Jun 1894, Johann Karl Christmann; 8 children; k. air raid Heilbronn, Neckarkreis, Württemberg, 4 Dec 1944 (FHL microfilm 68807, book 2, no. 246; FHL microfilm 25741; 1930 and 1935 censuses; IGI)

Rosa Christmann b. Heilbronn, Neckarkreis, Württemberg, 13 Sep 1903; dau. of Johann Karl Christmann and Marie Anna Braun; bp. 6 Jun 1925; conf. 6 Jun 1925; k. air raid 4 Dec 1944 (FHL microfilm 68807, book 2, no. 144; FHL microfilm 25741; 1930 and 1935 censuses; IGI)

Margareta Johanna Scholl b. Mannheim, Mannheim, Baden, 13 Nov 1900; dau. of Johann Martin Scholl and Elisabetha Ültzhöfer; bp. 1 May 1920; conf. 2 May 1920; m. Mannheim 30 Aug 1934, Gustav Heinrich Wacker; d. lung disease 13 Sep 1943 (FHL microfilm 68807, book 2, no. 601; FHL microfilm 245291; 1935 census; IGI; AF)

Anna Katharine Schulz b. Zazenhausen, Neckarkreis, Württemberg, 13 Sep 1896; dau. of Karl Schulz and Anna Schmidt; bp. 18 Sep 1930; conf. 18 Sep 1930; m. Heilbronn, Neckarkreis, Württemberg, 27 Dec 1916, Gotthilf Esslinger; d. cachexy 8 Mar 1940 (FHL microfilm 68807, book 2, no. 451; IGI)

Erwin Schulz b. Heilbronn, Neckarkreis, Württemberg, 27 Mar 1917; son of Karl Schulz and Anna Schmidt; bp. 18 Sep 1930; conf. 18 Sep 1930; k. in battle Russia, 2 Apr 1943 (FHL microfilm 68807, book 2, no. 454; FHL microfilm 245260; 1935 census; IGI)

Franz Schuwerk b. Altoberndorf, Schwarzwaldkreis, Württemberg, 4 Oct 1904; son of Josef Schuwerk and Anna Wolf; bp. 23 Jul 1927; conf. 23 Jul 1927; ord. deacon 2 Oct 1932; m. 15 Oct 1932, Anna Behr; d. in hospital in POW camp at Ogulin-Lika, Yugoslavia, 11 Nov 1945 (CHL microfilm 2458, form 42 FP, pt. 37, district list 218–19, district list 1947, 544–45; FHL microfilm 68807, book 2, no. 412; FHL microfilm 245260; 1930 and 1935 censuses; www.volksbund.de; IGI)

Notes

1. Presiding Bishopric, "Financial, Statistical, and Historical Reports of Wards, Stakes, and Missions, 1884–1955," 257, CHL CR 4 12.
2. West German Mission, branch directory, 1939, CHL 10045 11.
3. Heinz Mahler, interview by the author, Salt Lake City, June 13, 2006.
4. Helga Hock Seeber, interview by the author in German, Munich, Germany, August 21, 2008; unless otherwise noted, summarized in English by Judith Sartowski.
5. *100 Jahre Gemeinde Heilbronn* (Heilbronn: Gemeinde Heilbronn, 1999), 13; trans. the author.
6. Alex Christmann, telephone interview with Jennifer Heckmann in German, April 15, 2009.
7. Gisela Mahler Nitz, interview by Michael Corley, Salt Lake City, November 21, 2008.
8. *100 Jahre Gemeinde Heilbronn*, 13.
9. Helga Hock Seeber, autobiographical report (unpublished); private collection.
10. *100 Jahre Gemeinde Heilbronn*, 13.
11. *100 Jahre Gemeinde Heilbronn*, 14.

Reutlingen Branch

The members of The Church of Jesus Christ of Latter-day Saints living in Reutlingen were few in number in 1939. Although they lived only twenty miles from Stuttgart, they were not supported by American missionaries at the time and might well have felt a bit isolated from the Church.

Sacrament meeting took place at 10:30 a.m. in a room at Hohenzollernstrasse 1.[1] The branch directory also indicated that cottage meetings were being held at 8:00 p.m. on Mondays and Thursdays. With such a small branch population, it is likely that a single room could accommodate those who attended the meetings.

Reutlingen Branch[2]	1939
Elders	2
Priests	0
Teachers	0
Deacons	2
Other Adult Males	8
Adult Females	16
Male Children	1
Female Children	0
Total	29

Little is known about the general membership of the Reutlingen Branch, but documents found among the reports filed by president Erwin Ruf of the Stuttgart District show that several citizens of Reutlingen were required to officially withdraw (or be released) from the local Evangelical [Lutheran] Church in order "to join the Mormons" as of April 4, 1938:[3]

- Jud Friedrich [N.], born 1886, a master furniture maker
- Jud Amalie nee Reisch, born 1885
- Jud Anneliese [N.], born 1915, a seamstress
- Jud Helene [N.], born 1917, a franchise manager
- Jud Friedrich [N.], born 1923, attends school

The branch directory submitted to the mission office in June 1939 shows only one name: Friedrich Jud as branch president. Other than the names of two more members who died, the only other information available about this small branch during the years 1939 to 1945 is that the membership grew by two persons by November 1941—one elder and one male child.[4]

The general minutes of the Stuttgart District were kept conscientiously by president Erwin Ruf from November 1939 to June 1942 and include frequent notes of his visits among the Saints in Reutlingen.[5] On each occasion, he indicated which meeting he attended and provided the topic of the talk he gave. He also indicated that on a regular basis, he inspected the records of the branch. No other comments were recorded.

It is possible that the Reutlingen Branch discontinued meetings in early 1943. As of February of that year, Friedrich Jud began regular visits to and participation in meetings of the Göppingen Branch.[6] The distance from Reutlingen to Göppingen is only about thirty miles as the crow flies, but the trip by rail would have been indirect and likely took close to two hours in those days.

In Memoriam

The following members of the Reutlingen Branch did not survive World War II:

Friedrich Hans Jud b. Reutlingen, Schwarzwaldkreis, Württemberg, 27 Oct 1923; son of Friedrich Johannes Jud and Amalie Reisch; bp. 29 May 1932; conf. 29 May 1932; ord. deacon 2 Apr 1939; rifleman; d. in field hospital 3/619 at Taganrog, Russia, 25 Jan 1943 or 1945 (FHL microfilm 68807, book 2, no. 547; FHL microfilm 271374; 1930 and 1935 censuses; IGI; AF; www.volksbund.de)

Eva Maria Ulmer b. Willmandingen, Reutlingen, Schwarzwaldkreis, Württemberg, 16 May 1861; dau. of

Johannes Ulmer and Catharine Barbara Moek; bp. 17 May 1941; conf. 17 May 1941; m. 9 Feb 1892, Ludwig Eissler; d. old age 6 Jun 1943 (FHL microfilm 68807, book 2, no. 719; IGI; AF)

Albrecht Weichinger b. Boll, Schwarzwaldkreis, Württemberg, 11 Sep 1911; son of Joseph Weichinger and Wilhelmine Frank; bp. 9 Jun 1924; conf. 9 Jun 1924; d. murder 16 Oct 1941 (FHL microfilm 68807, book 2, no. 16; FHL microfilm 245296; 1930 and 1935 censuses; IGI)

Notes

1. West German Mission, branch directory, 1939, CHL 10045 11.
2. Presiding Bishopric, "Financial, Statistical, and Historical Reports of Wards, Stakes, and Missions, 1884–1955," 257, CR 4 12.
3. CHL MS 13360, 165.
4. Erwin Ruf, Stuttgart District statistics, CHL CR 16982 11.
5. Stuttgart District general minutes, CHL CR 16982 11.
6. Göppingen Branch general minutes, CHL LR 3235 11, vol. 15.

Stuttgart Branch

For centuries, the city of Stuttgart was the capital of Württemberg, the largest state in southwest Germany. In 1806, Napoleon raised Württemberg to the status of kingdom, and Stuttgart became home to royalty. Although relegated to secondary political status when the German Empire was founded in 1871, Württemberg remained a proud component of the new Germany, and Stuttgart was its principal jewel. In 1939, the city had more than 490,000 inhabitants.[1]

The Stuttgart Branch consisted of 197 registered members that year and was therefore the largest unit of the Church for miles around. One in six of those members held the priesthood, and with eighteen elders, the branch was in a position to render support to weaker units of the Stuttgart District.

The president of the Stuttgart Branch as World War II approached was Erwin Ruf. His counselors at the time were Karl Lutz and Wilhelm Ballweg. All leadership positions in the branch were filled: Karl Mössner (Sunday School), Friedrich Widmar (YMMIA), Erika Greiner (YWMIA), Julie Heitele (Primary), and Frida Rieger (Relief Society). Several other members were serving at the time in district leadership positions.[2]

Stuttgart Branch[3]	1939
Elders	18
Priests	0
Teachers	5
Deacons	10
Other Adult Males	21
Adult Females	110
Male Children	18
Female Children	14
Total	197

Branch meetings were held in rented rooms in a building at Hauptstätterstrasse 96. Sunday School began at 10:00 and sacrament meeting at 7:00 p.m. The Primary organization met on Tuesdays at 5:30 p.m. and the Mutual at 8:00. The Relief Society met on Thursdays at 8:00. The fast and testimony service was held once each month immediately following Sunday School, and a genealogical study group met at 8:00 p.m. on the first and second Tuesdays of the month.

The building at Hauptstätterstrasse 96 was less than one mile from the center of Stuttgart, and the branch had moved into the rooms there on February 14, 1926.[4] Walter Speidel (born 1922) recalled that the church rooms were upstairs above a factory and that the missionaries had lived in back rooms before their evacuation. "I was the Sunday School secretary when the war started, and I remember writing attendance numbers in the 120s often. There might have been seventy to eighty persons in the sacrament meetings."[5]

The Stuttgart Branch was one of only three in all of Germany that had a baptismal font in the meeting rooms.[6] This one was described by several eyewitnesses as a large tub. The chapel in the rooms at Hauptstätterstrasse 96 had a rostrum, according to Ruth Bodon (born 1927): "And my father donated a piano. The seats were individual chairs rather than benches. There was also a picture of Jesus on the wall, and I think there was a sign [with the name of the Church] out by the street."[7]

Esther Ruf (born 1929) recalled that there was also a pump organ in the main meeting room: "The piano was to the left at the front of the room and the pump organ to the right."[8] Dieter Kaiser (born 1939) recalled that when Maria Ruf was playing the piano, "I would run from the back of the room to the front, sit on her lap, and snuggle up to her because she smelled so good."[9]

Life for Germans in general was quite good in 1938, but this was not true for the Jews who had not yet left the country. Lydia Ruf (born 1923) recalled the event that signaled all-out war against the Jews in Nazi Germany—the Night of Broken Glass:

> Early in the morning [of November 10, 1938] I happened to go downtown in Stuttgart and saw the demolished windows of the Jewish shops. They were looted and merchandise strewn around. The news on the radio indicated that it was the rage of the German people against the Jews that caused them to destroy the Jewish shops. However, some of us knew very well that the [SA] troops were responsible and not the German people.[10]

With the departure of the American missionaries in August 1939, Erwin Ruf was called to serve as the president of the Stuttgart District. He in turn called Karl Lutz to lead the Stuttgart Branch. President Ruf then proceeded to write a history of the Stuttgart Branch under the title "Memorandum for the Celebration of Forty Years of History of Our Beloved Stuttgart Branch." With a date of 1899 for the founding of the branch, Ruf described in detail the challenges faced by the first missionaries and Saints in the city and in Württemberg. His final sentence reads: "I hope that [the Saints] will continue to sustain the new branch president, my former first counselor, and be obedient to him. If you do this, you are assured of the blessings of heaven."[11]

"I can still hear [in my mind] the radio announcement about the beginning of the war," recalled Walter Speidel: "'The Poles have finally attacked us, and as of 5:45 this morning we are shooting back.' We had thought that the Polish army would invade Germany, and one of my cousins had already been drafted." A month later, Walter was called to serve in the national labor force, and by January 1941 he was wearing the uniform of the Wehrmacht. Before leaving for basic training with the army, he was asked to speak in sacrament meeting, then was given a blessing by branch president Karl Lutz. In that blessing he was promised that he would return "without harm to body or spirit."

Maria Ruf (born 1923) recalled hearing the broadcast announcing the attack on Poland. She heard Hitler say that he would be joining his troops at the front. If something happened to him, he would be succeeded by Rudolf Hess, and if something happened to Hess, Hermann Goering would be the next leader. "Everybody was touched," she recalled, "It made you hope that nothing would happen to them. I came home to find out that my dad was drafted. That's what I remember from the first day of the war."[12]

Maria had finished high school and was hired as a secretary in a bank in the summer of 1939. She was still a member of the League of German Girls at the time and recalled that without that membership, she would not have gotten the job. Once employed, however, she wanted out of the league and managed to achieve her goal. At the same time, the office manager insisted that if she were not a member of the league or the National Socialist Party, she would forfeit her job. As it turned out, the league would not take her back. In total honesty, she insisted that even if she joined the party, she would not attend meetings. Before the manager could put more pressure on Maria, he was drafted into the army, and the matter was forgotten.

When she finished public school in 1941, Ruth Bodon was first called upon to serve her Pflichtjahr for the nation. She was assigned to work in a home and assist with domestic duties, as she recalled: "The man was an engineer, and the woman had two children. I went there in the morning and home in the evening. [The program] was Hitler's idea that you kind of get prepared for marriage and to be a good housewife." Following her year of service, Ruth began an apprenticeship as a dental assistant, and this training lasted for about a year.

After his selection for the Afrika Corps, Walter Speidel noticed odd reactions from German civilians when they saw his brown desert uniform, something quite foreign to the German army. By early 1942, he was ready for what promised to be a lengthy deployment in North Africa. Before leaving, Walter considered becoming engaged to a sweet young woman of the Stuttgart Branch whom he had known for years and seriously dated for several months. However, her mother objected to the union at that time. Walter described the hometown farewell from his sweetheart in these words:

> After MIA, and at the end of our walk home, we spent more time than usual to say good-bye in the dark entrance to the Gablenberg pharmacy. We held on to each other as if this would be the last time we would see each other ever again. She broke down several times and couldn't stop crying. But in the end, we knew we had to part. So, after a long time, we pulled ourselves together, and finally walked hand in hand to Gaishämmerstrasse. We embraced and kissed one last time, and then she ran into her building. I turned around and walked briskly back to my streetcar stop.[13]

Nephi Moroni Lothar Greiner (born 1929) was in trouble with the Hitler Youth when his father did not permit him to participate in activities on Sundays. He told the youth leaders, "I will raise my own son, and we go to church on Sunday!" The Hitler Youth leaders threatened action, as Lothar recalled, "They put me through a kind of humiliating ceremony; they took the insignia from my uniform—it was sort like being drummed out of camp. I can remember that very clearly."[14]

The records of the Stuttgart Branch in the Church History Library include two interesting documents issued by the office of the Lutheran Church in Stuttgart. The first bears the date October 22, 1941: "Anna Hilde Rügner née Armbruster, a bookbinder, born August 11, 1920, in Weil im Dorf has left the Lutheran Church. She plans to join the Mormons."[15]

A few months later, a report was sent from the office of St. Paul's Lutheran Church to the office of the Evangelical Lutheran Church District of Stuttgart. The report is a reminder that a change of heart (in either direction) can happen to LDS persons as well as persons of any faith:

> May 22, 1942: The person named below wishes to be allowed to enter the Lutheran Church again: Mrs. Meta Wagner née Manz, born 12 August 1908 in Stuttgart, residing at Augustenstrasse 131. She joined the Mormon Church in 1926 because she wanted to marry a man who was a member of that church. However, she eventually married a Catholic man. She had the child born to her in 1941 baptized in the Lutheran Church and now wishes to reenter the Lutheran Church. The attached document certifies that she has left the Mormon Church.[16]

The Erwin Ruf family were modest people who did not try to attract attention. Esther found that if she attended Jungvolk meetings on Wednesdays, she could skip them in favor of attending church on Sundays and nobody would report her ("I was kind of shy anyway.") In school her Old Testament (Jewish) given name could have been a reason for contention in Nazi Germany, but again she was able to avoid trouble. As she described the situation, "It wasn't too bad being a member of the Church, but as the years went by you said less and less about religion. They classified me as 'believing in God' [rather than as Catholic or Protestant]."

At the completion of their schooling, German teenagers were often given instruction in formal dance, but Maria Ruf's parents did not allow her to participate. Fortunately she was able to join with several other Latter-day Saints to learn under the tutelage of Max Knecht of the Stuttgart Branch.

They even staged a small prom, with phonograph records rather than a band. However, it turned out that some of the branch members did not approve of dancing in the church and voiced their protests. According to Maria, during the war "life got rather serious. I don't think I had a normal teenage life because of the war."

From March 8 to May 25, 1942, Walter Speidel and his comrades were moved from Germany through Italy to Tunisia in northern Africa. They saw many interesting and historic sites on the way and likely wondered what it would be like to fight the British in the desert. Serving under Field Marshall Erwin Rommel, the "Desert Fox," Walter was part of the communications team that worked to install and maintain radio systems and telephone lines.

Soon after his arrival, Walter was very close to the action. The German Afrika Corps was retreating slowly before the British from Egypt westward toward Tunisia, and soon the Americans approached their positions from the west. According to Walter, "The Afrika Corps was always desperate for fuel and ammunition because the British, destroyed 60 percent of it on its way across the Mediterranean Sea."[17]

Walter's description of the combat situation on July 11–12, 1942, reflects what many LDS German soldiers felt at one time or another during the war:

> The situation seemed hopeless. . . . For the first time, I thought that I might die. We knew we couldn't defend ourselves against tanks with our rifles and machine guns. . . . I thought of the blessing I had received before I left Stuttgart. I was promised that I would not have to shed blood, that my life would be protected and be spared in the end. With every breath, I sent up to heaven one Stossgebet [quick, desperate prayer] after the other. . . . There was only one thing I knew I could do: Pray, pray, and pray some more. My life was in His hands. Without His protection, I could not survive.[18]

Maria Ruf recalled the many ways in which civil defense authorities asked the Stuttgart civilians to prepare for air raids: "Each family [in the apartment building] had some kind of job," she explained:

> I was designated as the messenger; it was my job to run to the police station to report if anything happened to our building. We had water in the attic space in case a fire started there, and everybody was supposed to have a small suitcase packed with our best belongings to take to the basement during an alarm. We also had a [hole] from our basement into the next building in case our [exit] was blocked.

Nearly all the Latter-day Saints in Stuttgart lost their homes in the many air raids that plagued the city. Ruth Bodon was living in the home of her uncle when the bombs landed very close. However, Ruth and her cousin had not taken the sirens seriously; while others in the building went to the basement shelter, the two girls went back to sleep. "All of a sudden I woke up and all hell broke loose!" she recalled:

> We heard the bombs hitting and the antiaircraft shooting and we ran down to the basement in our nightgowns. My aunt who had so often made fun of us Mormons and Christians was down there praying to God for help. . . . Then the air raid warden came in and told us all to get out because the whole block was burning. . . . We had a container of water in the basement and we put our sheets in it and [put them over our heads and] then went out two at a time. We ran down the street and the houses were burning on both sides. It was just awful. My uncle's family lost everything.

To Lothar Greiner, the worst thing about the war was that his family was separated. During air raids, he and his father were required to stay in their apartment building to fight fires while his mother and his sister went down the street to a large bunker. After their building was hit and destroyed one night, Lothar went to the bunker: "It was my sad task to tell my mother that we had lost everything. I found her in the bunker, and she exclaimed joyfully, 'Lothar is here! Now we can go home!' I told her that we couldn't because there was nothing left but rubble." Sister Greiner and her daughter were then evacuated to Waldenburg, a few miles to the east, but Lothar and his father were not allowed to leave Stuttgart. "It became my greatest wish," he said, "to see my family united again."

Fig. 1. Kurt Ruf used this Russian booklet for his diary in 1941. Kurt crossed out the book's title and wrote "war journal, 1943, Kurt Ruf." (L. Ruf Wright)

Lydia Ruf had hoped that her brothers, Kurt and Alma, who were both employed by the Robert Bosch Company (an important war industry), would be exempt from military service. Alma had even obtained a patent for a measuring device, but their work did not keep the two out of the war for long. Kurt decided to volunteer in order to choose his unit; he selected the tank corps. Alma was not drafted until 1944, and Lydia remembered his departure:

> The last picture I have of him was taken at the [railroad station] in Stuttgart before he was shipped to Russia. There he stood in his uniform, leaning on his rifle—this fair-haired, young boy with the curly hair, who didn't have a single violent bone in his body, going to war. We knew, as we looked on his face, that he would not return. His expression seemed to say the same.[19]

During their contacts "nearly every day," Walter Speidel and field marshal Erwin Rommel learned that they were from the same part of Württemberg and enjoyed speaking their native Swabian dialect with each other. The field marshal also found out that Walter did not smoke or drink alcohol. In fact, on one occasion, the commander saw Walter's copy of the Book of Mormon, picked it up, thumbed through it for a few moments, and then asked if it was a Bible. Walter's response was a quick "Yeah, sort of," and that was the end of the discussion. "My friends all knew that I was a Mormon," he stated.[20]

District president Erwin Ruf was not allowed to leave Stuttgart, but he often sent his family away from the city to the safety of small communities. Anna Ruf had relatives in Deckenpfronn (twenty miles to the southwest), and she and her daughters spent significant time there. According to Esther, "I often took the train there by myself, even when I was only twelve. I thought I was all grown up. After getting off of the train, I still had to walk for an hour. It was kind of like a vacation for a few days. [But from Deckenpfronn] we could see Stuttgart burning [after air raids]."

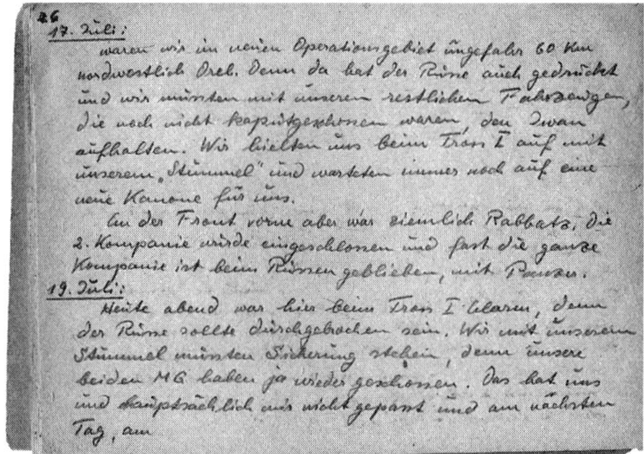

26
17. Juli:
waren wir im neuen Operationsgebiet ungefähr 60 km nordwestlich Orel. Denn da hat der Russe auch gedrückt und wir mussten mit unseren restlichen Fahrzeugen, die noch nicht kaputtgeschossen waren, den Iwan aufhalten. Wir hielten uns beim Tross I auf mit unserem „Stummel" und warteten immer noch auf eine neue Kanone für uns.
An der Front vorne aber war ziemlich Rabbatz, die 2. Kompanie wurde eingeschlossen und fast die ganze Kompanie ist beim Russen geblieben, mit Panzer.
19. Juli:
Heute abend war hier beim Tross I Alarm, denn der Russe sollte durchgebrochen sein. Wir mit unserem Stummel mussten Sicherung stehen, denn unsere beiden MG haben ja wieder geschossen. Das hat uns und hauptsächlich mir nicht gepasst und am nächsten Tag, am

Fig. 2. A page from the highly detailed diary of soldier Kurt Ruf. (L. Ruf Wright)

"Every night at about 2:00 a.m. the sirens would go off," recalled Harold Bodon (born 1936). "I was surprised that my dad let me go upstairs to watch the planes drop their bombs. I guess that was part of the curiosity factor." Harold recalled seeing phosphorus burning and hearing people screaming in the street below. "It was getting very dangerous in Stuttgart, and our [apartment] house was the only one on the street that wasn't destroyed." It was 1943, and for the family of Heinrich and Lina Bodon, it was time to leave Stuttgart. Brother Bodon received permission to move his business to his hometown of Waldsee, about one hundred miles southeast of Stuttgart.

Harold's younger brother, Karl-Heinz (born 1937), also had vivid memories of the air raids and preparing for them:

> Before we left [the apartment], we would go through a routine of covering all the windows and putting tape where there could have been some light seeping through. . . . I remember this old fellow who always came down into the basement shelter with some little toys, goodies, cookies, or what have you. It was all very orderly. Nobody seemed to get upset at all. We just all went down [to the basement]. We did it many, many times, and it was almost like a little get-together.[21]

The German Afrika Corps was eventually surrounded by Allied forces in Tunisia and Walter Speidel was taken captive by French Indochinese on May 12, 1943. Turned over first to the British and then to the Americans, he was transported by train through Algeria and Morocco, then to Tangier and Casablanca. A ship took him to New Jersey, and a train from there to Aliceville, Alabama, where he arrived on July 9.[22]

On the very day Walter was captured near the city of Tunis, his friend Kurt Ruf was thousands of miles away in the Soviet Union, writing the first entry in his new diary, entitled "My War Diary for the 1943 Campaign, Part I." The first entry gives important insights into his attitude at a time when in the minds of many German soldiers it was no longer a certainty that the Soviets would be conquered:

> May 12, 1943: I was just released from the field hospital after a week of reserve status. It is again time for me to serve. Today I joined with forty-nine other men for the trip to Russia. I cannot say that I was very happy about this because I really had it up to here with my first experience in Russia in 1942. But you have to obey in the army whether you want to or not. So I won't mope around and will do the best I can to enjoy life.

Kurt said good-bye to his family in Stuttgart and boarded a train for the long trip to the Eastern Front. His diary is very detailed and provides information about his locations and activities on a daily basis. As the radioman of a tank crew, his fate was connected to the status of his tank. The great majority of his time in the summer of 1943 was spent in radio training and in waiting for repairs to be made on his vehicle. Meals, sleeping quarters, and weather were frequent topics in his entries, but there were of course accounts of combat, adventure, and danger, as is seen in his report of July 6. When Kurt's crew encountered the Soviets that day, the Germans advanced with 104 tanks and "countless support vehicles." Of course, the Germans respected the Soviet T34 tanks that opposed them. After two hours of fire, during which Kurt could not determine whether the noise came from the tanks to either side or from the enemy, he received a radio message indicating that his crew was to pull "vehicle no. 441" out of a huge crater close to their position. Initially, the men hesitated to leave the safety of their tank:

> I said to myself, I have to go help my comrades. Who knows if some of them are wounded? So I decided to get out, and my heart was not even pounding. I opened my hatch, jumped out, and quickly got behind the tank. My buddies were right behind me—our commander and the other two crew members. Now there were four of us outside ready to help. We got our tow rope ready, but every time we stuck our heads out, the Russian sharpshooters were after us and we felt bullets whizzing by our ears. When we heard an artillery round coming our way, we hit the dirt and waited. Then we went to work again. I took one end of the chain, my buddy took the other, and we made ourselves as thin as possible and headed for the hook on the tank. The rope was too short, so we had to get another one. In the meantime, one of our crew got to the machine gun and kept the Russians busy for a few seconds. Finally we had the two tanks connected, and could start pulling him out. But, wouldn't you know it? Our tank wouldn't start. We had taken a hit from an artillery shell that knocked out our starter motor.[23]

Kurt's detailed report indicates that they eventually got their tank started and hauled their friends out of the bomb crater.

The next combat action came after only a few weeks of waiting while their tank was repaired. All summer long, Kurt's crew drove hundreds of miles as they maneuvered toward (and at times away from) the enemy. On one occasion, the crew accidentally filled their tank with diesel fuel instead of gasoline, and an officer accused them of treason. It turned out that a fuel depot assistant was the guilty party. It seemed that there was always something going wrong with the tank, and parts were extremely difficult to find.

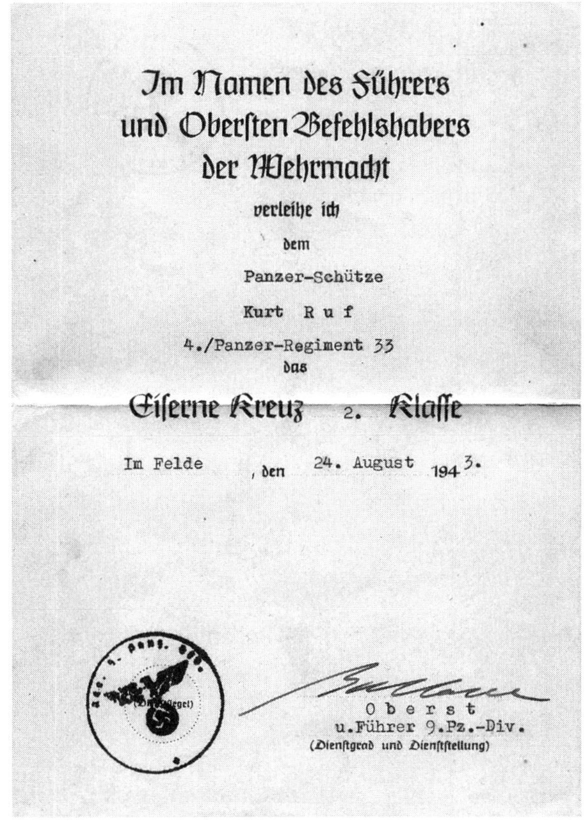

Im Namen des Führers
und Obersten Befehlshabers
der Wehrmacht
verleihe ich
dem
Panzer-Schütze
Kurt Ruf
4./Panzer-Regiment 33
das
Eiserne Kreuz 2. Klasse

Im Felde, den 24. August 1943.

Oberst
u.Führer 9.Pz.-Div.
(Dienstgrad und Dienststellung)

Fig. 3. Kurt Ruf was awarded the Iron Cross Second Class for valor in battle. (L. Ruf Wright)

On August 1, 1943, Kurt Ruf was promoted to corporal, but things were not going well for his tank division. Three days later he wrote, "Every day we move back and leave more territory to the Russians without a fight. We have been eating all of our chickens, geese, ducks, calves, and pigs. Anything that could not be consumed was destroyed, including gardens and crops." The Red Army pressed their enemy constantly, and Kurt was in combat on a regular basis. One day a cannon round penetrated his tank's armor plate and shrapnel flew inches past his head, hitting his comrade. He understood just how close he had come to dying.

The air raid that devastated large parts of Stuttgart on October 7–8, 1943, also destroyed the church rooms at Hauptstätterstrasse 96 that had served the Saints so well for seventeen years. After that, it was seldom known much in advance precisely where the meetings would be held. According to Lydia Ruf, meetings were held in the forest in good weather:

> Word got around that we should go to, say [streetcar] S-5 and the last station ["Georgsruh," according to Lothar Greiner]. There we would meet in the woods for sacrament meeting, check to see what happened to everybody, and thus keep track of each other. Church members became very, very close. Everybody helped each other. . . . It was a great time of togetherness. Also, after losing it all, those who had formerly been deemed wealthy were just like all the rest. Now we were all equal. No one had any more than anyone else. War is a great equalizer.[24]

"The new year [1944] is here, and the front is on fire everywhere," Kurt Ruf wrote. One of Kurt's battles in early 1944 was against his comrades' attempts to get him to drink alcohol. He resisted and ended up being the guardian of his drunken friends while his standards protected him. "I don't need alcohol to make me brave," he wrote, "I am my own master. I just had to laugh as I watched them break tables and chairs."

Alma Ruf did not last long as a soldier. On March 14, he was killed in battle in the Soviet Union. Lydia described the reaction of the Stuttgart Branch: "When we heard about his death, there was a memorial service at church. It is customary in Germany to wear black to a service of this kind, but I refused to wear black. Somebody accused me by saying, 'You're not even grieving for your brother.' I said nothing, but to myself I thought, 'I should wear white because I had known him.'"[25]

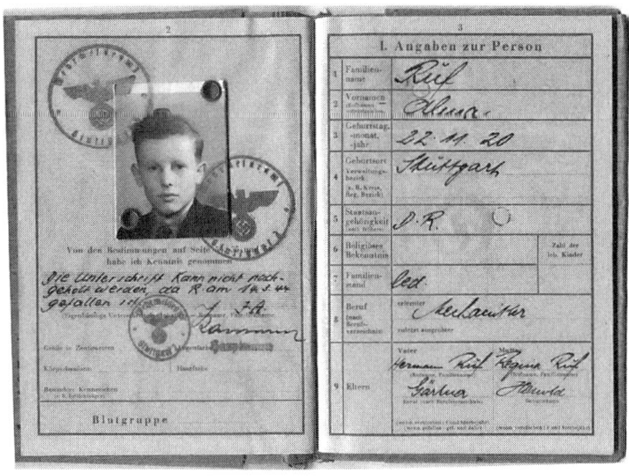
Von den Bestimmungen auf Seite … habe ich Kenntnis genommen

Die Unterschrift kann nicht nachgeholt werden, da R. am 14.5.44 gefallen ist

Blutgruppe

I. Angaben zur Person

1	Familienname	Ruf
2	Vornamen	Alma
3	Geburtstag, -monat, -jahr	22.11.20
4	Geburtsort	Stuttgart
5	Staatsangehörigkeit	D.R.
6	Religiöses Bekenntnis	
7	Familienstand	led.
8	Beruf	Mechaniker
9	Eltern	Vater: Hermann Ruf, Gärtner; Mutter: Regina Ruf

Fig. 4. The military ID of Alma Ruf. (L. Ruf Wright)

In distant Waldsee, Heinrich Bodon continued to operate his fur business. Young Karl-Heinz recalled the following about the business:

> People would bring us their dead foxes, . . . so we got all of those skins. Dad would work together with another firm to prepare the skins so that they could be made into fur coats. My mom and another lady sewed the furs together and made the coats. My dad and his brother took the coats to towns all around southern Germany and had two-day sales. They also sold muffs, caps, and collars.

Harold Bodon recalled that his father was also the town's civil defense director—possibly a commitment he accepted in order to get permission to move his family out of Stuttgart. Brother Bodon wore the small round Nazi Party lapel pin, but did not maintain any loyalty to the party. The family initially lived in the Hotel zur Sonne in Waldsee, but later moved into a house at Stadtgraben 14. Harold was baptized near there on June 28, 1944, as he recalled: "It was a little creek. I remember that we were all dressed in white, and there were a lot of people standing about two hundred feet away. I think my father and [my brother-in-law] Kurt Schneider did the ceremony."[26]

Heinrich and Lina Bodon were determined to raise their children in the gospel, despite the fact that Waldsee was a great distance from any branch of the Church. Every Sunday, they conducted a Sunday School in their home. According to young Harold, "My dad told us that if we participated [in Sunday School] he would take us either to a soccer game or to the movies in the afternoon. The soccer team was Schwarz-Weiss-Waldsee, and the movies were always about Hopalong Cassidy. That kept the family together. We learned a lot of good stuff, and eventually we made the right decisions [based on what we learned]." At the same time, the war went on, and Harold recalled that at school he and his classmates were given wooden rifles and taught to march: "We hoisted the swastika flag and goose-stepped and had a great time."

Toward the end of the war, Dieter Kaiser's father (not yet baptized) got in trouble with the strict Nazis at his work. He was employed in research and development, and his company employed several forced laborers from occupied countries. He had insisted to his superiors that the laborers needed better food and medical treatment, but his protests fell upon deaf ears. One night, an air raid threatened the prisoners, and Herr Kaiser let them out of their incarceration. In Dieter's recollection, "My dad came home with holes burned in his white shirt. If he had not let the prisoners out, they would have been killed by the bombs. The next day, I went with my father to the railroad station; he was now a private in the army and was headed to the Eastern Front." The message to troublemakers was clear: toe the party line or suffer the consequences.

Young Dieter understood the dangers of airplanes above Stuttgart. Barely five years old, he was once knocked off of a table during an air raid and needed stitches to close the gash on his head. While in the hospital, he managed to reopen the wound and needed more stitches. On another occasion, he was out fetching milk for his mother and was attacked by an American fighter plane. "The pilot fired at me with his machine gun, and I dove into a ditch to get out of his line of fire. I hit something hard and spilled the milk. When I got home, I had a bent milk can and my knee was bleeding. My mother [spanked] me because I hadn't been paying good enough attention."

The Erwin Ruf family experienced several terrifying nights when the bombs landed in their neighborhood. One bomb actually hit the corner of their building but did not explode. Another raid left their entire street on fire. When Lydia and her mother emerged from their basement shelter, her mother said that they had to leave the area immediately or they would not survive. Only five of the eighteen people in their shelter left in time; the others perished. Lydia described what happened next:

> The air was hot and thin. We stumbled over a couple of blackened, naked, hairless mannequins lying on the street. Timbers were falling and sparks threatened to ignite hair and clothing, so we wrapped our heads [with wet towels] and ran to the public shelter built into the mountain close by. Only later . . . did we realize that those were not mannequins but people who were not as lucky as we. When we returned the next morning, there was nothing. Not one stone above another. You could barely tell where the house had been.[27]

After her uncle's home was destroyed, Ruth Bodon went to live with her sister Charlotte, the wife of Kurt Schneider, president of the Strasbourg District. While in Strasbourg, she attended meetings of the branch with her sister's family. That French city was occupied by the German military, and the members of the small branch spoke both French and German. "We never talked about politics, Hitler, or the war," Ruth claimed.

Ruth was drafted into the national labor force, or Reichsarbeitsdienst, in the fall of 1944 and assigned to a factory in Kirchheim unter Teck, not far from home. She liked the factory work more than farmwork and enjoyed working at a manual knitting machine, making socks for soldiers. When that assignment ended after six months, Ruth thought she would be allowed to go home, but her term of service was not finished. Her next job was very unpleasant: she tested gas masks, putting them under pressure to determine if there were any leaks. "The gas made me deathly ill, but I only did that for a month. One day, our lead girl came in and told us: 'The war is coming to an end. Go home, but in groups. Don't go alone.'" Ruth decided to join her sister Charlotte, whose family had left Strasbourg when the American army approached and moved to a little town in the Black Forest.

Esther Ruf recalled that there were not many opportunities to enjoy life as a young teenager during the war: "I had the feeling that I couldn't really do the things that others my age did. Maybe that was because we weren't very well off. I could go swimming because there was a pool nearby. I remember reading two books every weekend. That was fun time for me. Every once in a while I could go to a movie, but we didn't go out that often."

In late May 1944, Kurt Ruf arrived in France with his tank division. A few days later, the Allies landed on the beaches of Normandy, but Kurt was as yet far from the action. He wrote to his father, Hermann (then the president of the Frankfurt Branch) on June 8 with very bad news:

> You have probably heard from Maria or from somebody else that Alma was killed on March 14 at Nikolajew [Russia]. This is a very painful loss, but who knows what will happen to all of us? He has it really good now. He certainly doesn't want to come back to this world with all of these evil people. I know that he's in a better place now, and I wish him all the best in heaven.[28]

Fig. 5. Kurt Ruf was a member of the crew of this tank when he was killed in France in August 1944. (L. Ruf Wright)

Fig. 6. Members of the Stuttgart Branch.

But the action caught up with Kurt, who wrote to his father on August 6, 1944: "I am writing you a quick note in haste. All of a sudden, I was in combat against the Americans. I'm very well right now. I hope that you're at least not any worse than before. I send you my best wishes. Your Kurt. Auf Wiedersehen!"[29] Four days later, Kurt was killed in battle.

The birth of a child in wartime Germany was an extraordinary challenge for many women—including Ute Auktor's mother. Ute was born in a Stuttgart hospital on September 28, 1944, but there was nothing typical about the process. Her mother explained the situation, and Ute related the events as follows:

> My mother was taken to the hospital for my birth. (My father was not there; he was out of town with the army.) Just as I was born, the doctor heard the air-raid sirens, which were going off all the time. I was 9½ pounds or something, a good-sized baby. And my mother was just a short lady, 4 foot 11, if she was that tall. They bundled me up, put me into her arms, and told her to go to the nearest air-raid shelter, which was down the street from the hospital, so she had to walk outside. She told me that one of the bombs landed not too far away from the building, and the force of it knocked her to the ground while she was still clutching me. A gentleman came up to her and offered to help. She was holding me so tightly that the poor man thought she was going to suffocate me. He had to finally just lift her up and get her to the air-raid shelter. And that was just about twenty or thirty minutes after I was born. It was kind of a rough entrance into the world.[30]

As a German POW in Alabama during the war, Walter Speidel had a rare treat—a visit from his sister. Elisabeth Speidel had married an American and immigrated to Utah before the war. When the Red Cross informed her of Walter's presence in Alabama, she requested and received permission to visit him there. According to strict regulations, an officer was assigned to be with the siblings and listen to all that was said. As Walter recalled:

> It was a little awkward at first, but Elisabeth handled the situation cleverly, putting the lieutenant at ease. . . . We talked and talked. First, about our parents and [my girlfriend], and Elisabeth's acquaintances in Stuttgart. . . . The few hours were gone too fast. We met the next one or two days. Towards the end, Elisabeth asked me what I would like her to send me. I told her that we actually had everything we needed. Perhaps, some personal things, church literature, etc. It was very difficult to say good-bye. Afterwards, everything appeared so unreal to me, like a "mirage" that now had all of a sudden disappeared.[31]

Erika Greiner Metzner (born 1919) was expecting her second child in July 1944 when her husband, Heinz, came home one evening with the announcement that she and their son, Rolf Rüdiger (born 1942), needed to leave Stuttgart at once. He helped her pack for the long trip of six hundred miles east to Silesia, where his relatives were surprised to see her but pleased to take them in. As much as she wished to stay with her husband (he was not allowed to leave), she knew that the chances for survival were much greater in the town of Frankenstein. Once there, she found life so peaceful and comfortable that she had "a bit of a guilty conscience."

Following the destruction of the branch meeting rooms on Hauptstätterstrasse, branch leaders spent a good deal of time seeking a suitable meeting place for this branch, which in the last two years of the war still enjoyed a large local population. An important document found among the papers of the Stuttgart Branch is remarkable:

> October 11, 1944 no. A.5303
>
> From the Lutheran Church Council in Grossheppach, Waiblingen County, to the office of the Lutheran Church District of Stuttgart: According to a report from your office, the representative of the Church of Jesus Christ (previously called Mormons) since their meeting hall in Stuttgart was destroyed and they cannot find a place to meet, has petitioned for the use of the hall in the Gaisburg Church each Sunday afternoon beginning at 3:00 p.m. until such time that they can find another place to meet. Although it has always been our practice to support churches that have lost their meeting places, the Lutheran Church District Office should consider declining this request, because allowing churches that are not solidly based on Christianity to meet in our buildings would send the wrong message to members of our church. Because this religious group is so small, it should be possible for them to find another location for their meetings.[32]

This is an important reminder that The Church of Jesus Christ of Latter-day Saints was generally not looked upon as a church (*Kirche*) anywhere in Germany at the time but rather as a sect (*Sekte*), a word that in the German language did not have a positive connotation.

Millions of German women gave birth during the war to children whose fathers were far from home in the service of their country. Erika Metzner was one of those women, but giving birth in a home or a hospital under planned conditions was one thing—going through the same process while trying to flee the invading Soviet army was quite another, as she recalled:

> It took us nearly an entire day to go the first twenty-five miles to Bad Landeck. I was helping to get our baggage off of the train when my water broke. . . . My sister-in-law turned pale when I told her. She ran off to find some assistance, and they found a car to take me to the [women's hospital]. I was very scared, because I didn't know what would become of my relatives and my little boy. That very night—February 15, 1945—I gave birth to a healthy little boy [Heinz Peter].[33]

Sister Metzner stayed in the hospital for ten days and was then sent to a mothers' home. This might normally have been a very pleasant experience, with mother and baby under the care of a nurse for a few weeks after birth, but it became a tragedy. As that terribly cold winter came to an end, there was no fuel left to heat the building. "Every day they carried out dead babies. They just weren't used to the cold," she explained. Her son was only three weeks old when he too passed away on March 10, 1945. A few weeks later, Erika Metzner and two-year-old Rolf Rüdiger boarded a train for home. The Soviet army was approaching, and it seemed that every German civilian in Silesia was determined to flee to the west rather than wait and see what the conquerors would do.

Traveling with Erika Metzner and her son were a sister-in-law and three children. It seemed like a miracle when they found passage together on a train to Vienna, where the tumult at the main station was daunting; again it seemed that everyone was headed west. From Vienna, another train took the six west to Fürstenfeldbrück, Germany, a town just outside of Munich. Seemingly stuck there as the war neared a conclusion, Sister Metzner had no way to proceed, but managed to write a letter to her husband back in Stuttgart. After about one week in Fürstenfeldbrück ("where we had a bed and water!" she rejoiced), Erika answered a knock at the door and opened it to see her brother Lothar Greiner. Only sixteen, he had left Stuttgart with the sole purpose of finding his sister and his nephew and taking them home. In Stuttgart, Erika found that her home was still standing. She described her feelings at the time: "I was so pleased to be home again with my dear family. But best of all, my husband showed up just a few weeks later. We were reunited, and what a blessing that was! And I was so happy to attend church again with my branch."

One day in April 1945, Lydia Ruf heard shooting and looked out the attic window. Seeing tanks rolling across fields in the distance, she hurried downstairs to tell her mother that the Americans were coming; it appeared that they would be in town soon. Regina Ruf quickly issued an order: "Let's kill the chickens!" The landlady was gone but had given instructions that the chickens in her coop should not fall victim to the invaders. According to Lydia:

> Mother went out to kill the chickens, brought them in, and we cooked them, put them in mason jars, and buried them in the garden. The next day the tanks rolled in. There was a little shooting in the streets, so mother and I hung out a white sheet, while our neighbor still displayed his flag with the swastika on it. . . . That same day . . . soldiers were coming through all the backyards looking for things like rabbits, chickens, or food of any kind. We felt so smug, since ours were already buried! I think the inspiration that my mother in many instances had, came from living the gospel.[34]

During his stay in three different POW camps in Alabama and North Carolina from 1943 to 1945, Walter Speidel was kept busy at many simple tasks, but there was also time for entertainment and academic pursuits. Walter busied himself studying the English language and became fairly proficient. At one point, he was given a physical examination, and the German physician determined that he was suffering from what was called Schlatter's disease. This meant that Walter could be classified as unfit for work, and soon he was put on a ship for transport across the Atlantic Ocean to France. He was fortunate to have the unfit classification, because many of the POWs who landed in the French port of LeHavre with him were taken by the French and put to work again; their "release" had been a deception.[35] Walter, on the other hand, proceeded to Marburg, Germany, where American military occupation officials gave him the necessary release papers and paid him $92.75 for the work he had done as a POW.[36]

When the end of the war approached, Ruth Bodon was the guest of the Schneider family in Schönwald, a ski resort town in the Black Forest. She liked the setting, but the entry of French troops in April 1945 was more excitement than she had bargained for. As it turned out, the troops entering the town under the French flag were anything but French. Ruth described the terrifying situation:

> I had never seen a Moroccan before. They were on horses and had turbans and big beards. They were awful-looking men, and we saw them through our window. All of a sudden, they came to a stop in the street right in front of our house. Apparently their officers were looking for quarters, and they stayed there for about a half hour. My sister was twenty-four, and I was eighteen. My sister said to her husband, "If they come in here, don't try to protect me. I don't want to be a widow, too." My brother-in-law prayed nonstop while they were outside in the street. He never stopped praying. And then they left. In the next town they raped every woman from thirteen to eighty. That would have been our experience if my brother-in-law had not prayed so hard for us to be safe.

After the arrival of the American army in Stuttgart, Lothar Greiner set off to find and rescue his mother and his sisters Edith and Ruth in the town of Waldenburg. Part of the journey was accomplished with the aid of an old bicycle, and part of it in the company of Polish laborers heading home ("I hoped they wouldn't speak to me."). He made it to Waldenburg and was united with his mother and sisters, then successfully escorted them home to Stuttgart. "It was wonderful to be together again," he explained.

Fig. 7. Little Dieter Kaiser with American soldiers in postwar Stuttgart. The second GI from the left is Alan Fry, who later married Maria Ruf, a daughter of the Stuttgart District president. (D. Kaiser)

Some of the first enemy troops to enter Stuttgart were French, as Dieter Kaiser recalled: "They were

French colonial troops, Moroccans. We used to bang on the lids of pots to cause distractions when those guys came around." Dieter was only six years old at the time and could not have known what molestations the soldiers were committing, but he apparently understood that their presence represented a great danger.

Esther Ruf explained that her family was never in danger when the enemy invaded Stuttgart. "We still lived in our home at the end of the war and my father was still employed. [The soldiers] never came into our home to steal our belongings or anything like that. Our home and our neighborhood had not been bombed; we just had some windows broken." Regarding her reaction to the news that Hitler was dead, she recalled: "I think that I was happy when I heard the news. Everything we had been told about him was a lie. I was glad to be a free person and not to live under a system of lies."

For the Bodon family in the town of Waldsee, the war ended with the arrival of the French army. Brother Bodon wanted to spare the town any damage from senseless defensive action, so he went out at night to remove antitank barriers. To do so during the day could have meant execution as a traitor and a defeatist. At the same time, other local residents believed in resisting the enemy. Harold Bodon recalled that several Hitler Youth boys were ordered to go to the nearby forest and prepare to fight against the invaders. "Of course the French didn't know that they were boys, so they started mowing down that forest and killed a lot of the kids."

Just before the French arrived, Brother Bodon loaded a small Bollerwagen with supplies and walked with his family to a farm just outside town, according to Karl-Heinz: "In our family prayers we had always asked to have the Americans occupy our area, so we were disappointed when the French came first. My dad didn't know if the enemy would come into Waldsee with guns ablazing or not. We hung out a huge white flag, and nothing happened where we were. But back in Waldsee there was a little damage done."

When the French army marched into Waldsee, the spectacle was frightening, according to Harold:

> The Africans came in on camels. They were the first blacks I'd ever seen [and they wore] turbans. The black men were very scary. They kept holding one hand on the little knives that they had on their belts. They would be walking down the street looking straight ahead, then they would suddenly turn and look at us and pull their knives out. I came close to fainting every time that happened.

With the French conquerors in town, Heinrich Bodon was most concerned for the safety of his wife and his daughter, Rosie. He quickly made a deal with the invaders that the family would cook and wash for them if the family were allowed to stay in their home. When it was all over, the worst losses they suffered were their radio, a camera, and a bicycle (all local families had to surrender such items to the French occupation forces). The Bodons lived in relative peace in Waldsee for seven more years.

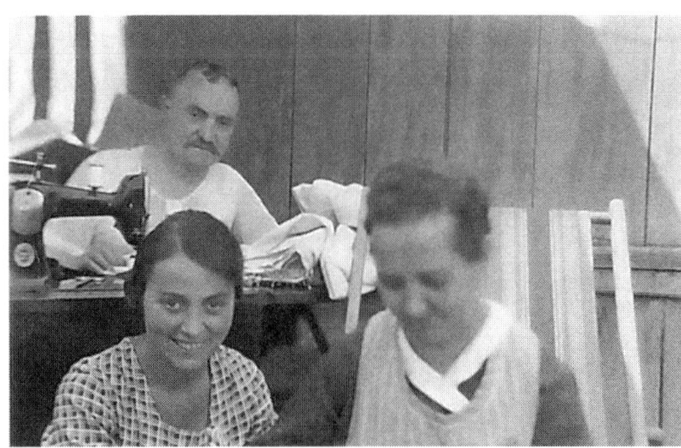

Fig. 8. Erna Lang Kaiser (left) of the Stuttgart Branch lost twenty-six close relatives (several of them LDS) during the war. Two of her relatives are shown here: Christian Lang (president of the Darmstadt Branch) and his wife, Anna Loeb Lang. Christian and Anna died in the firebombing of Darmstadt on September 11–12, 1944. (D. Kaiser)

Dieter Kaiser's mother did an excellent job in keeping her son fed, clothed, and sheltered while her husband was gone as a soldier. When the war ended, his whereabouts were not known, but eventually she learned that he was in a POW camp in Pennsylvania. She and Dieter were living in what was left of the family's apartment house. According to young Dieter, "a huge bomb destroyed one-half of the home. We could heat only one room after that, but we stayed in the home." Sister Kaiser's losses were much greater than property. No fewer than twenty-six close relatives had been killed in the war, including her parents. Her father, Christian Lang, was the branch president in Darmstadt and perished in his basement in the firebombing of that city on September 11–12, 1944, along with his wife and several other family members.

When Walter Speidel finally arrived home in Stuttgart after an absence of four years, he was surprised at the condition of the city, as he wrote:

> The whole area around the Hauptbahnhof all the way up to Wilhelmsbau, actually all of downtown Stuttgart, the whole inner city, was in ruins, just rubble, only some walls still standing here and there. Streetcars didn't have any glass, except up front, of course. What had been glass before was now boarded up with wood panels. [Arriving at my parents' apartment house] I woke up [everybody in the building] when I stomped up the stairs with my heavy American boots and my oversized duffle bag. Now, finally I was home. Was I, really? Or did I just dream?

Asked to speak in church on June 8, 1946, Walter mentioned the blessing in which he was promised he would return "without harm to body or spirit." Those remarks engendered some poor feelings among branch members in attendance. Several wondered why he had been given a special blessing promising his survival when a number of men and boys of the branch had perished in the war. "They were asking, 'Why didn't our sons receive that blessing?' I realized soon that I shouldn't have mentioned the blessing."[37]

The Latter-day Saints of the Stuttgart Branch had suffered substantial losses in life and property. Nearly all had lost their homes and were compelled to leave the city for at least a short time. It would be months and even years before some of them could return and join with their friends and family for worship services again.

In Memoriam

The following members of the Stuttgart Branch did not survive World War II:

Georg Andreas Konrad Bibinger b. Frankenthal or Gönkental, Pfalz, Bayern, 18 Apr 1884; son of Georg Bibinger and Anna Elisabeth Neufahrt; bp. 4 Jun 1921; conf. 4 Jun 1921; ord. deacon 29 Oct 1922; ord. teacher 23 Nov 1924; ord. priest 14 Oct 1928; ord. elder 2 Oct 1932; m. 28 Oct 1922, Rosine Fauser (div.); 2m. Stuttgart, Neckarkreis, Württemberg, 27 Jul 1931, Maria Luis Klink; d. heart attack Stuttgart, 10 Oct 1943 (FHL microfilm 68807, book 1, no. 200; FHL microfilm 25723; 1930 census; IGI)

Frida Luise Brosi b. Hohenhaslach, Neckarkreis, Württemberg, 24 May 1886; dau. of Gottlieb Brosi and Christina Frank; bp. 20 Jun 1918; conf. 20 Jun 1918; m. 2 Apr 1908, Gottlob Rieger; d. blood and liver poisoning 15 Sep 1939 (*Der Stern* no. 20, 15 Oct 1939, 323; FHL microfilm 68807, book 1, no. 637; FHL microfilm no. 271403; 1930 and 1935 censuses; IGI)

Emil Claude b. Donaueschingen, Villingen, Baden, 2 Feb 1871; son of Maria Claude; bp. 9 Aug 1924; conf. 9 Aug 1924; d. cerebral apoplexy 25 Oct 1939 (FHL microfilm 68807, book 2, no. 46; FHL microfilm 25741; 1930 and 1935 censuses; IGI)

Dieter Werner Fauser b. Stuttgart, Neckarkreis, Württemberg, 9 Sep 1935; son of Wilhelm Werner Fauser and Maria Barbara Katharina Soravia; d. diphtheria 15 May 1942 (FHL microfilm 68807, book 2, no. 633; FHL microfilm 25765; 1930 and 1935 censuses; IGI)

Maria Theresia Gommel b. Mengen, Donaukreis, Württemberg, 26 Sep 1875; dau. of Johannes Gommel and Pauline Schuhmacher; bp. 25 Jun 1911; conf. 25 Jun 1911; widow; d. dropsy 20 Dec 1944 (FHL microfilm 68807, book 1, no. 305; FHL microfilm 25775; IGI)

Johannes Albert Heil b. Stuttgart, Neckarkreis, Württemberg, 6 Sep 1912; son of Johann Wilhelm Heil and Friedrike L. Hohlweg or Hohlweger; bp. 17 May 1924; conf. 17 May 1924; k. in battle Italy 17 Sep 1943; bur. Cassino, Italy (CHL microfilm 2458, form 42 FP, pt. 37, 544–45; FHL microfilm 68807, book 1, no. 974; FHL microfilm 162780; 1935 census; www.volksbund.de; IGI)

Otto Friedrich Hertfelder b. Feuerbach, Württemberg, 8 Aug 1900; son of Ludwig Hertfelder and Berta Löffler; bp. 30 Apr 1921; conf. 30 Apr 1921; missing as of 20 Nov 1945 (FHL microfilm 68807, book 1, no. 314; FHL microfilm 162782; 1935 census)

Elise Anna Keller b. Buch, Frauenfeld, Thurgau, Switzerland, 28 Dec 1861; dau. of Johannes Keller and Barbara Leumann; bp. 21 May 1914; conf. 21 May 1914;

m. Ossweil, Ludwigsburg, Neckarkreis, Württemberg, 26 Oct 1884, Johann Friedrich Kahl; 6 children; d. senility Stuttgart, Neckarkreis, Württemberg, 23 Mar 1940 (FHL microfilm 68807, book 2, no. 280; FHL microfilm 271376; 1930 and 1935 censuses; IGI)

Regine Karoline Klink b. Alfdorf, Welzheim, Jagstkreis, Württemberg, 17 Dec 1873; dau. of Matthaeus Klink and Katharina Mueller; bp. 15 Apr 1922; conf. 15 Apr 1922; m. —— Loos; d. lung ailment 13 Dec 1944 (CR 375 8 2451, no. 379; FHL microfilm 271388; 1935 census; IGI)

Max Franz Knecht b. Schwäbisch Gmünd, Württemberg, 19 Feb 1910; son of Gottlieb Knecht and Christina Joos; ord. priest 1935; k. in battle. (M. Ruf Fry; FHL microfilm 271380; 1925 and 1935 censuses; IGI)

Christine Kurz b. Gniebel, Neckarkreis, Württemberg, 24 May 1865; dau. of Christian Kurz and Rosine Barbara Schäfer; bp. 4 Dec 1918; conf. 8 Dec 1918; m. Gniebel, Neckarkreis, Württemberg, 28 Nov 1895, Jakob Scholl; d. cerebral apoplexy Stuttgart, Württemberg, 27 Aug 1941 (FHL microfilm 68807, book 1, no. 541; FHL microfilm 245258, 1930 and 1935 censuses; IGI; AF)

Karoline Friedrike Lombacher b. Marbach or Steinheim, Neckarkreis, Württemberg 20 Dec 1864; dau. of Thomas Lombacher and Friederike Märtzirer or Märtyrer; bp. 9 Aug 1924; conf. 9 Aug 1924; m. 28 Sep 1889, Johann Friedrich Osswald; d. old age 24 Mar 1945 (FHL microfilm 68807, book 2, no. 42; IGI)

Horst Walter Lutz b. Stuttgart, Neckarkreis, Württemberg, 10 May 1924; son of Karl Wilhelm Lutz and Elisabeth Lutz; bp. 29 Mar 1935; conf. 29 Mar 1935; k. in battle Neustadt/Haardt, Pfalz, Bayern, 21 Mar 1945 (FHL microfilm 68807, book 2, no. 606; FHL microfilm no. 271390; 1935 census; IGI)

Pauline Auguste Neugebauer b. Schweidnitz, Schlesien, 27 Apr 1866; dau. of Pauline Neugebauer; bp. 18 Sep 1926; conf. 18 Sep 1926; m. —— Reicheneker; d. old age 29 Sep 1942 (FHL microfilm 68807, book 2, no. 201; FHL microfilm 271400; 1930 and 1935 censuses; IGI)

Hildegard Rieger b. Fellbach, Stuttgart, Neckarkreis, Württemberg 6 Sep 1908; dau. of Gottlob Rieger and Luise Frida Brosi; bp. 24 May 1932; conf. 24 May 1932; m. Stuttgart, 18 Jun 1932, Willy Fritz; d. meningitis Stuttgart, 21 May 1943 (FHL microfilm 68807, book 2, no. 539; FHL microfilm 25770; IGI)

Alma Helmuth Erwin Ruf b. Stuttgart, Neckarkreis, Württemberg, 22 Nov 1920; son of Hermann Otto Ruf and Regina Honold; bp. Stuttgart 30 Jun 1929; conf. 20 Jun 1929; ord. deacon 4 Oct 1934; ord. teacher 3 Dec 1939; ord. priest 29 Dec. 1940; radioman; k. in battle by Oktabriske sixty km east of Nikolajew, Russia, 14 Mar 1944 (L. Ruf-Wright; CHL CR 375 8 2451, no. 642; FHL microfilm 271407; 1930 and 1935 censuses; IGI)

Figs. 9 and 10. Brothers Kurt and Alma Ruf were both killed in battle in 1944. (L. Ruf Wright)

Kurt Walter Ruf b. Stuttgart, Neckarkreis, Württemberg, 10 May 1923; son of Hermann Otto Ruf and Regina Honold; bp. 30 May 1931 Stuttgart; conf. 30 May 1931; ord. deacon 22 May 1938; Waffen-SS lance corporal; tank crew; Iron Cross Second Class; k. in battle Noans or Alenson, France, 12 Aug 1944 (L. Ruf-Wright; CHL microfilm 2458, form 42 FP, pt. 37, district list 218–19, district list 1947, 544–45; FHL microfilm 68807, book 1, no. 818; FHL microfilm 271407; 1930 and 1935 censuses; IGI; AF)

Werner Hermann Widmar b. Stuttgart-Untertürkheim, Neckarkreis, Württemberg, 3 May 1921; son of Friedrich Widmar and Luise Frieda Rüdle; bp. 19 Jul 1930; conf. 19 Jul 1930; ord. deacon 4 Aug 1935; rifleman; k. in battle Naljiwajka (near present-day Trojanka Naljiwjka, Uman, Ukraine) 6 Aug 1941 (L. Ruf-Wright; www.volksbund.de; CHL CR 375 8 2451, no. 451; FHL microfilm 68807, book 1, no. 451; IGI)

Notes

1. Stuttgart city archive.
2. West German Mission branch directory, 1939, CHL LR 10045 11.
3. Presiding Bishopric, "Financial, Statistical, and Historical Reports of Wards, Stakes, and Missions, 1884–1955," 257, CR 4 12.
4. Erwin Ruf, "Denkschrift zur Feier des 40 jährigen Bestehens unsrer lieben Stuttgarter Gemeinde" (unpublished); private collection; trans. the author.
5. Walter Speidel, interview by the author, Provo, UT, February 23, 2007.
6. The other two branches were Hamburg-St. Georg and Essen.
7. Ruth Bodon Andersen, telephone interview with the author, August 13, 2009.
8. Esther Ruf Robinson, telephone interview with the author, April 13, 2009.

9. Dieter Kaiser, interview by the author, Salt Lake City, March 5, 2006.
10. Lydia Ruf Wright, "There Will Always Be Lilacs in August" (unpublished, 1992), 10; private collection.
11. Ruf, "Denkschrift."
12. Maria Ruf Fry, telephone interview with Jennifer Heckmann, December 8, 2008.
13. Walter Speidel, "Lebendig Gewordenes Gedächtnis" (unpublished), 123; private collection. The name of the young woman is withheld by request.
14. Lothar Greiner, interview with Jennifer Heckmann in German, Markgröningen, Germany, August 17, 2006, summarized in English by Judith Sartowski.
15. Stuttgart District records, 175, CHL MS 13360; trans. the author.
16. Ibid., 177.
17. Walter told a humorous story involving his father after the reunion in 1946: "My father told me he had seen a newsreel in the theater showing that it was so hot in Africa that German soldiers could cook an egg on the armor of a tank. I told my dad that the scene was only a trick, that there was actually a soldier underneath the tank with a blow torch to heat up the metal. My dad insisted that it was true because he had seen it on an official government newsreel. I had a hard time convincing him that it was all a ruse, a joke."
18. Speidel, "Lebendig," 153.
19. Wright, "Lilacs," 10.
20. Speidel, interview.
21. Karl-Heinz Bodon, telephone interview with the author, July 22, 2009.
22. Speidel, "Lebendig," 184–88.
23. Kurt Ruf, diary, July 6, 1943; used with permission of Lydia Ruf Wright.
24. Wright, "Lilacs," 11.
25. Wright, "Lilacs," 10.
26. Kurt Schneider (the husband of Harold's half-sister Charlotte) was the district president in Strasbourg, France, at the time. He enjoyed the use of a company car and traveled extensively in southwest Germany for church purposes.
27. Wright, "Lilacs," 11–12.
28. Kurt Ruf to Hermann Otto Ruf, June 8, 1944; used with permission of Lydia Ruf Wright.
29. Kurt Ruf to Hermann Otto Ruf, August 6, 1944; used with permission of Lydia Ruf Wright.
30. Ursula Auktor Augat, interview with the author, Salt Lake City, December 1, 2006.
31. Speidel, "Lebendig," 191. Walter's copy of the Book of Mormon had been taken by French guards when he was captured.
32. Stuttgart District records, 176.
33. Erika Metzner, "A Report of My Flight in the War Year of 1945 from Silesia to Stuttgart," (unpublished, 1981); used with permission of Rolf Rüdiger Metzner.
34. Wright, "Lilacs," 12–13.
35. Many thousands of German POWs (including several LDS men) were released by the Americans and British under the ruse of being sent home, only to be transferred to other POW camps in Belgium and France, where they stayed another year or more.
36. Speidel, "Lebendig," 199.
37. Speidel, interview.

VIENNA DISTRICT

West German Mission

The nation of Austria in 1938 consisted essentially of a remnant of the Hapsburg Empire, which had been known since 1866 as the Austro-Hungarian Empire. The Treaty of Versailles that concluded the Great War of 1914–18 took more than 80 percent of the empire's territory for the establishment of several new nations. The Austria that remained was the German-language territory of old; its neighbors were Germany to the northwest, Switzerland and Liechtenstein to the west, Italy to the southwest, Yugoslavia to the south, Hungary to the east, and Czechoslovakia to the northeast.

The government of the fledgling Austrian republic proved itself incapable of leading the nation to prosperity, and it came as no surprise that Austrians overwhelmingly voted to be annexed to Germany several times in the early 1920s. Of course, the League of Nations in Geneva would not allow such a union, and the country continued to lag behind Germany in economic growth. By the time Hitler's army marched across the borders into Austria on March 12, 1938, in yet another bloodless German conquest, many Austrians had become National Socialists in secret and were hoping that Germany would rescue their country soon from their sorrowful plight. The Wehrmacht troops that streamed across the border that morning were welcomed almost everywhere as liberators. Days later, Hitler appeared in person at the Heldenplatz in front of the Hofburg Palace in Vienna and was hailed by hundreds of thousands of Austrians as their new leader.

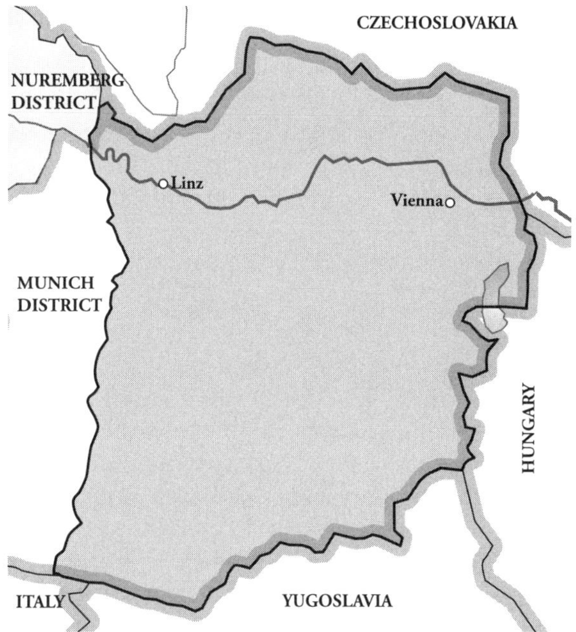

Fig. 1. The territory of the Vienna District was vast but mountainous and sparsely populated in 1939. There were no branches of the Church to the east or south of Austria.

The *Anschluss* (annexation) was the most momentous event in Austria between 1918 and 1945. Essentially all Austrians born before 1930 who are still alive remember where they were at the time. Below are the recollections of Latter-day Saints in three branches of the Church in Austria:

Alois Cziep (Vienna Branch, born 1893):

> [The Anschluss] brought many changes and transformations. Part of the citizens cheered the change and others expressed fearful apprehensions. At first things looked friendly! Suddenly there were no more unemployed! A sudden economic upswing, but it was unexplainable. However, soon we saw the other side of the coin. The first persecution of the Jews had started. . . . In my job the annexation was at first an advantage. The fish sales went up five times and it made an end to our constant need to conserve.[1]

Franz and Leopoldine Rosner (Haag am Hausruck Branch, born 1897 and 1894):

> Before the Anschluss, we could never travel to Germany. After that, we could go to Munich and Nuremberg for [church] conferences.[2]

Johann (John) Vazulik (Vienna Branch, born 1902):

> Swastika flags were hoisted and Nazis that had joined the party illegally in Austria between 1933 and 1938 surfaced and became quite active. . . . I kept on selling to my Jewish customers. . . . Traffic was changed from the left to the right as it was in Germany. Unemployment became rare and business picked up. The German salute "Heil Hitler" became the usual and the Nazis grew quite obnoxious.[3]

Gertrude Mühlhofer (Vienna Branch, born 1915):

> I had been without work for five years. Austria then became Germany on March [13]. I remember that everybody was excited because it meant that good things would happen and that conditions would be better for all of us. Everybody went to see Hitler speak. . . . I was not there in person, but I listened to it over the loudspeakers that were mounted in the trees.[4]

Walter Hirschmann (Vienna Branch, born 1921):

> We often heard that it would be good if everybody was finally able to get work and that Austria and Germany would be a larger territory now. . . . It did not bother us teenagers that Austria had a different name [*Ostmark*] all of a sudden. Maybe it bothered older people.[5]

Kurt Hirschmann (Vienna Branch, born 1921):

> I saw Hitler when he raised his hand [in the Nazi salute] and the people cheered him and I was there. I [cheered] too but not like most of the other people. . . . I was walking down the street when a Jehovah's Witness spoke to a man who was really yelling loud: "What will you do when Jesus Christ comes? Will you make this much noise for him?" The man answered, "Sure! Let him come!"[6]

Erwin Hirschmann (Vienna Branch, born 1924):

> On the day Hitler came to power in Austria, I was sent home from school because it was assumed that with my name, Hirschmann, I was Jewish. My father went to the school and explained to the administrators that we were in fact not Jewish. With this, they agreed to let [my brothers and me] return to school.[7]

Hildegard Dittrich (Haag am Hausruck Branch, born 1927):

> I remember when the German soldiers went through the town and the big tanks roared through the streets. It was very exciting and frightening. At first things looked friendly. No more unemployed people.[8]

Emmy Cziep (Vienna Branch, born 1928):

> I came home from school [that day] at lunchtime. My mother . . . was listening to the radio and she was crying; she was usually not that emotional. And as a child I was worried; I wondered what the problem was. I only remember her saying that [the Nazis] had taken Mr. Schuschnigg, who was the [Austrian] chancellor, and that the Nazis were going to take care of the country. She was trying to explain this to me a ten-year-old, but I did not understand what was going on. She said that force would be answered by force.[9]

The Church of Jesus Christ of Latter-day Saints had existed in Austria since the end of the nineteenth century, but only five branches were functioning in 1938: Vienna, Linz, Salzburg,

Frankenburg, and Haag am Hausruck. Prior to January 1, 1938, those branches belonged to the German-Austrian Mission, which was administered from Berlin, Germany. With the new year, a realignment of borders resulted in the establishment of the Swiss-Austrian Mission, with headquarters in Basel, Switzerland. However, due to the increasing difficulties encountered by American missionaries moving across the border between Switzerland and Austria after the Anschluss, as of November 1, 1938, missionary administration in Austria would be moved to the West German Mission, which was directed from the office in Frankfurt.

A district conference was held in Vienna on May 13–14, 1939, under the theme "Know the truth, and the truth shall make you free." District president Georg Schick presided at the conference. The attendance was recorded as follows: first session, sixty-five members and friends; leadership meeting, forty; Sunday School conference, seventy-one; fourth meeting, fifty; priesthood meeting, twenty-one; Relief Society meeting, thirty-one; and at the main session, seventy-four.[10] The mission history contains this statement regarding the conference: "Although the attendance in this district is not so large the audience was one of the most enthusiastic in the mission. All meetings were carried through in the regular order."[11]

During the conference it was announced that the district was to be disbanded. As of May 14, the presidents of the Linz and Vienna Branches were to answer directly to mission president M. Douglas Wood in Frankfurt. The small branches of Salzburg, Frankenburg and Haag am Hausruck were moved to the Munich, Germany District—principally because transportation to Munich was much more convenient than to Vienna. Georg Schick was released as district president after serving for six years.[12] The independent status of the Linz and Vienna Branches remained unchanged throughout World War II.

There are no official numbers for the populations of Saints in Linz and Vienna for the year 1939. Because of the transfer from one mission to another, reports sent to Salt Lake City after 1937 show only district membership. At the end of 1937, there were 281 members in the five Austrian branches. The three branches moved to the Munich District had a total of 120 members at the end of 1939, leaving approximately 160 in Linz and Vienna. Linz probably had only about thirty members on record, and Vienna perhaps 130.

Heinrich M. Teply described the condition of the Church in eastern Austria during the early war years in these words:

> For the most part the programs of the Church were carried out as before. Some of the terms had to be changed, such as *Versammlung* [meeting] to *Gottesdienst* [worship service] and *Verein* [society] to *Klasse* [class]. But those were just superficial changes. Of course, we were disappointed by the lack of literature and instructional materials, but we learned to get by with what we had. The West German Mission office tried to send us as much material as they could throughout the war years. In times of need, the members helped each other out. Families who lost their homes in air raids were taken in and cared for by others. In this regard the greatest assistance came from members in Upper Austria [Haag and Frankenburg Branches] who were less negatively affected by the war. Severe shortages were rarely the case, because the government provided the basic necessities right up until the end of the war.[13]

When World War II began on September 1, 1939, the Austrians found themselves in a contradictory situation: they were officially German citizens due to the Anschluss but were considered by the rest of the world to be victims of oppression—a conquered and occupied nation. The fact that the name Austria was replaced by *Ostmark* (the eastern realm) on German maps rankled many Austrians. However, some, including some members of the LDS Church, enjoyed their new status as citizens of a powerful country with an apparently promising future. At the same time, Austrian men did not always relish the idea of fighting battles in countries far away or dying for "Führer, Volk, und Vaterland."

Branch conferences of the Church were held in Vienna on a regular basis after the war began. A Sunday School conference was attended by fifty persons in February 1941, and one month later forty-five persons attended a Relief Society conference. A spring mission conference was held on June 7–8, 1941, under the leadership of mission supervisor Christian Heck, and several Saints from Austria took the train to Germany to participate. Branch leaders from Linz and Salzburg attended a conference in Munich in the fall of 1941. Mission records indicate that conferences were held in Vienna on April 3–4, 1943, and on October 2–3, 1943; mission leaders Christian Heck and Anton Huck presided, and Johann Thaller, president of the Munich District, was also in attendance.[14] It is clear that contacts with other districts and with the West German Mission office in Frankfurt were carefully maintained as long as possible.

At the conclusion of the war, Austria was divided into four regions for occupation by the victorious nations of Great Britain, the United States, France, and the Soviet Union. In the confusion, contact with the mission office in Frankfurt was interrupted, and the leaders of the five LDS branches in Austria wondered how they should proceed. They met in Haag am Hausruck in the summer of 1945 and decided to establish an Austrian administration of the Church; Anton Cziep of Vienna was selected as the leading elder of the organization until such time as the Church leadership in Salt Lake City could reestablish contact and provide instructions. This status prevailed only until May 1946, when Elder Ezra Taft Benson arrived to organize the Vienna District with Brother Cziep as president.[15]

The members of the five branches in Austria had fared somewhat better in the war years than their friends in the German branches, but there were losses and privations to overcome. Only the Linz Branch was without a real meeting venue in 1945, and all five branches were holding regular meetings. The spirit of the Church in Austria was very good, and several new branches were established in the next few years.

NOTES

1. Gayle Collette Hatch, *Alois and Hermine: A Cziep Family History, 1893–2005* (Durham, NC: G. C. Hatch, 2005), 77.
2. Franz and Leopoldine Rosner, interview by Douglas F. Tobler, Haag am Hausruck, Austria, March 16, 1974, 17, CHL MS 1882.
3. John Vazulik, "World War II Memories of John Vazulik" (unpublished manuscript); used with permission of Anton Vazulik.
4. Gertrude Mühlhofer Klein, interview by the author in German, Kiesling, Austria, August 9, 2008; unless otherwise noted, summarized in English by Judith Sartowski.
5. Walter Hirschmann, interview by the author in German, Munich, Germany, August 6, 2008.
6. Kurt Hirschmann, interview by the author, Ogden, UT, March 9, 2007.
7. Erwin Hirschmann, "A Life Well Lived" (unpublished autobiography).
8. Hildegard Dittrich Cziep, autobiography (unpublished); private collection.
9. Emmi Cziep Collete, interview by the author, Idaho Falls, ID, June 10, 2006.
10. Vienna Branch history, CHL LR 9781 11.
11. West German Mission quarterly report, 1939, no. 20, CHL LR 10045.
12. Anton F. Körbler, "Geschichte der Kirche Jesu Christi der Heiligen der letzten Tage in Österreich" (unpublished manuscript); private collection.
13. Heinrich M. Teply, "Bericht zur Kirchengeschichte in Österreich" (unpublished manuscript); private collection; trans. the author.
14. Vienna Branch history, CHL LR 9781 11.
15. Teply, "Bericht."

LINZ BRANCH

Located on the banks of the Danube River in the province of Upper Austria, the city of Linz was one of Austria's largest in 1938, with 123,000 inhabitants, but also home to a very small branch of The Church of Jesus Christ of Latter-day Saints.[1] There is no record of the actual number of branch members in Linz at the time, but several important documents have survived that describe the condition and activities of the branch during World War II.

Founded in 1921, the Linz Branch was led for many years by a professional soldier, Rudolf

Niedermair, who had joined the Church in the 1920s. According to Karl Schramm (born 1908), Niedermair was the commander of a local army post. Because Schramm was unemployed from 1931 to 1938, President Niedermair often gave him clothing no longer needed by the soldiers.[2]

The history of the Linz Branch provides the following description of the branch's condition just before the war:

> From 1933 to 1938 there was a serious economic crisis that caused hunger, illness and need among many families. When Hitler came to power in Austria in 1938, the Linz Branch was part of the Vienna District under the leadership of Georg Schick. On May 14, 1939, Linz and Vienna were designated as independent of the mission and remained so until 1946.[3]

Like many Austrians, Karl Schramm was pleased to see Hitler annex Austria in 1938: "I had a job by April 13, just one month later. I found a position in the field for which I was trained [cauldron smith]. Nobody was out of work any more. We had Hitler to thank for that."[4]

Fig. 1. Branch president Rudolf Niedermair was one of the first to join the Church in Linz. (G. Koerbler Greenmun)

According to the directory of the West German Mission, the Linz Branch held their Sunday School meetings in rooms on the second floor of a building at Landstrasse 49 during the summer of 1939. President Niedermair's counselors were Peter Mareska and Karl Schramm. No other men or women were listed as branch officers at the time. The directory indicates that only Sunday School was held at that location, whereas sacrament meeting took place at 7:30 p.m. in the fourth-floor apartment of a Sister Schleindl at Hofgasse 12. An entertainment evening was held on Wednesdays at 8:00 p.m. in the home of Brother Mareska.[5]

The condition of the branch in the first two years after Austria was annexed by Germany was described in detail by Karl Schramm in his memoirs:

> We were soon evicted from our rooms in the Vereinshaus and were compelled to find rooms in restaurants and other buildings. Thus began an endless search for suitable meeting places for our events. Many members offered their apartments and I will name just a few: Mareska, Schleindl, Scharinger, Pöschl, and Schramm. Special mention is due Sister Szigato who was so selfless in her service. Brother Niedermair led this branch with great care as it continued to shrink in size under these difficult circumstances. Little by little things began to change. We were forbidden to sing songs that glorified Zion or the Jewish religion. We were required to sing the Horst Wessel anthem and other such songs.[6] Brother Niedermair repeatedly testified to us that if we remained faithful, the Church would survive intact despite such chicanery. Then the shock came when we found ourselves at war against half of the world. The missionaries were pulled out and we were left to depend only on the Lord. Due to the blackout, we could no longer meet in the evenings and it became more difficult to get together. Some of the members were drafted and there were only about eight to ten members left and some of them were not coming regularly. By then, we were meeting in the home of eighty-year-old Sister Schleindl and Brother Niedermair was in charge.[7]

Rudolf Niedermair served as the branch president in Linz from 1924 to 1941. He was a loyal army officer who never spoke a word against the government, according to Karl Schramm, who also claimed that other branch members also refrained from making political statements during the war.[8]

According to the memoires of Karl Schramm, Rudolf Niedermair became seriously ill in 1941 at the age of fifty. His condition was not known until he suddenly missed church one Sunday. The members found him in the hospital suffering from blood poisoning. He told them that he was embarking upon a trip from which he would not return. His wife insisted that he was speaking nonsense in a fever, but two days later he passed away.[9]

When President Niedermair died on May 6, 1941, he received a military funeral. According to Anton F. Körbler, the funeral was a very large affair that was attended by thirty-five Latter-day Saints from several branches in Austria as well as by 350 friends. The religious portion of the ceremony was directed by former district president Georg Schick from Vienna and Alois Cziep, the president of the Vienna Branch.[10] The burial took place in the St. Barbara Cemetery in Linz.

Fig. 2. A career soldier, Rudolf Niedermair died of blood poisoning in 1941. (G. Koerbler Greenmun)

Karl Schramm, a priest in the Aaronic Priesthood, was then asked to see to the daily affairs of the branch but was not set apart as the branch president. He saw to these duties for the next eight months, during which time attendance decreased. The minutes of the Sunday School of the Linz Branch for the years 1941 and 1942 have survived. The number of persons attending was between three and eight for 1941 and decreased in 1942 to three to five persons each week.[11]

The records of the Linz Branch show that Heinz Jankowsky of Wels was set apart as branch president for Linz on April 18, 1943, by Alois Cziep, the president of the Vienna Branch. Brother Jankowsky served with the help of President Cziep and Georg Schick until the end of the war.[12] The branch history indicates that during the war the members held their meetings in the homes of members, in schools and restaurants, and in the Vereinshaus.[13] It was probably a difficult task to locate new places to meet while Linz was under Allied attack from the air in the last years of the war.

In February 1942, Karl Schramm was drafted into the Wehrmacht and sent to Russia, where he served for three and one-half years as a railroad worker. When he was released as a prisoner of war in 1945 and returned to Linz, he learned that his wife and his son had sought refuge among the Saints of the Haag am Hausruck Branch thirty miles to the west. Although they were not members of the Church, they were treated with such kindness by the Haag Branch that Frau Schramm asked to be baptized in August 1945, after which the Schramms returned to Linz.

From July 1944 until the end of the war, the city of Linz suffered under twenty-two air raids that took the lives of 1,679 residents. An estimated one-third of the dwelling space in the city was rendered useless by the time the American army arrived in the city on May 5, 1945.[14] It is not known if or how many of the Saints in Linz lost their homes.

With the arrival of the American army as the liberators and occupiers of the province of Upper Austria in May 1945, the Linz Branch began to be revived. Several of the American soldiers were Latter-day Saints, and they did what they could to ease the sufferings of the local Saints, who were subsisting on meager rations. On many Sundays, the soldiers invited three or four branch members to lunch at the post. Assistance also came from the Saints in Haag and Frankenburg, most of whom were farmers and thus had better access to food. The Saints in Linz were very grateful for the support as they continued to revive their branch after the war.

IN MEMORIAM

Only one member of the Linz Branch is known to have died during World War II:

Rudolf Niedermaier b. Wels, Oberösterreich, Österreich, 31 Oct 1888; son of Mathias Niedermaier and Anna Merfert; bp. 10 Jan 1909; conf. 10 Jan 1909; m. Anna Amalie Ring; 1 child; d. blood poisoning Linz, Oberösterreich, Österreich, 6 May 1941 (FHL microfilm 245242; 1925 and 1935 censuses)

Notes

1. Linz city archive.
2. Karl Schramm, interview by Jeff Anderson, Linz, Austria, 1991, CHL OH 1028.
3. *Gemeinde Linz, 1921–1986: 65 Jahre Kirchengeschichte* (1991), CHL LR 4931 21.
4. The Linz and Vienna Branches constituted the Vienna District after the branches in Salzburg, Haag am Hausruck, and Frankenburg were transferred to the Munich District in 1938.
5. Schramm, interview.
6. West German Mission branch directory, 1939, vol. 11, CHL LR 10045.
7. The Horst Wessel song was the anthem of the National Socialist Party; the text was written by Nazi martyr Horst Wessel.
8. Karl Schramm, "Die Geschichte der Mormonengemeinde in Linz, 1923–1956" (unpublished history, 1981); private collection; trans. the author.
9. Schramm, interview.
10. Schramm, "Geschichte der Mormonengemeinde."
11. Anton F. Köbler,"Geschichte der Kirche Jesus Christi der Heiligen der letzten Tage in Österreich" (unpublished manuscript).
12. Linz Branch records, CHL LR 4931 15.
13. Linz Branch records, CHL LR 9781 11, 66.
14. *Gemeinde Linz, 1921–1986.*
15. Linz city archive.

Vienna Branch

The Austro-Hungarian Empire was nearly four decades old when a branch of The Church of Jesus Christ of Latter-day Saints was established in the capital city of Vienna just after the turn of the century.[1] The city was the political, cultural, scientific, and industrial capital of the empire and attracted people from many lands speaking many languages. Years later, it would be commonly claimed that a genuine native of Vienna must have a Hungarian grandfather and a Bohemian grandmother. Vienna was at the same time the capital of Austria, a predominately Catholic country where German was the only official language.

By 1938, the Vienna Branch consisted of perhaps 130 members who lived in many of the twenty-three *Bezirke* (districts) of the metropolis. The home of the branch was Seidengasse 30 in District VII

Fig. 1. Seidengasse 30 in Vienna. The Church rooms were to the left of the main entry on the main and second floors. Note the sign in the first window left of the entry. (E. Cziep Collette)

(Neubau). The rooms were acquired in July 1935 and served their purpose well for five decades. According to branch president Alois Cziep (born 1893), the Church rented all of the rooms on the second floor as well as the rooms on the main floor to the left of the portal. Access to those rooms was a door to the left, just inside the portal.[2]

Gertrude Mühlhofer (born 1915) described the rooms rented by the branch at Seidengasse 30:

> We walked into the portal and on the left side was a door to our rooms. We then went up some stairs and reached the cloakroom. On the right side, there was the restroom. Then there was a small room in which the youngest children had their classes. On the right side, there were two smaller rooms also. There was also a large room for sacrament meeting. We had single chairs that could be connected and could not be moved easily. There were about sixty people there on a typical Sunday, and there were quite a few children.[3]

Gertrude had been out of work for five years when Austria was annexed by Germany. By a stroke of luck, she was offered employment in the parliament, as she later explained:

> I received very good training. I earned three hundred Marks a month and that was very good money back then. They also gave me extra money the first month so that I could

> buy myself something nice to wear. I had gone directly from babysitting to the new job and I looked pretty good. My task was to find all the legionnaires. I had a chauffeur who drove me everywhere to find the veterans jobs and places to live. I did this for five to six months, after which I became the secretary to the leader of the German Arbeitsfront. I stayed in Vienna and worked this job until I had my first baby [in September 1942].

Fig. 2. The main meeting room at Seidengasse 30. (E. Cziep Collette)

Young Emma (Emmy) Cziep (born 1928) recalled an interesting feature of the rooms at Seidengasse 30: "One of my favorite rooms was padded—one of those old-fashioned rooms where there was leather padding on the wall with buttons in them. I guess they used to call them smoking rooms. That was the priesthood and Sunday School room."[4] Emmy also recalled the stark contrast between those meeting rooms and the buildings in which her friends and neighbors worshipped: "We were sitting in this small apartment, and down the street was a huge cathedral."

Emmy's father, Alois Cziep, had been called to serve as branch president in 1933 and remained in that position until after the war. In September 1938, the Cziep family moved into a nice second-story apartment at Taborstrasse 20 in District II. President Cziep was the manager of a store in the Nordsee Seafood Company chain. Having lost an eye, he was classified as unfit for military duty and thus was able to remain in Vienna all during the war years.[5]

Members of the extended Hirschmann family lived in two five-story apartment buildings constructed by their father around 1900. Karl Hirschmann with his wife, Maria Huber, inhabited an apartment in the building at Linke Wienzeile 156 in District VI. Their children were Erwin, Walter, Charlotte, and Friedrich. Karl's building was back-to-back with a similar building that faced Mollardgasse. His brother Konrad lived in an apartment in that building with his wife Aloisia Huber. Their children were Kurt, Irmgard, Wilhelm, and Alfred. The two wives were sisters—daughters of Johann Huber, one of the great pioneers of the LDS Church in Austria. It was Johann's farm in Rottenbach, near Haag am Hausruck, where a number of significant events took place from his baptism in 1900 through the end of the war.[6] The Hirschmann children (and cousins) from Vienna were frequent visitors at the Huberhof over the years.[7]

Kurt Hirschmann (born 1921) explained that the family walked about fifteen minutes to church from the apartment houses on Linke Wienzeile and Mollardgasse because the streetcars did not run in the direction of the Seidengasse.[8] The attendance was sixty to seventy persons. Sunday School was held in the morning and sacrament meeting in the evening. MIA took place on Tuesday nights.

As an older teenager, Kurt could not get a job. Thus it happened that he was assigned by the government to work in faraway East Prussia. Very unhappy with the program ("five months of work and no pay"), Kurt learned that the trip home on the train would cost thirty-five marks and he wrote to his grandmother for the money. She sent it, and Kurt slipped away from the work camp one day and boarded the train for Vienna.

Before the war, the Vienna Branch had a small orchestra. Erwin Hirschmann (born 1924) recalled that he and his brother Walter both played the violin, as did Hans Vaculik and Heinz Teply. Erwin taught a Sunday School class for youth fourteen to sixteen and also served as the Sunday School president. As he recalled, "It was in this branch that I literally grew up. It was here that I became a deacon, a teacher, a priest and then after the war, an elder."[9]

The connection with Germany had an immediate impact on young Wilhelm Hirschmann (born 1930), as he explained:

> When Austria was annexed to Germany, I was eight years old and was immediately sent to Germany to live with a family. The government said that I would be safer there. My parents took me to the train station and said good-bye. We didn't know where I would be sent. There were not many children left on the train when it got to Wolfenbüttel. The Kletzer family took me in when I got off there. They were very nice to me. I stayed in Wolfenbüttel for six weeks. I liked the time there. I thought that I could tell the family a little about the Church I attended at home, but they were not interested.[10]

An enlightening report is found in the Church History Library in Salt Lake City detailing the home-teaching efforts of the Vienna Branch on September 17, 1939: nine brethren were assigned to visit a total of sixty-nine families. As of the date of the report, the home teachers had seen an average of seven families each month. This is the only such report filed in the West German Mission.[11]

Shortly after the Anschluss in 1938, the Straumer family arrived in Vienna from the Free City of Danzig.[12] Johannes Friedrich Straumer was a major in the German army and commanded a tank battalion stationed in Vienna. His family was assigned an apartment at Grinzinger Allee 17 in District XIX. His wife, Bertha Lisa, had joined the Church in 1926 and immediately sought contact with the Saints of the LDS branch at Seidengasse 30. Her daughters, Brigitta and Erika, also attended branch meetings and activities on occasion.[13]

Brigitta Straumer (born 1923) recalled that the Germans who arrived in 1938 to direct the transition of Austria into the National Socialist world were not resented by the local residents. In her recollection, "The Germans were the conquerors, but I don't think that the Austrians felt that they had been conquered. Many of them wanted us [Germans] there. They wanted to be part of Germany."[14]

Her sister Erika (born 1926) agreed that there was no animosity shown them as German citizens. However, she perceived a difference between her family and the local members of the Vienna Branch: "They were mostly poor and I looked down on them a bit because of our [higher] standing." The Straumers' neighborhood in District XIX featured higher-class buildings that allowed them a beautiful view north into the Vienna woods.[15]

Brigitta Straumer wanted to learn to dance and showed the necessary aptitude at an early age. By 1940, she had been accepted to the Academy for Music and Dramatic Arts in Vienna, where she studied under the famous Grete Wiesenthal. Johannes Straumer was not a member of the Church and felt that Brigitta should not be baptized until she was an adult, but she had been taught the principles of the gospel by her mother and practiced the LDS lifestyle—at times a challenge in the world of the performing arts. For the time being, it was still "Mutti's church" to Brigitta.[16]

Erika Straumer became a member of the BDM (League of German Girls) in 1940. She recollected:

> We had a big rally once in downtown Vienna and we had to march all the way there [from District XIX]. Eventually, I grew tired of the activities and began to stay away. But in order to receive my grades at the end of each semester, I had to tell [the school authorities] which group I belonged to, so I asked my friends to tell me what they had been doing recently. For a while, the BDM leaders kept track of me.

It appears that at Easter time in 1939, Gertrude Mühlhofer was living a charmed life. Given a comfortable vacation at a ski resort, she met a handsome young soldier, Fritz Klein, a native Berliner who had moved to Vienna. As she recalled, "He was not a member of the Church back then, and I told him there would be no hanky-panky before marriage. He respected that, and I give him credit for that to this day." Thus began a two-year long-distance courtship for Gertrude and Fritz. She returned to her work in Vienna, and he was sent to the Soviet Union.

The Mühlhofer-Klein wedding took place under irregular circumstances. Fritz had been severely wounded in Russia and wrote Gertrude in July 1941 that he had lost his left leg. She traveled to his hospital near Frankfurt, and they decided to marry. It was September 17, 1941, and she described the setting in these words: "They decorated a [hospital] room for us and it was really pretty. There were red roses on the walls and nice fabric as decoration. And there were gifts on the table from his comrades." Fritz was soon transferred to a hospital in Vienna, and the newlyweds went home soon thereafter.

After escaping from the work program in East Prussia, Kurt Hirschmann found a position in a trade school just two blocks from his home. From late 1938 to 1941, he attended school there and worked toward graduation as a machinist. Just a week after graduating, he received his draft notice and was mustered into an artillery unit of the German army on April 4, 1941. Initially, he was sent to Karlsruhe, Germany, for five months of training. While there, he attended meetings with the Karlsruhe Branch whenever possible and recalled singing enthusiastically "with mostly old people." In the fall of 1941, Kurt had three weeks of furlough and spent the time helping his Grandfather Huber on the farm at Rottenbach near Haag. From there, he was sent to the Soviet Union, where German forces were experiencing great success. As he recalled:

> It was [in Russia] that I learned that there is a God. You wonder sometimes how come you're still alive. One day we had stopped to arrest a man in a small house when dive-bombers swooped down to attack us. We were safe in the house, but bombs hit our car. When the attack was over, the motor was lying in the middle of the road and some tires were hanging in a tree. It all happened in a minute, and it was a very faith-promoting experience. . . . When God wants us to live, he finds a way for it to happen.

Walter Hirschmann (born 1921) finished his studies in an engineering school in Vienna in 1939 and found employment with the AEG Company. A year later, he was drafted and sent to Stuttgart, Germany, to be trained as a radio operator. By the fall of 1941, he was with the forces attacking Moscow, Russia. "When we reached that point [the outskirts of the city], we could not seem to go on," he recalled. Fortunately, he developed an abscess on his arm and was sent back to Austria for treatment. He was still there in January 1942 when his father passed away.[17]

Back in Russia a short time later, Walter stayed only six months. During that time, he fired his weapon only at night and "only as a kind of defensive measure," as he described it. He was never wounded, but there were instances where he thought it was his time to die. Fortunately, he was sent to Berlin to work with the Siemens Company, a huge electronics firm. "I kept my uniform but did not have to wear it. I worked in a department responsible for developing equipment to jam the navigation devices of British and American airplanes heading for German cities. We wanted to distract them from their bombing runs but were never able to carry out the plan." While in Berlin, Walter attended church meetings and was ordained a priest.

Wilhelm Hirschmann recalled a sign in the window announcing the presence of the Vienna Branch. He explained that the sign had a specific impact in one case:

> That sign attracted a family to the Church, and they joined during the war. They had been resettled from somewhere in Ukraine to Vienna because the government believed that they were in danger after the German army went through their area, maybe in 1941 or 1942. The mother of that family went looking for a church and saw our sign in the window. She knew instinctively that this was to be her church. Their name was Ivanitschi.

The family of Johann Friedrich Docekal was assigned a new apartment in 1941. His daughter Martha recalled that in November 1941, a woman who was assigned one of the rooms in their apartment told them, "They're coming to get *them* tonight," to which Maria Docekal responded, "I want to know what they're doing." Quietly opening their window, the Docekals watched as Jewish families living in apartments downstairs were taken from the house and put into an open truck. Each person was carrying a bundle. According to young Martha, "We knew that they were Jews, because we had seen them in the hall with the Star of David [on their coats]." Martha had seen Jews in the streetcars around town wearing the Star of David and had asked herself, "What have they done that they have to wear that?"[18]

For all practical purposes, there were three active holders of the Melchizedek Priesthood in the Vienna Branch who stayed at home during World War II—the branch presidency, consisting of Alois Cziep, Johann Ackerl, and Anton Körbler. The rest were serving in the military. Fortunately, several young men held the Aaronic Priesthood and attended meetings regularly, which was a great help to the branch presidency. During the war, two boys and one man were ordained deacons (Wilhelm Hirschmann, Heinz Martin Teply, and Stefan Meszaros), one was ordained a teacher (Josef Cziep), and four were ordained priests (Johann Schramm, Erwin Hirschmann, Roland Paleschka, and Stefan Meszaros). Johann Vaculik was the only man ordained to the office of elder. Attendance at priesthood meetings averaged about eight men during the war.[19]

Just as Alois Cziep worried about and cared for the members of the branch, his wife Hermine Cziep was the president of the Relief Society and had the same concerns. Throughout the war years, she walked countless miles across town to help the sisters with their babies, children, and illnesses when needed. She often expressed gratitude to her longtime counselors, Maria Hirschmann and Maria Docekal. The three were often seen in the branch rooms on Saturdays cleaning up and arranging things for the Sunday meetings.

Erwin Hirschmann had wanted to become a farmer (perhaps like his Grandfather Huber), but was a very good student as well. He finished public school with high marks and was enrolled in a state trade school, followed by a term of study at the Technical University of Vienna. Work internships took him for a few summer months to Friedrichshafen on Lake Constance and to Stuttgart, both in Germany. In March 1942, he went to work for Siemens and Halske in Vienna. On December 12, he was drafted into the Wehrmacht. Following boot camp in Braunschweig, Germany, he was sent to Belgium and then to France, where he became seriously ill with pleurisy. He was transfered to Vienna and then to a town close to Salzburg for nearly two months of treatment and recuperation.[20]

Membership in the Nazi Party was also the experience of several members of the Vienna Branch. At least two of the Hirschmann boys were required by their employers to join, but neither took part in Party meetings or activities. The branch president was not a member of the party, but according to his daughter, Emmy, one of his counselors was, and Brother Cziep had to deal with at least one political incident in Church during the war:

> Brother —— was a church leader who came to visit us from Germany. I remember his name, and I even remember what he looked like, . . . and he wore the Nazi Party button on his lapel. He came to our district meeting, and he gave a prayer and prayed for Hitler. My father got up right after him and said, "I'm sorry, Brother ——, but in this Church, in this branch, we do *not* pray for Hitler." That is the only political statement I remember hearing my father make. I heard this with my own ears, and it impressed me because I was a member of the Hitler Youth at the time.[21]

According to Emmy, her father instructed the Saints in Vienna that they were to pray for their families, the members of the Church, and the safety of the soldiers, "but not for Adolf Hitler!"

Nazi Party politics could not be totally avoided by the branch leaders. Alois Cziep recalled that "some of our best members were also party members or sympathizers and I had to go to great lengths to keep politics away from the Church."

One of his greatest challenges was to ask Sister Weiss and her son, who were Jews, to stay away from the meetings "because we would have lost our meeting place at once" if they were seen entering the building wearing the Star of David, as was required by law beginning in 1941. Brother Cziep visited Sister Weiss in her home until she and her son were deported to Poland, where he believed they were killed.[22]

Fig. 3. The Cziep family lived on the third floor to the right of the corner in this building on Taborstrasse. (E. Cziep Collette)

Like other young people in the Reich, Emmy Cziep was required to be a member of the Jungvolk, but while there were strict duties, there were also privileges. "We could ride the streetcar for free, get out of school for parades, and do all kinds of things. And who doesn't like a uniform when you're ten years old? I thought it was beautiful. We had a dynamic leader, and she was great. Had it not been for her, I probably wouldn't have liked it as much."

Looking back on the experience, Emmy realized that the girls were asked subtle questions that might have elicited dangerous answers, such as: What's your parents' favorite radio program? Who comes to visit and what do they talk about? What do you talk about at home?

Fig. 4. The presidency of the Vienna Branch. From left: second counselor Johann Ackerl, president Alois Cziep, first counselor Anton Franz Körbler. (G. Koerbler Greenmun)

Emmy did not recall any problems connected with her membership in the LDS Church, but there was an incident at school relating to religion. The teacher was dictating text to be written by each student and stated that there was no God and that Jesus was a figment of the imagination. Having learned many short quotations on religion from her parents, Emmy blurted out, "The glory of God is intelligence!" The teacher began to mock Emmy by asking her to explain the statement, which she could not do. "I had no way of explaining," she said, "so I felt like a fool."

As in other branches throughout Germany and Austria, this branch also celebrated births, baptisms, and weddings. Five children of record and converts were baptized during the war: Martha Docekal, Anton Alfred Vaculik, Marianna Przybyla, Brigitta Straumer, and Erika Straumer. Three weddings were also celebrated among the members of the branch: Gertrude Mühlhofer and Friedrich Klein (1941), Margarethe Czerney and Hans Wabenhauer (1941), and Johanna Mayer and a Mr. Richter (1942).[23]

Martha Docekal (born 1933) recalled her baptism in the Old Danube (an inactive arm of the Danube left over when the course of the river was regulated): "We were baptized, changed our clothes, and then we were confirmed at the same location." Anton Vaculik (born 1934) remembered that some friends of the branch owned a small cabin there and allowed the Saints to use it as a dressing room for baptismal ceremonies.[24]

In 1942, Johann Vaculik (born 1902) was drafted into the Wehrmacht and had to close his delicatessen store. At the age of forty, he found basic training to be very strenuous but was then assigned noncombat duty. Stationed in Vienna, he rode the train as an army policeman (*Zugwache*) who checked the papers of military travelers while looking for deserters and saboteurs. His travels took him to Germany, France, Bulgaria, Romania, and Greece. Brother Vaculik continued to enjoy duty away from the battlefield, being assigned to a supply company and doing guard duty in Russia and Poland in 1943.[25]

By the summer of 1942, Brigitta Straumer had progressed sufficiently in her dance studies to be sent with a group of dancers to perform for German soldiers in occupied Poland. The girls had to be cautious in the large city of Posen, because the Poles were understandably unhappy under the German occupation. Brigitta had no difficulties on the trip but recalled clearly the occasion when they boarded a streetcar for a ride through the Jewish ghetto and were told by German soldiers to not take any pictures:

> I will never forget that ride, what I saw and how I felt. . . . I was indoctrinated by Hitler and had certain feelings about the Jews. From the streetcar we could look and see the city streets and the people on the streets. I saw that many of the men wore long beards and black long coats, such a strange sight. . . . This was a ghetto for Jews. They couldn't leave the place. They were prisoners there. I did not feel sorry for them, but thought that it was all right to have all the Jews live together in one place. Oh, what had Hitler's teaching done to me, a nice 19-year-old girl? . . . I did not see the suffering of the people, nor did I want to.[26]

While still in Posen, Brigitta learned of the death of her brother, second lieutenant Hans-Joachim Straumer, in Russia. He was killed on August 8, 1942, not far from where his father was serving with a tank brigade. Bertha Straumer was devastated by the news but never faltered in her dedication to the Church and the branch. According to Brigitta, "The death of my brother started a slow change in me. I had been selfish, mostly thinking of myself, dancing and performing." Watching her mother serve without interruption after Hans-Joachim's death, Brigitta wondered where her mother received her strength. "Deep down, I knew the answer. It was the Savior, Jesus Christ, His love and atonement."[27]

The branch general minutes show that the leaders and members put forth a serious effort to maintain the programs of the Church during the war. For example, branch conferences were held the first week of December in 1941, in 1942 (with mission supervisor Christian Heck), and in 1943 ("an excellent success"). The MIA classes for young women and young men were combined in October 1942, and a study of the book *Teachings of the Gospel* by Joseph Fielding Smith was initiated. This was a great benefit to the youth, because MIA classes in most branches of the West German Mission had been discontinued by that time. The Sunday School also held periodic conferences and even organized a membership drive in November 1943.[28]

President Cziep wrote of the progress of the war in these words:

> At first it seemed that Germany was going to win. It didn't take long and no one could hide the hard facts! Food and necessities became scarcer and the black market was in full bloom. [Hitler was] always asking for more men and at last it was young boys and old men that were asked to bear arms. More and more wives and mothers heard the message that their husbands and sons were not going to return. As long as the bombing attacks were confined to the German cities, we viewed those people as heroes. But then when the hail of fire and iron fell over the cities of Austria, hopelessness, chaos and destruction became our reality. No one could dream of living a normal life![29]

In December 1942, Kurt Hirschmann came home to Austria on leave and married his sweetheart, Johanna Dietrich of the Frankenburg,

Austria, Branch. He had met her before the war when her family lived in Haag am Hausruck and attended church there. It would be nearly two years before he could see her again. In the meantime, his constant prayer had been answered: "I prayed that I would not be taken prisoner by the Russians. Maybe God could help me be wounded just badly enough that I would be sent away from Russia," he recalled. "On August 26, 1944, my prayer was answered when I was hit in the head by shrapnel." Loaded onto an ambulance wagon at the last second, he was saved from the advancing Red Army and was eventually sent to a hospital near Hanover in northern Germany.

Kurt's head wound was not serious and he assumed that he would be sent back to the fighting soon. Fortunately, an army doctor kept him in the hospital for a month and then transferred him to a second hospital for another month. "I didn't need to stay that long after he removed the piece of metal—two weeks at most. [While I was there,] my wife came from Austria to see me. When she walked in, she looked like an angel."

Fig. 5. Members of the Vienna Branch at the summer home of Maria Hirschmann in Purkersdorf in 1943. (E. Cziep Collette)

By the spring of 1943, Erwin Hirschmann had recovered from his bout with pleurisy and was assigned to a unit in Braunschweig again. He requested and was granted a transfer to Hanover and made the move just one day before his unit in Braunschweig was sent to a combat zone in Russia. He wrote, "I readily admit that this transfer to my reserve unit, as opposed to my combat unit, most likely saved my life. . . . In Hanover, our specialty was in the area of microwave communications . . . using magnetrons and klystrons for wireless transmissions." From Hanover, the group moved to Flensburg near the German-Danish border and from there to nearby Plön.[30]

From the summer of 1943 to the spring of 1944, Brigitta Straumer became increasingly interested in religion and her mother's church and attended LDS meetings more often than before. It took the Straumers forty-five minutes via streetcar to go to Church, and Sister Straumer often made extra trips. On one occasion, Brigitta was washing the big windows in the main meeting room and asked her mother, "Why do we have to do all this [cleaning]?" The humble answer was, "Tomorrow is conference, and the spirit of the Savior cannot dwell in an unclean building." Bertha Straumer always dressed in her finest for Church.[31]

On a cool day in May 1944, Brigitte Straumer was baptized in the Old Danube. It was raining, and she had prayed for a clear day. Her prayer was answered by the time she joined branch president Alois Cziep in the chilly water; the clouds parted and the rain stopped for a moment. After changing clothes, she sat on a chair under an umbrella while Anton Körbler confirmed her a member of the Church. "I had a wonderful feeling being so clean, all my sins were forgiven. I wanted to stay that way the rest of my life." Soon after her baptism, Brigitta was in the Netherlands on another dance tour and had the opportunity to successfully demonstrate her dedication to the Word of Wisdom while attending parties where alcohol was abundant.[32]

In early 1944, the officials of the Vienna city government anticipated frequent air raids and encouraged parents to take their children out of town to safer areas. Martha Docekal was taken by her mother to a small town about forty-five minutes from Frankenburg where there was an LDS branch. Martha was quite unhappy in the local school, where the teachers were not good as compared with her teachers in Vienna. To make matters worse, she was soon accused of skipping Jungvolk meetings, which could cause serious difficulties with local police. Her mother then gave her money for soup so that she could stay in town for the meetings. The long walk home in the dark of winter was hard for Martha, but she was soon pleased to learn that girls who lived more than a mile or two from Frankenburg were exempted from attending Jungvolk meetings.

Anton Vaculik turned ten in 1944 and was inducted into the Jungvolk. One major responsibility given the youngsters was to solicit funds for the Winterhilfswerk (winter relief fund). Anton recalled taking his little sister along when he attempted to fill his tin can with coins: "When the people saw this little girl, they were very generous in giving. I took her all around the Gürtel (one of the major streets around the city center), and we stood in front of every store. Pretty soon we had our can full of coins."

In general, Anton enjoyed the Jungvolk experience. The boys were encouraged to participate in sports, and he became very good at the long jump. This may have been a reason for Anton's candidacy for attendance at the famous Ordensschule in Sonthofen, Germany, where the next generation of Nazi leaders was to be trained. As he recalled, "One day, three men in uniform came to our school. They took [three of] us to the music room and told us to take our clothes off. It was cold in there, and we stood there stark naked in front of these three guys [for inspection]."[33] Anton was later informed that all three had been selected to attend the Ordensschule, but his mother strenuously objected and he remained in Vienna.

As the war dragged on, the number of attendees at Sunday meetings of the Vienna Branch decreased significantly. The branch general minutes show an average attendance at sacrament meeting of thirty for 1943 and twenty for the first few months of 1945. Many Saints who called Austria's capital city their home were at war all over Europe or had left the city in search of safer conditions. Others could no longer safely make the trip across town when public transportation was increasingly unreliable and the threat of attack ever present.

One of those families split apart by the war was that of Anton Körbler, a counselor to Alois Cziep in the branch presidency. Anton was a government employee and was thus required to remain in Vienna, but his wife, Stephanie, took their children, Gerliede and Peter, to the small town of Neuhaus on the German side of the Inn River. It was the fall of 1943, and while life was becoming increasingly challenging in Vienna, the war was still far away from Neuhaus, where the Körblers lived at the Fischer Inn. A year later, they moved across the river to house no. 248 in the Austrian town of Schärding. Totally isolated from the Church, Sister Körbler taught her children Bible stories and sang hymns with them. Gerliede (born 1936) recalled that there were many things to do in Schärding. She even saw Adolf Hitler there in the fall of 1944 when he made one of his last public appearances.[34] Sister Körbler only returned to Vienna on one short occasion before the war ended: Gerliede was baptized there by her father in the Old Danube in the fall of 1944.

When Vienna came under attack from the air, Alois Cziep was assigned as the air-raid warden for his building. It was his job to see that all twenty-eight residents went down into the basement each time an alarm sounded. When they left their apartment, they carried their most important papers along in case they had to find shelter away from home. At church, the sacrament meeting that had been held traditionally in the evening was moved to a time just after Sunday School so that branch members only had to make the walk to Church once each Sunday. Brother Cziep later wrote, "Many times we would have air raids in the middle of one of our meetings and I would lead the members to the shelter for safety."[35] The branch history lists alarms on February 12, 13, 14, 15, 17, and 18, 1945, and actual attacks on February 19–23.[36]

President Cziep kept a small metal box next to the door of the apartment and instructed his family to make sure that the box was taken by whomever was home into the basement shelter when an alarm sounded. The box contained membership records, tithing funds, and bank records. The branch president was determined to preserve order in the Church in Austria, no matter what happened to him or his apartment.[37]

By the time the air raids over Vienna were beginning to lay waste to large parts of the city, Anton Vaculik was ten years old. "After the first attack, I nearly had a nervous breakdown. I stared out the window all day long. In the evening I just broke down. . . . Our apartment house was damaged, and the building next door was totally destroyed. Seven dead people were pulled from the rubble there, and I watched [the rescuers] do it. Then my mother got angry because I was watching."

Anton specifically recalled Sunday, September 10, 1944:

> We never went to the shelter on Sunday because nothing ever happened. Suddenly the bombs hit, and I went down to the cellar with two big suitcases. I was right next to the cellar door when the bombs hit, and the pressure threw me into the cellar. So we were sitting in the cellar praying, and I said, "I'll be good, Father in Heaven. Don't let me die!"

According to Brigitta Straumer, the war came to Vienna "for real" in 1944. Sitting in air-raid shelters while bombs burst outside was frightening, and she wondered if her family members elsewhere in the city would survive and if their house would be standing after the attack. On at least one occasion, Brigitta and her mother made their way past burning buildings and saw people emerge from shelters in panic. The young convert recalled that church meetings were at times interrupted by sirens. When bombs landed in the yard of her home one day, it seemed as if she and her mother (who had delayed their trip to the shelter in the basement) would surely die.[38]

Fig. 6. This eight-story air-raid shelter/antiaircraft battery towers over Vienna's District VI near the Hirschmann home. (R. Minert, 1974)

Fig. 7. Alois Cziep kept Church records and money in this box in his apartment. (CHL)

Wilhelm Hirschmann's school in Vienna was closed in 1944, and he was sent to Haag am Hausruck to live with the family of branch

Fig. 8. This hole in the wall at Linke Wienzeile 156 led into the neighbors' basement, as required by civil defense regulations. (R. Minert, 2008)

president Franz Rosner. From there, he could take the bus to a school in nearby Ried. By February 1945, he was back at home and found that during his absence, two bombs had struck and partially damaged the adjacent buildings in which he and his cousins lived. He recalled how the families of those two buildings gathered in the basement with his Aunt Maria in Linke Wienzeile 156: "[During air raids] my aunt had us singing and praying when we sat in the basement. The other residents of the house were Catholic, but my aunt was our spiritual leader during those hours, and they respected her."

Walter Hirschmann never met another LDS soldier while at the front. His comrades knew that he did not drink alcohol or smoke, as did his colleagues at the Siemens Company, "and they respected that," he recalled. "Sometimes there were discussions about that topic, but they never made fun of me." By early 1945, Walter was back in Austria, near the city of Linz on the Danube River.

Having finished public school at age fourteen, Emmy Cziep was assigned service under the government's Pflichtjahr program. Fortunately, she found herself in the home of an LDS family with several children, where her presence enabled the mother to be employed. She lived with the family for a year and took the children to church on Sundays. "I was fortunate to have this assignment," she recalled. Her diary indicates that the Pflichtjahr lasted from July 17, 1943, to July 17, 1944.

The military experience of young Josef Cziep (born 1926), son of the branch president, began at age sixteen. He decided to enlist because this allowed him to choose the Luftwaffe (air force), where he was assigned as a truck driver. While serving on the Western Front, he wrote to his family in Vienna. Four of those letters reflect his state of mind in October 1944. From Detmold, Germany, on October 6, he informed them that he had been transferred to the Waffen-SS: "I at once went to the Lord and asked him to help me so I won't have to go to the SS. I also know that this prayer will be answered if it is the will of the Lord. . . . I have only one wish—to escape this chaos of war safe and sound and to be able to perfect myself in different areas."[39] Still agonizing about his involuntary move to the Waffen-SS, Josef wrote on October 12 from Freistadt, Germany: "A song from the Church keeps coming to my mind: 'If the way be full of trial, worry not, if it's one of sore denial, worry not.' I have nothing else but to trust the Lord in his help." Four days later, he wrote again: "I have been close to despair were it not for the support of the Church. The circumstances under which we live here are so very primitive. No water, no toilet, no beds, just straw spread out."[40]

Four days later, Josef Cziep had already been moved to Poland and wrote to his younger sister, Emmy. His spiritual orientation was still strong, as is clear from his instructions to her: "As you leave Vienna in January and are going to be only surrounded by your school friends you will have many occasions when you will be tempted and when prayer will be your support. That's when you will prove to yourself how strong you are in keeping the commandments. . . . Let the Lord help you in all things and be willing to acknowledge his help."[41]

The letter written by Josef on December 17, 1944, again reflects his peaceful inclinations. He had just been assigned to a sniper unit: "I hope never to be in this position, but should it occur I just don't know how I should act. I could never shoot a person. . . . I have [been inspired] to use all free minutes I might have in reading church books. . . . That we will soon be at the end [of the war] is clear to me."[42]

Fig. 9. Young Emmy Cziep sold such items as these (actual size) on the streetcars of Vienna to raise money for government programs. "Anybody who didn't buy one from me risked looking unpatriotic." The machine-stitched medallions show native Austrian costumes from various regions on the country. The booklet, The Führer and the Winter Relief Program, has thirty-two pages. (E. Cziep Collette)

Johann Vaculik was allowed a furlough at Christmas 1944 and was thus at home when his daughter, Marianne Christine, was born on December 23. His unit was then transferred to the Western Front to face the Americans in their steady advance toward the Rhine River. Just before the Americans captured the last bridge over the Rhine at Remagen on March 7, Brother Vaculik became a prisoner of war. He and his Austrian comrades were separated from the German POWs and sent to camps in Stenay and LeHavre, France. In a rare instance, he met another Austrian LDS soldier, Heinz Teply from Vienna. Their experience as POWs included the typical poor housing conditions and food, but having lost the war, they did not expect anything better.[43]

Fig. 10. The Cziep family: Hermine, Emmy, Mimi, Alois, and Josef. (E. Cziep Collette)

With Brother Vaculik gone most of the time, his wife depended heavily on her son, Anton. She even sent him to the office of the civil registrar to report the birth of her newest son. The name of the baby boy was supposed to be Johannes Bartel, but the registrar objected to the name. Thinking of the composer Wolfgang Amadeus Mozart, Anton selected the name Johannes Wolfgang for his infant brother.

In late 1944, Kurt Hirschmann was released from the hospital and rejoined his artillery unit near the city of Hamburg. There he attended meetings in the Altona Branch. A teacher in the Aaronic Priesthood, he had been away from Church meetings for nearly two years, and his only connection to religion had been personal prayer and a Bible he protected carefully. While in Hamburg, Kurt experienced the air raids that had terrorized the city's residents for years. He recalled the first such instance: "I had never seen anything like it. The basement walls shook just like a ship in a storm. I wondered how long it would last and if the whole building would collapse on top of us. This was a war against [women and] children."

Erika Straumer had enjoyed her life as a teenager in Vienna. She had advanced into a secondary school and had time to go to movies with friends. By the time she joined the Church in September 1944, she had also experienced a marked improvement in her attitude toward the gospel. During a vacation among relatives in Germany, she and Brigitta had become lost in a forest at night and prayed for direction. The answer reminded Erika that she too was dependent upon God, who answers prayers. However, in the fall of 1944, her life took on a more serious character when she was drafted into the national labor force and taken out of school. She was assigned to a camp at Buch near Innsbruck, Austria, where she and her comrades assembled small parts for aircraft. All her connections to the Church were suddenly lost.

Erika was given a new assignment in the Reichsarbeitsdienst in January 1945 and transferred to Rankweil, Austria, near the Swiss border. Three weeks later, word was received that the French army was approaching from the west and that the enemy soldiers had a very poor reputation for their treatment of conquered civilians. With the Soviets approaching Vienna from the east, Erika dared not go home but took a train to Innsbruck instead. Upon arrival, she called the home of a friend from her camp and asked to be taken in. They kindly agreed, but Erika had to leave when the American army arrived and quartered soldiers in the home. Her next refuge was a mountain home where she was required to work for her board, but at least she was safe. From there, she wrote to Franz Rosner of the Haag am Hausruck Branch for news about Vienna members; he knew nothing about her mother or sister in Vienna, but he informed her that her father was safe and living with the family of district president Johann Thaller in Munich.

The Klein household had been blessed with a son, Friedrich Heinz, on September 28, 1942. However, the fortunes of life apparently turned against Gertrude and Fritz when their son contracted tuberculosis. Expecting her second child in days, Gertrude demanded to take her sick son home from the hospital and succeeded despite the objections of the medical personnel. Gertrude felt that her son could pass away under better conditions at home than away and proceeded to push his baby carriage through the snow uphill to their apartment. "I talked to my son constantly, telling him to not fall asleep," she recalled, but he died on April 6, 1945. A few days later, her second child was born.

In January 1945, Emmy Cziep was in Gloggnitz, about fifty miles south of Vienna. She had been sent there with about one hundred schoolgirls (of whom she was one of the oldest) after their Vienna school had been destroyed. In Gloggnitz they heard loud noises in the distance and were initially told that it was the sound of German army maneuvers. Later, their leaders admitted that it was actually the Red Army approaching. The girls were then instructed to leave immediately in whatever direction they pleased and Emmy headed straight for home. "When I got back [to Vienna], the Russians were very close behind us. It was announced that they were at the outskirts of the city. I told my parents that we had to leave town, but my father said that as branch president he had to take care of the members and that we could not leave. He said that Father in Heaven would take care of us."

On April 5, 1945, a bomb struck the building in which the Cziep family lived. Fortunately, only the upper floors were damaged and the Czieps were not rendered homeless. Members of the branch spent a great deal of time in shelters praying for deliverance while the sirens wailed and bombs were heard landing all over town.[44] With the arrival of the Red Army in April 1945, street battles were the order of the day for an entire week. When the fighting subsided, one source of terror was simply replaced by another—the conquerors' search for booty and evil amusement.

Like thousands of other parents in Vienna, Alois and Hermine Cziep agonized about the safety of their daughters. Mimi and Emmy were twenty-one and seventeen respectively when the war ended and, as such, were prime targets of marauding soldiers. Fortunately, their hiding places were never discovered, and they managed to escape every threatening situation in a Vienna that seemed to have no rule of law for several weeks after it was conquered.[45]

"We went up to the [attic] time and again and hid behind the chimney because the Russians were raping everybody they could get their hands on. It was horrible. We had two sisters [in the branch] who were raped several times."

Just weeks before the war ended, the commander of Erwin Hirschmann's communications unit near Plön in northwestern Germany informed his men that the war was lost and issued them (illegal) release papers. They buried their weapons and equipment, found civilian clothing, and began to make their way to their various homes. Erwin's path led him south through areas conquered by the British and the Americans, while he carefully avoided any contact with the approaching Red Army. In the meantime, he and a comrade also had to keep a close watch for SS soldiers who were fanatically pressing German men and boys into a hopeless defensive effort and were quick to execute anybody who disobeyed. By July, Erwin had reached the German-Austrian border, where he was detained by American soldiers. Fortunately, he was able to convince them to call his uncle, Franz Rosner (the LDS branch president in Haag), who convinced the guards that Erwin was a native of Austria. The young former soldier then rode his bicycle to the Huber farm in Rottenbach, where he helped with the harvest of 1945. Erwin had never seen combat and had therefore never fired his rifle at an enemy.[46]

The war ended in a very peaceful fashion for little Gerliede Körbler in Schärding, Upper Austria. "It was kind of strange. We were not even home when the Americans came into town. We were out picking raspberries. When we came home, we found two bundles of our things in front of the house." When American soldiers moved into the building, Stephanie Körbler and her children were suddenly homeless. Competing with many other refugees in the area, she found several temporary quarters in succession while she also worked hard to gather enough food for the three of them. She was displaced a second time by American soldiers, and on another occasion she had to break into her own garden (locked up by the conquerors) to get food for her children. All the while, the Körblers had no contact with other Saints and did not see Anton until the late summer of 1945. He had lost his job with the government in Vienna. From Schärding he sought contact with the members of the Frankenburg, Haag am Hausruck, and Linz Branches in an attempt to help restore order there.

Fig. 11. Vienna Branch at the end of World War II. (E. Cziep Collette)

With the war over and a kind of disquieting peace settling over Vienna, the leaders of the branch were determined to gather their flock together again. President Cziep recalled that they had to go in search of the members on foot, assured that anybody riding a bicycle would lose it in minutes to Soviet soldiers. Local men were also being arrested and sent east as forced laborers. So it was that the brethren made their way through rubble-laden streets to the apartments of the Saints. "Imagine our joy when we would find a brother or sister and realize that almost none of the members had suffered seriously. How the Lord had his protecting hand over us."[47]

Anton Vaculik recalled how the Red Army soldiers searched the family apartment: "After only a few days, they came into our apartment with an Austrian interpreter. There were three Russians. We hurried out of the basement because the fighting was over, and we were told we could get out. The Russians came in with a long probe. They would open up the wardrobes and stick it in to find things we had hidden. My mother was really upset."

Walter Hirschmann was fortunate to avoid the fate of a prisoner of war. When hostilities ceased in

May 1945, he was still an employee of the Siemens Company and as such was not treated as a soldier by the invading Americans. Rather than leaving at once for Vienna (where the Soviet forces were in control), Walter stayed in the American occupation zone with his relatives in Rottenbach (Haag am Hausruck Branch). He did not see Vienna again for several years.

Somehow Josef Cziep had survived the end of the war on the Eastern Front and was back in Vienna by May 1945. However, his trials were not over, and his sister, Emmy, described what happened to him next: "May 8, 1945, Josef was abducted in Vienna by the Russians. Some holding areas were in open parks surrounded by barbed wire. We [Emmy and sister Mimi] looked for him in these prison yards but couldn't find him. Many young men like him were sent on trains to Siberia. We went from one camp to another trying to find him. We didn't know if he was still alive or not."

In an attempt to convince the Soviets that Josef had been forced against his will into the Waffen-SS, the Cziep sisters showed the Russians some of his letters (quoted above). The Soviets apparently assumed incorrectly that the Waffen-SS combat troops were similar to the SS police who had orchestrated the murder of millions of people in Eastern Europe. Fortunately, Josef eventually came home, as Emmy recalled: "Josef was released May 20, 1945, according to my diary. Josef couldn't tell us what happened. He was told if he did, they would come and kill him. All we knew was that he was hung from his feet upside down and beaten within an inch of his life."[48]

Bertha Straumer said many prayers for the safety of her daughters Brigitta and Erika when the Soviets arrived in Vienna. While Erika was still away from home, Sister Straumer devised hiding places for Brigitta in their apartment building. When soldiers searched for victims, Bertha Straumer was an equally enticing subject, but the safety of her daughter was her prime concern. On one occasion, soldiers beat her with the butts of their rifles and she suffered broken ribs. Another time, a soldier left his rifle in the family's apartment and Sister Straumer had to smuggle it out of the building so that she would not be suspected of killing a Russian or stealing Russian property.

Life during the first few weeks after the war meant constant terror for Brigitta. She was accosted several times by soldiers bent on taking such things as watches and bicycles. Once, soldiers who seemed to be drunk searched the family apartment. Brigitta and a girlfriend were hiding in the bathroom when a soldier entered. He looked straight at the girls but apparently did not see them. Brigitta was holding a Book of Mormon close and praying all the while for protection and was grateful to see her prayer answered so dramatically. One day, she went to a well for water when enemy soldiers came by. A neighbor who understood Russian heard the men speak of their plans to follow Brigitta home. The neighbor warned her to take a different route, which she did by means of many delays and detours. Fortunately, the soldiers were called away before they could discover where Brigitta lived. "When they were out of sight, I hurried home, shaking all over," she recalled.[49]

During the summer of 1945, Erika Straumer was able to travel to Salzburg, where she joined the LDS branch. A member of the branch took her in and, soon she was united with her father. Johannes Straumer had survived the war and contacted his wife in Vienna in August 1945. Unfortunately, he was imprisoned by the Americans for sneaking across the border from Germany into Austria. When Sister Straumer heard about this stroke of bad luck, she was convinced that he would become converted to the gospel while in prison. She told Brigitta, "This will be the way your father will be humbled, and then he will be ready to accept the Gospel of Jesus Christ."[50] He did soon thereafter.

Erika was finally able to join her family in Vienna in December 1945. She had traveled without legal papers from Linz in the American occupation zone to Vienna in the Soviet occupation zone, risking serious punishment if she were caught. "The people sitting next to me on the train had given me their permit so that I could get through. The Lord works in mysterious ways."

The branch meeting rooms at Seidengasse 30 survived the war intact, and the members of the Vienna Branch met for a testimony meeting on May 6, with twenty-three in attendance. They looked forward to a time when they could hold their worship services in peace. The first report of a major event in the branch tells of a spring conference held on July 1, 1945. The mission history has this comment: "Spring conference under the direction of Branch President Elder Alois Cziep. Theme: 'Repent, for the kingdom of Heaven is nigh at hand!' The pronounced influence of the Holy Ghost was felt by all present."[51]

Kurt Hirschmann was taken captive by the British near Lüneburg, Germany, in May 1945 and shipped to Belgium as a POW. He was not fed very well but knew instinctively that POWs in the Soviet Union were much worse off and was again grateful for the wound that had rescued him from duty at the front. His greatest trial as a prisoner was a lack of activity, so he sought opportunities to volunteer for work details. On March 14, 1946, he was released and sent by train back to Austria. There he saw for only the second time his two-year-old daughter, whom he hardly knew, and also visited his Grandmother Huber at the farm in Rottenbach. They had enjoyed a very close relationship, and he was pleased to see her just before she died.

Johann Vaculik was relieved to be put on a train bound from France to Austria in the fall of 1945. However, a cruel trick was played on him when the train stopped at the German-Austrian border by Salzburg and the POWs were transported back to Stenay, France. In February 1946, he was again heading east and made it all the way to Vienna. In Wegscheid, he was "fed by the Americans and brought up to a less-than-normal weight. They were embarrassed to show us off as skeletons when we came home to our families." Entering his neighborhood in Vienna, he found that his family's apartment had been damaged in the bombing and that the windows were covered by cardboard. He later wrote, "When I arrived it was quite a surprise for Maria and the children. The kids were quite underweight but had been helped by the LDS servicemen . . . with some of their own rations, coal, money, and lots of candy at Christmas." In church he had a "wonderful homecoming with my brothers and sisters in the gospel." With little delay, Brother Vaculik opened up his store again and began a new phase in his life.[52]

Anton Körbler brought his wife and two children back to Vienna in 1946. Their apartment was still there, but the windows had been shattered by the air pressure produced by bombs landing nearby. After three years of isolation, Sister Körbler and her children were very happy to be associated with the members of the Vienna Branch once more.

In Memoriam

The following members of the Vienna Branch did not survive World War II:

Karl Friedrich Hirschmann b. Vienna, Austria, or Rottenbach, Oberösterreich, Austria, 18 Oct 1892; son of Konrad Hirschmann and Anna Maria Zeh; m. 31 May 1920, Maria Huber; d. tumor Vienna 3 Jan 1942 (K. Hirschmann; AF, PRF)

Friedrich Heinz Klein b. 28 Dec 1942 Wien, Austria; d. tuberculosis 6 Apr 1945 Klosterneuburg, Niederösterreich, Austria (M. Mühlhofer Klein)

Florentine Sartori b. Wien, Austria, 4 Oct 1878; dau. of Edward Sartori and Barbara Kiessl; bp. 17 Oct 1928; conf. 17 Oct 1928; missing as of 20 Mar 1944 (CHL CR 375 8 2445, no. 782; FHL microfilm no. 245257; IGI)

—— **Sztraszeny** b. ca. 1915; m. ca. 1936–37; 2 children; k. in battle (E. Cziep Collette, M. Docekal Vaculik; M. Mühlhofer Klein)

Marianne Christine Vaculik b. Wien, Austria, 22 Dec 1944; d. Bad Hall, Austria, 23 May 1945 (Vazulik)

Notes

1. Anton Körbler, "Geschichte der Kirche Jesu Christi der Heiligen der letzten Tage in Österreich," (unpublished history, 1955). Used with the kind permission of Gerlinde Koerbler Greenmun.
2. Alois Cziep, autobiography (unpublished), 84.

3. Gertrude Mühlhofer Klein, interview by the author in German, Kiesling, Austria, August 9, 2008; unless otherwise noted, summarized in English by Judith Sartowski.
4. Emmy Cziep Collette, interview by the author, Idaho Falls, ID, June 10, 2006.
5. Cziep, autobiography, 74, 87.
6. See the Haag am Hausruck Branch chapter for more about Johann Huber.
7. Eric Hirschmann provided the genealogical details presented in this paragraph.
8. Kurt Hirschmann, interview by the author, Ogden, UT, March 2007.
9. Erwin Hirschmann, "A Full Life Well Lived" (unpublished autobiography); private collection.
10. Wilhelm Hirschmann, interview by the author in German, Vienna, Austria, August 9, 2008;
11. Vienna Branch general minutes, CHL LR 9781 11.
12. For a description of the Anschluss (the annexation of Austria by Germany), see the Vienna District chapter.
13. Brigitta Straumer Clyde, "Biography of Brigitta Emmy Maria Straumer Clyde" (unpublished autobiography, 1996), 30.
14. Brigitta Straumer Clyde, interview by the author, Logan, UT, July 29, 2008.
15. Erika Straumer Anderson, telephone interview with Roger P. Minert, March 31, 2009.
16. "Biography of Brigitta Emmy Maria Straumer Clyde," 27.
17. Walter Hirschmann, interview by the author in German, Munich, Germany, August 6, 2008.
18. Martha Docekal Vazulik, interview by the author, Draper, UT, March 7, 2007.
19. Vienna Branch general minutes.
20. Hirschmann, "A Full Life Well Lived."
21. The name of the man was given in the interview but is withheld here by the author.
22. Cziep, autobiography, 81. Several eyewitnesses recalled the Weiss family, several members of which attended meetings of the Vienna Branch. Sometime during the war, the Weiss' disappeared. Nothing is known about their origins or their fate.
23. Vienna Branch general minutes.
24. Anton Vazulik, interview by the author, Draper, UT, March 7, 2007. The surname was spelled "Vaculik" in Austria.
25. Johann (John) Vazulik, "World War II Memories of John Vazulik" (unpublished history); private collection. Used with permission of Anton Vazulik.
26. Clyde, "Biography of Brigitta Emmy Maria Straumer Clyde," 40–41.
27. Ibid., 41.
28. Vienna Branch general minutes.
29. Cziep, autobiography, 87.
30. Hirschmann, "A Full Life Well Lived."
31. Clyde, Biography of Brigitta Emmy Maria Straumer Clyde, 45.
32. Ibid., 43.
33. Anton later learned that the men were likely determining that none of the boys had been circumcised—something very rarely done among Christians at the time.
34. Gerliede Körbler Greenmun, telephone interview with the author, January 12, 2009. Hitler returned to Berlin in January 1945 and never again left his headquarters in the city's center for another large public event.
35. Cziep, autobiography, 88.
36. Vienna Branch general minutes.
37. Emmy Cziep Collette donated that valuable heirloom to the LDS Church History Museum.
38. Clyde, "Biography of Brigitta Emmy Maria Straumer Clyde," 45
39. Josef ("Joschi") Cziep, letter to his parents October 6, 1944, cited in Emma Esther Cziep Collette, *Glen and Emmy Collette Family History* (Brigham Young University Press, 2007), 226.
40. Josef Cziep to his parents, October 12 and 16, 1944.
41. Josef Cziep to Emma Cziep, October 1944.
42. Josef Cziep to Alois Cziep, December 17, 1944.
43. Johann (John) Vazulik "World War II Memories."
44. Cziep, autobiography, 89.
45. Cziep, autobiography, 92–93.
46. Hirschmann, "A Full Life Well Lived."
47. Cziep, autobiography, 97.
48. Emma Esther Cziep Collette, *Glen and Emmy Collette Family History*, 226.
49. "Biography of Brigitta Emmy Maria Straumer Clyde," 48.
50. Ibid., 49.
51. Vienna Branch general minutes.
52. Johann (John) Vazulik, "World War II Memories."

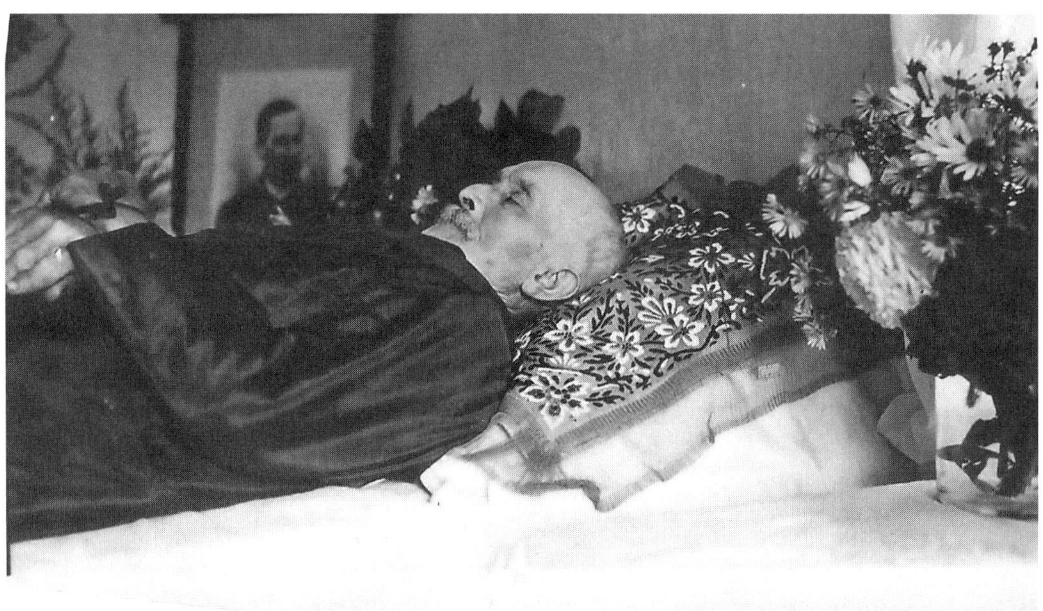

Johannes Huber (1861-1941) was possibly the best known member of the Church in Austria. From the time of his conversion, at the turn of the century, to his death in 1941, he and his family contributed greatly to the growth of the Church. Many of the Austrian saints spent vacation and holidays on his farm near Haag.

WEIMAR DISTRICT

West German Mission

In the very center of 1939 Germany is what was known to Latter-day Saints as the Weimar District. Located as it was at the junction of the East and West German Missions, it was apparently the most convenient group of branches to move from the East German Mission to the West German Mission at the dawn of the year 1938. The following report is found in the history of the West German Mission: "Saturday, January 1, 1938: the entire Weimar District is transferred from the East German Mission to the West German Mission, including missionaries in Erfurt, Gotha, Weimar, Gera and Nordhausen."[1]

The reasons for the transfer are not provided in the mission history, but it is relatively certain that the move was made to bring the respective mission populations into closer balance. The district on the whole was also slightly closer geographically to Frankfurt than to Berlin.

The Weimar District consisted primarily of the territory of Thuringia in the south and a portion of Prussian Saxony to the north. The Church administrative units surrounding the Weimar District in 1939 were as follows: the Nuremberg District to the south, the Frankfurt District to the southwest, the Hanover District to the northwest, and the East German Mission to the northeast and east. Travel from Weimar to the other four branches in the district was not difficult: Erfurt is thirteen miles to the west and Gotha twenty-six miles west; Nordhausen is forty-five miles to the northwest and Gera thirty-two miles directly east.

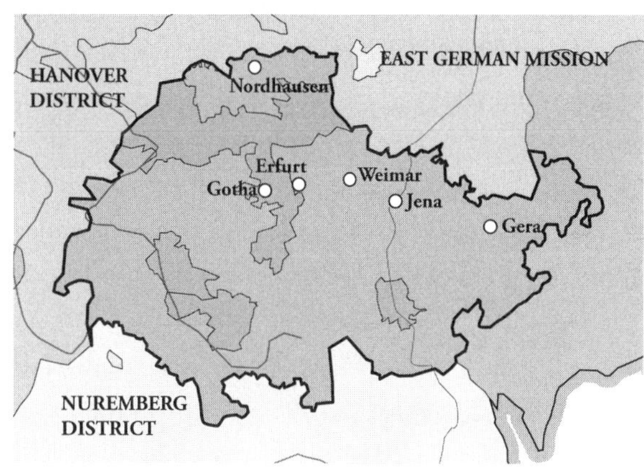

Fig. 1. The Weimar District was in the very heart of Germany.

That region of Germany was sparsely populated at the time. The largest city was Erfurt with 165,615, and no other city had more than one hundred thousand inhabitants.[2] The membership of the Weimar District at the end of the year 1939 was reported as 337, but no details are available for any of the five branches.[3] Regarding the spiritual state of affairs among the members after the transfer, only one paragraph in the records of the West German Mission provides insight:

> Sunday, October 9, 1938: On Saturday, October 8, and today the Weimar District conference was held in Gera under the direction of District President Elmer R. Tueller [US missionary]. The advance group of missionaries having just returned on October 4 [from Copenhagen], it was possible for President and Sister M. Douglas Wood and Elders Osmond L. Harline and J. Richard Barnes to be in attendance at this conference which was well attended and a most wonderful spirit prevailing.[4]

A similar report was filed five months later when the Saints of the Weimar District gathered in Erfurt for a conference: "Sunday, March 12, 1939: Weimar District conference in Erfurt. 515 attended. The meetings of this conference were especially interesting and the Saints received them in one of the most humble, eager and enthusiastic receptions of any conference for a long time."[5] The attendance of 515 is the equivalent of every member of every branch and one friend for every two members (153 percent of the official district membership). Because 100 percent attendance among members is not probable, the percentage of friends was high.

In the months just before the German invasion of Poland, most of the leaders of the Weimar District actually lived in Erfurt. American missionary Darrell Robins was the district president, and his counselors were Willy Brachmann and Karl Krummrich, both from Erfurt. Brother Brachmann was also responsible for the Sunday School, and Brother Krummrich for the YMMIA. Elly Schneider of Gera was the leader of the YWMIA, and Elsa Maiwald, also of Gera, guided the Primary organization. Elisabeth Köcher of the Weimar Branch was the president of the Relief Society.[6]

Willi Brachmann of Erfurt was asked to serve as district president after Elder Robins left Germany in August 1939. According to his own statement, Brachmann served in that capacity until the last months of the war. He did not explain why his tenure in that calling ceased at that time.[7]

Although the city of Weimar was the seat of the Church district, conferences were often held in Erfurt. According to Ursula Schlevogt (born 1926), district gatherings were held in the Hinterhaus at Johannesstrasse 136 until too many of the leading men were drafted into military service.[8]

Notes

1. West German Mission quarterly report, 1938, no. 4, CHL LR 10045 2.
2. Erfurt city archive.
3. Presiding Bishopric, "Financial, Statistical, and Historical Reports of Wards, Stakes, and Missions, 1884–1955," 257, CR 4 12.
4. Weimar District quarterly report, 1938, no. 36, LR 9986, QR 1938:36.
5. West German Mission quarterly report, 1939, no.11, CHL LR 10045 2.
6. West German Mission branch directory, 1939, no. 11, CHL LR 10045.
7. Willi Brachmann to Walter E. Scoville, February 3, 1947, Walter E. Scoville, papers, CHL MS 18613.
8. Ursula Schlevogt Herold, interview by the author in German, Weimar, Germany, August 17, 2008; summarized in English by Judith Sartowski.

Erfurt Branch

Formerly a district capital in the Prussian province of Saxony, the city of Erfurt was the largest (165,615 inhabitants) and most important city in the region in 1939. Although no records regarding the population of the Erfurt Branch in that year have survived, the branch directory lists leaders for every organization but the Primary. It would appear that the branch had at least seventy-five members.

Karl Müller was the branch president, and his only counselor was Karl Krummrich. Willi Brachmann directed the Sunday School, Alexander Ludwig the YMMIA, and Ella Possner the YWMIA. Erna Brachmann was the Relief Society president, and Louis Trefflich was responsible for both *Der Stern* magazine and genealogical instruction in the branch.

Meetings of the Erfurt Branch were held in rented rooms in a Hinterhaus at Johannesstrasse 136. The first meeting on Sunday was Sunday School at 10:00 a.m., and later a genealogy class began at 6:00 p.m. and sacrament meeting at 7:30 p.m. MIA met on Tuesdays at 8:00 p.m., and both the priesthood and Relief Society meetings took place on Thursdays at 8:00 p.m.

The daughter of the branch president, Margot Krummrich (born 1935), described the meeting rooms:

> There was a large room on the main floor. On the [rostrum] stood the pump organ and the piano. The pulpit was also in the front. There were some pictures of Christ in the main room. There were also classrooms. During the war, we might have had four to ten people in the meetings. It was actually a large branch, but most of the members could not attend.[1]

Just before the war began, Margot was hospitalized with diphtheria. At the point when she was almost paralyzed, a most remarkable thing occurred: her father wanted to give her a priesthood blessing but was not allowed to be in her room. He then stood outside the room and pronounced the blessing. She was healed by the next day.

Fig. 1. The Johannesstrasse in Erfurt as it looks today. (R. Freitag)

The history of the Erfurt Branch offers only one statement regarding the life of the Latter-day Saints in that city during World War II. Brigitte Loch explained, "During the war the members held meetings in various homes and taught and edified each other."[2]

Margot Krummrich had looked forward to being baptized in November 1944, but wartime conditions delayed the event until January 13, 1945. The baptism took place in a small pool in the local hospital. "It was cold," she recalled, but she was fortunate that her father, who was home on leave, could perform the ceremony.

The American army entered the region in April 1945. According to Margot, there was no fighting when they arrived. Shortly thereafter, the GIs left the region, and the Soviet occupation forces took over. She recalled that the Americans had conducted themselves fairly well among the locals, but the same could not be said of the Soviets later on: "They did not treat the women with any respect."

"My father was gone from home for about a year and a half, but he returned in May 1945," recalled Margot. The family had been evacuated to the town of Möbisburg (just five miles south of Erfurt) for a few months, but with Karl's return, they went home to their apartment at Johannesstrasse 131, just down the street from the branch rooms. The family's return was timely, because the branch was nearly evicted from the building. Margot explained the odd circumstances:

> A family from the Cottbus Branch came to town and needed a place to stay. My father decided that they could live in one of the classrooms. But they wanted all the branch rooms, which we of course couldn't give them. The family then said that they would take our apartment if we moved somewhere else. We had a beautiful and large apartment. We then lived together for a while but that didn't work, so we left our apartment and moved into the Church meeting rooms. [The guest family] said that if we didn't give them our apartment, they would tell the housing authority that the branch rooms weren't being used and other people could move in. My father was quick to decide that we would move into the branch rooms.[3]

Thus the church meeting place was preserved, and the members of the branch began again to worship together. Their numbers increased as soldiers returned and evacuated members found their way back to the city that had since lost many of its residential buildings to air raids.

Two years after the war, branch president Willi Brachmann wrote a letter to former missionary Walter E. Scoville, who was attempting to determine the status of LDS families in branches in which he had served just before the war. The following is an excerpt from that letter:

> Well, the war is now over and it really took its toll. Even though we were never in favor of war, we too must pay the price. I lost my only son (Horst) in the last days of the war. He was 17½. Six young men of the Erfurt Branch were killed in battle. Alex Ludwig is still a POW of the French in Africa. Brother Wittmer spent 1½ years in prison. He had been sentenced to five years for helping American POWs to escape. I was assigned to be the president of the Weimar district and I served as such until just before the end of the war. All [*sic*] of our members made it through the war fairly well. After the war, we all began anew to do the work of the Lord.[4]

Brother Brachmann's letter was very optimistic. As a point of fact, the Erfurt Branch alone had lost six men in combat situations, and another eight members died at home.

In Memoriam

The following members of the Erfurt Branch did not survive World War II:

Horst Brachmann b. Erfurt, Erfurt, Sachsen, 10 May 1927; son of Willi August Walter Brachmann and Erna Amalie Scharf; bp. 22 June 1935; conf. 23 June 1935; k. in battle 25 Mar 1945 (FHL microfilm 25728; 1930 census; FS)

Karl Eichler b. Erfurt, Erfurt, Sachsen, 15 Jul 1907; son of Wilhelm Wärtzburg and Elly Eichler; bp. 26 Jun 1920; conf. 26 Jun 1920; lance corporal; d. wounds at H. V. Pl. Sanko 432 at Friedland, Korfantow, Poland, 8 Feb 1945 (FHL microfilm 68808, no. 61; FHL microfilm 25760; 1935 census; www.volksbund.de; IGI)

Emma Therese Pauline Käferhaus b. Allstedt, Weimar, Sachsen-Coburg-Gotha 8 Oct 1874; dau. of Herrmann Käferhaus and Lütowine Reime; bp. 1 May 1924; conf. 1 May 1924; m. 24 Apr 1909, —— Markhardt; d. old age 4 Dec 1941 (FHL microfilm 68808, no. 198; FHL microfilm 245226; 1930 and 1935 censuses)

Johannes Friedrich Koch b. Erfurt, Erfurt, Sachsen, 28 Apr 1916; son of Wilhelm Louis Koch and Anna Therese Hopfe; bp. 29 May 1925; conf. 29 May 1925; ord. deacon 7 Apr 1935; m. 19 Oct 1939, Ruth Tiehle; lance corporal; d. wounds in field hospital 161 at Babino 2 Jun 1942; bur. Sologubowka, St. Petersburg, Russia (FHL microfilm 68808, no. 129; FHL microfilm 271380; 1930 and 1935 censuses; www.volksbund.de; IGI)

Hulda Emilie Louise Krummrich b. Alach, Erfurt, Sachsen, 11 Mar 1869; dau. of Johann Friedrich Wilhelm Krummrich and Emilie Luise Eva Engelhardt; bp. 1 May 1924; conf. 1 May 1924; m. Hugo Weigand; 1 child; m. Alach 20 Aug 1893, Heinrich Friedrich Julius Gräfe; six children; d. old age Erfurt, Erfurt, Sachsen, 12 Mar 1945 (FHL microfilm 68808, no. 87; FHL microfilm 25776; 1930 and 1935 censuses; IGI; AF)

Therese Auguste Ortlepp b. Waltershausen, Gotha, Sachsen-Coburg-Gotha, 19 Apr 1862; dau. of Heinrich Wilhelm Ortlepp and Friederike Kutt or Cott; bp. 28 May 1927; conf. 28 May 1927; m. —— Franz; d. old age 24 Nov 1942 (FHL microfilm 68808, no. 72; FHL microfilm 25769; 1935 census; IGI)

Adam Johann Reichert b. Erfurt, Erfurt, Sachsen, 27 Nov 1872; son of August Reichert and Mathilde Kühn; bp. 22 Sep 1920; conf. 22 Sep 1920; d. old age 16 Oct 1940 (FHL microfilm 68808, no. 421; FHL microfilm 271400; 1930 census)

Alfred Edmund Schumann b. Zorbau, Querfurt, Sachsen, 13 Mar 1871; son of Herrmann Schumann and Thekla Munkelt; bp. 1 May 1924; conf. 1 May 1924; d. bilious complaints 7 Dec 1941 (FHL microfilm 68808, no. 426; FHL microfilm 245260; 1930 and 1935 censuses)

Heinz Karl Stoll b. Erfurt, Erfurt, Sachsen, 18 Sep 1919; son of Karl Ernst Stoll and Minna Schröter; bp. 14 Jun 1930; conf. 14 Jun 1930; ord. deacon 3 Nov 1935; ord. teacher 23 Apr 1939; d. larynx cancer 9 Feb 1940 (FHL microfilm 68808, no. 365; FHL microfilm 245276; 1930 and 1935 censuses)

Walter Helmuth Stoll b. Erfurt, Erfurt, Sachsen, 1 Nov 1922; son of Karl Ernst Stoll and Minna Schröter; bp. 4 Jul 1931; conf. 5 Jul 1931; k. in battle Eastern Front 30 Jul 1943 (FHL microfilm 68808, no. 261; FHL microfilm 245276; 1930 and 1935 censuses)

Elsa Martha Stüllein b. Klosterfeldsdorf, Thüringen, 20 Jul 1883; dau. of Georg Stüllein and Emilie Braun; bp. 7 Sep 1908; conf. 7 Sep 1908; m. 19 Jan 1911, A. Ludwig; d. uterine cancer 6 Sep 1941 (FHL microfilm 68808, no. 174; FHL microfilm 271389, 1930 census)

Louis Hermann Trefflich b. Großhettstedt, Schwarzburg-Rudolstadt, 10 Aug 1870; son of Emma Treffliche; bp. 20 Feb 1934; conf. 20 feb 1934; ord. deacon 9 Dec 1934; ord. teacher 3 Jan 1937; ord. priest 12 Dec 1937; ord. elder 13 Jul 1941; m. 23 Apr 1923, Friederike Christiane Sander; d. heart attack 7 Mar 1942 (FHL microfilm 68808, no. 431; FHL microfilm 245287; 1935 census)

Walter Paul Voigt b. Erfurt, Erfurt, Sachsen, 12 Nov 1920; son of Paul Karl Voigt and Frieda Verges; bp. 14 Jun 1930; conf. 14 Jun 1930; k. in battle 5 Jul 1944 (FHL microfilm 68808, no. 299; FHL microfilm 245291; 1930 and 1935 censuses)

Willi Carl Georg Voigt b. Erfurt, Erfurt, Sachsen, 28 Feb 1919; son of Paul Karl Voigt and Frieda Verges; bp. 2 Jan 1917; conf. 2 Jan 1917; m. 8 Jun 1942, Dorothea Schöne; k. in battle Eastern Front 28 Dec 1944 (FHL microfilm 68808, no. 297; FHL microfilm 245291; 1930 and 1935 censuses)

Notes

1. Margot Krummrich Gurney, telephone interview by the author in German, July 10, 2007; summarized in English by Judith Sartowski.
2. *Jahre Gemeinde Erfurt* (2007), 23.
3. The name of the offending family is known, but there is no compelling reason to reveal that name here. Margot expressed no bitterness toward them. The incident simply serves as evidence that even Latter-day Saints can be selfish when under the stress of losing their homes. Margot stated that her family consisted of the parents and seven children at the time; it is not likely that the two branch rooms included a bath, so giving up their apartment to another family would have been a genuine sacrifice.
4. Willi Brachmann to Walter E. Scoville, February 3, 1947, Walter E. Scoville, papers, CHL MS 18613.

Gera Branch

The city of Gera is located on the main railroad route from Dresden in eastern Germany to Weimar, Erfurt, Eisenach, and Frankfurt to the west. In 1939, the city had a population of 81,931.[1] No report on the population and constitution of the Gera Branch of the Latter-day Saints was filed in the mission office at the end of 1939, but it can be assumed that the branch numbered fewer than fifty persons.

The branch president in July 1939 was American missionary Harold E. Kratzer. He was serving at the time without counselors. The Sunday School was directed by Hermann Kirst, and the YMMIA by Wilfred Wegener, also an American missionary. The YWMIA was not functioning then, but the Relief Society was led by Emma Zemisch, and the Primary by Else Maiwald. The *Stern* magazine representative was Lottie Sonntag, and the position of genealogical instructor was vacant.[2]

Sunday School was scheduled for 10:00 a.m., priesthood meeting for 11:30 p.m., and sacrament meeting for 8:00 p.m. The Relief Society members gathered on Tuesdays at 8:00 p.m. Both the Primary and MIA met on Thursdays, the former at 2:30 p.m. and the latter at 8:00 p.m. The meeting schedule shows an "entertainment" program scheduled for Saturdays at 8:00 p.m.

The branch meetings were held in rented rooms at Humboldstrasse 25 in Gera. As of this writing, no description of the rooms is available. The only eyewitness report related to the Gera Branch comes from Elder Kratzer's journal. He wrote that in August 1939, Elder Wegener was transferred and replaced by Elder Richard Glade.

> On my birthday, August 23, 1939, the Kretchmar family invited my new companion, Elder Glade, and me to dinner. They lived in the outskirts of Gera. The family was more active than the father. He tolerated the missionaries, something was bothering him. He didn't know how to cope with it. We couldn't seem to help him. . . . We had a very delicious dinner. Most of all we had an interesting political discussion with Brother Kretchmar. He told us it was just a matter of time before Germany would be at war. He said a boy who has an overabundance of toys would start to play with them sooner or later. Hitler was that boy. When we left the Kretchmars, we were wondering when that would happen. As we stepped out of the door, we saw rows of double blue lights coming over the hill on the local Autobahn. Both lanes of the newly constructed super highways were full of war machines on their way to the Polish front. . . . It was sight to see. Something we had never seen before.[3]

Two days later, the missionaries received a telegram instructing them to leave immediately. According to Elder Kratzer, "We ordained Brother Kirst a priest the night before we left and made him the branch president. . . . There was no doubt in my mind that he was the right man for that responsibility. He accepted the call." The missionaries called a meeting of all members and did their best to contact every one of them personally.

The meeting took place on August 27 or 28. The missionaries ordained Hermann Kirst a priest in the presence of the entire branch, and then proposed that he be sustained as the branch president. (They had no authority to ordain him an elder.) There were no opposing votes, and as reported in Elder Kratzer's journal, "There wasn't a dry eye in those present. The die was cast. The Gera Branch had new leadership."

There is currently no way to know how well or how long Hermann Kirst carried out the duties of branch president in Gera. No eyewitness reports for the war years have been located. The city itself was subjected to punishment from the Allied forces. Twelve air raids were recorded during the war, and at least 548 civilians were killed. On April 14, 1945, when the American army arrived, 846 buildings with 1,118 apartments had been destroyed.[4] It is likely that some Latter-day Saints of the Gera Branch were among those residents who lost their property.

In Memoriam

The following members of the Gera Branch did not survive World War II:

Emilie Pauline Behr b. Crimla, Sachsen-Weimar-Eisenach, 13 Jun 1860; dau. of Karl Friedrich Behr and Emilie Augusta Thienemann; bp. 28 May 1907; conf. 28 May 1907; d. old age 7 Apr 1943 (FHL microfilm 68808, no. 47; FHL microfilm 25721; 1930 census; IGI)

Bertha Barbara Bernklau b. Regensburg, Oberpfalz, Bayern, 3 Sep 1864; dau. of Katherine Bernklau; bp. 25 Jul 1924; m. 11 Sep 1916; Ernst Timper; d. old age 30 Apr 1940 (FHL microfilm 68808, no. 294; FHL microfilm 245286; 1930 and 1935 censuses)

Ernestine Böhme b. Falken, Mühlhausen, Sachsen, 16 Jan 1850; dau. of Franz Böhme and Erdmude Werbahn or Urban; bp. 6 May 1926; conf. 6 May 1926; m. 16 Jul 1872, Heinrich Böhme; d. old age 28 Jan 1940 (FHL microfilm 68808, no. 53; FHL microfilm 25726; 1930 census; IGI)

Pauline Karoline Boxhorn b. Lausnitz, Neustadt Orla, Sachsen-Weimar-Eisenach, 14 Nov 1865; dau of Julius Boxhorn and Pauline Günther; bp. 8 Jun 1921; conf. 8 Jun 1921; m. 22 Dec 1904, Karl Kanis; d. old age 15 Mar 1944 (FHL microfilm 68808, no. 541; FHL microfilm 271376; 1930 and 1935 censuses)

Katharine Filbig b. Marktleugast, Bayern, 9 Oct 1866; dau. of Magerete Filbig; bp. 26 Jun 1926; conf. 26 Jun 1926; m. 4 Jan 1908, Hermann Schröder; d. old age 1944 (FHL microfilm 68808, no. 284; FHL microfilm 245258; 1930 and 1935 censuses; IGI)

Pauline Agnes Hempel b. Gera, Reuß, j. L., 6 Oct 1851; dau. of Karl Hempel and Emilie Dötz; bp. 25 Jul 1924; conf. 25 Jul 1924; m. 25 Aug 1874, Hermann Theilig; d. old age 21 Oct 1939 (FHL microfilm 68808, no. 295; FHL microfilm 245283; 1930 and 1935 censuses)

Erich Kütterer b. Leutzsch, Leipzig, Sachsen, 14 Mar 1910; son of Kurt Friedrich Kütterer and Wilhelmine Eggert; bp. 30 Oct 1920; conf. 30 Oct 1920; rifleman; k. near Cesena, Italy, 7 Nov 1944; bur. Futa-Pass, Italy (FHL microfilm 68808, no. 147; www.volksbund.de; CHL 2458, form 42 FP, pt. 37, 138–39; FHL microfilm 271382; 1935 census; IGI)

Minna Anna Schubert b. Roda, Sachsen-Altenburg, 2 Sep 1881; dau of Friedrich Karl Schubert and Emilie Pfan; bp. 20 Feb 1926; conf. 20 Feb 1926; m. 24 Oct 1905, Otto Brauer; d. accident 8 Jun 1943 (FHL microfilm 68808, No. 52; FHL microfilm No. 25728 1930 census; IGI)

Sophie Henriette Süssengut b. Lobenstein, Reuß, i. L., 2 Mar 1864; dau. of Ernstine Süssengut; bp. 6 May 1926; conf. 6 May 1926; m. 24 Oct 1886, Adolf Schade; d. old age 1944 (FHL microfilm 68808, no. 282)

Notes

1. Gera city archive.
2. West German Mission branch directory, 1939, CHL LR 10045 11.
3. Harold Eugene Kratzer, journal, 1937–39, CHL MS 19552.
4. Gera city archive.

Fig. 1. This photograph was taken when missionary Erma Rosenhan visited the Gotha Branch in June 1939. The adults in the back row are (from left) Sister Walter, Sister and Brother Meissinger, Sister Schindler, and Sister Rosenhan. (E. Rosenhan)

Gotha Branch

The city of Gotha in the state of Thuringia had a population of 51,995 when World War II began in September 1939. It is not known how many of those inhabitants were Latter-day Saints, because the necessary reports were not submitted to the mission office at the end of that year.

Meetings were held in rented rooms at Hünerdorfstrasse 9 in Gotha. The Saints in that city met formally only on Sundays, holding Sunday School at 10:00 a.m. and sacrament meeting at 11:00. The branch directory for July 1939 lists only one leader: American missionary T. Frank Swallow as the branch president.[1]

Karl Heimburg (born 1924) and his family were members of the Gotha Branch until they moved to Frankfurt in 1938. He recalled the following about the meeting rooms in Gotha: "We met [in 1938] at Hünersdorfstrasse in a Hinterhaus. There was a big room which was our chapel, and we had some smaller rooms for the different classes of the Sunday School."[2]

The only information available about the Gotha Branch at that time is taken from the missionary diary of Erma Rosenhan of Salt Lake City: "Sunday, June 4: Walked from Siebleben to Gotha to attend Sunday School. There were 4 grownups and about 4 children, Bro. Swallow from Erfurt and myself. Bro. and Sis. Meissinger knew father and Sis. Meissinger knew mother. . . . She seems to be a devout Mormon."[3]

Because no eyewitnesses or eyewitness testimony could be found at the time of this writing, the fate of the members of the LDS Gotha Branch during World War II is not known.

In Memoriam

The following members of the Gotha Branch did not survive World War II:

Franz Stephan Gothe b. Mühlhausen, Sachsen, 10 Mar 1889; son of Christian Gothe and Johanne Genzel; d. 17 Aug 1944 (CHL CR 375 8, no. 2458, 856–57)

Frieda Rose Montag b. Wandersleben, Erfurt, Sachsen, 22 Dec 1903; dau. of Paul Montag and Therese Pachtner; bp. 2 Apr 1927; conf. 2 Apr 1927; m. 8 Jun 1927, Karl August Hering; d. tuberculosis 1 Dec 1940 (FHL microfilm 68808, no. 399; FHL microfilm no. 162782; 1930 and 1935 censuses)

Notes

1. West German Mission branch directory, 1939, CHL CR 10045 11.
2. Karl Ernst Heimburg, interview by the author, Sacramento, California, October 24, 2006.
3. Erma Rosenhan, papers, CHL MS 16190. Sister Rosenhan had received permission from the mission president to visit the area in order to gather genealogical information about her ancestors. (Siebleben is only one mile east of Gotha.) Her parents had grown up there but had since immigrated to Salt Lake City.

Nordhausen Branch

Perhaps the most isolated of the Latter-day Saint branches in the Weimar District was the branch in Nordhausen. The city is located in the Harz Mountains at a point almost as close to the Hanover District as to the Weimar District.

Clark Hillam, a missionary from Brigham City, Utah, was assigned to work in Nordhausen in early 1938. He had the following recollections:

> On a given Sunday, we would have quite a few visitors and about twenty-five people total. Sister Kopp, who was a nonmember, played the organ for us. It was a pump organ. In this branch, we met in the mornings and then again in the evenings. Sunday School was held during the morning hours, and then everybody came back for sacrament meeting in the evening. I remember having Primary and Relief Society during the week, but as I can recall we didn't have MIA. There were mostly adults in this branch but also a few children. During sacrament meeting, we usually only had adults attending.[1]

A year later, the branch president was an American missionary, Louis J. Haws. The only other persons listed in the branch leadership directory in July 1939 were Maria Hoffmann as secretary of the Sunday School, and Maria Helene Schirmer and Augusta Ortlieb as the leaders of the Primary organization.[2] The meeting schedule showed only Sunday School at 10:30 a.m. and sacrament meeting at 7:00 p.m., with the Primary meeting on Thursdays at 3:00 p.m.

Agnes Fuchs (born 1928) recalled the branch in the early years of the war: "There would have been eight to ten adults in the meetings. We also had many children—sometimes even twenty (many of whom were not members). I liked that atmosphere. Brother [Karl] Brachmann from Erfurt was responsible for us. We really didn't have any [Nordhausen] men in the branch."[3]

In May 1938, the missionaries had been able to find a relatively nice place for the branch to hold its meetings. Clark Hillam and his companion had secured the new meeting rooms: "We moved from an older building to a newer one, essentially a pub. The missionaries were responsible to find the new building. I was so heartsick because I wanted to be there for the first meeting in the new meeting rooms. I had worked so hard to find those rooms, and they transferred me the day before the first meeting."

Fig. 1. Clark Hillam took this picture of missionaries and a friend moving chairs into the new meeting rooms at Waisenstrasse 5 in May 1938. (C. Hillam)

Regarding the meeting rooms, Agnes Fuchs recalled the following: "We also had a piano on which we could play some hymns. Most of the members could not play, so we just sang without the accompaniment. We did not have any pictures or decoration on the wall. If we wanted to use some pictures, we would bring them and take them home after we were done."

Fig. 2. Members of the Nordhausen Branch celebrating Easter in 1938. (C. Hillam)

Agnes recalled her fondness for Sisters Ortlieb and Schirmer, essentially the only adults who consistently attended church meetings during the war. They held gatherings in their homes on occasion and were always surrounded by numerous children.

Fig. 3. Missionaries and branch members cleaned the meeting rooms at Waisenstrasse 5 before the chairs were delivered in May 1938. The branch met there throughout the war years. (C. Hillam)

A young teenager during the war, Agnes was one of a generation of German historians would later call the *Jugend ohne Jugend* (youth without a youth). The typical activities common among children and adolescents were simply not available very often under wartime conditions: "We could do things like going to the movies, but often those activities were interrupted by air raids, and we had to find the nearest shelter. That is what made it less fun for us, so we decided to stay home most of the time. We had our friends from school also, but most importantly we had each other as siblings." Her siblings still at home during the war were Horst, Hermann, and Linda. The two boys were drafted in the later war years, as was their father, Emil Fuchs, who was not a member of the Church. He was employed in a local tobacco factory and was drafted despite his age (he was born in 1901). The family believed that his draft notice had come as a result of the fact that Emil had refused to join the Nazi Party.

Just two miles northwest of Nordhausen was a large underground aircraft factory called Dora.[4] Once the Allies learned of its existence, they made many attempts to destroy it, and the resulting air raids caused great damage in nearby Nordhausen. As Agnes recalled:

> Nordhausen suffered from three air raids, of which two were very severe. I was nearly killed during one of them. I was asked to go [from Dora] into the city to get some medical records, and then the sirens sounded. I knew that I had to go into the shelter whenever we heard the sirens. But because nothing had happened before when we heard them, I continued my walk toward the downtown. I thought I would be back by the time the alarm was over. On my way, the [air-raid wardens] grabbed me and told me to go back into the basement immediately. I did not want to listen and started walking another way. But they still found me and made sure that I went home to be in the basement with my mother and siblings. That was one of the two large attacks on Nordhausen. Had I not gone back into the basement, something serious might have happened to me. In order to get the medical records, I would have had to go to the city center, where the largest destruction took place. Nothing stood anymore at the end of that attack. That was in April 1944.

Agnes was indeed fortunate. Her family lived on the outskirts of town in a neighborhood that was not seriously damaged. She recalled that bombs landed in front of and behind her home but left no more damage than broken windows. Her home was still standing when the war ended: "Our basement was officially designated an air-raid shelter, but it was not at all safe. It was not built especially for air raids in any way. It would have protected us against shrapnel at best. All in all, we were very blessed so many times."

The city of Nordhausen was not as fortunate in general. According to official records, seventy-five percent of the structures were destroyed. At least 8,800 people (among a prewar population of 42,316) were killed during the night of April 3–4, 1945, alone. The city suffered a total of thirteen attacks.[5]

Emil Fuchs was killed in Hungary in 1944.[6] Back at home, his widow, Gertrud, did her best to protect her daughters as Hitler's Third Reich came crashing down around them. When the American army approached Nordhausen in April 1945, Frau Fuchs and her daughters joined many Nordhausen residents who heeded the recommendation of the mayor to take shelter in the underground facility called the *Felsenkeller.* There was no significant fighting when the city was invaded. Agnes recalled the day when the mayor of the city announced that it was safe to leave the shelter and return to their homes:

> One day, we heard that we were able to go home, so we put my mom [who was a sickly woman] on the handcart again and went home. We found our home in a little bit of a mess because people had looked through everything, but we were so glad to finally be home again. Some of our things were gone, and that might have been because people tried to look for things to exchange for food.[7]

Although Emil Fuchs did not survive the war, his sons Horst and Hermann returned to their mother and their sisters unscathed. The family apartment was intact, and life could begin again for them and the other survivors of the Nordhausen Branch. The American invaders had been replaced by Soviet occupation forces, but even that would be tolerated with time. Fortunately the meeting rooms at Waisenstrasse 5 had also survived the war and continued to serve as the home of this very small group of Saints.

No members of the Nordhausen Branch are known to have died during World War II.

Notes

1. Clark Hillam, interview by the author, Brigham City, UT, August 20, 2006.
2. West German Mission branch directory, 1939, CHL LR 10045 11.
3. Agnes Fuchs Richter, telephone interview with the author in German, April 29, 2009; summarized in English by Judith Sartowski.
4. Readers may recognize the name by association with the concentration camp Dora-Mittelbau, which was established close to the factory. Many camp inmates worked in the aircraft factory, but of course they were not free to go to Nordhausen.
5. Nordhausen city archive.
6. Emil had not been baptized into the Church. His wife, Gertrud, joined the Church after the war.
7. Some of those people may have been inmates of the concentration camp at Dora-Mittelbau; they escaped or were released when the Americans entered the area.

Weimar Branch

Two of Germany's greatest literary men, Johann Wolfgang von Goethe and Friedrich Schiller, once lived in Weimar, and their legacy has given this small Thuringian city the air of intellectual greatness since then. It was that sense of intellectual greatness that prompted the German government to move the parliament from Berlin to Weimar in 1920 when the capital was besieged by revolutionaries (hence the name "Weimar Republic" for the German state from 1920 to 1933).

The branch of The Church of Jesus Christ of Latter-day Saints in Weimar might have numbered one hundred members in 1939, but no records have survived to establish the population. It is known that the branch held its meetings in the building at Seminarstrasse 4 downtown.[1] Katharina Dietrich (born 1922) recalled the setting as a Hinterhaus: "There was a factory on the bottom floor. It was fine inside [our rooms]. It looked well maintained, and there was a pump organ and French-style chairs. There were about thirty or forty persons in attendance—maybe even more if you counted all of the children."[2]

Ruth Schlevogt (born 1926) added the following to the description of the branch rooms: "When we separated for class, we closed the curtain in the large hall and could hold two classes in the same room. There was another church congregation next door to us, but we never bothered each other."[3] Ruth's twin sister, Ursula, recalled that the neighbors were Adventists and that the restrooms for the branch members were outside.[4]

The family of Fritz and Alma Schlevogt lived nearly three miles away on the eastern outskirts of Weimar. They walked to church in the morning, then home for lunch, then back to town for sacrament meeting. They carried a lantern while walking in the dark and made it to church "in all kinds of weather," according to Ruth. "We did not miss our meetings." Ursula stated that many of the branch members lived in the suburbs rather than the center of Weimar.

Fig. 1. The main meeting hall of the Weimar Branch decorated for Mother's Day 1938. (E. Horn Pruess)

In the months immediately prior to the outbreak of war, the president of the Weimar Branch was missionary Ellis Rasmussen of Redmond, Utah. His counselors were Karl Wolff and Fritz Schlevogt. The former was also the leader of the Sunday School, and the latter the leader of the YMMIA. Klara Margarete Hess directed the YWMIA, and Elisabeth Köcher the Relief Society. There was no Primary organization at the time.

The Weimar Branch meeting schedule was a modest one, with only two meetings on Sunday: Sunday School at 10:00 a.m. and sacrament meeting at 8:00 p.m. The Relief Society sisters met on Thursdays at 8:00, and the MIA met on Tuesdays at 8:00 p.m., after which an entertainment gathering was scheduled.

Whereas the number of persons attending meetings in 1939 can only be estimated, there is some information available about who attended. Elder Rasmussen recorded in his journal the names of families represented on a typical Sunday by at least two members each: Barth, Blietz, Dempe, Dietrich, Fernstädt, Hess, Hönig, Köcher, Köhler, Rauch, Schlevogt, Semmler, Steinbrück, Thiemann, and Wolff.[5]

Walter Horn, an elder in the Weimar Branch, had what his daughter Evelyn (born 1932) described as a "horrific experience" one evening as he walked home from a meeting:

> It was dark, and he was walking home to where we lived, a little bit outside of Weimar, and he ran into a transport of Jews who were herded from the railway station and pushed and shoved onto big trucks. He said they were all ages—young, older children, older, really old people. And when he came home his face was as white as a sheet, and he was shaking. It was a horrible, horrible experience to see that, because outside of Weimar there was Buchenwald, the concentration camp. It was still secret, so they did their transports late at night so that nobody would see it.[6]

Ursula Schlevogt explained that while the people of Weimar knew of a prison camp at Buchenwald, they assumed that the inmates were average criminals who had committed offenses against the system. She noted, "We knew it was a place where nasty things happened. Sometimes we even saw workers [from the camp] in the streets, and people secretly gave them food. We never went to Buchenwald."[7]

With a negative attitude toward the government, Walter Horn was not interested in joining the Nazi Party. When a high-ranking party member pressured him to do so in early 1939, he responded by finding employment in Goslar, a town some eighty miles to the northwest. He moved his family there

Fig. 2. Members of the Weimar Branch on an outing in 1938. (E. Horn Pruess)

and survived the war in relative peace. He had successfully outrun the long arm of the party.[8]

When Elder Rasmussen was instructed to leave Weimar for Copenhagen, Denmark, on August 26, 1939, he may not have designated any of the local brethren as leader of the branch. According to Katharina Dietrich, the branch was not able to hold meetings for very long after the war started. The members were instructed to travel to Erfurt (twenty-five miles to the west) and attend meetings there. Initially, that was no major difficulty, but it became increasingly difficult as the war continued.

"We never had any disturbances while holding our meetings," recalled Helmut Wolff (born 1926). However, the same could not be said of the Jehovah's Witnesses who met upstairs. "We had seen how they were banned in 1937." Helmut also recalled that the meetings were discontinued just after the war began. He was fourteen by then and did not attend any more church meetings before leaving his hometown in 1943.[9]

Otto Dietrich, a veteran of the Great War, was a member of the Stahlhelm Party, a conservative group of veterans not appreciated by Adolf Hitler. Brother Dietrich was thus not free with his political opinions during the years of the Third Reich. He and others recognized that war was imminent when the American missionaries left Germany.

Katharina Dietrich said, "We had to be careful after the war started; you couldn't show your sympathies for America." The Dietrich family had maintained contact with a great aunt who had immigrated to Salt Lake City, but the correspondence between the two families ended when Germany and the United States exchanged declarations of war after Pearl Harbor in December 1941. The isolation from the Church increased with decreasing opportunities to travel to Erfurt for church meetings.

A dental office employee in 1939, Katharina was admitted to a dental school in Dresden and left home to study in that famous city. It was there that she met the brother of a classmate and fell in love

Fig. 3. Another outing of the Weimar Branch in the spring of 1938. (E. Horn Pruess)

with him. He had been wounded in Russia and was home on recuperative leave. Raised in the Lutheran Church, he was what she called "very religious," and she married him. During the last years of the war, Katharina was a mother and was concerned both about her child and the status of her soldier husband.

Alma Schlevogt was not enthusiastic about Hitler's government and staunchly refused to greet people with the expected "Heil Hitler!" Her daughter Ruth recalled that "people used to say that if she didn't say 'Heil Hitler!' she would eventually be arrested." When it came time for Ruth to join the Jungvolk, her parents declined to give her permission to attend the meetings. There were no negative repercussions. Regarding politics in church, Ursula Schlevogt recalled that whereas nobody prayed for Adolf Hitler in the meetings, they did pray for their branch members serving in the military.

After finishing public school, Ruth was employed as a salesperson at Hekra-Hepprich in downtown Weimar. She rode her bicycle to work every day. That was no challenge, except when air raids caused damage to the downtown and she was forced to make long detours on her way back home. When the sirens sounded, Ruth found her way to the basement of the company's warehouse. In her recollection, the branch meeting rooms were not destroyed, nor was her home damaged, but the beautiful city theater was destroyed.

Regarding the life of the young people of the Weimar Branch, Ruth Schlevogt made the following comment:

> I cannot say that all the things we did during the war were very serious. We found a way to have fun. There were many members who were willing to meet in the evenings so that we could play

> games. I had my friend with whom I could do many things. I also had friends from outside the Church. We didn't always just think about the war—it was not always that serious in our area.

In 1943, Helmut Wolf was drafted into the Reichsarbeitsdienst. A veteran of the Jungvolk, he had managed to avoid joining the Hitler Youth, but service in the national labor force was inevitable. His father, Karl, was already away from home, serving in Lithuania with the construction corps known as the *Organisation Todt*. By the time Helmut finished with the labor force, he knew that a summons to the army would arrive soon. He chose to enlist in the Waffen-SS instead, preferring to exercise some degree of choice in his military assignment. He was to experience a nomadic career, being trained in Poland before serving in France, Belgium, Luxembourg, Germany, Austria, and Czechoslovakia. He recalled, "I traveled a lot but didn't fight much."

A call to the national labor force arrived in the Schlevogt mail box in March 1944, and Ursula soon found herself on a train bound for Czechoslovakia. For the next six months, she worked on a farm in Moravia: "In the morning, we went to the farm to help and usually spent the entire day there until we went back to our bedrooms at night. We slept in sheds and wore uniforms." In October, Ursula and her friends were transferred to Prague, the capital of occupied Czechoslovakia, where she was assigned to an office. Regarding her experiences there, she said:

> We didn't have to wear a uniform this time and slept in a school. My job was to inspect all the armaments. We lived in the Mariankerschule, which was located a little on the border of the city. There were many young women with whom I could go to work and back to the school. I even had contact with the Church while I was in Prague. I wrote to Frankfurt, and they mailed me the address of a meetingplace in Prague. It was a small group, and I always went whenever I had my Sundays off. We met in the city center of Prague in the homes of members. The leader of the district there even gave me some books to read. During the night, there were always men who protected us while we were sleeping. They stayed outside of the school and took care of us.

By the last year of the war, meetings at Seminarstrasse 4 apparently had been discontinued. Eyewitnesses were not able to explain the change, because the building was still standing. Some at least recalled holding meetings in the apartments of various branch members.

Helmut Wolff's Waffen-SS unit was sent from the Eastern Front to an area near Paris in 1944, but arrived too late to keep the Allies out of the French capital. A few months later, he participated in the Battle of the Bulge in Belgium and Luxembourg. Surviving a direct hit on his tank there, he was next sent toward Berlin to help save the Reich's capital city from the advancing Red Army. At the last moment, another transfer sent his unit to Austria and then on to Hungary. When the war ended for Helmut in April 1945, his unit was somewhere in Austria near the Czechoslovakian border—directly between the Soviets and the Americans. "Our only goal was to get home as soon as possible," Helmut explained. "We left everything behind and walked through fields. Soon we crossed paths with some American soldiers, and that was the end of our trip home." As a POW, Helmut was shipped to France and eventually "sold" by the Americans to the French government.

"At the end of March 1945, we were released [from the Reichsarbeitsdienst] just barely before the war ended," recalled Ursula Schlevogt. After a two-day trip back to Weimar through the ashes of firebombed Dresden, she found that just a few of the Saints were still meeting but only on Sundays. The sole priesthood holder left in the city was old Brother Köhler. Fritz Schlevogt had been away in military service but was transferred to Weimar, where he worked in a hospital in the final months of the war. He was not free on Sundays.

Ruth Schlevogt described the arrival of the Americans in Weimar:

> I remember watching them when they walked down the street. We were so excited that the war was finally over and we were not afraid of the Americans. They were very nice to us, didn't take away our property, and even gave candy to the children. They had orders to not have contact with the Germans because all of us were considered to be Nazis. We didn't hang out anything white. They also didn't shoot at us.

As the American army approached Weimar from the west and the Red Army from the east, Elise Dietrich decided to take her youngest children and move west toward the Americans. Daughter Katharina joined the group with her own infant. They had wanted to travel with the last train headed in that direction but were too late and had to walk. Their destination was Kumberg, about twenty miles distant. Along the way, they encountered long lines of German soldiers retreating from the advancing GIs. Many were wounded, and some were trying hurriedly to exchange their uniforms for civilian clothing.

"About halfway to Kumbach, a wheel on my baby carriage broke. We couldn't fix it, so I continued on three wheels," explained Katharina. On several occasions, American fighter planes swooped down to attack the soldiers and civilians, and Katharina's party took refuge in the brush by the road. They escaped harm, but her youngest sister (approximately the age of Katharina's own daughter) contracted measles along the way. With no available medical assistance, the little girl died after two weeks. Katharina had additional reasons to be discouraged, for she had not heard from her own husband since January. As it turned out, he had been captured by the Americans in Italy.

Shortly after the end of the war, Katharina and her mother, Elise Dietrich, returned with their children to their home on the outskirts of Weimar and found that it had not been seriously damaged. To their surprise and delight, Katharina's husband soon showed up, having been released from an American POW camp.

In one of the countless tragedies of the long war, two boys of the Weimar Branch became some of the last victims. On Mother's Day 1945, Karl Heinz Wolff (born 1931) and his brother Gerhard (born 1935) were searching for flowers for their mother in a forest near Weimar. One of them stepped on a mine hidden there by the invading American army, and both boys were killed instantly. According to Helmut Wolff, the death of his brothers was nearly too much for his mother to handle, coming as it did at a time when the whereabouts of Sister Wolff's husband and an older son were still a mystery. As far as she was concerned, they too might be dead.

On July 1, 1945, the Thuringian territory of eastern Germany was transferred from the Americans to the Soviets in accordance with Allied stipulations. The peaceful times of the American occupation were over, as Ruth Schlevogt recalled, "When the Russians came into Weimar, they came into our store and destroyed everything. It was horrible behavior." The residents of Weimar may have thought that the war was over by then. Regarding the revelations of Nazi atrocities in extermination camps in Poland and concentration camps in Germany, Ruth, like many other German civilians, claimed that she had no idea what was going on in camps such as Buchenwald.

Helmut Wolff had survived the war, but captivity among the French was no particular pleasure for him. However, with time, his existence there became more tolerable, and he eventually met and fell in love with a sweet French girl. He received permission to marry her in November 1948 and decided not to return to Germany. By then, he had established correspondence with his parents (his father had indeed survived) and told them that they would not see him again soon. Regarding his status as a member of the Church during the war, Helmut observed:

> When I was a soldier, I never met another member of the Church, not even while I was a captive of the Americans. I was also not able to attend any meetings of the Church anywhere. As soon as I left home, I seemed to have danger around me constantly. I was so glad and grateful that I always made it through. Many things happened that cannot logically be explained, but I believe that Heavenly Father protected me in many situations.

According to Ursula Schlevogt, regular church meetings resumed in Weimar after her father Fritz came home in the early summer of 1945. The building used by the church at the beginning of the war still stood but was in very poor condition.

IN MEMORIAM:

The following members of the Weimar Branch did not survive World War II:

Klara Margaretha ——; m. —— Hess; k. air raid Weimar, Thüringen, 1944 (Ursula Schlevogt)

Gertrude Dietrich b. about Jun 1944; dau. of Max Karl Otto Dietrich and Hewig Isa Else Stock; d. measles Thüringen, Apr 1945 (K. Dietrich Voigt)

Rolf Herbert Heinz Dietrich b. Weimar, Sachsen-Weimar-Eisenach, 1 Apr 1925; son of Max Karl Otto Dietrich and Hewig Isa Else Stock; bp.; conf.; ord. deacon; corporal; d. 10 April 1944; bur. Andilly, France (FHL microfilm no. 25755, 1930 census; www.volksbund.de; IGI)

Selma Bertha Anna Eberitsch b. Beutelsdorf, Sachsen-Altenburg, 8 May 1870; dau. of Johann Friedrich Eberitsch and Christiana Schrak; bp. 27 Aug 1929; conf. 27 Aug 1929; m. —— Barth; d. pneumonia 18 Dec 1940 (FHL microfilm 68808, no. 465; FHL microfilm no. 25718, 1930 census)

Elisabeth Maria Magdalene Gäbler b. Leipzig, Sachsen, 27 Jul 1893; dau. of Gottlieb Bernhard Gäbler and Augusta Goldhorn; bp. 6 Dec 1931; conf. 6 Dec 1931; m. 5 Oct 1918, Karl Becker; k. in air raid 27 Nov 1944 (FHL microfilm 68808, no. 627)

Minne Else Hasse b. Weimar, Sachsen-Weimar-Eisenach, 21 Nov 1876; dau. of Anthon Hasse and Emma Mayberg; bp. 31 Mar 1927; conf. 31 Mar 1927; m. August or Gustav Bruno Rauch; d. heart condition 19 Feb 1941 (FHL microfilm 68808, no. 230; FHL microfilm 271399, 1930 and 1935 censuses)

Olga Friedricke Kirschner b. Hyn [?], Fieselbach [?], Germany, 18 Apr 1863; dau. of Theodor Kirschner and Louise Ginozel; bp. 25 May 1921; conf. 25 May 1921; m. —— Schulze; d. old age 3 Dec 1941 (FHL microfilm 68808, no. 246)

Maria Emma Knopf b. Schönborn, Germany, 30 Jun 1863; dau. of Karl Knopf and Wilhelmine Bergner; bp. 27 Mar 1910; conf. 27 Mar 1910; m. 7 Jul 1889; Hermann Neudorf or Neundorf; d. old age 30 Mar 1943 (FHL microfilm 68808, no. 216)

Marie Helene Kolba b. Ohrdruf, Sachsen-Coburg-Gotha, 26 Apr 1889; dau. of Hugo Kolba and Helene Roth; bp. 11 Jul 1936; conf. 11 Jul 1936; m. —— Walter; d. gall stone surgery 8 Apr 1944 (FHL microfilm 68808, no. 454)

Maria Antonia Rumel or Rummel b. Hohenlaum [?], Weida, Sachsen-Weimar-Eisenach, 13 Feb or Mar 1855; dau. of Christian Rumel and Ernestine Diebler; bp. 25 Jul 1924; conf. 25 Jul 1924; m. 23 Sep 1915, Christian Friedrich Buchner; d. old age 10 Feb 1945 (FHL microfilm 68808, no. 48; IGI)

Werner Semmler b. Weimar, Sachsen-Weimar-Eisenach, 2 Jan 1924; son of Otto Semmler and Helene Spiegler; private; k. 10 Apr 1945 (CHL CR 375 8 #2459, 1146–47; volksbund.de)

Paul Peter Welzel b. Neustadt, Schlesien, 21 Sep 1919; son of Paul Peter Welzel and Hedwig Anna Krebs; bp. 15 Jun 1929; conf. 15 Jun 1929; k. in battle 27 Jun 1941 (FHL microfilm 68808, no. 553)

Gerhard Wolff b. Oberweimar, Sachsen-Weimar-Eisenach, Thüringen 6 August 1935; son of Karl Herman Wolff and Klara Marie Gumpert; k. by land mine Weimar, Thüringen, 21 May 1945 (H. Wolff; FS)

Karl Heinz Wolff b. Oberweimar, Sachsen-Weimar-Eisenach, 9 February 1931; son of Karl Herman Wolff and Klara Marie Gumpert; bp. 13 May 1940; conf. 13 May 1940; k. by land mine Weimar, Thüringen, 21 May 1945 (H. Wolff; FS)

NOTES

1. West German Mission branch directory, 1939, CHL LR 10045 11. The postwar address of the building was on Gropiusstrasse; the structure was razed in 1978, according to a report from the city office dated July 31, 2008.
2. Katie Dietrich Voigt, telephone interview with Jennifer Heckmann, October 24, 2008.
3. Ruth Schlevogt Bode, interview by the author in German, Erfurt, Germany, August 17, 2008; unless otherwise noted, summarized in English by Judith Sartowski.
4. Ursula Schlevogt Herold, interview by the author in German, Weimar, Germany, August 17, 2008.
5. Ellis T. Rasmussen, journal (unpublished); private collection.
6. Evelyn Horn Pruess, interview by the author, Salt Lake City, December 1, 2006. The Buchenwald concentration camp was located just four miles northwest of the city, but a small mountain stood between the two and helped conceal the former from the latter.
7. Apparently the Schlevogt family members were not among the Weimar residents forced by American soldiers to walk up the hill to Buchenwald to view the camp after its liberation and before many of the bodies of inmates had been removed.
8. The Goslar Group chapter features the interesting story of the Horn family.
9. Helmut Wolff, telephone interview with the author in German, January 14, 2009.

CONCLUSION

To say that the German and Austrian members of The Church of Jesus Christ of Latter-day Saints experienced difficult times during World War II would be an understatement. I have presented the first-person stories of more than 240 eyewitnesses. The episodes included represent what I consider to be the most significant among the thousands of incidents recounted by those eyewitnesses. Many survivors had experiences that could be presented sufficiently only in book-length format. I leave that daunting task to other authors.

The experiences of these Saints are unique in the history of the Church since the era of Joseph Smith. To be sure, other groups of Saints have suffered harrowing trials, including those who lived in the countries attacked, conquered, and occupied by the German Wehrmacht during World War II. Their stories, too, remain to be told and will likely mirror in many respects the accounts on the foregoing pages.

Without any attempt to present the Latter-day Saints in the West German Mission exclusively as martyrs or victims of the war, I offer below some observations about their experiences in general.

German Latter-day Saints as Outsiders

The German citizenry during World War II belonged principally to the Catholic and Protestant churches. Latter-day Saints represented one of the tiniest religious groups in the nation. Several eyewitnesses admitted being somewhat ashamed to tell friends and relatives that the local branch met not in a large and beautiful church but in a Hinterhaus, often a former restaurant or office building or a backstreet factory. Unlike their neighbors of other faiths, the Saints attended church services twice on Sunday and met for activities as often as four times during the week.

Latter-day Saint youth were often left out of religious instruction in school because they did not fit either the Catholic or the Protestant mold. To serve a mission (usually within the borders of their native land), they separated themselves from their non-LDS friends and appeared to be fanatics. When it came time to marry, LDS young adults looked to distant branches for partners or chose non-LDS spouses, hoping for a subsequent conversion. Many longed for the day when they could enter the temple in Salt Lake City (the closest one to Germany at the time) to be married in Church ordinances valid for all time.[1] No Saints residing in the West German Mission when the war began are known to have participated in temple ordinances.

Just as the Saints could not point to ostentatious meetinghouses, neither could they identify members of the Church in the higher socioeconomic strata. This investigation has not yielded evidence of Latter-day Saints as doctors, lawyers, or teachers; university graduates were extremely rare. The men of the Church in the West German Mission were primarily laborers and craftsmen. A few owned shops. Several were supervisors in local factories, but there is no evidence of Church members who sat on boards of directors or owned industries and department stores. As the war escalated, many of the men in the Church who were not drafted were required to increase their work weeks to sixty hours or more, and many were compelled to work on Sundays.

Latter-day Saints and the German Experience in World War II

As mentioned, the population of Germany in 1939 was approximately eighty million. Just over 13,500 of the inhabitants of the Reich were members of The Church of Jesus Christ of Latter-day Saints. It appears that they shared nearly all of the experiences of their neighbors—the average citizens and families in Germany. Just as their non-Mormon countrymen, Latter-day Saints attended schools, worked in factories, lived in huge apartment complexes in large cities, bought their food in small specialty shops, participated in local harvest festivals, and swam in city lakes. They dreamed of owning their own home or an automobile or of enjoying the convenience of a telephone in the home.

Most Latter-day Saints attended parades and watched Hitler and his troops pass in review. Some raised their arms in the Nazi salute and greeted friends and strangers alike with the obligatory "Heil Hitler!" They sang the national anthem in movie theaters with their neighbors and in schools with their classmates. Some believed that Hitler's plans to regain German territory from neighboring countries (especially from Poland and Czechoslovakia) were justified and his methods appropriate.

A few members of the Church belonged to the Nazi Party, but most avoided political involvement and seldom spoke of Hitler at home. Most Latter-day Saint boys and girls wore the uniforms of various branches of the Hitler Youth for a year or longer. Young men and young women answered the call to serve in government labor programs such as Pflichtjahr and Reichsarbeitsdienst. Most recalled enjoying their term of service and believed it to be an important contribution to their nation, though it usually meant a delay in their occupational progress. Declining to serve in Hitler's Germany was not an option.

Under the universal conscription laws passed in Germany in 1935, Latter-day Saint men served in the German army, navy, and air force, as well as in elite combat forces such as Heinrich Himmler's Waffen-SS and as paratroopers. They were there when Germany mounted offensives against Poland, France, and the Soviet Union, and were still there when the Allies struck back and invaded the fatherland. Just as their Catholic and Protestant comrades, Latter-day Saint German soldiers were buried where they fell. Some lost limbs and returned home as invalids, while others suffered for years from wounds unseen. They died as prisoners of war thousands of miles from home. The final resting places of many LDS soldiers remain unknown.

Latter-day Saint men too old to be drafted were pressed into service as local auxiliary police (e.g., Eugen Hechtle of the Mannheim Branch, Karlsruhe District) and saw combat anyway. Others were assigned to the Volkssturm (home guard) as the Third Reich experienced its last painful hours. For most of them, this was something to be avoided, and some were able to do so (thanks to the confusion that reigned in the final months of the war). Women, too, were compelled to serve in soup kitchens, refugee shelters, and in other critical war capacities. Many had to leave the home and replace men as full-time employees in factories and offices. Some were pressed into temporary service in hospitals or in constructing fortifications around the cities.

Some female Church members were honored by the government with the Mutterkreuz for giving birth to five or more children (but there is no evidence that LDS women gave birth to children specifically for their country). They bore children without the attendance of their husbands and raised those children for years in the absence of the fathers. LDS women contributed to relief programs with donations of money, goods, or labor. To provide for their families they stood in long lines to purchase food on ration coupons and made do with less and less as the war drew to a close.

When Germany came under attack from the air, Latter-day Saint civilians huddled in air raid shelters, praying for heavenly protection. They endured more than two hundred attacks in such cities as Cologne and Hanover alone. They were also numbered among the thousands of their countrymen who were killed in those raids—some as family groups such as the Lang family of the Darmstadt Branch. Other Saints were killed in artillery barrages or by invading soldiers just hours before the war ended. Many Latter-day Saints witnessed the horrific firebombings of Hamburg, Darmstadt, Pforzheim, and Heilbronn and several disappeared forever in those attacks.

Hundreds of Church members in western Germany lost their homes and property in the first two years of the war and moved to different homes and in some cases even to different cities. Many changed local addresses several times, trying to stay away from or at least a step ahead of the incessant attacks from above. Where possible, they repaired damaged apartments, but building materials were generally not to be found and broken panes of glass were usually replaced only by cardboard. The lack of fuel to heat an apartment was of little consequence when the apartment had no roof or was missing an exterior wall.

Like their neighbors, German and Austrian Latter-day Saints often endured without medical and dental services for long periods of time. Illnesses that in most modern countries were rare or even unknown became challenges again. Poor sanitation conditions caused by destruction of housing and utilities gave rise to disease and contagion. Taking a drink of water or walking down the street amid ruins became challenging, hazardous, and even life-threatening activities. Rich and poor, old and young alike suffered as they eked out their existence among the ruins of their once-picturesque cities.

The relief felt by the survivors when they realized that the war was truly over was often quickly forgotten when they were confronted by conquerors in their streets and in their apartments. Even in peacetime, wounds and injuries caused by military devices were supplanted by wounds and injuries caused by individuals armed only with thoughts of conquest or revenge. Many Allied soldiers enjoyed for the first time the power and opportunity to exercise control over others and to inflict harm on persons and property at will. Several Latter-day Saint women—both young and old—suffered physical abuse at the hands of their conquerors, resulting in mental scars that in some cases never disappeared.

Latter-day Saints assisted in fighting fires and rescuing neighbors after air raids and from other life-threatening calamities. They carried children, old folks, and valuable furniture out of burning buildings and recovered and buried the bodies of fellow Saints and longtime neighbors. They suffered together when loved ones departed for distant battlefields and wept together after official letters and Nazi Party representatives appeared at the door with the news of the dead and the missing.

Probably three-quarters of the members of the Church in the West German Mission lost the homes they inhabited in 1939. Many more lost personal property—in some cases their most cherished possessions. They lost pets, farm animals, photographs, heirlooms, genealogical documents, personal scriptures, the money in their savings accounts, silverware—everything but the clothes on their backs. Most of the buildings in which they held their meetings were destroyed or confiscated. Membership records, hymnals, pump organs, chairs, and pulpits vanished and usually could not be replaced for years.

German citizens who were not of "Aryan" (Caucasian) ancestry were subjected to the same poor treatment as Jews all over the country, as is evident in the experience of Salomon Schwarz in the Barmbek Branch of the Hamburg District and the Weiss family of the Vienna Austria Branch. Citizens who criticized Hitler's government were subject to incarceration in jails and concentration camps, as was the case of the three youths of the St. Georg Branch of the Hamburg District. Thousands of mentally or physically infirm persons became victims of government sterilization and euthanasia programs; at least three young Saints of the West German Mission were among the mentally impaired taken from their homes and families for "treatment" in hospitals in remote locations. In each case, a terse message informed the family of the death of the inmate under suspicious circumstances.[2]

In short, nearly everything experienced by the general populace in Hitler's Third Reich was experienced by one or more members of The Church of Jesus Christ of Latter-day Saints in the West German Mission.

Lest the impression be made that the war years meant nothing but death and suffering for the Saints of western Germany and Austria, it should be clearly stated that they enjoyed good times as well. Eyewitnesses often told of joyous occasions in the home or with other church members—visits by soldier fathers and brothers on leave, Christmas holidays, wedding celebrations, the births of sons and daughters, and baptismal ceremonies for member children and converts. One of the most frequently and fondly mentioned church events was the district conference that usually lasted two days and to which members traveled substantial distances. Those from out of town were commonly housed in the homes of local members, and friendships were born and cultivated. Such events were especially meaningful for young adults. Life for the Saints in many locations in Germany did not involve personal daily suffering until the final stages of the war.

Like their neighbors, the German and Austrian Latter-day Saints cultivated hobbies, developed talents, courted and married, pursued educational goals, started businesses, saved money for nice furniture, looked for larger apartments or garden plots to rent, and in general were determined to enjoy life as best they could under the circumstances. One of the finest ways for Latter-day Saints to preserve life and lifestyle was to sustain the local branch by holding regular meetings. Eyewitness accounts make it clear that the Saints in Germany and Austria achieved that goal.

Final Comments

One of the goals of this research was to ascertain how members of The Church of Jesus Christ of Latter-day Saints in the West German Mission fared during the years 1939 to 1945. It would be interesting to know how they interacted with the Nazi Party. Another goal was to determine the losses they suffered as individuals, families, and branches. In this regard, I offer the following conclusions based on the testimonies of eyewitnesses and the examination of surviving documents.

The National Socialist Party and the Latter-day Saints of the West German Mission

A few adult Latter-day Saints joined the National Socialist Party. Others were asked to do so but found ways to quietly decline the invitation or avoid the issue altogether. Some were pressured to join but declined and suffered penalties for their opposition. Of those who joined, some did so only because it was required of them as employees of the government. Based on the statements of eyewitnesses, it appears that less than 3 percent of the Latter-day Saints in the West German Mission joined the Nazi Party. Douglas F. Tobler, a professor of German history, estimated that "only about five percent of Mormon adults either joined the party or its various organizations. . . . The overwhelming majority of German Mormons remained apolitical and quiescent."[3] There is no indication that any Latter-day Saint had a significant leadership position within the Party. Reports of Party members making overt political statements in branch meeting facilities are too infrequent to suggest a pattern. Even rarer than Nazi Party members in Church were the Saints who belonged to other political parties.[4]

Eyewitnesses are in agreement that some of those Saints who were known to be members of the Nazi Party were enthusiastic about Adolf Hitler's leadership in the early years and were convinced that the Führer had the answers to Germany's problems, but those individuals did not often promote their political views in Church meetings.[5] Only in rare instances was a portrait of Adolf Hitler seen in a Church facility and never on a lasting basis. Only two references to the person of Adolf Hitler have been found in Church meeting records (see the Kassel and Vienna Branch sections).

Photographs of Latter-day Saint homes (interior and exterior) rarely show pictures of Adolf Hitler or the German swastika flag.[6] However, to avoid flying the flag on specific occasions meant to risk incurring the wrath of a fanatical neighbor (and there was often one living close by). Eyewitnesses told of parents who did their best to simply keep out of sight rather than to openly oppose the government. Survivors also recalled hearing infrequent criticism of Hitler or the Party from their parents, but understood that they dare not repeat such criticism outside of the home.

While it could be suggested that Latter-day Saints should have opposed the rise of Hitler in the 1930s through political activism, historians generally agree that such opposition could only have led to personal and collective suffering for the dissidents and their families (and possibly for the Church).[7] Any overt or violent resistance after 1933 could have merited capital punishment, as is evident from the deaths of thousands of alleged revolutionaries in Germany, especially after the abortive plot to assassinate Hitler on July 20, 1944. Some have suggested that the average German (and by extension the average LDS German) should have risen up in rebellion against the evil German government. If they should have (and I do not agree with the premise) and did not, they certainly paid a high price for their inaction: their nation was destroyed, and millions of Germans died.

On the other hand, civil disobedience comes in various forms. Several eyewitnesses have admitted that one or more of their parents listened to broadcasts of BBC London. Such actions were, of course, illegal under National Socialism, but there is no record of any Latter-day Saint being charged with that crime (with the exception of St. Georg Branch youths). In all other cases, it was believed that information received through this medium was never transmitted to persons outside of the immediate family—even to trusted friends at church.

In many ways, it appears that the leaders of the mission, the districts, the branches, and the families increased their efforts to safeguard the Saints and support the branches during the war years. They could neither stop nor (as they learned later) win the war, but they could care for the members, maintain Church worship services and programs and in general keep the Church alive until the war ended. In this regard, they were immensely successful.

In general, German Latter-day Saints found it possible to live their lives as good German citizens who had no valid reason to rebel against the government, even if it meant leaving their homes, loved ones and church callings to fight and die in distant lands. According to eyewitnesses, most adult Saints did not like Adolf Hitler in 1939, because they saw in his overt militarism the prospect of another devastating war. Regarding military service, they often quoted the LDS twelfth Article of Faith ("We believe in being subject to kings, presidents, rulers, and magistrates . . .") to justify serving Hitler's government. Latter-day Saint soldiers often expressed a hope for two things: that they would not be compelled to hurt their fellow man and that they might return to their families in good health. For many, the first wish was fulfilled, for most the second as well.

The Latter-day Saint Family Under Fire

As Hitler and his cronies gained power in the nation, the family came under increasing pressure. National Socialist philosophy emphasized the importance of the Party over that of the family and the Church. Organizations such as the Hitler Youth served in part to take young Germans from their homes and place them into a setting where they could be schooled carefully in the Nazi concept of patriotism and the philosophies of the Party. Children were raised to serve *Führer, Volk und Vaterland* rather than God, church, and family. Fortunately, it seems that in many cases, the goal was not achieved among Latter-day Saint youths.

It is evident that many parents in the Church understood that while some aspects of the Hitler Youth program were positive, others were sinister. In some cases, the parents of eyewitnesses forbade their children to join the Hitlerjugend or the Bund Deutscher Mädel at age fourteen, insisting that the programs of the Church would provide the necessary education, training, and entertainment. Although such noncompliance was not tolerated under the law, many Latter-day Saint parents got away with it. According to eyewitnesses, punishments for noncooperation were rare and seldom had any lasting effect.

Another method used by the Party to weaken the influence of parents in the lives of their children was the program under which children were moved as school classes to rural settings. Under the auspices of protecting the children from harm through air raids by Allied forces, teachers (required by law to be members of the Party) and Party leaders often used the setting to indoctrinate the children. The program was called Kinderlandverschickung, and in the case of nearly every eyewitness interviewed, this absence from home prevented any contact with the Church.[8] When Latter-day Saint mothers independently took their children away from the big cities, they rarely had the opportunity to attend Church services. The absence from Church was perceived as a very negative aspect of life during the war. The corresponding decline in member populations also had a negative effect on the programs of the local branches.

The national labor service required of teenage boys and girls (under programs called Reichsarbeitsdienst and Pflichtjahr/Landjahr) also separated family members. For as much as a year at a time, Latter-day Saint youth lived too far from home to visit their families and were totally subject to the leadership of Party officials. Few of the eyewitnesses reported ever having had the opportunity to attend church during this period of their lives and few were able to take along and study the holy scriptures.

Any time a country goes to war, fathers are removed from their homes. When a lengthy war is fought and lost, many fathers do not return to their families. When German Saints were away at the front, their wives and children survived without the presence of patriarchal and priesthood leadership in the home—in some instances for as long as eight to ten years. The eyewitnesses expressed universal sadness regarding this aspect of their lives. Furloughs granted Latter-day Saint soldiers were rare and brief—sometimes just long enough to produce another child who was then brought into the world and raised by a mother without a father. Several children of Latter-day Saint soldiers from Germany and Austria never knew their fathers.

The West German Mission in Isolation

After the United States and Germany declared war upon each other in December 1941, communications between the office of the East German Mission in Berlin and the headquarters of the

Church in Salt Lake City were interrupted. This state of isolation persisted until the summer of 1945 (forty-two months), when attempts were made to reestablish the connection. President Max Zimmer of the Swiss Mission traveled into Germany to inquire regarding the status of both German missions and their leaders.[9] Several American soldiers who had served in the German missions before the war were allowed to travel to Frankfurt and Berlin to ascertain the fate of the members.[10] Elder Ezra Taft Benson of the Church's Quorum of the Twelve Apostles arrived in Europe in the fall of 1945 to establish a system through which welfare supplies could be distributed to the surviving Latter-day Saints in Germany and other war-torn nations.[11]

It was learned in 1945 that the German Saints had maintained meeting schedules and branch activities as consistently as possible since 1939—at times under challenging conditions. There is no evidence that Church procedures or practices were altered or allowed to deviate from the established norms. Tithing funds were paid, collected, and transferred to the mission office carefully until the final months of the war, when the postal system began to break down. Church literature was produced and distributed faithfully until paper shortages or government regulations hindered the effort.

The work of the priesthood was carried on faithfully and correctly throughout the war. Babies were blessed, children and converts were baptized, blessings of healing and comfort were given, and miracles were performed. The priesthood was conferred upon worthy brethren all over the mission. Priesthood leaders who were absent or killed were replaced via the standard processes. Meetings were conducted and presided over by the proper authorities. In cases where no priesthood holders were present to preside over the ordinance of the sacrament, there simply was no such ordinance. In the absence of priesthood leadership, women did not usurp authority or stewardship but simply held study groups, Primary classes, and choir rehearsals in an attempt to maintain the community of the Saints.[12]

Eyewitnesses attested to the dedication of the Saints to the branches and programs of the Church. In cases where the branch organization broke down totally, individual members prayed, read the scriptures, fasted, and taught their families the gospel. Many eyewitnesses told of their attempts to find a branch of the Church wherever they might be. For them, life was not complete without regular interaction with the Saints.

A short explanation regarding priesthood ordinations in those days is warranted. Ordinations were not done primarily on the basis of age but rather on the basis of need in the branch. Whereas some young men were ordained deacons soon after turning twelve, advancement within the Aaronic Priesthood followed no regular pattern thereafter. Almost exactly one-half of the male members over twelve years of age in 1939 were not holders of the priesthood, though some were quite active in the branch.

Ordination to the Melchizedek Priesthood took place when the man was needed as a branch leader. Many men became elders after the age of thirty or forty. Because there was no stake of Zion in Germany or Austria until 1961, there were no bishops, high priests, or patriarchs in those countries during the war.

The German Government and the West German Mission

From the testimony of eyewitnesses and the surviving records of the West German Mission, it is evident that the government of Germany made no attempt during the Hitler era to shut down The Church of Jesus Christ of Latter-day Saints in that nation. The only substantiated intervention by the government came when the Berlin police instructed leaders of the East German Mission to have the members avoid singing hymns containing words associated with the Jewish culture, such as *Zion* and *Israel*.[13] In fact, with the exception of rare and short-lived episodes of police inquiries and the occasional private harassment of individual Saints by local Nazi Party leaders, members of the Church and the branches to which they belonged in the West German Mission were never at risk of extinction. The government either had no intention at the time of erradicating the Church or did not consider the 13,500 members of the Church in Germany worthy of special attention.

Investigations by the secret state police (Gestapo) involved the following leaders of the Church in the West German Mission: Christian Heck (mission office, 1942), Otto Berndt (Hamburg District, 1942), Anton Huck (mission office, 1943) and Ilse Brünger Förster (mission office, 1943). The details of those investigations are provided in the corresponding chapters of this book. The tragic case of the Helmut Hübener group of the St. Georg Branch is summarized in the Hamburg District chapter.

Several eyewitnesses told of seeing official observers in church meetings across the mission. Such observers always entered without fanfare, were recognizable as "strangers," inevitably sat on the back row, and avoided any kind of participation. Not one account of an interruption of meetings by such officials was proffered.[14]

Changes in the Mission, the Districts, and the Branches During World War II

As can be seen in previous chapters, the West German Mission leadership continued to function with dedication and efficiency throughout the war. Despite the fact that mission supervisors Friedrich Ludwig Biehl and Christian Heck had to be released when called into active duty in the German army, mission leaders were true to their stewardship.[15] Following the departure of foreign (principally American) missionaries in August 1939, only female German Saints were called as full-time missionaries in the West German Mission. By 1940, all male missionaries had been released, and there were only a few women left in these callings. According to eyewitnesses and available documents, those young women performed admirably.

The number of Church districts actually increased from thirteen in 1939 to fourteen in 1943 with the formation of the Strasbourg District (including territory in German-occupied France). Surviving mission records allow the assumption that all districts were holding semiannual conferences as late as 1944 and some even in the spring of 1945. All fourteen districts were under the direction of faithful presidents—four of whom were called into active duty and had to be replaced: Alwin Brey (Hamburg), Willi Wille (Hanover), Eugen Hechtle (Karlsruhe) and Robert Salopiata (Schleswig-Holstein). All former district presidents survived the war. Many eyewitnesses reported seeing members of district presidencies visiting the weaker branches to offer priesthood support and the branch meeting minutes confirm such reports. Conditions during the war sometimes required district leaders to travel to outlying branches via bicycle.

Nearly every branch in the West German Mission (sixty-nine in number when the war broke out in 1939) was still holding meetings in 1943. By that time, several already had lost their meeting facilities (through destruction or confiscation) but had found other rooms. By the end of the war, at least three-quarters of the branches had lost their meeting places (and some interim locations) and could hold services only in the homes of members and on an irregular basis. Branches without priesthood leadership often held only Sunday School meetings. With few exceptions, meetings were still held across the mission as late as April 1945, and in a few cases, there were no interruptions at all.

The Effects of the War on the Programs of the Church

As previously mentioned, sacrament and Sunday School meetings survived the war in most branches, but this is not true with other meetings.

The Primary organization was weakened or even discontinued in branches in cities where the Jungvolk units were very active. However, the resourcefulness of the members came into play when the Primary meetings no longer took place: the adults invested their energies in the education of the children in Sunday School classes. It should be noted, of course, that the small number of children shown in the membership tables explains the lack of any Primary organization in several branches.

The Mutual Improvement Association (Gemeinschaftliche Fortbildungsvereinigung) in German branches included essentially every unmarried member over the age of twelve. Many married members also participated in the activities of the MIA. As might be expected, the absence of young men who were serving in the military and young women performing their duties under the Pflichtjahr program weakened the branches' MIA groups considerably. As the privations of war increased, there were also few resources available to support the cultural activities of the MIA (typically musical and theatrical performances, outings, dances, and dinners). Only the largest few branches in the mission were still holding MIA meetings in 1945.

The Relief Society groups survived the war in nearly all branches. The sisters intensified their compassionate service during the first years of the war, but as they left the big cities with their children, lost their homes, became widows, or were otherwise distracted by the challenges of daily survival, their service to others did in many cases decline. In the last year of the war, even those sisters still carrying out their society duties had little to offer others in the way of welfare items and food. Eyewitness reports make it clear that most of those who still had the means to survive were willing to share whatever they had (see the Wuppertal Branch, Ruhr District). In the very least, they could meet to discuss important topics, as is seen in the case of the Michelstadt Branch of the Frankfurt District.

Military Losses among Latter-day Saints of the West German Mission

Prophets and Apostles of The Church of Jesus Christ of Latter-day Saints have never taught that members of the Church would be spared trials and sufferings in this life. Indeed, Church doctrine holds that negative experiences are an integral part of life. It can come as no surprise that hundreds of Saints of the West German Mission lost their lives during the war. In addition to the first two German mission supervisors, Friedrich Ludwig Biehl and Christian Heck, several branch presidents or their counselors perished under various circumstances.

It is probable that more than nine hundred members of the Church in the West German Mission served in the various branches of the German armed forces (Wehrmacht). Fewer than fifty were in the navy, approximately 130 in the Luftwaffe (mostly ground personnel), and the rest in the army. Several dozen served in various police assignments. An additional one to two hundred older male members of the Church were inducted into the Volkssturm after October 1944.

Of those German and Austrian Saints of the West German Mission in German military service, 155 died in wartime (by May 8, 1945) and 33 more died by the end of 1950.[16] Available data suggest that more than 50 percent of those men had been ordained to the priesthood, the majority holding offices in the Aaronic Priesthood. For purposes of this discussion, all soldiers reported missing in action are assumed to have died by 1955, when the last German prisoners of war were officially released from incarceration in the Soviet Union.

Except for those whose wounds were debilitating, no Latter-day Saint men in uniform in 1943 were released before the end of the war. Many who were drafted as early as 1940 served for the duration; several were drafted before the war and did not come home until after the war. From eyewitness testimony, it is clear that only a few Latter-day Saint German soldiers escaped being taken prisoner by war's end. Rare are the stories of soldiers who in May 1945 simply went home and became civilians again, as did Manfred Gellersen of the Stade Branch, Hamburg District. If all needed data were available to investigate this matter, we might see that at least 90 percent of the regular Wehrmacht soldiers in the Church spent time behind barbed wire. At least seven died while incarcerated. The majority of the Latter-day Saint POWs were held in camps in the Soviet Union, but significant numbers spent time in the United States, Canada, Great Britain, France, and Belgium. Very few returned as early as 1945, several in 1946, most in 1947, and many in 1948. The last Latter-day Saint POW is believed to have returned to Germany in 1950.

German and Austrian Latter-day Saints Who Died in Military Service in World War II	
Killed in battle or died of wounds	155
Missing in action*	26
Died as prisoners of war	7
Total deaths	188

*It is assumed that all soldiers missing in action were in fact killed in battle or died later.

Due to the confusion existing in German military units toward the end of the war and the lack of records in POW camps, it is very probable that several more LDS men died during their military service.

Civilian Losses among Latter-day Saints

The primary cause of many deaths among Latter-day Saint civilians cannot be directly attributed to the war. However, as explained earlier in the Memorial Book, some nonviolent deaths among members of the Church would certainly not have happened in peacetime. Many Saints died due to what in German is called Kriegseinwirkung (enemy action). Among those whose deaths came through enemy action, the most common cause was the Allied air war over their cities. The second most common cause of death through enemy action occurred when the American, British, and French armies invaded Germany from the west beginning in the fall of 1944. The third category of civilian losses includes those members who died while fleeing the invaders. In most such cases, the survivors were allowed to return to the town of their choice, but conditions prevented some from doing so for several years.

Latter-day Saint Civilians Who Died as a Result of World War II	
Killed in air raids and by invasion forces	85
Died from diseases or starvation	226
Died from other causes	145
Died in concentration camps or euthanasia facilities	5
Missing	64
Total deaths	525

As was the case among the soldiers, it is very likely that dozens more civilian deaths actually occurred among the general membership of the West German Mission.

While it comes as no surprise that members of The Church of Jesus Christ of Latter-day Saints in Germany and Austria were not spared sacrifice, suffering, and death, there are hundreds of stories told by survivors who believe that they were shielded from harm on specific occasions—some of them more than once. Soldiers and civilians alike told of occasions when they "should have been killed" or at least when their survival or rescue defied human explanation. For example, a freak accident could easily have taken the life of little Vera Uhrhan of the Frankfurt/Main Branch. Some Saints later connected the moment of impending death to the moment when a family member at home was extending to God an extraordinary plea for the safety of a soldier son (such as happened to Walter Speidel of the Stuttgart Branch).

Deaths in the West German Mission	
Total LDS military deaths	188
Total LDS civilian deaths	525
Total LDS deaths	713

German Latter-day Saints and the Crimes of Nazi Germany

Several eyewitnesses stated that they were aware before the war that Jewish neighbors and business acquaintances were being mistreated. The events of Reichkristallnacht (the Night of Broken Glass) on November 9–10, 1938, shocked Latter-day Saints as much as they did millions of Germans across the Reich. Saints saw some of the destruction of Jewish businesses as it happened. Others noticed that Jews they knew disappeared soon after that fateful night. The fact that some children in German schools were subjected to vicious anti-Semitic propaganda is confirmed by several eyewitnesses.

No members of the Church in the West German Mission are known to have served as guards in concentration or extermination camps during the Hitler era. None are known to have used the power of the military to wantonly or intentionally take the life of an innocent person. However, by the very nature of such crimes, it is highly unlikely that a man who committed such a crime would confess to it. While the debate over the awareness of the German citizenry of the crimes committed by Germany during the war may be diminishing in intensity, there are still many who do not believe the simple claim that typical Germans had no way of knowing that Jews, foreigners, prisoners of war, and persons of minority status were being mistreated and murdered under the swastika flag.

Several Latter-day Saints recalled seeing labor groups near camps or even in towns; in all cases, they noted that the prisoners appeared to be in poor health. In all cases, it was clear that passersby were not allowed to give the prisoners as much as a crumb to eat and must not talk with them. Even young eyewitnesses concluded that something was amiss. Hans Pohlsander was eighteen when Jews on their way to the Bergen-Belsen concentration camp escaped from guarded trains during an air raid; he recalled how those Jews were hunted down in and around the city of Celle and some of them shot.

The West German Mission at the End of World War II

The territory of the West German Mission was intact when Germany surrendered on May 8, 1945. Of the seventy-one branches, more than sixty were still meeting at least monthly. Mission supervisor Anton Huck and his office staff continued in their administrative duties in the office at Schaumainkai 41 (though they were displaced by American soldiers during May and June). Most of the branches no longer had meeting rooms large enough to accommodate the active branch population. Many branches were led by aging priesthood holders, while a few branches held only Sunday school meetings (essentially study groups) maintained by the surviving women while they hoped and waited for their husbands to return.

In many surviving or newly-acquired meeting rooms, there were no glass windows left; the materials used to cover the openings were opaque, and the rooms were dark. At many such locations, there was also no functional supply of electricity, gas, or water. Meetings taking place in the late afternoon or evening often required the use of candlelight. These conditions may have given rise to the commonly held Latter-day Saint misconception that members of the Church in wartime or postwar Germany using candles on the sacrament table had adopted deviant practices and rituals during the time when the German missions were out of contact with Church leaders in Salt Lake City.[17]

The population of Saints in the West German Mission had been reduced from 5,795 in 1939 to approximately 5,100 by May 1945. Of the survivors, at least 60 percent (and possibly as many as 70 percent) no longer had a home of their own. Most of those who had lost their homes were crowded into rooms provided by relatives or friends. Some found temporary quarters on farms (often in a barn) and in attics and basements where no utilities were available. Some lived in the ruins of large buildings (such as Seith family of the Karlsruhe Branch). Some were assigned housing by local government and were not welcomed by their hosts who resented the imposition.

Hundreds of LDS families subsisted without fathers (at least temporarily) in the summer of 1945. In those families, the mothers were usually gone during the day—working, looking for work, or searching for food and fuel. Many of the men who were fortunate to have come home from the war were busy with the same daily tasks. Most healthy LDS men had found employment by the end of that first postwar summer.

Nearly two thousand Latter-day Saints of the East German Mission were living within the borders of the West German Mission by the end of 1945. They had come as refugees trying to stay out of reach of the invading Red Army. Most arrived with nothing but the clothes on their backs, but they usually sought out the Church as soon as they found a place to live. This led to the enlargement of several branches and the founding of a few dozen more in western Germany.

A unique part of this LDS migration history took place in the town of Langen, nine miles south of Frankfurt. The Moderegger family of the Tilsit Branch in distant East Prussia found work in a Langen landscaping company and moved there in the summer of 1945. Always on the lookout for ways to help their fellow Saints, the Modereggers located additional employment opportunities and invited other LDS refugees to join them in Langen. By 1950, more than three hundred Latter-day Saints from eastern Germany had crowded into the small town and the new branch became one of the largest in the West German Mission. By 1953, they had constructed a nice building in which to conduct their meetings and other activities.

It seems that wherever they found themselves, the surviving Saints of the West German Mission began in May 1945 to pick up the pieces of their branches or to join and strengthen whichever branch was close at hand. By the fall of that year, several young men (most of them veteran soldiers) had been called as full-time missionaries—charged first and foremost with the task of helping Church members recover from the war. The Church was in good hands and conditions steadily improved.

According to the statements of eyewitnesses, the general state of mind of Church members in the West German mission in the summer of 1945 encompassed both sadness and relief. Hundreds of members were dead or still missing, men were in short supply, homes and meetinghouses had been destroyed or damaged, food was scarce, utilities were interrupted, and transportation was unreliable. Nevertheless, most Saints were alive and had maintained their testimonies of the gospel of Jesus Christ, or, as many survivors remembered, their testimonies had maintained them. World War II had weakened the Church in certain physical respects, but the faith of individuals was alive and well. Years would pass before some of the bad memories faded, but the work of the kingdom of heaven on the earth was carried forth with dedication by Saints who praised God for preserving their lives.

NOTES

1. Marriage ceremonies conducted for LDS Church members in church buildings or homes were purely symbolic in nature. No representatives of any church in Germany or Austria were allowed to conduct marriages after 1938 (in compliance with civil law).
2. See the stories of Harald Ludwig Adam of the Saarbrücken Branch (Karlsruhe District) and Herbert Eduard Fiedler of the Düsseldorf Branch (Ruhr District).
3. Douglas F. Tobler, "German Mormons as 'Righteous Gentiles': Trying to Save a Few Jewish Friends" (unpublished manuscript, 1995), 7; private collection.
4. After the Reichstag (parliament building) fire of 1933, Hitler had used the German government to legally outlaw the Communist Party and to severely repress other political parties.

Activity in any but the Nazi Party was thus grounds for suspicion on the part of the state.

5. Several eyewitnesses stated emphatically that Anton Huck of the mission leadership and St. Georg Branch president Arthur Zander were members of the Party who wore the official lapel pin and openly discussed national political issues.
6. See related photographs and stories in the chapters of the Munich and Essen Branches.
7. The chapter on the Hamburg St. Georg Branch in the West German Mission provides the only known example of serious resistance to Hitler's regime by Latter-day Saints—the case of teenagers Helmut Hübener, Karl-Heinz Schnibbe, and Rudi Wobbe.
8. Exceptions are noted in the stories of the Essen, Göppingen, and Munich Branches, where determined (and homesick?) boys located and attended church meetings with Saints near the Kinderlandverschickung facility.
9. See Roger P. Minert, "Succession in German Mission Leadership during World War II," in *A Firm Foundation: Church Organization and Administration* (Provo, UT: Religious Studies Center, Brigham Young University, 2011), 552–571.
10. J. Richard Barnes, a veteran of the West German Mission, was an officer with the US Army forces that entered Germany in 1945. Several of his reports on the status of the Church in Germany were published in the *Deseret News* in the summer of 1945.
11. See Frederick W. Babbel, *On Wings of Faith* (Salt Lake City: Bookcraft, 1972).
12. The calling of Karoline Müller of the Bad Homburg Branch, Frankfurt District, was perhaps unique in its scope.
13. Roger P. Minert, *In Harm's Way: East German Latter-day Saints in World War II* (Provo, UT: Religious Studies Center, Brigham Young University, 2009), 29.
14. Indeed, the only interruptions described by eyewitnesses occurred after the war, principally under the occupation of the Russian army.
15. See Roger P. Minert, "Succession in German Mission Leadership."
16. See Roger P. Minert, "German and Austrian Latter-day Saints in World War II: An Analysis of Casualties and Losses," in *Mormon Historical Studies* 11, no. 2 (Fall 2010): 1–23.
17. Eyewitness Ruth Schumann Hinton of the Chemnitz Schloss Branch (East German Mission) offered this explanation years later: "How were the brethren to read the sacrament prayers in those dark rooms without light? With the power out, we had to use candles." See Minert, *In Harm's Way*, 188.

GLOSSARY

Civilian Programs of the Third Reich

Bund Deutscher Mädel (League of German Girls): Beginning at age fourteen, all German girls were to join the Bund Deutscher Mädel (BDM) for two or three years. Like the boys of the same age, many girls were already employed or in occupational training and thus not free to attend the meetings. BDM girls were trained extensively in domestic skills such as baking and sewing, but were also carefully schooled in patriotic virtues and taught to prepare to be model German mothers who would bear children for the state. Their uniforms reflected conservative standards of virtue and discipline. Meetings were often held on Sundays.

Jungvolk (Young People): All German boys and girls were to be inducted into the Jungvolk at the age of ten. The program was organized through the public schools, and participation was required. There were official penalties for noncompliance, but some Latter-day Saint parents were able to invent excuses for the absence of their children from Jungvolk activities. Jungvolk groups wore uniforms, marched in parades, memorized nationalistic songs and details of Hitler's life, and engaged in wholesome activities, often out of town. Meetings were held weekly, but usually not on Sundays.

Hitler Jugend (Hitler Youth): All German boys were expected to enroll in the Hitler Jugend (HJ) when they turned fourteen years of age. Since some boys had already finished public school and were busy in apprenticeships, it was not as easy for local officials to determine whether a certain boy was attending his HJ meetings. Again, penalties were promised those who did not comply. Activities included sports, war games, political lectures, political rallies, and camping. HJ members wore a distinctive uniform, were taught to observe strict health standards, to deport themselves as gentlemen, and to act in every way as loyal citizens of the National Socialist state. Quite a few HJ units conducted meetings and activities on Sundays. Training with actual weapons was not common among HJ units.

National Sozialistische Deutsche Arbeiter Partei (National Socialist German Workers Party, or Nazi Party): Founded in Munich in 1920, the party attracted far-right reactionaries who were antirepublican, anticommunist, and rabidly anti-Semitic. Adolf Hitler joined the party early and soon became its leader. By 1929, the Nazi Party was one of the largest political parties in Germany. It steadily gained power until in 1932 it earned the greatest number of seats in the parliament. As the leader of the Nazi Party, Hitler was appointed chancellor of Germany in January 1933.

Pflichtjahr (duty/service year): Because so many young men were taken from the local economy to serve in the military, the program known as Pflichtjahr was introduced to provide substitutes. Each teenage girl in Nazi Germany could expect to be inducted into the Pflichtjahr program, which would usually require her to render service in one or two capacities: as a farm laborer or as a domestic helper in a home without a father. The call to begin Pflichtjahr service came in the form of a draft notice, and the term of service lasted from six months to one year. During the Pflichtjahr, many girls had Sundays free, but Latter-day Saint girls were usually too far from a branch of the Church to attend meetings. Service on a farm within this program was often called Landjahr.

Reichsarbeitsdienst (Reich labor force): Preparing for and waging war required all the manpower Germany could muster. Thus the Reichsarbeitsdienst (RAD) was formed early on to provide that labor and simultaneously to prepare young men for military service. The call to the RAD came to seventeen-year-olds in the form of a draft notice. They wore uniforms very similar to those of the army, marched with shovels rather than with rifles, and lived in camps that closely resembled boot camps. The most common activity for RAD units was the construction of roads, airfields, harbor facilities, and fortifications—often in foreign countries. A full term with the RAD was one year, and a young man could expect to be drafted into the military very soon after he returned home.

Military Organizations of the Third Reich

Geheime Staatspolizei or Gestapo (secret state police): Under the command of one of Hitler's closest cronies, Heinrich Himmler, the Gestapo was reponsible for the identification and arrest of enemies of the Nazi Party and the state in general. Known for their long leather coats, Gestapo agents instilled terror in the hearts of German citizens by their mere presence. They were occasionally seen in LDS branch meetings but came and went in silence, never causing any interruptions or cancelations of meetings.

Luftwaffe: The German air force.

Marine: The German navy.

Polizei: Police; the term was also used to designate military police and police officials stationed in occupied territories, where they assisted the military.

Volkssturm: home guard; these were civilians inducted toward the end of the war to defend the fatherland; they were often more than sixty years old and, in some cases, younger than seventeen.

Waffen-SS: The elite combat forces under the command of Heinrich Himmler, whose personal titles included "Reichsführer-SS and Chief of the German Police." Waffen-SS troops wore black uniforms (with the SS lightning bolt insignia), fought on various fronts, and enjoyed better living conditions (see the story of Lothar [John] Flade in Chemnitz Center Branch, Chemnitz District). The term Waffen-SS is often confused with the regular SS—police units whose infamous duties included the command of concentration camps and death camps.

Wehrmacht: Technically referring to all armed forces together, the word *Wehrmacht* was also used to describe the regular army, i.e., the land forces (officially *Heer*).

Other Items of Interest

Adolf Hitler: Born in Braunau, Austria, on April 20, 1889, Hitler was a decorated veteran of World War I and became a member and leader of the Nazi Party in the early 1920s. His rise to power in German politics culminated in the combination in his person of the office of Reichskanzler (chancellor) and Präsident (president) in 1934. He was the so-called Führer (leader) of the German nation until he committed suicide in Berlin on April 30, 1945.

Hinterhaus: In German cities, Hinterhäuser were buildings constructed in the space behind the main buildings on the block. The tradition of building Hinterhäuser dates back to the Middle Ages. Access to such a building was usually gained through a portal in the main building at that address. In some cases, one went through the entry hall of the main building, out the back door, and then across a courtyard (Hinterhof) to the Hinterhaus. In the largest cities, there were often several Hinterhäuser within a given block; they were usually designated Hof I, Hof II, and so forth (see Forst Branch Chapter, Spreewald District).

Kinderlandverschickung: As early as 1941, German city leaders found it advisable to send children to rural areas where their lives would not be threatened by enemy air raids. The program had two aspects: the transfer of entire classes of schoolchildren (from eight to fourteen years of age) with their respective homeroom teachers to hotels in tourist regions, and the evacuation of mothers with small children to the homes of relatives in rural regions. Under this program, school children were often away from their parents for a year or more. Many families disapproved of the program but did not wish to see their children in danger at home.

Mein Kampf **(My Struggle):** This autobiography of Adolf Hitler was written while he was incarcerated in Landsberg following a failed coup against the government of Bavaria in Munich. The book was published after he left prison in 1925. Although some statements made in the book proved prophetic, the work was not popularly read. It was often given by the civil registrar to newlyweds.

Reich (Empire): This term was exalted to prominence during the Hitler regime (*das Dritte Reich* or "the Third Reich") of 1933–45. The word was frequently used in connection with other nouns describing government programs, such as Reichsarbeitsdienst (described above).

Reichskristallnacht (Night of Broken Glass): Ostensibly as a spontaneous reaction to the assassination of the German ambassador to France, Nazi Party strongmen (SA members) attacked hundreds of Jewish synagogues and thousands of Jewish-owned businesses all over Germany during the night of November 9–10, 1938. Nearly one hundred Jews were killed. Most Germans were shocked by the open violence, but it was finally clear that there was no longer a place for Jews in Hitler's Germany.

INDEX
of Personal Names

A woman who married before the war began in 1939 is listed under her married name.

A woman who married after the war began is listed under her maiden name as well as her married name, as shown in this example of Edith Rehbein, who married Hans Marquardt in 1940:

Rehbein Marquardt, Edith, 144, 166, 188
Marquardt, Edith Rehbein. *See* Rehbein Marquardt, Edith

Names containing the German umlaut characters *ä, ö,* or *ü* are alphabetized as if those characters were spelled *ae, oe* or *ue,* respectively.

Adult LDS Church members for whom no given name is known are listed as (*Brother*) or (*Sister*) after the surname. American missionaries whose given names are unknown are listed as (*Elder*) or (*Sister*).

For those listed in the In Memoriam sections, only the principal is included in this index—not his or her parents or spouse(s).

Page numbers in italics refer to images.

F

G

L